U.S. Government on the Web

U.S. Government on the Web

Getting the Information You Need

Third Edition

Peter Hernon

Robert E. Dugan

John A. Shuler

LIBRARIES UNLIMITED

U N L I M I T E D

A Member of the Greenwood Publishing Group

Westport, Connecticut • London

Library of Congress Cataloging-in-Publication Data

Hernon, Peter.
    U.S. government on the web : getting the information you need / Peter
Hernon, Robert E. Dugan, John A. Shuler.—3rd ed.
      p. cm.
    Includes bibliographical references and indexes.
    ISBN 1-59158-086-2
    1. Electronic government information—United States—Directories. 2. Web sites—
United States—Directories. 3. Electronic government information—United States. 4.
Web sites—United States. I. Dugan, Robert E., 1952– . II. Shuler, John A.
ZA5075.H47 2003
025.04—dc21   2003051584

British Library Cataloguing in Publication Data is available.

Library of Congress Catalog Card Number: 2003051584
ISBN: 1-59158-086-2

First published in 2003

Libraries Unlimited, Inc., 88 Post Road West, Westport, CT 06881
A Member of the Greenwood Publishing Group, Inc.
www.lu.com

Printed in the United States of America

The paper used in this book complies with the
Permanent Paper Standard issued by the National
Information Standards Organization (Z39.48-1984).

10   9 8 7 6 5 4 3 2 1

Contents

Chapter 13 (*Cont.*)

Preface

The question is not what you look at, but what you see.

Henry David Thoreau, *Journals* (November 16, 1830).[1]

A number of people proclaim that the era of "Big Government" is over, and they point to a marked decrease in the size and role of the national government. Nonetheless, as perusal of this encyclopedic guide indicates, the federal government remains large by any standard, and, to some, its presence on the World Wide Web (Web) is overwhelming. The Web is the primary means by which the national government communicates many of its information resources to the governed. At the same time, the government offers a number of services to the public and special communities (e.g., the business community) over the Web.

Government Web sites, collectively and individually, provide invaluable information resources and services to the American public and the international community. Even with the availability of some good search engines, it is virtually impossible to conduct a comprehensive search among all publicly available sites to uncover everything produced and distributed electronically. In addition, search engines may miss some items and de-emphasize some important ones. Within such an environment, the *U.S. Government on the Web* offers a road map for those wanting to navigate the government's presence on the Web. Although the coverage is not (and cannot be) comprehensive, the intent of this guide is to present options for conducting a search: use of search engines or "portals," approaching government by its three branches or by a particular body (e.g., Congress, department, agency, or office), browsing so-called one-stop shopping sites, or searching for a type of information resource (e.g., statistics or maps) or selected subject (e.g., health and medical resouces or genealogy).

Of course, competing guides also present government resources on the Web. Unlike others, this one is more than a mere listing of Web sites. Except for Chapters 5, 12, and 13, we do not present sources within an artificial subject arrangement. To do so would ignore the fact that many people may focus their attention on a few government bodies and that it is virtually impossible to predict which body will necessarily publish information on which subject. For example, the president, Congress, and some of their support agencies are not limited on the subjects that they can address. Thus, the strength of this guide is that it serves as a pointer through the maze of the government's structure and various information resources. At the same time, it shows that the government communicates with all age groups over the Web, including the youth of the nation (see

Chapter 13). Chapter 12 and Appendix C serve to compensate for the lack of a subject focus to much of this book.

U.S. Government on the Web is intended to appeal to a diverse audience, especially those individuals who do not deal with government information on the Web regularly or to a great extent. The audience includes undergraduate and graduate students (including library school students), academics, teachers in public and private schools, high school students, parents, librarians (e.g., those not serving as government documents librarians), and anyone needing information produced by (and available from) the government.

A question that readers may raise is, "Why do we need a print guide to government resources on the Web?" The answer is that, because of the complexity of the government, there is a distinct advantage to having a print source to consult and review, as information seekers decide how to conduct a search that will have the best chance of locating something that meets their need. Second, bypassing a guide such as this one and searching independently requires knowledge of government structure and types of publications (see Chapter 2), terminology, specific titles (e.g., the *Congressional Record* and the *Federal Register*), and how government functions. Without prior awareness of these issues, it is easy to look at a Web site and miss some valuable content. For example, in dealing with congressional information resources, it is important to be able to differentiate between a *report* and a *hearing*. In the case of the executive branch, information seekers need an elementary understanding of the Freedom of Information Act and the difference between a *publication* and a *record*. Furthermore, the Government Printing Office's GPO Access is not an easy portal to navigate. It includes many services but does not lay them out easily for a novice searcher to follow. FirstGov (see Chapter 3) is a portal that enables information seekers to search across Web sites and, to some extent, branches of government. The results may appear overwhelming, however, even though they are not comprehensive. Readers may be confused by an often long list of presumed relevant sources. Complicating matters, proponents of FirstGov claim that this portal provides (or will provide in the future) comprehensive access to all government information. Because much information still has not been tagged for inclusion, including that contained in serial volumes (e.g., the *Congressional Record*), no single source will be able to provide comprehensive access to digital information resources available on the Web.

Third, this guide serves as a snapshot in time of an ever-moving and elusive target, and thus partially documents changes in the government's presence on the Web and how a body presents itself to the public. There is no standardization of Web sites across branches of government, departments, or even agencies within departments. For example, the federal judiciary regards the Web as an important resource for those individuals dealing with it and needing access to rules, opinions, and other types of publications. Yet there are variations among the courts regarding what they make available and how they display information. Nonetheless, the courts' presence on the Web is becoming more diverse and significant.

Two other questions that readers may raise are "Why do I need government information at all?" and "Can't I find the same content in nongovernment sites?" Chapters 1–3 address these questions, and the other chapters provide evidence of the wealth of information resources available from the government. These chapters underscore something that graduate students over the past twenty-eight years (which is how long I have been teaching about government information policies, services, practices, and resources) have told me: "I had no idea that the government produced such publications. I wish that I had known about these treasures—ones supported by tax dollars—years ago."

For those readers wanting to know the major differences between this edition and the previous one, let us offer some highlights:

- The content has been updated to spring 2003.

- We include coverage of the unfolding of the newly created Department of Homeland Security.

- Two new appendices have been added: one that identifies the government's e-commerce activities and one that attempts to provide general subject access to agency publishing programs. Although far from being comprehensive, this appendix serves as a general pointer to key bodies that publish information resources on general topics.

During the time that this guide book was being revised, several significant laws were enacted that will have a great impact on the provision of federal government information in a Web environment. President Bush signed into law the *E-Government Act of 2002,* H.R. 2458 (Public Law 107-347), on December 17, 2002. This law accelerates the shift to electronic distribution of public information into high gear and institutionalizes several initiatives launched in the mid-1990s; Chapter 14 discusses the related policy instruments. The *E-Government Act* furthermore must be placed within the context of two other significant policy developments that were a direct result of the September 11, 2001, terrorist attacks: the *USA PATRIOT Act,* H.R. 3162 (Public Law 107-173), and the creation of the Homeland Security Department (Public Law 107-296). These three laws generate further levels of complexity into the provision of electronic government information. Suffice it to say that the struggle over new electronic government initiatives will be waged within a changed framework of policies involving privacy, national security (secrecy), and intelligence gathering within the current war on terrorism.

The new *E-Government* law legislates into existence several new interagency committees, calls for further standards on privacy involving electronic information resources, goes further in clearly asking for standards on the naming and organization of electronic information records, and invites closer examination of preservation and archival issues. What is particularly encouraging is that, for the first time, the issues of geographic information science and the growing web of federal judicial information are specifically mentioned as part of the law. Earlier legislation either left these aspects out of the legislative language or treated them with unclear direction. Title II of the act supersedes Title X of the *Homeland Security Act,* which was a new version of the old *Government Information Security Reform Act of 2000* (114 Stat. 1654-266). Also of interest in the new law is the reference to "sensitive information" (undefined) in section 208(b) (1) (C). Most curiously, section 892 of the *Homeland Security Act* empowers the president, when prescribing and implementing information sharing procedures, to identify and safeguard homeland security information that is sensitive but unclassified (undefined). Clearly, we are preparing the third edition of this guide and snapshot of government Web sites in 2003 at a time of flux when new laws are unfolding and a new department (Department of Homeland Security) is materializing. Obviously, future editions will document their impact on public access to digital government information.

An issue that has received scant attention in the discussion of digital or electronic government is the fact that although Web sites change and improve, the government has constantly changed Web addresses for many of the information resources included on their pages. For the potential of e-government to be realized, there must be much more stability in those addresses over time. Until this is accomplished, it is our intent to provide monthly updates that identify changes in the Web addresses listed in this biennial guide. Those updates can be found on the home page of Libraries Unlimited: **http//www.lu.com/lu/idu.html**. In that e-government and the Department of Homeland Security are continuing to unfold and will continue to do so for years, the publisher's home page will serve as a mechanism for updating content on both of these areas between the biennial revision of this guide.

Finally, it merits mention that Libraries Unlimited has published a complementary work, *United States Government Information* (2002), that focuses on information policies and sources. A companion 1,800-page CD-ROM provides key policy documents, learning exercises, and primary source material. This source and the CD-ROM look at government information policies currently and historically, thereby placing *U.S. Government on the Web* in historical perspective.

Peter Hernon

NOTE

1. The quotation is taken from William Bernhardt, *Dark Justice* (New York: Ballantine Books, 1999), n.p.

Chapter 1

Government Information and Its Importance

The federal government routinely "collects, maintains, uses, disseminates, saves, loses, and destroys vast quantities of information,"[1] a large portion of which is or may become *public* assuming it has not been lost or destroyed. Public information includes information products that the government imparts on its own initiative or that is required to release (e.g., through the *Freedom of Information Act*; FOIA), whereas *nonpublic* information is meant solely for use within government and is not for public consumption. Because it is held in confidence, for example, for reasons of predecision, security, or personal privacy, or protective stipulations in administrative or statutory law, nonpublic information is not released under the FOIA or other "open government" laws.

Public information comes from not only government bodies located in the nation's capital, but also regional offices of federal departments and agencies located throughout the United States as well as branch offices located in other countries. Public information not available through the FOIA may be *published*—placed on department or agency World Wide Web (Web) sites or released as a printed document. As more agencies print on demand (upon request) or disseminate more publications through the Web, the number of print publications will continue to decline, sometimes dramatically so.

The amount of public and nonpublic information that the federal government collects and produces during any one year is unknown and probably unquantifiable because there is neither a standard of measure nor an attempt to compile a definitive number. The number of print publications, however, must be enormous—perhaps in the hundreds of thousands. With the inclusion of publications (and other resources) on the Web, that number increases manyfold. One conservative estimate is that "the government has created more than 20,000 Web sites containing more than 100 million pages."[2] The Smithsonian Institution has placed so much information on its Web site that it would require approximately 35 hours to read it all! This fact illustrates the problems in both providing a brief snapshot of the federal government's enormous, promi-

1

nent, and ever-developing presence on the Web and producing a comprehensive portal that identifies and retrieves all government information resources available in digital form.

The number of electronic records increased from a "few thousand to several hundred thousand" over the 1990s, according to reporter William Matthews, and has continued to grow in the new millennium. He also noted that archivists expect the "growth to accelerate in the future" and that the U.S. State Department estimated it has at least 25 million diplomatic messages to archive. Furthermore, the Clinton administration produced "millions of e-mail messages, presidential memorandums, documents, National Security Council cable traffic, the president's daily diary and more."[3] In all likelihood, the Bush administration has already produced as much, if not more, information resources, many of which are not intended for public consumption.

DEFINITIONS: PUBLICATION, INFORMATION, DATA, AND RECORDS

One complexity in dealing with government information involves a definition of key terms. A *publication,* presenting public information, is commonly viewed as "informational matter which is published as an individual document at government expense, or as required by law."[4] In recent years, that definition has been interpreted to include *information products*, a term that encompasses CD-ROMs and other electronic formats. Libraries in the federal depository program of the U.S. Government Printing Office receive government *publications* or *products* other than those "determined by their issuing components [the department or agency] to be required for official use only or for strictly administrative or operational purposes which have no public interest or educational value and publications classified for reasons of national security."[5] Thus, for instance, internal manuals, declassified records, and agency forms are excluded from this distribution program.

This definition treats "informational matter" as a *public* thing or object (e.g., report or hearing) and as a document, but it does not specify the medium in which the publication appears—print, audiovisual, video, electronic, and so on. A publication is intended to be informative or instructive, to provide information or data, or to impart knowledge. It is intended to meet one of the following functions: the administration of federal laws and regulations, advancement of the legislative process, reporting on government activities, and informing the public about the nature and activities of government, the conduct of research, and the provision of service.[6]

In today's environment of a global, interconnected Internet and World Wide Web, the word *published* no longer refers solely to an ink-on-paper process. The Web is a means of publication: the articles, books, images (e.g., photographs, motion pictures, satellite imagery, filmstrips, and videos), and other "informational matter" placed on the Web for the public's benefit. Such matter has "public interest" or "educational value," but, in some instances, may comprise internal or administrative documentation.

Data, or a collection of raw numbers perhaps in an electronic data base, are a type of "informational matter" that might be published, especially as more government bodies place data on their Web sites. For instance, the government releases vast amounts of statistical data covering most facets of life and public administration but frequently does not make available documentation—codebooks—that explains the layout, quality, and usability of the data.

The federal government, like most governments, creates *records* in the course of conducting its official business and shares those records with the parties to that business. A record may be a matter, physically, of defined space in a medium, such as a piece of paper. It may also be undefined, as in some electronic records. A record should be recognized less for its form or format and more for its context. In some federal offices, routing slips do not comprise records; they are temporary documents to assist with the distribution of other "records." For security purposes, however, routing slips may be retained as a records in some offices to monitor the flow of, and accountability for, sensitive documents. In brief, in a policy context, a record is "what I say it is" (i.e., a document or format that contains information that is a matter of record or information in need of preservation).[7]

Presidential records are materials created by (perhaps on behalf of or at the direction of) or received by the president, his immediate staff, or someone in an agency of the Executive Office of the President, that relate to the official duties of the president. Not all publications, information, and data comprise records: "being transacted in a particular business context is crucial to a record, thus an adequate record will contain evidence of the context of its creation."[8] Government departments and agencies are placing some records, especially those reflecting past activity, on the Web.

The Archivist of the United States approves the terms under which agencies decide how to handle a particular set of records. These terms, known as schedules, stipulate whether records are considered *temporary* or *permanent* and, if regarded as temporary, how long agencies need to retain them before they can be destroyed (see **http://www.archives.gov/**). In the fall 2002, the National Archives and Records Administration (NARA) announced that it plans to narrow its focus, carefully examining only three classes of records: those that protect individual rights, ensure agency accountability, and have continuing value for documenting the national experience. Everything else, it seems, will be left to agency discretion, perhaps even automated processing.

It merits mention that with the exception of two Office of Management and Budget (OMB) memorandums concerning the personal privacy of visitors to federal agency Web sites, there is no explicit policy concerning the life-cycle management of "records" posted on such Web sites. The amendments to the *Electronic Freedom of Information Act of 1996* indicate that so-called electronic reading rooms can be made available to the public through Web sites, but those amendments leave the determination of what records will be made available through such reading rooms to individual agencies. Of late, this determination has been tempered by "homeland security" considerations—the protection of sensitive but unclassified information.

Apart from Web site materials, NARA has issued policy guidance on the preservation of records in electronic forms and medium, including, when appropriate, e-mail communiqués. Furthermore, NARA is actively building an Electronic Records Archive (ERA; see Chapter 6), and the Library of Congress is actively building an electronic library of records, documents, periodicals, and books that have been created in electronic form.

In summary, the Web offerings of a government body comprise virtual publications, and an increasing number of official Web sites contain a diverse and expansive set of publications—more so than ever released in print form. Indeed, the Web environment, with its multiple types of information resources aimed at a diverse population, differs significantly from the more restrictive paper environment. The definition of a government publication is definitely expanding as more diverse "informational matter" becomes electronically available for a worldwide population. A publication might be something to read, but it also might be something to see, listen to, or interact with.

EXAMPLES

Government information on the Web includes, for instance, the text of reports, studies, and legislation (see Chapter 2); games; interactive maps; images; and tours of historic sites. The Bureau of Consular Affairs of the Department of State, for example, provides travel warnings, information sheets, and public announcements relating to international travel (e.g., related to voting assistance abroad and lists of doctors and hospitals in other countries). The site (**http://travel.state.gov/**) even provides information on international adoption and international parental child abduction. Individuals traveling to areas of political upheaval are well advised to check out this site before their departure.

The Chesapeake Bay Program, a partnership that the Environmental Protection Agency leads, focuses on the Chesapeake Bay watershed, which encompasses more than 64,000 square miles that drain into the bay and its rivers. Its Web site (**http://www.chesapeakebay.net**) covers, for instance, Bay restoration, water quality, fisheries, habitats, and pollution reduction, and it provides maps, tables, charts, and other information arranged by zip code, watershed name, county, and city.

The U.S. Mint, within the Department of Treasury, has a Web site of games and "fun facts." There is a "puzzle mint," "coin memory machine," "golden dollar puzzle," and other activities (see **http://www.usmint.gov/kids/index.cfm?flash=yes&Filecontents= kids/games/index.cfm**).

As discussed in Chapter 13, the Central Intelligence Agency (CIA) has a Web site for the nation's youth, the purpose of which is to dispel myths about the agency—not to recruit future generations of CIA employees. The Internal Revenue Service's (IRS) Web site offers income tax forms and other publications that can be downloaded for printing and for electronic completion and returning to the agency (**http://www.irs. ustreas.gov/formspubs/index.html**).

Examples of the images offered by government sites include photographic images of Mars taken from the Mars Global Surveyor. There is a gallery of more than 93,000 images, as well as weather reports, the latest images, pictures for sale, and an archival collection containing additional images (**http://www.msss.com/mars_images/**).

Agencies use Shockwave, a browser plug-in, to provide the public with animation, movies, self-guided tutorials, and training exercises. For instance:

- The U.S. Geological Survey has interactive and multimedia maps that include national geospatial and geostatistical data sets that, for instance, show elevation and vegetation growth (**http://www-atlas.usgs.gov/atlasvue.html**).

- The National Park Service has a virtual tour of historic Harpers Ferry, West Virginia (**http://www.nps.gov/hafe/home.htm**).

- The Environmental Protection Agency (EPA) offers "Clean up Dumptown," a game that promotes recycling (**http://www.epa.gov/recyclecity/**).

Two other examples of interactive maps are available at the Web site of the International Trade Administration within the Department of Commerce. A world map identifies the countries that have imported the highest values of U.S. paper products. Another display identifies those countries that have experienced the greatest increases in imports of electronic products from California (see **http://ese.export.gov/**). The second example is GeoMAC, a collaborative effort involving the U.S. Geological Survey, the Forest Service, and other agencies. This mapping tool designed for coordinating firefighting efforts is publicly available (**http://www.geomac.gov/**).

The national government offers both information resources and services on the Web. By providing online services, it meets the information needs of a population that is making greater use of microcomputers for business, economical, political, daily life, and recreational purposes. There is an increased opportunity for government officials and policy makers to communicate directly with the public and to ascertain their viewpoints. Government officials, members of Congress, and government agencies, for example, maintain e-mail addresses and encourage the public to communicate with them. Some other services include online forms, electronic town meetings, online press conferences, the online discussion of government policy and practices, and so on (see Appendix A). FirstGov, a portal (see Chapters 3 and 9), is envisioned as a way for the public to navigate the maze of federal agencies to find needed information.

☞ Some So-called Best and Popular Sites

From 1997 to 2000, GovExec.com (**http://www.govexec.com/bestfeds/**) conducted an annual competition to recognize the *best* government Web sites for their excellent customer service, their business practices, and their use of technology. The awards were discontinued in the belief that government sites were no longer "cutting edge in online technology." Nonetheless, examples of past winners include the following:

- U.S. Mint (**http://www.usmint.gov/**), which offers e-commerce (for coins), lesson plans for teachers and games for budding collectors, and information about coinage

- Bureau of the Census (**http://www.census.gov/**), which provides economic, population, and housing data

- Small Business Administration (**http://www.sbaonline.sba.gov/starting/**), which helps people start their own businesses

Various lists of the most popular government sites have been produced, with popularity being defined in terms of high numbers of visits. The Environmental Protection Agency (EPA) home page (**http://www.epa.gov/**), for instance, draws 1.4 million hits and 600,000 requests for customer maps per month. Some other popular sites are the following:

- National Oceanic and Atmospheric Administration, **http://www.noaa.gov/**

- National Institutes of Health, **http://www.nih.gov/**

- Department of the Treasury, **http://www.ustreas.gov/**

- Department of Army, **http://www.army.mil/**

- Department of Navy, **http://www.navy.mil/**

- National Aeronautics and Space Administration, **http://www.nasa.gov/home/ index.html**

- House of Representatives, **http://www.house.gov/**

WHY IS GOVERNMENT "INFORMATIONAL MATTER" SO IMPORTANT?

The previous examples should correct any misperceptions that the federal government only (or largely) produces "informational matter" that is trivial, unnecessary, poorly written, duplicative of what the private sector produces, and of little interest or value to anyone outside the employees and contractors of a particular government body. It is hoped that the educational and informative examples highlighted in this chapter put to rest any claim that all government publications waste taxpayer dollars and are of lesser importance than what the private sector offers. Government sources recount government policies, the development of statutory and administrative law, research findings, the administration's position as well as that of Congress on issues, congressional oversight of the executive branch, court renderings, and so on. These sources enable members of the public to hold government accountable and to advance their business, educational, recreational, and other interests. In a number of instances, the private sector offers no counterpart, or private sector sources draw on (or reprint) government publications. Commercial portals might even rely on interactive maps produced by the government but not acknowledge the fact that the government created and maintains those maps at its own Web sites.

Many printed government publications are not styled for the mass public—those reading at grade level eight or under. Pamphlets explaining services and how to apply for federal benefits may be written for lower grade level comprehension, and perhaps in languages other than English, however. The majority of printed government publications may also be technical and not that useful to the layperson, and they may be difficult to read and understand. Government Web sites, however, speak to a more diverse population, including the nation's youth, parents, and teachers, as well as to those needing government services. For example, the home page of the Library of Congress (**http://www.loc.gov/**) arranges different information resources "Especially for . . . Researchers, Law Researchers, Librarians & Archivists, Teachers, Publishers, Persons with Disabilities, and Blind Persons."

The EPA is an example of an agency wanting to communicate with the segment of the population that does not speak, or prefers not to speak, English. It has a Web page devoted to publications appearing in Spanish (*Recursos en Español,* **http://www.epa.gov/espanol/**). The home page for the Department of Interior appears at **http://www.doi.gov/**, but a mirror page appears in Spanish (**http://www.doi.gov/ doipress/spanish/main.htm**).

GENERAL ISSUES TO BE AWARE OF WHEN USING GOVERNMENT "INFORMATIONAL MATTER" AND GOVERNMENT WEB SITES

A number of issues have arisen concerning the availability and accessibility of information resources released on the Web, including the duration of accessibility. These issues also relate to the public's right to know and to individual's privacy rights. Web sites may not directly address these issues, but that does not diminish their importance. As one public policy analyst notes,

 Information is the currency of democracy. And an informed citizenry is, indeed, the bulwark of a democracy. There are many assistants and auxiliaries in the creation and maintenance of a knowledgeable populace. But, a truly sovereign people must be able to obtain information, of their own volition, from their government for minimal reasons of protecting their individual rights as well as preserving the well-being of the larger community or society.[9]

Government policies regarding information dissemination through the Web are still evolving. Electronic dissemination through the Web saves agencies substantial printing costs. The National Science Foundation, for example, estimates, for one year, a savings of $750,000 for its most frequently requested publications.[10] At the same time, because of an amendment to a 2001 appropriations bill, OMB, within the Executive Office of the President, is required to issue directives "for ensuring and maximizing the quality, objectivity, utility, and integrity of information (including statistical information) disseminated by federal agencies."[11] As J. Timothy Sprehe, president of Sprehe Information Management Associates, observes, the draft guidelines represent "motherhood and apple pie," but with a "political agenda." Each agency is expected to create administrative grievance processes for addressing any data quality complaints from the public. Opponents to proposed administrative rules can challenge the data quality supporting the rule and "conceivably drag out final regulatory adoption for months or years."[12] Since Sprehe made his critique, the OMB, in October 2002, issued the final guidelines, which proclaimed that "Anyone seeking the correction of information has the burden of proof with respect to the necessity for correction as well as with respect to the type of correction desired." The ability to challenge data quality would probably still be of concern to Sprehe and others. At any rate, the U.S. State Department is one example of a body that is implementing those guidelines (see **http://www.state.gov/misc/13864.htm**).

Robert Gellman, a privacy and information policy consultant, raised some important questions, ones that have not been satisfactorily and completely answered despite OMB's policy advice. He asked, "Is there a time requirement to maintain online access to all Web pages and documents? Can an agency dispose of Web documents? If so, when?" He noted that "many federal Webmasters operate without considering these questions. Agency Web sites have proliferated with scant central control, legal consultation or long-range planning. Still, the rapid acceptance by agencies of the Internet as a means for public access has been a positive development."[13]

⟋⟍ **Digital Government**

Digital or electronic government is an evolving concept that currently includes four areas: (1) the delivery of services (government-to-citizen), (2) providing information to the public, (3) facilitating the procurement of goods and services (government-to-business and business-to-government), and (4) facilitating efficient exchanges within and between agencies (government-to-government). Subordinate to the four areas is a fifth one, the government as an online retailer (see Appendix B). E-government and the related information policies expand the five areas into eleven purposes:

1. Communication between an agency and the public, and communication among government bodies

2. Information access and meeting the information needs of the American public, from the nation's youth to senior citizens

3. Service delivery and the provision of online services, including online sales

4. Procurement or the purchase of services and goods from the private sector

5. Security, including the protection of Internet transactions among government entities and between those entities and the public against obstruction, diversion, interception, and falsification. Security also extends to protection against hacking of home pages and safeguarding Web sites and computers against viruses. Furthermore, security pertains to the storage of electronic information so as to ensure its integrity and prevent unauthorized disclosure

6. Privacy of personally identifiable information and unauthorized use of cookies that can be attached to computers so that agencies can monitor the public's use of their Web sites

7. Management of e-government operations and related matters

8. Maintenance of information technology systems that underlie e-government

9. Reducing the so-called digital divide—the perceived disparity that results from portions of the population not having the ability to use information technology because of a lack of access, skill, or both. This is why government agencies use standard plug-ins that the public can freely download from the Web, or agencies provide free access to plug-ins that they specially created for some of their products

10. Emergency response, or dealing with a sudden crisis that threatens the nation. For example, following September 11, the public used government Web sites to monitor the situation and report alleged terrorist sightings to the appropriate agency. Special institutions, such as the Federal Emergency Management Agency (FEMA), have been created to respond to and plan for national emergencies, as well as coordinate the efforts of other responding agencies. Such institutions have coordinated and contributed to the preparation and maintenance of emergency plans, such as the federal response plan for the delivery of federal disaster assistance, and standby directives, such as Executive Order 12656 of November 18, 1988, assigning emergency

preparedness responsibilities among the federal departments and agencies. In addition, Congress has enacted various laws that provide the president ready authority to address an emergency, as well, as some standby statutory powers that may be selectively activated under the terms of the *National Emergencies Act of 1976,* as amended

11.   Oversight of the development of e-government by both the executive branch and Congress

In a management agenda, released in August 2001, President Bush declared that his first priority was to make government citizen-centered. An editorial in *Federal Computer Week* challenged whether this declaration is the cornerstone of administration policy, however. It stated that the policy "has so far rung hollow" and noted the increasing gap between citizens and decision makers regarding access to public information. The editorial even noted that government information technology (IT) managers "fear reprisal" from the administration if they shared best practices or discussed "IT information technology policies and programs in their agencies."[14]

In October 2001, OMB proposed 24 government projects to bring electronic services to the public, and in April 2002, it selected five e-government initiatives that would share $4.15 million in funding. One initiative, for instance, will enable state and local governments to apply online for grants. To develop a more cohesive, cross-government approach to technology management, OMB expects government bodies to pursue a complex strategy of relying on "plug-and-play e-government" that focuses on component-based architecture, the purpose of which is to encourage them to rely on software that others have used. The assumption is that these bodies can plug their e-government strategy into something already in use and make preexisting software useful. The climate noted here also has a negative impact on e-government. At the same time, agencies typically have not gathered relevant data to determine if their e-government projects support their mission and improve service to the public.[15]

Nevertheless, under the rubric of e-government, the government has undertaken more activities that, in past years, have largely been reserved for the private sector. Because it enabled researchers to examine more than 1,400 peer-reviewed journals free of charge, PubScience, a Web page of the Department of Energy, was a good test of the extent to which the government might *compete* with commercial services. If government employees prepare the abstracts, does this practice duplicate what the private sector does? Is such a value-added function permissible to serve the public, including scientists, better? In November 2002, the department answered these questions by terminating PubScience.

The *E-Government Act of 2002* (Public Law 107-347) treats agencies as publishers and expects them to improve public access to their information resources. Agencies will have to follow standards in organizing information and making it easily searchable, and to provide basic information on agency mission, structure, and strategic plans. The government intends to develop a portal that organizes *all* government information by type, not by the agency that produces it, and the act extends existing rules for security, expands the role of the National Institute for Standards and Technology in setting security policy, creates an Office of Electronic Government within OMB to set uniform Web standards, provides a formal management structure for different e-government concepts and initiatives, and creates a process for deciding what information gets posted online. One provision requires that all agencies publish rules and regulations on their home pages as well as in the *Federal Register.*

The act also directs the chief justice of the United States, the chief judge of each circuit and district, and the chief bankruptcy judge of each district to ensure that court Web sites contain the following information or links to Web sites with the following information:

- Location and contact information for the courthouse, including the telephone numbers and contact names for the clerk's office and justices' or judges' chambers

- Local rules and standing or general orders of the court

- Access to docket information for each case

- Access to the substance of all written opinions issued by the court, regardless of whether such opinions are to be published in the official court reporter, in a text searchable format

- Access to all documents filed with the courthouse in electronic form

- Any other information (including forms in a format that can be downloaded) that the court determines useful to the public

More than likely, it will take several years, for the detailed road map specified in the legislation to materialize and for a definition of "sensitive information" to emerge and be consistent with section 892 of the *Homeland Security Act,* which has yet to define "sensitive but unclassified information." Nonetheless, as this edition of the guide illustrates, the government has made great progress independent of the *E-Government Act* in organizing and presenting its information resources. The complication is that portals and other general guides do not (and are not likely to) displace the Web presence of individual agencies and other bodies within the three branches of government. The public will still have to be knowledgeable about government structure and the roles of each branch of government.

There is a general belief that government Web sites are "generally more difficult to navigate than private-sector sites." Despite the fact that 68 million Americans have used government Web sites (see **http://www.pewtrust.org/pdf/vf_pew_internet_e-citizens.pdf**) and the heavy use of the Internet following September 11, "many Americans are unaware there is a dot-gov domain name—when asked a tax question, subjects mostly checked out www.irs.com, a commercial Web site. Interestingly Air Force and Coast Guard job sites have a dot-com domain name."[16] Contrary to the popular impression (and the *E-Government Act*), more government bodies are making their Web sites easier to navigate and retrieve needed information; an exception might relate to information "archived" at a site. Clear presentation of all resources on a home page can be a difficult feat to achieve given the vast amount of information that departments and agencies make available on a home page. The Library of Congress, for instance, provides access to more than 20,000 Web pages on its home page. This example is not intended to show that government Web sites have reached their full potential; rather, it indicates that they are still evolving.

Examples of services provided by digital government include the following:

- Bureau of the Public Debt (**http://www.publicdebt.treas.gov/**) and the purchase of t-treasury bills and bonds online

- Department of Housing and Urban Development (**http://www.hud.gov/ homes/homesforsale.cfm**) and buying homes from the government

- Bureau of Land Management (**http://www.adoptahorse.blm.gov/**) and adopting wild horses and burros

- Federal Aviation Administration (**http://www.fly.faa.gov**) and up-to-the-minute information on airport delays

- Department of Education (**http://fafsa.ed.gov/**) and online filing for financial aid

Another use of e-government is to embrace e-learning for those in the federal workforce. The Department of Defense, for instance, offers courses online. The National Technical Information Service in the Department of Commerce intends to partner with a company to develop and deliver a hosted e-learning and knowledge management service for high-security agencies.

Finally, from the fall of 1996 through 2001, the Bureau of Labor Statistics, within the Department of Labor, asked a group of researchers to examine how the agency could improve access to its Web site (**http://www.bls.gov/**). The purpose of the study was twofold: "to gain a better understanding of how nonspecialists think about, access, and use statistical data," and "to understand and document . . . how the agency adopts and adapts technologies to better serve the needs of diverse communities." The study relied on interviews with users and agency staff, as well as data collected by means of transaction log analysis, to document patterns of user behavior.

Among the findings were a marked increase in the number of e-mail requests "with relatively constant phone volume," and, over time, users' comments about how to improve the Web interface. Users became more dependent on the Web site over the last five years, while the site became more customer-focused and able to serve high-tech users. At the same time, the site was better able to meet the needs of nonspecialists and to help them navigate the various offerings for needed information. The agency improved the presentation of its information resources.[17] As a result, e-government has become more of a reality to the public because it provides universal access for an increasing user population and an agency able to improve its home page while planning better to provide future services. In essence, the agency is probably well on its path to meeting the requirements of the *E-Government Act.*

Persons with Disabilities. The Center for Information Technology, in the General Services Administration's Office of Governmentwide Policy, educates the federal workforce and builds the infrastructure to support implementation of Section 508 of the *Workforce Investment Act of 1998.* Using the Web site **http://www.section508.gov/**, both federal employees and the public can locate resources to understand and implement the requirements of the section. Under that section, government agencies cannot buy, develop, maintain, or use electronic and information technology that is inaccessible to people with disabilities. This includes people who have vision or hearing disabilities, who have limited use of their hands, or who suffer from color blindness, photosensitive epilepsy triggered by rapidly flashing lights, and so on.

Because by law government Web sites must be accessible to people with disabilities, agencies must ensure that their home pages and their twenty most frequently visited pages are in compliance with the requirements of Section 508. Undoubtedly, agency compliance will be closely monitored, especially because members of the public and government employees with disabilities have the right to sue agencies in federal court and to file administrative complaints for noncompliance.

A problem for some agencies is that documents in portable documents format (.pdf) may not be readable by the current generation of screen readers or translated for Braille displays. Adobe Systems is developing a new version of its Acrobat Reader, however, that will enable screen readers to comprehend a number of .pdf files that, at present, those with disabilities cannot read. Currently the company has a Web site (**http://access.adobe.com**) that converts .pdf documents into HTML (hypertext markup language) or plain text so that screen readers can interpret them.

Dot-Coms. Because the government lacks a sufficient staff with the technical knowledge and experience to manage numerous online services, and because agencies cannot afford to hire all of the staff with such knowledge and experience, agencies may be forced to outsource some services to various companies in the private sector that want to assist the government in its transition to digital government. Assuming that issues (e.g., consumer protection, computer security, and privacy) can be resolved, these e-companies, or "dot-coms," might be able to leverage their experience with commercial e-commerce technology and create new services for businesses and the public conducting financial transactions with the government.

These dot-coms, on the whole, are outside the scope of this book. An exception that merits mention is the U.S. Postal Service (USPS; **http://www.usps.com**). This site reflects the agency's move to electronic commerce; the agency provides business-to-business services and supports online communications. The USPS offers electronic postmarks and certified delivery for e-mail, as well as an e-bill service so that customers can pay bills online through a secure portal. Its PC Postage service enables customers to purchase stamps online and to print them directly onto envelopes or labels.

What Are Government Web Sites and Web Pages?

As previously noted, there are various estimates about the number of government Web sites and Web pages. A first reaction on hearing any number is, "I had no idea how large the presence is!" Behind these estimates is a complex issue, one that the government and others have yet to acknowledge: those making the estimates may be confusing terminology. The most basic document on the Web is a "Web page." It is a single document that can be viewed without linking to any other document. Characteristically, the Web page has a unique Web address, known as the URL (uniform resource locator), which oftentimes ends with the extension ".htm" or ".html." Other extensions include ".pdf" and ".asp."

A "Web presentation" is a collection of Web pages designed to be linked to each other to convey an idea(s), a product(s), or a service(s). Web page designers employ numerous Web pages in a presentation instead of a single page to facilitate navigation between and among Web pages and to reduce the time necessary for the viewer to download each page onto the local computer from the World Wide Web.

A "Web site" may be one Web presentation, or a collection of two or more Web presentations. There may be little, if any, contextual relationship of the Web presentations among and between each other. Or a Web site may include two or more Web presentations that are dependent on each other for content and context.

A Web site is usually a destination (e.g., **http://www.whitehouse.gov/**), and it is anchored by the site's "home page." A home page is the Web designer's preferred starting point for a Web site. It oftentimes serves as the organizing page, such as an electronic table of contents, and as the start of the site's navigational buttons linking the home page to one or more Web pages in one or more Web presentations.

Pages and presentations on a Web site are frequently arranged in a hierarchical manner, resembling a pyramid, with the home page at the top. HTML, the scripting language most commonly used on today's Web, allows the Web designer to incorporate links on the home page to any other page in the presentation, to other presentations on the Web site, or to other Web sites. Finally, it should be noted that a Web site is not necessarily a discrete, physical object. A physical Web server, the machine that stores and presents the Web pages, may host one Web site or thousands of them.

Freedom of Information Act

At least two national laws advance the public's right to know: the *Freedom of Information Act* (FOIA; 5 *United States Code* 552) and the *Privacy Act* (5 *United States Code* 552a; see next section). The FOIA, which became operative law in July 1967, establishes procedures for gaining access to reproductions of records created and maintained by executive branch agencies. The FOIA, which "is exclusively a disclosure statute,"[18] was intended to serve primarily as a means of access to relatively current records (paper documents, films, tapes, and other materials created or obtained by an agency as part of its official duties), rather than to large numbers of decades-old records of permanent historic value. It does not apply to the president or vice president or to the legislative and judicial branches of government. Under FOIA, agencies must disclose records unless they fall within one of the nine exemptions (e.g., specifically authorized under criteria established by an executive order to be kept secret in the interest of national defense or foreign policy, and security classified as such; related solely to the internal personnel rules and practices of any agency; specifically exempted from disclosure by statute; personnel or medical files; records or other information compiled for law enforcement purposes; and geological and geophysical information and data).

The FOIA has been amended at various times since its enactment (see Chapter 14). The 1996 *Electronic Freedom of Information Act* amendments (E-FOIA) made clear that records also include electronically created information (e.g., databases, word-processed documents, and e-mail). The act also stipulated that executive departments and agencies should create online reading rooms to house (1) inventories of all major information and records locator systems; (2) records created since November 1, 1996; and (3) often-requested documents, defined as documents that "the agency determines have become or are likely to become the subject of subsequent requests for substantially the same records."

Although executive branch departments and agencies place some of their declassified records in E-FOIA public reading rooms, there remains great variation among them regarding the extent of their compliance with the law. Some agencies broadly embrace the E-FOIA and use the opportunity to make more records and information publicly available on the Web, whereas others have been less forthcoming, especially following September 11.

The guidelines issued by Attorney General John Ashcroft on October 12, 2001, contrast sharply with those issued by his predecessor, and it "endorses far more restrictions to access than any previous administration over the past 35 years," according to Lotte E. Feinberg, professor of public administration at John Jay College of Criminal Justice, the City University of New York. Feinberg continues as follows:

> The more significant change is the new, very different, standard the Justice Department plans to use to defend agency decisions to withhold records. An agency can be "assured" . . . that Justice attorneys "will defend your decisions unless they lack a sound legal basis or present an unwarranted risk of adverse impact" on other agencies' abilities to protect their records." . . . Clearly, Congress and others will monitor how agencies manage FOIA requests and make litigation decision under the new guidelines.[19]

Agencies, such as the National Aeronautics and Space Administration (NASA), accept FOIA requests electronically through their Web sites. Placing requests electronically does not, however, expedite the process or guarantee a favorable outcome. The National Archives and Records Administration has "the NARA Freedom of Information Act (FOIA) Homepage" (**http://www.archives.gov/research_room/foia_reading_room/foia_reading_room.html**), which, among other things, leads to an electronic reading room and a page titled "Public Availability and Use of Federal Records," which covers the agency's regulations for access to its holdings (**http://www.archives.gov/about_us/regulations/part_1250.html**). Finally, it merits mention that the Department of Justice has an FOIA page that provides links to principal FOIA contacts within executive agencies, other federal agencies FOIA Web sites, annual FOIA reports, reference materials, FOIA reading rooms in the department, and so on (**http://www.usdoj.gov/04foia/index.html**).

✒ Privacy

As noted by one specialist in government information policy,

> While the FOI Act has been characterized as an access law standing in the tradition of the First Amendment, the Privacy Act may be described as a fair information practice law standing in the tradition of the Fourth Amendment and its generalized "right of the people to be secure in their persons, houses, papers, and effects." But the statute is, as well, an amalgam of ideas concerning the still evolving concept of privacy.[20]

The 1974 *Privacy Act* is dated legislation, is not comprehensive, and does not thoroughly cover the electronic environment. It is, however, the cornerstone of fair information practices and other privacy law in the United States. Privacy is not "an interest that outweighs other social values and objectives. The controversies arise over the details of the balancing" between the surveillance powers of government and the privacy rights and interests of the public.[21]

The OMB has directed government bodies to post clear and easy-to-find privacy policies on their Web sites. The policies must appear on the department or agency's principal Web site and explain what information is collected, why that information is collected, and how the government body plans to use it. Agencies must also add privacy policies to other government sites that link to their home pages.[22]

Agencies might collect and store information on individuals who use their home pages; however, any information collected should not impinge on the public's right to privacy. In the past, some agencies were criticized for gathering information that they should not have collected. Any survey attached to a government Web site that is designed to gather information voluntarily should not violate privacy rights protected by federal statute. Agencies might collect information on the types of domain from which people access the Web (e.g., *.edu* for a college or university or *.gov* for a person from a government site), the date and time of access, and the screen or information sought.

Some agencies still use *cookies,* which are small computer files placed on a Web site visitor's hard drive that track that user's travels on the Web to determine who visited the site recently and how that person got there. A cookie should neither gather invasive information about the public and its online behavior nor track behavior without user consent. Thus, *session cookies,* ones that expire when the user closes the Web browser at the end of an online session, do not pose the threat that *persistent cookies,* ones that are stored on a user's computer and expire after a specific time, do.

According to OMB, persistent cookies may threaten individual privacy, and therefore agencies and their contractors should notify visitors if a Web site uses them. OMB informed agencies that they should not use cookies "unless the following conditions are met:

- There is a compelling need to gather the data on the site

- The agency takes the appropriate and publicly disclosed privacy safeguards for handling of information derived from cookies

- The Web site administrators have received approval from the head of the agency" [23]

Agencies can use session cookies to help them personalize their Web sites for the benefit of their users. In accordance with OMB policy, agencies must clearly present and make easily accessible their privacy policy.

The U.S. Mint has one of the few Web sites to announce publicly its use of cookies (see the partially eaten cookie at the lower left-hand corner of Figure 1.1). It uses a cookie.

Figure 1.1. Example of a Cookie

(United States Mint, **http://www.usmint.gov/index. cfm?flash=yes**).

to keep you connected to our site during your session, to operate our shopping cart online retail and certain forms, or to count the number and type of visitors to different pages on our site. We don't use cookies to store individually-identifiable information, or to track your actions over time or across Web sites. You can configure your browser to accept or decline cookies, or to alter you when cookies are in use. You don't have to accept cookies from us, but if you choose not to, some of the functions on our site may not be available to you. Once your transaction is completed and confirmed, you may delete any USMint.gov cookies from your hard drive (see **http://www.usmint.gov/policy/policy/ index.cfm?action=full#cookies**)

As this quote clearly indicates, the user has the obligation to remove or not accept a cookie. The agency does not aid that person by explaining how to remove a cookie. Removal is a complex issue because a cookie may not reside in any particular place on the browser.

In conclusion, in a survey of Internet users, it was found that "Americans have a generally positive outlook on government services moving to the Internet but are very concerned about the privacy of their personal information." Their concerns centered on the possibility of hackers breaking into government computers and of government employees misusing personal information in violation of existing laws.[24]

Archival Sources

A Web site might serve as a permanent repository for a period of time or, more likely, as a transient bulletin board containing an assortment of information resources having momentary interest or relevance, covering, for example, the last six months. NARA preserves historically valuable government records and other source material, but on a selective basis; agencies preserve their own operative records. NARA has preserved the White House Web site from the Clinton presidency by taking a snapshot of the White House site once every two years of his administration (see **http://www. clinton.archives.gov/**).

If a publication, or even a record, is changed—for instance, a word-processed paper that undergoes various drafts—is it important (or possible) to track the various drafts, seeing the evolution of policy or a change in procedures? Furthermore, a Webmaster might remove government publications from the Web. What becomes of them? Is it possible to retrieve information resources once they are removed? The answer may well be that the publications are lost or destroyed and that there is no archival record of them. This is not to say that there necessarily should be an archival version. Clearly, some government bodies provide an historical archive, and others do not. If such an archive exists, how comprehensive is it?

E-Records

The policies governing the preservation of records tend to focus on paper documents, and many valuable electronic records evade notice, capture, and custody of the National Archives and Records Administration. As Matthews observed, "federal agencies crank out electronic records by the billions," resulting in an "e-records avalanche." Furthermore, "records that are essential to the government accumulate in office computers, reside in agency tape libraries and often are lost when systems are replaced or shut down."[25]

There is concern that "today's electronic documents will become unreadable as new hardware and software systems are developed and old ones are abandoned."[26] This happened in the past with census data that can no longer be read by technology of the 1980s and later. One pundit characterized the problem with document and data migration as the present day *Titanic*.[27]

The government is still trying to determine how to preserve the millions of electronic documents that departments and agencies produce annually, and, at the same time, to continue to provide public access to these files. Government officials have struggled with this problem since at least 1985, when a federal panel warned that the nation was "in danger of losing its memory" through the transition to the use of computers in creating records and documents. Thus, the issue remains unresolved, and part of the country's memory is being (and has been) lost.

The Web versus Secrecy

On one hand, "public access to government information resources is viewed as a service to the citizen and a bulwark of democracy"; on the other, it "has become synonymous with giving aid and comfort to our enemies. Public access, it seems, is not an unalloyed good; access has a dark side."[28] Those benefiting from access to these resources, it is presumed, could be terrorists or hackers seeking to "cause mischief, destroy valuable data, and threaten national security."[29]

Since the emergence of e-government, hackers have penetrated numerous federal computer systems and defaced agency Web sites. Digital graffiti—incorrect information inserted—has appeared on sites such as THOMAS (Congress), the Office of the

General Counsel (Department of Energy), Department of Justice, and NASA's Ames Research Center. The products of hackers may remain on the site for only a short time; still, any of us could be unaware that the information that we are retrieving is imaginary. Indeed, everyone should be cautious about any information used—electronic or paper, Web- or non-Web-based, government or nongovernment—and not assume that it is necessarily accurate.[30]

In some instances, hackers have captured sensitive information.[31] On the Web, there may also be sources of *misinformation* (honest mistakes) and *disinformation* (part of a governmental campaign to misinform, e.g., hostile governments). For instance, the Bureau of Labor Statistics, during fall 1998, suspended the posting of some supplementary economic data on its Web site until new posting rules could be developed. The reason was that bureau staff inadvertently placed "sensitive employment data on the bureau's Web site a day and a half before the data was scheduled for release. The mistake sparked a miniature bond rally as investors traded on the information."[32]

Agencies may place draft publications on the Web for public comment. Some of these incorrectly place quotation marks around passages that are not identical to the original source, some are factually incorrect, and some draw incorrect inferences from a legal source, for example.[33] Yet a reader may assume that the information presented is correct. Unless the government, or any Web site, stands behind the authority of the information provided, nobody should assume that the contents are necessarily official and accurate.

Much government and other information presented on the Web is unfiltered, and, as the previous example indicates, there may be a desire to deceive or confuse—to shape and sway public opinion in the United States or elsewhere. The Web is a means to convey information, data, and messages—truthful, deceptive, or somewhere in between—to an audience. Some education researchers and social scientists, for instance, have charged that the Department of Education is limiting information and research on specific issues for ideological reasons—they do not reflect the conservative ideology of the Bush administration.[34] An editorial appearing in the *Boston Globe* echoed the same sentiment but this time noted that the ideology was reflected on the home pages of the National Cancer Institute and the Centers for Disease Control and Prevention.[35] Thomas Oliphant, an editorial page columnist for the *Boston Globe,* noted that the Bush administration placed "insurance propaganda on a government Web site falsely claiming that the 'average' jury award had risen by" a much larger percentage (75 percent) than it actually did (6.4 percent) for the years 1996 through 1999. He mentioned that premiums on health insurance or prices for prescription drugs rose at a higher percentage than the jury awards.[36] Disinformation placed on government Web sites could undermine the public's trust in the reliability of information presented on government home pages.

The Web, especially following September 11 (see the next section, "Homeland Security"), "continues to challenge government security practices and to disturb the official equilibrium between secrecy and disclosure." Questions arise about what information the federal government should provide and to whom, how to strike a balance between openness and secrecy, who should determine that balance, and what knowledge or insights can be gained from combining a variety of information resources. Fortunately, the government releases extensive amounts of government information, but, at the same time, it has increased the amount of information withdrawn from public scrutiny.[37]

Homeland Security

As Relyea notes,

> in the aftermath of the September 11, 2001, terrorist attacks on the World Trade Center in New York City and the Pentagon in suburban Washington, DC, the phrase "homeland security" has come into popular use in discussions of protecting against, and combating, terrorism. It is a nebulous concept, without public policy definition, although and Office of Homeland Security has been established within the Executive Office of the President, a Homeland Security Council has been created, and presidential directives are being issued in its name.[38]

Relyea also shows that, "compared with national security, the concept of internal security appears to have no history of intellectual development" and that "the concept of homeland security—preservation of the security of the homeland—appears to be rooted in past efforts at civil defense."[39]

L. Elaine Halchin, an analyst in American National Government with the Congressional Research Services, points out that the government has responded to the possibility that compromising information resides on departmental and agency Web sites by removing or modifying information; establishing firewalls around, or limiting access to, some data; or, in cases in which old information is of use, updates are not available. "While the Bush Administration has not issued a policy on agency Web sites and the proper way to handle sensitive information (reportedly, a set of guidelines is forthcoming), the Federal Bureau of Investigation (FBI) has issued an Internet content advisory, and Attorney General John Ashcroft's memorandum on the . . . FOIA . . . signals the administration's approach to information disclosure post–September 11."[40]

In an advisory dated January 17, 2002, the FBI offered guidance to government bodies on their Web site content. Seven questions posed in the advisory may assist government officials in evaluating their departmental and agency home pages:

1. Has the information been cleared and authorized for public release?

2. Does the information provide details concerning enterprise safety and security? Are there alternative means of delivering sensitive security information to the intended audience?

3. Is any personal data posted (such as biological data, addresses)?

4. How could someone intent on causing harm misuse this information?

5. Could this information be dangerous if it were used in conjunction with other publicly available data?

6. Could someone use the information to target your personnel or resources?

7. Many archives sites exist on the Internet, and that information removed from an official site might nevertheless remain publicly available elsewhere. [41]

Halchin believes that "the steps taken by government following 9-11 reflect a change in the balance between security and the right to information. For the foreseeable future, it appears that safeguarding the nation—an undertaking that has many components, including scrubbing potentially compromising information from government Web sites—will continue to trump other objectives and other values."[42]

In conclusion, the Bush administration has advanced two competing messages on e-government: (1) widespread dissemination of information and services to the public and government accountability to the governed and (2) permitting the removal and withholding of information once considered public and cautioning executive departments and agencies about the unintended consequences of releasing information. "Both messages have value, but the administration has failed to fashion a coherent message that incorporates both perspectives."[43] The contradictory messages "may thwart the promise of e-government."[44]

Department of Homeland Security. The congressional elections of November 2002 gave the Republican Party a clear majority in Congress and consolidated its control over the executive and legislative branches. One consequence was the easy passage of homeland security legislation and enactment of the Department of Homeland Security, which combined twenty-two agencies and was sought by a president who came to office seeking to diminish the role of government in the lives of Americans.

The newly created department (see Chapters 5 and 12) will have a profound impact on government on the Web as agencies leave their present home, enter the new department, and assume new responsibilities. For example, the Secret Service, formerly part of the Department of Treasury, will try to maintain its core missions (protecting the president, vice president, heads of state, and others) while reporting to a new secretary. A competition for money could threaten duties, such as investigating financial crimes and cyberattacks on the nation's banking and telecommunications infrastructure. The Federal Emergency Management Agency, formerly an independent agency, must coordinate the initial response of emergency service workers after a terrorism strike, while maintaining adequate funding for other federal disasters.

The General Accounting Office has predicted that it will take the new department at least ten years to function properly. Thus, to update this guide between its biannual publication, the Web site mentioned in the Preface will provide updated coverage of homeland security.

Electronic-Mail Messages

Most government bodies offer their Web site users an opportunity to send e-mail messages to their public information units or personnel. In an experiment conducted in 1998, *Government Computer News* tested how quickly twenty-six agencies responded to a request for information. "A dozen agencies responded almost immediately, but 10 agencies had not responded after two weeks."[45] The staff performing the test discovered that "there are few formal policies or procedures on dealing with e-mail questions from the public [, and,] in most cases, there's no structure in place as to who the e-mail should be referred to." Furthermore, only a "few agencies . . . see a flood of e-mail via their Web sites."[46] Have the results changed since this experiment was conducted? If the answer is negative, here is another complication in the achievement of e-government.

The option to send e-mail messages to an agency may not produce the results that the public expects. Sending e-mail messages to members of Congress, most likely, results in the receipt of a response via snail mail. If e-mail comprises records, then government bodies should preserve them; however, information requests do not comprise records. Readers interested in the issue should consult NARA for information on General Records Schedule 20 (GRS 20), which offers agencies guidance on how to maintain and release electronic records (for records schedules, see **http://www.archives.gov/records_ management/records_schedules.html**).

Closing Department of Interior Web Sites

Unrelated to the terrorist attacks of September 11, U.S. District Court Justice Royce Lamberth ordered Web sites of the Department of the Interior shutdown in December 2001 after it was alleged that, for years, the department had mismanaged funds intended for American Indians and after a computer security firm broke into departmental computer funds and reportedly cut a check from trust funds held for American Indians.[47] It took months for some agencies within the Department of the Interior to gain permission from the court-appointed special master to reopen their Web sites and restore e-mail capabilities. As of spring 2003, the home page of the Bureau of Indian Affairs remains closed. (For source material on the Indian Trust Assets Management, see **http://www.doi.gov/indiantrust/**.)

Web Sites Do Not Convey "Official" Information

Users of government Web sites might assume that the "informational matter" provided is the official version—in other words, the government stands behind the authority and reliability of all information and data presented. In fact, this is often not the case. A government body may retain a presentation copy of a print publication as the authentic version or the source of record. If there is no paper counterpart and if different versions exist, the questions becomes, "What version does the government stand behind?" The answer is often not apparent from using a Web site. More than that, a government body may not have developed a satisfactory answer to the question. Still, Web users should check the opening screens of a site, or the frequently asked questions, to see if the issue is addressed and what the answer is.

Digital watermarking is one means of ensuring the security and authenticity of digital photographs by embedding an encrypted image in the photograph, similar to the watermarks used on the redesigned $20, $50, and $100 bills. Other ways to combat fraud and enhance security exist and apply mostly to e-commerce. The information presented on the Web is not so protected, and thus the integrity of that information might be questioned.

Intellectual Property Rights

Publications coming from work prepared by U.S. government employees as part of their official duties tend not to be copyrighted. Anyone can use and reuse the information without having to gain permission from the issuing body or author. The same applies to data, even when the government makes those data available to a private publisher. That publisher might turn around and copyright the publication; however, the publisher is really copyrighting any value-added features (such as an introduction), any analysis of the data, data that the publisher compiled independently, and an index. If other publishers were to ask the issuing body for the same nonproprietary data, that body would probably comply with the request. One significant exception to this would be consulting and other contracted reports that the funding body lets the author have published as scholarly articles or as commercial books, thereby more broadly disseminating the results. Another exception is for software produced by government employees; in these instances, the government or the employee may be the copyright holder.

Free or Fee

Many government publications are publicly available free of charge. The Government Printing Office (GPO), however, maintains a sales program for some congressional and other publications, and the National Technical Information Service also sells information resources (see Chapters 3 and 4). STAT-USA, a collection of statistical data on trade that the Department of Commerce offers for Web users, is fee-based (see Chapter 8). To some extent, the public may bypass STAT-USA's fee by visiting a depository library because these libraries can provide free access on two workstations. (For the nearest depository, see "Locate Federal Depository Libraries by State or Area Code," **http://www.gpoaccess.gov/libraries.html**).

Clarity of URL Addresses

As this encyclopedic guide illustrates, access to government information resources can be complex. General government Web addresses tend to be intuitive, however. For example, the federal judiciary can be found at **http://www.uscourts.gov/** and, for Congress, the House of Representatives is at **http://www.house.gov/** and the Senate is at **http://www.senate.gov/.** A number of executive departments and agencies appear under **http://www.____.gov**. In the blank space, the information seeker inserts the abbreviation or name of the department (e.g., commerce) or agency (e.g., census and epa [for the Environmental Protection Agency]). The Department of Treasury, however, requires the insertion of *ustreas* in the blank space. Chapters 4 through 13 illustrate more complex addresses.

Navigating government Web sites is not necessarily intuitive. There is no standardized layout among them. There may or may not be a site map. Even when such a map exists, some resources may be difficult to find. Clearly, anyone using a government site should spend some time browsing it and seeing how the site presents information resources. Subsequent chapters will explain key terminology.

Congress, the judiciary, and the president may address any issue they choose. Likewise, the jurisdiction of departments and agencies may also be broad, making it difficult to anticipate with any degree of certainty what subjects they will address. Thus, it is impossible to produce a definitive subject categorization that defines the range of subjects with which a particular government body automatically deals. Consequently, those seeking government information may benefit from consulting the *United States Government Manual* (see **http://www.archives.gov/federal_register/ publications/government_manual.html**).

⟲ The Web in Political Campaigns

Beginning with the 1996 presidential and congressional elections, candidates used the Web to organize campaign events, send supporters e-mail updates, advance their positions, and define their opposition. With the primaries leading to the 2000 elections, candidates, such as John McCain, also used the Web to solicit campaign contributions and to recruit volunteers to their campaign. Now campaign Web sites frequently identify a candidate's position on numerous issues, offer press releases and news articles, provide surveys so that site visitors can express their views on various issues, offer photo opportunities, encourage people to work for the candidate, and enable visitors to sign up for e-mail updates and make campaign contributions, discover the candidate's campaign schedule, and find press information and opportunities to debate issues. Clearly, no serious candidate—or political party—would forego the use of the Internet as part of a campaign strategy, including taking out paid advertising that identifies the candidate's positions. At the same time, those navigating government sites must be aware of parodies of Web sites and of sites containing unsubstantiated stories. No doubt, once elected, these individuals will most likely regard the Internet as an essential means of communicating with those they represent. They may also demand that agencies expand their digital services to their constituents.

SUMMARY

The U.S. government actively disseminates a variety of publications—information, data, and records—to the public through the Web. These publications are delivered in various media (e.g., textual, video, or audio). There is, however, no guarantee that a publication will appear on a Web site for a long time or that all publications will be (or have been) preserved. Sites tend to be in a state of flux, adding new features and eliminating or consolidating old ones. Complicating matters, the public may experience problems in identifying the diverse array of information resources contained on a home page, especially those contained in a departmental or agency *library*—an archive of resources that may not be searchable by subject.

Even if the Web's role as the predominant means of delivering publications directly to the public continues to develop (see Chapter 14 for a detailed analysis of electronic government), it is highly doubtful that print publication will fade away entirely. Such publication remains a means (perhaps a secondary one) of informing the public. Nonetheless, Web resources, as already noted, represent more than just the equivalent to the print publication. There are government images, data sets, interactive maps, and other resources on the Web that have no print counterpart. Clearly, the information made available does more than promote the services and programs of government bodies. It informs the public and enables us to be more knowledgeable citizens, consumers, and voters. Furthermore, people use government Web sites to complete transactions (e.g., get or renew a passport or secure benefits). As some writers have noted, "according to an IRS news release of April 26, 2002, 39.5 million Americans filed their 2001 income taxes electronically in 2002, 6.6 million of these used home computers—a one-third jump from the previous year." They hypothesize that "linked to direct deposit and other commercial transaction systems, increasing numbers of citizens are avoiding long lines, complicated phone menu systems, and postal delays by using government transaction processing systems."[48]

Although the OMB has not done so, it could require executive departments and agencies to register with and report to the director of the OMB all existing Web sites that they create and subsequently maintain. "Beyond this requirement, agencies might be obligated to obtain OMB approval of new websites they propose to create." The director might also be "authorized to issue explicit website management guidelines for agency compliance. Such guidelines might be required to specify basic expectations concerning web site accessibility to the public, content, organization and layout, and information security and personal privacy."[49] Until some requirements are implemented, the guidelines and best practices issued by the World Web Federal Consortium will have to suffice. This document covers the development, maintenance, and enhancement of executive branch Web sites.[50]

Anyone visiting a government Web site appreciates an easy-to-follow layout that displays a site map and enables him or her to connect seamlessly to resources of that government department or agency. A site should offer appropriate links to related agencies and resources and a list of frequently asked questions, identify key services, and enable the visitor to conduct a search of the site by keyword. Items should not be buried in a searchable archive, and it should be possible to contact the Webmaster or other agency personnel if questions arise and then to receive a timely response. A privacy statement should be prominently displayed, and the site should not abuse the public's trust (e.g., by using persistent cookies). There should also be good access to the site and its resources for those with disabilities, so that the site complies with federal law. Furthermore, explanation of the FOIA should be prominently displayed, as should any electronic records. When the organizational structure of a department or agency is complex and consists of subunits that have a presence on the Web, it should be easy to determine the type of activity in which each subunit engages. Hot links should be available to relevant sites, and those links should not be obsolete. When exiting a Web site or page, using the "back" function, the user should be able to do so and not be locked into one site or page. The government is making progress in addressing some of these points, but there is still no uniformity in site presentation within and across branches of government. Such uniformity, however, would be difficult to create and enforce. Agencies are also providing more digital resources in Spanish and other languages.

Finally, significant attention and resources have focused on the development of a government wide portal (see Chapter 3) and the improvement of agency search engines. Still, the capability of those search engines may be limited. Users may not be able to place much confidence in their ability to search the thousands of pages at that site. Compounding the problem, individual search engines use different terminology, and it may take some time to identify the proper term. Clearly, the search ability of a number of people far exceeds the capability of a number of agency search engines. More attention should be directed at the improvement of these search engines, because no governmentwide portal will totally replace the value of having such search engines.

Increased Web usability would require a significant outlay of resources, such as that anticipated with the *E-Government Act of 2002,* as well as staff training, a commitment to "customer service, and follow through to make information as easy to find as possible." A good model is a site of the National Cancer Institute (**http://www.cancer. gov/**), which has received usability awards (see **http://www.usability.gov/**).

NOTES

1. Gary D. Bass and David Plocher, "Finding Government Information: The Federal Information Locator System (FILS)," *Government Information Quarterly* 8 (1991): 13.

2. William Matthews, "Access Denied," *Federal Computer Week* 14 (May 29, 2000): 21.

3. William Matthews, "Archives Predicts Deluge," *Federal Computer Week* 14 (July 10, 2000): 14.

4. 44 *United States Code* 1901.

5. 44 *United States Code* 1902.

6. LeRoy C. Merritt, *The United States Government as Publisher* (Chicago: University of Chicago Press, 1943).

7. According to 44 *United States Code* 3301, " 'records' include [*sic*] all books, papers, maps, photographs, machine readable materials, or other documentary materials, regardless of physical form or characteristic, made or received by an agency of the United States Government under Federal law or in connection with the transaction of public business and preserved or appropriate for preservation by that agency or its legitimate successor as evidence of the organization, functions, policies, decisions, procedures, operations, or other activities of the Government or because of the informational value of data in them. Library and museum material made or acquired and preserved solely for reference or exhibition purposes, extra copies of documents preserved only for convenience of reference, and stocks of publications and of processed documents are not included."

   For examples of government records, see 44 *United States Code* 3301 (federal records), 44 *United States Code* 2203 (presidential records), and 44 *United States Code* 2201 (personal records of the president). The index to the *United States Code* identifies other types of records.

8. David Bearman and Jennifer Trant, "Electronic Records Research Working Meeting, May 28–30, 1997: A Report from the Archives Community," *Bulletin of the American Society for Information Science* 24 (February/March 1998): 14.

9. Harold C. Relyea, "Public Access through the Freedom of Information and Privacy Acts," in *Federal Information Policies in the 1980's: Conflicts and Issues*, eds. Peter Hernon and Charles R. McClure (Norwood, NJ: Ablex, 1987): 52.

10. Bill Murray, "Web Site Saves Money for NSF," *Government Computer News* 17 (October 26, 1998): 32.

11. Office of Management and Budget, "Information Quality" (October 1, 2002): 5. Available: **http://www.whitehouse.gov/omb/inforeg/igg-oct2002.pdf.**

12. J. Timothy Sprehe, "Data Quality Politics," *Federal Computer Week* 16 (July 29, 2002): 36.

13. Robert Gellman, "Agencies Need to Ponder Web's Long-term Role," *Government Computer News* 17 (October 12, 1998): 22.

14. "This Is Citizen-Centered?" *Federal Computer Week* 16 (December 9, 2002): 3.

15. See General Accounting Office, *Electronic Government: Selection and Implementation of the Office of Management and Budget's 24 Initiatives*, GAO-03-229 (Washington, D.C.: GAO, November 2002). Available: **http://www.gao.gov/ cgi-bin/getrept?GAO-03-229.**

16. Steve Kelman, "Broadening E-gov's Reach," *Federal Computer Week* 16 (September 2, 2002): 52. See also William Matthews, "Survey: Fed Web Sites Still Need Work," *Federal Computer Week* 16 (August 16, 2002): 13.

17. Gary Marchionini, "Co-evolution of User and Organizational Interfaces: A Longitudinal Case Study of WWW Dissemination of National Statistics," *Journal of the American Society for Information Science and Technology* 53 (December 2002): 1192–1209.

18. *Chrysler Corporation v. Brown,* 441 U.S. 281 at 292 (1979).

19. Lotte E. Feinberg, "Homeland Security: Implications for Information Policy and Practice—First Appraisal," *Government Information Quarterly* 19 (2002): 269, 270.

20. Relyea, "Public Access," 66.

21. Robert Gellman, "Perspectives on Privacy and Terrorism: All Is not Lost—Yet," *Government Information Quarterly* 19 (2002): 261.

22. Jacob J. Lew, "Memorandum for the Heads of Executive Departments and Agencies: Privacy Policies on Federal Web Sites" (June 2, 1999). Available: **http://www.whitehouse.gov/omb/memoranda/m99-18.html.** See also Jacob J. Lew, "Memorandum for the Heads of Executive Departments and Agencies: Privacy Policies and Data Collection on Federal Web Sites" (June 22, 2000). Available: **http://www.whitehouse.gov/omb/memoranda/m00-13.html.**

23. Diane Frank, "OMB Counters 'Cookies,' " *Federal Computer Week* 14 (June 26, 2000): 10. See also Diane Frank, "Congress: Stay out of the Cookie Jar," *Federal Computer Week* 14 (July 31, 2000), 50. Please note that section 501 of the Transportation Appropriation law (December 2000) set a cookies prohibition for the agencies funded by the Treasury Appropriations tile of that statute, which includes entities within the Executive Office of the President .

    Section 501, to be more precise, prohibits funds appropriated by the legislation to be used by any executive agency to (1) collect, review, or create any aggregate list, derived by any means, that includes the collection of any personally identifiable information relating to an individual's access to or use of any federal government Internet site of the agency; or (2) enter into any agreement with a third party, including another government agency, to collect, review, or obtain any aggregate list, derived from any means, that includes the collection of any personally identifiable information relating to an individual's access to or use of any nongovernmental Internet site. These limitations do not apply to any (1) record of aggregate data that does not identify particular persons; (2) voluntary submission of personally identifiable information; (3) action taken for law enforcement, regulatory, or supervisory purposes, in accordance with applicable law; and (4) action that is a system security action taken by the operator of an Internet site and is necessarily incident to the rendition of the Internet site services or to the protection of the rights or property of the provider of the Internet site.

24. Ben White, "Americans Favor U.S. Web Services," Washingtonpost.com, 29 September 2000, p. A31. Available: **http://www.washingtonpost.com/wp-dyn/articles/ A40872-2000Sep28.html.**

25. William Matthews, "NARA Rethinks E-records," *Federal Computer Week* 16 (August 19, 2001): 48.

26. William Matthews, "First Y2K, Now 'Titanic,' " *Federal Computer News* 14 (March 20, 2000):14.

27. Ibid.

28. J. Timothy Sprehe, "Find a Balance between Information Access, Security," *Federal Computer Week* 13 (August 2, 1999): 25.

29. Ibid.

30. See Ellen Altman and Peter Hernon, *Research Misconduct* (Norwood, NJ: Ablex, 1997); and Anne P. Mintz, ed., *Web of Deception: Misinformation on the Internet* (Medford, NJ: Information Today, 2002).

31. "Hackers can gain access to sensitive medical and financial information on nearly every American because of widespread security weaknesses in agency computer systems." See "GAO: Public Info Open to Hackers," *Federal Computer Week* 12 (September 28, 1998): 1.

32. Merry Mayer, "Statistics Bureau Will Post No Data before Its Time," *Government Computer News* 17 (November 23, 1998): 1, 8.

33. See Peter Hernon, "Disinformation and Misinformation through the Internet: Findings of an Exploratory Study," *Government Information Quarterly* 12 (1995): 133–39.

34. Richard Monastersky, "Research Groups Accuse Education Department of Using Ideology in Decisions about Data," *The Chronicle of Higher Education* (November 25, 2002). Available: **http://chronicle.copm/daily/2002/11;2002112501n.htm**.

35. "Unscientific Findings" (editorial), *The Boston Globe* (January 17, 2003), p. A18.

36. Thomas Oliphant, "Opinion: An Effort to Deceive Hospital 'Reform,' " *Boston Globe,* 21 January 2003, p. A11.

37. See Harold C. Relyea, ed., "Symposium Issue: Issues in Homeland Security and Information," *Government Information Quarterly* 19 (2002): 213–88; Carl Peckinpaugh, "FOIA on the Block," *Federal Computer Week* 16 (October 14, 2002): 46. OMB Watch keeps a list of information removed from government Web sites following 9-11. Available: **http://www.ombwatch.org/article/ articleview/213/1/104/**.
      Examples include President Bush's reinterpretation of the *Presidential Records Act* to place new restrictions on the release of records from previous White House administrations; consideration of replacing new restrictions on "sensitive but unclassified information (it is left to agencies to determine what fits into this category); and draft rules on the disclosure of some sensitive research (limit publication of some federal research and other government-owned data that would be classified as "sensitive homeland security information." See also William Matthews, "Removal of Web Info Concerns Democrats," *Federal Computer Week* 16 (November 4, 2002): 45. Most relevant to any discussion of classification policy is President Bush's Executive Order 13292 on classified national security information, signed March 23, 2003 (see **http://www.fas.org/sgp/bush/eoamend.html**).

38. Harold C. Relyea, "Homeland Security and Information," *Government Information Quarterly* 19 (2002): 213.

39. Ibid., 217, 218.

40. L. Elaine Halchin, "Electronic Government in the Age of Terrorism," *Government Information Quarterly* 19 (2002): 245.

41. Ibid., 247. Federal Bureau of Investigation, National Infrastructures Protection Center, Internet Content Advisory: Considering the Unintended Audience, Advisory 02-002 (January 17, 2002). Available: **http://www.nipc.gov/warnings/advisories/2002/02-001.htm**.

42. Halchin, "Electronic Government in the Age of Terrorism," 248.

43. Ibid., 251.

44. Ibid., 249.

45. Christopher J. Dorobek, "GCN Test: Agencies Vary in Handling of Online Queries," *Government Computer News* 17 (September 7, 1998): 1, 83.

46. Ibid., 83.

47. The Individual Indian Monies is a series of accounts started in 1887 when the federal government forced Indian tribes off ninety million acres of their land. In return, they and their heir were granted royalties from the sale of oil, gas, timber, mineral, and other rights on an additional eleven million acres. The fund now generates more than $500 million a year to at least 300,000 account holders, although many records have been lost or incompetently kept for decades that the government cannot provide an accurate history for a single account.
   In 1996, Indians filed suit and claimed that the government owes them at least $10 billion in lost or missing funds. The case still resides in federal District Court.

48. Gary Marchionini, Hanan Samet, and Larry Brandt, "Digital Government," *Communications of the ACM* 46 (January 2003): 26.

49. Harold C. Relyea, "Paperwork Reduction Act Reauthorization and Government Information Management Issues," unpublished (Washington, D.C.: Congressional Research Service, 2000).

50. World Wide Web Federal Consortium, "Guidelines and Best Practices" (1995) and revised in November 1996. Available: **http://www.dtic.mil/staff/cthomps/ guidelines/**. This document was revised in July 1999 (**http://www.oip.usdoj.gov/ oa/fedweb.guide/**).

URL Site Guide for This Chapter

Home Page
Department of State
http://www.state.gov/

Headlines: Global Alert and Consular Services
http://travel.state.gov/

Information Quality
http://www.state.gov/misc/13864.htm

Chesapeake Bay Program
http://www.chesapeakebay.net

Home Page
National Aeronautics and Space Administration
http://www.nasa.gov/home/index.html

Mars images
http://www.msss.com/mars_images/

Home Page
Environmental Protection Agency
http://www.epa.gov/

Clean up Dumptown
http://www.epa.gov/recyclecity/

Recursos en Español
http://www.epa.gov/espanol/

Home Page
Department of the Interior
http://www.interior.gov/

Mirror Site (Spanish)
http://www.doi.gov/doipress/spanish/main.htm

Maps of Elevation and Vegetation Growth
Geological Survey
http://www-atlas.usgs.gov/atlasvue.html

Virtual Tour of Historic Harpers Ferry (WV)
National Park Service
http://www.nps.gov/hafe/home.htm

Bidding on Wild Horses and Burros

Bureau of Land Management
http://www.adoptahorse.blm.gov/

Indian Trust Assets Management
http://www.doi.gov/indiantrust/

Best Sites

GovExec.com
http://www.govexec.com/bestfeds/

Home Page
Department of the Treasury
http://www.ustreas.gov/

Coinage
United States Mint
http://www.usmint.gov/

Games for Kids
United States Mint
http://www.usmint.gov/kids/index.cfm?flash=yes&Filecontents=kids/games/index.cfm

Home Page
Internal Revenue Service
http://www.irs.gov/

Income Tax forms
Internal Revenue Service
http://www.irs.ustreas.gov/formspubs/index.html/

Online Purchases (e.g., t-bills)
Bureau of the Public Debt
http://www.publicdebt.treas.gov/

Home Page
Commerce Department
http://www.commerce.gov/

Statistical Data
Bureau of the Census
http://www.census.gov/

Home Page
National Oceanic and Atmospheric Administration
http://www.noaa.gov/

Starting a Businesses
Small Business Administration
http://www.sbaonline.sba.gov/starting/

Home Page
National Institutes of Health
Department of Health and Human Resources
http://www.nih.gov

Home Page
Department of the Army
Department of Defense
http://www.army.mil

Home Page
Department of the Navy
Department of Defense
http://www.navy.mil

Buying Property from Government (Homes)
Department of Housing and Urban Development
http://www.hud.gov/homes/homesforsale.cfm

Information on Airport Delays
Department of Transportation
Federal Aviation Administration
http://www.fly.faa.gov/

Health
Healthfinder®
http://www.healthfinder.gov/

Student Financial Aid
Department of Education
http://www.fafsa.ed.gov/

Acrobat Reader
Adobe Systems Inc.
http://access.adobe.com

Electronic Commerce
U.S. Postal Service
http://www.usps.com

Home Page
Bureau of Labor Statistics
Department of Labor
http://www.bls.gov/

Cookie policy: U.S. Mint
Department of the Treasury
http://www.usmint.gov/policy/policy/index.cfm?action=full#cookies
http://www.usmint.gov/index.cfm?flash=yes

Home Page
White House
http://www.whitehouse.gov/

Home Page
National Archives and Records Administration
http://www.archives.gov/

Clinton Presidential Materials Project
http://www.clinton.archives.gov/

NARA Freedom of Information Act (FOIA) Home Page
http://www.archives.gov/research_room/foia_reading_room/foia_reading_room.html

Public Availability and Use of Federal Records
http://www.archives.gov/about_us/regulations/part_1250.html

Records Schedules
http://www.archives.gov/records_management/records_schedules.html

United States Government Manual
http://www.archives.gov/federal_register/publications/government_manual.html

Section 508
(Workforce Investment Act)
General Services Administration
http://www.section508.gov/

Mapping Tool

GeoMAC
http://www.geomac.gov/

Interactive Maps

International Trade Administration
Department of Commerce
http://ese.export.gov/

FOIA Page

Department of Justice
http://www.usdoj.gov/04foia/index.html

CIA for Kids
Central Intelligence Agency
http://www.odci.gov/cia/ciakids/

Congress

House of Representatives
http://www.house.gov/

Senate
http://www.senate.gov/

Home Page
Library of Congress
http://www.loc.gov

Locate Federal Depository Libraries by State or Area Code

Government Printing Office
http://www.gpo.access.gov/libraries.
html/

Home Page
Judicial Branch
http://www.uscourts.gov/

FirstGov
http://www.firstgov.gov/

Home Page
National Cancer Institute
http://www.cancer.gov/

Usability Focus
http://www.usability.gov/

Internet Survey
http://www.pewtrust.org/pdf/vf_pew_internet_
e-citizens.pdf

Chapter 2

Government: Structure and Types of Information Sources

Understanding and using information or publications produced by the U.S. government requires knowledge about how the federal government functions on a constitutional and political level. Regardless of whether one is searching for information on the Web or through traditional print sources, many of these works can be used effectively if one understands how different types of publications relate directly to the structure and process of the government itself. This chapter briefly explains how the federal government works and the types of publications that it produces.

The U.S. federal government, as set by the Constitution,[1] creates two political centers: one central and the other regional. The central realm refers to the national government, and the regional includes subnational state and local governments. The central government consists of three branches: the legislative, the executive, and the judiciary. Furthermore, the Constitution gives specific roles, as well as shared obligations, to these three branches. These roles and obligations are enforced through a system of "checks and balances" designed by the nation's founders to ensure the proper distribution of power, consultation, and information sharing among the three and with the people. The primary activity of Congress is legislative (including oversight, initiating legislation, and appropriating funds), and that of the executive branch is administration (carrying out the policies established by Congress and the president). Of course, the executive branch is also involved in policy determination and execution, and Congress has administrative responsibilities. The judicial branch interprets the Constitution and the laws, thereby guiding the other two branches.

LEGISLATIVE BRANCH

The legislative branch consists of Congress—the House of Representatives and Senate— and its support agencies. Article I, section 8, of the Constitution gives Congress the sole power to assess and collect taxes, to regulate both interstate and foreign commerce, to coin money, to establish post offices and post roads, to establish courts inferior to the Supreme Court, to declare war, and to raise and maintain an army and navy. Congress is also empowered to "provide for calling forth the Militia to execute the Laws of the Union, suppress Insurrections and repell Invasions" and to "make all Laws which shall be necessary and proper for carrying into Execution the foregoing Powers, and all other Powers vested by this Constitution in the Government of the United States, or in any Department or Officer thereof." Congress also has the right to propose amendments to the Constitution, to call a constitutional convention if two-thirds of the state legislatures want changes to the Constitution, and to oversee the administrative organization of the government. "Congress' power of the purse is one of its greatest prerogatives and consumes a large portion of the institution's time."[2]

The Senate approves or disapproves most high-level presidential appointments and all treaties. The House has the sole power to impeach and the Senate tries impeachments. In addition to the standing committees (see Figure 2.1 for a list), the House and Senate have committees of the whole and each may use special or select committees. Some panels—known as joint committees—include representatives from both chambers. "Committees have rightly been called the 'workshops' of Congress. It is in committee that most of the legislative detail work takes place."[3] Committees also have oversight and informing functions.

Other areas rich in public information, and vital to keep the public informed, come from the daily transcripts of each chamber's floor proceedings (as captured by the daily publication of the *Congressional Record*). Further information about the structure and function of either chamber can be found in the respective offices of the party leadership.[4] Several congressional support agencies (see Figure 2.1) provide information services, manage printing and distribution of publications, analyze the budget, conduct audits, and so on.

Figure 2.1. Examples of Legislative Branch Bodies.

House (Standing Committees)
- Committee on Agriculture
- Committee on Appropriations
- Committee on Armed Services
- Committee on the Budget
- Committee on Education and the Workforce
- Committee on Energy and Commerce
- Committee on Financial Services
- Committee on Government Reform
- Committee House Administration
- Committee on International Relations

- Committee on the Judiciary
- Committee on Resources
- Committee on Rules
- Committee on Science
- Committee on Small Business
- Committee on Standards of Official Conduct
- Committee on Transportation and Infrastructure
- Committee on Veteran Affairs
- Committee on Ways and Means

House (Special, Select, and Other)
- Permanent Select Committee on Intelligence
- Select Committee on Homeland Security

Senate (Standing Committees)
- Committee on Agriculture, Nutrition, and Forestry
- Committee on Appropriations
- Committee on Armed Services
- Committee on Banking, Housing, and Urban Affairs
- Committee on Budget
- Committee on Commerce, Science, and Transportation
- Committee on Energy and Natural Resources
- Committee on Environment and Public Works
- Committee on Finance
- Committee on Foreign Relations
- Committee on Governmental Affairs
- Committee on Health, Education, Labor and Pensions
- Committee on Judiciary
- Committee on Rules and Administration
- Committee on Small Business and Entrepreneurship
- Committee on Veterans' Affairs

Senate (Special, Select, and Other)
- Senate Select Committee On Intelligence
- Senate Select Committee On Ethics
- Senate Committee On Indian Affairs
- Senate Special Committee On Aging

Joint Committees
- Joint Committee on Taxation
- Joint Committee on the Library
- Joint Economic Committee
- Joint Committee on Printing
  There are also leadership offices for both chambers

Figure 2.1. (*Cont.*)

House
- Office of the Speaker
- Office of the Majority Leader
- Office of the Minority Leader
- Office of the Majority Whip
- Office of the Democratic Whip

Senate
- Majority Leader
- Minority Leader
- Assistant Majority Leader
- Assistant Minority Leader

Legislative Agencies and Commissions
- Library of Congress
- Government Printing Office
- General Accounting Office
- Congressional Budget Office
- Architect of the Capitol
- Office of Compliance
- Medical Payment Advisory Commission
- National Bipartisan Commission on the Future of Medicare

EXECUTIVE BRANCH

The executive branch is a dynamic political organization. Its policy structure constantly adapts to the following changes in the national political agenda as

- Presidents assume and leave office

- Department secretaries and other top personnel leave office

- Executive issues and congressional priorities shift in order to deal with current national problems

- Members of the public demand new or improved public services

- Inefficiencies are identified

- The inability of agencies to meet their responsibilities is identified

The executive's traditional organizational unit is a department more or less responsible for a homogeneous group of programs established by Congress and the president to support the major obligations of national government responsibility as outlined by public laws enacted legislative session. The department's head, called a secretary, is usually a member of the president's "cabinet." Currently, this body of senior presidential advisors consists of fifteen departments (see Figure 2.2).

Figure 2.2. Examples of Executive Branch Bodies.*

Executive Office of the President
> Council of Economic Advisors, Council on Environmental Quality, Domestic Policy Council, National Security Council, Office of Administration, Office of Management and Budget, Office of National Drug Control Policy, Office of Science and Technology Policy, Office of the United States Trade Representative, White House Office

Cabinet Level Offices

Department of Agriculture
> Agricultural Research Service; Cooperative State Research, Education, and Extension Service; Economic Research Service; Education & Extension Service; Farm Service Agency; Forest Service; National Agricultural Library; National Agricultural Statistics Service; Natural Resources Conservation Service; Risk Management Agency

Department of Commerce
> Bureau of the Census, Bureau of Economic Analysis, Bureau of Industry and Security, Economic & Statistics Administration, International Trade Administration, National Institute of Standards & Technology, National Ocean Service, National Oceanic & Atmospheric Administration, National Technical Information Service, National Telecommunications & Information Administration, National Weather Service, Patent and Trademark Office

Department of Defense
> Air Force, Army, Defense Technical Information Center, Joint Chiefs of Staff, Marine Corps, National Imagery and Mapping Agency, Navy

Department of Education
> Educational Resources Information Center, National Library of Education

Department of Energy
> Energy Information Administration; Los Alamos National Laboratory; Office of Economic Impact and Diversity; Office of Environment, Safety and Health; Office of Science; Office of Scientific and Technical Information; Southwestern Power Administration

Department of Health and Human Services
> Agency for Healthcare Research and Quality, Centers for Disease Control, Food and Drug Administration, National Institutes of Health (including the National Library of Medicine), Office of Research Integrity

Department of Homeland Security
> Federal Emergency Management Agency, U.S. Customs Service, U.S. Secret Service, and other agencies will relocate to this site

Figure 2.2. (*Cont.*)

Department of Housing and Urban Development
> Housing and Urban Development Library

Department of the Interior
> Bureau of Indian Affairs; Bureau of Land Management; Bureau of Reclamation; Minerals Management Service; National Park Service; Office of Surface Mining; U.S. Fish and Wildlife Service; U.S. Geological Survey

Department of Justice
> Federal Bureau of Investigation, Federal Bureau of Prisons

Department of Labor
> Bureau of Labor Statistics, Mine Safety and Health Administration, Occupational Safety and Health Administration, Women's Bureau

Department of State
> Bureau of Consular Affairs, Freedom of Information Office, Historian's Office

Department of Transportation
> Bureau of Transportation Statistics, Federal Aviation Administration, Federal Railroad Administration

Department of the Treasury
> Bureau of Engraving and Printing, Internal Revenue Service, U.S. Mint

Department of Veterans Affairs

Major Independent Establishments and Government Corporations

> African Development Foundation
> American Battles Monument Committee
> Central Intelligence Agency
> Commodity Futures Trading Commission
> Consumer Product Safety Commission
> Corporation for National Service
> Defense Nuclear Facilities Safety Board
> Environmental Protection Agency
> Equal Employment Opportunity Commission
> Export-Import Bank of the United States
> Farm Credit Administration
> Federal Communications Commission
> Federal Depository Insurance Corporation
> Federal Election Commission
> Federal Energy Regulatory Commission
> Federal Housing Finance Board
> Federal Labor Relations Authority
> Federal Maritime Commission
> Federal Reserve System

Federal Trade Commission
General Services Administration
Institute of Museum and Library Services
Inter-American Foundation
Merit Systems Protection Board
National Aeronautics and Space Administration
National Archives and Records Administration
National Commission on Libraries and Information Science
National Credit Union Administration
National Endowment for the Arts
National Endowment for the Humanities
National Mediation Board
National Railroad Passenger Corporation
National Science Foundation
National Transportation Safety Board
Nuclear Regulatory Commission
Office of Government Ethics
Office of Personnel Management
Office of Special Counsel
Overseas Private Investment Corp.
Peace Corps
Pension Benefit Guarantee Corporation
Postal Rate Commission
Securities and Exchange Commission
Selective Service System
Small Business Administration
Social Security Administration
Tennessee Valley Authority
Trade and Development Agency
United States Agency for International Development
United States Architectural and Transportation Barriers Compliance Board
United States Civil Rights Commission
United States Holocaust Memorial Museum
United States International Trade Commission
United States Postal Service
United States Trade and Development Agency
Voice of America

Quasi-Official Agencies

Legal Services Corporation
Smithsonian Institution
United States Institute of Peace

Boards, Commission, and Committees

Advisory Council on Historic Preservation

*The *United States Government Manual* provides additional examples.

A special political and administrative enclave, the Executive Office of the President, contains "personnel, fiscal, and planning management entities to assist the president."[5] For instance, the Office of Management and Budget and the Council of Economic Advisors are part of the Executive Office.

Complicating this administrative picture are numerous independent executive establishments and regulatory agencies. A large portion of rules and regulations created by these noncabinet agencies regulate members of the public whose activity might come under their authority. There are many boards and commissions that have no consequential regulatory responsibilities but serve as information-gathering and storage institutions. Other quasi-official agencies serve as public corporations to deliver specific educational or nonprofit purposes Still other government corporations have revenue-producing potential because they recover fees or specific taxes tied to particular industries or commercial activities. Regarding corporations, there is no commonly accepted doctrine that guides their structure or activities. Examples include the Federal Deposit Insurance Corporation and the Tennessee Valley Authority.[6]

JUDICIAL BRANCH

As specified in Article III, section 1, of the Constitution, "The judicial Power of the United States, shall be vested in one supreme Court, and in such inferior Courts as the Congress from time to time ordain and establish." Unlike the president and Congress, courts do not initiate actions; they dispose of matters brought before them on the initiative of outsiders. They exercise judicial power through their ability to "decide 'cases' and 'controversies' in conformity with law and by the methods established by the usages and principles of law."[7] Figure 2.3 provides an overview of the structure of the national judicial system.

COMPLEXITY OF THE STRUCTURE

Anyone who seeks access to federal government information resources, whether in print or on the Web, cannot simply go to a single finding aid, search engine, or Web site and request everything available on a given subject. Instead, one must have some knowledge of the organizational structure of government and then, for instance, proceed to the Web site of a particular body or unit in the hope that a particular department or agency has organized its information usefully.[8] As discussed in Chapter 3, finding aids" and search engines perform a useful function in that they cut across this complicated organizational structure to bring widely distributed information resources together through one search structure. Nonetheless, those tools useful for conducting subject searches tend to be selective and do not disclose the full range of *public* information products and services that the federal government offers. Therefore, it is critical that users understand the specific types of publications and information resources produced.

Figure 2.3. Examples of Judicial Branch Bodies.*

Courts
- Supreme Court
- U.S. Circuit Court of Appeals
- District and Bankruptcy Courts
- Special courts, that is, Court of International Trade, Territorial Courts, U.S. Court of Appeals for the Armed Services, U.S. Court of Federal Claims, U.S. Tax Court, U.S. Court of Appeals for Veterans Claims

Administration of the Courts
- Administrative Office of the United States Courts
- Federal Judicial Center
- The Judicial Conference of the United States
- U.S. Sentencing Commission

*The *United States Government Manual* provides additional examples.

TYPES OF PUBLICATIONS

The federal government produces at least twenty-six types of publications that it publishes and might place on the Web. As Figure 2.4 indicates, the executive branch, followed by the legislative branch, offers the widest variety. Given that the judicial branch interprets laws, it is not surprising that it offers the fewest types. No type of publication is unique to one branch of government. Although bills and resolutions originate in Congress, the administration often plays a role in shaping legislation and offers suggested language for draft legislation. Many executive agencies issue bulletins and technical documentation. In the legislative branch, the General Accounting Office, the Congressional Budget Office, and the Library of Congress (LC) issue bulletins, and the LC also offers technical documentation. Each chamber of Congress produces a journal (the Senate also has an executive journal) and transcripts of floor proceedings—the *Congressional Record*—and the comparable executive "journal" or gazette is the *Federal Register*.

Bills and Resolutions

Bills and resolutions are the formal documents that Congress uses when it is drafting and enacting specific legislation. Written by members of Congress, their staff, special interest groups, or the administration, these documents may become statutory law, or the so-called law of the land. As such, they are primary source material, critical for research and investigation and for the public to understand the framework of rules and regulations that the executive and legislative branches propose and use to conduct their mutual business.

Figure 2.4. Types of Government Publications.*

Executive Branch	Legislative Branch	Judicial Branch
Presidential directives, orders, and OMB circulars	Bills and resolutions	Orders
Bulletins	Bulletins	
Catalogs (bibliographies, abstracts, lists, and indexes)	Catalogs (bibliographies, abstracts, lists, and indexes)	
Circulars, directives, rules, and regulations	Circulars, directives, rules, and regulations	Rules
Decisions and opinions	Decisions and opinions	Decisions and opinions
Directories	Directories	Directories
Flyers, brochures, booklets, pamphlets, and fact sheets	Flyers, brochures, booklets, pamphlets, and fact sheets	Flyers, brochures, booklets, pamphlets, and fact sheets
Forms (e.g., survey, grants, and compliance—tax)	Forms	Forms
Handbooks, manuals, and guides	Handbooks, manuals, and guides	Handbooks, manuals, and guides
Hearings	Hearings	Hearings
(*Federal Register*)	Journals and proceedings	
Laws (statutory and administrative)	Laws (statutory and administrative)	
Maps, atlases, and charts	Maps, atlases, and charts	
Monographs (substantial publications)—books	Monographs (substantial publications)—books	
Motion pictures and sound recordings	Motion pictures and sound recordings	
Patents	(copyrights)	
Periodicals and newspapers (published on a periodic basis; more substantial than newsletters and bulletins), and newsletters	Periodicals and newsletters	Periodicals and newsletters
Photographs and images (e.g., satellite)	Photographs	Photographs
Posters	Posters	
Proceedings of symposia, workshops, conferences, hearings, etc.	Proceedings of symposia, workshops, conferences, hearings, etc.	Proceedings of symposia, workshops, conferences, hearings, etc.

Executive Branch	Legislative Branch	Judicial Branch
Public notices and news (press) releases	Public notices and news (press) releases	Public notices and news (press) releases
Reports (one time and recurring)	Reports (one time and recurring)	Reports (one time and recurring)
Statistics	Statistics	Statistics
Technical documentation (e.g., relating to software)	Technical documentation (e.g., relating to paper)	
Treaties and international agreements	Treaties and international agreements	

*Adapted from "Types of Publications Included in the Depository Library Program,"
Administrative Notes [Office of the Superintendent of Documents, Government Printing Office]
11, no. 14 (June 30, 1990): 3–8 (Appendix II).

Congress provides access to bills and resolutions via the Web (through **http://www.gpoaccess.gov/bills.index.html**). The Government Printing Office (GPO), through its sales program, sells copies of bills and resolutions (see **http://bookstore.gpo.gov/**), but congressional committees provide paper copies of them for free as long as supplies last. The bills may also be identified using the congressional Web page THOMAS (see **http://thomas.loc.gov/**). The House of Representatives has a Documents Room (telephone: 202-225-3456), which provides one copy of a House bill or resolution free of charge; the Senate also has a Documents Room, but it does not directly serve the public. Another alternative is to contact a member of Congress—a representative or Senator—for a paper copy.

⬦ Bulletins

Many executive departments and agencies publish "bulletins," which are recurring publications in a series that convey research, specialized information, or specific legal/regulatory information (see also the section on "circulars") . For instance there is the *U.S. Geological Survey Bulletin* (**http://pubs.usgs.gov/products/books/bulletins.html**) and the *NLM* [National Library of Medicine] *Technical Bulletin* (**http://www.nlm.nih.gov/pubs/techbull/tb.html**).

⬦ Catalogs

This category actually encompasses catalogs, bibliographies, abstracts, lists, and indexes. Executive departments and agencies, as well as congressional committees and agencies, issue lists of their respective publications or bibliographic guides to research they conduct. These, however, are not always comprehensive or current. An example of a general, but still not comprehensive, index is the GPO's *Catalog of United States Government Publications* (see **http://www.gpoacces.gov/cgp/index.html**). The GPO also has a *Sales Product Catalog* (**http://www.bookstore. gpo.gov/**) for items in its sales program; information on GPO's home page explains how to place orders. Department and agency Web sites often have "libraries" or collections of their publications. A number of these publications, available in .pdf, can be downloaded and then read using the Adobe Acrobat Reader (government sites provide instructions on how to do so).

↗ Circulars, Directives, Rules, and Regulations

Like bulletins, circulars are recurring publications in a series. The Office of Management and Budget regards both circulars and bulletins as

 major tools used by the Executive Office of the President to exercise managerial and policy direction over federal agencies. Circulars and Bulletins generally promote government effectiveness by providing uniform guidance to agencies. They provide policy guidance or processes over a broad range of subjects, ranging from detailed instructions on preparing agency budget requests to principles for determining allowable research costs at universities.[9]

Rules and regulations, often referred to as administrative law, represent the procedures by which an agency in the executive or legislative branch administers statutory law. Agencies frequently release draft regulations for public comment. Draft and final rules and regulations appear in the *Federal Register* (**http://www.gpoaccess.gov/fr/index.html**), and, when finalized, they are integrated into the *Code of Federal Regulations* (**http://www.gpoaccess.gov/cfr/index.html**).

Article I, section 5, of the Constitution, authorizes each chamber of Congress to determine the rules that will govern its respective proceedings. For example, the rules of the House of Representatives are found at **http://clerkweb.house.gov/** and are adopted for each session of Congress. Senate standing rules (**http://rules.senate.gov/senaterules/menu.htm**) continue from one Congress to another but are subject to change; these precedents encompass a broader concept; the precedents of the Senate comprise procedural law under which that chamber conducts its business. This type of law consists of standing rules, ad hoc orders, unanimous consent agreements of the Senate, and relevant statutory and constitutional provisions. The House has published precedents and a manual of procedure. The federal rules of civil and criminal procedure are in the *United States Code* (**http://www.gpoaccess.gov/uscode/index.html**).

↗ Decisions and Opinions

The courts, regulatory agencies, the attorney general, the military, and the comptroller general (General Accounting Office) produce official decisions and opinions for interpreting public laws and regulations.

↗ Directories

These publications identify officials of government agencies, agency resources, government bodies, places, and organizations. Web sites contain many such lists for answering "fact-type" questions and for making referral. One example is the *Congressional*

Directory (**http://www.gpoaccess.gov/cdirectory/index.html**),which provides an overview of Congress—the committees, members, and assorted other information about the legislative branch, the press, and so on. Increasingly, however, many agencies and offices are offering databases of personnel and office descriptions that slowly replace these earlier forms of published directories.

☞ Flyers, Brochures, Booklets, Pamphlets, and Fact Sheets

This type of publication offers overviews, explanations, and procedures (e.g., for applying for assistance). Such publications inform the public about government programs and services, and might offer suggestions, ideas, and techniques for how people can lead better, or at least more comfortable or enjoyable, lives.

☞ Forms

These constitute the data or paperwork members of the public must complete to be in compliance with federal laws, regulations, or gain eligibility to participate in the many government programs or services. Income tax forms and census surveys are examples. The U.S. Postal Service also has special forms, printed by the GPO, for mailing and certifying the receipt of a package or letter.

☞ Handbooks, Manuals, and Guides

This type provides synopses, descriptions, or analyses of significant developments and issues. These publications may provide a general overview of a topic or represent a compilation of factual information.

☞ Hearings

Congressional hearings are held either in public or in closed session. They enable members of Congress to determine whether a particular action is necessary, to see whether legislation is warranted, or to draw public attention to an issue. They afford an opportunity to collect information from informed sources, to present a variety of viewpoints, to educate the public about an issue, or to call attention to the consequences of an action. Congressional hearings are either for an *oversight* purpose (i.e., to review existing laws, program effectiveness, or administrative actions or indiscretions) or a *legislative* purpose (i.e., to examine legislation before Congress or a subject on which legislation is contemplated). There are also investigative or fact-finding hearings. Congressional committees place prepared statements from numerous hearings on their Web sites, and usually do so in a timely manner. These statements are included in subsequently published hearing transcripts.

Executive agencies also hold hearings, but these are infrequently published and may remain in transcript form in the office files of the agency or at the National Archives and Records Administration (NARA), where the public can inspect them at a later date. Courts of the judicial branch may also conduct hearings and occasionally releases them (or related attorney briefs) through the Web.

ᗕ Journals and Proceedings

These serve as the records of each session of Congress (see Chapter 4 on the legislative branch). The journals are the minutes or summary of the actions and activities of each chamber of Congress (e.g., the *House Journal* and the *Senate Journal*), and proceedings (e.g., the *Congressional Record;* **http://www.gpoaccess.gov/crecord/index. html**) contain the debates and speeches delivered on the floor of each chamber, as well as assorted other material (for monitoring the progress of legislation through Congress).

ᗕ Laws

Statutes, the culmination of the legislative process, provide the content of enacted public laws. The *Statutes at Large* is a chronological reprinting of the laws as enacted in each session of Congress. It includes the complete text—all the sections and provisions. The *United States Code,* on the other hand, distributes federal statutes by placing their provisions in the organized code of operative law.

ᗕ Maps, Atlases, and Charts

Government agencies, such as the U.S. Geological Survey, the National Oceanic and Atmospheric Administration, and the National Imagery and Mapping Agency, produce maps, charts, and some atlases (see Chapter 11). Some Web sites provide interactive maps, and both NARA and the LC have historical maps.

ᗕ Monographs

This type refers to the many books that the government produces. These books cover a wide variety of topics and can be quite substantial in length.

ᗕ Motion Pictures and Sound Recordings

LC is a major repository for this type of government publication. For instance, its American Memory covers "historical collections for the national digital library" (**http://memory.loc.gov/ammem/amhome.html**). The "motion picture collections" (**http://memory.loc.gov/ammem/papr/mpixhome.html**) covers "early motion pictures, 1897–1920." One subset of this collection is "the Spanish-American War in motion pictures, 1898–1901:" fifty-five films of the war showing "scenes of troops, ships, notable figures, parades, and other war-time events."

This type of publication might also include videotapes and audio recordings; the government produces an extensive array of audiovisual resources. Chapter 6, for example, covers the National Technical Information Service and its National Audiovisual Center.

☞ Patents

A patent for an invention is a grant by the federal government of exclusive rights to an inventor. Awarded by the Patent and Trademark Office, the patent right extends to the entire United States and its territories and possessions for a period of seventeen years.

☞ Periodicals, Newspapers, and Newsletters

The federal government is a major producer of periodicals. Varying in content, appearance, value, and purpose, they range from those aimed at a narrow audience to titles having a broad appeal. The gamut of periodical types include research journals, popular periodicals on specific topics, scenic or travel periodicals, and so forth. Many agencies produce newsletters that inform readers about recent activities and planned events. Newsletters are informative and may present the agency in its best light.

☞ Photographs and Images

In addition to motion pictures and sound recordings, the government maintains an extensive collection of photographs and images. The LC's American Memory is one example, and NARA's presidential libraries maintain extensive Web-based collections of photographs (see Chapter 6). Other types of images extend to the galaxies, space probes, and declassified and nonclassified satellite imagery of the earth's surface. The Smithsonian Institution also contains numerous images.

☞ Posters

This type relates to popular culture and the intent of the government to announce, inform, influence, and create impressions. NARA and LC hold numerous historical posters, such as those from both world wars.

☞ Proceedings of Symposia and Other Conferences

Unlike the congressional proceedings mentioned earlier, this category refers to the reports of special conferences, seminars, or workshops hosted by many executive agencies or departments. Their purpose is to inform government officials or special interest groups about various facets of a topic, or to report on the exchange of ideas. The Bureau of the Census, for example, releases proceedings related to the planning and evaluation of a decennial census.

☞ Public Notices and News Releases

These publications provide current information and identify agency activities, source material, publicly held meetings, proposed rules and regulations, and speeches delivered by important officials within a department or agency. Like newsletters—a similar type of publication—they may be subjective and intended to advance a particular point of view.

⟍ Reports

This type of publication includes administrative, committee or commission, and research reports. Many government agencies issue an annual or other periodic report covering their accomplishments during the past year and their proposed budget and activities for the upcoming year. These reports frequently contain organizational charts, list the services provided, and summarize major agency activities.

Both Congress and the president establish special committees and commissions to examine and report on significant economic, foreign policy, political, or social concerns or issues. Congressional committees often issue reports when they release legislation for floor debate and action. These reports review legislative history, identify amendments, and convey legislative intent, showing how a committee majority (and perhaps minority) interpret key provisions.

The executive or legislative branch might release a report containing the results of a research study. Research may be conducted on a list of myriad topics, including health care, nuclear energy, space exploration, agriculture, labor trends, electronic commerce and government, and so on.

⟍ Statistics

The government is the largest collector, tabulator, and publisher of statistical data in the world. (Chapter 8 reviews the major statistical reporting agencies.) Government departments and agencies may release statistics on various topics, and, at other times, they publish large data sets on the Web and by CD-ROM so that researchers can examine and massage the data and make detailed comparisons.

Agencies may combine maps with statistical data by enabling the public to select and display certain statistics from among a set of predefined maps. For instance, the Bureau of the Census profiles congressional districts and provides reference and thematic maps (see **http://www.census.gov/geo/www/maps/CP_MapProductions.htm**; **http://www. census.gov/geo/www.mapGallery/index.html**).

As discussed in Chapter 11, geographic information systems (GISs) capture, store, display, analyze, and model data references to locations on the earth's surface. Such systems enable researchers, policy analysts, and others to link different data sets to a common referent (e.g., street address, voting or congressional district, census tract, zip code, or telephone exchange) and to produce visual and statistical profiles of those data.

⟍ Technical Documentation

Machine-readable data files may require technical documentation that explains the layout and content of data fields, the reliability of the data, and so on. Many of these files, available from the National Technical Information Service, the Census Bureau, and some other agencies, have such documentation. For many other government data files available on the Web, such documentation is absent.

⟗ Treaties and International Agreements

This type of publication refers to foreign policy and the agreements that the government enters into with other governments and international bodies (e.g., the United Nations). The Senate must ratify treaties, but both chambers convey their concerns and points of view on a variety of international issues to the administration. Thus, some people monitor the issues leading up to the signing and ratification of a treaty, as well as compliance with previously signed treaties. Within the executive branch, international issues are not the sole responsibility of the State Department. They may relate to areas involving the jurisdiction of the Departments of Agriculture, Commerce, Defense, Treasury, and so on.

KEY PUBLICATIONS

Anyone who does not have a strong background in U.S. government and civics, or anyone needing a refresher course, might benefit from an examination of sources such as the following:

- *Understanding the Federal Courts* (**http://www.uscourts.gov/UFC99.pdf**). This resource explains the "federal judicial branch," "state and federal courts," and the "structure of the federal courts." It also discusses the administration of the courts

- *The United States Government Manual* (**http://www.gpoaccess.gov/gmanual/index. html**) is an official government handbook that provides an overview (i.e., purpose, function, programs, and activities) and other information (e.g., key officials and brief history) on many agencies within the three branches of government. It also covers quasi-official agencies, international organizations in which the United States participates, and boards, commissions, and committees.

- For an overview of the legislative process, there is *How Our Laws Are Made* (produced by the House of Representatives, **http://thomas.loc.gov/home/ lawsmade.toc.html**). For a further explanation of the legislative process in the House (a series of reports from the Congressional Research Service), see **http://www.house.gov/rules/95-563.htm.**

- For an explanation of the legislative process in the Senate as well as a flow chart documenting the process, see **http://www.senate.gov/pagelayout/legislative/ d_three_sections_with_teasers/process.htm**.

- The House has published miscellaneous publications (see **http://www.access. gpo.gov/congress/house/index.html**).

- The Immigration and Naturalization Service (INS) produces excellent introductions to U.S. civic life through guides designed to assist individuals involved in the naturalization process (**http://www.immigration.gov/graphics/ services/natz/require.htm**).

SUMMARY

Anyone searching for government publications or information on the Web cannot depend on a general search engine. He or she must gain some knowledge of the federal government's structure along with the types of publications (or information products) created to support the myriad purposes and programs of that structure. When one considers legislation, for instance, it is important to know how bills are introduced in Congress and referred to committees and understand that each is given a unique number. Hearings, if held, occur before committees. If committees release legislation for floor consideration, then, most likely, a report is produced (again with a unique number necessary to find the report). Journals and proceedings also provide useful insights as legislation moves to its final result—either demise or enactment as public law. Because most legislation never becomes law and because the legislative process involves the use of special terminology, it is important to understand the process and to review the types of sources mentioned as "Key Publications." Clearly, when dealing with government, one must realize that a source might be a combination of different types of publications. Nonetheless, the depiction of types suggests that terminology is important and that the publishing programs of government bodies are diverse.

The overarching principle to remember is that there is a patchwork quilt of access to government information resources. Some agencies make their resources publicly accessible on a broad scale, and others do not. Those that do may merely release resources but not provide any explanation of content and utility nor, most likely, make any connections to work done by other government bodies or even within the issuing body. Complicating matters, there is, in fact, more than one quilt, and the various "pieces—the different agency Web sites—are not stitched together into a whole."[10] As discussed in the next chapter and in Chapter 9, however, FirstGov (**http://www.firstgov.gov/**) continues to provide a mechanism that attempts to stitch these multitude of patches into one quilt of information. Until that mechanism is perfected, access to *published* government publications, information, data, and records might be characterized as an enormous maze: Where do we enter? How do we proceed? How might we conduct a search effectively and efficiently? These are some of the questions that this guide attempts to address.

©Linsay Hernon

NOTES

1. See the discussion of the several fundamental founding documents of American federal government on the U.S. National Archives Web pages: **http://www.archives.gov/ exhibit_hall/index.html**

2. U.S. Congress. House. *Organization of the Congress. Final Report of the House Members of the Joint Committee on the Organization of Congress* (Washington, D.C.: Government Printing Office, 1993): 4.

3. Ibid., 5.

4. The leadership of both the House and Senate changes and is led by the party that has the majority of members elected to either chamber. In this way, the Congress could be dominated by two parties and the White House by either party.

5. Harold C. Relyea, "Preface," in *The Executive Office of the President*, ed. Harold C. Relyea (Westport, CT: Greenwood Press, 1997): xi. This excellent work provides "a historical, biographical, and bibliographic guide" to the office.

6. See Ronald C. Moe, *Administering Public Functions at the Margin of Government: The Case of Federal Corporations* (Washington, D.C.: Library of Congress, Congressional Research Service, 1983).

7. E. S. Corwin, *The Constitution and What It Means Today* (Princeton, NJ: Princeton University Press, 1948), p. 117.

8. See the National Archives and Records Administration, *The United States Government Manual* in the section "Key Publications."

9. See "Office of Management and Budget's "Bulletin" and "Memoranda" at **http:www. whitehouse.gov/omb/**.

10. Patrice McDermott, "Letter: GILS Not Superfluous," *Federal Computer Week* 12 (September 21, 1998): 20.

URL Site Guide for This Chapter

GPO Access
http://www.gpoaccess.gov/

> **Bills and Resolutions**
> http://www.gpoaccess.gov/bills/
> index.html
>
> **Catalog of United States Government Publications**
> Superintendent of Documents
> Government Printing Office
> http://www.gpoaccess.gov/cgp/index.
> html
>
> **Sales Product Catalog**
> **Bookstore**
> **Superintendent of Documents**
> http://bookstore.gpo.gov/
>
> **Rules and Regulations**
> **Federal Register**
> http://www.gpoaccess.gpo.gov/fr/index.
> html
>
> **Code of Federal Regulations**
> http://www.gpoaccess.gov/cfr/index.html
>
> **Congressional Directory**
> http://www.gpoaccess.gov/cdirectory/
> index.html
>
> **Congressional Record**
> http://www.gpoaccess.gov/crecord/index.
> html
>
> **The United States Government Manual**
> http://www.gpoaccess.gov/gmanual/index.
> html

Rules (House of Representatives)
> **Clerk of the House**
> http://clerkweb.house.gov/

Rules (Senate)
> **Office of the Secretary**
> http://rules.senate.gov/senaterules/menu.htm

U.S. Geological Survey Bulletin
http://pubs.usgs.gov/products/books/
bulletins.html

NLM Technical Bulletin (National Library of Medicine)
http://www.nlm.nih.gov/pubs/techbull/
tb.html

American Memory

> **Library of Congress**
> http://memory.loc.gov/ammem/
> amhome.html
>
> **Motion Picture Collection**
> http://memory.loc.gov/ammem/papr/
> mpixhome.html

Census Maps

> **Bureau of the Census**
> http://www.census.gov/geo/www/maps/
> CP_MapProductions.htm

Understanding the Federal Courts
http://www.uscourts.gov/UFC99.pdf

THOMAS (Library of Congress)
http://thomas.loc.gov/

> **How Our Laws Are Made**
> http://thomas.loc.gov/home/lawsmade.toc.
> html
> http://www.access.gpo.gov/congress/house/
> index.html
>
> **Enactment of a Law**
> http://thomas.loc.gov/home/enactment/
> enactlawtoc.html
>
> **Legislative Process**
> **House**
> http://www.house.gov/rules/95-563.htm
>
> **Senate**
> http://www.senate.gov/pagelayout/
> legislative/d_three_sections_
> with_teasers/process.htm

United States Code

http://www.gpoaccess.gov/uscode/index.html

INS Naturalization Guides

http://www.immigration.gov/graphics/services/natz/require.htm

FirstGov

http://www.firstgov.gov/

Circulus, Bulletins, Memorandom

Office of Management and Budget

http://www.whitehouse.gov/omb/

Online Exhibits

National Archives and Records Administration

http://www.archives.gov/exhibit_hall/index.html

Chapter 3

Search Engines:
Navigating the Information Maze

The federal government produces a considerable amount of *public* information products. The actual number, past or present, is unknown and undeterminable. Complicating any precise count is the fact that the three branches do not share a central printer or distribution and dissemination mechanism. Furthermore, federal offices and other subunits are located throughout the United States and around the globe, further frustrating attempts to count and retrieve all electronic and print publications and to rely on a single printer or distributor. Congress often favors decentralization and does not support government information management through a single body; rather, it prefers a competitive publishing environment.

When it comes to government information or data, people may know the producing or disseminating agency or body. On the other hand, they might not, or they might want to conduct a general subject search across all branches of government. Given the size and complexity of the government, as well as the fact that Congress, the federal courts, the White House, and departments and agencies consider a wide variety of issues and problems, it would be impossible to predict where to limit such a subject search.

The ultimate questions about searching for federal government information might simply be, "Why should one bother? What does the government know that I can't find in nongovernment sources?" As already noted, the answers to these questions rest on the critical roles that the federal government plays in our daily lives. We live in a global economy, and government policies have broad ramifications, consequences, and impacts. It is impossible to pick up a newspaper or listen to a news program (radio, television, or Web page) without some reference to government policies, practices, and services. By refusing to visit government sites and use the information provided, one ignores a considerable body of information paid for by public funds and often the only source of information that is free, unbiased, and accurate. These Web sites are not filled with self-serving nonsense; rather, they contain information that will assist the public in holding government accountable; in improving the environment, the economy, and society itself; and in understanding and challenging government practices and policies. These sites also provide services as the government wants the

American public to rely more on its Internet services. Furthermore, through e-government the federal government plays an active role in providing the public with information, services, and e-commerce, as well as enabling us to participate in e-democracy.

When engaged in subject searching, the question also becomes, "To what extent do the Web's general search engines focus exclusively on government-produced products?" Users cannot rely exclusively on the general subject searching offered by most commercial Web search engines to uncover the diverse wealth of federal information resources. These search engines often fail to help the user understand the complex structure of the federal government, as well as the organization of a particular executive department. The public may fail to identify some basic titles as they try to navigate government Web sites, and they may not understand the complex terminology used, for instance, to distinguish common legislative publications such as bills, hearings, committee prints, and reports from other information sources produced by Congress. Commercial search engines may also be unable to conduct a more complete and focused search, while evaluating the value of the information found. How significant is that information? Where does it stand in comparison to other information issued by the government?

The assumption of this guide, of course, is that individuals want government, as opposed to nongovernment, information, or that they want their pool of source material to include government products. Clearly, no search engine provides a comprehensive search of the Web and all products available for general use. The most relevant information on a topic might only be available at the Web site of a department agency or congressional committee. Nonetheless, some search engines are better than others at providing access to executive branch publications. But before we can explain the differences between government and commercial Web search engines, we need some background on the approaches developed over the last decade as the federal government sought to bring some order and standardization to its information resource management.

GOVERNMENT INFORMATION LOCATOR SERVICES: ORGANIZING FEDERAL INFORMATION BEFORE THE WEB

Over several decades, a considerable number of public laws, rules, and regulations have attempted to bring both order and accessibility to federal government information production, distribution, dissemination, and organization. For instance, the *Paperwork Reduction Act of 1995* (109 Stat. 163) specifies that each agency, "with respect to information dissemination," will

- "Ensure that the public has timely and equitable access to the agency's public information"

- "Regularly solicit and consider public input on the agency's information dissemination activities"

- "Provide adequate notice when initiating, substantially modifying, or terminating significant information dissemination products"

As a result, government agencies were mandated to recognize their individual and collective roles and responsibilities to keep the public informed about its activities and business. This does not mean, however, that the government is always forthcoming in the release of public information.

Also in the mid-1990s, with the growing use of electronic information technology and distribution networks, Congress and some officials within the executive branch pressed for a Government Information Locator Service (GILS) as a structure to identify, locate, and describe publicly available information resources. "GILS is a decentralized collection of agency-based information locators using network technology and international standards to direct users to relevant information resources within the . . . government."[1]

Through GILS, the government and the public should be able to learn about the types of resources produced and how to obtain the information as well as how to benefit from well-designed, easy-to-use links to the desired information (see **http://www.gils.net/index.html**). Yet governmentwide implementation of GILS remains limited and uneven; some listings are current and extensive (or even complete), whereas others are incomplete and outdated. At any rate, agency home pages may contain information about GILS records. Thus, anyone conducting a comprehensive search should be alert to announcements about such records.

DEVELOPMENT OF COMPREHENSIVE GOVERNMENT SEARCH ENGINES AND PORTALS

Realizing that access to Web-based government information is comparable to finding one's way through a maze of undeterminable size and shape, the Clinton administration sought to create a single search engine designed to integrate nearly all federal Web pages. WebGov, originally intended to be a portal, evolved into FirstGov, a search engine that allowed users to search through broad subjects (e.g., farming, medicine, and information about foreign countries). Such a tool, many argued, would be useful because "the compilers of the FirstGov database [have] discovered that the federal government has posted about 40 million pages on the Internet."[2] FirstGov (**http://www.firstgov.gov/**) has evolved considerably since its introduction several years ago. It relies on partnerships with a group of "Certified Partners" to organize and present federal information and services for specific users. Partners include businesses, universities, or individuals. FirstGov also depends on a sophisticated database structure.

FirstGov performs a valuable service for individuals either familiar or unfamiliar with the organization and structure of the government, and its creators maintain that "the portal search function can comb through 500 million pages of text in a quarter of a second, conduct 200,000 searchers simultaneously and 100 million searches daily."[3] Furthermore, "FirstGov will search all .gov and .mil pages on the Web and search .com pages of the U.S. Postal Service."[4] Other reported benefits include the promotion of a new generation of multiagency Web sites that focus on government services, rather than the offerings of a particular agency, and showing government departments, agencies, courts, and congressional committees how they can serve the public better. As well, FirstGov "will force federal agencies to be more open by making their online information far easier for the public to find. It also will direct the public to agency sites where online transactions can be carried out, helping to lay the foundation for electronic government."[5] Through its first couple of years of service, many observers held equal parts of praise and scorn for the new service. Many hoped that the "public's interest" would not be measured through a tally of the number of visitors to a government Web site.[6] Naturally, there will be variation among agencies regarding their cooperation with a "click-through" service.[7] Anyone searching comprehensively for electronic government information will still have to consider other search options: searching by government body or retrieving titles not included within FirstGov that provides key information. Before FirstGov, there was little interconnectivity among departmental and agency Web sites, and FirstGov, in its early years, might have been a good place to begin a search. The vast number of references resulting from a search on FirstGov often produced *information overload*, however. Moreover, the information-seeking public often found itself with unfamiliar departments and little understanding of how they could find the information they requested within their respective Web sites. Such knowledge is vital for those not well versed in the structure of government and the jurisdiction of specific bodies and for those attempting to conduct a comprehensive subject search of the Web for government information. It is important to remember, even with great improvements that have taken place since the last edition of this guide, that the layout and organization of federal Web sites have not been standardized. Thus, the information seeker must rely on the following chapters to negotiate this department- or agency-centric mode of information resources (as well as on the updated list of Web addresses maintained on the publisher's home page—see the preface).

By late 2002, however, FirstGov had evolved sufficiently into a general "portal" for all the federal government (and state governments), to overcome many of these initial problems. As a portal, FirstGov now includes other significant ways to access government information—not only from its original innovative search engine but also through the creation of groups of related Web sites that seek to benefit seniors, students, small businesses, and other specific communities. It has also extended its reach to include government information from state, local, and international government bodies, in addition to various profit and nonprofit groups with contracts and connections to provide particular government programs, services, or research. Organizing information is no longer enough for FirstGov; it now promotes itself as the best overall "gateway" to public information on the Web, offering current news, promoting government programs, and providing users many ways to customize the Web interface to meet their individual needs.

GENERAL SEARCH ENGINES
AND INTERNET PORTALS

The commercial firms that design and manage the most popular Web search engines (e.g., Lycos, Netscape, Google, and Yahoo!) view their services less as general tools and more as portals. Users can locate current news and coverage of assorted topics, as well as perform a general subject searches throughout the World Wide Web. Like FirstGov, these nongovernment Web search engines and portals have evolved, and, in fact, several of them featured in earlier editions of this guide no longer exist. Commercial Web portals attempt to appeal to the largest audience as possible, and, at the same time, capture *audience share* from other commercial Internet portal providers. In a real sense, then, they are no longer *general* Web search engines, and their usefulness regarding government information remains challenged by not only the complexity of the government's presence on the Web, but also the fact that the searching *resources* are increasingly segmented to reach particular audiences or market segments. Indeed, only three or four of the commercial Web sources actually have organized directories that focus on the Web pages of the federal government, and even these do not compare to the level of consistency or depth of FirstGov. Only one, Google's UncleSam search engine, even comes close. Also, featured Web pages that are part of many of these commercial Web sites databases (again, with the exception of Google) pay an extra fee to be listed at the top of the search results, regardless of the relevance of the Web resources to the original search terms used by the user. Thus, the results retrieved mix government and nongovernment information resources, with emphasis on the latter. Using these search engines or portals, one might search by

- Agency name

- General subject likely to pull up government sites

- Specific event or issue

Still, these general search engines (see Figure 3.1) often have limited value in retrieving the names of government agencies and for general subject searching for government information.

Figure 3.1. General Search Engines.

Name	URL
AltaVista	http://www.altavista.com
Excite	http://www.excite.com
Go Network	http://www.go.com
Google	http://www.google.com/
LookSmart	http://www.looksmart.com
Lycos	http://www.lycos.com
Netscape	http://www.netscape.com
NBCi	http://www.nbci.com/
Webcrawler	http://www.webcrawler.com/
Yahoo!	http://www.yahoo.com

MORE "TARGETED" SEARCH ENGINES

Figure 3.2 identifies search engines that concentrate on government information. Although none of them provides comprehensive access, such search engines may make a good starting point if one wants to search by subject—keyword or phrase. They enable a person to make a quick connection to home pages unknown to the information navigator.

Figure 3.2. Search Engines for Government Information.

Name	URL
DOTbot	http://search.bts.gov/ntl/index.html
Federal Web Locator	http://www.infoctr.edu/fwl/
FedWorld	http://www.fedworld.gov/
FirstGov	http://www.firstgov.gov/
Google's Uncle Sam	http://www.google.com/unclesam
GovEngine.com	http://www.govengine.com
GovSpot	http://www.govspot.com/
GPO Access	http://www.access.gpo.gov/
PubMed	http://www.ncbi.nlm.nih.gov./entrez/query.fcgi
THOMAS	http://thomas.loc.gov/
Yahoo!	http://dir.yahoo.com/Government/U_S_Government

☞ DOTbot

In August 1998, the Department of Transportation (DOT) launched DOTbot, which indexes documents in the files of more than one hundred DOT Web sites. It does not, however, identify information that the Department has not published on the Web.

☞ Federal Web Locator

The Federal Web Locator is intended as the one-stop shopping point for federal government information on the Web. It can be searched by the "Latest Additions," "Federal Quick Jumps," and "Federal Government Web Servers," which approaches government information by categorizing sites according to branch of government; independent agencies; quasi-official agencies; federal boards, commissions, and committees; and nongovernment federally related sites.

☞ FedWorld

The National Technical Information Service (NTIS), an agency in the Department of Commerce, is an official source of government-sponsored scientific, technical, engineering, and business-related information produced in the United States and elsewhere. For a number of its products, NTIS is required to recover its costs, thereby fulfilling its congressional mandate to be self-sustaining. In 1992, it started FedWorld as a online locator service for electronic information products disseminated by the federal government that also assists agencies in meeting the information needs of their staff and constituents.

⇗ Google's Uncle Sam

Of the commercial Web sites mentioned in this chapter, Google's Uncle Sam is the best in terms of results and ease of use. When combined with FirstGov, users can be assured, with a fair degree of confidence, that they have searched the thousands of federal Web sites as completely as one can expect given the level of technology, the vast distribution of information, and those resources tagged for retrieval from such tools. Whereas FirstGov delivers its search results using a technique that gives the highest relevance to Web sites in which the search terms occur most often or in the way they were entered into the system, Uncle Sam lists the pages according to the number of links that other Web sites have made to the pages in which the search terms occur. In this sense, Uncle Sam allows builders of Web pages to choose the most relevant Web sites based on this complicated arrangement of mutual linking and acknowledgment. Both methods, when used together, provide an effective way of screening "information overload." For instance, searching the terms "cancer rate" as a phrase turns up two lists of possible hits (3,410 in Uncle Sam and more than 1,000 in FirstGov); fortunately, both search engines offer specific ways to narrow these vast numbers through "advanced searching techniques."

⇗ GovEngine.com

Billing itself as the "premiere federal, state & local government site on the Internet," this portal is managed by a Florida based non-profit organization with the primary objective of promoting electronic government. Unlike other search engines, it does not rely on text searching, but on an organizational structure that provides a clear way to navigate its information links as if they were structured through a government organization manual: executive branch, legislative branch, and judicial branch. There is no attempt to interpret or organize the links according to subject. Still, it is a useful Web site for a no-frills look at the complexity of governance from all levels. Its most useful search function involves a map of the United States that allows a person to click on a state and to get all the government agencies operating at a regional, state, or local levels. GovEngine.com is most useful, for instance, when someone is trying to get a sense of the various federal, state, and local court systems.

⇗ GovSpot

Under "Gov't Online," GovSpot provides access to government Web sites by branch of government as well as to sites of state and local government, and world government. There is also access to government employees, a short list of "must see" sites (some agencies, sources, and FirstGov), and quick access to certain types of information (e.g., the "Top Federal Contractors").

⇗ GPO Access

GPO Access, which the Government Printing Office (GPO), a legislative branch agency, maintains, offers the *Catalog of United States Government Publications,* an index to publications GPO prints and often distributes. It is possible to search this index, since January 1994, by fields such as keyword, title, superintendent of documents classification number, and depository item number (see **http://www.gpoaccess.gov/ cgp/index.html**).

Publications contained in GPO Access might be available electronically or through the GPO's depository library program. For example, once someone has searched the database and found a hit, there will be an indication of whether that publication or a summary is available in text or .pdf (portable document format) format online. If there is no online availability, the searcher is informed that the publication is likely to be in a depository library and is instructed on how to find the nearest such library (see **http://www.gpoaccess.gov/libraries.html**).

The GPO also offers an online bookstore (**http://bookstore.gpo.gov/**) and has compiled approximately 150 *Subject Bibliographies* "to assist in the identification of publications, subscriptions and electronic products that can be purchased from GPO" (see **http://bookstore.gpo.gov/sb/index.html**).

GPO Access has "Core Documents of U.S. Democracy" (**http://www.gpoaccess. gov/coredocs.html**) that includes the following:

- Legislative and Legal: Articles of Confederation, the Bill of Rights; congressional documents and debates, 1774–1873; congressional bills, *Congressional Directory*; *Congressional Pictorial Directory*; *Congressional Record*; the Constitution of the United States; the Constitution, analysis and interpretation; the Declaration of Independence; the Federal Papers; public laws, Supreme Court decisions, 1937–1975, 1992/93–; and the *United States Code*

- Regulatory: *Federal Register* and *Code of Federal Regulations*

- Executive Office of the President: *Budget of the United States Government*, codified presidential proclamations and executive orders, and the *Weekly Compilation of Presidential Documents*

- Demographic: *American Factfinder* and *Statistical Abstract of the United States*

- Economic: *Catalog of Federal Domestic Assistance*, *Commerce Business Daily*, economic indicators, and *Economic Report of the President*

- Miscellaneous: the Gettysburg Address, the Emancipation Proclamation, the *Catalog of United States Government Publications*, and the *United States Government Manual*

Moreover, GPO Access provides no-charge public access to more than seventy agency databases, GILS records, and *Privacy Act* notices.

GPO Access hosts some Web sites of government agencies. For a list, see **http://www.access.gpo.gov/su_docs/sites.html**. There are also links to thirty-six agency GILS databases (**http://www.access.gpo.gov/su_docs/gils/index.html**). Furthermore, "GPO Access points to over 115,000 electronic government publications. More than 15 million items are downloadable monthly by the public."[9] Furthermore, "over 4,500 individual federal agency files, in a variety of formats, are available for free download from the Federal Bulletin Board (FBB)"[10] (see **http://fedbbs.access. gpo.gov/**).

↗ PubMed

A service from the U.S. National Library of Medicine, PubMed offers access to more than 12 million citations, back to the mid-1960s, for both medical and life science journals. PubMed includes links to many sites providing full text articles and other related resources.

↗ THOMAS

THOMAS is frequently not regarded as a general gateway, but, as shown in Chapter 4 and Figure 4.1, it provides access to bills, the *Congressional Record*, roll call votes, public laws, hearing transcripts (selective), reports, and more. It is also possible to search the database by word or phrase and to obtain a list of frequently asked questions and House and Senate directories. There are also links to both chambers, legislative branch agencies, historical documents, and links to the executive and judicial branches. THOMAS, as a result, is the best single source of information for all the steps in the legislative process.

↗ Yahoo!

Yahoo! provides access to the three branches of the U.S. government at **http://dir.yahoo.com/Government/U_S__Government/**. Under each of the branches, it organizes the Web resources into several broad subject categories. For instance, under the executive branch, it offers the following categories:

- Awards
- Camp David
- Departments and Agencies
- George W. Bush Administration
- History
- Presidential Inaugurations
- Presidential Powers
- White House, The

© Linsay Hernon

SUMMARY

In our opinion, the best general search engines for government resources are the following: FirstGov, GPO Access, Google's Uncle Sam, Yahoo!, THOMAS, and FedWorld. DOTbot is excellent but in a narrower context. GPO Access also enables subject searching of specific databases and is broad in its scope. PubMed is an excellent example of how the federal government can provide general public access to the specialized literature of medicine and science. Users, however, must know something about the contents of many of these databases if they intend to perform a comprehensive search of available resources. FedWorld often leads to fee-based and subscription services. THOMAS concentrates on one branch of government, but it does lead the information seeker to the other branches. The other search engines are all excellent for anyone navigating through the sites of various government bodies for the first time or who does not intend to develop expertise in searching for and retrieving government information. Clearly, users attempting extensive or comprehensive searches for government information must have some knowledge of the government's structure and the types of information resources produced, and this is the central logic behind the organization of this guide. Furthermore, many of these search engine functions are being displaced by governmentwide portals, which will be discussed more fully in Chapter 9.

NOTES

1. GPO Access, "What Is GILS?" Available: **http://www.access.gpo.gov/su_docs/ gils/whatgils.html**.

2. William Matthews, "The End of Government as We Know It," *Federal Computer Week* 14 (September 18, 2000): 20.

3. Ibid.

4. Ibid.

5. Ibid., 17

6. Ibid.

7. See Patrice McDermott, "FirstGov: All Bark, No Bite," *Federal Computer Week* 14 (August 14, 2000), p. 58.

8. Matthews, "The End of Government as We Know It," 18.

9. See *Administrative Notes* [Office of the Superintendent of Documents] 19(14) (November 15, 1998): 14.

10. See "About GPO Access," **http://www.access.gpo.gov/su_docs/whatis.html**.

URL Site Guide for This Chapter

(Figure 3.1 Contains Additional URLs)

DOTbot
http://search.bts.gov/ntl/index.html

Federal Web Locator
http://www.infoctr.edu/fwl/

FedWorld
National Technical Information Service
http://www.fedworld.gov/

FirstGov
http://www.firstgov.gov/

GovEngine.com
http://www.govengine.com

GovSpot
http://www.govspot.com/

PubMed
http://www.ncbi.nlm.nih.gov./entrez/
   query.fcgi

THOMAS
Library of Congress
http://thomas.loc.gov/

Uncle Sam
Google
http://www.google.com/unclesam

Yahoo!
http://dir.yahoo.com/Government/U_S_Gover
   nment/

Government Information Locator
   Service
   http://www.gils.net/index.html

GPO Access
http://www.gpoaccess.gpo.gov/
http://www.access.gpo.gov/su-docs/
   whatis.html

   Catalog of United States Government
     Publications
   http://www.gpoaccess.gov/cgp/
     index.html

   Location of Nearest Depository
     Library
   http://www.gpoaccess.gov/libraries.html

   Online Bookstore
   Superintendent of Documents
   http://bookstore.gpo.gov/

   Subject Bibliographies
   Superintendent of Documents
   http://bookstore.gpo.gov/sb/

   Core Documents of U.S. Democracy
   http://www.gpoaccess.gov/coredocs.html

   Hosting Government Web sites
   http://www.access.gpo.gov/su_docs/
     sites.html

   Federal Bulletin Board
   http://fedbbs.access.gpo.gov/

   Links to GILS Database
   http://www.access.gpo.gov/su_docs/gils/
     index.html

Chapter 4

Legislative Branch

Congress and its support agencies have developed a substantial presence on the World Wide Web. Like the executive branch, Congress views the Web as a primary means of information dissemination and of direct communication with the public. Members of Congress tend to have their own Web sites, but the information conveyed is not always current; it may also be self-serving. Each chamber (the House of Representatives and the Senate) divides its tasks among more than two hundred committees and subcommittees:

Committees are subsidiary organizations . . . established for the purpose of considering legislation, conducting hearings and investigations, or carrying out other assignments as instructed by the chamber. "Standing" committees generally have legislative jurisdiction, and most operate with subcommittees that handle a committee's work in specific areas. "Select" and "Joint" committees are chiefly for oversight or housekeeping tasks.[1]

The committee chair "and a majority of . . . [a committee's] members come from the majority party. The chair primarily controls a committee's business. Each party is predominantly responsible for assigning its members to committees, and each committee distributes its members among its subcommittees." Committees decide which measures they will consider, thus "determining the fate of measures and, in effect, helping to set a chamber's agenda make committees powerful."[2]

When a committee or subcommittee favors a measure, it usually

- "Asks relevant executive agencies for written comments on the measure"

- "Holds hearings to gather information and views from non-committee experts"[3]

- "Meets to perfect the measure through amendments, and non-committee members sometimes attempt to influence the language"

- "Sends the measure back to the chamber [when language is agreed upon], usually along with a written report describing its purpose and provisions and the work of the committee thereon"[4]

"The influence of committees over measures extends to their enactment into law. A committee that considers a measure will manage the full chamber's deliberations on it. Also, its members will be appointed to any conference committee created to reconcile the two chambers' differing versions of a measure."[5] In addition to being aware of committee activities, the public should be able to monitor the progress of legislation through Congress, floor activities, debates, and roll call votes.

The Web plays an important role in presenting the following committee activities: hearings, reports, and other publications. The *Congressional Record* and C-SPAN record floor activities, and the *Congressional Record* accounts for legislation. Although another part of this chapter discusses the various Web sites that offer a way of examining the information and data produced during the legislative process, THOMAS (discussed in the next section) remains the single best source of information that includes all the legislative steps in a single structure and search engine. It links to the relevant portions of the *Congressional Record*, as well as to reports, votes, and other legislative actions.[6]

OVERVIEW

A good introductory site on the legislative branch (**http://thomas.loc.gov/home/ legbranch/legbranch.html**) provides links to the

- United States Congress (House of Representatives; individual representatives; Clerk of the House; Senate; individual senators; *Congressional Directory* since the 104th Congress; *Congressional Pictorial Directory* for the current Congress; the U.S. Congress—its history, operation, and composition; and the Capitol Building—art and architecture)

- Legislative agencies and commissions (Library of Congress, General Accounting Office, Architect of the Capitol, Medical Payment Advisory Commission, Government Printing Office, Congressional Budget Office, Office of Compliance, and Office of Technology Assessment)

The "U.S. Congress—its history, operation, and composition," under United States Congress (see **http://thomas.loc.gov/home/legbranch/uscong.html**), for instance, provides information on the institution from Grolier online encyclopedia (with links to other articles) and the *United States Government Manual*, Capitol Questions (a C-SPAN scholar asks various questions about Congress), "Current Congressional Profile" (provided by the Office of the Clerk of the House), "Learn about Congress" (information from Indiana University's Center for Congress), and the "History of Congress" (links to historical, biographical, and election information).

A directory of current senators is available at **http://www.senate.gov/general/ contact_information/senators_cfm.cfm**. A similar directory for the House of Representatives can be found at **http://www.house.gov/house/MemberWWW.html**.

⟋⟍ Congressional Directory

The *Congressional Directory*, the official almanac of Congress, complements the *U.S. Government Manual*. The *Directory* provides short biographies on members of Congress, along with their committee memberships, terms of service, addresses, and telephone numbers. It also covers executive officials and federal judges, foreign diplomats, and news media personnel and provides other general information. The *Directory,* together with its online revision, is available through GPO Access (**http://www.gpoaccess.gov/cdirectory/index.html**).

⚞ THOMAS

Named after Thomas Jefferson, THOMAS (**http://thomas.loc.gov/**) is a gateway to the legislative process that provides access to legislation, the *Congressional Record,* committee information, as well as links to information about the gateway, frequently asked questions , Congress and its support agencies, discussion of the legislative process in both the House and the Senate, the workload of Congress and the number of days in session for each session of Congress, the home pages of the other branches of government, and home pages of state and local government. There are also historical documents (see Figure 4.1).

Figure 4.1. THOMAS: Legislative Information on the Web.

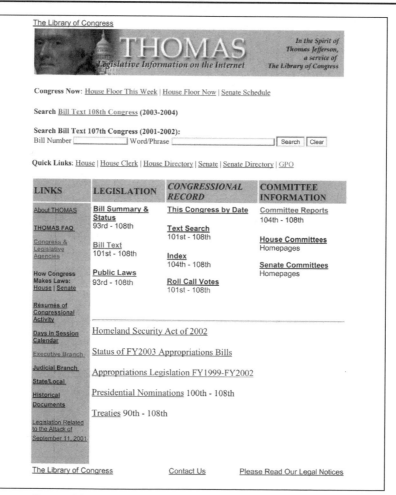

Source: Library of Congress, THOMAS (**http://thomas.loc.gov/**).

With the 108th Congress, the look of THOMAS has been revised. The readability and usefulness of the "Bill Text," "Bill Summary and Status Congressional Record," and "Committee Reports" pages has been improved. The search capabilities and functionality remained unchanged.

Under the heading for the *Congressional Record,* THOMAS presents the most recent issue, a text search (1989–), the index (1994–), and roll call votes. The historical documents include the Constitution of the United States of America, the Bill of Rights, the Federalist Papers, the Declaration of Independence, broadsides from the Continental Congress and Constitutional Convention, the papers of Thomas Jefferson, and "A Century of Lawmaking for a New Nation: U.S. Congressional Documents and Debates, 1774–1873." This set includes journals of Congress; the *Annals of Congress* (1789–1793), a predecessor to the *Congressional Record*; and other early documents.

THOMAS provides access to two well-known pamphlets, *How Our Laws Are Made*, which the House parliamentarian prepared, and *Enactment of a Law,* which the Senate parliamentarian authored. For anyone unfamiliar with the legislative process, these pamphlets are essential reading.

It merits mention that the congressional publications listed in GPO Access's "Legislative" page (**http://www.access.gpo.gov/su_docs/legislative.html**) complement the coverage provided in THOMAS. For instance, the Government Printing Office (GPO) offers congressional hearings (105th Congress forward), the *Congressional Record* (since 1994), a history of bills (1983 forward), and reports and treaty documents (since the 104th Congress).

HOUSE OF REPRESENTATIVES

The House has a general Web site (**http://www.house.gov/**), which links to member, committee, and leadership offices; to "Other Organizations, Commissions, & Task Forces"; and to media galleries. There is also a "House Directory" (directory of phone numbers and addresses), links to the Office of the Clerk, "House Operations" (rules), "Search House Sites," "Schedule Information" (e.g., "This Week on the House Floor," and "Committee Hearing Schedules & Oversight Plans"), "Legislative Information" (e.g., "Find Vote Information"), and "General Information" (e.g., "Employment Information"), and more.

↗ Standing Committees

Figure 4.2 presents the committees and examples of the types of resources that they make available online. Committees tend to provide hearing transcripts, thereby ensuring public access to hearings before they are printed, and to indicate what legislation has been marked up for consideration. They also present committee schedules and Webcast hearings (a Webcast is an audiovisual presentation that can be viewed online in real time or archived for later viewing).

Furthermore, the home pages provide links to subcommittees and related sites. In the 108th Congress, the House created the Select Committee on Homeland Security but limited its existence to that one Congress (the years 2003–2004). The committee has oversight responsibilities and can develop corrective legislation related to homeland security. Its home page (**http://hsc.house.gov/**) provides information about committee membership, news, a schedule of activities, links, an opportunity to register for e-mail updates or to contact the committee, and a listing of the subcommittees and their jurisdiction.

Figure 4.2. Types of Information Available from House Committees.

Committee	URL	Types of Information Available
Committee on Agriculture	**http://agriculture.house.gov/**	About the committee, access to subcommittees, facts, news and press releases, hearings, publications, and archives (1997–), and so on
Committee on Appropriations	**http://www.house.gov/ appropriations/**	News releases, bills, membership, schedule of hearings, markups; link to Minority Web page, and more
Committee on Armed Services	**http://armedservices.house.gov/**	Chairman's welcome, about the committee, news, hearing schedules and transcripts, publications, press releases, about the committee, bills and reports, ranking minority members' page, a mailing list, site search, and Webcasts
Committee on the Budget	**http://www.house.gov/budget/**	Assorted resources on the budget (e.g., budget links), a schedule, hearings, news, e-mail notices, "What's New," stories information on committee staff, a list of committee members, photos, rules, minority home page, and so on
Committee on Education and the Workforce	**http://edworkforce.house.gov/**	Members, committee schedule, history, issues, press, what's new, status of legislation, markups, hearings, internships and fellowships, publications, history, and more
Committee on Energy and Commerce	**http://energycommerce.house. gov/**	Weekly schedule, e-mail updates, hearings, news releases, publications, membership, jurisdiction, in the news, recent action, issues, audio broadcasts, minority Web site, and so

Figure 4.2. (*Cont.*)

Committee	URL	Types of Information Available
Committee on Financial Services	**http://financialservices.house.gov/**	Chairman's home page, information about the committee, subcommittees, bills referred, bills and summaries, hearings and legislation, documents, meetings, news membership, printed hearings, reports, rules, schedule, Democrats' view, and site search
Committee on Government Reform	**http://www.house.gov/reform/**	Introduction, members and subcommittees, rules, oversight, press releases, hearings and reports, related links, minority office, and schedule
Committee on House Administration	**http://www.house.gov/cha/**	About the committee, members, schedule, legislation, hearings, jurisdiction, committee business, rules of procedure, history, publications, and so
Committee on International Relations	**http://wwwa.house.gov/international_relations/**	Schedule, current issues, hearings and markups, activities, documents, press releases, oversight plan, jurisdiction, reports, newsletters, rules, history, other sites, Democratic members, and contacting the committee
Committee on Judiciary	**http://www.house.gov/judiciary/**	Membership, Minority Web page, press releases, schedule, legislative hearings, meetings and markups, intern program, congressional links, judiciary Democrats page, and more
Committee on Resources	**http://resourcescommittee.house.gov/**	Schedule, news, press releases, sign up for e-news, frequently asked questions, site map, minority page, committee news, jurisdiction, publications, and more

Committee	URL	Types of Information Available
Committee on Rules	**http://www.house.gov/rules/**	Committee schedule, special rules, special announcements, parliamentary outreach program, log-in form, legislation, information on the committee and on how Congress works, and a site search
Committee on Science	**http://www.house.gov/science/welcome.htm**	Members and committee information, press releases, hot topics, speeches, hearings, markups, documents, bills and publications, information technology, hearings oversight plan, weekly schedule, science policy study, science education, congressional links, minority site, frequently asked questions, site search, Democratic Office, and so on
Committee on Small Business	**http://www.house.gov/smbiz/**	Biography of chair, contact information, schedule, hearings, legislation, press releases, minority site, newsletter, special projects, committee and subcommittee membership, small business facts, related links, oversight plan, budget views and estimates, rules, Webcasts, and site search
Committee on Standards of Official Conduct	**http://www.house.gov/ethics/**	Ethics manual, gifts and travel booklet, campaign booklet, highlights of the ethics rules, financial disclosure information, press releases, investigative reports, information on the committee and its membership, a site search, and more
Committee on Transportation and Infrastructure	**http://www.house.gov/transportation/**	Top stories, weekly schedule, site map, press gallery, hot issues, current news, links to other resources, minority site, hearings, legislation, publications, and more

Figure 4.2. (*Cont.*)

Committee	URL	Types of Information Available
Committee on Veterans' Affairs	**http://veterans.house.gov/**	Members, committee information and news, legislation, hearings, veterans' information, links to other sites, minority site, and contact the committee
Committee on Ways and Means	**http://waysandmeans.house.gov/**	About the committee, press releases, what's new, schedule, prints and publications, rules and jurisdiction, legislative resources, site search, issues committee members, chairman's portrait page, hearings, legislation and accomplishments, subcommittees, and more
Permanent Select Committee on Intelligence	**http://intelligence.house.gov/**	Information on the chairman and ranking Democrat, committee membership, subcommittees, documents, and press releases
Select Committee on Homeland Security	**http://hsc.house.gov/**	News, legislation, information about the committee, schedule of upcoming committee events, documents, and guiding principles for a Department of Homeland Security

The Committee on Rules offers a set of links and information on "How Congress Works":

• Rules and Precedents of the House

• Parliamentary Terms and Definitions

• General Parliamentary Procedure

• The Budget Process

• House Committee Procedures

• House Floor Procedures

• Resolving Differences with the Senate

• Parliamentary Outreach Program

• Congressional Research Service (CRS) Reports

• Joint Committee on the Organization of Congress

Various reports of the CRS explain "Congress: The House," "House Floor Proceeding," "Introduction and Origins of Legislative Measures," "House Committees," "Special Rules and the Rules Committee," the "Budget Process," "Congress: The Senate," "Relations with the Senate," and "Presidential Relations." Examples cover House and Senate rules of procedure, "questions of privilege in the House," "private bills: procedure in the House," "how measures are brought to the House Floor: A brief introduction," and "decorum in House debates" (**http://www.house.gov/rules/crs_reports.htm**). For anyone dealing with the federal budget and in need of a tutorial, the Committee on the Budget provides such a tool, budget.house.gov (**http://www.budget.house.gov/budgettutorial.htm**).

At **http://www.house.gov/house/CommitteeWWW.html**, there is access to the standing committees as well as an opportunity to search all committee sites or get "quick links" to the membership of a specific committee; to a subcommittee, a committee's hearing schedule, hearings, or jurisdiction; or to hot topics.

⟐ Office of the Clerk

The Office (**http://clerkweb.house.gov/**) provides "What's New," "The Office of the Clerk," "Member Information," "Committee Information," "Legislative Activities," "Historical Highlights" (**http://clerk.house.gov/histHigh/index.php**; e.g., "Historical Facts," an online biographical directory of more than 11,500 people who have served in Congress since 1789, a list of the Speakers of the House since 1789, and the names of all women who have served or are serving in the House), "Public Disclosure," "Educational Resources" (**http://clerk.house.gov/eduRsrcs/index.php**), and a search of the site. Other resources include a site for youth (Kids in the House, see Chapter 13), "What's New," and "Quick Links" to

- House Floor Proceedings
- Roll Call Votes
- Bill Summaries and Status
- Congressional Biographical Directory
- Congressional Calendar
- Congressional Record
- Discharge Petitions
- Federal Depository Libraries (GPO)
- Federal Register
- House Calendar
- How Our Laws Are Made
- Library Services (Congressional Staff)
- Lobbying Registration Information
- Members' Web Sites

- Official Lists of Members
- Member Office Mailing Labels
- Write Your Representative

Speaker of the House

Speaker J. Dennis Hastert has a site (**http://speaker.house.gov/**) that covers news, issues, features, documents, and related Web links, and there are stories about (and statements by) him. Furthermore, the public can send e-mail messages to the Speaker and subscribe to an e-mail service that provides the latest news.

Office of the Majority Leader

The Web site of House majority leader (**http://www.majorityleader.gov/**) covers floor action, "Quick Links," and news.

Office of the Majority Whip

This site (**http://majoritywhip.house.gov/**) provides the majority whip's perspective on issues, news, information about him (Tom Delay), resources, how to contact him, an opportunity to receive e-mail updates, legislative resources (e.g., "GOP Talk Radio Topics"), a search of the site, the House calendar, and links to floor proceedings.

Office of the Minority Leader

Minority leader Nancy Pelosi's site (**http://democraticleader.house.gov/**) contains a "Leader's Corner" (the party's agenda), "Media Center" (e.g., press releases), "In the News," "Issues and Answers," headline news, and an opportunity to sign up for e-mail updates.

House Democratic Whip

The Democratic whip (currently Steny H. Hoyer), which is the second-ranking position among House Democrats, has a Web site (**http://democraticwhip. house.gov/**) that provides information about the individual as well as press resources, e-mail updates, coverage of issues, and more.

Office of the Inspector General

This office was established in the 103rd Congress and reestablished in the 104th Congress. This site (**http://www.house.gov/IG/**) contains documentation on that establishment, reports (in HTML or .pdf format, or both, dating from 1995), employment opportunities, a search of the site, and a link to "IGnet for directory of Federal Inspectors General & related organizations, plus IG community news."

☞ Caucuses

The word *caucus* has three meanings. First, it refers to the official organization of each party in each chamber (i.e., party caucus). Second, it is the official title of the organization of House Democrats (House and Senate Republicans, and Senate Democrats, call their organizations "conferences"). Third, caucus is a term for an informal group of members who share legislative interests. Several of these use the term in their titles.

Democratic Caucus. This Web site (**http://dcaucusweb.house.gov/**) presents information on the caucus, a calendar, issues (comparison of positions between both political parties), a directory of House Democratic members, news, task forces (a directory of eighteen task forces), press releases, "House Facts," a site search, and an opportunity to receive e-mail updates.

House Republican Policy Committee. The committee "is the policy-making arm of the House Majority. It is comprised of the House Leadership (the Speaker, the Majority Leader, the Majority Whip, the Conference Chairman, the Policy Chairman, the Conference Vice Chairman, the Conference Secretary, the NRCC Chairman, and the elected leaders of the Junior, Sophomore, and Freshmen classes), the chairmen of key standing committees of the House, and Members elected by region and seniority. The Committee meets weekly to consider legislation and issues of national importance." The Web site (**http://policy.house.gov/**) presents information about the caucus and its subcommittees, reports, key issues, policy statements, news releases and reports, the leadership agenda, publications, related Web links, "What's New," photographs, and general information, including how to send e-mail messages to the Committee.

House Republican Conference. The conference's Web site (**http://www.gop.gov/**) contains information about key issues and members of Congress and news releases. At **http://www.gop.gov/**, the House Republican Committee informs the public about the activities of House Republicans and legislation under consideration on the floor. There is an opportunity to register for e-mail updates.

Congressional Black Caucus. This home page (**http://www.house.gov/ebjohnson/cbcmain.htm**) contains information about the caucus, tributes, news, views, coverage of issues, history, related Web links, membership and profiles, and more.

Congressional Hispanic Caucus. This organization's Web site (**http://www.house.gov/reyes/CHC/**) offers news, coverage of task forces, media, and information about the caucus.

Western Caucus. This home page (**http://www.house.gov/cannon/wc.htm**), which covers the western states, provides articles, letters, statements membership information, and related Web links.

The Congressional Internet Caucus Advisory Committee. The committee is "a diverse group of public interest, nonprofit, and industry groups working to educate the Congress and the public about important Internet-related policy issues." This site (**http://www.netcaucus.org/**) contains information about the caucus and its activities (e.g., issues, events, briefing books, statistics, and event schedule).

Congressional Rural Caucus. This bipartisan coalition of House members is committed to assisting "agricultural and rural America build strong, more prosperous futures for those living on farms, ranches, and rural communities." The Web site (**http://www.house.gov/emerson/crc/**) contains press releases, links to rural sites, and an overview (e.g., members, mission, and organization).

Congressional Progressive Caucus. This group examines problems confronting the nation and the world. The Web site (**http://bernie.house.gov/pc/**) offers coverage of a wide range of issues, including, for example, education, corporate welfare, energy, and the federal budget. There are also issue briefs and alerts, as well as daily updates on the issues.

⟲ Other

For access to House commissions (e.g., National Commission on Restructuring the Internal Revenue Service) and House organizations (e.g., Chief Administrative Officer), see **http://www.house.gov/house/Party_organizations.html**.

THE SENATE

The home page for the Senate (**http://www.senate.gov/**) covers

- "Senators:" A list of members (alphabetical order, state, and party)

- "Committees": Explanation of the committee system, list of committees, committee assignments, committee and subcommittee membership, and the Caucus on International Narcotics Control. There is access to historical links on the Senate legislative process and Senate rules

- "Legislation & Records": How members voted, nominations, *Congressional Record,* treaties, bills and resolutions, appropriations bills, lobbying disclosure, and legislative process (guides to the Senate covering the legislative process, standing rules of the chamber, a ill search option, access to the Office of the Public Record, coverage of landmark legislation, and more)

- "Art & History": Senate history, sculptures, paintings, historical minute essays, exhibits, people, and so on

- "Visiting the Senate": Information about visiting the nation's Washington, D.C., and the U.S. Capitol. It is possible to take a virtual tour of the Capitol

- "Visitors Center": Provides the e-mail and office address for each senator

- "Reference": A virtual reference desk (access to information on topics such as "cloture," "nominations," "publications," "rules and procedure," and "traditions"), books, bibliographies, "Is it true that . . . ," "How to find . . ." (e.g., bills, committee reports and conference reports), or "How to research the collections of former senators"), a glossary, the Senate's organization, and access to the United States Constitution

- The Senate Historical Office, which is located under "Art & History," "collects and provides information on important events, precedents, dates, statistics, and historical comparisons of current and past Senate activities for use by members and staff, the media, scholars, and the general public. The office advises senators and committees on cost-effective disposition of their noncurrent office

files, assists researchers seeking access to Senate records, and maintains automated information databases detailing locations of former members' papers.
Since 1976, the office has conducted a series of oral history interviews with former senators and retired members of the Senate staff. Both biographical and insti-
tutional in scope, these interviews include personal recollections of careers within
the Senate and discussions of how Congress has changed over the years. With the
online publication of a 1989 interview with Senator George A. Smathers
(D-Florida), the Historical Office initiated a project that will eventually provide
Internet access to its complete oral history series." Those transcripts available
online can be found at **http://www.senate.gov/artandhistory/history/common/
generic/Senate_Historical_Office.htm**.

Also in the section on "Art & History," the Senate Historical Office provides the
Biographical Directory of the United States Congress, which offers historical news,
archival, biographical, and bibliographical information on each current and former
senator (see **http://bioguide.congress.gov/biosearch/biosearch.asp**). An institu-
tional bibliography of the Senate covers items published since 1789.

Committees

Figure 4.3 identifies examples of the types of resources that the standing, special,
and select committees issue. As with the House of Representatives, committees tend to
provide hearing transcripts, Webcasts, and schedules of committee meetings, as well
as links to related sites. Clearly, the Web offers a rich variety of information on the
Senate, much of which tends to be current.

Leadership

For an identification of the leadership (the majority leader, the minority leader,
the assistant majority leader, and the assistant minority leader, as well as a discussion
of their responsibilities and an organizational chart (see **http://www.senate.gov/senate.
gov/pagelayout/senators/a_three_sections_ with_teasers/leadership.htm**).

Officers and Staff

The site (**http://www.senate.gov/pagelayout/history/one_item_and_teasers/
officers.htm**) provides access to home pages for the vice president of the United
States, who is also president of the Senate; the president pro tempore; the secretary of
the Senate; the sergeant at arms; party secretaries; the Senate chaplain; and the secretary of state.

Figure 4.3. Types of Information Available from Senate Committees.

Committees	URL	Types of Information Available
Committee on Agriculture, Nutrition, and Forestry	**http://agriculture.senate.gov/**	Membership, rules, press releases, hearings, topical coverage (nutrition, food safety, and forestry), legislation, committee briefs, oversight, resources, links, history, and so on
Committee on Appropriations	**http://appropriations.senate.gov/**	General information (membership and jurisdiction), subcommittees news, legislation, floor schedule, the budget process, hearings, markup, and more
Committee on Armed Services	**http://armed-services.senate.gov/**	Membership, hearings, publications, press releases, and about the committee
Committee on Banking, Housing, and Urban Affairs	**http://banking.senate.gov/**	Membership, hearings (including video archive of selected hearings), from the chairman, news releases, committee information, nominations, documents, links, banking's legislative milestones, "from ranking minority," and schedule
Committee on Budget	**http://budget.senate.gov/**	Information about the committee, hearings and testimony, and links to a majority and to a minority Web site
Committee on Commerce, Science, and Transportation	**http://commerce.senate.gov/**	Issues, press releases, legislation, upcoming events, audio of all hearings (see CapitolHearings.com), hearing archive, schedule, about the committee, and how to contact committee
Committee on Energy and Natural Resources	**http://energy.senate.gov/**	About the committee, hearings, schedule, legislation, major issues, contact information, other resources, and issues

Committees	URL	Types of Information Available
Committee on Environment and Public Works	**http://epw.senate.gov/**	Subcommittees, environmental law, rules, press releases, nominations, meeting notes, membership, hearings, jurisdiction, and schedule
Committee on Finance	**http://finance.senate.gov/**	Hearings, legislation, other links, about the committee, news, weekly schedule, and opportunity for public comment
Committee on Foreign Relations	**http://foreign.senate.gov/**	Using AltaVista's translation service, the information (news, hearings, publications) can be translated into French, German, Italian, Portuguese, or Spanish
Committee on Governmental Affairs	**http://govt-aff.senate.gov/**	Membership, hearings, key legislation, jurisdiction, press statements, video of selected hearings, special investigations and reports, Internet sites of interest, and subcommittees
Committee on Health, Education, and Human Resources	**http://labor.senate.gov/**	Hearings and Webcasts, press releases, legislation, membership, subcommittees jurisdiction, links, and "Previous Congresses" (coverage of the committee for the 105th and 106th Congresses)
Committee on Indian Affairs	**http://indian.senate.gov/**	Hearings (past, upcoming, and postponed), news, membership, briefings, staff, internships, links, history, press, and more
Committee on Judiciary	**http://judiciary.senate.gov/**	Membership, subcommittees, hearings, nominations, business meetings, press releases, week's schedule, instruction on ordering a document, committee information, frequently asked questions, site search, and an online library (e.g., legislation, hearings, and reports)

Figure 4.3. (*Cont.*)

Committees	URL	Types of Information Available
Committee on Rules and Administration	**http://rules.senate.gov/**	Purpose and jurisdiction, rules, membership, and hearings
Committee on Small Business and Entrepreneurs	**http://sbc.senate.gov/**	Legislation, members, news (including a news archive), hearings, jurisdiction, rules, Democrat's Web site, photographs, information on committee and its chairman, and so on
Committee on Veterans' Affairs	**http://veterans.senate.gov/**	About the committee, hearings, membership, legislation, resources and publications, press releases, schedule, and contact the committee
Select Committee on Ethics	**http://ethics.senate.gov/**	(There is a choice of a text or graphics on this site.) Membership, ethics manual, public finance disclosure, reports, forms, joining a mailing list, and related links
Select Committee on Intelligence	**http://intelligence.senate.gov/**	Membership, jurisdiction, legislation, hearings, press releases, publications, links, and "Statutes/Laws/Executive Orders"
Special Committee on Aging	**http://aging.senate.gov/**	"What's New?," headlines, about the committee, committee events, Elder Justice Center, Boomer Center, coverage of issues, useful links, Fraud Hotline, and more

⤳ Other

There is also the

- Senate Republican Policy Committee: "composed of GOP Senate leaders and the chairmen of the Senate standing committees, it assists GOP senators and their staffs with all aspects of the legislative process" (**http://www.senate. gov/~rpc/**)

- Senate Democratic Leadership Committee, which "provides information to Democratic Senators, their staffs, the press and the public. Reports range from weekly floor and hearing schedules, to detailed legislative analyses" (**http://democrats.senate.gov/leadership.html**)

- Senate Republican Conference, which "assists Republican Senators by providing a full range of media related services in the areas of television, radio, and graphics" (**http://www.senate.gov/~scr/home/index.cfm**)

Also worthy of mention is the Senate Caucus on International Narcotics Control, which is the only official caucus of the Senate. The caucus's Web site (**http://drugcaucus.senate.gov/**) identifies its members, hearings, events, news items, and so on.

JOINT COMMITTEES (OF BOTH CHAMBERS)

➹ Joint Economic Committee

The Joint Economic Committee (JEC) reviews economic conditions and offers recommendations for achieving full employment. The home page (**http://jec.senate.gov/**) specifies "What's New" about the Committee and its members and provides access to hearings, press releases, reports, and research and studies. It also allows user to sign up to receive e-mail notices and to search the site.

➹ Joint Committee on Taxation

This Web site (**http://www.house.gov/jct/**) contains selective publications, such as the Committee's *General Explanation of the Joint Committee on Taxation.*

➹ Joint Committee on Printing

"The principle purpose of the Joint Committee on Printing is to oversee the functions of the Government Printing Office (GPO) and general printing procedures of the federal government." The home page (**http://jcp.senate.gov/**) identifies committee members and the mission and "business" (organizational meeting) of the committee. There are also committee rules and inspector general reports and audits.

➹ Joint Committee on the Library

This committee deals with the Library of Congress. There is a listing of its membership (see **http://www.senate.gov/general/committee_membership/committee_memberships_JSLC.htm**).

SUPPORT AGENCIES

☞ Architect of the Capitol

"The Architect of the Capitol is both the person and the title of the agency responsible to Congress for the structural and mechanical care of the Capitol, the legislative office buildings, the Library of Congress buildings, the Supreme Court buildings, the surrounding grounds, and other elements of the Capitol Complex. The Architect is also responsible for the care and conservation of numerous works of art." The Web site (**http://www.aoc.gov/**) provides "an overview of the capitol and its function, the building's construction history, its architectural features and historic spaces, its architects, and the Capitol Grounds." It also contains information about the congressional office buildings, current and recent projects, works of art, and answers to frequently asked questions.

"Established by Congress in 1820, the United States Botanic Garden [a component of the Architect of the Capitol] is the oldest botanic garden in North American. The garden's first greenhouse was constructed in 1842; since 1849 the Garden has been located at the eastern end of the Mall." The home page (**http://www.usbg.gov/**) provides information about the garden and its projects (e.g., there is a virtual tour).

☞ Congressional Budget Office

The Congressional Budget Office (CBO) provides Congress "with objective, timely, nonpartisan analyses needed for economic and budget decisions and with the information and estimates required for the Congressional budget process." The home page (**http://www.cbo.gov/**) offers information about the agency, publications, congressional testimony, cost estimates, a site map, employment opportunities, technical papers, links to related sites, " "Historical Budget Data," the agency's record on economic forecasts, and more.

☞ General Accounting Office

The General Accounting Office (GAO), "the investigative arm" or "watchdog agency" of Congress, is a nonpartisan agency that helps "Congress oversee federal programs and operations to assure accountability to the American people. . . . GAO accomplishes its mission through a variety of activities including financial audits, program reviews, investigations, legal support, and policy/program analyses." Furthermore, "GAO's findings and recommendations are published as reports to congressional members or delivered as testimony to congressional committees."

GAO's Web site (**http://www.gao.gov/**) provides access to

- "From the Comptroller General"

- GAO's strategic plan, etc.

- GAO Reports (updated daily; Today's Reports, Testimony, Month in Review, Annual Indexes, Special Publications. *Subscribe to daily e-mail alert for newly released GAO products)*

- Order GAO Products (order printed copies of GAO reports, request reference services)

- Other Publications (policy, the *Yellow Book*, methodology, documentation, software, guidance, financial report of the U.S. government, GAO strategic plan)

- Employment Opportunities (current job vacancies, recruitment information, divisions and offices within the GAO)

- Careers at GAO (employment opportunities)

- About GAO (mission, history, annual report, organization, and photographs)

- For the Press (e.g., subscribe to e-mail alerts)

- GAO Legal Products (updated daily; legal decisions and opinions about appropriations, bid protests, and major federal agency rules)

- GAO's Performance and Accountability Series and High Risk Update

- Help Using This Site (how to find reports, help for the visually impaired, how the site was created, and privacy policy)

- Market Mechanism for Student Loans (a study group)

- FraudNet (report allegations of fraud, waste, abuse, or the mismanagement of federal funds)

- Commercial Activities Panel (includes *Federal Register* notice and request for comments)

- In the News

There is an opportunity to search the site, and there is a site map (**http://www.gao.gov/sitemap.html**). GPO Access covers GAO reports and testimony (**http://www.access.gpo.gov/su_docs/aces/aces160.shtml**) and comptroller general decisions (**http://www.access.gpo**. gov/su_docs/aces/aces170.shtml). Sixty days of current comptroller general decisions are kept on the GAO site, and older decisions are retained on GPO Access.

Figure 4.4 illustrates the wide variety of topical areas covered in GAO reports and congressional testimony. For any or all of these topical areas, as well as decisions of the comptroller general, the public can subscribe to e-mail alerts whereby the agency will send daily e-mail announcements of any report or testimony issued in the selected topical area(s) (see **http://www.gao.gov/subtest/subscribe.html**).

Government Printing Office

The Government Printing Office (GPO) prints, binds, and distributes government publications, and, through its Office of Superintendent of Documents, sells selected publications, manages GPO Access for distributing electronic media, administers the Federal Depository Library Program, and performs related services.

In December 2002, GPO printed the administration's next fiscal year budget (for 2004). What makes this printing noteworthy is that for the first time since the initial budget was printed in 1921, GPO had to gain the contract through competitive bidding.

It won the contract with an offer of $387,000; the previous year the cost for printing the budget was more than $500,000. The administration celebrated the savings and, declaring the competition showed that its price could not be beaten, GPO likewise declared a victory.

Figure 4.4. GAO Reports by Topic.*

Agriculture and Food	Housing
Budget and Spending	Income Security
Business, Industry, and Consumers	Information Management
Civil Rights	International Affairs
Economic Development	Justice and Law Enforcement
Education	National Defense
Employment	National Resources
Energy	Science, Space, and Technology
Environmental Protection	Social Services
Financial Institutions	Special Publications
Financial Management	Tax Policy and Administration
Government Operations	Transportation
Health	Veterans Affairs
Homeland Security	

*See **http://www.gao.gov/subtest/subscribe.html**.

GPO's home page (**http://www.gpo.gov/**) provides information about the agency, including its leadership, mission, organizational structure, and so on. A "Sights and Sounds" file offers video coverage of the Web offset presses that the GPO "purchased to improve print quality of [the] *Congressional Record* and *Federal Register.*" The file also shows the "adhesive binding line which gathers signatures, trims, covers, adhesive binds, addresses and bundles the finished products" (**http://www.access.gpo.gov/demo/vap.html**).

GPO's Office of Congressional and Public Affairs "serves as the principal contact with the Congress, the news media, other Government entities, private sector organizations and the general public." The home page (**http://www.gpo.gov/public-affairs/index.html**) provides general and legislative information, publications (including the GPO *Newsletter* and annual report), fact sheets, news releases, official biographies of GPO's senior-level personnel, congressional testimony, and media contacts.

GPO Access (**http://www.gpoaccess.gov/**) provides information resources by branch of government, a "Featured Item," "What's New?," an "A–Z Resource List," "Locate a Federal Depository Library" (**http://www.gpoaccess.gov/libraries.html**), "U.S. Government Online Bookstore" (**http://bookstore.gpo.gov/**), "Ben's Guide to U.S. Government" see (Chapter 13), "GPO Access User Support," a site search, and pull-down menus for resources by topic, and "Federal-wide Resources." Under "Official Federal Government Information at Your Fingertips" (**http://www.access.gpo.gov/su_docs/**), GPO Access provides similar information, a site search, site contents, an online bookstore, findings aids, library services, "What's New Archive," "What's New on GPO Access," a link to Ben's Guide and

- Quick Links . . .

  Code of Federal Regulations and *Federal Register* (administrative law or rules and regulations)

  Congressional Record (for the legislative process and occurrences of the floor of both the House and Senate)

  United States Code (for public laws)

  Congressional bills

  Catalog of United States Government Publications (formerly titled the *Monthly Catalog of United States Government Publications*)

- Other databases

- What's Available . . .

  Legislative

  Executive

  Judicial

  Regulatory

  Administrative Decisions

  Core Documents of U.S. Democracy

  Hosted Federal Web Sites

Each of these options leads to specific titles and search options. For example, under "Legislative," there are choices such as

- Congressional bills

- Committee prints

- *Congressional Directory*

- Congressional documents

- Congressional hearings

- *Congressional Pictorial Directory*

- *Congressional Record* and *Congressional Record Index* (**http://www.gpoaccess. gov/crecord/index.html**)

- Congressional reports

- *Deschler's Precedents of the U.S. House of Representatives*

  Economic Indicators

  History of bills

  House calendar and journal

  House, Senate, and executive reports

House, Senate, and treaty documents

Public laws

Senate calendar

United States Census Monitoring Board

United States Code

U.S. Constitution

Miscellaneous House and Senate publications and committees

Among the titles under "Executive" are, for instance, the

- *Budget of the United States Government*

- *Public Papers of the Presidents of the United States* (at present, coverage is very selective; see also the presidential libraries administered by the National Archives and Records Administration in Chapter 6)

- *United States Government Manual* (covers federal departments and agencies, giving their enabling legislation, purpose, functions, activities, and key contacts)

- *Weekly Compilation of Presidential Documents* (a significant listing of presidential statements, proclamations, speeches, executive orders, nominations, press conferences, and press releases)

"Core Documents of U.S. Democracy" (**http://www.gpoaccess.gov/coredocs.html**) groups publications by eight categories: "Cornerstone Documents," "Congressional," "Presidential," "Judicial," "Regulatory," "Demographic," "Economic," and "Miscellaneous." The first category includes, for example, the Articles of Confederation, the Bill of Rights, and The Federalist Papers; examples in the last category are the Emancipation Proclamation and the Gettysburg Address.

The "A–Z Resource List" includes, among other items, the *Catalog of United States Government Publications* (CGP; **http://www.gpoaccess.gov/cgp/index.html**), which provides bibliographic information to assist in the identification, location, and access to information products offered through the GPO. Some of the publications in the *Catalog* are available online, whereas others require a visit to a depository library. (see **http://www.gpoaccess.gov/libraries.html**).

The FDLP Desktop (**http://www.access.gpo.gov/su_docs/fdlp/index.html**) provides locator services and tools, information about the depository library program, a site index, and other resources available for use by depository library staff. *Browse Topics* (**http://www.access.gpo.gov/su_docs/locators/topics/index.html**), a partnership service developed by the Oklahoma State University Library, "provides topical pathfinders to U.S. government information. . . . This list of topics is derived from the approximately 150 subject bibliographies that are used to categorize the publications, subscriptions, and electronic products for sale by the Superintendent of Documents." A service, *New Electronic Titles* (NET) (**http://www.access.gpo.gov/su_docs/locators/net/index.html**), which started in January 2000, "is a finding aid used to locate, by month, online Federal Government publications that were acquired for the Federal Depository Library Program Electronic Collection." GPO Access identifies other "Locator Tools and Services" at **http://www.access.gpo.gov/su_docs/fdlp/lts.html**.

FDLP's Electronic Collection Archive (**http://www.access.gpo.gov/su_docs/locators/net/net_archive/index.html**) provides electronic publications no longer available from the issuing agency. The purpose is to complement the holdings of depository libraries and ensure public access to a wider array of government information products (see also "Other PPA Resources" of the Permanent Public Access [PPA] to U.S. Government Information Working Group, **http://www.gpo.gov/ppa/resources.html**). This page covers, for instance, digital archiving.

The John C. Stennis Center for Public Service

Created in 1988, the center strives "to promote and strengthen public service leadership in America at all levels of government" and "to carry on the commitment to public service exemplified by the life and work of Senator J. C. Stennis of Mississippi." The home page (**http://www.stennis.gov/**) provides the center's mission, programs, a biography of the former senator, and other information about the center. There is also a selective list of Web sites "for those who are interested in public service."

Library of Congress

The Library of Congress (LC) has assorted divisions, services, and publications on its Web site. The home page (**http://www.loc.gov/**) provides general information about the LC, its services, reading rooms, catalog of books and other holdings, thesauri, resources for researchers and information professionals, and hours during which the reading room is open. There is also an opportunity to search the database, except such a search will not be comprehensive of the site. Other choices from the home page include

- American Memory ("primary source and archival material relating to American culture and history")
- THOMAS
- Copyright Office
- The Library Today (e.g., news and events)
- Help & FAQs (general information)
- Exhibitions (an online gallery)
- American's library ("Fun site for kids & families")
- A site map
- Information resources targeted for specific audiences (e.g., researchers, parents, and teachers)
- A gift shop

LC's Serial and Government Publications Division maintains an eight-page "Browse Government Resources" (**http://lcweb.loc.gov/rr/news/extgovd.html**), which lists a number of gateways, portals, one-stop shopping sites, and other useful sites for access to legal information. It also has links to selected agencies, sources monitoring the legislative process within Congress and politics, and links to resources from some governments outside the United States.

American Memory. Dedicated to digitizing and preserving information that has unique value to American history, the site (**http://memory.loc.gov/**) stores digitized documents and sheet music, images (e.g., the 1906 San Francisco earthquake and fire), manuscripts, films, photographs, sound recordings (e.g., folk music), and maps. For example, there are more than 2,100 baseball cards, dating from 1887 and coverage of the origins of American animation.

The motion picture collection, as another example, contains collections related to "Early Motion Pictures, 1897–1919." One of these collections covers the Spanish-American War. Film crews dispatched to cover the war for the Edison Manufacturing Company and the American Mutoscope & Biograph Company produced motion pictures of the war in Cuba, and the subsequent Philippine Revolution, from 1898 to 1901. This war was the first one "in which the motion picture camera played a role." The complete collection, which "will include 68 motion pictures and a selection of sound recordings related to the war," shows "troops, ships, notable figures, and parades, as well as reenactments of battles and other war-time events" (**http://memory. loc.gov/ammem/sawhtml/sawhome.html**). Brief essays explain the historical content of the films. For instance, there is coverage of Theodore Roosevelt's Rough Riders, the construction of a military road, an ambush, and the wreck of the battleship *Maine*.

American Memory also explains how to order film reproductions and a variety of other resources on the war, including maps, still photographs, biographies of leading figures, and documents. There are also indexes of some of the Library of Congress holdings that are not online, such as accounts of the war by Americans, Cubans, Filipinos, and Spaniards.

Another example covers "The Last Days of a President: Films of McKinley and the Pan-American Exposition." Twenty-eight films in this collection provide "footage of William McKinley at his second inauguration, the Pan-American exposition, and . . . the President's funeral after his assassination." Other examples include the operations of a factory, Westinghouse Works, in 1904; "early motion pictures and sound recordings from the Thomas A. Edison Companies"; New York City, 1898-1906; and "vaudeville and popular entertainment, 1870-1920." On the lighter side, American Memory offers Coca-Cola television commercials of the past fifty years.

American Memory has a Learning Page (**http://memory.loc.gov/ ammem/ndlpedu/index.html**), which offers resources for "students, teachers, and life-long learners." There are activities, lessons, programs, research tools, features, a historical time line, and coverage of topics such as elections, women pioneers, and presidential inaugurations.

Moreover, America's Story from America's Library (**http://www.americaslibrary. gov/cgi-bin/page.cgi**) promotes LC and its collections, as well as American Memory. It includes odds and ends about the nation's past, including some pictures, and encourages the more serious searcher to visit American Memory. For a discussion of the Library of Congress digital collections, of which American Memory is just one, see **http://www.loc.gov/library/libarch-digital.html**.

Exhibitions. Here are all kinds of theme-linked online collections (**http:// www.loc.gov/exhibits/**). Some rotate, and others are on permanent view. "Bob Hope and American Variety" offers a rich history of American comedy over a number of years. The designs of Frank Lloyd Wright are celebrated from 1922–1932. The fascinating sketches and plans here first appeared in a museum exhibit that closed in 1997. Some of the other collections are "Blondie Gets Married! Comic Strip Drawings by Chic Young," "Religion and the Founding of the American Republic," "Sigmund Freud: Conflict & Culture," and "The Wizard of Oz: An American Fairy Tale." The exhibitions also include Thomas Jefferson's handwritten draft of the Declaration of Independence.

Congressional Research Service. CRS's home page (**http://lcweb.loc.gov/crsinfo**) focuses exclusively on employment opportunities, including recruiting, internship, and visiting scholar programs. It does not provide access to the wealth of information that the CRS generates on behalf of Congress. Selected reports and *Issue Briefs*, however, are available from the House Committee on Rules (**http://www.house. gov/rules/crs_reports.htm**) and other congressional committees (see also p. 83 of the companion book to this volume, *United States Government Information,* mentioned in the Preface.)

The Library of Congress Country Studies. These studies (**http://lcweb2.loc.gov/ frd/cs/cshome.html**) comprise a continuing series of books prepared by the Federal Research Division of the Library of Congress under the Country Studies/Area Handbook Program sponsored by the Department of the Army. This online series presently contains studies of 101 countries and regions in "lesser known areas of the world or regions in which U.S. forces might be deployed. . . . Notable omissions include Canada, France, the United Kingdom, and other Western nations, as well as a number of African nations." The books tend to

deal with a particular foreign country, describing and analyzing its political, economic, social, and national security systems and institutions, and examining the interrelationships of those systems and the ways they are shaped by cultural factors. Each study is written by a multidisciplinary team of social scientists. . . . Particular attention is devoted to the people who make up the society, their origins, dominant beliefs and values, their common interests and the issues on which they are divided, the nature and extent of their involvement with national institutions, and their attitudes toward each other and toward their social system and political order.

A cautionary note explains that "the books represent the analysis of the authors and should not be construed as an expression of an official United States government position, policy, or decision. The authors have sought to adhere to accepted standards of scholarly objectivity." Funding for the program was cut in the late 1990s, however, and the existing collection will no longer be updated. Nonetheless, it remains a valuable historical collection.

Digital Library Federation. Founded in 1995, the Digital Library Federation (DLF) is a

consortium of libraries and related agencies that are pioneering in the use of electronic-information technologies to extend their collections and services. Through its members, the DLF provides leadership for libraries broadly by

- Identifying standards and "best practices" for digital collections and network access

- Coordinating leading-edge research-and-development in libraries' use of electronic-information technology

- Helping start projects and services that libraries need but cannot develop individually

The home page (**http://www.diglib.org/dlfhomepage.htm**) explains the DLF and covers "What's New," "Architecture," "Preservation," "Collections," "Standards & Practices," "Use & Users," "Roles & Responsibilities," "Forums," "Publications & Resources," and site "Search."

National Film Preservation Board. The NFPB, a public advisory group, "works to ensure the survival, conservation and increased public availability of America's film heritage, including: advising the Librarian [of Congress] on the annual selection of films to the National Film Registry, and counseling the Librarian on development and implementation of the national film preservation plan." The home page (**http://lcweb.loc.gov/film**) provides basic information on the NFPB and covers its members, preservation research a list of titles on the National Film Registry, the National Film Preservation Foundation, "Other Film Resources," and "Moving Image Archive."

National Library Service for the Blind and Physically Handicapped. The home page for the National Library Service (**http://lcweb.loc.gov/nls/**) contains basic information (including press releases, frequently asked questions, and "What's New"), a draft standard for digital talking books, a sample talking book (in RealAudio format), catalogs and book listings, fact sheets, directories, reference publications, identification of NLS services, newsletters, technical papers, information about how to contact NLS, and so on.

United States Copyright Office. The office has the following responsibilities:

- To provide expert assistance to Congress on intellectual property matters

- To advise Congress on anticipated changes in U.S. copyright law

- To analyze and assist in the drafting of copyright legislation and legislative reports and to provide and undertake studies for Congress

- To offer advice to Congress on compliance with multilateral agreements such as the Berne Convention for the Protection of Literary and Artistic Work

- To work with the State Department, the U.S. Trade Representative's Office, and the Patent and Trademark Office in providing technical expertise in negotiations for international intellectual property agreements; and provides technical assistance to other countries in developing their own copyright laws

- Through its International Copyright Institute, to promote worldwide understanding and cooperation in providing protection for intellectual property

Furthermore,

The Copyright Office is also an office of record, a place where claims to copyright are registered and where documents relating to copyright may be recorded when the requirements of the copyright law are met. The Copyright Office furnishes information about the provisions of the copyright law and the procedures for making registration, explains the operations and practices of the Copyright Office, and reports on facts found in the public records of the Office. The Office also administers various compulsory licensing provisions of the law, which include collecting royalties. Additionally, the Copyright Office and the Library of Congress administer the Copyright Arbitration Royalty Panels, which meet for limited times for the purpose of adjusting rates and distributing royalties.

The Web site (**http://www.loc.gov/copyright/**) provides

- What's New
- About the Office
- News
- Publications (application forms, information circulars, form letters, office reports and studies, federal regulations, and "Compendium II, Copyright Office Practices")
- Laws
- Licensing
- Searching Copyright Records (e.g., registration)
- Laws and Policy (e.g., copyright law, new and pending regulations, current legislation)
- How to Register a Work
- How to Record a Document
- Related Links

NewsNet is a news bulletin that covers current and past issues. There is also a calendar (see **http://copyright.gov/newsnet/**).

OTHER AGENCIES

Office of Compliance

Established by the *Congressional Accountability Act of 1995*, the Office of Compliance (CAA) generally extends the right and protections of 11' employment and labor laws to covered employees in the legislative branch of the federal government. The CAA also makes it unlawful for any employing office to intimidate, retaliate against, or otherwise take negative action against a covered employee for opposing an unlawful practice, initiating proceedings or bringing a claim under the CAA, or for testifying, assessing, or participating in a proceeding under the CAA. The CAA only applies to alleged violations occurring on or after January 23, 1996. Workplace practices can be challenged only if they violate a statutory requirement or prohibition of the CAA.

The Web site (**http://www.compliance.gov/**) provides press releases, contact information sheets, reports decisions, general information, and more.

Medicare Payment Advisory Commission

Congress merged the Physician Payment Review Commission and the Prospective Payment Assessment Committee, as part of the *Balanced Budget Act of 1997,* to create the Medicare Payment Advisory Commission (MedPAC). The Commission advises Congress on Medicare payment policies. The site (**http://www.medpac.gov/**) presents information about the agency, announcement of public meetings, publications, job opportunities, a mailing list, and useful Web links.

National Bipartisan Commission on the Future of Medicare

Created by Congress in the *Balanced Budget Act of 1997,* the commission is charged with examining the Medicare program and making recommendations to strengthen and improve it. The home page (**http://rs9.loc.gov/medicare/**) provides "Key Documents," news and information about the Commission, "Commission Proceedings," and "The Facts about Medicare."

Office of Technology Assessment

Now defunct (it ceased in 1995), the Office of Technology Assessment, a nonpartisan analytical agency, produced a number of reports and background papers that, although now outdated, provide an excellent background analysis of some issues that are still relevant today. A number of the studies present the results of some large-scale research studies that congressional committees requested be conducted. An archive of publications still on the Web is available through the GPO (**http://www.access.gpo. gov/ota/index.html**) and the University of North Texas Libraries (see below).

Some Other Defunct Agencies

The University of North Texas Libraries, in cooperation with the Government Printing Office, provides Cybercemetery (**http://govinfo.library.unt.edu/cc_AtoZ. html**), which offers access to the electronic files of some agencies that have ceased operation. Examples include the Advisory Commission on Intergovernmental Relations (**http://www.library.unt.edu/gpo/ACIR/acir.html**), the Web site for the Vice President Al Gore's National Partnership for Reinventing Government, which, for instance, provides documents on the development of the Internet during the Clinton administration, and the Office of Technology Assessment.

SOME NONGOVERNMENTAL WEB SITES

FedNet

FedNet (**http://www.fednet.net/**) gives live and archived audio and video coverage of congressional activities, including House and Senate floor debates, hearings, and press conferences. FedNet also provides "today's schedule" for debates and hearings and a hearing, press, and event archives.

The Hill

The Hill (**http://www.hillnews.com/**), a weekly subscription service (billed with the first issue), "reports and analyzes the actions of Congress as it struggles to reconcile the needs of those it represents with the legitimate needs of the administration, lobbyists and the news media. We explain the pressures confronting policy-makers, and the ways—often unpredictable—that decisions are made." Features include stories, pundit speaks, classifieds, advertising, subscription information, daily briefings, and so on.

Roll Call

Roll Call (**http://www.rollcall.com/**) presents recent news, policy briefings, commentary and politics, "news, congressional developments, editorial commentary and opinion," and so on.

TRACING LEGISLATION

Chapter 4 of *United States Government Information* (see Preface), as well as its companion CD-ROM, discusses the legislative history process and provides detailed coverage of the related sources. This section offers a brief sketch of those sources relevant to tracing the role of Congress in this process. THOMAS, GPO Access, and the Web sites of congressional committees play an important role regarding this process. Legislative histories result in the enactment of public laws, as reported, for instance in the *United States Code,* which the Office of the Law Revision Counsel of the U.S. House of Representatives, prepares and publishes. One database (**http://www.gpoaccess.gov/uscode/index.html**) contains the general and permanent laws of the United States. More precisely,

- For the *United States Code* (1994), the general and permanent laws are in effect as of January 4, 1995

- For the *United States Code* (1994, supplement 1), the general and permanent laws are in effect as of January 16, 1996

- For the *United States Code* (1994, supplement 2), the general and permanent laws are in effect as of January 6, 1997

- For the *United States Code* (1994, supplement 3), the general and permanent laws are in effect as of January 26, 1998

- For the *United States Code* (1994, supplement 4), the general and permanent laws are in effect as of January 5, 1999

- For the *United States Code* (1994, supplement 5), the general and permanent laws are in effect as of January 23, 2000

- For the *United States Code* (2000), the general and permanent laws are in effect as of January 2, 2001

GPO Access (**http://www.access.gpo.gov/**) has the Public and Private Laws database, a collection of laws enacted from the 104th Congress forward (see also **http://www.gpoaccess.gov/plaws/index.html**).

Other resources related to passage of legislation by Congress and action taken by the President include:

- Bills (the text of legislation)

    GPO Access provides the text of bills (**http://www.gpoaccess.gov/bills/ index.html**); bills can be downloaded

    LOCIS (of the Library of Congress) provides bills since 1973 by subject, keyword, sponsor, and stage of legislative process

    Clerk of the House

    THOMAS

- Bill Status

    THOMAS

- Documents (miscellaneous information compiled by a committee, as well as executive branch communications)

    GPO Access, **http://www.gpoaccess.gov/serialset/cdocuments/index.html** (and GPO's *Catalog of United States Government Publications*,[7] if the documents have been printed)

    Figures 4.2 and 4.3 (individual committee home pages)

    Clerk of the House

- Hearings (testimony before committees)

    Figures 4.2 and 4.3 (individual committee home pages)

GPO Access, **http://www.access.gpo.gov/congress/cong017.html** (and GPO's *Catalog of United States Government Publications,* if the hearings have been published)

THOMAS

- Reports (contain the text of legislation coming from a committee, together with the interpretation of the majority (those favoring the legislation) and perhaps minority (those in opposition)

  Figures 4.2 and 4.3 (individual committee home pages)

  THOMAS

  GPO Access, **http://www.gpoaccess.gov/serialset/creports/index.html** (and GPO's *Catalog of United States Government Publications*, if the report has been published)

- Prints (produced by committees—their staff or a body such as the Congressional Research Service; prints comprise research reports and convey background information on selected issues)

  Figures 4.2 and 4.3 (individual committee home pages)

  GPO Access, **http://www.gpoaccess.gov/cprints/index.html** (and GPO's *Catalog of United States Government Publications*, if the prints have been published)

- Calendars and Schedules

  GPO Access, **http://www.gpoaccess.gov/calendars/index.html** (beginning with the 104th Congress, 1995–1996)

  Figures 4.2 and 4.3 (individual committee home pages)

  Home pages for the House and the Senate

  THOMAS

- Floor Debates

  Congressional Record (available through GPO Access, **http://www.gpoaccess.gov/crecord/index.html**; **http://www.gpoaccess.gov/cri/index.html**)

  THOMAS

- Roll Call Votes

  Congressional Record (available through GPO Access)

  Home pages for the House and the Senate

  THOMAS

- Text of Public Laws

  United States Code

  Public and Private Laws database (THOMAS and GPO Access)

• Presidential Statements, Including Vetoes

White House Web site

Weekly Compilation of Presidential Documents, **http://www.gpoaccess. gov/wcomp/index.html**

Public Papers of the President (annual accumulation of *Weekly Compilation of Presidential Documents*), **http://www.access.gpo.gov/nara/pubpaps/ srchpaps.html**

See also presidential libraries (National Archives and Records Administration, see Chapter 6)

SUMMARY

Like the executive branch, the legislative branch addresses a wide set of issues and topics. A quick perusal of Figures 4.2 and 4.3 illustrate that the standing committees of Congress have broad jurisdiction both for legislative and oversight purposes. In addition, on the floor of Congress, members treat a wide set of topics and issues on a daily basis, as is reflected in the *Congressional Record*. Congressional committees may ask the GAO to investigate an issue or problem and report back its findings through testimony and reports. Thus, the GAO also covers a wide-ranging list of subjects. The same is true of the Library of Congress, the Web site of which covers intellectual property rights, popular culture, history, and the legislative process. Finally, the GPO prints and distributes publications and provides a record of its publishing from the *Catalog of United States Government Publications*. The GPO also maintains an online bookstore offering sales of publications from the three government branches and a depository library program that offers access to a wide assortment of publications covering topics ranging from the humanities to the social and behavioral sciences, as well as health sciences and the physical sciences.

NOTES

1. See **http://www.house.gov/rules_org/95-591.htm#1**.

2. Ibid.

3. Other types of hearings focus on the implementation and administration of programs (*oversight*) or allegations of wrongdoing (*investigative*).

4. See **http://www.house.gov/rules_org/95-591.htm#1**.

5. Ibid.

6. A conference committee contains members from both Chambers and seeks a legislative compromise acceptable to Congress and the White House.

7. The Web version of the *Congressional Record* is not comparable to the paper edition. One could say that this is a problem with many traditional publications as they migrate to the Web, but, in many instances, the Web offers a .pdf version that recreates the intellectual content in a traditional package. With the *Congressional Record*, that does not occur. A reader is forced to "page" through HTML links. On the surface, there may not seem to be a

great difference, but readers must negotiate a series of disjointed texts or Web pages accessible through GPO Access. The bottom line is that, in some significant ways, the *Congressional Record* does not exist on the Web. In other words, the legislative process via the Web is best represented by THOMAS, not the *Congressional Record.*

8.   See Cathy Nelson Hartman, "Storage of Electronic Files of Federal Agencies That Have Ceased Operation: A Partnership for Permanent Access," *Government Information Quarterly* 17 (2000): 299–307.

9.   Many publications listed in GPO's *Catalog of United States Government Publications* are available in depository libraries.

URL Site Guide for This Chapter

Congress

List of Senators
http://www.senate.gov/general/contact_
information/senators_cfm.cfm

List of Representatives
http://www.house.gov/house/MemberW
WW.html

House of Representatives
Home Page
http://www.house.gov/

Committees

Committee Office Web Services and Searching across Sites
http://www.house.gov/house/
CommitteeWWW.html

Agriculture
http://agriculture.house.gov/

Appropriations
http://www.house.gov/appropriations/

Armed Services
http://armedservices.house.gov/

Budget
http://www.house.gov/budget/

Budget.house.gov
http://www.budget.house.gov/
budgettutorial.htm

Education and the Workforce
http://edworkforce.house.gov/

Energy and Commerce
http://energycommerce.house.gov/

Financial Services
http://financialservices.house.gov/

Government Reform
http://www.house.gov/reform/

House Administration
http://www.house.gov/cha/

International Relations
http://wwwa.house.gov/international_
relations/

Judiciary
http://www.house.gov/judiciary

Resources
http://resourcescommittee.house.gov/

Rules
http://www.house.gov/rules/

CRS Reports
http://www.house.gov/rules/crs_
reports.htm

Science
http://www.house.gov/science/
welcome.htm

Small Business
http://www.house.gov/smbiz/

Standards of Official Conduct
http://www.house.gov/ethics/

Transportation and Infrastructure
http://www.house.gov/transportation/

Veterans' Affairs
http://veterans.house.gov/

Ways and Means
http://waysandmeans.house.gov/

Permanent Select Committee on Intelligence
http://intelligence.house.gov/

Select Committee on Homeland Security
http://hsc.house.gov/

Congressional Black Caucus
http://www.house.gov/
ebjohnson/cbcmain.htm

Congressional Hispanic Caucus
http://www.house.gov/reyes/CHC/

**Congressional Internet Caucus
     Advisory Committee**
http://www.netcaucus.org/

Congressional Progressive Caucus
http://bernie.house.gov/pc/

Congressional Rural Caucus
http://www.house.gov/emerson/crc/

Democratic Caucus
http://dcaucusweb.house.gov/

Democratic Leadership
http://www.democraticleader.house.gov/

Democratic Whip
http://democraticwhip.house.gov/

House Republican Conference
http://www.gop.gov/

House Republican Policy Committee
http://policy.house.gov

Office of the Clerk
http://clerkweb.house.gov/

> **Educational Resources**
> Http://clerk.house.gov/eduRsrcs/
>   index.php

> **Historical Highlights**
> http://clerk.house.gov/histHigh/
>   index.php

Office of Inspector General
http://www.house.gov/IG/

Office of the Majority Leader
http://www.majorityleader.gov/

Office of the Majority Whip
http://majoritywhip.house.gov/

Office of the Minority Leader
http://democraticleader.house.gov/

Speaker of the House
http://speaker.house.gov/

Western Caucus
http://www.house.gov/cannon/wc.htm

**House Organizations, Commissions,
     and Task Forces**
http://www.house.gov/house/Party_
     organizations.html

Senate
Home page
http://www.senate.gov/

> **Leadership**
> http://www.senate.gov/pagelayout/
>   senators/a_three_sections_with_
>   teasers/leadership.htm

> **Officers and Staff**
> http://www.senate.gov/pagelayout/
>   history/one_item_and_teasers/
>   officers.htm

Committees

> **Agriculture, Nutrition, and
>   Forestry**
> http://agriculture.senate.gov/

> **Appropriations**
> http://appropriations.senate.gov/

> **Armed Services**
> http://armed-services.senate.gov/

> **Banking, Housing, and Urban
>   Affairs**
> http://banking.senate.gov/

> **Budget**
> http://budget.senate.gov/

> **Commerce, Science, and
>   Transportation**
> http://commerce.senate.gov/

> **Energy and Natural Resources**
> http://energy.senate.gov/

> **Environment and Public Works**
> http://epw.senate.gov/

> **Finance**
> http://finance.senate.gov/

> **Foreign Relations**
> http://foreign.senate.gov/

> **Government Affairs**
> http://govt-aff.senate.gov/

> **Health, Education, Labor and
>   Human Resources**
> http://labor.senate.gov/

> **Indian Affairs**
> http://indian.senate.gov/

Judiciary
http://judiciary.senate.gov/

Rules and Administration
http://rules.senate.gov/

Small Business and Entrepreneurship
http://sbc.senate.gov/

Veterans' Affairs
http://veterans.senate.gov/

Select Committee on
Aging
http://aging.senate.gov/

Ethics
http://ethics.senate.gov

Intelligence
http://intelligence.senate.gov/

Senate Caucus on International
Narcotics Control
http://drugcaucus.senate.gov/

Senate Historical Office
Biographical Directory of the United
States Congress
http://bioguide.congress.gov/biosearch/biosearch.asp

Oral History Program (Online)
http://www.senate.gov/artandhistory/
history/common/generic/Senate_
Historical_Office.htm

Senate Republican Policy Committee
http://democrats.senate.gov/leadership.html

Senate Democratic Leadership
Committee
http://democrats.senate.gov/leadership.html

Senate Republican Conference
http://www.senate.gov/~scr/home/
index.cfm

Joint Committees

Joint Economic Committee
http://jec.senate.gov/

Joint Committee on Printing
http://jcp.senate.gov/

Joint Committee on Taxation
http://www.house.gov/jct/

Joint Committee on the Library
http://www.senate.gov/general/
committee_membership/
committee_memberships_JSLC.htm

Legislative Agencies

Architect of the Capital
http://www.aoc.gov/

United States Botanic Garden
http://www.usbg.gov/

Congressional Budget Office
http://www.cbo.gov/

General Accounting Office
http://www.gao.gov/

Site Map
http://www.gao.gov/sitemap.html

GAO Access Coverage
http://www.access.gpo.gov/su_docs/
aces/aces160.shtml
http://www.access.gpo.gov/su_docs/
aces/aces170.shtml

Subscribe to GAO E-mail Alerts
http://www.gao.gov/subtest/subscribe.
html

Government Printing Office
Home Page
http://www.gpo.gov/

Sights and Sounds
http://www.access.gpo.gov/demo/vap.html

Office of Congressional and Public
Affairs
http://www.access.gpo.gov/
public-affairs/index.html

Office of the Superintendent of
Documents
http://www.access.gpo.gov/su_docs

Bookstore
http://bookstore.gpo.gov/

102

Browse Topics
http://www.access.gpo.gov/su_
    docs/locators/topics/index.html

**Catalog of United States
    Government Publications**
http://www.gpo.gov/su_docs/
    locators/cgp/index.html

**Core Documents of U.S.
    Democracy**
http://www.gpoaccess.gov/
    coredocs.html

FDLP Desktop
http://www.access-gpo.gov/su_
    docs/fdlp/index.html

Electronic Collection Archive
http://www.access.gpo.gov/su_docs/
    locations/net/net/archive/index.
    html

PPA Resources
http://www.gpo.gov/ppa/resources.
    html

**Federal Depository Library
    Program Electronic
    Collection Archive**
http://www.access.gpo.gov/su_
    docs/fdlp/cc/ecarc.html

**Locate a Federal Depository
    Library**
http://www.gpoaccess.gov/libraries/
    html

Locator Tools and Services
http://www.access.gpo.gov/su_docs/
    fdlp/lts.html

Legislative Resources
http://www.access.gpo.gov/su_docs/
    legislative.html

New Electronic Titles
http://www.access.gpo.gov/su_docs/
    locators/net/index.html

**Official Federal Government
    Information at Your
    Fingertip**
http://www.access.gpo.gov/
    su_docs/

GPO Access
http://www.gpoaccess.gov/

Comptroller General's Decisions
http://www.access.gpo.gov/su_
    docs/aces/aces170.shtml

Congressional Record
http://www.access.gpo.gov/su_docs/
    aces/aces150.html
www.gpoaccess.gov/crecord/index.
    html

United States Code
http://www.gpoaccess.gov/uscode/
    index.html

**Weekly Compilation of
    Presidential Documents**
http://www.gpoaccess.gov/wcomp/
    index.html

Public Papers of the President
http:www.access.gpo.gov/nara/
    pubpaps/srpaps.html

GAO Reports and Testimony
http://www.access.gpo.gov/su_docs/
    aces160.shtml

Public and Private Laws
http://www.gpoaccess.gov/plaws/
    index.html

Congressional Directory
http://www.gpoaccess.gov/cdirectory/
    index.html

John C. Stennis Center for Public
    Service
Home Page
http://www.stennis.gov/

Library of Congress
Home Page
http://www.loc.gov/

Site Map
http://www.loc.gov/help/sitemap.html

**America's Story from America's
    Library**
http://www.americaslibrary.gov/cgi-bin/
    page.cgi

American Memory
http://memory.loc.gov/

Spanish-American War
Pictures
http://memory.loc.gov/ammem/sawhtml/
sawhome.html

Learning Page
http://memory.loc.gov/ammem/ndlpedu/
index.html

Browse Government Resources
http://lcweb.loc.gov/rr/news/extgovd.html

Congressional Research Service
Home Page
http://lcweb.loc.gov/crsinfo

Digital Collections and Programs
http://www.loc.gov/library/libarch-digital.
html

Digital Library Federation
http://www.diglib.org/dlfhomepage.htm

Exhibitions
http://www.loc.gov/exhibits/

Library of Congress Country Studies
http://lcweb2.loc.gov/frd/cs/cshome.html

Library of Congress Exhibitions
http://lcweb.loc.gov/exhibits

National Film Preservation Board
http://lcweb.loc.gov/film

**National Library Service for the Blind
    and Physically Handicapped**
http://lcweb.loc.gov/nls

Siberia (Meeting of Frontiers)
http://frontiers.loc.gov/

United States Copyright Office
http://www.loc.gov/copyright/

> **NewsNet**
> http://www.copyright.gov/newsnet/

> **U.S. Legislative Branch**
> http://lcweb.loc.gov/global/
>   legislative/congress.html

**Medicare Payment Advisory
    Commission**
Home Page
http://www.medpac.gov/

**National Bipartisan Commission of
    the Future of Medicare**
http://rs9.loc.gov/medicare/

Office of Compliance
http://www.compliance.gov/

**Office of Technology Assessment
    (defunct)**
http://www.access.gpo.gov/ota
http://govinfo.library.unt.edu/cc_
    AtoZ.html

THOMAS
http://thomas.loc.gov/

> **Introduction to Legislative Branch**
> http://thomas.loc.gov/home/legbranch/
>   legbranch.html

> **Legislative Branch Internet Resources**
> http://thomas.loc.gov/home/legbranch/
>   legbranch.html

> **The U.S. Congress (Overview)**
> http://thomas.loc.gov/home/legbranch/
>   uscong.html

White House
Home Page
http://www.whitehouse.gov/

Congressional Directory
http://www.gpoaccess.gov/cdirectory/
    index.html

Some Nongovernment Sites

> **The Hill on the Net**
> http://www.casey.com/hill/

> **FedNet**
> http://www.fednet.net/

> **The Hill**
> http://www.hillnews.com/

Roll Call
http://www.rollcall.com/

University of North Texas
Advisory Commission on
　　　Intergovernmental Relations
　　　and Other Defunct Agencies
http://www.library.unt.edu/gpo/
　　　ACIR/acir.html

Cybercemetery
http://govinfo.library.unt.edu/cc_
　　　AtoZ.html

Chapter 5

Executive Branch

The executive branch consists of fifteen departments within the President's Cabinet, the White House management offices, and the Executive Office of the President, as well as independent agencies and commissions (see Chapter 6). These various executive departments consist of thousands of subunits (e.g., agencies, offices, and bureaus). In fact, their number is so extensive that this chapter, and indeed this book, only provides selective coverage. It is important to remember that the Web site for a particular department identifies the subunits that have Web sites and offers direct links to them. In some instances (e.g., the Department of Energy), however, the information seeker may have to use the search index (A–Z) to locate subordinate units within the various departments. It is also useful to remember, if the user wants an overview of all executive government agencies and their relationships with other branches of government, that a useful organizational chart of the U.S. government can be found at **http://usinfo.state.gov/products/pubs/outusgov/govchart.pdf**.

Furthermore, with the establishment of the new Department of Homeland Security in January 2003, a new executive branch structure will emerge more fully over the next several years. Thus, until the next revision of this guide, the publisher's home page will update the content of the Department of Homeland Security and its impact on other Web resources from other parts of the executive branch.

DEPARTMENT OF AGRICULTURE

The site of the Department of Agriculture (USDA; **http://www.usda.gov/**) provides the following pages: "Welcome," "Newsroom," "What's New," "Agencies, Services & Programs," "USDA Offices," "Subject," and "Search/Help." Other site features include "Events," "Top Stories," the "Freedom of Information Act" (FOIA), a site search, Web policies such as for privacy and security, and "Issues." Some of the issues covered are "Biotechnology," "Black Farmer Consent Decree," "Civil Rights," "Drought," "e-Government Program," "Energy and Agriculture," "Food Safety,"

"Home Gardening," "Mad Cow Disease," "Meat Product Recalls," "Sustainable Development," and "Workplace Violence Prevention."

The "Newsroom" covers events, speeches, congressional testimony, reports, releases (national, agency, and media information), the FOIA, the Office of Communications, publications, and "For Your Information." "Broadcast News" (**http://www. usda.gov/agency/oc/vtr/broadcastnews.htm**) provides current and archived news releases as well as "broadcasters letter" (video, radio, and television).

There are also links to individual USDA offices (**http://www.usda.gov/offices. html**), and, under "Agencies, Services & Programs" (**http://www.usda.gov/services. html**), the USDA provides links to

- Opportunities

- Farm & Foreign Agricultural Service

- Food Nutrition and Consumer Services

- Employment

- For Employers

- Food Safety

- Marketing and Regulatory Programs

- Natural Resources & Environment

- Other Services

- Rural Development

- Research, Education, and Economics

- Other Services

Thanks to this helpful grouping, this section of the chapter only highlights the research, education, and economics agencies and a few other agencies, such as the Forest Service. It merits mention, however, that the "Partnership for Food Safety Education" (**http://www.fightbac.org/main.cfm**) provides information on food-borne illnesses for consumers, educators, and the media (e.g., "Four Steps" to keep food safer from bacteria: "Clean," "Separate," "Cook," and "Chill"; "Success Stories," a site map, and related links). There is even mention of the USDA's Meat and Poultry Hotline (800-535-4555) and the Food and Drug Administration's (FDA) Food Safety Information Hotline (888-SAFEFOOD).

↗ The Research, Education, and Economics Agencies

Four agencies fall within this area of the department's mission: (1) the Agricultural Research Service (ARS); (2) Cooperative State Research, Education, and Extension Service (CSREES); (3) Economic Research Service (ERS); and (4) National Agricultural Statistics Service (NASS). The ARS home page (**http://www.ars. usda.gov/**), which is the USDA's primary in-house research agency, explains that body's organization, discusses news, and provides information, coverage of research programs, access to offices (ARS area offices and the office of the ARS administrator) and programs, a site search and site map (for access to research programs), other research (e.g., linkage to the National Technical Information Service), and more. Some of the research programs relate to animal health, food safety, global change, human nutrition, water quality and management, air quality, integrated agricultural systems, plant diseases, crop production, and crop production and quarantine.

The National Agricultural Library (NAL) is part of the ARS. The Web site (**http://www.nalusda.gov/**) provides general information about library collections, publications, databases (e.g., agricultural images), and services, and it explains what is available for general use. The site provides access to AGRICOLA (AGRICultural On-Line Access), a bibliographic database of citations to agricultural literature created by the library and its cooperators. Before searching the database, however, information seekers should see "AGRICOLA: Frequently Asked Questions" (**http://www.nal.usda. gov/general_info/agricola/agricola.faq.html**).

The Library Web site also provides a link to the Agriculture Network Information Center (AgNIC; **http://www.agnic.org/**), which "is a discipline-specific distributed network that provides access to agriculture related information, subject area experts, and other resources. It was established by an alliance of the National Agricultural Library, land grant universities, and other organizations committed to facilitating public access to agricultural and related information." It uses librarians and subject specialists to provide online reference assistance, and AgNIC covers subjects such as

- Agricultural and applied economics
- American cranberry
- Animal welfare
- Asparagus
- Bees and pollination
- Blueberries (cultivated and wild)
- Chile peppers
- Entomology systematic
- Food and nutrition
- Food marketing
- Forestry
- Maple syrup
- Rangeland management
- Subtropical forestry
- Sustainable agriculture
- Tree fruits
- Turfgrass
- USDA statistics
- Water quality

The Cooperative State Research, Education, and Extension Service (**http://www. reeusda.gov/**) provides access to program information, state partners, legislation and budget information, human resources, funding opportunities, news and information, job opportunities, and award administration. There is also an opportunity to explore the individual units of the agency and to visit the site map and related links.

The department also offers "Agriculture in the Classroom," which the CSREES sponsors; it is managed though a cooperative agreement with Utah State University. The page provides state agricultural profiles, teacher resources, links to a site for the nation's youth (see Chapter 13), a site map, access to state programs, a national conference, and a screen saver that anyone can download. There is also linkage to "Space Agriculture in the Classroom" (**http://www.agclassroom.org/**), a partnership between the USDA and the National Aeronautics and Space Administration.

The Current Research Information System (CRIS) is the department's documentation and reporting system for ongoing and recently completed research projects in agriculture, food and nutrition, and forestry. The page (**http://cris.csrees.usda.gov/**) covers these projects, many of which are conducted or supported by the USDA's research agencies, state agricultural experiment stations, state land-grant universities, other cooperating state institutions, and participants in many USDA research grants programs. There is a manual of classification, coverage of funding sources, and a site search feature. Before using the CRIS system, see **http://crs.crees.usda.gov/star/ system.html**.

Another useful site, "e-answers," is a "searchable Web site that provides reliable, research-based information on a wide range of Extension or Outreach-oriented subjects." It covers topics such as fishing, family and consumer issues, laws and gardens, child development, 4-H/youth, the environment, public policy, economics, water quality, and communities (see **http://128.227.242.197/**).

The Economic Research Service is the "main source for economic information and research" on agriculture, food, natural resources, and rural development. The site (**http://www.ers.usda.gov/**) covers "Key Topics," "Briefing Rooms," "Publications," "Data," a site map, information about the agency, and "Research Emphases," which presents the ERS's major research areas. Key topics offer "a significant body of research and analysis" on crops, food safety, international agriculture, policies, rural America, and more. Using a pull-down menu, there are also quick links to topics and shortcuts (e.g., finding state facts). Briefing rooms (**http://www.ers.usda.gov/Briefing/**) take a topic and typically provide an overview of it, profiles, readings, related links, and maps and images. Furthermore, these Briefing Rooms contain maps, photographs, and state fact sheets ("information on population, employment, income, farm characteristics, and farm financial indicators for each state"). Entering "maps" in the agencywide search index quickly produces a number of maps and map galleries (see **http://search.ers.usda.gov/**).

The National Agricultural Statistics Service (NASS; **http://www.usda.gov/nass/**) provides "Statistical Information" (publications, graphics, historical data, state information, statistical research and information about the conduct of the Census of Agriculture, and an opportunity to search the site) and "Agency Information" (upcoming events and news, agency information, customer service, other links, and NASS Kids). NASS issues national and state level agricultural statistics in various reports (see "Publications") for many commodities and data series. County-level data are also available;

"the county query is limited to five years because the dataset may be very large." There are also district forecasts for selected states beginning with winter wheat in May (see **http://www.nass.usda.gov:81/ipedb/**). Some of the data are part of historical series dating back to 1866 (see **http://www.usda.gov/nass/pubs/histdata.htm**). The Agricultural Use Database covers commodity acreage and active ingredient agricultural chemical use data from 1990–2001, with annual updates. The data might be presented through maps or graphical reports (**http://www.pestmanagement.info/nass/**).

Farm Service Agency

The mission of the Farm Service Agency (FSA) relates to "stabilizing farm income, helping farmers conserve land and water resources, providing credit to new or disadvantaged farmers and ranchers, and helping farm operators recover from the effects of disaster." The Web site (**http://www.fsa.usda.gov/pas/default.asp**) contains information about the agency, news releases (electronic subscription is available), coverage of services, links to local FSA offices, online forms, and commodity information. There is coverage of agricultural programs, farm loan and conservation programs, employment information, and compliance with civil rights laws. "Quick Search" permits subject searching. Because "most of FSA's work is done at the agency's service centers," the Office Locator provides a link to the service centers from a map of the United States.

The agency has a page covering "Drought Information" (**http://www://drought.fsa.usda.gov/**) that provides news, weather and climate conditions, disaster designations, and assistance information. Another page covers trade and agriculture, with trade data, fact sheets, current issues, other links, and coverage of import programs, buying American products, exporter assistance, news, and more (**http://www.fas.usda.gov/ustrade.html**). FAS Online (**http://www.fas.usda.gov/data.html**) leads to the agency's Production, Supply and Distribution (PS&D) online database, which "contains current and historical official USDA data on production, supply and distribution of agricultural commodities for the United States and key producing and consuming countries." There are also import and export data, market reports, and fact sheets.

Another Web site, the Hay Net (see **http://www.fsa.usda.gov/haynet/**), lists information about hay and its availability for producers. There is a choice of "need hay" or "have hay."

Risk Management Agency

The Risk Management Agency provides news, crop policies, data, regulations, crop weather, information about the agency, links to its library, frequently asked questions, "Today's Events," "Pilot Programs," "Agent Locator," "Producer Training," a quick search of the site (with accompanying search tips), and more (see **http://www.act.fcic.usda.gov/**).

⇗ Forest Service

This agency, which was established in 1905, is discussed in Chapters 11 and 13. The agency's Webmaster is currently revising the entire national Web site. The current home page (**http://www.fs.fed.us/**) discusses the agency, employment opportunities, maps and brochures, passes and permits, photo and video galleries, projects and policies, publications, recreational activities, research and development, and state and private forestry. There is also a site search as well as budgetary, historical, and other information, including guides and visitor maps to national forests and grasslands, and topographic maps, which may be purchased from the U.S. Geological Survey (Department of the Interior).

A useful site, "Current Wildlife Fire Information" (**http://www.nifc.gov/information. html**), provides "current information," "weather, outlooks and assessments," and "other information resources" for the "Wildland Fire Season." Additional features address related links, safety, prevention, education, science and technology, and the National Interagency Coordination Center.

⇗ Natural Resources Conservation Service

The Natural Resources Conservation Service (NRCS) "works in partnership with the American people to conserve and sustain our natural resources." The Web site (**http://www.nrcs.usda.gov/**) provides information about the agency; a keyword search of the site; "Quick Access" (e.g., to a photo gallery, a plants database, publications, and local service centers); "Features;" a newsroom; coverage of programs, partnerships, technical resources, and agency contacts; and frequently asked questions. There is information specifically for communities, farmers and ranchers, homeowners, agency staff, policy makers, and teachers and students.

⇗ Other

Nutrition.Gov provides food facts, coverage of food safety, issues for people (arranged by the age of the individual), a site search, health management, food assistance, research, and resources. Other features include news and basic explanations of public health issues such as diabetes (see **http://www.nutirition.gov/home/index.php3**).

The USDA has a partnership with land-grant universities in each state that relates to science and education. For coverage of this partnership, see **http://www.reeusda. gov/success/impact.htm**.

DEPARTMENT OF COMMERCE

The site for the Department of Commerce (DOC; **http://www.commerce.gov/**) provides information about DOC, a newsroom, job opportunities, coverage of stories (top stories and success stories), popular departmental sites, the role of DOC as a steward for coastal and maritime resources, Webcasts (current and archived), coverage of free trade, innovation (technology, patents and trademarks, and telecommunications), a site search and a site map (e.g., see "Commerce Organization," for links to subordinate agencies, and "Commerce Offices and Services Near You" for offices and services arranged by state), a person finder, key indicators, and more. The newsroom contains a library of new releases as well as the texts of speeches and congressional testimony, audio sound bites, and news reports that can be redistributed on television, radio, and the Internet.

Bureau of Economic Analysis

This agency, discussed in Chapter 8, seeks to strengthen the understanding of the U.S. economy and its competitive position by providing the most accurate and relevant gross national product and economic accounts data in a timely and cost-effective manner. The Bureau of Economic Analysis (BEA) prepares national, industry, international, and regional accounts that present essential information on such issues as economic growth, regional economic development, interindustry relationships, and the nation's position in the word economy. The bureau makes many of its products available through its Web site (**http://www.bea.gov/**), but it also offers many of them for sale.

Bureau of Industry and Security

The Bureau of Industry and Security, which was formerly known as the Bureau of Export Administration, has as its mission "to advance U.S. national security, foreign policy, and economic interests." The agency's activities include

regulating the export of sensitive goods and technologies in an effective and efficient manner; enforcing export control, antiboycott, and public safety laws; cooperating with and assisting other countries on export control and strategic trade issues; assisting U.S. industry to comply with international arms control agreements; monitoring the viability of the U.S. defense industrial base; and promoting federal initiatives and public-private partnerships across industry sectors to protect the nation's critical infrastructures.

The Web site (**http://www.bxa.doc.gov/**) discusses the bureau and provides access to agency news, upcoming training programs, programs, "Export Administration Regulations and Lists," "Getting Help and Contacting Us," and events.

International Trade Administration

The International Trade Administration (ITA) is "dedicated to helping U.S. businesses compete in the global marketplace." Its home page (**http://www.ita.doc.gov/**) covers the agency, trade data, state export data, the trade information center, Export America Magazine, "ITA's Key Links," press releases, "Upcoming Trade Missions," "Locate ITA Employees," "Jobs & Internships," the Office of Administration and the Office of Chief Information Officers, and more. The trade data include reports on U.S. trade, global data links, U.S. industry and trade outlook, U.S. foreign trade highlights, U.S. industry sector data, and more.

One site, Buy USA.com (**http://www.buyusa.com/page/my_gtn/splash.asp**) identifies trade services, success stories, participants in the program, membership services, "Search for New Trade Leads," "List Your Company for Free," and free tools and services for "International Companies." Another site, TIC 1-800-USA-TRADE of the Trade Information Center (**http://www.trade.gov/td/tic/**), provides industry information, trade events, a list of trade offices nationwide, export resources, tariff and tax information, a guide to export programs, country information, and answers to export questions.

National Institute of Standards and Technology

The National Institute of Standards and Technology (NIST), created in 1901, is a nonregulatory agency that develops standards and guidelines for information systems and that works "with industry to develop and apply technology, measurements and standards." NIST is developing guidelines for enhancing the overall security of federal information technology systems. Its home page (**http://www.nist.gov/**) provides access to information about the agency, programs, a pull-down menu to NIST "Laboratories' Web Sites," a site search, the Malcolm "Baldrige Quality Program," the "Manufacturing Extension Partnership" ("technical and business assistance to smaller manufacturers"), the "Advanced Technology Program" ("partners with the private-sector to develop broadly beneficial technologies"), products and services (e.g., software, standards, databases, and computer security), an "A–Z Subject Index," NIST conferences, instructions on contacting agency staff and programs, frequently asked questions, news, videos, publications, and a "Guide to NIST" (a catalog of agency programs, projects, and services), and the official U.S. time by time zone (**http://www.time.gov/**).

It is possible to see how NIST has made a connection to our everyday lives by taking a tour of a city (**http://www.nist.gov/public_affairs/nhouse/ccity/ccity.htm**), a home (**http://www.nist.gov/public_affairs/nhouse/index.html**), or a community (**http://www.nist.gov/public_affairs/licweb/niychome.htm**). A NIST Physics Laboratory presents "A Walk through Time" showing the evolution of time measurement from ancient calendars to NIST time calibration (see **http://physics.nist.gov/GenInt/Time/time.html**).

For access to various NIST scientific data bases, see **http://www.nist.gov/srd/**. One database relates to human and computer interactions data and another to international comparisons.

National Oceanic and Atmospheric Administration

The National Oceanic and Atmospheric Administration (NOAA) collects an extensive array of data and images as part of its mission to monitor, assess, and predict oceanic and atmospheric conditions. The Web site (**http://www.noaa.gov/**) provides access to a site map, site search, news (including a news archives), information about the agency, *NOAA Magazine,* storm watches (e.g., weather forecasts, snow cover satellite images, current satellite images, and archived images of significant events). One of the online articles from *NOAA Magazine* discusses the joint venture between NOAA and the U.S. Navy to raise the turret of the USS *Monitor,* the Civil War ironclad, from the floor of the Atlantic Ocean. The article concludes with "Relevant Web

Sites." The home page also has "Cool NOAA Web Sites" (e.g., "Live North Pole Web Cam," which tracks "the latest snow cover and weather conditions on the North Pole"; and "NOAA Photo Library," which contains "more than 20,000 public domain photos" of animals reefs, coastal scenes, etc.), "Check This Out . . .," and agency resources grouped by

- Weather

- Ocean

- Satellites

- Fisheries

- Climate

- Research

- Coasts

- Charting and Navigation

For instance, "Climate" covers El Niño and La Niña, global warming, drought, climate prediction, archived weather data, and paleoclimatology; "Ocean" includes coral reefs, tides and currents, buoys, marine sanctuaries, estuaries, diving, and oil and chemical spills. Each of the thirteen marine sanctuaries that NOAA maintains around the United States has a Web page.

NOAA has also grouped Web sites by "Media Advisories," "Opportunities" (e.g., "Business & Grants"), and "Organizations," which includes components of the agency that have Web sites and "media contacts and background information," such as news releases. Examples of those components are the National Weather Service; National Environmental Satellite, Data, & Information Service; National Marine Fisheries Service; National Ocean Service; and NOAA Research.

NOAA's National Data Centers comprise the National Oceanographic Data Center (NODC), the National Geophysical Data Center (NGDC), and the National Climatic Data Center (NCDC). The centers acquire and preserve the nation's atmospheric, climatic, geophysical, and oceanographic data. NODC's oceanographic data are available at **http://www.nodc.noaa.gov/**. NCDC "is the world's largest active archive of weather data," and its geophysical data are available at **http://www.ngdc.noaa.gov/**. NCDC's atmospheric and climatic data are at **http://lwf.ncdc.noaa.gov/oa/ ncdc.html**, and the NCDC has the Historical Significant Events Imagery database (HSEI), which "contains satellite images capturing some of the more important weather and environmental events over the last 30 years" (**http://www.ncdc.noaa. gov/oa/ncdc.html**). It is possible to obtain the image details and to order print copies of the images. For example, there is a color image of Hurricane Lili over the Louisiana coast in October 2002.

NOAA's Aquarius project (**http://www.uncwil.edu/nurc/aquarius/**) is an underwater ocean laboratory located offshore at a depth of sixty feet, and it houses scientists and researchers for up to seven days at a time. The project offers information about the mission, a series of lessons, and an ocean observatory.

The mission of NOAA's National Hurricane Center (**http://www.nhc.noaa. gov/index.shtml**) is "to save lives, mitigate property loss, and improve economic efficiency by issuing watches, warnings, forecasts, and analyses of hazardous tropical weather." As a consequence, the site offers the latest information on hurricanes; it provides storm information, products, forecasts, satellite imagery, aircraft reconnaissance, storm warnings, graphical representation of actual hurricanes, and detailed descriptions. A cumulative wind distribution chart shows how the size of a storm changes, the areas affected by tropical storm winds, and the location of hurricane-force winds. There are also links to the Central Pacific Hurricane Center and the Joint Typhoon Warning Center.

The National Weather Service (**http://www.nws.noaa.gov/**) provides "Current Watches, Warnings, Statements, and Advisories" for anywhere in the United States. The site also covers flash flood warnings, freeze warnings, flood warnings and watches, winter storm watches, wind advisories, nonparticipation statements, flood statements, special weather statements, an hazardous weather outlook, gale warnings, small craft advisory, marine weather statement, and short-term forecasts. There are also "observations" (e.g., by satellite), forecasts (including maps and models), weather safety information, educational and career resources, an information center (publications, glossaries, and past weather information), and an opportunity to contact the agency or to peruse frequently asked questions.

An Interactive Weather Information Network (IWIN; **http://iwin.nws. noaa.gov/**) offers an animated graphics version (high-speed Internet connections), Enhanced Graphics version (midspeed Internet connections), text version (useful for disabled access, wireless devices, and low-speed Internet connections), All National Weather Service home pages, and IWIN links (live computer data broadcasts via, for instance, satellite, radio, and the Internet).

Weather.gov (**http://iwin.nws.noaa.gov/**), which has more than 10,000 Web sites linked to it, provides access to the IWIN. There are live computer data broadcasts and access to the home pages of the National Weather Service. By the way, this site has had more than one billion hits since 1997.

NOAA hosts the National Environmental Data Index (NEDI; **http://www. nedi.gov/**), which serves as the "yellow pages" for environmental data. NEDI provides a listing and description of environmental and scientific information (e.g., on weather, water quality, vegetation, and wetlands) held by different government departments and agencies as well as a link to where the actual information can be located. In some cases, the information seeker can connect directly to an actual publication.

NOAA has a central library (**http://www.lib.noaa.gov/**) that connects to various agency home pages and that provides information about the library and its services. There are collections of photographs, maps, and charts. The photographs illustrate meteorology and climatology, geodetic and hydrographic surveying, fisheries science, marine biology, geophysics, and the military use of these disciplines. The historical maps and charts date from the mid-1800s through the early 1990s. The library's WINDandSEA locator service has more than a thousand links to science and policy sites organized by topic and alphabetical within topic (see **http://www.lib.noaa. gov/docs/windandsea.html**). Furthermore, a Heritage Page provides access to historical documents and collections. A series of "tales" (Alaska, ocean, personal, Philippine, technology, war, and western tales) offers insights based on the writings of coast and geodetic survey offices as well as other government bodies.

⇗ National Ocean Service

As discussed in Chapter 11, the National Ocean Service (NOS) is one of the government's principal mapping agencies (see **http://www. nos.noaa.gov/**) and the site map (**http://oceanservice.noaa/mapfinder**). One of its products is Mapfinder (**http://oceanservice.noaa.gov/mapfinder/**), which "provides 'one-stop shopping' for images and data from a number of . . . NOS offices." Mapfinder offers products "by theme (e.g., coastal aerial photography, low resolution nautical charts, coastal survey maps, environmental sensitivity index atlases, hydrographic survey outlines, historical maps, water level station data, geodetic control points, and estuarine bathymetry data)."

A Coral Reef Information System (CoRIS) Web site "provides access to 19,000 aerial photos, 400 preview navigational charts, tide stations, paleoclimatological studies, photo mosaics, coral reef monitoring, bleaching reports, and other information." The NOS home page also identifies popular Web sites of the agency (e.g., one for marine protected areas and another for oil and chemical releases).

⇗ National Technical Information Service

This clearinghouse was created in 1970, but its predecessors date back to the 1940s. As discussed in Chapter 3, the National Technical Information Service (NTIS) has a portal entitled FedWorld (**http://www.fedworld.gov/**) that provides access to its diverse collection of information resources. Because NTIS has a congressional mandate that primarily requires it to be financially self-supporting, many of its products and services are fee-based.

More than 750,000 resources—for engineering, physical and health sciences, behavioral and social sciences—are available through FedWorld and the NTIS Web site (**http://www.ntis.gov/**). NTIS identifies "Hot Products," which are the most requested or popular items in its database. At **http://tradecenter.ntis.gov/**, NTIS has an online bookstore that offers a collection of trade and business publications from both the public and private sectors. NTIS also has a Gov.Research_Center (**http://grc.ntis.gov/**), which is a partnership with the National Information Services Corporation to provide a single access point to databases in agriculture, energy, technology, nuclear science, and other fields. This partnership, in effect, results in an online subscription service to some well-known databases. There is also access to databases of the National Institute for Occupational Safety and Health. One database provides access to federal research in progress.

NTIS also houses the National Audiovisual Center (NAC) (**http://www.ntis.gov/ products/types/audiovisual/index.asp?loc=4-4-1**), which is a collection of more than nine thousand federally developed training and education materials. The training materials cover "occupational safety and health, fire services, law enforcement, and foreign languages. Information and educational materials include areas such as history, health, agriculture, and natural resources."

⟋ National Telecommunications and Information Administration

The National Telecommunications and Information Administration (NTIA) "is the executive branch's principal voice on domestic and international telecommunications and information technology issues." Its Web site (**http://www.ntia.doc.gov/**) discusses the agency and presents publications, press releases, employment information, "What's New?," a site map, new developments, coverage of grants programs and the telecommunications research lab, access to some of its subbodies, and other information. At **http://www.ntia.doc.gov/startingpoints.htm**, NTIA offers "Starting Points," which lays out nicely agency resources and various search options for the "Assistant Secretary," "Domestic Policy," "Spectrum Management," "Telecom Research," "Internet Issues," "International Policy," "Grants Program," and "Other Information."

DEPARTMENT OF DEFENSE

DefenseLINK (**http://www.defenselink.mil/**), the portal of the Department of Defense (DOD), is the starting point for finding U.S. military information online. It covers news, images, publications and "special reports," current developments, and frequently asked questions. There is a site map, site search, information on the Department (e.g., information about the Pentagon, the Defense Almanac and the Quadrennial Defense Review, and a tour), and links to the Web sites, for instance, for

- Air Force
- Anthrax
- Army
- Budget
- Business Opportunities
- Civilian Job Opportunities
- Coast Guard
- Combined Federal Campaign
- Defend America
- Enduring Freedom
- Environment
- Facts and Statistics
- *Freedom of Information Act*
- Guantanamo
- Homeland Security
- Joints Chiefs of Staff
- Marine Corps

- Navy

- Terrorism and Terrorists

Before beginning a search of the DOD for the first time, it is advisable to browse the site map (**http://www.defenselink.mil/sitemap.html**) and its explanation of publicly available sites. By the way, the Defense Technical Information Center (DTIC) is the central DOD "facility for providing access to and facilitating the exchange of scientific and technical information." A large portion of its information resources are not open to the general public. Nonetheless, it provides various products and services that are publicly available. For example, DTIC provides numerous publicly accessible resources, some of which are available on the Internet (see **http://www.dtic.mil/dtic/links.html**). Finally, the Defense Visual Information Center "is the official records center for the storage and preservation of visual information . . . records of the U.S. military. Our holdings include motion picture film, videotape, still photography, and CD-ROM stock photo collections for use by . . . DoD . . . customers in support of mission requirements. Most of our imagery is made available to the public on a cost-recovery fee basis" (**http://www.defenselink.mil/multimedia/archive.html**).

The Missile Defense Agency is charged with developing internal missile defense capabilities and with "meeting the near-term ballistic missile threat to our homeland, our deployed forces, and our friends and allies." The home page (**http://www.acq.osd.mil/bmdo/bmdolink/html/**) discusses the agency and provides news, resources, an overview, and more.

DEPARTMENT OF EDUCATION

The opening screen (**http://www.ed.gov/**) offers access to the "No Child Left Behind" Web site, which is for parents, policy makers, and educators, or the Departmental Web site (**http://www.ed.gov/index.jsp**). The departmental site "draws a wide range of visitors, including college students seeking loan information and researchers looking up the latest Education policies."[1] As reporter L. Scott Tillett notes, the site

contains links to such nuggets as how to find money to pay for college or whether fourth-grade girls, on average, score higher than boys on reading tests (they do). The site includes an interactive budget calculator for students and enables members of the public to apply online for direct loans to consolidate their education debt.[2]

Along the top of the page of the opening screen is "About ED" [about the department itself], "A–Z Index," "Search," "Site Map," "Information for . . ." (specifically aimed at students, parents and families, teachers, principals, higher education administrators, or grantees and assistance providers), "Grants & Contracts," "Financial Aid," "Education Resources," and "Research & Statistics." There is also coverage of news releases and "Policy," which covers legislation, regulations, policy guidance, speeches and initiatives, and state organizations. My.ED.gov enables users to "personalize this site to see your favorite topics each time you visit."

The department "houses and supports a number of organizations that provide research, evaluation, and statistical information," including the autonomous Institute of Education Sciences, which replaced the Office of Educational Research and Improvement in the fall 2002 and has the goal of infusing federal education research with "scientific rigor." The Institute functions as a separate office under the direction of a fifteen-member National Board for Education Sciences, whose members are appointed by the president and confirmed by the Senate. The board advises and consults with the institute director in setting the institute's policies and priorities.

Some of the other research, evaluation, and statistical units within the department include the National Center for Education Statistics, the National Institute on Disability and Rehabilitation Research, the Office of Special Education Programs, and the National Research and Dissemination Centers for Career and Technical Education.

For an quick overview of "Publication and Products," see **http://www.ed.gov/about/pubs.jsp**. This page leads to "newsletters and journals from the department," "collections of research synopses" ("concise, research-based synopses and literature reviews of major educational topics"), "guides to the U.S. Department of Education" ("general overviews of the Department and road maps to its programs and offices"), "ED pubs online ordering system" ("to identify and order current U.S. Department of Education publications and products"; **http://www.edpubs.org/webstore/Content/search.asp**), and a "database of ED publications in ERIC" ("a searchable bibliographic database of more than 28,000 publications produced or funded by ED since 1980") .

A listing of "ED-Funded Internet Resources" provides access to departmental supported centers and clearinghouses" and to "Other Government Internet Resources for Education and Libraries" (see **http://www.ed.gov/EdRes/EdFed/index.html**). Another page covers the same listing as well as identifies "State Agencies and Resources," "Educational Institutions and Education Support Institutions," "Libraries," and "Educational Associations and Organizations" (see **http://www.ed.gov/about/organizations.jsp**).

The home page of the National Library of Education (**http://www.ed.gov/NLE**) covers the library and its resources and services. Among the services are the

- Gateway to Educational Materials, which is a "one-stop, any-stop access to high quality lesson plans, curriculum units, and other educational resources on the Internet" (see **http://www.thegateway.org/**)

- Virtual Reference Desk, which "is dedicated to the advancement of digital reference and the successful creation and operation of human-mediated, Internet-based information services" (**http://www.vrd.org/**)

- United States Network for Education Information (USNEI), which is "an interagency and public/private partnership whose mission is to provide official information assistance for anyone seeking information about U.S. education and for U.S. citizens seeking authoritative information about education in other countries" (**http://www.ed.gov/NLE/USNEI/**)

- Educational Resources Information Center (ERIC) and its many resources (see **http://www.eric.ed.gov/**).[3] ERIC is a national information network that acquires, catalogs, summarizes, and provides access to educational information The ERIC system includes sixteen subject-specific clearinghouses (see **http://search.edu/gov/csi/eric/html**), the ERIC Processing and Reference

Facility, and ACCESS ERIC, which provides introductory services. AskERIC is an electronic question answering service for teachers on the Internet (see **http:// askeric.org/**). There are also links to the U.S. Network for Education Information and the National Clearinghouse for Educational Facilities (**http://www. edfacilities.org/**).

DEPARTMENT OF ENERGY

The opening screen of the Web site for the Department of Energy (DOE) (**http://www.energy.gov/**) features information related to "Health," "House," "Transportation," "School," "Business," "Community," "World," and "Future." It also covers "Headlines" and news, as well as information about the department, "Career Opportunities," "Press Room," "Energy and . . . ," "Data and Prices," "Efficiency," "Environmental Quality," "National Security," "Science and Technology," publications and other resources, "Free Subscriptions," "National Library," a site search and an advanced search, "Kidz Zone" (see Chapter 13), the "FOIA," and an "A–Z" index. By using the "A–Z" index, the information seeker can identify various agencies such as the Energy Information Administration. A number of headquarter, field, and regional offices can be found in the index under "Offices." The Web site also includes more than eight hundred links to relevant sites.

"Data & Prices" leads to Country Analysis Briefs, International Energy Outlook, Annual Energy Outlook, Energy Demand, and gasoline prices. "National Security" covers "Computer Science," "Emergency Response," "Nonproliferation," "Our History," "Safety Resources," "Security," "Stockpile Stewardship," and "Bright Ideas." "Our History," a subheading of "National Security," covers "Atomic History, "Cold War File," "Locator," "Declassified Documents," "Historical Films," and "Nuclear Testing." "Declassified Documents" leads to OpenNet (**http://www.osti.gov/opennet/**), which is the department's database for documents declassified since October 1, 1994. OpenNet has information on early nuclear weapons testing, human radiation experiments, and many other areas such as health, environmental, and safety issues. Another searchable database is the Historical Records Review Database (see **http://www.osti.gov/ opennet/nsi.html**).

✍ Energy Information Administration

The Energy Information Administration (EIA; **http://www.eia.doe.gov/**) is a statistical agency that provides policy-independent data, forecasts, and analyses to promote sound policy making, efficient markets, and public understanding regarding energy and its role in the economy and the environment (see Chapter 8). The site provides energy information for petroleum, gasoline, diesel, natural gas, electricity, coal, nuclear power, renewable energy, and alternative fuels. Information is arranged by geographical location, fuel, and sector; or by subject (process, environment, and forecast). Other choices are "Energy: Subjects A–Z, Quick Stats, Glossary"), "What's New," "About Us/Jobs," "Press Releases," "Country Analysis Briefs," a kid's page (see Chapter 13); current and upcoming publications; historical data; an opportunity to register for e-mail updates or to contact an expert; energy links; presentations; energy events; and more. Those energy experts (for coal, electric power, international coverage, natural gas, petroleum, uranium, economic and financial matters, forecasts, multifuel consumption, nuclear power, and renewable energy) are available by telephone or fax (see **http://www.eia.doc.gov/contacts/main.html**). The EIA site also provides monthly statistics, annual data, and projections, as well as country analysis briefs and coverage of states.

Los Alamos National Laboratory

The Los Alamos National Laboratory is a partnership between the government and the University of California that resulted in the production of the atomic bomb and the hydrogen bomb. The university has run the lab for the government since the lab was created during World War II as the headquarters of the secret Manhattan Project to build the bomb. Today, "the Laboratory's central mission is to reduce the global nuclear danger." The site (**http://www.lanl.gov/worldview/**), for example, discusses the Laboratory, news, science and technology, the community served, employment opportunities, and more.

Office of Economic Impact and Diversity

Created in 1993, the Office of Economic Impact and Diversity addresses "the needs of small business, minority educational institutions and the DOE workforce and bring[s] about change through strategic partnerships with our customers." The home page (**http://www.hr.doe.gov/ed/index.html**) covers those units of the Office that have Web sites, "Minority Education," "Minority Business," "Bank Deposit Program," "Informal Complaints [of] Racial Profiling," "Mentor Protégé Program," "Prime and Subcontracting Opportunities Database," "Minority Economic Research," "Civil Rights & Diversity," and "Whistleblower: Safety, Health, and Security Disputes." Moreover, there is information "About Us," "The Director," "Program Offices," "ED Staff," "Secretarial Diversity Notices," "Calendar of Events," "Publications," "DOE Locator," "Links," and "Contacting Us."

Office of Environment, Safety and Health

This office provides environmental, safety, and health information (ES&H). The site (**http://tis.eh.doe.gov/portal/home.htm**) covers features and news, an archives, conferences, publications, a resource center, and ES&H knowledge management tools.

Office of Science

The Office of Science, formerly the Office of Energy Research, supports and conducts basic research in the physical sciences, and it contributes to other scientific fields, including advanced computing and mathematics and the life sciences. The home page (**http://www.sc.doe.gov/**) covers the agency, a calendar of events, ten national laboratories, grants and contracts, occasional papers, the budget, key projects, and news. Other choices include "Biology & Environment," "Basic Energy Science," "Fusion Energy Science," "High Energy & Nuclear Physics," "Advanced Scientific Computing," and "Science Education."

☞ Office of Scientific and Technical Information

The Office of Science and Technical Information (OSTI) leads DOE's "e-government initiatives for disseminating R&D [research and development] information." The agency's goal "is a fully searchable dynamic information resource that provides organized access to a comprehensive resource of scientific and technical information in physics and other disciplines of concern to the Department of Energy." For an excellent introduction to and overview of those resources, see **http://www.osti.gov/resource.html**. This page covers "Gray Literature," "Preprint Literature," "Journal Literature," "R&D Announcement Sites," "Specialized Information Resources and Software," "Customized Information Tools," and an "E-News Service."

Examples of the resources available on the page (**http://www.osti.gov/**) include

- DOE Information Bridge: "Searchable and downloadable bibliographic records and full text of DOE research report literature from 1995 forward" (**http://www.osti.gov/bridge/**)

- PrePRINT Network: "A searchable gateway that provides access to preprint servers from around the world by which scientists communicate their findings covering such disciplines are physics, mathematics, chemistry, and other topics"

- Energy Citations Database: "Bibliographic records for energy and energy-related scientific and technical information"; this database provides citations from 1948 to the present (**http://www.osti.gov/energycitations/**)

- GrayLIT Network: "The world's most comprehensive portal to over 130,000 full-text technical reports"

- EnergyFiles: The Virtual Library Collections of Energy Science and Technology (**http://www.osti.gov/EnergyFiles**) provides information and resources on energy science and technology

☞ Southwestern Power Administration

The Southwestern Power Administration (SWPA) "is responsible for marketing the hydroelectric power produced at twenty-three U.S. Army Corps of Engineers multipurpose dams." The Web site (**http://www.swpa.gov/**) covers the agency, employment with the agency, "Generation," "Interconnecting," "Acquisitions," "Competing Uses," publications, questions, rates, "System Maps," and more.

DEPARTMENT OF HEALTH AND HUMAN SERVICES

The Web site for the Department of Health and Human Services (HHS) (**http://www.os.dhhs.gov/**) clearly arranges its resources by the following headings: "Diseases & Conditions," "Safety & Wellness," "Drug & Food Information," "Disasters & Emergencies," "Grants & Funding," "Reference Collections," "Families & Children," "Aging," "Specific Populations," "Resource Locators," "Policies & Regulations," "About HHS," "News," and "Features." Each of these headings is subdivided for quick perusal. For example, "Resource Locators" covers "nursing homes," "physicians, other healthcare providers, and health care facilities," and "Reference Collections" includes "dictionaries, libraries, databases," "publications, fact sheets," and "statistics." The site map provides further subdivisions for each category. By the way, there is also a list of frequently asked questions and an opportunity to contact the Webmaster.

Healthfinder® (**http://www.healthfinder.gov/**) is a free gateway to reliable consumer health and human services information. It provides convenient access to resources for specific age and gender groups and covers minority health and family health. There is a Web page devoted entirely to smallpox (**http://www.os. dhhs.gov/smallpox/index.html**).

The category "About HHS" includes a "Topic List" (e.g., bioterrorism and the FOIA, as well as access to the department's agencies, regional, and other offices). Examples of HHS agencies are the Administration for Children and Families (**http://www.acf.hhs.gov/**), which funds state, local, and tribal organizations to provide family assistance (welfare), child support, child care, Head Start, child welfare, and other programs relating to children and families. Its Web site covers the agency and its programs, contacts, grants, and job opportunities. Other options are state and local resources, research, publications and statistical data, budget and policy, conferences, the *Freedom of Information Act,* questions, and a site index and a site search. The site also covers adoption, foster care, child abuse and neglect, child care, child support enforcement, and other programs.

The Administration on Aging, another agency, has a home page (**http://www. aoa.gov/network/default.htm**) that provides a quick index; a site index and site search; an opportunity to contact the agency; "What's New;" information about the agency and its programs, press releases, statistics; "Alzheimer's Resource Room"; "Aging Related Web sites"; "Elder Abuse Prevention"; and other information useful to "older people and their families." One of the options from the opening screen is the Aging Network, which contains fact sheets, tables and spreadsheets, and assorted information and resources.

The Agency for Healthcare Research and Quality, which was created in 1989 as the Agency for Health Care Policy and Research, supports "research designed to improve the outcome and quality of health care, reduce its costs, address patient safety and medical errors, and broaden access to effective services." Its home page (**http://www.ahcpr.gov/**) provides access to research, information about the agency, surveys and report tools, and subunits of the agency (e.g., evidence-based practice centers and task forces).

The Office of Public Health and Science has an Office of Population Affairs, which includes a National Women's Health Information Center, "a one-step gateway for women seeking answers to critical health questions. The Web site called 4women.gov links to a wide array of reliable women's health material" (see **http://opa.osophs.dhhs.gov/other-sites.html**). The National Adoption Information Clearinghouse provides a national adoption directory, databases, publications, laws, statistics, conferences, and more, including resources for gay and lesbian adoptive parents (see **http://www.calib.com/naic/pubs/f_gay.cfm**).

The following sections highlight some other examples of HHS agencies.

Centers for Disease Control and Prevention

The Centers for Disease Control and Prevention (CDC) promotes "health and quality of life by preventing and controlling disease, injury, and disability." Its home page (**http://www.cdc.gov/**) contains an extensive array of information resources intended for public use, but some pages require authorized access: log-in and use of a password. Some items are available on subscription to the public; CDC has a mailing list (sent via e-mail) covering different diseases and other topics (see **http://www. cdc.gov/subscribe.html**).

The site discusses the agency and provides announcements, current news, funding opportunities, "Highlighted Resources" (e.g., "terrorism and public health"), access to the Emerging Infectious Diseases Journal, coverage of "Hoaxes and Rumors" ("information about hoaxes or rumors that may be prevalent on the Internet or other sources of communication"), data and statistics, identification of "Other Sites" ("Information Networks and Other Information Sources"), "Publications, Software and Other Products," training and employment, "Travelers' Health" ("how to protect yourself from disease when traveling outside the U.S. and alerts about disease outbreaks"), "Health Topics A–Z" ("fact sheets, disease prevention and health information from A to Z [e.g., Anthrax, Cancer, Drownings, Zoster]"), and more. For an excellent overview of some of the available resources and a direct link to them, see "Data and Statistics" (**http://www.cdc.gov/scientific.htm**). One example is surveillance reports, which the Division of Sexually Transmitted Diseases has provided since 1993 (**http://www.cdc.gov/nchstp/dstd/Stats_Trends/Stats_and_Trends.htm**).

The CDC includes eleven centers, institutes, and offices. For access to them, see **http://www.cdc.gov/aboutcdc.htm**. The page for "Tobacco Industry Documents" (**http://www.cdc.gov/tobacco/industrydocs/index.htm**) provides public access to industry documents, a glossary of terms, a list and description of industry document Web sites, a citation index to industry documents, and links to a smoking and health database. It is also possible to search the set of Minnesota documents on a selective basis.

Centers for Medicare and Medicaid Services

As of the summer 2001, the Health Care Financing Administration became the Centers for Medicare & Medicaid Services. Its home page (**http://cms.hhs.gov/**) provides information for consumers, professionals, and the news media. There is headline information; a set of frequently asked questions; coverage of programs, topics, initiatives, resources, and tools; a site map; and a site search.

Food and Drug Administration

The Food and Drug Administration (FDA) "assures the safety of foods and cosmetics, and the safety and efficacy of pharmaceuticals, biology products, and medical devices." Its Web site (**http://www.fda.gov/**) covers the agency and interacting with it, news and hot topics (e.g., bioterrorism, buying medicines online, and cell phones), "Enforcement Activities," "Products Regulated by FDA." "Major Initiatives/Activities," publications, and information about the Web site. Another option is to retrieve

"Information for Specific Audiences: AIDS Patients, Cancer Patients, Consumers, Health Professionals, Industry, International, Kids, Seniors, Small Business, State and Local Offices, Press, Women."

The products that the FDA regulates include

- Allergy Therapies

- Animal Drugs and Food

- Aquaculture

- Bioengineered Food

- Biologics

- Blood

- Breast Implants

- Cell Phones

- Cosmetics

- Dietary Supplements

- Drugs

- Food

- Gene Therapy

- LASIK

- Mammography Facilities

- Medical Devices

- Orphan Products (drugs and devices)

- Radiation-Emitting Electronic Products

- Tattoos

- Tissue for Transplantation

- Whole-Body CT (computed tomography) Scans

- Xenotransplanation

Furthermore, there is a site index (see **http://www.fda.gov/oppacom/ hpchoice.html**), a site map and site search, "A–Z Index," and coverage of food safety (**http://www.foodsafety.gov/**). There are even specialized site maps for the Center for Biologics Evaluation & Research, Center for Drug Evaluation & Research, Center for Devices & Radiological Health, Center for Food Safety & Applied Nutrition, Center for Veterinary Medicine, and National Center for Toxicological Research (see **http://www.fda.gov/siteindex.html**). The Center for Food Safety & Applied Nutrition (**http://vm.cfsan.fda.gov/**) provides "Recent News," coverage of "Program Areas," "Overview," "National Food Safety Programs," and "Special Interest Areas,"

"Interacting with the Center," "Obtain FDA Documents," and "Other Sources of Food Information" (**http://www.cfsan.fda.gov/**).

National Institutes of Health

The site for the National Institutes of Health (NIH; **http://www.nih.gov/**) covers "What's New," "Health Information," "Grants and Funding Opportunities," "News & Events," "Scientific Resources" (e.g., NIH research laboratories on the Web), "Institutes, Centers & Offices" (see also **http://www.nih.gov/icd/**), information about the agency, questions and answers, career information, coverage of clinical trials, a search of the site and a site map, information for employees (e.g., assistance for persons with disabilities).

NIH also has a search engine (see **http://search.nih.gov/**) and information on stem cells (**http://www.nih.gov/news/stemcell/index.htm**). NIH launched ClincalTrials.gov (**http://www.clinicaltrials.gov/**), which provides "patients, family members and members of the public [with] current information about clinical research trials."

Within the NIH is the National Library of Medicine (**http://www.nlm.nih.gov/**), which offers various resources on health information and well as coverage of library services, research programs (**http://www.nlm.nih.gov/resprog.html**), news and announcements, exhibits, and general information. The library offers MEDLINE, MEDLINEplus, NIHSeniorHealth, and other resources on diseases, health care, and so on (see **http://www.nlm.nih.gov/siteindex.html**). MEDLINEplus provides the latest medical research and health information to the layperson, and its Web page (**http://medlineplus.gov/**) collects information on common diseases and conditions and offers numerous reference tools used by medical librarians. A page (**http://www.nim.nih.gov/hinfo.htm**) offers information and Web links by subject (e.g., Arctic health, bioethics, space life sciences, and the history of medicine).

The Gateway (**http://gateway.nlm.nih.gov/gw/Cmd**) lets NLM users search multiple retrieval systems: MEDLINE/Pub Med, OLDMEDICINE, LOCATORplus, MEDLINEplus, DIRLINE, AIDS Meetings, Health Services Research Meetings, Space Life Sciences Meetings, and HSRProj.

Office of Research Integrity

This office within the Public Health Service deals with scientific misconduct (fraudulent and falsified research). It investigates those cases brought to its attention and publicizes the cases in which misconduct was and was not found. Thus, the home page (**http://ori.hhs.gov/html/programs/instructresource.asp**) provides a tentative record of the seriousness of the problem. It also covers the responsibilities of mentors, protecting human subjects, conflicts of interest, the results of investigations from 1993–1997, handling misconduct, and scientific misconduct regulations.

DEPARTMENT OF HOMELAND SECURITY

This department, which was legislated into official existence on January 25, 2003, became the second largest cabinet-level office in the federal government. It includes more than 170,000 employees and represents the most significant government reorganization since the late 1940s, when the Department of Defense was fashioned out of the Departments of War, Navy, and the Army. The Homeland Security Department has three primary missions: to prevent terrorist attacks within the territories of the United States, to reduce threats from acts of terror, and to minimize the damage that might come from potential terrorist attacks (along with natural disasters).

Its Web site (**http://www.dhs.gov/dhspublic/**) includes links that explain the department's structure (**http://www.dhs.gov/dhspublic/theme_home1.jsp**); information for citizens (**http://www.dhs.gov/dhspublic/display?theme=36**) on how they can help in the fight to make America's homeland secure; advice to the private sector (**http://www.dhs.gov/dhspublic/display?theme=37**) on how they can contribute to national security, as well as how to do business with the department; links for other government agencies that work with the Homeland Security Department (**http://www.dhs.gov/dhspublic/display?theme=38**); and a series of information links for Homeland Security employees (**http://www.dhs.gov/dhspublic/display?theme=39**) and others interested in the department's mission. It also includes links to news releases and other official announcements, as well as the national terrorist threat level indicator system (**http://www.dhs.gov/dhspublic/display?theme=29&content=320**).

The department's five major divisions, called "directorates," are largely drawn from twenty-two existing federal agencies and bureaus reorganized under the responsibility of Homeland Security. These include the following (the former government office location given in parentheses):

Border and Transportation Security (BTS): This directorate is responsible for the security of the nation's borders and transportation systems. The largest of the five Homeland Directorates, it houses the following functions transferred from other parts of the federal government:

- Within BTS, three agencies are now managed through the **Bureau of Immigration and Customs Enforcement (ICE)**, **http://www.bice.immigration. gov/graphics/index.htm**

  - The U.S. Customs Service (Treasury), now called Customs and Border Protection, **http://www.customs.gov/xp/cgov/home.xml**

  - The Immigration and Naturalization Service [part] (Justice), now called Bureau of Citizenship and Immigration Services, **http://www.immigration. gov/ graphics/index.htm**

  - The Federal Protective Service (General Services Administration [GSA]), **http://www.bice.immigration.gov/graphics/fps.htm**

ICE will be responsible for several areas of law enforcement and border security:

- Immigration Investigations—responsible for investigating violations of the criminal and administrative provisions of the Immigration and Nationality Act and other related provisions of the *United States Code*

- Customs Investigations—responsible for investigating a range of issues including terrorist financing, export enforcement, money laundering, smuggling, fraud including Intellectual Property Rights violations, and cybercrimes

- Customs Air and Marine Interdiction—responsible for protecting the nation's borders and the American people from the smuggling of narcotics, other contraband, and terrorist activity with an integrated and coordinated air and marine interdiction force

- Federal Protective Service—responsible for providing a safe environment in which federal agencies can conduct their business by reducing threats posed against the more than 8,800 GSA-controlled facilities nationwide

- Detention and Removal—responsible for safely and humanely detaining, transporting, processing, and supervising illegal aliens who are awaiting removal or other disposition of their case

- Immigration Intelligence—responsible for the collection, analysis, and dissemination of intelligence to immigration staff at all levels to aid in making day-to-day, midterm, and long-term operational decisions; acquiring and allocating resources; and determining policy

- Customs Intelligence—responsible for the collection, analysis, and dissemination of strategic and tactical intelligence data for use by the operational elements of customs enforcement

- The Transportation Security Administration (Transportation), **http://www.tsa.gov/public/index.jsp**

- Federal Law Enforcement Training Center (Treasury), **http://www.fletc.gov/**

- Animal and Plant Health Inspection Service (Agriculture), **http://www.aphis.usda.gov/**

- Office of Domestic Preparedness (Justice), **http://www.ojp.usdoj.gov/odp/**

Emergency Preparedness and Response (EPR): This directorate will ensure that the nation is prepared for catastrophes, whether natural disasters or terrorist assaults. Not only will the directorate coordinate with first responders, it will oversee the federal government's national response and recovery strategy. To fulfill these missions, EPR will incorporate the following existing federal offices and bureaus:

- The Federal Emergency Management Agency (FEMA; **http://www.fema.gov/**) see Chapter 6.

- Strategic National Stockpile and the National Disaster Medical System (HHS)

- Nuclear Incident Response Team (Energy), **http://www.dhs.gov/dhspublic/display?theme=17&content=368**

- Domestic Emergency Support Team (Justice)

- National Domestic Preparedness Office (Federal Bureau of Investigation, FBI)

Science and Technology (S&T): This directorate is the department's primary research and development arm. The S&T Directorate will organize the vast scientific and technological resources of the United States to prevent or mitigate the effects of catastrophic terrorism against the United States or its allies. It will unify and coordinate much of the federal government's efforts to develop and implement scientific and technological countermeasures, including channeling the intellectual energy and extensive capacity of important scientific institutions, such as the national laboratories and academic institutions. One priority of the directorate will be to sponsor research, development, and testing to invent new vaccines, antidotes, diagnostics, and therapies against biological and chemical warfare agents. Current federal offices and bureaus to be include in this directorate:

- CBRN Countermeasures Programs (Energy)
- Environmental Measurements Laboratory (Energy)
- National BW Defense Analysis Center (Defense)
- Plum Island Animal Disease Center (Agriculture; **http://www.ars.usda. gov/plum/**)

Information Analysis and Infrastructure Protection (IAIP): IAIP will fuse and analyze information from multiple sources pertaining to terrorist threats. The directorate will be a full partner and consumer of all intelligence-generating agencies, such as the National Security Agency, the Central Intelligence Agency (CIA), and the FBI. The directorate's threat analysis and warning functions will support the president and, as he directs, other national decision makers responsible for securing the homeland from terrorism. To further ensure such protections, DHS will establish an office for a chief privacy officer. It will bring together into the new bureau the following existing federal functions:

- Critical Infrastructure Assurance Office (Commerce)
- Federal Computer Incident Response Center (GSA)
- National Communications System (Defense)
- National Infrastructure Protection Center (FBI)
- National Infrastructure Simulation and Analysis Center (Energy)
- Energy Security and Assurance Program (Energy)

Management: This directorate is responsible for budget, management, and personnel issues in DHS.

Along with these new directorates, several other existing agencies were moved from other agencies and made part of the new Homeland Security Department.

United States Coast Guard (USCG): The commandant of the Coast Guard will report directly to the secretary of homeland security. The USCG will also work closely with the undersecretary of border and transportation security and maintain its existing independent identity as a military service. Upon declaration of war or when the president so directs, the Coast Guard will operate as an element of the Department of Defense, consistent with existing law (**http://www.uscg.mil/USCG.shtm**).

United States Secret Service: The primary mission of the Secret Service is the protection of the president and other government leaders, as well as security for designated national events. The Secret Service is also the primary agency responsible for protecting U.S. currency from counterfeiters and safeguarding Americans from credit card fraud (**http://www.secretservice.gov/index.shtml**).

Bureau of Citizenship and Immigration Services: Although the BTS will be responsible for enforcement of the nation's immigration laws, the Bureau of Citizenship and Immigration Services will provide efficient immigration services and ease the transition to American citizenship. The director of citizenship and immigration services will report directly to the deputy secretary of homeland defense.

The legislation also created two new independent offices within the organizational structure.

Office of State and Local Government Coordination: This office sustains close coordination between local, state, and federal governments. It will ensure that close coordination takes place with state and local first responders, emergency services, and governments.

Office of Private Sector Liaison: This office provides America's business community a direct line of communication to the department. The office will work directly with individual businesses and through trade associations and other nongovernmental organizations to foster dialogue between the private sector and the Department of Homeland Security on the full range of issues and challenges faced by America's business sector in the post–September 11 world.

The department's information is organized into several general categories:

- Emergencies and Disasters (**http://www.dhs.gov/dhspublic/theme_home2.jsp**): This page describes the various programs, resources, and efforts to coordinate a national response to a terrorist attack, natural disaster, or any other large-scale emergency demanding a coordinated response among all levels of government. Examples include fires, floods, hurricanes, tornados, and other severe weather. Resources also include sources of information about government responses and recovery assistance, as well as how to prepare for the impact of weapons of mass destruction.

- Travel & Transportation (**http://www.dhs.gov/dhspublic/theme_home3.jsp**): This contains information about the department's efforts to secure national borders, including all coastal, river, and lake areas. Additional responsibilities describe the department's oversight of the national transportation infrastructure, and international trade across U.S. borders.

- Immigration and Borders (**http://www.dhs.gov/dhspublic/theme_home4.jsp**): Programs include the management of all travel and immigration of foreign nationals within the United States, as well as regulation of specific animal and plant products and their inspection at the national borders.

- Research & Technology (**http://www.dhs.gov/dhspublic/theme_home5.jsp**): Programs listed under this topic describe the different efforts to support the research and organization of scientific, engineering, and technological resources to help protect the nation. "Universities, the private sector, and the federal laboratories will be important DHS partners in this endeavor. Another DHS priority is the creation of the Advanced Research Projects Agency to jump-start and facilitate early research and development efforts to help address critical needs in homeland defense on the scientific and technological front."

- Threats and Protection (**http://www.dhs.gov/dhspublic/theme_home6.jsp**): This page explains efforts and programs designed to "anticipate, preempt, and deter threats to the homeland whenever possible, and the ability to respond quickly when such threats do materialize." Resources include information technology, coordinated intelligence gathering and organization with other federal agencies, along with a national system of public alerts and advisories.

- Working with DHS (**http://www.dhs.gov/dhspublic/theme_home7.jsp**): This page describes specific ways members of the public, private sector firms, and other government agencies can work with the department.

- Press Room (**http://www.dhs.gov/dhspublic/theme_home8.jsp**): This page includes archives for the department's press releases, news articles, speeches, press conferences, testimony, legislation, and library.

Finally, at Ready.Gov, the Department of Homeland Security provides information for the public to prepare for (and be informed about) a security threat (see **http://www.ready.gov/**).

DEPARTMENT OF HOUSING AND URBAN DEVELOPMENT

The department's mission is "a decent, safe, and sanitary home and suitable living environment for every American." The Web site (**http://www.hud.gov/**) covers homes and communities and provides information about the department, press releases, coverage of "Homes" (buying, selling, renting, homeless, home improvements, HUD homes, fair housing, FHA refunds, foreclosure, and consumer information), "Communities" (about communities, volunteering, organizing, and economic development), "Working with HUD" (e.g., grants, work online, and complaints), "Resources" (library, handbooks and forms, and common questions), and "Tools" (e.g., Webcasts and mailing lists). Some information is arranged by state and for specific groups: "Citizens" (e.g., homebuyers, veterans, and senior citizens), "Housing Industry" (e.g., lenders and brokers), and "Other Partners" (e.g., grantees and Congress). "Complaints," for example, is subdivided into

- Housing discrimination

- Bad landlords in federal housing

- Manufactured housing

- Land sales

- Deceptive contractors

- Fraud, waste, and abuse

There are many online systems available for citizens and HUD business partners. Most helpful is the grouping of these systems by a matrix indicating their relevance for each audience group (e.g., see **http://www.hud.gov/systems/housing.cfm**; **http://www.hud.gov/systems/citizens.cfm**).

Another useful grouping of Web pages can be found in the library (see "Resources"). To assist those navigating the home page, the library contains nineteen bookshelves, which identify various Web pages by a common theme. For example, the first bookshelf identifies the most requested HUD pages (**http://www.hud.gov/library/bookshelf01/index.cfm**). Incidentally, the second bookshelf pertains to the *Freedom of Information Act,* the third covers research, and the twelfth addresses legal information produced by the department. Bookshelf seven addresses "Brownfields," which are abandoned, idled, or underutilized real property where expansion or redevelopment is complicated by real or perceived contamination.

There is an opportunity to search the site, and the site index (**http://www.hud.gov/assist/siteindex.cfm**) lays out information for quick retrieval.

Ginnie Mae, which was created in 1968 as a wholly owned corporation with HUD, is intended "to promote accessibility to affordable housing for all Americans." The home page (**http://www.ginniemae.gov/**) "provides information to our customers and provides Ginnie Mae with opportunities to increase our mission in working with the mortgage industry to provide more affordable housing for the homebuyers of today and tomorrow." The page, for instance, offers a site map, an opportunity to search the site, information about Ginnie Mae and home ownership, resources, financial information, an investment center, "Mortgage-backed Securities," "e-commerce (EDI)," publications (e.g., Ginnie Mae memoranda), and more.

DEPARTMENT OF THE INTERIOR

The home page of the Department of the Interior (DOI; **http://www.doi.gov/**) groups its resources under "DOI Officials," "News," "About DOI," "Bureaus/Offices," "Contact," "Hot Topics," "Collaborative Efforts," "American Indians," "Fish/Wildlife," "National Parks," "Public Lands," "Energy," "Science," and "Water." There are also links to Web pages for teachers and kids (see Chapter 13), FIREWISE (preparing homes to withstand forest fires; **http://www.firewise.org/usa/title.htm**), recreation (**http://www.recreation.gov/**), and volunteers.

"Bureaus/Offices" leads to home pages for the department's substructure (see **http://www.doi.gov/bureaus.html**). Some of the major subunits (bureaus) include

- United States Fish and Wildlife Service (**http://www.fws.gov/**)

- U.S. Geological Survey (**http://www.usgs.gov/**)

- Bureau of Land Management (**http://www.blm.gov/nhp/index.htm**)

- Minerals Management Service (**http://www.mms.gov/**)

- National Park Service (**http://www.nps.gov/**)

- Bureau of Reclamation (**http://www.usbr.gov/**)

- Office of Surface Mining (**http://www.osmre.gov/osm.htm**)

Chapter 11 covers the U.S. Geological Survey, which provides scientific information to "describe and understand the Earth; minimize loss of life and property from natural diseases; manage water, biological, energy, and mineral resources; and enhance and protect our quality of life." This section also omits coverage of the Bureau of Indian Affairs (BIA), which, as noted in Chapter 1, does not have a Web site in operation at the time that this guide was written. The bureau's Web site currently reads as follows:

The BIA website as well as the BIA mail servers have been temporarily unavailable due to the Cobell Litigation. Please continue to check from time to time. We have no estimate on when authorization will be given to reactivate these sites.
Here are some alternate ways to get BIA-related information:
For general BIA information: 202 208-3710
For Tribal Leaders Directory: 202 208 3711

Although it is not mentioned on the BIA site, additional information is available on DOI's home page under "American Indians," which discusses Indian Trust Assets Management and related court decisions.

U.S. Fish and Wildlife Service

The major responsibilities of the agency "involve migratory birds, endangered species, certain marine mammals, and freshwater and anadromous fish—as well as people, of course." The service's "mission is, working with others, to conserve, protect and enhance fish, wildlife, and plants and their habitats for the continuing benefit of the American people." The home page contains "portal links" to

- Birds
- Contaminants
- Contracts
- Endangered Species
- Fire
- Fisheries
- Grants
- Habitat
- History
- Hunting
- Images
- Index

- International
- Jobs
- Kids/Educators (see Chapter 13)
- Law Enforcement
- Information Quality
- Guidelines
- Legislation
- News
- Offices (those within the agency)
- Partnerships
- Permits
- Planning
- Policies
- Questions?
- Refuges
- Species
- Training
- Volunteers
- Wetlands

The portal for "Endangered Species," for example, provides a list of threatened and endangered species, species information, species in the spotlight, laws and policies, information about the agency's role, an endangered species bulletin and other publications, and more.

⬆ Bureau of Land Management

The Bureau of Land Management (BLM) "administers 264 million acres of land, located primarily in the 12 Western States. The BLM sustains the health, diversity, and productivity of the public lands for the use and enjoyment of present and future generations." The agency is also "responsible for wildfire management and suppression on 388 million acres." The home page covers news (e.g., news releases and legislative actions), information (e.g., about the agency and areas under its jurisdiction and on FOIA), publications, frequently asked questions, offices and centers within BLM, permits, employment opportunities, bureau telephone directories, maps of public lands, maps depicting points of interest in a state (**http://www.blm.gov/nhp/map/natmap. html**), and so on. A most helpful feature is "Browse," which serves as a site map that, for example, provides access to the online bookstore, statistics, and a video conference.

The *Wild Free-Roaming Horse and Burro Act of 1971* directs BLM to manage and protect wild horses and burros on public lands. Because the current population exceeds the rangeland carrying capacity, BLM operates an adoption program. The Wild Horse and Burro Page (**http://www.wildhorsandburro.blm.gov/**) discusses adoption procedures.

Minerals Management Service

The Minerals Management Service (MMS) manages "the mineral resources of the Outer Continental Shelf in an environmentally sound and safe manner" and collects, verifies, and distributes "mineral revenues from federal and Indian lands." The home page has a "Director's Page" as well as a "Topic Index," information about the agency, and "What's New." Other options are "Strategic Planning," "Minerals Revenue," "Offshore Program," "Newsroom," "Congressional Affairs," "Advisory Committees," "Library," "Info Quality Guidelines," "FOIA," "Kids' Page" (see Chapter 13), "Privacy Act/Disclaimers," "Links," "Products & Services," "Job Opportunities," "Navigation Tips," "Contact Us," "Deepwater Environment," "Deepwater Exploration/Development," "Industry Awards," "Oil Valuation," and "Reengineering."

Deepwater environmental information, for instance, covers the Gulf of Mexico region, which "has emerged as an important oil and gas province and therefore has experienced a substantial increase in leasing, exploration, development, and production activities." The option for "Links" covers Web sites related to MMS activities and responsibilities. These sites come from the federal and state government, international bodies, professional associations, nongovernment organizations, and they cover "Information Resources" (oil and gas) and "Natural Resources, Earth Sciences, and Offshore Environment."

It is possible to conduct a search of the Web site. Before doing so (or, in fact, before using the Web site), however, it might be advisable to peruse "Navigation Tips," because the MMS "Website contains thousands of pages."

National Park Service

The opening screen of the Web site, which is called ParkNet, covers "Visit Your Parks," "Links to the Past" ("histories, cultures, & places"), "Nature Net" ("nature & science in the parks"), "Learn NPS" ("for teachers and learners"), and "Info Zone" ("servicewide information"). Other choices are the bookshop, news, contacting the agency, a site search, and the FOIA.

"Links to the Past" covers, for instance, cultural resources for exploring America's past. Those resources relate to "Archeology," "Historic Buildings & Structures," "History," "Maritime," "Museums & Collections," "Publications," and more. It merits mention that the NPS's Archeology and Ethnography Program provides guidance to decision makers regarding the preservation of the diverse cultures and cultural heritage found in the parks. A page (**http://www.cr.nps.gov/aad/index.htm/**) encourages visitors to explore, learn, and participate. Pathfinders identify anthropological sites and projects, museums, exhibits, and other links.

NatureNet (**http://www.nature.nps.gov/**) has the following components for the National Parks:

- Air

- Biology

- Geology

- Social Science

- Water

- Science

- Educational Opportunities

- Partnerships

- Publications

Under "Air," AIRWeb (**http://www2.nature.nps.gov/ard/**) addresses air quality and other topics related to those parks and refuges under the jurisdiction of NPS's Air Resources Division and the Fish and Wildlife Service's Air Quality Branch. Under "Geology," there is, for instance, "Park Geology," which covers geology and soils programs, hot topics, an online museum, and more (see **http://www2.nature.nps. gov/grd/tour/index.htm**). "After seven years of compiling data from twenty museums, the database of Florissant type and published specimens now lives on the web! It includes all 1700 species from Florissant, photo images for most specimens, and digital copies of many of the publications."

﹖ Bureau of Reclamation

Established in 1902, the Bureau of Reclamation, a water management agency, is "the largest wholesaler of water in the country." Its home page explains what the Bureau of Reclamation does and offers a "Newsroom" (speeches and reference material) "Programs" (which also addresses initiatives and activities), "DataWeb," "Feature," coverage of the water supply, congressional testimony, publications, employment opportunities, "comments" directed to the agency, and a search of the site. DataWeb provides information on reclamation reservoirs, dams, and facilities; water data; and engineering data. It also contains interactive maps and information on power plants and projects.

The bureau also manages cultural resources, "the physical remains of a people's way of life that archaeologists and historians study to try to interpret how people lived." This page (**http://www.usbr.gov/cultural/**) provides publications, coverage of reclamation activities under the *Native American Graves Protection and Repatriation Act,* and more.

﹖ Office of Surface Mining

The office, in cooperation with the states and Indian tribes, is responsible for the protection of "citizens and the environment during coal mining and reclamation," and it reclaims mines abandoned before 1977. The home page contains a "Welcome" and provides announcements, news releases, information and publications (e.g., about historic and cultural preservation), statistics (e.g., for coal production), a slide show, a postcard, and "Subscribe":

In an effort to make the Office of Surface Mining information more accessible to the public, a subscription service is being offered that will automatically send you, via e-mail, copies of News Releases (in electronic format) and/or notification of mountaintop mining information or published reports when they become available. Based on past experience it is expected that a News Release subscription will result in approximately three or four messages per month, a Mountaintop Mining information subscription in two or three notifications per month, and a Published Reports subscription in five notification per year.

The form to subscribe or to unsubscribe is then provided.

The opening screen contains a "Subject Index" ("most frequently requested topics"), "Regulation of Active Mines" ("protecting citizens and the environment during coal mining"), "Abandoned Mine Reclamation" ("reclaiming land affected by past coal mining practices"), "Finance and Administration" ("budget, grants, and fee collection"), "Links to Information" ("connection to coal mining and reclamation Web sites"), and "Other Information" ("quick-links to important pages on this web site"). The site maps breaks down many of above categories.

DEPARTMENT OF JUSTICE

The Web site of the Department of Justice (DOJ; **http://www.usdoj.gov/**) covers "About DOJ" (e.g., alphabetical list of components, organization chart, general information, and budget information), "Publications and Documents" (e.g., annual reports of the attorney general, legal documents, and strategic plan), employment information, the FOIA, "Doing Business with DOJ," "Grants," "Fugitives & Missing Persons," "Other Federal Sites," "Press Room," "Justice for Kids & Youth" (see Chapter 13), and an archive of several offices and divisions. There is also "Information for Individuals and Communities" that covers

- Civil Rights & Liberties Violations

- Disabilities

- Dispute Resolution

- Domestic Violence

- Elder Justice

- Faith-Based & Community Initiatives

- Fraud

- Immigration Information

- Prison and Parole Information

- Safe Communities

- Youth Violence

- Victims of Crime

The alphabetical list of components, **http://www.usdoj.gov/02organizations/ 02_1.html**, for example, leads to the Federal Bureau of Prisons (**http:// www.bop.gov/**), which offers press releases, "Quick Facts and Statistics," a weekly population report, publications, inmate information, the FOIA, and so on. The United States Marshals Service, which protects the federal courts (**http://www.usdoj. gov/marshals/**), offers "Current News," the most wanted fugitives, "Major Fugitive Cases," publications, newsletter, and other information resources.

DOJ "Publications and Documents" are grouped into five categories ("AG [Attorney General] Annual Reports," "Legal Documents," "Reports and Publications," "Strategic Plan," and "U.S. Attorneys' Manual"):

 Many of the Departments publications and documents can be found online. Departmental briefs in major cases, regulations, business review letters, memoranda, and opinions are among the items that will be found in Legal Documents. Research, statistical, and special reports, newsletters, and general publications are in Reports and Publications. The FBI's Uniform Crime Reports, and the U.S. Attorneys Manual are just some of the various items that can be found in this portion of the Web site.

Additional publications can be found at the National Criminal Justice Reference Service Web site and at the National Institute of Corrections Publications Web site.

Created in 1984, the Office of Justice Programs (OJP) "works within its established partnership arrangements with federal, state and local agencies and national and community-based organizations to develop, fund and evaluate a wide range of criminal and juvenile justice programs." The office's "mission is to provide federal leadership in developing the nation's capacity to prevent and control crime, administer justice and assist crime victims." The home page (**http://www.ojp.usdoj.gov/**) covers the agency, "What's New," "Grants/Funding," "OJP Publications—A to Z," press releases, "Technical Assistance Guide," "Hot Topics," employment opportunities, a site map and a site search, and links to related Web sites. "Funding, Training, Programs, Statistics and Research" covers the justice system, crime victims, and fighting crime.

A history of DOJ and its agencies can be found at **http://www.usdoj.gov/ 02organizations/dojhistory.htm**. This page includes a list of past Attorneys General.

Drug Enforcement Administration

The DEA's Web site (**http://www.usdoj.gov/dea/**) covers the agency and its programs, and it offers a site search, news, and stories. "Briefs & Background" covers drug trafficking and abuse, law enforcement, drug policy, and resources for contractors, job applicants, law enforcement, legislators, parents and teachers, physicians and registrants, and students. There are also statistics for drug and law enforcement and for overview drug use in the United States.

Federal Bureau of Investigation

The FBI's site (**http://www.fbi.gov/**) covers the agency, "Most Wanted," "Terrorism," "Employment," "Press Room," "For the Family," "Interagency Programs,"

"Library & Reference," a site search and a site map, "FBI E-News," the FOIA, related Web links, and more. "Resources" includes business opportunities, frequently asked questions, legal attaché offices (overseas FBI representation), field offices, and more. Among the publications is the Uniform Crime Reports, an annual reporting of crime in the United States and statistics such as on hate crimes and "Law Enforcement Officers Killed and Assaulted."

The FBI's electronic reading room contains frequently requested documents released under the Freedom of Information Act. The site (**http://foia.fbi.gov/**) contains the following categories: "Alphabetical Listing," "Espionage," "Famous Persons," "Gangster Era," "Historical Interest," "Unusual Phenomena," and "Violent Crime." Under "Unusual Phenomena, the FBI has released documents relating to Project Blue Book," which was an Air Force program for the investigation of Unidentified Flying Objects (UFO; see **http://foia.fbi.gov/bluebook.htm**). Here, therefore, are declassified documents giving, for instance, the number of UFO sightings from 1947 through 1969—the year in which the Air Force discontinued the program. Some of the "Famous Persons" are Lucille Ball, William Faulkner, Errol Flynn, Robert F. Kennedy, Malcolm X, Marilyn Monroe, Pablo Piscasso, Elvis Presley, and Will Rogers. For example, some people reported their concern that Elvis was corrupting American youth and that Malcolm X advocated violence.

National Criminal Justice Reference Service

The Service (NCJRS) "is a federally sponsored information clearinghouse for people around the country and the world involved with research, policy, and practice related to criminal and juvenile justice and drug control." "Anyone interested in the fields of criminal and juvenile justice and drug policy can use or request NCJRS services and assistance." The home page (**http://www.ncjrs.org/**) covers "What's NEW," statistics, "Corrections," "Courts," "Drugs and Crime," "International," "Juvenile Justice," "Law Enforcement," "Victims of Crime," "More Issues in Criminal Justice," "In the Spotlight" (e.g., school safety, club drugs, and hate crime), a calendar of events, grants and funding opportunities, and various publications. It is possible to search full-text publications and an abstracts database (containing summaries of more than 170,000 criminal justice publications), and to subscribe to JUSTINFO, a newsletter.

National Institute of Justice

This agency, which is DOJ's research, development, and evaluation agency, examines crime control and justice issues. The home page (**http://www.ojp.usdoj.gov/nij/**) discusses the agency and presents "What's New," "Programs," "Funding Opportunities," "Highlights," publications, and contacting the agency.

In 1997, the agency's Mapping and Analysis for Public Safety (MAPS) replaced the Crime Mapping Research Center. Its goal "is to promote research, evaluation, development, and dissemination of GIS [geographic information system] technology for criminal justice research and practice." MAPS' home page (**http://www.ojp. usdoj.gov/**) presents "Headline News," "Mapping Tools," publications, frequently asked questions, conferences, funding, and "Bibliography."

Office of the Pardon Attorney

In consultation with the attorney general or his designee, the office

assists the President in the exercise of executive clemency as authorized under Article II, section 2, of the Constitution. Under the Constitution, the President's clemency power extends only to federal criminal offenses. All requests for executive clemency for federal offenses are directed to the Pardon Attorney for investigation and review. The Pardon Attorney prepares the Department's recommendation to the President for final disposition of each applicant. Executive clemency may take several forms, including pardon, commutation of sentence, remission of fine or restitution, and reprieve.

The home page (**http://www.usdoj.gov/pardon/index.html**) provides application forms, standards for consideration of clemency petitions, clemency regulations, clemency statistics, a list of clemency recipients, and access to the *Freedom of Information Act.*

DEPARTMENT OF LABOR

The home page for the department (**http://www.dol.gov/**) highlights key information related to the department, and it arranges information "by topic," "by audience," "by top 20 requested items," "by form," and "by organization." Other choices include frequently asked questions, the FOIA, elaws advisors, agency contacts, statistics, publications, a site search, an "A–Z Index," and more. Employment Laws Assistance for Workers and Small Businesses (elaws) "is an interactive system designed to help employers and employees understand and comply with numerous employment laws enforced by the Department of Labor. Each elaws Advisor gives advice and provides information on a specific law or regulation based on the user's particular situation." The home page (**http://www.dol.gov/elaws/**) has icons for Advisors on "Retirement and Health Benefits Standards," "Safety and Health Standards," "Wage, Hour, and Other Workplace Standards," and "All Advisors." Furthermore, there is also a media page, an opportunity to search by keyword and by agency, a "Summary of the Major Laws Administered by DOL," and so forth.

Among the "top 20 requested items" are America's Job Bank, which provides guidance in job seeking and encourages employers to post job vacancies; the *Occupational Outlook Handbook*, which provides overviews of different professional careers, consumer price indexes, employment projections, state labor offices and state laws, and so on.

DOL has a list of its subagencies (offices, bureaus, and agencies) that provides links to their Web sites and access to their mission statements, organizational chart, and list of key personnel (see **http://www.dol.gov/dol/organization.htm**).

⟲ Bureau of Labor Statistics

This agency, which is discussed more thoroughly in Chapter 8, collects and provides statistical data on the labor force. The home page (**http://stats.bls.gov/**) covers "Programs & Surveys," various workforce indices, "What's New," the "Most Requested BLS Statistics," publications, a glossary, "What's New," and more. For various topics ("Employment & Unemployment," "Prices & Living Conditions," "Compensation & Working Conditions," "Productivity & Technology," and "Regional Resources") and the subtopics listed, there might be "Special Notices" as well as an indication of the "Most Requested Statistics" and an opportunity to "Create Customized Tables (One Screen)" or "Create Customized Tables (Multiple Screens)." Some of the subtopics are available as "flat files;" "Given the limitations on the amount of data which can be extracted using any of the applications provided on the Web site, the FTP [file transfer protocol] server can be ideal for those users requiring large volumes of timeseries data." Thus, flat files provide a link to the BLS FTP server.

⟲ O*NET Project

"The O*NET Project supports and is supported by numerous related workforce development initiatives that are sponsored by the Department of Labor, the Employment and Training Administration, and other DOL agencies." Icons from the opening screen of this open page (**http://www.doleta.gov/programs/onet/**) cover "Business," "Grants & Contacts," "Job Seekers," "Research," "Workforce Community," "Youth," a site search, "Related Documents," "Related Links," "What's New with O*Net," and more. There is an online guide to tests and other means of assessment and explanations of O*Net's uses and of how to use the resource (see also **http://www.doleta.gov/programs/onet/onet_default.asp**).

⟲ Mine Safety and Health Administration

The Mine Safety and Health Administration (MSHA) administers the *Federal Mine Safety and Health Act of 1977* and "enforces compliance with mandatory safety and health standards as a means to eliminate fatal accidents; to reduce the frequency and severity of nonfatal accidents; to minimize health hazards; and to promote improved safety and health conditions in the Nation's mines." The home page (**http://www.msha.gov/**) covers the agency, "Education & Training," "Fatal Alert Bulletins," rules and regulations, FOIA reading room, forms and online filings, media information (e.g., press releases, congressional testimony, and speeches), a mining industry directory, "Program Areas," "Office of the Solicitor," "Safety and Health Information," frequently asked questions, statistics, interactive tools and streaming media files (video), links to related Web sites, a translation site (translate some agency information into Spanish), news "Highlights," mine rescue and emergency information, hazard alerts and bulletins, "General Information," and fatality statistics. It is also possible to conduct a site search. By the way, the Office of the Solicitor maintains a home page for kids (see Chapter 13).

↗ Occupational Safety and Health Administration

The mission of the agency "is to save lives, prevent injuries and protect the health of America's workers." The home page (**http://www.osha.gov/**) provides a site search and site index ("A-Z Index"), information about the agency, subscription services, publications and posters, facts, announcements, regulations, standards, a news room (e.g., press releases), statistical data, and research studies. There are links to OSHA advisors and offices. Also posted are a reading room (e.g., FOIA, manuals, statistics and inspection data), compliance assistance, and more.

↗ Women's Bureau

This bureau "is the single unit at the Federal government level exclusively concerned with serving and promoting the interests of working women." The home page (**http://www.dol.gov/wb/welcome.html**) discusses the agency and provides a library of resources (e.g., statistics and data); a news room; and coverage of initiatives, frequently asked questions, and FOIA. There is access to regional information, press releases, publications, and more.

DEPARTMENT OF STATE

The Department of State is the oldest executive-level office in the president's cabinet. The department's core responsibilities are to manage and direct the country's official relationships with other national governments and international organizations. Through its global network of embassies, consulates, and foreign missions, the State Department's Web site (**http://www.state.gov/**) is a rich source of information about other countries and is the single best source for understanding the official foreign policy of the United States. The department is also responsible for a variety of services and support for citizens who travel overseas (passports, visas, marriage and divorce, and health issues) and for people who have particular questions about the United States or want to visit or become U.S. citizens.

The Web site provides information, for example, about the department and its bureaus, offices, and embassies; press releases, daily press briefings, and an electronic subscriptions service (**http://www.state.gov/www/listservs_cms.html**); information about travel and living abroad; countries and regions (including country background notes); international topics and issues; history, education, and culture; country commercial guides, contracting opportunity, and per diem rates; other services; and the FOIA (**http://foia.state.gov/**).

The section on "Countries and Regions" (**http://www.state.gov/countries/**) presents the principal bureaus that cover the nation's global relationships: African Affairs, East Asian and Pacific Affairs, European and Eurasian Affairs, Near Eastern Affairs, South Asian Affairs, and the Western Hemisphere Affairs. Each of these is the touchstone between the policy developed by president and the secretary of state in Washington, D.C., and the immediate reporting and observations of hundreds of U.S. foreign missions around the globe.

If one were planning a trip to Fiji, a quick look at the European Affairs Bureau's Country Background Notes would provide information on that country's history, economy, people, government, political condition, and so on. In fact, each of the State Department's regional bureaus have created these kinds of notes on nearly every country that enjoys diplomatic relations with the United States. The document on Fiji, as well as a complete list of these background notes, can be found at (**http://www.state.gov/r/pa/ei/bgn/**).

"International Topics and Issues" covers "Topics and Issues A–Z," which covers arms control, HIV/AIDS, the Holocaust, human rights, legal issues, religious freedom, security (diplomatic, embassy, and international), trafficking in persons, war crime issues, women's issues, and so on. Note that for the time period before January 20, 2001(or the inauguration of the Bush administration), topics and issues can be found at **http://www.state.gov/www/policy.html**. In addition, various archived sources are available at **http://www.state.gov/index.html** (see the previous edition of this guide).

"History, Education and Culture" leads to the department's Office of the Historian, which, among other things, prepares the *Foreign Relations of the United States* (**http://www.stte.gov/r/pa/ho/frus/**), a series which began in 1861 that contains declassified records "from all foreign affairs agencies." Of the more than 350 volumes produced, the more recent ones are available online. The Office of the Historian also produces a list of "U.S. Visits by Foreign Heads of State and Government," since 1874, and assorted other historical publications (see **http://www.state.gov/r/pa/ho/pubs/**), including a "time line of U.S. diplomatic history and "U.S. Concern over the Fate of Nazi German Looted Gold, German External Assets, and Related Subjects."

The FOIA Electronic Reading Room complements the *Foreign Relations of the United States*, and it identifies different collections that are available, including declassified press releases and statement for Argentina and Chile (see **http://foia.state.gov/SearchColls/Search.asp**).

For Americans traveling abroad, "Travel and Living Abroad" offers important information about the opportunities and challenges of visiting and living in other countries (see Chapter 12). This includes a range of information on marriage or divorce oversees, oversees schools, dual citizenship, births oversees, and so on. There is an explanation of specific emergency services available to American citizens traveling overseas, along with the complicated process of obtaining a passport. In addition, globe-trotting citizens may find the information about which American embassies and consular offices are on the Web particular useful (**http://usembassy.state.gov/**). One of the most popular services offered by the Consular Affairs is their hundreds of notices and warnings advising U.S. citizens of the multitude of dangers that may exist in particular countries.

The Bureau of Arms Control develops "policy in the areas of conventional, chemical/biological, and nuclear forces, for supporting arms control negotiations, for implementing existing agreements in these areas, and for advising the Secretary [of State] on related national security issues such as nuclear testing and missile defense." The home page (**http://www.state.gov/t/ac/**) covers bureau offices and an organizational chart, biological and chemical weapons convention, missile defense, treaties, an archive (1997–2000), and more.

DEPARTMENT OF TRANSPORTATION

The Department of Transportation's (DOT) Web site (**http://www.dot.gov/**) covers the department, "DOT News," "Doing Business with DOT," "Safety" ("the primary safety sites within the DOT"), "Dockets" (regulations), "Jobs and Education," "FOIA," Web links, and "Spotlight" (current information), "Quick Answers" and "Other Questions?," a list of frequently asked questions, the TranStats-New Intermodal database, and more. "About DOT" identifies and links to DOT agencies, and to "useful" government and nongovernment links. Examples of those agencies include the Bureau of Transportation Statistics (see Chapter 8), Federal Aviation Administration, Federal Highway Administration, Federal Railroad Administration, Maritime Administration, Federal National Highway Traffic Safety Administration, Office of the Inspector General, Office of the Secretary of Transportation, Research and Special Programs Administration, St. Lawrence Seaway Development Corporation, Surface Transportation Board, Transportation Administrative Service Center, Transportation Security Administration, and the U.S. Coast Guard.

"Doing Business with DOT" provides "business opportunities and vendor information." It discusses DOT online transactions' policies and services. "DOT is committed to transforming the way we do business by utilizing the power of the Internet to allow citizens to transact business on-line 24 hours a day, 7 days a week. This on-line transaction capability, which is commonly referred to as E-Government, will enable you to perform such tasks as making payments and accessing DOT databases" (**http://www.dot.gov/business.html**).

The National Transportation Library (**http://ntl.bts.gov/**) contains documents and databases provided free of any restriction on reproduction. The library also has TRIS Online, which is "the largest and most comprehensive source of information on published transportation research" on the Web (**http://199.79.179.82/sundev/search. cfm**). The National Transportation Library also provides "Quick Answers" (e.g., related to "new car rollover ratings," "moving companies," and "file an airline complaint") and a list of frequently asked questions (**http:// ntl.bts.gov/cgi-bin/ref/ ref.cgi**). It is possible to send an e-mail comment or question to the Library reference service (**http://ntl.bts.gov/cgi-bin/ref/ref.cgi**).

Federal Aviation Administration

The Federal Aviation Administration's (FAA) Web site (**http://www.faa.gov/**) provides information for

- Airline Operators
- Airport Operators
- Educators
- FAA Employees
- General Aviation
- International

- Kids (see Chapter 13)

- News Media

- Mechanics

- Military

- Pilots

- Space Transportation

- Students

- Travelers

There is also "General Information"; a newsroom; "Traveler Briefings" and alerts; forms; current information; coverage of "Aviation Safety," rules and regulations; certification; "Air Traffic"; and a section on "How Do I" that covers

- Become (e.g., a pilot or air traffic controller)

- Get (e.g., a copy of my pilot certification or publications)

- Find (e.g., FAA offices, jobs, contracting opportunities, or training facilities)

- Report (e.g., a safety violation or an air travel service problem)

☞ Federal Railroad Administration

The home page of this agency (**http://www.fra.dot.gov/site/index.htm**) covers the agency, "Safety," "Railroad Development," "Passenger Rail," "Regulations & Legislation," "Data Central" (e.g., safety data), "Studies & Publications," "Press Room," and a site search. Other options include the receipt of information about employment opportunities, coverage of doing business with the agency and of issues, the FOIA, and "Kids & Education" (see Chapter 13).

☞ National Highway Traffic Safety Administration

The home page (**http://www.nhtsa.dot.gov/**) covers "Recalls," "Buying a Safer Car," "Service Bulletins Database," "Impaired Driving," "Hot at NHTSA," "Crash Tests," press releases, news, and a site map. There are also publications, an Auto-Safety Hotline, the telephone number for the agency's toll-free hotline, and an opportunity to search the site. "Popular Information" covers topics such as air bags, child seat inspections, grants, press releases, real video, a publications' catalog, recalls, and school buses. "Star Ratings," one of the topics under "Popular Information," rates cars, trucks, vans, and sport utilities for "frontal crash protection:" "you can access crash test scores or safety features."

DEPARTMENT OF TREASURY

This Web site (**http://www.ustreas.gov/**) covers the secretary, news, "Key Topics" (e.g., "Currency & Coins," "General Interest," "Small Business," and "Taxes"), Webcasts, e-mail subscription services, press releases, "Education," "Direct Links" (e.g., frequently asked questions, employment opportunities, and seized property auctions), site search and site index, FOIA, and "Offices" and "Bureaus." The headings for "Offices" (**http://www.ustreas.gov/offices/index.html**) and "Bureaus" (**http://www.ustreas.gov/bureaus/index.html**) provide access to the divisions of the department. For example, among the bureaus are the following:

- **Bureau of Alcohol, Tobacco & Firearms,** which "is responsible for enforcing and administering firearms and explosives laws, as well as those covering the production, use and distribution of alcohol and tobacco products" (**http://www.atf.treas.gov/**).

- **Bureau of Engraving and Printing,** which designs and manufactures U.S. currency, many stamps, securities, and other official certificates and awards. The agency "serves as the federal government's most secure and efficient source of vital Government securities" (**http://www.bep.treas.gov/; http://www.moneyfactory.com/**).

- **Bureau of the Public Debt,** which "borrows the money needed to operate the Federal Government. It administers the public debt by issuing and servicing U.S. Treasury marketable, savings and special securities" (**http://www.publicdebt.treas.gov/**).

- **Financial Crimes Enforcement Network,** which "supports law enforcement investigative efforts and fosters interagency and global cooperation against domestic and international financial crimes. It also provides U.S. policy makers with strategic analyses of domestic and worldwide trends and patterns" (**http://www.fincen.gov/**).

- **Financial Management Service,** which "receives and distributes all public monies, maintains government accounts, and prepares daily and monthly reports on the status of government finances" (**http://www.fms.treas.gov/**).

- **Internal Revenue Service,** "which is the largest of Treasury's bureaus. It is responsible for determining, assessing, and collecting internal revenue in the United States" (**http://www.irs.gov/**).

- **Office of the Comptroller of the Currency,** which "charters, regulates, and supervises national banks to ensure a safe, sound, and competitive banking system that supports the citizens, communities, and economy of the United States" (**http://www.occ.tres.gov/**).

- **Office of Thrift Supervision,** which "is the primary regulator of all federal and many state-chartered thrift institution, "including savings banks and savings and loan associations" (**http://www.ots.treas.gov/**).

• **U.S. Mint,** which "designs and manufactures domestic, bullion and foreign coins as well as commemorative medals and other numismatic items. [The] Mint also distributes U.S. coins to the Federal Reserve banks as well as maintains physical custody and protection of our nation's silver assets" (**http://www. usmint.gov/**).

Internal Revenue Service

The Internal Revenue Service's (IRS) Web site provides information about the agency, "Tax Stats," career information, coverage of the FOIA, a newsroom, a site search and a site map, a search for forms and publications, tax help, and information about resolving a tax matter, obtain a refund, tax scams and fraud, "Check Your Withholding," and more. There is also information aimed at "Individuals," "Businesses," "Charities & Non-Profits," "Government Entities," "Tax Professionals," and "Retirement Plans." There are online instructions for completing a tax return and other advise and guidance.

DEPARTMENT OF VETERANS AFFAIRS

The Web site (**http://www.va.gov/**) of the Department of Veterans Affairs asks "How May We Serve You?" and arranges answers by the following topics: "Burial & Memorial Benefits," "Health Benefits & Services," "Compensation & Pension Benefits," "Home Loan Guaranty Services," "Education Benefits," "Appeals: Board of Veterans' Appeals," "Life Insurance Program," and "Vocational Rehab & Employment Services."

The site also provides a site map and search of the site, a facilities locator, as well as coverage of "Online Applications," "Hot Topics," "Special Programs," and "Today's VA," which, for instance, covers "Veteran Data," and "What's New." The Department has launched an online benefit application system (Veterans ON-line Application Website) to help veterans handle the process electronically and to reduce the waiting time to receive a check (**http://www.vabenefits.vba.va.gov/vonapp/main.asp**).

WHITE HOUSE

This Web site (**http://www.whitehouse.gov/**) covers the "President," "Vice President," "First Lady," "Mrs. Cheney," "News & Policies," "Your Government," "History & Tours," "Kids" (see Chapter 13), "Appointments" (application and nominations), "Contact," speeches, photographs, a history of the West Wing, and "Tours." Some of the highlighted policies relate to national, homeland, and economic security. It is possible to search the site, receive e-mail updates, and gain access to speeches, announcements, nominations, radio addresses, and so on. "Your Government" links to the cabinet departments and other parts of the executive branch as well as to the other two branches of government.

EXECUTIVE OFFICE OF THE PRESIDENT

For an excellent historical overview of the executive office, readers should consult the encyclopedic guide titled *The Executive Office of the President*.[4] Included under "Your Government" (White House Web site) are links to the agencies that comprise the Executive Office of the President. These are the following:

- **Council of Economic Advisors (CEA),** which "analyzes and interprets economic developments, appraises the programs and activities of the Government, and then advises the President on national economic policy." The Web site (**http://www.whitehouse.gov/cea/**) explains the Council of Economic Advisors and provides publications (**http://www.whitehouse.gov/cea/pubs.html**) and a link to GPO Access and the *Economic Report of the President*, which explains economic developments and trends for the nation (**http://w3.access. gpo.gov/eop/index.html**).

- **Council on Environmental Quality (CEQ),** which "coordinates federal environmental efforts and works closely with agencies and other White House offices in the development of environmental policies and initiatives." The Web site (**http://www.whitehouse.gov/ceq/**) provides an overview of the Council, presents news, internships, annual reports, and more.

- **Domestic Policy Council (DPC),** which "coordinates the domestic policy-making process in the White House and offers policy advice to the President. The DPC also works to ensure that domestic policy initiatives are coordinated and consistent through federal agencies. . . . [T]he DPC monitors the implementation of domestic policy, and represents the President's priorities to other branches of government."

  The DPC also "oversees major domestic policy areas such as education, health, welfare, justice, federalism, transportation, environment, labor, and veterans affairs. The **Office of National AIDS Policy** (ONAP; **http://www.whitehouse. gov/onap/ aids.html**), the **Office of National Drug Control Policy** (ONDCP; **http://www.whitehousedrugpolicy.gov/**), and the **Office of Faith-Based and Community Initiatives** (OFBCI) (**http://www.whitehouse.gov/government/ fbci**) are also affiliated with the Domestic Policy Council. The . . . Council's formal membership includes the cabinet Secretaries and Administrators of federal agencies that impact the issues addressed by the DPC" (for DPC, see **http://whitehouse.gov/dpc/**).

- **National Economic Council,** which "coordinates policy-making for domestic and international economic issues, coordinates economic policy advice for the President, ensures that policy decisions and programs are consistent with the President's stated economic goals, and monitors implementation of the President's economic policy agenda" (**http://www.whitehouse.gov/nec/l**).

- **National Security Council (NSC),** which was established by the *National Security Act of 1947* and, in 1949, as part of the Reorganization Plan, was placed in the Executive Office of the President. The NSC "is the President's principal forum for considering national security and foreign policy matters with his senior national security advisors and cabinet officials" (**http://www.whitehouse.gov/nsc/**).

- **Office of Administration (OA),** which "provides administrative support services to all units within the Executive Office of the President. The services provided include information, personnel, and financial management; data processing; library services; records maintenance; and general office operations, such as mail, messenger, printing, procurement, and supply services" (**http://www.whitehouse.gov/oa/**).

- **Office of Management and Budget (OMB),** which has as its "predominant mission . . . to assist the President in overseeing the preparation of the federal budget and to supervise its administration in executive branch agencies. In helping to formulate the President's spending plans, OMB evaluates the effectiveness of agency programs, policies, and procedures; assesses competing funding demands among agencies; and sets funding priorities." Furthermore, "OMB ensures that agency reports, rules, testimony, and proposed legislation are consistent with the President's budget and with Administration policies. In addition, OMB oversees and coordinates the Administration's procurement, financial management, information, and regulatory policies." (**http://www. whitehouse.gov/omb/**).

- **Office of Science and Technology Policy (OSTP),** which was created in 1976 "to provide the President with timely policy advice and to coordinate the science and technology investment," advances "the Bush Administration's agenda in fundamental science, education and scientific literacy, investment in applied research, and international cooperation." The home page (**http://www.ostp. gov/**) covers the agency and "What's New." It also provides links to the home page of the National Science and Technology Council (NSTC) and the President's Committee of Advisors on Science and Technology (PCAST). NSTC "is the principal means for the President to coordinate science, space, and technology to coordinate the diverse parts of the Federal research and development enterprise" (**http://www.ostp.gov/NSTC/html/NSTC_Home.html**), while PCAST (**http://www.ostp.gov/PCAST/pcast.html**) advises the president on "technology, scientific research priorities, and math and science education."

- **President's Foreign Intelligence Advisory Board (PFIAB),** which "provides advice to the President concerning the quality and adequacy of intelligence collection, of analysis and estimates, of counterintelligence, and of other intelligence activities. The PFIAB, through its Intelligence Oversight Board, also advises the President on the legality of foreign intelligence activities" (**http://www.whitehouse.gov/pfiab/**)

- **Office of the United States Trade Representative,** the head of which is the U.S. trade representative (USTR)—the nation's chief trade negotiator and the principal trade policy advisor to the president. In this role, the USTR and the Agency's staff are responsible for developing and implementing trade policies that promote world growth and create new opportunities for American businesses, workers, and agricultural products (**http://www.ustr.gov/**).

The White House Military Office (**http://www.whitehouse.gov/whmo/**) has assorted pages such as coverage of Air Force One (**http://www.whitehouse.gov/ whmo/af1.html**) and Marine Helicopter Squadron One (**http://www.whitehouse. gov/whmo/hmx1.html**).

Some additional remarks about the home pages of OMB and USTR follow.

Office of Management and Budget

The OMB's Web site (**http://www.whitehouse.gov/omb/**) posts information about the agency, budget and legislative information, "Federal Management," "Office of Information and Regulatory Affairs," "Communications & Media," news releases, statements of the administrator (head of OMB), and "Information for Agencies." Other choices include "The Budget in Progress," "Regulatory Oversight in Action," "The Wastebasket," "The President's Management Work," "OMB Locator," a site search and site map, job opportunities, and the FOIA. There is excellent coverage of the policy "instruments" developed by the Office of Information and Regulatory Affairs to guide the executive branch. One of these instruments is called a circular (instructions or information issued by OMB to federal agencies that are expected to have a continuing effect of two or more years; see **http://www.whitehouse.gov/omb/circulars/ index.html**).

Office of the United States Trade Representative

The USTR's home page (**http://www.ustr.gov/**) covers "Monitoring & Enforcement," "Trade & Development," "Outreach," "About USTR," "WTO & Multilateral Affairs," "World Regions," "Sectors," "Trade & Environment," a site search and a site map, "Resources" (e.g., press releases, reports, speeches, and congressional testimony), "Hot Topics," news, press releases, employment opportunities, and rules and regulations. "Sectors," for instance, leads to "Agriculture," "Services," "Investment," "Intellectual Property," "Industry & Telecommunications," and "Textiles;" and "World Regions" consists of "Africa," "Asia and the Pacific," "China, Hong Kong, Mongolia, and Taiwan," "Europe and the Mediterranean," "Japan," and "Western Hemisphere."

OTHER

This section gives some indication of other units in the executive branch that might be of interest to some users of this guide.

Chief Information Officers Council

The CIO Council, established in 1996,

serves as the principal interagency forum for improving practices in the design, modernization, use, sharing, and performance of Federal Government agency information resources. The Council's role includes developing recommendations for information technology management policies, procedures, and standards; identifying opportunities to share information resources; and assessing and addressing the needs of the Federal Government's IT [information technology] workforce.

The Web site (**http://www.cio.gov/**) offers quick links that feature short Web addresses and that link users directly to the desired information. More specifically, there is coverage of "Hot Items," "Best Security Practices" (**http://www.cio.gov/index.cfm?function=documents&section=best%20practices**), the Council and its committees, documents, and more.

National Security Agency

The agency "coordinates, directs, and performs highly specialized activities to protect U.S. information systems and produce foreign intelligence information. A high-technology organization, the National Security Agency (NSA) is on the frontiers of communications and data processing. It is also one of the most important centers of foreign language analysis and research within the government." The home page (**http://www.nsa.gov/**) presents the agency, public information release, employment opportunities, the agency's cryptologic history, and the National Cryptologic Museum.

Under Executive Order 12958 (dated April 17, 1995), which applies to classified national security information, "NSA is reviewing for declassification all permanently classified documents 25 years or older. This declassification effort, which NSA has named OPENDOOR, will include information about all documents declassified and made available to the public under E.O. 12958. Because these documents are declassified, they will be turned over to the National Archives and Records Administration" (see Chapter 6; **http://www.nsa.gov/programs/opendoor/Scope.html**).

SUMMARY

The portal THOMAS identifies a number of agencies within the executive branch departments (see **http://lcweb.loc.gov/global/executive/fed.html**). Likewise, the "U.S. Federal Government Agencies Directory" of Louisiana State University Libraries (**http://www.lib.lsu.edu/gov/fedgov.html**) provides an excellent introduction to the executive branch, with an extensive list of subunits (e.g., agencies) arranged by department. Despite the invaluable contribution that such lists make, it is often beneficial to examine the Web site of a department and to peruse those subunits having Web sites.

Although FirstGov (see Chapter 3) pulls together an overwhelming number of information resources on a particular topic, information still remains "buried" within the Web sites of agencies, bureaus, offices, and institutes. For example, Air Force Link (**http://www.af.mil**) of the Department of Defense presents that branch of the armed forces through images, careers, news, and stories. There are also publications and other resources. In 1994, "the Office of the Secretary of the Air Force concluded an exhaustive search for records in response to a General Accounting Office . . . inquiry of an event popularly known as the 'Roswell Incident,' " which pertains to the alleged crash and recovery by the government of an space vehicle and its alien occupants near Roswell, New Mexico, in 1947. Although not settling the matter for some people, Air Force Link provides photographs and film footage showing that it was possible to have mistaken high-altitude balloons, anthropomorphic test dummies as a "crash and recovery" effort by the "government."[5] These resources are contained in the Air Force's library of resources (see **http://www.af.mil/lib/roswell**). Without prior knowledge about their existence and location on the Web, these resources would be difficult to locate and retrieve.

NOTES

1. L. Scott Tillett, "Popularity a Mixed Blessing at Education Site," *Federal Computer Week* 13 (February 1999): 23.

2   Ibid.

3. In April 2003, the Department of Education announced that with the current contracts for the sixteen clearinghouses soon to expire, it would seek to consolidate the clearinghouse into a single database administered by one contractor. The proposal is available online at **http://www.eps.gov/spg/ED/OCFO/CPO/Reference-Number-ERIC2003/Attachments.html**

4. *The Executive Office of the President: A Historical, Biographical, and Bibliographic Guide,* Harold C. Relyea, ed. (Westport, CT: Greenwood Press, 1997).

5. "Claims of 'alien bodies' at the Roswell Army Field hospital were most likely a combination of two separate incidents: (1) a 1956 KC-97 aircraft accident in which 11 Air Force members lost their lives; and (2) a 1959 manned balloon mishap in which two Air Force pilots were injured" (see **http://www.af.mil/ lib/roswell;** February 20, 2001).

URL Site Guide for This Chapter

Home Page
Department of Agriculture
http://www.usda.gov/

Agencies, Services, and Programs
http://www.usda.gov/services.html

Offices
http://www.usda.gov/offices.html

Broadcast News
http://www.usda.gov/agency/oc/vtr/
broadcastnews.htm

E-Answers
Extension and Outreach Subjects
http://128.227.242.197/

Current Research Information System
http://cris.csrees.usda.gov/
http://cris.csrees.usda.gov/star/system.
html

Agriculture Research Service
http://www.ars.usda.gov/

National Agricultural Library
http://www.nalusda.gov/

AGRICOLA
http://www.nal.usda.gov/general_
info/agricola/agricola_faq.html

Agriculture Network Information Center (AgNIC)
http://www.agnic.org/

Cooperative State Research, Education, and Extension Service
http://www.reeusda.gov/

Space Agriculture in the Classroom
http://www.agclassroom.org/

Economic Research Service
http://www.ers.usda.gov/

Briefing Rooms
http://www.ers.usda.gov/Briefing/

Site Search (for Maps)
http://search.ers.usda.gov/

National Agricultural Statistics Service
http://www.usda.gov/nass

Agricultural Statistics Database
http://www.nass.usda.gov:81/ipedb/
http://www.pestmanagement.info/
nass/

Historical Data
http://www.usda.gov/nass/pubs/
histdata.htm

Farm Service Agency
http://www.fsa.usda.gov/pas/default.asp

Drought Information
http://drought.fsa.usda.gov/

Hay Net
http://www.fsa.usda.gov/haynet/

Trade and Agriculture
http://www.fas.usda.gov/ustrade.html

Trade Data
FAS Online
http://www.fas.usda.gov/data.html

Forest Service
http://www.fs.fed.us/

Current Wildland Fire Information
http://www.nifc.gov/information.html

National Resources Conservation Service
http://www.nrcs.usda.gov/

Nutrition.Gov
http://www.nutrition.gov/home/index.
php3

Partnership for Food Safety Education
http://www.fightbac.org/main.cfm

Risk Management Agency
RMA Online
http://www.act.fcic.usda.gov/

Science & Education Impact
(Partnerships)
http://www.reeusda.gov/success/impact.
htm

Home Page
Department of Commerce
http://www.commerce.gov/

Bureau of Economic Analysis
http://www.bea.gov/

Bureau of Industry and Security
http://www.bxa.doc.gov/

International Trade Administration
http://www.ita.doc.gov/

BuyUSA.com
http://www.buyusa.com/page/my_
gtn/splash.asp

TIC1-800-USA-TRADE
Trade Information Center
http://www.trade.gov/td/tic/

National Institute of Standards and
Technology
http://www.nist.gov/

Time (U.S.)
http://www.time.gov/

City Tour
http://www.nist.gov/public_affairs/
nhouse/ccity/ccity.htm

Home Tour
http://www.nist.gov/public_affairs/
nhouse/index.html

A Walk through Time
http://physics.nist.gov/Genlnt/Time/
time.html

NIST Databases
http://www.nist.gov/srd/

NIST in Your Community
http://www.nist.gov/public_affairs/srd/

National Oceanic and Atmospheric
Administration
http://www.noaa.gov/

National Ocean Service
http://www.nos.noaa.gov/

Mapfinder
http://oceanservice.noaa.gov/
mapfinder

Site Map
http://www.nos.noaa.gov/sitemap.
html

National Weather Service
Http://www.nws.noaa.gov/

National Data Centers

National Oceanographic Data
Center
http://www.nodc.noaa.gov/

National Geophysical Data
Center
http://www.ngdc.noaa.gov/

National Climatic Data Center
http://lwf.ncdc.noaa.gov/oa/ncdc.html

Historical Significant Events Imagery
National Climate Data Center
http://www.ncdc.noaa.gov/oa/ncdc.html

Aquarius Project
http://www.uncwil.edu/nurc/aquarius/

National Hurricane Center
http://www.nhc.noaa.gov/index.shtml

Interactive Weather Information
Network
http://iwin.nws.noaa.gov/

Weather.gov
http://iwin.nws.noaa.gov/

National Environmental Data Index
http://www.nedi.gov/

Library
http://www.lib.noaa.gov/

WINDandSEA
http://www.lib.noaa.gov/docs/
windandsea.html

National Technical Information
Service
http://www.ntis.gov/

FedWorld
http://www.fedworld.gov/

National Audiovisual Center
http://www.ntis.gov/prodcuts/types/
audiovisual/index.asp?loc=
4-4-1

Trade and Business Publications
http://tradecenter.ntis.gov/

Gov.Research_Center
?http://grc.ntis.gov

National Telecommunications and
Information Administration
http://www.ntia.doc.gov/

Starting Points
http://www.ntia.doc.gov/startingpoints.
htm

Department of Defense
DefenseLINK
http://www.defenselink.mil/

Air Force Link
http://www
http:/www.af.mil/

Roswell Incident
http://www.af.mil/lib/roswell

Site Map
http://www.defenselink.mil/sitemap.html

Defense Technical Information Center
Web Links
http://www.dtic.mil/dtic/links.html

Defense Visual Information Center
http://www.defenselink.mil/multimedia/
archive.html

Missile Defense Agency
http://www.acq.osd.mil/bmdo/bmdolink/
html/

Department of Education
http://www.ed.gov/index.jsp

No Child Left Behind
http://www.ed.gov/

National Library of Education
http://www.ed.gov/NLE

ERIC
http://www.eric.ed.gov/

ERIC Clearinghouses
http://www.eric.ed.gov/

Ask ERIC
http://askeric.org/

Gateway to Educational Materials_
http://www.thegateway.org/

National Clearinghouse for
Educational Facilities
http://www.edfacilities.org/

United States Network for Education
Information
http://www.ed.gov/NLE/USNEI/

Virtual Reference Desk_
http://www.vrd.org/

Online Educational Resources
http://www.ed.gov/about/organizations
.jsp
http://www.ed.gov/EdRes/EdFed/index.
html

Publications and Products
http://www.ed.gov/about/pubs.jsp

ED PUBS (online ordering system)
http://www.edpubs.org/webstore/
Content/search.asp

Home Page
Department of Energy
http://www.energy.gov/

Energy Information Administration
http://www.eia.doe.gov/

EIA Energy Experts
http://www.eia.doe.gov/contacts/
main.html

Los Alamos National Laboratory
http://www.lanl.gov/worldview/

Office of Economic Impact and
Diversity
http://www.hr.doe.gov/ed/index.html

Office of Environment, Safety and Health
http://tis.eh.doe.gov/portal/home.htm

Office of Science
http://www.sc.doe.gov/

Office of Scientific and Technical Information
http://www.osti.gov/

> **DOE Resource Descriptions**
> http://www.osti.gov/resource.html
>
> **Energy Files**
> Virtual Library of Energy Science and Technology
> http://www.osti.gov/EnergyFiles
>
> **Energy Citations Database**
> http://www.osti.gov/energycitations/
>
> **DOE Information Bridge**
> http://www.osti.gov/bridge/
>
> **OpenNet**
> http://www.osti.gov/opennet/
>
> **Historical Records Review Database**
> http://www.osti.gov/opennet/nsi.html

Southwestern Power Administration
http://www.swpa.gov/

Home Page
Department of Health and Human Services
http://www.os.dhhs.gov/

> **Healthfinder®**
> http://www.healthfinder.gov/
>
> **HHS Agencies**
> http://www.hhs.gov/agencies
>
> **Adoption**
> National Adoption Information Clearinghouse
> http://www.calib.com/naic/pubs/f_gay.cfm
>
> **Smallpox page**
> http://www.os.dhhs.gov/smallpox/index.html

Administration for Children and Families
http://www.acf.hhs.gov/

Administration on Aging
http://www.aoa.gov/network/default.htm

Agency for Healthcare Research and Quality
http://www.ahcpr.gov/

Centers for Disease Control and Prevention
http://www.cdc.gov/

> **Mailing List**
> http://www.cdc.gov/subscribe.html
>
> **Data and Statistics**
> http://www.cdc.gov/scientific.htm
>
> **Subunits of Agency**
> http://www.cdc.gov/aboutcdc.htm
>
> **Subunits of Agency**
> http://www.cdc.gov/aboutcdc.htm
>
> **Surveillance Reports**
> Division of Sexually Transmitted Diseases
> http://www.cdc.gov/nchstp/dstd/Stats_Trends/Stats_and_Trends.htm
>
> **Tobacco Industry Documents**
> http://www.cdc.gov/tobacco/industrydocs/index.htm

Centers for Medicare & Medicaid Services
http://cms.hhs.gov/

Food and Drug Administration
http://www.fda.gov/

> **Site Index**
> http://www.fda.gov/opacom/hpchoice.html
>
> **Site Map**
> http://www.fda.gov/sitemap.html
>
> **Food Safety**
> http://www.foodsafety.gov/
>
> **Center for Food Safety & Applied Nutrition**
> http://vm.cfsan.fda.gov/

National Institutes of Health
http://www.nih.gov/

> **Links to Other Agency Sites**
> http://www.nih.gov/icd/
>
> **Search engine**
> http://search.nih.gov/

ClinicalTrials
http://www.clinicaltrials.gov/

Stem Cell Information
http://www.nih.gov/news/stemcell/
index.htm

National Library of Medicine
http://www.nlm.nih.gov/

> **Site Map**
> http://www.nlm.nih.gov/siteindex.
> html
>
> **Gateway**
> http://gateway.nlm.nih.gov/gw/
> Cmd
>
> **Health Information (Sites and Subjects)**
> http://www.nlm.nih.gov/hinfo.html
>
> **MEDLINEplus**
> http://medlineplus.gov/
>
> **Research Programs**
> http://www.nlm.nih.gov/resprog.
> html
>
> **Resources**
> http://www.nlm.nih.gov/sitemap.
> html

Other sites
Office of Population Affairs
http://opa.osophs.dhhs.gov/other-sites.
html

Office of Research Integrity
http://ori.hhs.gov/html/programs/
instructresource.asp

Home Page
Department of Homeland Security
http://www.dhs.gov/dhspublic/

Site Index
http://www.dhs.gov/dhspublic/sitemap
.jsp

Frequently Asked Questions
http://www.dhs.gov/dhspublic/faq.jsp

Bureau of Customs and Border Protection
http://cbp.customs.gov
http://www.customs.gov/xp/cgov/
home.xml

Bureau of Citizenship and Immigration Services
http://www.immigration.gov

Bureau of Immigration and Customs Enforcement
http://www.bice.immigration.gov/
graphics/index.htm

Federal Protective Service
http://www.bice.immigration.gov/
graphics/fps.htm

The Transportation Security Administration
http://www.tsa.gov/public/index.jsp

Federal Law Enforcement Training Center
http://www.fletc.gov/

DHS Structure
http://www.dhs.gov/dhspublic/theme_
home1.jsp

Emergencies and Disasters
http://www.dhs.gov/dhspublic/theme_
home2.jsp

Information (Agency Staff)
http://www.dhs.gov/dhspublic/display
?theme=39

Information (Citizens)
http://www.dhs.gov/dhspublic/display
?theme=36

Information (Private Sector)
http://www.dhs.gov/dhspubli/display
?theme=37
http://www.dhs.gov/dhspublic/display
?theme=38

Public Announcements
http://www.dhs.gov/dhspublic/display
?theme=29+content=320

Travel & Transportation
http://www.dhs.gov/dhspublic/theme_
home3.jsp

Immigration and Borders
http://www.dhs.gov/dhspublic/theme_
home4.jsp

Research & Technology
http://www.dhs.gov/dhspublic/theme_
home5.jsp

Ready.Gov
http://www.ready.gov/

Threats and Protection
http://www.dhs.gov/dhspublic/theme_
home6.jsp

Working with DHS
http://www.dhs.gov/dhspublic/theme_
home7.jsp

Press Room
http://www.dhs.gov/dhspublic/theme_
home8.jsp

**Animal and Plant Health Inspection
Service [part] (Agriculture)**
http://www.aphis.usda.gov/

**Office of Domestic Preparedness
(Justice)**
http://www.aphis.usda.gov/odp/

**The Federal Emergency Management
Agency (FEMA)**
http://www.fema.gov/

**Nuclear Incident Response Team
(Energy)**
http://www.dhs.gov/dhspublic/
display?theme=17&content=368

**Strategic National Stockpile and the
National Disaster Medical
System (HHS)**
http://www.cdc.gov/nceh/radiation/
response.htm

**National Domestic Preparedness
Office (FBI)**

http://www.ojp.usdoj.gov/odp/

**Plum Island Animal Disease Center
(Agriculture)**
http://www.ars.usda.gov/plum/

**Critical Infrastructure Assurance
Office (Commerce)**
http://www.ciao.gov/

**Federal Computer Incident Response
Center (GSA)**
http://www.fedcirc.gov/

**National Communications System
(Defense)**
http://www.ncs.gov/

**National Infrastructure Protection
Center (FBI)**
http://www.nipc.gov/

**National Infrastructure Simulation
and Analysis Center (Energy)**
http://www.sandia.gov/CIS/NISAC.htm

**Energy Security and Assurance
Program (Energy)**
http://oea.dis.anl.gov/home.htm

United States Coast Guard
http://www.uscg.mil/USCG.shtm

United States Secret Service
http://www.secretservice.gov/index.shtml

Home Page
**Department of Housing and Urban
Development**
http://www.hud.gov/

Site Index
http://www.hud.gov/assist/siteindex.cfm

Most Requested Pages
http://www.hud.gov/library/bookshelf01/
index.cfm

Online Systems
http://www.hud.gov/systems/housing.
cfm
http://www.hud.gov/systems/citizens.
cfm

Ginnie May
Home page
http://www.ginniemae.gov/

Home Page
Department of the Interior
http://www.doi.gov/

> **Bureaus/Offices/Committees**
> http://www.doi.gov/bureaus.html

> **United States Fish and Wildlife Service**
> http://www.fws.gov/

> **U.S. Geological Survey**
> http://www.usgs.gov/

> **Bureau of Land Management**
> http://www.blm.gov/nhp/index.htm

>> **Points of Interest Maps**
>> http://www.blm.gov/nhp/map/natmap.html

>> **The Wild Horse and Burro Page**
>> http://www.wildhorseandburro.blm.gov/

> **Minerals Management Service**
> http://www.mms.gov/

> **National Park Service**
> http://www.nps.gov/

> **National Park Geology**
> http://www2.nature.nps.gov/grd/tour/index.htm

> **NatureNet**
> http://www.nature,nps.gov/

> **AIRWeb**
> http://www2.nature.nps.gov/ard/

> **Archeology and Ethnography Program**
> http://www.cr.nps.gov/aad/index.htm/

> **Bureau of Reclamation**
> http://www.usbr.gov/

> **Cultural Resources Management**
> http://www.usbr.gov/cultural/

> **Office of Surface Mining**
> http://www.osmre.gov/osm.htm

FIREWISE
http://www.firewise.org/usa/title.htm

Home Page
Department of Justice
http://www.usdoj.gov/

> **Alphabetical List of Agencies**
> http://www.usdoj.gov/02organizations/02_1.html

> **Departmental History**
> http://www.usdoj.gov/02organizations/dojhistory.htm

> **Office of Justice Programs**
> http://www.ojp.usdoj.gov/

> **Drug Enforcement Administration**
> http://www.usdoj.gov/dea/

> **Federal Bureau of Investigation**
> http://www.fbi.gov/

>> **FBI's Electronic Reading Room**
>> http://foia.fbi.gov/

>> **Project Blue Book**
>> http://foia.fbi.gov/bluebook.htm

> **National Criminal Justice Reference Service**
> http://www.ncjrs.org/

> **National Institute of Justice**
> http://www.ojp.usdoj/.gov/nij/

> **Mapping and Analysis for Public Safety**
> http://www.ojp.usdoj.gov/

> **Office of the Pardon Attorney**
> http://www.usdoj.gov/pardon/index.html

Home Page
Department of Labor
http://www.dol.gov/

> **Elaws**
> http://www.dol.gov/elaws/

> **Agency List**
> http://www.dol.gov/dol/organization.htm

> **Bureau of Labor Statistics**
> http://stat.bls.gov/

Mine Safety and Health Administration
http://www.msha.gov/

Occupational Safety and Health Administration
http://www.osha.gov/

O*NET Project
http://www.doleta.gov/programs/onet/
http://www.doleta.gov/programs/onet/onet_default.asp

Women's Bureau
http://www.dol.gov/wb/welcome.html

Home Page
Department of State
http://www.state.gov/

> **Archived Site**
> http://www.state.gov/www/policy.html

> **Countries and Regions**
> http://www.state.gov/countries/

> **Background Notes**
> http://www.state.gov/r/pa/ei/bgn/

> **Electronic Reading Room (FOIA)**
> http://foia.state.gov/

>> **Document Collections**
>> http://foia.state.gov/SearchColls/Search.asp

> **Foreign Relations of the United States**
> http://www.state.gov/r/pa/ho/frus

> **Organizational chart (U.S. government)**
> http://usinfo.state.gov/products/pubs/outusgov/govchart.pdf

> **Publications of the Office of the Historian**
> http://www.state.gov/r/pa/ho/pubs/

> **Embassies and Other Diplomatic Missions**
> http://usembassy.state.gov/

> **Subscription Services**
> http://www.state.gov/www/listservs_cms.html

Bureau of Arms Control
http://www.state.gov/t/ac/

Citizenship and Nationality
http://travel.state.gov/acs.html#cit

Home Page
Department of Transportation
http://www.dot.gov/

> **Table of Contents**
> http://www.bts.gov/contents1.html

> **E-Government Transactions**
> http://www.dot.gov/business.html

> **National Transportation Library**
> http://ntl.bts.gov/

> **Reference Services**
> http://ntl.bts.gov/cgi-bin/ref/ref.cgi

> **Quick Answers**
> http://ntl.bts.gov/faq/index.html

> **TRIS Online**
> http://199.79.179.82/sundev/search.cfm

> **Federal Aviation Administration**
> http://www.faa.gov/

> **Federal Railroad Administration**
> http://www.fra.dot.gov/site/index.htm

> **National Highway Traffic Safety Administration**
> http://www.nhtsa.dot.gov/

Home Page
Department of the Treasury
http://www.ustreas.gov/

> **List of Bureaus**
> http://www.ustreas.gov/bureaus/index.html

> **List of Offices**
> http://www.ustreas.gov/offices/index.html

> **Bureau of Alcohol, Tobacco and Firearms**
> http://www.atf.treas.gov/

> **Bureau of Engraving and Printing**
> http://www.bep.treas.gov/
> http://www.moneyfactory.com/

161

Bureau of the Public Debt
http://www.publicdebt.treas.gov/

Financial Crimes Enforcement Network
http://www.fincen.gov/

Financial Management Service
http://www.fms.treas.gov/

Internal Revenue Service
http://www.irs.gov/

Office of the Comptroller of the Currency
http://www.occ.treas.gov/

Office of Thrift Supervision
http://www.ots.treas.gov/

U.S. Mint
http://www.usmint.gov/

Home Page
Department of Veteran's Affairs
http://www.va.gov/

   Online Benefit Applications
   http://www.vabenefits.vba.va.gov/
   vonapp/main.asp

White House
Home page
http://www.whitehouse.gov/

Executive Office of the President

Council of Economic Advisors
http://www.whitehouse.gov/cea/

Publications
http://www.whitehouse.gov/cea/pubs.html

Economic Report of the President
http://w3.access.gpo.gov/eop/index.html

Council on Environmental Quality
http://www.whitehouse.gov/ceq/

Domestic Policy Council
http://www.whitehouse.gov/dpc/

   Office of Faith-Based and Community Initiatives
   http://www.whitehouse.gov/
   government/fbci/

Office of National AIDS Policy
http://www.whitehouse.gov/
onap/aids.html

Office of National Drug Control Policy
http://www.whitehousedrugpolicy.
gov/

National Economic Council
http://www.whitehouse.gov/nec/

National Security Council
http://www.whitehouse.gov/nsc/

Office of Administration
http://www.whitehouse.gov/oa/

Office of Management and Budget
http://www.whitehouse.gov/omb/

Circulars
http://www.whitehouse.gov/omb/
circulars/index.html

Office of Science and Technology Policy
http://www.ostp.gov/

   National Science and Technology Council
   http://www.ostp.gov/NSTC/html/
   NSTC_Home.html

   President's Council of Advisors on Science and Technology
   http://www.ostp.gov/PCAST/pcast.
   html

Office of the United States Trade Representative
http://www.ustr.gov/

President's Foreign Intelligence Advisory Board
http://www.whitehouse.gov/pfiab/

White House Military Office
http://www.whitehouse.gov/whmo/

   Air Force One
   http://www.whitehouse.gov/whmo/
   af1.html

   Marine Helicopter Squadron One
   http://www.whitehouse.gov/whmo/
   hmx1.html

Home Page
Chief Information Officers Council
http://www.cio.gov/

> **Best Security Practices**
> http://www.cio.gov/index.cfm?function=
> document&section=best%
> 20practices

Home Page
National Security Agency
http://www.nsa.gov/

> **OPENDOOR**
> http://www.nsa.gov/programs/opendoor/
> Scope.html

THOMAS (Library of Congress)
http://thomas.loc.gov/

> **Identification of Executive Sites**
> http://lcweb.loc.gov/global/executive/
> fed.html

Directory of Government Agencies
Louisiana State University Libraries
http://www.lib.slu.edu/gov/fedgov.html

FirstGov
http://www.firstgov.gov/

Chapter 6

Independent Establishments and Quasi-Government Agencies

Agencies may be found in all three branches of the federal government. Within the legislative branch, for example, Congress is supported by agencies such as the Congressional Budget Office, the General Accounting Office, and the Library of Congress (see Chapter 4). Within the judicial branch, the courts are assisted by agencies such as the Administrative Office of the United States Courts and the Federal Judicial Center (see Chapter 7). Within the executive branch, in addition to the entities of the Executive Office of the President and the cabinet-level departments, there are various independent establishments and government corporations. These entities are "independent," to one extent or another, of control by other executive officials, such as the president and the cabinet secretaries. Many of them have a regulatory mission, exercising quasi-legislative and quasi-judicial powers.

There is also a group of agencies that have a quasi-official status—"organizations that are not Executive agencies under the definition in 5 *U.S.C.* 105 but that are required by statute to publish certain information on their programs and activities in the *Federal Register*."[1] Examples of quasi-official agencies include the Legal Services Corporation, the Smithsonian Institution, and the United States Institute of Peace.

Agencies may be structured in various ways (e.g., single head, collegial leadership, or corporate model) and variously denominated (e.g., a board, commission, foundation, or system). Moreover, during the past forty years, the heads of some agencies, at the time of their nomination, have been vested with cabinet rank by the president, which means those officials regularly attend and participate in meetings of the traditional cabinet and receive all documentation surrounding those sessions. For a list of the Bush cabinet, including those members holding cabinet rank but who are not cabinet secretaries, see the White House Web site under "Your Government" (**http://www.whitehouse.gov/government/**).

This chapter does not distinguish among the various types of agencies; rather, it presents agencies (ones not covered in Chapter 5) that publish information resources on the Web that potentially have general interest to the readership of this guide. To know more about an agency's structure, jurisdiction, or type or to discover additional

165

agencies, primarily ones without a Web presence, consult the *United States Government Manual*. (**http://www.gpoaccess.gov/gmanual/index.html**; editions at this location date from 1995–96).

To assist readers in negotiating the diverse array of agencies presented in this chapter, the agencies have been arranged according to a general subject classification. Development of an all-encompassing classification is impossible given the multiple jurisdictions that agencies serve; however, Appendix C may be helpful.

AERONAUTICS, SPACE FLIGHT, AND SPACE RESEARCH

➔ National Aeronautics and Space Administration

NASA's Web site (**http://www.nasa.gov/home/index.html**), which is partially covered in Chapters 11 and 13, is rich in information content and visual presentations. The site, which requires Flash Player 6, is well organized and easy to navigate. Information resources are arranged by groups: kids, students, educators, and media and press. There is also coverage of the agency, "News & Features," "Events," "Multimedia," and "Missions." Other options include "Improve Life Here" (news and photographs), "Extend Life to There" (e.g., Mars exploration), "Find Life Beyond," "NASA Careers," and "NASA TV." There is also access to NASA research centers, the FOIA, and, for instance,

- Greatest images of NASA
- Human spaceflight Web
- Lift off to Learning
- Mars exploration
- NASA education program
- NASA history
- NASA image exchange
- NASA kids (see Chapter 13)
- NASA spacelink
- *Planetary Photojournal*
- Science@NASA

The *Planetary Photojournal* (**http://photojournal.jpl.nasa.gov/**) covers Earth, the planets, our solar system, stars and galaxies, technology, spacecraft and telescopes, the universe, technology, history, and people and facilities. This page contains a wide assortment of photographs, and it explains credits and copyright relating to those photographs.

NASA also has an Educator Astronaut Site (**http://edspace.nasa.gov/**) that provides useful information for classroom teachers. One example is "living in space."

Commission on the Future of the United States Aerospace Industry

Section 1092 of the *National Defense Authorization Act* for Fiscal Year 2001 (P.L. 106-398) established the commission to "study the issues associated with the future of the United States aerospace industry in the global economy, particularly in relationship to the United States national security; and assess the future importance of the domestic aerospace industry for the economic and national security of the United States." The home page (**http://www.aerospacecommission.gov/**) discusses the commission and its commissioners and provides press releases, information on public meetings, reports, and links to related sites.

AFRICA

The African Development Foundation

The African Development Foundation (ADF) "promotes broad-based, sustainable development in sub-Saharan Africa." The home page (**http://www.adf.gov/**) discusses the agency, its strategy and results, as well as business opportunities, country program profiles, participatory development, business partnerships, business partnerships, project descriptions, publications, photographs, and country liaison officers. There are also frequently asked questions.

AGRICULTURE

Farm Credit Administration

The Farm Credit Administration (FCA) regulates and examines the banks, associations, and related entities that comprise the Farm Credit System (FCS). The home page (**http://www.fca.gov/**) covers career opportunities, borrower rights, procurement opportunities, the *Freedom of Information Act,* publications (including an archives), news and events, the office of the inspector general, legal information (e.g., legal opinions), FCS institutions (e.g., Farmer Mac), and so on.

THE AMERICAS

The Inter-American Foundation

The Inter-American Foundation's home page (**http://www.iaf.gov/**) provides information about the agency and covers news and events, fellowships, grants, publications, a photo essay, and frequently asked questions. There are also related links and a site map.

BANKING

Export-Import Bank of the United States

The Export-Import Bank, known as the Ex-Im Bank:

> was created in 1934 and established under its present law in 1945 to aid in financing and to facilitate U.S. exports. Its creation was spurred by the economic conditions of the 1930's when exports were viewed as a stimulus to economic activity and employment. A primary aim of Ex-Im Bank was to foster trade between the United States and the Soviet Union. During the post–World War II era, Ex-Im Bank helped U.S. companies participate in the reconstruction of Europe and Asia. Ex-Im Bank is encouraged to supplement, but not compete with private capital. Over the years, the private sector, Congress and the executive branch have debated Ex-Im Bank's role in a free market economy, where the private sector handles the majority of export financing. According to supporters, Ex-Im Bank has historically filled gaps created when the private sector is reluctant to engage in export financing. Ex-Im Bank provides guarantees of working capital loans for U.S. exporters, guarantees the repayment of loans or makes loans to foreign purchasers of U.S. goods and services and provides credit insurance against non-payment by foreign buyers for political or commercial risk. Ex-Im Bank must also balance its mandate, that there exists a reasonable assurance of repayment. (**http://www.exim.gov/history.html**)

The home page (**http://www.exim.gov/**) covers the agency, "What's New," new and small businesses, products and services, partners, country and fee information, links to other sites, a site search and site index, forms, news and events, contacts, information quality guidelines, policies, publications and resources, and so on. The bank has an "Environmental Exports Program." which supports exporters of environmentally beneficial good and services, as well exporters participating in foreign environmentally beneficial projects (see **http://www.exim.gov/products/special/environment.html**).

Federal Deposit Insurance Corporation

The Web site of the Federal Deposit Insurance Corporation (FDIC) (**http://www.fdic.gov/**) covers "Deposit Insurance," "Bank Data," "Regulations & Examination," "Consumers & Communities," "Buying from, Selling to FDIC,"

"Newsroom, Events & FOIA," and "About FDIC." Other choices include a site map and a site search, "What's New," and "Topics of Interest," Examples of those topics include the following:

- FDIC Real Estate Retrieval System (a "searchable database of property for sale by property type, state, site, cost, other criteria. Updated weekly")

- Institution Directory (a "searchable directory of FDIC-insured institutions by name, city, or state")

- Quarterly Banking Profiles ("summary of financial results from all insured commercial banks and savings institutions—analyses, graphs, and statistical tables")

- Statistics on Banking ("quarterly publication of aggregate financial and structure information on FDIC-insured institutions; summary totals by state and charter type")

Federal Financial Institutions Examination Council

The Council (FFIEC) is a formal interagency body empowered to prescribe uniform principles, standards, and report forms for the federal examination of financial institutions by the Board of Governors of the Federal Reserve System, the Federal Deposit Insurance Corporation, the National Credit Union Administration, the Office of the Comptroller of the Currency, and the Office of Thrift Supervision. It also makes recommendations to promote uniformity in the supervision of financial institutions.

Its home page (**http://www.ffiec.gov/**) provides "Quick Links"; explains "What's New" and the Council's charge; provides press releases, reports, reporting forms, handbooks and catalogs, and "Enforcement Actions and Orders;" and covers "On-line Information Systems" and "Other FFIEC Sites."

The *Community Reinvestment Act* (CRA; 12 *U.S.C.* 2901; and implemented by 12 *CFR* parts 25, 228, 345, and 563e) encourages "depository institutions to help meet the credit needs of the communities in which they operate." The CRA's home page (**http://www.ffiec.gov/cra/**), which is within that of the council, provides information on the regulation and its interpretation, as well as on CRA examinations. There are instructions on how to report CRA data, reports, and ordering information for CRA public data. The reports "provide information regarding CRA lending activity, as well as census demographic information that can be used for data analysis."

Federal Reserve System

Founded in 1913, the Federal Reserve System, as the nation's central bank, executes monetary policy. It also supervises and regulates banks; protects the credit rights of consumers; maintains the stability of the nation's financial systems; and provides financial services to the U.S. government, the public, financial institutions, and foreign official institutions. The system consists of the Board of Governors and 12 district banks (Boston, New York, Philadelphia, Cleveland, Richmond, Atlanta, Chicago, St. Louis, Minneapolis, Kansas City, Dallas, and San Francisco). The Board of Governors of the Federal Reserve System has broad supervisory powers; determines general monetary, credit, and operating policies for the Federal Reserve System; and formulates the rules and regulations necessary to carry out the requirements of the *Federal Reserve Act.*

The Web site for the Federal Reserve Board is found at **http:// federalreserve.gov/**. However, first-time users might first visit the site map (**http:// federalreserve.gov/sitemap.htm**), which breaks the major categories ("About the Fed," "Press Releases," "Testimony and Speeches," "Monetary Policy," "Banking Information and Regulation," "Payment Systems," "Economic Research and Data," "Consumer Information," "Community Development," "Reporting Forms," "Publications and Education Resources," and "Career Opportunities") into subcategories, making the site much easier to navigate. "Publications and Education Resources," for example, includes articles from the *Federal Reserve Bulletin*, which, in general, reports and analyzes economic developments, discusses bank regulatory issues, and presents new data). *Fed in Print* is a database of the Federal Reserve Systems' economic research. It is possible to search the database by keywords, titles, author, bank, publication year, or publication name (**http://www.frbsf.org/publications/ fedinprint/index.html**).

The Federal Reserve System has a public information catalog that "is a comprehensive guide and online ordering facility for all publications and materials available from the Federal Reserve System. Most items are free of charge and many are available online in Adobe Acrobat format to view or download" (**http://app.ny. frb.org/cfpicnic/main.cfm**). The Federal Reserve Board also offers "Statistics: Releases and Historical Data," arranged according to daily, weekly, monthly, quarterly, and annual releases (**http://www.federalreserve.gov/releases/**). By the way, some Federal Reserve data are available from the Department of Commerce's *STAT-USA* (see **http://www.stat-usa.gov/**).

Federal Reserve Banks. Each Federal Reserve Bank and the Board of Governors have Web sites offering information specific to their districts or the board, such as publications, speech texts, news releases, statistics, and services for financial institutions (see site map of the Federal Reserve Bank of Minneapolis; **http:// minneapolisfed.org/sitemap2.cfn**).

National Credit Union Administration

The National Credit Union Administration (NCUA) "supervises and insures 6,981 federal credit unions and insures 4,257 state-chartered credit unions. It is entirely funded by credit unions and receives no tax dollars." The home page (**http://www.ncua.gov/**) explains credit unions and the agency's organization. It also provides, for instance, current news, documents, credit union data, press releases, speeches, "Recently Posted" information, "Reference Information," a site search, and more.

BORDER DISPUTES

⟋ International Joint Commission

The commission "prevents and resolves disputes between the United States of America and Canada under the 1909 boundary Waters Treaty and pursues the common good of both countries as an independent and objective advisor to the two governments." Its Web site (**http://www.ijc.org/ijcweb-e.html**) discusses water quality issues for the Great Lakes, studies of the Upper Great Lakes and of Lake Ontario–St. Lawrence, Great Lake Water exports, announcements, and the Montreal Public Forum.

CIVIL LEGAL ASSISTANCE

⟋ Legal Services Corporation

The Legal Services Corporation (LSC), headed by a bipartisan board of directors, seeks "to ensure equal access to justice under the law for all Americans by providing civil legal assistance to those who otherwise would be unable to afford it." This private, nonprofit corporation "provides grants to independent local programs chosen through a system of competition." The home page (**http://www.lsc.gov/**) explains the agency's grant competitions and how to get help from the agency. Other choices include a press room, a map of LSC programs, a FOIA site, publications, a site index, a search of the site, employment opportunities, links to related sites, and so on.

CIVIL RIGHTS

⟋ U.S. Civil Rights Commission

The U.S. Civil Rights Commission is a bipartisan agency first established in 1957 and reestablished in 1983. It is directed to

- Investigate complaints alleging that citizens are being deprived of their right to vote by reason of their race, color, religion, sex, age, disability, or national origin or by reason of fraudulent practices

- Study and collect information relating to discrimination or a denial of equal protection of the laws under the Constitution because of race, color, religion, sex, age, disability, or national origin, or in the administration of justice

- Appraise federal laws and policies with respect to discrimination or a denial of equal protection of the laws because of race, color, religion, sex, age, disability, or national origin, or in the administration of justice

- Serve as a national clearinghouse for information in respect to discrimination or a denial of equal protection of the laws because of race, color, religion, sex, age, disability, or national origin

- Submit reports, findings, and recommendations to the president and Congress

- Issue public service announcements to discourage discrimination or a denial of equal protection of the laws

Its Web site (**http://www.usccr.gov/**) provides information about the commission, regional offices, the commission's meeting calendar, employment opportunities, and filing a complaint. There are also publications, news releases, public affairs information, multimedia presentations of Civil Rights events, and more.

COMMUNICATIONS MARKETS

Federal Communications Commission

The mission of the Federal Communications Commission (FCC) "is to encourage competition in all communications markets and to protect the public interest." Furthermore, "the FCC develops and implements policy concerning interstate and international communications by radio, television, wire, satellite, and cable." The home page (**http://www.fcc.gov/**) provides information on the agency, auctions, community meetings, employment opportunities, headlines, forms, and "Priority Issues." There is also a site search and a site map, information for consumers, coverage of initiative, e-flings, updates, and contacts within the agency. Another useful feature is the links to FCC bureaus and offices. and resources (including, for example, speeches, the agenda for the next open meeting, daily business files, FCC weekly calendar, FCC weekly filings, statistics, consumer issues, the annual report, and forms). The *Daily Digest* "provides a brief synopsis of Commission orders, news releases, speeches, public notices and all other FCC documents that are released each business day." The *Digest* "is released on paper, via email, and on the FCC Web Site (click on calendar dates at left)" (**http://www.fcc.gov/Daily_Releases/Daily_Digest/2003/**). (Note that the last four digits in the URL change annually according to the year.) To subscribe to the *Digest* by e-mail, send the following message to subscribe@info.fcc.gov: **subscribe** digest Your-first-name Your-last-name.

Anyone planning to conduct business with the FCC must register on the Commission Registration System (CORES; **https://svartifoss2.fcc.gov/cores/CoresHome.html**).

COMMUNITY SERVICE

Corporation for National and Community Service

The corporation's home page (**http://www.cns.gov/**) discusses the agency, news ("What's Hot") , e-grants, service programs (e.g., AmeriCorps and Senior Corps), and opportunities, including employment, fellowships, internships, scholarships, and honors recognition. There are also press releases, research and other materials, a site map, and so on.

CONSUMERISM

Consumer Product Safety Commission

The Consumer Product Safety Commission (CPSC), "an independent federal regulatory agency, helps keep American families safe by reducing the risk of injury or death from consumer products." The Web site (**http://www.cpsc.gov/**) explains what the agency does and what services it offers. It also provides information for consumers, a press room, recalls/news, a site map, and site search, an electronic reading room for fostering public availability of FOIA records, linkage to a home page for kids (see Chapter 13), "business," a public calendar (agendas for CPSC meetings), an opportunity to report unsafe products, and so on.

DISABILITY

National Council on Disability

The National Council on Disability (NCD) "is an independent federal agency making recommendations to the President and Congress on issues affecting 54 million Americans with disabilities."

NCD's overall purpose is to promote policies, programs, practices, and procedures that guarantee equal opportunity for all individuals with disabilities, regardless of the nature of severity of the disability; and to empower individuals with disabilities to achieve economic self-sufficiency, independent living, and inclusion and integration in all aspects of society.

The home page (**http://www.ncd.gov/**) contains a site map, newsroom, frequently asked questions, resources (e.g., brochures), and links to federal agencies.

United States Architectural and Transportation Barriers Compliance Board

The U.S. Access Board, as the agency is also known,

develops minimum guidelines and requirements for standards issued under the Americans with Disabilities Act (ADA) and the Architectural Barriers Act (ABA), develops accessibility guidelines for telecommunications equipment and customer premises equipment under the Telecommunications Act, develops accessibility standards for electronic and information technology . . . , provides technical assistance on those guidelines and standards, and enforces the Architectural Barriers Act.

The home page (**http://www.access-board.gov/**) discusses the board and offers building and facility design guidelines and standards, "Enforcement," publications, training, research, rules, a news archive, best practices, technical assistance, links to related sites, and so forth.

DISTRICT OF COLUMBIA PLANNING

National Capital Planning Commission

The commission "provides overall planning guidance for federal land and buildings in the National Capital region, which includes the District of Columbia; the city of Alexandria; Prince George's and Montgomery Counties in Maryland; Arlington, Fairfax, Prince William, and Loudoun Counties in Virginia; and the cities and towns with these counties. Through its planning policies and review of development proposals, the commission seeks to protect and enhance the extraordinary historical, cultural, and natural resources of the Nation's Capital." The home page (**http://www.ncpc.gov/**) discusses the commission, its members, and key staff, and it presents a history of planning in the District of Columbia, meeting information, Commission actions, press releases, publications, information for submitting agencies, employment opportunities, and related links.

ECONOMIC GROWTH AND DEVELOPMENT

Commodity Futures Trading Commission

The Commodity Futures Trading Commission (CFTC), a regulatory agency for futures trading, analyzes economic issues affected by (or affecting) futures trading. The home page (**http://www.cftc.gov/cftc/cftchome.htm**) explains the CFTC's role and programs, the commitments of traders, "Exchanges & Products," "Before You Trade," "Customer Protection," "Market Oversight," "Law & Regulations," news items, the FOIA, reports and publications, forms, a site map and site search, and more.

Federal Maritime Commission

The Federal Maritime Commission regulates shipping in the foreign trade of the United States. The home page (**http://www.fmc.gov/**) introduces the commission and presents forms and publications, complaint filing, "Recent Significant Issuances," news releases, employment opportunities, the text of the 1984 *Shipping Act,* information about how to initiate proceedings, area representatives, public information (e.g., FOIA), rules, speeches, notices, frequently asked questions, "What's New," and more.

Federal Trade Commission

The Federal Trade Commission seeks "to maintain competitive enterprise as the keystone of the American economic system, and to prevent the free enterprise system from being fettered by monopoly or restraints on trade or corrupted by unfair or deceptive trade practices. The Commission is charged with keeping competition both free and fair." Its home page (**http://www.ftc.gov/**) contains information about the agency, antitrust and competition, legal framework, and consumer protection; offers business guidance; covers economic issues as well as formal actions, opinions, and activities; and provides links to regional offices and related sites. There are also news releases, publications, speeches, and more.

Overseas Private Investment Corporation

The Overseas Private Investment Corporation (OPIC), a government corporation, provides risk insurance and loans to assist American businesses in investing and competing "in more than 140 emerging markets and developing nations worldwide.... By charging user-fees, OPIC operates at no net cost to U.S. taxpayers." Its home page (**http://www.opic.gov/Main.htm**) explains what the agency does, how to do business with it, and the agency's role with small business and with the environment. There are also press releases, publications, a list of frequently asked questions, employment information, a site map and search of the site, and so on. As shown in Chapter 13, OPIC has a Web site for kids. An "Information Gateway" provides business, economic, and political information on the emerging markers and developing nations.

Tennessee Valley Authority

The Tennessee Valley Authority (TVA) "conducts a unified program of resource development for the advancement of economic growth in the Tennessee Valley region. The Authority's program of activities includes flood control, navigation development, electric power production, fertilizer development, recreation improvement, and forestry and wildlife development." The Web site (**http://www.tva.gov/**) discusses the agency and covers investor information, "News," contacts within the agency, publications, the environment, lake levels and water release schedules, employment opportunities, legal notices, economic development, recreation, a search of the site, and so on.

U.S. Agency for International Development

"U.S. foreign assistance has always had the twofold purpose of furthering America's foreign policy interests in expanding democracy and free markers while improving the lives of the citizens of the developing world." Within this context, USAID extends "assistance to countries recovering from disasters, trying to escape poverty, and engaging in democratic reforms." Those countries are locate din Sub-Saharan Africa, Asia and the Near East, Latin America and the Caribbean, and Europe and Eurasia. The home page (**http;//www.usaid.gov/**) provides frequently asked questions, the agency's organization and contact information, USAID's accomplishments and disability policy, public opinion related to the agency's activities, speeches and congressional testimony, a brief history of foreign assistance under the Marshall Plan, and more.

U.S. Trade and Development Agency

The Trade and Development Agency's (TDA) mission "is to promote economic development in, and simultaneously export U.S. goods and services to, developing and middle-income nations in . . . Africa/Middle East, Asia/Pacific, Central and Eastern Europe, Latin America and the Caribbean, and the New Independent States." TDA assists U.S. companies to pursue overseas business opportunities. The Web site (**http://www.tda.gov/**) highlights the agency and how to do business with it, trade and export news, publications, employment opportunities, a site index, related links, the TDA Pipeline (activities by region and sector), and so forth.

United States International Trade Commission

The United States International Trade Commission (USITC) is an independent, quasi-judicial federal agency that offers "objective trade expertise to both the legislative and executive branches of government, determines the impact of imports on U.S. industries, and directs actions against certain unfair trade practices, such as patent, trademark, and copyright infringement." Its "analysts and economists investigate and publish reports on U.S. industries and the global trends that affect them. The agency also updates and publishes the Harmonized Tariff Schedule of the United States."

The Web site (**http://www.usitc.gov/**) introduces the agency and covers news and events, dockets, the FOIA, headlines, publications, a site map and site search. It also covers recent filings, *Federal Register* notices and rules of practice and procedure, statistics, and more. DataWeb (see **http://dataweb.usitc.gov/**) provides industry information, regional or country information, trade assistance, data sets, economic development, and so on. It enables users to obtain data on U.S. imports and exports, and to examine the values of commodities for specific countries. It is possible to produce a "Percent Distribution of Values within Year." There is also a tariff database, data on planned general U.S. tariff reductions by product, coverage of production sharing (U.S. imports), data on selected countries and country groupings, and detailed tables of trade data.

ELECTIONS (PRESIDENTIAL AND CONGRESSIONAL)

Federal Election Commission

The Federal Election Commission (FEC) administers and enforces the *Federal Election Campaign Act,* which governs the financing of federal elections. The FEC's Web site (**http://www.fec.gov/**) provides insights into the agency and using its services; "What's New," news releases; financial information about candidates, political parties, and political action committees (PACs); assistance for candidates, parties, and PACs; publications; a site map; and more. Information is arranged by three broad guides: "Citizen Guide," "Media Guide," and "Candidate and Committee Guide."

EMERGENCY ASSISTANCE/PREPARATION

↗ Federal Emergency Management Agency

The Web site of the Federal Emergency Management Agency (FEMA) will move to the Department of Homeland Security (see Chapter 5). Until the transfer, however, it can be found at **http://www.fema.gov/**; this site provides information about agency services, news releases, emergency personnel, a list of declared disasters, a breakdown of activities by geographical regions, hazards assistance, emergency prevention and preparedness, response and recovery, emergency planning, victims, as well as up-to-date information on threatening weather conditions, weather maps, a site map, and storm watches. There is also information for the media.

Information seekers can view the history of tornadoes, hurricanes, hailstorms, earthquakes, windstorms, and floods for any area in the United States. This mapping project is part of Project Impact, which was created to encourage the development of plans for local disaster prevention. For flood and other maps, some of which are interactive, see **http://www.fema.gov/maps.shtm**. There are also links to related sites and a Photo Library, which can be searched by keyword, disaster type, location, and other choices.

One of the links is to the U.S. Fire Administration (**http://www.usfa.fema.gov/**), the mission of which "is to reduce life and economic losses due to fire and related emergencies, through leadership, advocacy, coordination, and support." The Web site explains "What's New" and provides access to publications, fact sheets, and so forth.

EMPLOYMENT

↗ U.S. Equal Employment Opportunity Commission

The Equal Employment Opportunity Commission (EEOC) promotes "equal opportunity in employment by enforcing the federal civil rights employment laws through administrative and judicial actions, and education and technical assistance." The site (**http://www.eeoc.gov/**) covers the commission's mission, authority, staffing, and press releases; information (for employers and employees); laws, regulations and policy guidance; publications; enforcement statistics; outreach and training programs; related links; and so on.

ENERGY

☞ Federal Energy Regulatory Commission

The Federal Energy Regulatory Commission (FERC), an independent regulatory agency within the Department of Energy, "regulates the transmission and sale for resale of natural gas in interstate commerce," "the transmission of oil by pipeline in interstate commerce," and "the transmission and wholesale sales of electricity in interstate commerce." The FERC also "licenses and inspects private, municipal and state hydroelectric projects," "oversees related environmental matters," and "administers accounting and financial reporting regulations and [reviews the conduct] of jurisdictional companies."

The FERC Web site (**http://www.ferc.gov/**) introduces the commission and offers a calendar of events, news and reports, documents and filings, legal and other resources, and employment opportunities. There are "Featured Topics," notices, orders, meetings, speeches, docket sheets, and service lists. Most helpful is the grouping of offerings around four areas of regulation

- Electric Power: "The Commission approves rates for wholesale electric sales of electricity and transmission in interstate commerce for private utilities, power marketers, power pools, power exchanges and independent system operators." There are standards of conduct, reports, links to other sites, and other information resources.

- Natural Gas: "The Commission regulates both the construction of pipeline facilities and the transportation of natural gas in interstate commerce. Companies providing services and constructing and operating interstate pipelines must first obtain Commission certificates of public convenience and necessity." There are links to the Office of Energy Projects and the Office of Markets, Tariffs & Rates, as well as standards, publications, seminars, rules and other policy statements, forms, a list of natural gas pipeline company Web sites, and more.

- Hydropower: There is a discussion of the origin of hydroelectric regulation and other general information, coverage of dam safety and inspections, and licensing and compliance.

- Oil: "The Commission does not oversee the construction of oil pipelines or regulate the supply and price of oil or oil products. Rather, it helps to assure shippers equal access to pipeline transportation, equal service conditions on a pipeline, and reasonable rates for moving petroleum and petroleum products by pipeline."

☞ Nuclear Regulatory Commission

The Nuclear Regulatory Commission (NRC) "licenses and regulates civilian use of nuclear energy to protect public health and safety and the environment." Its Web site (**http://www.nrc.gov/**) discusses the agency and what it does; covers nuclear reactors, nuclear materials, radioactive waste, public involvement, an electronic reading room (i.e., FOIA), the Office of the Inspector General, a site search and a site map, rule making, and publications.

U.S. Nuclear Waste Technical Review Board

The board (NWTRB) provides "independent scientific and technical oversight of the U.S. program for management and disposal of high-level radioactive waste and spent nuclear fuel from civilian nuclear power plants." Its home page (**http://www.nwtrb.gov/**) presents the board's mission and members, reports, correspondence, congressional testimony, press releases and meeting announcements, a calendar of future board meetings and events, transcripts of board and panel meetings, strategic and performance plans, a site map, and links to other nuclear waste Web sites.

ENVIRONMENT

Environmental Protection Agency

The Environmental Protection Agency (EPA) has a well-laid-out and easy-to-navigate Web site (**http://www.epa.gov/**) that explains the agency and the scope of its jurisdiction, as well as offers a search of the site, a kids' page (see Chapter 13), announcements, and stories. The general headings of the opening screen are

- Key Topics and Browse EPA Topics
- Current Issues
- Newsroom
- Laws & Regulations
- Where You Live
- Information Sources
- Educational Resources
- About EPA
- Programs
- Business Opportunities
- Employment Opportunities
- Resources Available in Spanish

Each of these headings leads to subheadings and various search choices. For example, "Laws and Regulations" covers new regulations, proposed rules, codified regulations, public laws, current legislation, and dockets, which "contain information and supporting documentation related to the rulemaking process." There is an excellent introduction to laws and regulations that explains the process by which legislation becomes public law (Chapter 4) as well as the process by which agencies create rules (**http://www.epa.gov/epahome/law.intro.htm**; see Chapter 12).

"Information Sources" covers clearinghouses, hotlines, dockets, publications, newsletters, the FOIA Office, databases and software, test methods and models, frequently asked questions, and more. "Where You Live" includes "Search Your Community" ("enter your zip code and choose from four databases to retrieve environmental information about your community"), state environmental agencies, EPA regional offices, and the following databases:

- **Envirofacts:** "Provides access to several EPA databases to provide you with information about environmental activities that may affect air, water, and land anywhere in the United States."

- **Window to My Environment:** "Use interactive maps and tools to answer popular questions about environmental conditions affecting air, land and water in your community; and learn what is being done locally to protect the environment."

- **AIRNOW:** "Search the Air Quality Index and find ozone maps to learn more about air quality and air pollution."

- **Toxic Release Inventory:** "Search the TRI and find information regarding toxic chemicals that are being used, manufactured, treated, transported, or released into the environment."

- **National Superfund Sites:** "Get information about Superfund sites in your community."

- **Watershed Information Network:** "Get involved in your watershed."

"Browse Topics" leads to the following:

- Air: Acid rain, global warming, and emissions
- Cleanup: Brownfields, Superfund, and corrective action
- Compliance and Enforcement: Complaints and compliance assistance
- Economics: Cost-benefit analysis, grants, and financing
- Ecosystems: Wetlands, watersheds, and endangered species
- Emergencies: Reporting, oil spills, and accidents
- Environmental Management: Livable communities and risk management
- Human Health: Children's health, risk assessment, and exposure
- Industry: Small business, permits, and reporting
- International Cooperation: Border issues and technical assistance
- Pesticides: Insecticides, registration, and food safety
- Pollutants/Toxics: Lead, dioxins, chemicals, and radiation
- Pollution Prevention: Recycling, conservation, and energy
- Research: Publications, laboratories, and models
- Treatment and Control: Treatment technologies and pretreatment

- Wastes: Hazardous wastes, landfills, and treatment

- Water: Wastewater, drinking water, and ground water

The Global Warming Site (**http://www.epa.gov/globalwarming/**) covers the climate, emissions, impacts, and actions. There are news items, lists of upcoming events, publications, presentations, online tools, science questions and answers, a visitor's center, "uncertainties," a site map, Web links, and more. The site uses icons to help different segments of the population (e.g., public officials, industry, concerned citizens, and health professionals).

U.S. Chemical Safety and Hazard Investigation Board

The board was created by the *Clean Air Act Amendments of 1990,* but, due to a lack of funding, it did not begin operations until 1998, This independent, scientific investigatory agency, which does not have regulatory or enforcement capability, promotes the prevention of major chemical accidents at fixed facilities. The home page (**http://www.chemicalsafety.gov/**) discusses the board and provides chemical incident data, a strategic plan, headlines, and a staff directory.

U.S. Global Change Research Program

The USGCRO "was created as a high-priority national research program to address key uncertainties in Earth's global environmental system, both natural and human-induced; monitor, understand, and predict global change; and provide a sound scientific basis for national and international decision-making." The home page (**http://www.usgcrp.gov/**) provides news, a library of resources, highlights, calls for proposals, assessments (major studies), "Focus Areas," announcement of events, links to related sites, a site map, and information about the initiative.

EUROPE

Commission on Security and Cooperation in Europe

This independent agency monitors and encourages compliance with the *Helsinki Final Act* and other commitments of the countries participating in the Organization for Security and Cooperation in Europe. The home page (**http://www.csce.gov/helsinki. cfm**) provides information by country, coverage of issues, a subscription service, contact information, press releases, events, publications (including hearings and briefings), and related links.

FEDERAL EMPLOYMENT

Federal Labor Relations Authority

The Federal Labor Relations Authority (FLRA) administers "the labor-management relations program for 1.9 million federal employees worldwide. . . . Its mission is to promote stable and constructive labor-management relations that contribute to an efficient and effective government." The home page (**http://www.flra.gov/**) introduces the agency and how to file a case; identifies statutes, regulations, and decisions; provides court opinions and the Office of the Solicitor; contains news, publications (e.g., *FLRA News* [historical] and the *FLRA Bulletin* [1996–]), and a link to the Office of General Counsel and the Federal Service Impasses Panel; explains arbitration appeals, negotiation and representation issues, unfair labor practices, and collaboration and alternative dispute resolution services; and training opportunities.

Federal Retirement Thrift Investment Board

The board (FRTIB) "was established to administer the Thrift Savings Plan (TSP), which provides Federal employees the opportunity to save for additional retirement security. The TSP is a tax-deferred defined contribution plan similar to a private sector 401(k) plan." The Web site (**http://www.frtib.gov/**) covers the electronic reading room, provides procurement information, and discusses employment opportunities. There is a separate home page for the Thrift Savings Plan (**http://www.tsp.gov/**).

Merit Systems Protection Board

The Merit Systems Protection Board (MSPB) "protects the integrity of federal merit systems and the rights of federal employees working in the systems." The home page (**http://www.mspb.gov/**) discusses the agency, provides a link to the regional offices, and presents "What's New," forms, publications and studies, decisions, the FOIA, a site map, and sources of additional information. Furthermore, there are instructions on how to file an initial appeal, and a petition for review (challenging an initial decision) and for court review of a final board order. The text of Title 5, *Code of Federal Regulations,* Part 1200 (the agency's regulations), is reproduced.

Office of Government Ethics

The mission of the Office of Government Ethics (OGE) is "not only to prevent and resolve conflicts of interest and to foster high ethical standards for federal employees but also to strengthen the public's confidence that the Government's business is conducted with impartiality and integrity." The home page (**http://www.usoge.gov/**) discusses the agency, its jurisdiction and program areas; presents information resources related to the executive branch ethics program; and provides electronic links to other online ethics resources, including international sites. There is legal information as well as information on recent developments in the ethics program; training, educational, and research materials; and other services provided by the OGE. For example, there are policy memoranda, known as DAEOGRAMS, that the OGE sends to each executive branch designated agency ethics official (DAEO) "providing guidance on how to interpret and comply with modifications or new issuances of conflict of interest, post-employment, standards of conduct, or financial disclosure policies and procedures." These DAEOGRAMS that are available online date from 1992 (see **http:// www.usoge.gov/pages/daeograms/daeograms.html**).

Office of Personnel Management

The Office of Personnel Management (OPM) "administers a merit system to ensure compliance with personnel laws and regulations and assists agencies in recruiting, examining, and promoting people on the basis of their knowledge and skills, regardless of their race, religion, sex, political influence, or other nonmerit factors." Furthermore, among its other roles, OPM provides guidance to agencies in operating human resources programs and supports program managers in their human resources management responsibilities.

The Web site (**http://www.opm.gov/**), for instance, provides "What's New," news releases, upcoming events, publications, headlines, employment opportunities, a site search, USAJOBS (see **http://www.usajobs.opm.gov/**), which is "the U.S. Government's official site for jobs and employment information provided by the United States Office of Personal Management." The site also gives statistics on the federal workforce and directs visitors to the Bureau of Labor Statistics for information on the U.S. workforce and the Department of Defense for statistics on the military. Furthermore, OPM has a page on "Veterans" and a "Quick Index" to topics such as "Accountability," "Disability," "Family Friendly Workplace," "Family Leave Policies," "FOIA," and "Welfare-to-Work." There are diversity profiles, which are statistical profiles, for example, of "African-Americans," "Hispanics," "Persons with Disabilities," "Women," and "Native Americans" (see **http://www.opm.gov/employ/diversity/ stats/profiles.htm**).

Office of Special Counsel

The Office of Special Counsel (OSC) "is an independent federal investigative and prosecutorial agency. Our primary mission is to safeguard the merit system by protecting federal employees and applicants from prohibited personnel practices, especially reprisal for whistleblowing." The Web site (**http://www.osc.gov/**) is part of an "effort to reach out to federal employees and others served by OSC and to tell them about the ways in which OSC can help them—including by enforcement of legal protections against prohibited personnel practices (including reprisal for whistleblowing), and by advice about allowable and unallowable political activities." There is an introduction to the agency, a description of prohibited personnel practices, whistleblower disclosures, press releases, the FOIA, forms and publications, employment opportunities, other links, and so on.

GAMING

⤳ National Indian Gaming Commission

This independent regulatory agency regulates "gaming activities on Indian lands for the purposes of shielding Indian tribes from organized crime and other corrupting influences; ensuring that Indian tribes are the primary beneficiaries of gaming revenues; and assuring that gaming is conducted fairly and honesty by both operations and players." The home page (**http://www.nigc.gov/nigc/index.jsp**) discusses the commission and covers laws and regulations, the FOIA, tribal data, commission actions, regulations, and press releases. There are links to the regional field offices.

HISTORIC PRESERVATION

⤳ Advisory Council on Historic Preservation

The Advisory Council on Historic Preservation (ACHP) promotes "the preservation, enhancement, and productive use of our Nation's historic resources, and advises the President and Congress on national historic preservation policy." It encourages the government to be a responsible steward for future generations as specified in the *National Historic Preservation Act* (1966) and in subsequent amendments. The ACHP's home page (**http://www.achp.gov/**) discusses the agency and covers "top stories." The site includes news, the Native Historical Preservation Program, section 106 reviews ("the federal review process designed to ensure that historic properties significant to the American people . . . are fully considered during federal or federally assisted planning and decisionmaking"); state, tribal, and federal agency programs and Web links; a site index; assorted publications on historic preservation; and more. (For additional information, see "Historic Preservation" in Chapter 12.)

HOUSING

⤳ Federal Housing Finance Board

The board, an independent regulatory agency, regulates the Federal Home Loan Banks "that were created in 1932 to improve the supply of funds to local lenders that, in turn, finance loans for home mortgages." The home page (**http://www.fhfb.gov/**) discusses the agency, its programs, and career opportunities; and it provides news, regulatory reporting, press and reading rooms (e.g., for the FOIA), an employee directory, a list of the banks, and a monthly interest rate survey.

✄ Office of Federal Housing Enterprise Oversight

The Office (OFHEO), an independent agency within the Department of Housing and Urban Development, "promotes housing and a strong economy by ensuring the safety and soundness of Fannie Mae [Federal National Mortgage Association] and Freddie Mac [Federal Home Loan Mortgage Corporation] and fostering the strength and vitality of the nation's housing finance system."

The Web site (**http://www.ofheo.gov/**) provides information on the agency and an organizational chart. It also has job postings, public documents, related links, and a quarterly *House Price Index* (**http://www.ofheo.gov/house/**).

HUMANITIES

✄ National Endowment for the Arts

The mission of the National Endowment for the Arts (NEA) is to enrich "our nation and its diverse cultural heritage by supporting works of artistic excellence, advancing learning in the arts, and strengthening the arts in communities throughout the country." The home page (**http://arts.endow.gov/**) provides information about the NEA, "Endowment News," applications and grant forms, publications, and "NEA Partnerships." Other features include

- Explore: "Arts features, interviews, new work in the Gallery and Writers' Corner. Learn about the exceptional work being done by artists and arts organizations across the country."

- Art Forms: "Choose an Art Form to find resources, links, field reports, and features on artists and arts organizations."

- Cultural Funding: Federal Opportunities: "Federal funding available for arts initiatives through national, state and local funding programs."

- FOIA Guide

- Site Search and Site Map

✄ National Endowment for the Humanities

The National Endowment for the Humanities (NEH) "supports learning in history, literature, philosophy, and other areas of the humanities. We fund research, education, museum exhibitions, documentaries, preservation, and activities in the states." The site (**http://www.neh.fed.us/**) covers "Who We Are," grants and applications, exhibitions, a mail advisory, state humanities councils, a list of the "best of humanities on the web," news and publications, NEH projects, grant deadlines, online subscription to the *Humanities* magazine, and more.

INTELLIGENCE COMMUNITY

◿ Central Intelligence Agency

The home page (**http://www.odci.gov/**) encompasses the

- Directorate of Intelligence
- Directorate of Science & Technology
- The Center for the Study of Intelligence
- Office of General Counsel
- Office of Military Affairs
- Office of Public Affairs
- Director of Central Intelligence
- Overview of the Intelligence Community (see Figure 6.1, beginning on p. 201)
- National Intelligence Council
- FOIA Electronic Reading Room
- CIA's Home Page for Kids (see Chapter 13)

The site for the CIA provides information about the agency employment, press releases, speeches, "What's New," publicly available congressional testimony, publications, and related Web links. Publications include, for instance, the *World Factbook*, one of the premiere sources of information on every country in the world; the *Factbook on Intelligence*; maps (see Chapter 11); a list of chiefs of state and cabinet ministers; and so forth. "Related Links" (**http://www.odci.gov/cia/other_links.other.html**) provides access to sources in other agencies (e.g., Department of State and U.S. Geological Survey).

The Office of Public Affairs for the Director of Central Intelligence and Central Intelligence Agency provides a Web Site Update Service, which is an e-mail notification service for new documents or new pages to the Web site, excluding the FOIA Electronic Reading Room (see **http://www.odci.gov/cia/update_service.html**).

The Electronic Reading Room offers access to annual reports, frequently requested records, and information on filing a FOIA or *Privacy Act* request (see **http://www.foia.cia.gov/**). The frequently requested records cover unidentified flying objects (UFOs), the Bay of Pigs, Guatemala, prisoners of war and those missing in action (POW/MIA), Human Rights in Latin America, Ethel and Julius Rosenberg, the U-2 spy incident during the Eisenhower administration, and a Western spy in the Soviet Union (**http://www.foia.cia.gov/records.asp**). There are also links to relevant historical collections outside the agency.

LABOR RELATIONS

⟳ Federal Labor Relations Authority

See the section of this chapter titled "Federal Employment."

⟳ National Labor Relations Board

Created in 1935, the National Labor Relations Board (NLRB) enforces the *National Labor Relations Act* by conducting "secret-ballot elections to determine whether employees want union representation" and investigates and remedies "unfair labor practices by employers and unions." The home page (**http://www.nlrb.gov/**) discusses the agency, employee rights under the act and other labor laws, and how to file a charge or election petition (see "Help Desk" button). Other options provide fact sheets on the agency, the NLRB's organization, a "Weekly Summary" of NLRB cases ("all published NLRB decisions in unfair labor practice and representation election cases, except for summary judgment cases. It also lists all decisions of NLRB administrative law judges"), the Office of the Inspector General, and e-flings. There are also forms, press releases, decisions, public notices, rules and regulations, publications, coverage of the FOIA, employment opportunities, and materials available in Spanish.

LIBRARIES AND MUSEUMS

⟳ Institute of Museum and Library Services

The Institute of Museum and Library Services (IMLS), an independent agency created by the *Museum and Library Services Act of 1996,* "provides distinct programs of support for libraries and museums and also encourages partnerships between museums and libraries." That support includes grant awards. The home page (**http://www.imls.gov/**) introduces the agency and its services (e.g., grants programs) and publications. There is a site map.

⟳ National Commission on Libraries and Information Science

The National Commission on Libraries and Information Science (NCLIS), established in 1970, advises "the executive and legislative branches on national library and information policies and plans." According to *the Museum and Library Services Act of 1996,* NCLIS advises "the Director of the Institute of Museum and Library Services (IMLS) on general policies with respect to the duties, powers and authority of the IMLS relating to library services." NCLIS's home page (**http://www.nclis.gov/index. cfm**) covers the agency, news, the FOIA, selected government information policies (those NCLIS is trying to influence), libraries nationally and internationally, statistics and surveys, and the "Millennium." There are a site map and a site search.

↗ Smithsonian Institution

The Smithsonian Institution (SI), created more than 150 years ago, "is an independent trust instrumentality of the United States that fosters the increase and diffusion of knowledge." SI includes museums and galleries, the National Zoo, and research facilities, and it is dedicated to public education, national service, and scholarship in the arts, history, and the sciences.

The home page (**http://www.si.edu/**) features the museums and research centers, their history, collections, exhibitions, services, events, activities, shops, memberships, "What's New," and some basic resources (e.g., the *Smithsonian Magazine*). The Virtual Smithsonian highlights more than 360 artifacts in the museums and has a virtual walk to a castle. Most relevant to this guide is the list of Smithsonian research centers (**http://www.si.edu/research/**) and museums (**http://www.si.edu/museums/**).

↗ United States Holocaust Memorial Museum

Charted by an act of Congress in 1980, the United States Holocaust Memorial Museum "is America's national institution for the documentation, study, and interpretation of Holocaust history, and serves as this country's memorial to the millions of people murdered during the Holocaust." The primary mission of the museum "is to advance and disseminate knowledge about this unprecedented tragedy; to preserve the memory of those who suffered; and to encourage its visitors to reflect upon the moral and spiritual questions raised by the events of the Holocaust as well as their own responsibilities as citizens of a democracy." The well-laid-out Web site (**http://www.ushmm.org/**) provides museum, educational, and research information. There are remembrances, a site search, an opportunity to join the Museum or make a donation, and more. The Holocaust Learning Center provides an introduction to the Holocaust and covers topics such as racism, anti-Semitism, mosaic of victims, the camp system, forced labor, ghettos, and much more (**http://www.ushmm.org/wlc/en/**).

LITERACY

↗ National Institute for Literacy

Created by the *National Literacy Act of 1991,* the National Institute for Literacy (NIFL) "serves as focal point for public and private activities that support the development of high-quality regional, state, and national literacy services." It "is administered by the Secretaries of Education, Labor, and Health and Human Services, who make up the governing Interagency Group." The home page (**http://novel.nifl.gov/**) discusses the NIFL, provides grants and contacts, programs and services, publications, a mailing list, and frequently asked questions.

MANAGING GOVERNMENT PROPERTY AND BUSINESS

General Services Administration

According to the *United States Government Manual,* the General Services Administration (GSA),

> establishes policy for and provides economical and efficient management of Government property and records, including construction and operation of buildings; procurement and distribution of supplies; utilization and disposal of real and personal property; transportation, traffic, and communications management; and management of the governmentwide automatic data processing resources program. Its functions are carried out at three levels of organization: the central office, regional offices, and field activities.[2]

The home page (**http://www.gsa.gov/Portal/home.jsp**), which will be redesigned to be "more useful, efficient, and user-friendly," covers the agency, news, "Buying to through GSA," "Selling to the Government," events, media relations, "Also of Interest," and "Contacts." There is also a site map, a site search, and an opportunity to personalize communication (MyGSA). "Key Information" is arranged by topics such as

- Catalog of Federal Domestic Assistance
- Federal Forms
- Public Buildings
- Report Waste, Fraud, and Abuse
- Travel on Government Business
- Employment

Another topic deals with e-government (e-commerce and e-real estate). The agency "is the managing partner for the following eGov initiatives which support President Bush's Management and Performance Plan for Expanding Electronic Government":

- eAuthentication
- eTravel
- Federal Asset Sales
- Integrated Acquisition Environment
- USA Services

The GSA also has the Federal Consumer Information Center in Pueblo, Colorado. The Center's Web site (**http://www.pueblo.gsa.gov/**) contains a site map and buttons for "Cars," "Children," "Computers," "Education," "Employment," "Federal Programs," "Food," "Health," "Housing," "Money," "Small Business," "Travel," "[safety] Recalls," and so on. There is consumer information, such as a catalog that includes publications on numerous topics that can be downloaded or acquired free of charge.

MANAGING GOVERNMENT RECORDS

➤ National Archives and Records Administration

According to the *United States Government Manual*, the National Archives and Records Administration (NARA)

> ensures, for citizens and federal officials, ready access to essential evidence that documents the rights of American citizens, the actions of federal officials, and the national experience. It establishes policies and procedures for managing U.S. government records and assists federal agencies in documenting their activities, administering records management programs, scheduling records, and retiring noncurrent records to federal records centers. . . . [NARA] accessions, arranges, describes, preserves, and provides access to the essential documentation of the three branches of government; manages the Presidential Libraries system; and publishes the laws, regulations, and Presidential and other public documents. It also assists the Information Security Oversight Office, which manages federal classification and declassification policies, and the National Historical Publications and Records Commission, which makes grants nationwide to help nonprofit organizations identify, preserve, and provide access to materials that document American history.[3]

In addition to a site map and site index, the home page (**http://www.archives.gov/**) covers

- Welcome
- About NARA
- Research Room
- Records Management
- Records Center Program
- The Federal Register
- NHPRC [National Historical Publications and Records Commission] and Other Grants
- Exhibit Hall
- Digital Classroom
- Records of Congress
- Presidential Libraries

Particularly helpful is that, for each of these topics, the relevant Web page clearly lays out the search choices. "Research Room," for instance, provides news and events, resources, "sections" (areas to check), records of concern, and information about a in-person visit. Three of the choices in "sections" are "Genealogy," "Research Paths," and "Archival Research Catalog (ARC)."

ARC (**http://www.archives.gov/research_room/arc/index.html**) "is the online catalog of NARA's nationwide holdings in the Washington, DC area, Regional Archives and Presidential Libraries." Replacing its prototype, the NARA Archival Information Locator (NAIL), it contains descriptions of a diverse assortment of records, photographs (e.g., of two lifeboats carrying survivors after the *Titanic* sunk), and posters from World War II depicting women in the workforce (e.g., "Rosie the Riveter—the strong, competent woman dressed in overalls and bandanna—was introduced as a symbol of patriotic womanhood"). ARC also includes text, maps and charts, sound recordings, films, architectural drawings, and videos.

"Genealogy," which is located in the "Research Room," identifies guides and other publications. Workshops, related Web resources, information on "Beginning Your Genealogical Research," and more.

The "Federal Register" leads to "resources" such as

- The Federal Register
- Code of Federal Regulations
- Presidential Documents
- Public Laws
- *U.S. Government Manual*
- Document Drafting Handbook

"Our documents," a page for teachers, provides one hundred milestone documents from American History and other resources (**http://www.ourdocuments.gov/**).

NARA has issued policy guidance on the preservation of records in electronic forms and formats, including, when appropriate, e-mail communiqués. Furthermore, the agency is actively building an Electronic Records Archive (ERA; see **http://www.archives.gov/electronic_records_archives/**). For a discussion of NARA's role in the e-government strategy of the Bush administration, see **http://www.archives.gov/records_management/initiatives/erm_overview.html**.

The National Historical Publications and Records Commission (NHPRC), which is NARA's grant-making affiliate, "makes grants nationwide to help identify, preserve, and provide public access to records, photographs, and other materials that document American history." The home page (**http://www.archives.gov/grants/index.html**) introduces the NHPRC and its staff and provides information for grant applicants, publications (e.g., annual reports, press releases, and in-house publications), status reports on funded projects, and links to related organizations.

The *President John F. Kennedy Assassination Records Collection Act* (Public Law 102-526) "mandated that all material related to the assassination . . . be housed in a single collection in . . . [NARA]. On December 28, 1992, NARA established the John F. Kennedy Assassination Records Collection." As agencies complete the reviews of their collections and transfer newly opened records to NARA, the holdings becomes more extensive (see **http://www.archives.gov/research_room/jfk/jfk_search.html**).

A Web page guides researchers to records about finances and other assets looted by the Nazis during the Holocaust (**http://www.archives.gov/research_room/holocaust_era_assets/**). Finally, *Prologue,* the quarterly and scholarly journal of NARA, is available online, as is *The Record*, NARA's newsletter.

Presidential Libraries. Under the direction of the Office of Presidential Libraries, NARA manages ten presidential libraries and museums; the Nixon Presidential Materials Staff, which hold the presidential material of former President Richard M. Nixon,[4] and the Clinton Presidential Materials Staff. For a list of these libraries (their mailing addresses, telephone and fax numbers, and e-mail addresses), together with links directly to the sites, see **http://www.archives.gov/presidential_libraries/addresses/addresses.html**. On the other hand, for a brief introduction to "access to presidential records," see **http://www.archives.gov/presidential_libraries/presidential_records/presidential_records.html**.

Three of these libraries (Lyndon B. Johnson, Gerald Ford, and George H. W. Bush) list documents that the president or his national security advisors issued to federal agencies to either relay policy statements to request action programs. These issuances might be referred to as National Security Action Memoranda, and a number of them have been declassified, their images scanned, and included at the home page.

Information Security Oversight Office. This office, which receives program guidance from the National Security Council and NARA's administrative component, has responsibility for the policy oversight of the governmentwide security classification system and the National Industrial Security Program. This site (**http://www.archives.gov/isoo/**) provides relevant executive orders on policies related to national security and national industrial security classification. There are annual reports and other information.

MEDIATION

✈ National Mediation Board

The National Mediation Board (NMB), the "national mediator for the airline and railroad industries," plays a critical role in arbitration to resolve railroad grievances. The home page (**http://www.nmb.gov/**) explains the NMB's role, offers a directory of its officials, and provides services, public information (e.g., representation, forms, documents, "What's New"), and links to related Web sites.

MONUMENTS

✈ American Battle Monuments Commission

The commission honors the accomplishments of the American armed forces since World War I. The Web site (**http://www.abmc.gov/**) discusses the commission and provides the annual report and details on the American Battle Monuments Commission cemeteries and memorials. There is also coverage of the "War Dead" honored at the cemeteries, services available to the public, Memorial Day activities, and commemorative events associated with D-Day. Additional information relates to the new World War II Memorial in Washington, D.C., and the Vietnam Veterans Memorial Plague.

MUTUAL UNDERSTANDING WITH PEOPLE OF OTHER COUNTRIES (COMMUNICATION)

International Broadcasting Bureau

Founded in 1994, the International Broadcasting Bureau (IBB) is composed of the Voice of America (VOA), Radio Sawa, Radio and TV Marti, WORLDNET Television and Film Service, and an Engineering Directorate that maintains transmitting facilities and provides support for the agency's broadcasting elements. The home page (**http://www.ibb.gov/**) explains the agency and offers engineering and program support to Radio Free Europe and Radio Liberty, and Radio Free Asia; news releases, editorials, and other information.

The home page of Voice of America (**http://www.voa.gov/index.cfm**) has a press room, a program schedule, language services, information (e.g., a virtual tool), and more.

NUCLEAR HEALTH AND SAFETY

Defense Nuclear Facilities Safety Board

The Defense Nuclear Facilities Safety Board provides "independent, external oversight of all activities in DOE's [Department of Energy] nuclear weapons complex affecting nuclear health and safety." The home page (**http://www.dnfsb.gov/**) discusses the board and includes frequently asked questions, a site search, "What's New," resources, and more.

PENSION PLANS

Pension Benefit Guaranty Corporation

The Pension Benefit Guaranty Corporation (PBGC) "guarantees payment of nonforfeitable pension benefits in covered private-sector defined benefit pension plans." The home page (**http://www.pbgc.gov/**) provides information about the agency legal information and coverage of FOIA, forms, news, contact information, retirement planning, and publications. There is a site guide and information on participant services, plan administration, conducting a pension search, searching for trustee plan information, searching the site, and searching for information by topic.

POSTAL SERVICE

Postal Rate Commission

The Postal Rate Commission makes recommendations to the Postal Service Governors on postal rates, fees, and mail classifications. The home page (**http://www. prc.gov/**) introduces the Commission and conveys postal rates and fees, decisions, press releases, congressional submissions, coverage of FOIA and the *Privacy Act,* employment opportunities, docketed cases, the domestic mail classification schedule, employment information, a calendar of scheduled events, Post Office data files, a search of the site, and more. There are also online filing and coverage of consumer advocacy.

United States Postal Service

Both Chapters 10 and 13 discuss this agency, which provides mail processing and delivery services (see **http://www.usps.com/**). For example, the agency has increased its portfolio of online services by making it possible to send and receive certified e-mail, purchase stamps, purchase Post Service merchandise, calculate postage, find zip codes, track mailings and confirm receipt, and so on.

RAILROAD TRAVEL AND WORKERS

National Railroad Passenger Corporation

Amtrak is a registered service mark of the National Railroad Passenger Corporation. The home page (see **http://www.amtrak.com/**) provides a reservation service and listing of destinations, information on savings and promotions, assistance in planning a trip, a guide of services, information for frequent travelers, a press room, and more.

Railroad Retirement Board

The Railroad Retirement Board "administers comprehensive retirement-survivor and unemployment-sickness benefit programs for the Nation's railroad workers and their families." The home page (**http://www.rrb.gov/**) offers "What's New," a site map and search of the site, links to related sites, online services, "Benefit Programs," "News and Publications" (e.g., news releases, statistical information, and congressional testimony), "Recent Updates," "Frequently Requested Information," and "FYI: Spotlighting Information on the Website." The site also discusses the agency and how to contact it.

SCIENCE AND ENGINEERING

🖙 National Science Foundation

The National Science Foundation (NSF) promotes science and engineering. Its home page (**http://www.nsf.gov/**) discusses the agency, grants and awards, legislative and public affairs, science statistics, news and media, a search of the site and a site map, contracting opportunities, custom news service, publications, "Highlights," "NSF Staff & Organizations," and "Specialized Info for [topical areas]." Some of the other options include a strategic plan, publications (e.g., grant proposal guide), and "Program Areas: Overview of Programs" including the following:

- Biology

- Computer, Information Sciences

- Crosscutting

- Education

- Engineering

- Environmental Research and Education

- Geosciences

- International

- Math, Physical Sciences

- Polar Research

- Social, Behavioral, Economic Sciences

There is an index to NSF publications, which has different search choices (e.g., by type which leads to reports and other resources; see **http://www.nsf.gov/pubsys/**).

SECURITY MARKETS

🖙 Securities and Exchange Commission

The Securities and Exchange Commission (SEC) "administers federal securities laws that seek to provide protection for investors; to ensure that securities markets are fair and honest; and, when necessary, to provide the means to enforce securities laws through sanctions." The home page (**http://www.sec.gov/**) covers "About the SEC," "Investor Information," "Filings and Forms (EDGAR [Electronic Data Gathering, Analysis and Retrieval system])," "Regulatory Actions," "News and Public Statements," "Litigation," and "Staff Interpretations." Other choices include employment information, forms, links to related sites, forms, and contact information. Some of the information found at these pages are the *SEC News Digest* (**http://www.sec.gov/ news/digest.shtml**), a periodical and daily information on recent commission actions, including enforcement proceedings, rule filings, policy statements, and upcoming meetings.

The SEC requires "all public companies (except foreign companies and companies with less than $10 million in assets and 500 shareholders) to file registration statements, periodic reports, and other forms electronically through EDGAR. Anyone can access and download this information for free." The relevant links (**http://www.sec.gov/edgar.shtml**) are

- QUICK EDGAR Tutorial
- Search for Company Filings
- Descriptions of SEC Forms
- About EDGAR
- FTP [file transfer protocol] Users (indices and documentation for EDGAR data dissemination before September 28, 1995)
- SIC Codex
- Information for EDGAR Filers

SELECTIVE SERVICE (FOR MILITARY)

Selective Service System

This site of the Selective Service System (**http://www.sss.gov/**) provides information about online registration for possible training and service in the armed forces. Other resources presented include information about the agency, news and publications, "Fast Facts," an explanation of "What Happens in a Draft," and an opportunity to check a registration. There is also a section on history and records, and an opportunity to conduct a search of the site.

SMALL BUSINESS INTERESTS

Small Business Administration

The home page (**http://www.sbaonline.sba.gov/**) discusses the agency, "Headline News," "What's New?," "Calendars," "Site of the Week," and "Answer Desk." Other options are coverage of FOIA; an opportunity to report fraud, waste, or abuse; frequently asked questions, a site map, links to local and regional offices; contact the agency; and

- Starting Your Business
- Financing Your Business

- Business Opportunities
- Offices and Services
- Your Local SBA Offices
- Pro-Net
- Laws and Regulations
- Disaster Assistance
- SBA Classroom
- Business Cards
- Ombudsman
- Outside Resources
- Online Library
- Subscriptions

The Online Library, for instance, covers forms, loans information, programs, publications, reports, statistics, shareware, and so on. Pro-Net "is an electronic gateway of procurement information—for and about small businesses. It is a search engine for contracting officers, a marketing tool for small firms and a 'link' to procurement opportunities and important information. It is designated to be a 'virtual' one-stop-procurement-shop" (**http://pro-net.sba.gov/index2.html**).

The home page also identifies "Frequent Requested Services" and guides users on "How can SBA help you?," which is arranged by topic. Furthermore, there are links to business resources (**http://www.sbaonline.sba.gov/hotlist/**), such as those related to "Franchising," "International Trade," "Legal and Regulations," "Minorities," "Non-profit," "Trade Shows," "Travel," "Welfare to Work," and "Women in Business."

SOCIAL SECURITY

Social Security Administration

According to the *United States Government Manual,* the Social Security Administration (SSA)

manages the Nation's social insurance program, consisting of retirement, survivors, and disability insurance programs, commonly known as Social Security. It also administers the supplementary Security Income program for the aged, blind, and disabled. The Administration is responsible for studying the problems of poverty and economic insecurity among Americans and making recommendations on effective methods for solving these problems through social insurance. The Administration also assigns Social Security numbers to U.S. citizens and maintains earnings records for workers under their Social Security numbers.[5]

Social Security Online, the SSA's Web site (**http://www.ssa.gov/SSA_Home.html**), resembles a tabloid. Across the top are "Forms," "Top 10 [Services]," "Other Sites," "Search Site," "Site Map," and "Privacy." Below these categories are ("eNews: subscribe . . . It's free") "Benefits Planners," "Online Services," "Social Security Statement, and "Medicare Replacement." On the next line, is a site search by category. The rest of the opening three pages have "Quick Start" ("Understanding Social Security," "How to . . . ," "Search," "Services Online," and "Contact Us") . There is "Benefits Information," Benefit Payments," "Special Gateway Pages" (e.g., in Spanish and covering "Immigration") , "About SSA," "Online Direct Services," "Services for Businesses," "Research and Data," "Financing, Planning, and Budget," "SSA Program Rules," "Reporting Fraud," news, and more.

The "Top Ten Services" (**http://www.ssa.gov/top10.html**) include the following:

1. Apply for Social Security benefits online

2. Request a replacement Medicare card online

3. 2003 Cost of Living information

4. Prepare and place for your future financial security

5. How to replace, correct, or change your name on your social security card

6. Benefit information publications

7. Request a social security statement

8. If you have already received a social security statement and have questions about it, try our My Statement page

9. Have you tried our new Searchable Frequently Asked Questions database?

10. How to contact a local office

The Office of the Chief Actuary (**http://www.ssa.gov/OACT**) reviews "the balance between future benefit liabilities and future tax collections" and "evaluates the cost impact of the many proposals to change the Social Security program." It offers trust fund data, publications, beneficiary data, coverage of automatic increases in benefits, an opportunity to "compute your own benefit," and actuaries at SSA.

The Office of Policy (**http://www.ssa.gov/policy/**) serves as the SSA's "focal point for policy development, policy analysis and research, evaluation, and statistics." The site provides publications and coverage of programs, "Policy Areas," other links, employment information, and research information.

TRANSPORTATION

The National Transportation Safety Board

The jurisdiction of the National Transportation Safety Board extends to aviation, highways, water, "pipelines & hazardous materials," and railroads. The home page (**http://www.ntsb.gov/**) provides information about the agency (e.g., history and mission, board members, office locations, and organization chart), news and events, data and information products, and information sources and contacts within the agency, employment opportunities, related sites, a site map, and most wanted transportation safety improvements. There is coverage of the investigative process, accident investigation hearings, tables and charts depicting Safety Board statistical information, and other sources of information.

The center part of the home page arranges resources related to transportation safety by

- Aviation
- Highway
- Marine
- Pipeline and Hazardous Materials
- Railroad

"Aviation," for instance, includes accident synopses and statistics and procedures and forms for reporting an accident.

WORKPLACE

Occupational Safety and Health Review Commission

The Occupational Safety and Health Review Commission (OSHRC) "is an independent Federal agency created to decide contests of citations or penalties results from OSHA inspections of American workplaces. The Review Commission, therefore, functions as an administrative court, with established procedures for conducting hearings, receiving evidence and rendering decisions by its Administrative Law Judges (ALJs)."

The home page (**http://www.oshrc.gov/**) covers the agency and provides procedural rules, decisions, publications (including the strategic plan and performance reports), press releases, coverage of the budget, the FOIA, related Web sites, "What's New," and a site search.

WORLD PEACE AND FRIENDSHIP

Japan-U.S. Friendship Commission

This independent agency supports training and provides information to help Americans meet the challenges and opportunities that the U.S.-Japanese relationship presents. The home page (**http://www.jusfc.gov/commissn/commissn.html**) covers grant programs to support Japanese studies in the United States, public affairs and education, the arts, and the study of the United States.

◿ Peace Corps

Established in 1961, "the Peace Corps' purpose is to promote world peace and friendship, to help other countries in meeting their needs for trained men and women, and to promote understanding between the American people and other peoples served by the Peace Corps." There is a "commitment toward programming to meet the basic needs of those living in the countries where volunteers work."

The home page (**http://www.peacecorps.gov/index.cfm**) contains news and an applicant's toolkit, and it covers diversity, assignments, countries, benefits, information about the agency, and more. There is also an opportunity for individuals to join the Peace Corps and information on how to obtain a graduate school education with Peace Corps enlistment.

◿ United States Commission on International Religious Freedom

This independent agency has a home page (**http://www.uscirf.gov/index.php3? SID=a5eof61f6297ece5a001293abc75e250**) that provides frequently asked questions, information about the commissions, press releases, reports, material displayed by country, and more.

◿ United States Institute of Peace

The mission of the United States Institute of Peace, an independent, nonpartisan agency, "is to strengthen the nation's capabilities to promote the peaceful resolutions of international conflicts." Established in 1984, it has "an array of programs, including grants, fellowships, conferences, and workshops, library services, publications, and other educational activities." The home page (**http://www.usip.org/**) reflects these programs. It offers information about the agency, highlights, publications, discussion of research areas, education and training, grants, fellowships, an event archive, related links, and more.

SUMMARY

The more than sixty agencies discussed in this chapter play important roles—advisory, regulatory, judicial, and other. Additional independent establishments and quasi-official agencies appear at the excellent "U.S. Federal Government Agencies Directory" of Louisiana State University (**http://www.lib.lsu.edu/gov/fedgov.html**).

NOTES

1. *United States Government Manual 1998/99* (Washington, D.C.: Government Printing Office, 1998): 723.

2. *United States Government Manual 1997/98* (Washington, D.C.: Government Printing Office, 1997): 568.

3. Ibid., 589.

4. For an introduction to presidential libraries and materials, see two symposia issues of *Government Information Quarterly* 11, no. 1 (1994); 12 no. 1 (1995). By the way, a later issue of that journal (13, no. 2, 1996) carries Michele F. Pacifico's "The National Archives at College Park" (117–31), which discusses the new archives facility.

5. *United States Government Manual 1997/98,* 671.

Figure 6.1. The U.S. Intelligence Community.

A member is a federal government agency, service, bureau, or other organization within the executive branch that play a role in the business of national intelligence. The Intelligence Community (IC) comprises fourteen such organizations, eight of them within the Department of Defense (DoD), which receive 85 percent of the intelligence budget.

The DoD IC members are

- Defense Intelligence Agency (DIA): Provides timely and objective military intelligence to warfighters, policy makers, and force planners

- National Security Agency (NSA): Collects and processes foreign signals intelligence information for the nation's leaders and warfighters, and protects critical U.S. information security systems from compromise

- National Reconnaissance Office (NRO): Coordinates collection and analysis of information from airplane and satellite reconnaissance by the military services and the CIA

- National Imagery and Mapping Agency (NIMA): Provides timely, relevant, and accurate geospatial intelligence in support of national security

- Army, Navy, Air Force, and Marine Corps Intelligence Agencies: Each collect and process intelligence relevant to their particular Service needs

The non-DoD members are

- Central Intelligence Agency (CIA): Provides accurate, comprehensive, and timely foreign intelligence on national security topics to national policy and decision makers

- State Department: Deals with information affecting U.S. foreign policy

- Energy Department: Performs analyses of foreign nuclear weapons, nuclear nonproliferation, and energy security–related intelligence issues in support of U.S. national security policies, programs, and objectives

- Treasury Department: Collects and processes information that may affect U.S. fiscal and monetary policy

- Federal Bureau of Investigation: Deals with counterespionage and data about international criminal cases

- United States Coast Guard: Deals with information related to U.S. maritime borders and Homeland Security

All the responsibilities of the CIA, DIA, NSA, NRO, and NIMA are concerned with intelligence. Therefore, each of these organizations in its entirety is considered to be a member of the IC. The other nine organizations are concerned primarily with missions and business other than intelligence but do have intelligence responsibilities. In these cases, only the part of the organization with the intelligence responsibility is considered to be a part of the IC. In the case of the U.S. Navy, for instance, only its Office of Naval Intelligence is an IC member. The rest of the navy supports the DoD in missions other than intelligence.

Source: Central Intelligence Agency (http://www.intelligence.gov/1-members.shtml; see also http://www.intelligence.gov/1-deinition.shtml).

URL Site Guide for This Chapter

U.S. Government Manual
http://www.gpo access.gov/gmanual/
    index.html

Your Government
White House
http://www.whitehouse.gov/government/

Home Page
National Aeronautics and Space
    Administration
http://www.nasa.gov/home/index.html

> **Educator Astronaut site**
> http://edspace.nasa.gov/
>
> **Planetary Photojournal**
> http://photojournal.jpl.nasa.gov/

Home Page
Commission on Future of the U.S.
    Aerospace Industry
http://www.aerospacecommission.gov/

Home Page
The African Development Foundation
http://www.adf.gov/

Home Page
Farm Credit Administration
http://www.fca.gov/

Home Page
The Inter-American Foundation
http://www.iaf.gov/

Home Page
Export-Import Bank of the United States
http://www.exim.gov/

> **Environmental Exports Program**
> http://www.exim.gov/products/special/
>   environmental.html

Home Page
Federal Deposit Insurance Corporation
http://www.fdic.gov/

Federal Financial Institutions
    Examination Council
http://www.ffiec.gov/

Community Reinvestment Act
http://www.ffiec.gov/cra/

Federal Reserve System
Federal Reserve Board
http://federalreserve.gov/

> **Fed in Print**
> http://www.frbsf.org/system/fedinprint/
>   index.html
>
> **Federal Reserve Bank of Minneapolis**
> http://minneapolisfed.org/sitemap2.cfm
>
> **Information Catalog**
> http://app.ny.frb.org/cfpicnic/main.cfm
>
> **Site Map**
> http://federalreserve.gov/sitemap.htm
>
> **Statistics: Releases and Historical**
>   **Data**
> http://www.federalreserve.gov/releases/

STAT-USA
Department of Commerce
http://www.stat-usa.gov/

Home Page
National Credit Union Administration
http://www.ncua.gov/

Home Page
International Joint Commission
http://www.ijc.org/ijcweb-e.html

Home Page
Legal Services Corporation
http://www.lsc.gov/

Home Page
U.S. Civil Rights Commission
http://www.usccr.gov/

Home Page
Federal Communications Commission
http://www.fcc.gov/

> **CORES**
> https://svartifoss2.fcc.gov/cores/
> CoresHome.html

> *Daily Digest*
> http://www.fcc.gov/Daily_Releases/
> Daily_Digest/2003/

Home Page
**Corporation for National and Community
Service**
http://www.cns.gov/

Home Page
Consumer Product Safety Commission
http://www.cpsc.gov/

Home Page
National Council on Disability
http://www.ncd.gov/

Home Page
**U.S. Architectural and Transportation
Barriers Compliance Board**
http://www.access-board.gov/

Home Page
National Capital Planning Commission
http://www.ncpc.gov/

Home Page
Commodity Futures Trading Commission
http://www.cftc.gov/cftc/cftchome.htm

Home Page
Federal Maritime Commission
http://www.fmc.gov/

Home Page
Federal Trade Commission
http://www.ftc.gov/

Home Page
Overseas Private Investment Corporation
http://www.opic.gov/Main.htm

Home Page
Tennessee Valley Authority
http://www.tva.gov/

Home Page
U.S. Agency for International Development
http://www.usaid.gov/

Home Page
U.S. Trade and Development Agency
http://www.tda.gov/

Home Page
**United States International Trade
Commission**
http://www.usitc.gov/

DataWeb
http://dataweb.usitc.gov/

Home Page
Federal Election Commission
http://www.fec.gov/

Home Page
Federal Emergency Management Agency
http://www.fema.gov/

> **Maps**
> http://www.fema.gov/maps.shtm

> **U.S. Fire Administration**
> http://www.usfa.fema.gov/

Home Page
**U.S. Equal Employment Opportunity
Commission**
http://www.eeoc.gov/

Home Page
Federal Energy Regulatory Commission
http://www.ferc.gov/

Home Page
Nuclear Regulatory Commission
http://www.nrc.gov/

Home Page
**U.S. Nuclear Waste Technical Review
Board**
http://www.nwtrb.gov/

Home Page
Environmental Protection Agency
http://www.epa.gov/

Global Warming Site
http://www.epa.gov/globalwarming/

Introduction to Laws and Regulations
http://www.epa.gov/epahome/
lawintro.htm

Home Page
**U.S. Chemical Safety and Hazard
Investigation Board**
http://www.chemsafety.gov/

Home Page
U.S. Global Change Research Program
http://www.usgcrp.gov/

Home Page
**Commission on Security and Cooperation
in Europe**
http://www.csce.gov/helsinki.cfm

Home Page
Federal Labor Relations Authority
http://www.flra.gov/

Home Page
**Federal Retirement Thrift Investment
Board**
http://www.frtib.gov/

Thrift Savings Plan
http://www.tsp.gov/

Home Page
Merit Systems Protection Board
http://www.mspb.gov/

Home Page
Office of Government Ethics
http://www.usoge.gov/

DAEOGRAMS
http://www.usoge.gov/pages/daeograms/
daeograms.html

Home Page
Office of Personnel Management
http://www.opm.gov/

Diversity Profiles
http://www.opm.gov/employ/diversity/
stats/profiles.htm

USJOBS
http://www.usajobs.opm.gov/

Home Page
Office of Special Counsel
http://www.osc.gov/

Home Page
National Indian Gaming Commission
http://www.nigc.gov/nigc/index/jsp

Home Page
Advisory Council on Historic Preservation
http://www.achp.gov/

Home Page
Federal Housing Finance Board
http://www.fhfb.gov/

Home Page
**Office of Federal Housing Enterprise
Oversight**
http://www.ofheo.gov/

House Price Index
http://www.ofheo.gov/house/

Home Page
National Endowment for the Arts
http://arts.endow.gov/

Home Page
National Endowment for the Humanities
http://www.neh.fed.us/

Home Page
Central Intelligence Agency
http://www.odci.gov/

Electronic Reading Room
http://www.foia.cia.gov/

Frequently Requested Records
http://www.foia.cia.gov/records.asp

Intelligence Community
http://www.intelligence.gov/
1-members.shtml
http://www.intelligence.gov/
1-definition.shtml

Related Links
http://www.odci.gov/cia/other_links/
other.html

Web Update Service
http://www.odci.gov/cia/update_
service.html

Home Page
National Labor Relations Board
http://www.nlrb.gov/

Home Page
Institute of Museum and Library Services
http://www.imls.gov/

Home Page
**National Commission on Libraries and
Information Science**
http://www.nclis.gov/index.cfm

Home Page
Smithsonian Institution
http://www.si.edu/

Museums
http://www.si.edu//museums

Research Centers
http://www.si.edu/research

Home Page
United States Holocaust Memorial Museum
http://www.ushmm.org/

Holocaust Learning Center
http://www.ushmm.org/wlc/en/

Home Page
National Institute for Literacy
http://novel.nifl.gov/

Home Page
General Services Administration
http://www.gsa.gov/Portal/home.jsp

**Federal Consumer Information
Center**
http://www.pueblo.gsa.gov/

Home Page
**National Archives and Records
Administration**
http://www.archives.gov/

Archival Research Catalog
http://www.archives.gov/research_room/
arc/index.html

Our Documents
http://www.ourdocuments.gov/

Electronic Records Archives
http://www.archives.gov/electronic_
records_archives/

**Electronic Records Management
Initiative**
http://www.archives.gov/records_
management/initiatives/erm_
overview.html

Information Security Oversight Office
http://www.archives.gov/isoo/

Holocaust-era Assets
http://www.archives.gov/research_room/
holocaust_era_assets/

JFK Assassination Records
http://www.archives.gov/research_room/
jfk/jfk_search.html

**National Historical Publications and
Records Commission**
http://www.archives.gov/grants/

Presidential Libraries (Listing)
http://www.archives.gov/presidential_
libraries/addresses/addresses.html

Presidential Records
http://www.archives.gov/presidential_
libraries/presidential_records/
presidential_records.html

**National Historical Publications and
Records Commission**
http://www.nara.gov/nhprc/grants/
index.html

Home Page
National Mediation Board
http://www.nmb.gov/

Home Page
American Battle Monuments Commission
http://www.abmc.gov/

Home Page
International Broadcasting Bureau
http://www.ibb.gov/

> **Voice of America**
> http://www.voa.gov/index.cfm

Home Page
Defense Nuclear Facilities Safety Board
http://www.dnfsb.gov/

Home Page
Pension Benefit Guaranty Corporation
http://www.pbgc.gov/

Home Page
Peace Corps
http://peacecorps.gov/index.cfm

Home Page
Postal Rate Commission
http://www.prc.gov/

Home Page
United States Postal Service
http://www.usps.com

Home Page
National Railroad Passenger Corporation
http://www.amtrak.com/

Home Page
Railroad Retirement Board
http://www.rrb.gov/

Home Page
National Science Foundation
http://www.nsf.gov/

> **Publications Index**
> http://www.nsf.gov/pubsys/

Home Page
Securities and Exchange Commission
http://www.sec.gov/

> **EDGAR**
> http://www.sec.gov/edgar.shtml

> *SEC News Digest*
> http://www.sec.gov/news/digest.shtml

Home Page
Selective Service System
http://www.sss.gov/

Home Page
Small Business Administration
http://www.sbaonline.sba.gov/

> **Outside Resources and Great Business Hotlinks**
> http://www.sbaonline.sba.gov/hotlist/

> **Pro-Net**
> http://pro-net.sba.gov/index2.html

Home Page
Social Security Administration
http://www.ssa.gov/SSA_Home.html

> **Top Ten Services**
> http://www.ssa.gov/top10.html

> **Office of Policy**
> http://www.ssa.gov/policy/

> **Office of the Chief Actuary**
> http://www.ssa.gov/OACT

Home Page
National Transportation Safety Board
http://www.ntsb.gov/

Home Page
Occupational Safety and Health Review Commission
http://www.oshrc.gov/

Home Page
Japan-US Friendship Commission
http://www.jusfc.gov/commissn/commissn.html

Home Page
Peace Corps
http://www.peacecorps.gov/index.cfm

Home Page
United States Commission on International Religious Freedom
http://www.uscirf.gov/index.php3?SID=a5eof61f6297ece5a001293abc75e250

Home Page
United States Institute of Peace
http://www.usip.org/

Home Page
**Federal Financial Institutions Examination
Council**
http://www.ffiec.gov/

Community Reinvestment Act
http://www.ffiec.gov/cra/

**U.S. Federal Government Agencies
Directory**
Louisiana State University
http://www.lib.lsu.edu/gov/fedgov.html

Chapter  7

Judiciary Branch

As explained in *Understanding the Federal Courts,*

 the powers of the U.S. courts are limited first to the powers granted to the federal government by the U.S. Constitution and second to judicial powers. . . . Judicial powers and judicial work involve the application and interpretation of the law in the decision of real differences; that is, in the language of the Constitution, the decision of cases and controversies. The courts cannot be called upon to make laws, which is the function of the legislative branch, or be expected to enforce and execute laws, which is the function of the executive branch.[1]

Although each jurisdiction has its own system of court organization, the typical organization at both the federal and state levels is a trial court and appellate court. Although that structure has changed over time, the Supreme Court is at the top level. At the level below are the intermediate appellate courts (the courts of appeals), which are lower than the Supreme Court but higher than the district courts.

The U.S. Court of Appeals for the Federal Circuit considers appeals in cases from the United States Court of International Trade, the United States Court of Federal Claims, and the U.S. Court of Veterans Affairs, as well as from the International Trade Commission, the Board of Contract Appeals, the Patent and Trademark Office, and the Merit Systems Protection Board. The court also "hears appeals from certain decisions of the secretaries of the Department of Agriculture and the Department of Commerce, and cases from district courts involving patents and minor claims against the federal government."[2]

At the bottom level, there are district courts and specialized courts. "Most federal cases are initially tried and decided in the U.S. district courts of general trial jurisdiction."[3] Each district court "has a bankruptcy unit that hears and decides petitions of individuals and businesses seeking relief from bankruptcy."[4] Regarding the specialized courts, the

- United States Court of International Trade deals with cases involving international trade and customs' duties. Its Web site (**http://www.cit.uscourts.gov/**) offers a calendar, a directory, employment opportunities, the judges, Office of the Clerk, rules and forms, a site map, Case Management/Electronic Cases File (CM/ECF), "What's New," slip opinions, and other resources.

- United States Court of Federal Claims "has nationwide jurisdiction over a variety of cases, including tax refunds, federal taking of private property for public use, constitutional and statutory rights of military personnel and their dependents, back-pay demands from civil servants claiming unjust dismissal, persons injured by childhood vaccines, and federal government contractors suing for breach of contract. Most suits against the government for money damages in excess of $10,000 must be tried here."[5] The Web site (**http://www.uscfc.uscourts.gov/**) includes a welcome, announcements, opinions, "WINSTAR" (published decisions), rules, biographies, bar information, history of the Court, general orders, forms, and Office of the Special Masters.

Other specialized courts include the following:

- United States Court of Appeals for the Armed Forces, which deals with questions of law arising from trials by court martial in the armed services in which the death sentence is imposed. The court also has worldwide jurisdiction in cases certified for review by the Judge Advocate General or cases in which the accused facing a severe sentence petitions the Court and shows good cause for further review. (The U.S. Court of Military Appeals was created in 1951 and, in 1994, renamed the United States Court of Appeals for the Armed Services). The home page (**http://www.armfor.uscourts.gov/**) covers the establishment and its history, jurisdiction, judges, opinions and digest, *Daily Journal*, annual reports, scheduled hearings, court rules, bar, Judicial Conference, Clerk's Office, Library, and links to other Web sites.

- United States Court of Appeals for Veterans Claims, which has "exclusive jurisdiction over the decisions of the Board of Veterans' Appeals on the motion of claimants. Such cases include all types of veterans' and survivors' benefits, mainly disability benefits, and also loan eligibility and educational benefits."[6] The home page (**http://www.vetapp.uscourts.gov/**) provides information about the court (e.g., facts and annual reports), court rules and procedures, a public list of practitioners, stay order, forms and fees, case dockets, decisions and opinions, a calendar, career opportunities, news and announcements, and so on.

- United States Tax Court, which decides "controversies between taxpayers and the Internal Revenue Service involving underpayment of federal income, gift, and estate taxes."[7] The home page (**http://www.ustaxcourt.gov/ustcweb.htm**) covers opinions (today's and historical), press releases, forms, docket inquiry, frequently asked questions, rules, phone numbers, and fees and charges.

To summarize, the federal district courts are the trial courts. Generally, the facts of the case give rise to an issue that is based on a legal rule or principle. When a case is appealed it is not, in fact, retried. The federal appellate court only decides questions of law, and its opinion is based on the trial transcript from below. The trial court is where the parties appear and the evidence is presented.

COURT PRESENCE ON THE WEB

Although more courts are developing Web sites and placing assorted information resources there, their administrative agencies, together with law schools, the media, and the not-for-profit and for-profit sectors still perform an essential role in access to court information and publications. Through Project Hermes, named after the ancient Greek messenger of the gods, the Supreme Court transmits electronically the text of its decisions within eight hours of their release for inclusion on the Federal Bulletin Board (FBB) and availability to a consortium of information-providing organizations using the Web.[8] Access to court decisions, as a consequence, is available from a variety of consortium channels. For an list of court opinion publishers that is updated annually, see the .pdf document "Where to Find Supreme Court Opinions" (**http://www.supremecourtus.gov/opinions/opinions.pdf**). This list covers print and electronic sources, both official and unofficial.

The main value of the Web's coverage of the judiciary is that a court provides information about itself, doing business with it, and its products (decisions and opinions). There also might be useful information about the judges, as well as miscellaneous publications. If someone did not know the jurisdiction of a case and wanted to conduct a general search or a subject search, however, similar to what that person could do using FirstGov (see Chapter 3), government sites would not be helpful. Rather, that person would be more likely to turn to WESTLAW and other products. It is outside the scope of this book to present the complex, vast array of print and other general reference and research aids for monitoring various facets of the legal system, including WESTLAW (subscribers: **http://www.westlaw.com**) and LEXIS-NEXIS (subscribers: **http://www.lexis.com/xchange**).

ELECTRONIC PUBLIC ACCESS SERVICES

The Administrative Office of the U.S. Courts operates the PACER Service Center, which is "The Federal Judiciary's centralized registration, billing, and technical support center for electronic access to U.S. District, Bankruptcy, and Appellate court records." At **http://pacer.psc.uscourts.gov/**, there is an overview of PACER (Public Access to Court Electronic Records), an opportunity to register for the service, "Links to PACER Web Sites," "Account Information," "PACER Documents." "What's New," announcements, and frequently asked questions. There is also a link to the *U.S. Party/Case Index*, which is a national index for U.S. district, bankruptcy, and appellate courts. This index allows searchers to determine whether or not a party is involved in federal litigation almost anywhere in the nation. The *U.S. Party/Case Index* provides the capability to perform national or regional searches on party name and social security number in the bankruptcy index, party name and nature of suit in the civil index, and party name in the criminal and appellate indices. A search will provide a list of case numbers, filing locations, and filing dates for those cases matching the search criteria.

The PACER Service Center's Web-PACER Training Site is a "demonstration and training site for PACER Web applications": "you may use this site to become familiar with the appellate, district, and bankruptcy applications" (**http://pacer.psc.uscourts.gov/announcements/general/pacer_train.html**).

For other information about electronic access to the courts, see **http://www. uscourts.gov/electaccrt.html**. This page explains public access fees and provides access to the "Judiciary Privacy Policy Page" (**http://www.privacy.uscourts.gov/**, solicits comments on proposed policy options on privacy and public access to electronic case files, and provides the actual policy, "News Releases," "Recent Additions," and the "Case Management/Electronic Case Files" (CM/ECF), which applies to the U.S. Court of International Trade (see **http://www.cit.uscourts.gov/cmecf/ cm-ecf.htm**). For any other services provided by the judiciary, see the home page of a particular court.

THE U.S. FEDERAL COURTS

Figure 7.1 illustrates the structure of the federal judiciary, with the Supreme Court at the top and other entities falling below it.

Figure 7.1. The United States Federal Courts.

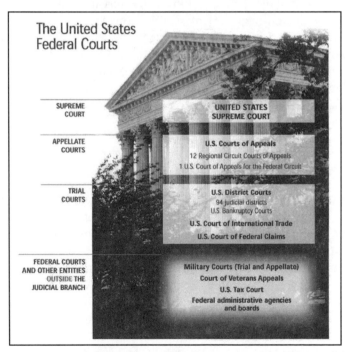

Source: The Federal Judiciary Website: Source: **http://www.uscourts.gov/outreach/structure.jpg**

Supreme Court

The Supreme Court consists of the chief justice of the United States and eight associate justices. At its Web site (**http://www.supremecourtus.gov/**), the Supreme Court provides a site search and icons for "About the Supreme Court," "Docket," "Oral Arguments," "Bar Admissions," "Court Rules," "Case Handling Guides," "Opinions," "Orders and Journal" (the Journal "contains the official minutes of the

Court"), "Visiting the Court," "Public Information," and "Related Websites." "About the Supreme Court," for instance, includes a brief overview of the Court, "The Justice's Caseload," "The Court and Constitutional Interpretation," "Biographies of Current Members of the Supreme Court, Members of the Supreme Court (1789 to Present)," "Circuit Assignments of Justices," "The Court and Its Traditions," and "The Court as an Institution."

"Opinions" (**http://www.supremecourts.gov/opinions/opinions.html**) includes those issued since 2000, sliplists, a counsel listing, "Where to Obtain Supreme Court Opinions," and other resources. Some of these listings even discuss the importance of paper products as the source of record. For information on the Supreme Court Fellows Program, see **http://www.fellows.supremcourtus.gov/**.

Appellate Courts

Figure 7.2, taken from the Federal Judiciary home page, displays a map of the United States that divides the states into circuits. The ninety-four U.S. judicial districts are organized into twelve regional circuits, each of which has a U.S. court of appeals:

Figure 7.2. Court Links (Appellate and Trial Courts).

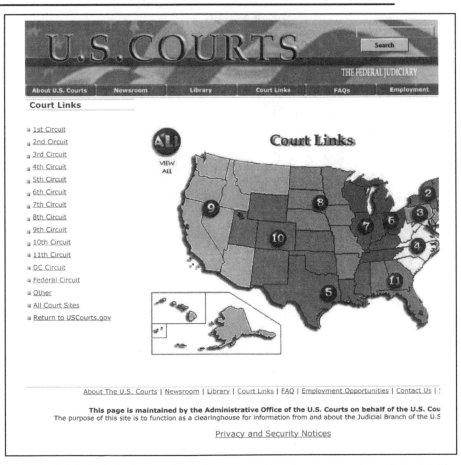

Source: "Links" (the Federal Judiciary home page, **http://www.uscourts.gov/links.html**).

A court of appeals hears appeals from the district courts located within its circuit, as well as appeals from decisions of federal administrative agencies. In addition, the Court of Appeals for the Federal Circuit has nationwide jurisdiction to hear appeals in specialized cases, such as those involving patent laws and cases decided by the Court of International Trade and the Court of Federal Claims. (**http://www.uscourts.gov/courtsofappeals.html**)

By clicking on the appropriate state, the information seeker is connected to the appropriate courts (appellate, district, and bankruptcy court). For a specific appellate court, see the following:

- First U.S. Circuit (**http://www.ca1.uscourts.gov/**): party/case/index, local rules, court procedures and guidelines, forms, and opinions

- Second U.S. Circuit (**http://www.ca2.uscourts.gov/**): site search, speeches, general information, legal job postings, information about the judges and about oral argument from remote video-argument centers, decisions, court information, other search engines, Federal Court Index (which provides a link to all appellate courts), and so on

- Third U.S. Circuit (**http://www.ca3.uscourts.gov/**): death penalty information, opinions and dockets, rules and procedures, information and forms, frequently asked questions, other resources (e.g., links to other sites), task force reports, online chambers, and mediation

- Fourth U.S. Circuit (**http://www.ca4.uscourts.gov/**): information, opinions, docket information, mediation, argument calendar, rules and procedures, forms and notices, cases of public interest, and court links

- Fifth U.S. Circuit (**http://www.ca5.uscourts.gov/**): opinions (published opinion search), event notification registration, docket information, Clerk's Office, position vacancies, status of "CJA [*Criminal Justice Act*] vouchers," court calendars, forms, judges' biographies, a site map, court links, calendars, and so on. The University of Texas maintains a page for the Fifth U.S. Circuit (**http://www.law.utexas.edu/us5th/us5th.html**) that provides opinions (1992 to the present) and other information

- Sixth U.S. Circuit (**http://www.ca6.uscourts.gov/**): court information, local rules, opinions, notices and forms, circuit executive (e.g., procedures for jury selection), and court links

- Seventh U.S. Circuit (**http://www.ca7.uscourts.gov/**): case information calendar, rules and guides, forms, CJA information, court news, contact information, and more

- Eighth U.S. Circuit (**http://www.ca8.uscourts.gov/index.html**): today's opinions, a directory, case information, calendars, court rules, "One Stop Search" ("allows you to access all documents available for a case from a single page"), and so on

- Ninth U.S. Circuit (**http://www.ca9.uscourts.gov/**): mission, court information, calendar, documents, frequently asked questions, employment opportunities, court links, news, and orders

- Tenth U.S. Circuit (**http://www.ck10.uscourts.gov/**): attorney admissions, Appellate Bulletin Board Service, bankruptcy appellate panel, clerk's office mission and vision statements, court calendar, career opportunities, general information and fee schedule, court judges, presenting videoconferenced arguments, published opinions, Tenth Circuit Courts, Tenth Circuit Judicial Conference, rules and forms, a travel guide, and more

- Tenth U.S. Circuit (Hugh F. Macmillan Law Library of Emory University School of Law; **http://www.law.emory.edu/10circuit**): decisions (August 1995–October 1997)

- Eleventh U.S. Circuit (**http://www.ca11.uscourts.gov/**): opinions and rules, about the court, documents, court officials, human resources, related and "most requested" links, and more

- District of Columbia Circuit (**http://www.cadc.uscourts.gov/**): forms, news and information, job vacancies, case information, opinions, rules and procedures, calendar and courtroom, court offices, judge's library, news and announcements, selected documents, an oral argument calendar, contacts, links, news, a site map, and so on

The U.S. Court of Appeals for the Federal Circuit (**http://www.fedcir.gov/**) offers rules and internal operating procedures, court calendar and dispositions, opinions and decisions, employment information, a search of the site, directories, rules and forms, information and statistics, and so on. Since August 1995, the Emory University Courts Publishing Project (**http://www.law.emory.edu/fedcircuit/**) and the Edward Bennett Williams Law Library, Georgetown University Law School (**http://www. ll.georgetown.edu/Fed-Ct/cafed.html**) have provided searchable sites for circuit court opinions.

Office of the Circuit Executive: United States Courts for the Ninth Circuit. "The Ninth Circuit, the largest of the 13 federal circuits, includes all federal courts in California, Oregon, Washington, Arizona, Montana, Idaho, Nevada, Alaska, Hawaii, Guam and the Northern Mariana Islands." The Office of the Chief Executive maintains a home page (**http://www.ce9.uscourts.gov/**) that provides publications and resources, news, court restructuring issues, resources, frequently asked questions, information on the judges, manuals (e.g., one on jury trial procedures), links to other sites, "contact us," circuit opinions, and so on.

Trial Courts

The home pages for the district courts, most typically, contain information about the court, jury information, and resources such as dockets, opinions, fee schedules, forms, and rules. The U.S. District Court, Eastern District of Pennsylvania, is unique in offering a "Frames Version." It also takes "standing orders" and offers microfiche reports, access to a video teleconferencing pilot program, and other services (see **http://www.paed.uscourts.gov/**). Following is a list of the sites (again, these are also available in Figure 7.2):

- **First Circuit**

  Maine District Court (**http://www.med.uscourts.gov/**)

Massachusetts District Court (**http://www.mad.uscourts.gov/**)

New Hampshire District Court (**http://www.nhd.uscourts.gov/**)

Puerto Rico District Court (**http://www.prd.uscourts.gov/**)

Rhode Island (**http://www.rid.uscourts.gov/USDCPR/home.htm**)

- **Second Circuit**

  Connecticut District Court (**http://www.ctd.uscourts.gov/**)

  New York Eastern District Court (**http://www.nyed.uscourts.gov/**)

  New York Northern District Court (**http://www.nynd.uscourts.gov/**)

  New York Southern District Court (**http://www.nysd.uscourts.gov/**)

  New York Western District Court (**http://www.nywd.uscourts.gov/**)

  Vermont District Court (**http://www.vtd.uscourts.gov/**)

- **Third Circuit**

  Delaware District Court (**http://www.ded.uscourts.gov/**)

  New Jersey District Court (**http://pacer.njd.uscourts.gov/**)

  Pennsylvania Eastern District Court (**http://www.paed.uscourts.gov/**)

  Pennsylvania Middle District Court (**http://www.pamd.uscourts.gov/**)

  Pennsylvania Western District Court (**http://www.pawd.uscourts.gov/**)

  Virgin Islands District Court (**http://www.vid.uscourts.gov/**)

- **Fourth Circuit**

  Maryland District Court (**http://www.mdd.uscourts.gov/**)

  North Carolina Eastern District Court (**http://www.nced.uscourts.gov/**)

  North Carolina Middle District Court (**http://www.ncmd.uscourts.gov/**)

  North Carolina Western District Court (**http://www.ncwd.uscourts.gov/**)

  South Carolina District Court (**http://www.scd.uscourts.gov/**)

  Virginia Eastern District Court (**http://www.vaed.uscourts.gov/**)

  Virginia Western District Court (**http://www.vawd.uscourts.gov/**)

  West Virginia Northern District Court (**http://www.wvnd.uscourts.gov/**)

  West Virginia Southern District Court (**http://www.wvsd.uscourts.gov/**)

- **Fifth Circuit**

  Louisiana Eastern District Court (**http://www.laed.uscourts.gov/**)

  Louisiana Middle District Court (**http://www.lamd.uscourts.gov/**)

  Louisiana Western District Court (**http://www.lawd.uscourts.gov/**)

Mississippi Northern District Court (**http://www.msnd.uscourts.gov/**)

Mississippi Southern District Court (**http://www.mssd.uscourts.gov/**)

Texas Eastern District Court (**http://www.txed.uscourts.gov/**)

Texas Northern District Court (**http://www.txnd.uscourts.gov/**)

Texas Southern District Court (**http://www.txs.uscourts.gov/**)

Texas Western District Court (**http://www.txwd.uscourts.gov/**)

- **Sixth Circuit**

  Kentucky Eastern District Court (**http://www.kyed.uscourts.gov/**)

  Kentucky Western District Court (**http://www.kywd.uscourts.gov/**)

  Michigan Eastern District Court (**http://www.mied.uscourts.gov/index.html**)

  Michigan Western District Court (**http://www.miwd.uscourts.gov/**)

  Ohio Northern District Court (**http://www.ohnd.uscourts.gov/**)

  Ohio Southern District Court (**http://www.ohsd.uscourts.gov/**)

  Tennessee Eastern District Court (**http://www.tned.uscourts.gov/**)

  Tennessee Middle District Court (**http://www.tnmd.uscourts.gov/**)

  Tennessee Western District Court (**http://www.tnwd.uscourts.gov/**)

- **Seventh Circuit**

  Illinois Central District Court (**http://www.ilcd.uscourts.gov/**)

  Illinois Northern District Court (**http://www.ilnd.uscourts.gov/**)

  Illinois Southern District Court (**http://www.ilsd.uscourts.gov/**)

  Indiana Northern District Court (**http://www.innd.uscourts.gov/**)

  Indiana Southern District Court (**http://www.insd.uscourts.gov/**)

  Wisconsin Eastern District Court (**http://www.wied.uscourts.gov/**)

  Wisconsin Western District Court (**http://www.wiw.uscourts.gov/**)

- **Eighth Circuit**

  Arkansas Eastern District Court (**http://www.are.uscourts.gov/**)

  Arkansas Western District Court (**http://www.arwd.uscourts.gov/**)

  Iowa Northern District Court (**http://www.iand.uscourts.gov/**)

  Iowa Southern District Court (**http://www.iasd.uscourts.gov/**)

  Minnesota District Court (**http://www.mnd.uscourts.gov/**)

  Missouri Eastern District Court (**http://www.moed.uscourts.gov/**)

  Missouri Western District Court (**http://www.mow.uscourts.gov/**)

Nebraska District Court (http://www.ned.uscourts.gov/)

North Dakota District Court (http://www.ndd.uscourts.gov/

South Dakota District Court (http://www.sdd.uscourts.gov/)

- **Ninth Circuit**

    Alaska District Court (http://www.akd.uscourts.gov/)

    Arizona District Court (http://www.azd.uscourts.gov/)

    California Central District Court (http://www.cacd.uscourts.gov/)

    California Eastern District Court (http://www.caed.uscourts.gov/)

    California Northern District Court (http://www.cand.uscourts.gov/)

    California Southern District Court (http://www.casd.uscourts.gov/)

    Guam District Court (http://www.gud.uscourts.gov/)

    Hawaii District Court (http://www.hid.uscourts.gov/)

    Idaho District Court (http://www.id.uscourts.gov/)

    Montana District Court (http://www.mtd.uscourts.gov/)

    Nevada District Court (http://www.nvd.uscourts.gov/)

    Northern Mariana Island District Court (http://www.nmid.uscourts.gov/)

    Oregon District Court (http://www.ord.uscourts.gov/)

    Washington Eastern District Court (http://www.waed.uscourts.gov/)

    Washington Western District Court (http://www.wawd.uscourts.gov/)

- **Tenth Circuit**

    Colorado District Court (http://www.co.uscourts.gov/dindex.htm; http://www.co.uscourts.gov/)

    Kansas District Court (http://www.ksd.uscourts.gov/)

    New Mexico District Court (http://www.nmcourt.fed.us/dcdocs/)

    Oklahoma Eastern District Court (http://www.oked.uscourts.gov/)

    Oklahoma Northern District Court (http://www.oknd.uscourts.gov/)

    Oklahoma Western District Court (http://www.okwd.uscourts.gov/)

    Utah District Court (http://www.utd.uscourts.gov/)

    Wyoming District Court (http://www.ck10.uscourts.gov/wyoming/district/index.html)

- **Eleventh Circuit**

    Alabama Middle District Court (http://www.almd.uscourts.gov/)

Alabama Northern District Court (**http://www.alnd.uscourts.gov/**)

Alabama Southern District Court (**http://www.als.uscourts.gov/page.cfm?page=1**)

Florida Middle District Court (**http://www.flmd.uscourts.gov/**)

Florida Northern District Court (**http://www.flnd.uscourts.gov/**)

Florida Southern District Court (**http://www.flsd.uscourts.gov/**)

Georgia Middle District Court (**http://www.gamd.uscourts.gov/**)

Georgia Northern District Court (**http://www.gand.uscourts.gov/**)

Georgia Southern District Court (**http://www.gasd.uscourts.gov/**)

- District of Columbia Circuit Court (District Court) (**http://www.dcd.uscourts.gov/**)

Federal District-Court Civil Trials. The Web page for Federal District-Court Civil Trials (**http://teddy.law.cornell.edu:8090/questtr2.htm**) maintains "a database of about 3.7 million federal district-court civil cases terminated over the last 17 fiscal years. The data were gathered by the Administrative Office of the United States Courts, assembled by the Federal Judicial Center, and disseminated by the Inter-university Consortium for Political and Social Research."

With the data set, anyone can compile statistics on federal civil cases by

- Specified categories (e.g., 140 negotiable instruments, 110 insurance, or 152 recovery of defaulted student loans)

- Jurisdictional basis

- Amount demanded

- "Case's origin in the district as original or removed or transferred"

- Dates of filing and termination in the district

- "Procedural stage of the case at termination (including whether it was tried by a judge or jury)"

- "Procedural method of disposition"

- "When a judgment was entered, who prevailed, and any amount awarded in damages or other relief"

Bankruptcy Courts. On the Web, the bankruptcy courts might provide, for example, case information, rules, fee instructions, forms, general information, and general information. Following is a list of home pages for those courts that have Web sites:
- **First Circuit**

Maine Bankruptcy Court (**http://www.meb.uscourts.gov/**)

Massachusetts Bankruptcy Court (**http://www.mab.uscourts.gov/**)

New Hampshire Bankruptcy Court (**http://www.nhb.uscourts.gov/**)

Puerto Rico Bankruptcy Court (**http://www.prb.uscourts.gov/**)

Rhode Island Bankruptcy Court (**http://www.rib.uscourts.gov/**)

- **Second Circuit**

  Connecticut Bankruptcy Court (**http://www.ctb.uscourts.gov/**)

  New York Eastern Bankruptcy Court (**http://www.nyeb.uscourts.gov/**)

  New York Northern Bankruptcy Court (**http://www.nynb.uscourts.gov/**)

  New York Southern Bankruptcy Court (**http://www.nysb.uscourts.gov/**)

  New York Western Bankruptcy Court (**http://www.nywb.uscourts.gov/**)

  Vermont Bankruptcy Court (**http://www.vtb.uscourts.gov/**)

- **Third Circuit**

  Delaware Bankruptcy Court (**http://www.deb.uscourts.gov/**)

  New Jersey Bankruptcy Court (**http://www.njb.uscourts.gov/**)

  Pennsylvania Eastern Bankruptcy Court (**http://www.paeb.uscourts.gov/**)

  Pennsylvania Middle Bankruptcy Court (**http://www.pamb.uscourts.gov/**)

  Pennsylvania Western Bankruptcy Court (**http://www.pawb.uscourts.gov/**)

- **Fourth Circuit**

  Maryland Bankruptcy Court (**http://www.mdb.uscourts.gov/default.asp**)

  North Carolina Eastern Bankruptcy Court (**http://www.nceb.uscourts.gov/**)

  North Carolina Middle Bankruptcy Court (**http://www.ncmb.uscourts.gov/**)

  North Carolina Western Bankruptcy Court (**http://www.ncwb.uscourts.gov/**)

  South Carolina Bankruptcy Court (**http://www.scb.uscourts.gov/**)

  Virginia Eastern Bankruptcy Court (**http://www.vaeb.uscourts.gov/**)

  Virginia Western Bankruptcy Court (**http://www.vawb.uscourts.gov/courtweb/enter1.html**)

  West Virginia Northern Bankruptcy Court (**http://www.wvnb.uscourts.gov/**)

  West Virginia Southern Bankruptcy Court (**http://www.wvsb.uscourts.gov/bakruptcy/index.htm**)

- **Fifth Circuit**

  Louisiana Eastern Bankruptcy Court (**http://www.laeb.uscourts.gov/**)

  Louisiana Middle Bankruptcy Court (**http://www.lamb.uscourts.gov/**)

  Louisiana Western Bankruptcy Court (**http://www.lawb.uscourts.gov/**)

  Mississippi Northern Bankruptcy Court (**http://www.msnb.uscourts.gov/**)

  Mississippi Southern Bankruptcy Court (**http://www.mssb.uscourts.gov/**)

  Texas Eastern Bankruptcy Court (**http://www.txeb.uscourts.gov/**)

Texas Northern Bankruptcy Court (**http://www.txnb.uscourts.gov/index.jsp**)

Texas Southern Bankruptcy Court (**http://www.txs.uscourts.gov/**)

Texas Western Bankruptcy Court (**http://www.txwb.uscourts.gov/**)

- **Sixth Circuit**

  Kentucky Eastern Bankruptcy Court (**http://www.kyeb.uscourts.gov/**)

  Kentucky Western Bankruptcy Court (**http://www.kywb.uscourts.gov/ fpweb/**)

  Michigan Eastern Bankruptcy Court (**http://www.mieb.uscourts.gov/**)

  Michigan Western Bankruptcy Court (**http://www.miwb.uscourts.gov/**)

  Ohio Northern Bankruptcy Court (**http://www.ohnb.uscourts.gov/**)

  Ohio Southern Bankruptcy Court (**http://www.ohsb.uscourts.gov/**)

  Tennessee Eastern Bankruptcy Court (**http://www.tneb.uscourts.gov/**)

  Tennessee Middle Bankruptcy Court (**http://www.tnmb.uscourts.gov/**)

  Tennessee Western Bankruptcy Court (**http://www.tnwb.uscourts.gov/**)

- **Seventh Circuit**

  Illinois Central Bankruptcy Court (**http://www.ilcb.uscourts.gov/**)

  Illinois Northern Bankruptcy Court (**http://www.ilnb.uscourts.gov/**)

  Illinois Southern Bankruptcy Court (**http://www.ilsb.uscourts.gov/**)

  Indiana Northern Bankruptcy Court (**http://www.innb.uscourts.gov/**)

  Indiana Southern Bankruptcy Court (**http://www.insb.uscourts.gov/**)

  Wisconsin Eastern Bankruptcy Court (**http://www.wieb.uscourts.gov/**)

  Wisconsin Western Bankruptcy Court (**http://www.wiw.uscourts.gov/ bankruptcy/**)

- **Eighth Circuit**

  Arkansas Eastern and Western Bankruptcy Court (**http://www.arb. uscourts.gov/**)

  Iowa Northern Bankruptcy Court (**http://www.ianb.uscourt.gov/**)

  Iowa Southern Bankruptcy Court (**http://www.iasb.uscourts.gov/ webpages/home/default.asp**)

  Minnesota Bankruptcy Court (**http://www.mnb.uscourts.gov/**)

  Missouri Eastern Bankruptcy Court (**http://www.moeb.uscourts.gov/**)

  Missouri Western Bankruptcy Court (**http://www.mow.uscourts.gov/**)

  Nebraska Bankruptcy Court (**http://www.neb.uscourts.gov/**)

North Dakota Bankruptcy Court (**http://www.ndb.uscourts.gov/**)

South Dakota Bankruptcy Court (**http://www.sdb.uscourts.gov/**)

• **Ninth Circuit**

Alaska Bankruptcy Court (**http://www.akb.uscourts.gov/**)

Arizona Bankruptcy Court (**http://www.azb.uscourt.gov/**)

California Central Bankruptcy Court (**http://www.cacb.uscourts.gov/**)

California Eastern Bankruptcy Court (**http://www.cacb.uscourts.gov/**)

California Northern Bankruptcy Court (**http://www.canb.uscourts.gov/**)

California Southern Bankruptcy Court (**http://www.casb.uscourts.gov/**)

Hawaii Bankruptcy Court (**http://www.hib.uscourts.gov/**)

Idaho Bankruptcy Court (**http://www.id.uscourts.gov/**)

Montana Bankruptcy Court (**http://www.mtb.uscourts.gov/**)

Nevada Bankruptcy Court (**http://www.nvb.uscourts.gov/**)

Oregon Bankruptcy Court (**http://www.orb.uscourts.gov/**)

Washington Eastern Bankruptcy Court (**http://www.waeb.uscourts.gov/**)

Washington Western Bankruptcy Court (**http://www.wawb.uscourts.gov/**)

• **Tenth Circuit**

Colorado Bankruptcy Court (**http://www.cob.uscourts.gov/bindex.htm**)

Kansas Bankruptcy Court (**http://www.ksb.uscourts.gov/**)

New Mexico Bankruptcy Court (**http://www.nwcourts.fed.us/bkdocs/**)

Oklahoma Eastern Bankruptcy Court (**http://www.okeb.uscourts.gov/**)

Oklahoma Northern Bankruptcy Court (**http://www.oknb.uscourts.gov/**)

Utah Bankruptcy Court (**http://www.utb.uscourts.gov/**)

Wyoming Bankruptcy Court (**http://www.wyb.uscourts.gov/**)

• **Eleventh Circuit**

Alabama Middle Bankruptcy Court (**http://www.almb.uscourts.gov/**)

Alabama Northern Bankruptcy Court (**http://www.alnb.uscourts.gov/**)

Alabama Southern Bankruptcy Court (**http://www.alsb.uscourts.gov/**)

Florida Middle District Court (**http://www.flmb.uscourts.gov/**)

Florida Northern District Court (**http://www.flnb.uscourts.gov/**)

Florida Southern District Court (**http://www.flsb.uscourts.gov/**)

Georgia Middle District Court (**http://www.gamb.uscourts.gov/wwwgamb/**)

Georgia Northern District Court (**http://www.ganb.uscourts.gov/**)

Georgia Southern District Court (**http://www.gasb.uscourts.gov/**)

• District of Columbia Circuit (Bankruptcy Court; **http://www.dcb.uscourts.gov/**)

American Bankruptcy Institute. The American Bankruptcy Institute (**http://www.abiworld.org**) has an extensive collection of bankruptcy court decisions sorted by state (see the site map). It is also possible to conduct a general search for bankruptcy opinions.

Pretrial Services and Probation Courts. The court links available through Figure 7.2 identify some pretrial services and probation courts on the Web. However, some of these are under construction and, for others, the link did not result in a connection. Nonetheless, some of those services and courts have an online presence.

First, in the First Circuit, the home page of the Puerto Rico Pretrial Services Office (**http://www.prpt.uscourts.gov/home.htm**) offers general information, an office directory, special projects, related sites, and "Meet Puerto Rico." In the Third Circuit, the Pretrial Services Agency for the District of New Jersey (**http://www.njpt.uscourts.gov/**) provides information about itself, employment, internships, and so on. In the Fourth Circuit, the page of the Virginia Eastern Pretrial Services Office (**http://www.vaept.uscourts.gov/**) introduces the agency, and the page for the West Virginia Southern Probation Office (**http://www.wvsd.uscourts.gov/probation/index.html**) provides office and personnel information, and a record check directory. In the Fifth Circuit, the Web sites of the Louisiana Eastern Pretrial Services Office (**http://www.laept.uscourts.gov/**) and the Texas Eastern Probation Office (**http://www.txep.uscourts.gov/**) introduce the agencies.

In the Sixth Circuit, the page of the Ohio Southern Probation Office (**http://www.ohsp.uscourts.gov/**) covers local rules, student programs, application for federal employment, job vacancies, and a monthly supervision report. In the Seventh Circuit, the home page of the U.S. Probation Office and Pretrial Services for the Northern District of Indiana (**http://www.innp.uscourts.gov/**) has office locations, documents, court links, "defendant" frequently asked questions, an employment listing, and information about both pretrial services and the court. At **http://www.insp.uscourts.gov/**, the probation office has a map, list of officers, special instructions for other offices, pretrial services reporting instructions, and so on. The Probation Office for the Southern District of Illinois (**http://www.ilsd.uscourts.gov/uspo/default.html**) provides maps, general information, reporting instructions, employment opportunities, and court related Web sites. The Wisconsin Western Probation Office has a page (**http://www.wiw.uscourts.gov/agencies.htm**) that covers "What's New," court offices, about the agency, PACER, related sites, and so on.

In the Eighth Circuit, the page of the Pretrial Services for the Eastern District of Missouri (**http://www.moept.uscourts.gov/**) has general information, documents, frequently asked questions, locations, a jobs listing, a telephone list, and links to other Web sites. The page of the Missouri Eastern Probation Office (**http://www.moep.uscourts.gov/**) covers general information, investigation documents, job listings, supervision documents, frequently asked questions, locations, orientation to the supervision manual, a telephone list, and links to related Web sites.

In the Ninth Circuit, the page of Probation Office of California's Eastern District (**http://www.caep.uscourts.gov/**) provides "What's New," "Information about Us," "Photos," and "Related Links." The Probation Office for the Southern District of California has a simple home page that identifies its locations, hours of operation, and chief probation officer (**http://www.caqsp.uscourts.gov/home.html**). Finally, in the Tenth Circuit, the page of the New Mexico Pretrial Services (**http://www.nmcourt. fed.us/ptdocs/**) identifies the offices statewide and employment opportunities, briefly discusses the agency, and highlights the city of Albuquerque. The home page of the New Mexico Probation Office (**http://www.nmcourt.fed.us/pbdocs/**) provides a mission statement, history of the office, related links, and an opportunity to give "Feedback" to the Office.

⬈ Military Courts

As discussed at the beginning of the chapter, the United States Court of Appeals for the Armed Forces has a Web site (**http://www.armfor.uscourts.gov/**) that provides assorted information, including information about the Judicial Conference of the United States Court of Appeals for the Armed Forces, which "is an annual conference for all judges and practitioners, military and civilian, with an interest in the military justice system." Its Web site (**http://www.armfor.uscourts.gov/ConfPage.htm**) provides a schedule of events.

ADMINISTRATION OF THE U.S. COURTS

"In addition to the courts themselves, the judicial branch . . . includes several bodies that provide for its administration and self-government."[9] These include the

- Judicial Conference of the United States: Created in 1922, the conference is composed of the Chief Justice of the United States and twenty-six other federal judges. It "meets twice yearly to consider policy issues affecting the federal courts, to make recommendations to Congress on legislation affecting the judicial system, to propose amendments to the federal rules of practice and procedure, and to consider the administrative problems of the courts."[10]

- Administrative Office of the United States Courts: Established in 1939, the agency provides "administrative support, program management, and policy development. It is charged with implementing the policies of the Judicial Conference of the United States and supporting the network of Conference committees. And, it is the focal point for Judiciary communication, information, program leadership, and administrative reform."[11] Among its activities, the Administrative Office develops and executes the courts' budget, researches and analyzes matters for the Judicial Conference committees to consider, audits the courts financial operations, and monitors the performance of programs and the use of resources

- Federal Judicial Center: Created in 1967, the Center (**http://www.fjc.gov/**), which is the education and research agency for the federal courts, conducts research and studies the operation of the federal courts; develops and presents for consideration by the Judicial Conference recommendations for improvement of the administration of the federal courts; develops and conducts programs of continuing education and training for personnel of the judicial branch; provides, if requested by the Conference or a committee chair, staff assistance to the Judicial Conference and its committees; and cooperates with the State Justice Institute in the establishment and coordination of research and programs concerning the administration of justice."[12] The center's home page provides publications, history of the federal judiciary, and educational programs and materials (**http://www.fjc.gov/newweb/jnetweb.nsf/**).

- United States Sentencing Commission: It is an independent agency in the judicial branch; "its principal purposes are: (1) to establish sentencing policies and practices for the federal courts, including guidelines prescribing the appropriate form and severity of punishment for offenders convicted of federal crimes; (2) to advise and assist Congress and the executive branch in the development of effective and efficient crime policy; and (3) to collect, analyze, research, and distribute a broad array of information on federal crime and sentencing issues, serving as an information resource for Congress, the executive branch, the courts, criminal justice practitioners, the academic community, and the public." The home page (**http://www.ussc.gov/**) covers "What's New," general information, notices in the *Federal Register*, "Guidelines, Manuals & Amendments," reports to Congress, publications, organizational guidelines and compliance, guideline training and education, federal sentencing statistics, committee meeting information, hearing transcripts and testimony, and links to related sits.

- Judicial Councils: Each circuit has a council that takes the necessary steps to manage efficiently the caseload of the district courts and courts of appeal.

The Federal Judiciary home page (**http://www.uscourts.gov/**), maintained by the Administrative Office of the United States Courts, provides access to the home pages for the Supreme Court, the appellate courts, and the district and bankruptcy courts. It also explains the role of the Administration Office and covers "Educational Outreach," "Electronic Access to Courts," "Federal Rulemaking," and "Judicial Conference." "Educational Outreach" leads to "Courts to Classes," which is designed to assist educators in teaching about the federal court system by providing "classroom resources." The newsroom (**http://www.uscourts.gov/news.html**) provides news releases, a listing of judicial vacancies, and publications.

A page (**http://www.uscourts.gov/rules/index.html**) covers "Federal Rulemaking." It "provides access to the national and local rules currently in effect in the federal courts, as well as background information on the federal rules and rulemaking process."

LAW SCHOOLS

The home pages of many law schools also provide a wealth of legal resources, many of which are beyond the scope of this book. For example, Washburn University's School of Law provides access to each appellate court, resources arranged by topic (e.g., "law journals," "legal dictionaries," and "executive law"), resources of some states, and so on (**http://www.washlaw.edu/**). Cornell Law School (**http://**

www.law.cornell.edu/) supports *LII* (Legal Information Institute), which provides access to an extensive collection of decisions of the Supreme Court and other resources. Northwestern University (**http://oyez.nwu.edu**) presents *The Oyez Project*, which is a multimedia database on the Supreme Court: opinions, information about the justices, a virtual tour, and so on. Villanova University has the "Internet Legal Research Compass," which links to a "Federal Court Locator," "State Court Locator," "Federal Web Navigator," "Tax Law Locator," and more (**http://vls.law.villanova.edu/compass/**).

OTHER WEB SITES

Anyone seeking a good introduction to the U.S. legal system should see sources such as *Understanding the Federal Courts*, one of the publications available at the Federal Judiciary Homepage. An excellent companion source is a mock trial based on the actual events of the *Titanic* disaster. That site, *AKO Titanic Virtual Trial* (**http://www.andersonkill.com/titanic/home.htm**), covers the trial and the judicial process.

⟲ Library of Congress

The Library of Congress maintains the Global Legal Information Network (GLIN) (**http://www.loc.gov/law/glin/**), which

is a database of laws, regulations, and other complementary legal sources. The documents included in the database are contributed by the governments of the members from the original, official texts which are deposited, by agreement of the members, in a server presently located at the Library of Congress. . . . Anyone may sign on to the system as a guest and view the summaries and citation information for the laws and legal writings in the database. Searchers can be done by jurisdiction, subject, date, or type of legal instrument, or by a combination of these elements.

⟲ Federal Panel on MultiDistrict Litigation

The panel's home page (**http://www.jpml.uscourts.gov/**) provides general and hearing information, rules, links, and other information.

⟲ Office of the Federal Public Defender

Created in 1991, the Office of the Federal Public Defender for the District of Columbia "represents indigent defendants before the U.S. District Court for the District of Columbia." Representation includes counsel and investigative, expert and other services necessary for an adequate defense. The home page (**http://www.dcfpd.org/**) provides information related to its function, a "BriefBank," a library of assorted resources, links, sentencing information, and more.

The Judicial Fellows Program

This site (**http://www.ussc.gov/jdfellow/JDFELLOW.HTM**) explains the program and identifies the judicial fellows for the year, the selection process, and so on.

Federal Court Clerk's Association

The association, which promotes the professionalism and integrity of the federal judiciary, has a Web site (**http://www.id.uscourts.gov/fcca.htm**) that covers the association, its committees, treasurer's report, and so on.

Supreme Court Historical Society

The society, a private nonprofit organization, supports work on the history of the Supreme Court. It offers public and educational programs, as well as general interest and scholarly publications. The Web site (**http://supremecourthistory.org/**) explains the society's mission and membership, covers the history of the court, explains on the court works, and provides access to a gift shop, society awards, researching he court, and the Learning Center. There are also online publications.

American Judicature Society

The society, a nonpartisan organization, "works to maintain the independence and integrity of the courts and increase public understanding of the justice system." The Web site (**http://www.ajs.org/**) discusses the organization and its activities, "What's New," publications, and other resources.

FindLaw

FindLaw (**http://www.findlaw.com/**) is a searchable database of Supreme Court decisions rendered since 1893. It can be browsed by year and *U.S. Reports* volume number and is searchable by citation, case title, and full text. *U.S. Reports*, by the way, is a published source containing Supreme Court decisions. *FindLaw*, which is a free service, also contains a library of circuit court and district court opinions, and the annotated U.S. Constitution produced by the Congressional Research Service (Library of Congress), with links to cited Supreme Court cases.

Law.com

In addition to providing access to a Supreme Court monitor (current information), this service (**http://www.law.com/index.shtml**) provides other information for the legal professional, such as breaking developments in the law, research issues and cases, and online continuing legal education seminars. Perusal of the site map indicates how much material this site covers.

⟫ FedLaw

FedLaw of the General Services Administration (**http://www.thecre.com/fedlaw/ default.htm**) directs its users to legal resources: decisions of the Supreme Court, circuit courts, and district and bankruptcy courts, as well as to a "Topical and Title Index" (alphabetical list of subjects in FedLaw), "Federal Laws and Regulations" (by subject), "Arbitration and Mediation" (federal laws, arbitration and mediation rules, and alternate dispute resolution), "How-to-Legal-related Sites," and more. It is aimed at those looking up points of law, and it even provides access to the *United States Code* and decisions of the Comptroller General (General Accounting Office).

⟫ CataLaw

This site (**http://www.catalaw.com/**) covers legal topics and offers access to legal resources from different countries and to other resources (e.g., a list of legal periodicals).

⟫ Examples of Fee-based and Subscription Services

In addition to the sites discussed thus far, fee-based and subscription services are also available. Examples include the following:

- USSC+ (InfoSynthesis, Inc.; **http://www.usscplus.com/**), which provides Supreme Court opinions, a CD-ROM database, and other resources

- *Westlaw* (**http://web2.westlaw.com/signon/default.wl?newdoor=true**), which is a credit card document retrieval service provided by West Group for the retrieval of legal documents

- LEXIS-NEXIS (**http://www.lexis-nexis.com/**), which provides assorted legal and legislative documents

SUMMARY

A number of Web sites cover the judicial branch, thereby offering choices about which site or sites to use. The courts offer a number of services so that the public can receive up-to-date information. Although not all of the courts that exist at the federal level have a Web presence, it is clear that the court system has gained an even more notable presence on the Web since the publication of the first edition of this guide. The judicial sites clearly offer a much broader array of information resources than just court decisions or opinions. As discussed in Chapters 1 and 14 and in the Preface, the *E-Government Act of 2002* includes coverage of the judicial branch and the types of information that court Web sites must cover. In fact, many of the sites already provide such information.

NOTES

1. *Understanding the Federal Courts* (**http://www.uscourts.gov/UFC99.pdf**).

2. Ibid.

3. Ibid.

4. Ibid.

5. "However, the district courts have exclusive jurisdiction over tort claims (a civil wrong or breach of duty) and concurrent jurisdiction over tax refunds" (Ibid.).

6. Ibid.

7. Ibid.

8. For an excellent and fascinating article analyzing the emergence of Project Hermes, see Bruce D. Collins, "SCON Is Dead! . . . Long Live Project Hermes!" *Government Information Quarterly* 10 (1993): 415–42.

9. *Understanding the Federal Courts.*

10. Ibid.

11. Ibid.

12. Ibid.

URL Site Guide for This Chapter

Graphic Depiction of Court Structure (Figure 7.1)
http://www.uscourts.gov/outreach/structure.jpg

Federal Judiciary HomePage
http://www.uscourts.gov/

Electronic Access to Courts
http://www.uscourts.gov/electaccrt.html

Federal Rulemaking
http://www.uscourts.gov/rules/index.html

Judiciary Privacy Policy Page
http://www.privacy.uscourts.gov/

Newsroom
http://www.uscourts.gov/news.html

PACER Service Center
http://pacer.psc.uscourts.gov/

Web-PACER Training Site
PACER Service Center
http://pacer.psc.uscourts.gov/announcements/general/pacer_train.html

Court Opinions (Electronic Services)
http://pacer.psc.uscourts.gov/pubaccess.html

Supreme Court
http://www.supremecourtus.gov/

Fellows Program
http://www.fellows.supremecourtus.gov/

Opinions
http://www.supremecourtus.gov/opinions/opinions.html

Where to Find Supreme Court Opinions
http://www.supremecourtus.gov/opinions/opinions.html

United States Court of International Trade
http://www.cit.uscourts.gov/

Case Management/Electronic Case Files
http://www.cit.uscourts.gov/cmecf/cm-ecf.htm

United States Court of Federal Claims
http://www.uscfc.uscourts.gov/

United States Court of Appeals for the Armed Forces
http://www.armfor.uscourts.gov/

United States Court of Appeals for Veterans Claims
http://www.vetapp.uscourts.gov/

United States Tax Court
http://www.ustaxcourt.gov/ustcweb.htm

Appellate Courts

First U.S. Circuit Court
http://www.ca1.uscourts.gov/

Second U.S. Circuit Court
http://www.ca2.uscourts.gov/

Third U.S. Circuit Court
http://www.ca3.uscourts.gov/

Fourth U.S. Circuit Court
http://www.ca4.uscourts.gov/

Fifth U.S. Circuit Court
http://www.ca5.uscourts.gov/
http://www.law.utexas.edu/us5th/us5th.html

Sixth U.S. Circuit Court
http://www.ca6.uscourts.gov/

Seventh U.S. Circuit Court
http://www.ca7.uscourts.gov/

Eighth U.S. Circuit Court
http://www.ca8.uscourts.gov/index.html

Ninth U.S. Circuit Court
http://www.ca9.uscourts.gov/

Tenth U.S. Circuit Court
http://www.ck10.uscourts.gov/
http://www.law.emory.edu/10circuit

Eleventh U.S. Circuit Court
http://www.ca11.uscourts.gov/

D.C. Circuit Court
http://www.cadc.uscourts.gov/

The United States Court of Appeals for the Federal Circuit
http://www.fedcir.gov/

> **Searchable Sites for Circuit Court Opinions**
> http://www.law.emory.edu/fedcircuit/
> http://www.ll.georgetown.edu/Fed-Ct/cafed.html

> **Jurisdiction**
> http://www.uscourts.gov/courtsofappeals.html

Office of the Circuit Executive: United States Courts for the Ninth Circuit
http://www.ce9.uscourts.gov/

District Courts

Alabama

> **Middle District**
> http://www.almd.uscourts.gov/

> **Northern District**
> http://www.alnd.uscourts.gov/

> **Southern District**
> http://www.alsd.uscourts.gov/page.cfm?page=1

Alaska
http://www.akd.uscourts.gov/

Arizona
http://www.azd.uscourts.gov/

Arkansas
Eastern District
http://www.are.uscourts.gov/

> **Western District**
> http://www.arwd.uscourts.gov/

California

> **Central District**
> http://www.cacd.uscourts.gov/

> **Eastern District**
> http://www.caed.uscourts.gov/

> **Probation Office (Eastern)**
> http://www.caep.uscourts.gov/

> **Northern District**
> http://www.cand.uscourts.gov/

> **Southern District**
> http://www.casd.uscourts.gov/

> **Probation Office (Southern District)**
> http://www.casp.uscourts.gov/home.html

Colorado
http://www.co.uscourts.gov/dindex.htm
http://www.co.uscourts.gov/

Connecticut
http://www.ctd.uscourts.gov/

Delaware
http://www.ded.uscourts.gov/

District of Columbia
http://www.dcd.uscourts.gov/

Florida

> **Middle District**
> http://www.flmd.uscourts.gov/

> **Northern District**
> http://www.flnd.uscourts.gov/

> **Southern District**
> http://www.flsd.uscourts.gov/

> **Middle District**

Georgia

> **Middle District**
> http://www.gamd.uscourts.gov/

Northern District
http://www.gand.uscourts.gov/

Southern District
http://www.gasd.uscourts.gov/

Guam
http://www.gud.uscourts.gov/

Hawaii
http://www.hid.uscourts.gov/

Idaho
http://www.id.uscourts.gov/

Illinois

Central District
http://www.ilcd.uscourts.gov/

Northern District
http://www.ilnd.uscourts.gov/

Southern District
http://www.ilsd.uscourts.gov/

Probation Office (Southern District)
http://www.ilsd.uscourts.gov/uspo/default.html

Indiana

Northern District
http://www.innd.uscourts.gov/

Probation Office/Pretrial Services
http://www.innp.uscourts.gov/

Southern District
http://www.insd.uscourts.gov/

Probation Office (Southern District)
http://www.insp.uscourts.gov/

Iowa
Northern District
http://www.iand.uscourts.gov/

Southern District
http://www.iasd.uscourts.gov/

Kansas
http://www.kds.uscourts.gov/

Kentucky

Eastern District
http://www.kyed.uscourts.gov/

Western District
http://www.kywd.uscourts.gov/

Louisiana

Eastern District
http://www.laed.uscourts.gov/

Pretrial Services Office (Eastern District)
http://www.laept.uscourts.gov/

Middle District
http://www.lamd.uscourts.gov/

Western District
http://www.lawd.uscourts.gov/

Maine
http://www.med.uscourts.gov/

Maryland
http://www.mdd.uscourts.gov/

Massachusetts
http://www.mad.uscourts.gov/

Michigan

Eastern District
http://www.mied.uscourts.gov/index.html

Western District
http://www.miwd.uscourts.gov/

Minnesota
http://www.mnd.uscourts.gov/

Missouri

Eastern District
http://www.moed.uscourts.gov/

Pretrial Services Office (Eastern District)
http://www.moept.uscourts.gov/

Probation Office (Eastern District)
http://www.moep.uscourts.gov/

Western District
http://www.mow.uscourts.gov/

Mississippi

Northern District
http://www.msnd.uscourts.gov/

Southern District
http://www.mssd.uscourts.gov/

Montana
http://www.mtd.uscourts.gov/

Nebraska
http://www.ned.uscourts.gov/

Nevada
http://www.nvd.uscourts.gov/

New Hampshire
http://ww.nhd.uscourts.gov/

New Jersey
http://pacer.njd.usourts.gov/

Pretrial Services Agency
http://www.njpt.uscourts.gov/

New Mexico
http://www.nmcourt.fed.us/dcdocs/

U.S. Pretrial Services
http://www.nmcourt.fed.us/ptdocs/

Probation Office
http://www.nmcourt.fed.us/pbdocs/

New York

Eastern District
http://www.nyed.uscourts.gov/

Northern District
http://www.nynd.uscourts.gov/

Southern District
http://www.nysd.uscourts.gov/

Western District
http://www.nywd.uscourts.gov/

North Carolina

Eastern District
http://www.nced.uscourts.gov/

Middle District
http://www.ncmd.uscourts.gov/

Western District
http://www.ncwd.uscourts.gov/

North Dakota
http://www.ndd.uscourts.gov/

Northern Mariana Island
http://www.nmid.uscourts.gov/

Ohio

Northern District
http://www.ohnd.uscourts.gov/

Southern District
http://www.ohsd.uscourts.gov/

Probation Office (Southern District)
http://www.ohsp.uscourts.gov/

Oklahoma

Eastern District
http://www.oked.uscourts.gov/

Northern District
http://www.oknd.uscourts.gov/

Western District
http://www.okwd.uscourts.gov/

Oregon
http://www.ord.uscourt.gov/

Pennsylvania

Eastern District
http://www.paed.uscourts.gov/

Middle District
http://www.pamd.uscourts.gov/

Western District
http://www.pawd.uscourts.gov/

Puerto Rico
http://www.prd.uscourts.gov/USDCPR/home.htm

Pretrial Services Office
http://www.prpt.uscourts.gov/home.htm

Rhode Island
http://www.rid.uscourts.gov/

South Carolina
http://www.law.scd.uscourts.gov/

South Dakota
http://www.sdd.uscourts.gov/

Tennessee

Eastern District
http://www.tned.uscourts.gov/

Middle District
http://www.tnmd.uscourts.gov/

Western District
http://www.tnwd.uscourts.gov/

Texas

Eastern District
http://www.txed.uscourts.gov/

Probation Office (Eastern District)
http://www.txep.uscourts.gov/

Northern District
http://www.txnd.uscourts.gov/

Southern District
http://www.txs.uscourts.gov/

Western District
http://www.txwd.uscourts.gov/

Utah
http://www.utd.uscourts.gov/

Vermont
http://www.vtd.uscourts.gov/

Virgin Islands
http://www.vid.uscourts.gov/

Virginia

Eastern District
http://www.vaed.uscourts.gov/

Pretrial Services Office (Eastern District)
http://www.vaept.uscourts.gov/

Western District
http://www.vawd.uscourts.gov/

Washington

Eastern District
http://www.waed.uscourts.gov/

Western District
http://www.wawd.uscourts.gov/

West Virginia

Northern District
http://www.wvnd.uscourts.gov/

Southern District
http://www.wvsd.uscourts.gov/

Probation Office (Southern District)
http://www.wvsd.uscourts.gov/
probation/index.html

Wisconsin

Eastern District
http://www.wied.uscourts.gov/

Western District
http://www.wiw.uscourts.gov/

Probation Office (Western Office)
http://www.wiw.uscourts.gov/
agencies.htm

Wyoming
http://www.ck10.uscourts.gov/
wyoming/district/index.html

Federal District-Court Civil Trials
http://teddy.law.cornell.edu:8090/
questtr2.htm

Bankruptcy Courts

Alabama

Middle District
http://www.almb.uscourts.gov/

Northern District
http://www.alnb.uscourts.gov/

Southern District
http://www.alsb.uscourts.gov/

Alaska
http://www.akb.uscourts.gov/

Arizona
http://www.azb.uscourts.gov/

Arkansas
http://www.akb.uscourts.gov/

California

> **Central District**
> http://www.cacb.uscourts.gov/

> **Eastern District**
> http://www.caeb.uscourts.gov/

> **Northern District**
> http://www.canb.uscourts.gov/

> **Southern District**
> http://www.casb.uscourts.gov/

Colorado
http://www.cob.uscourts.gov/bindex.htm

Connecticut
http://www.ctb.uscourts.gov/

Delaware
http://www.deb.uscourts.gov/

Florida

> **Middle District**
> http://www.flmb.uscourts.gov/

> **Northern District**
> http://www.flnb.uscourts.gov/

> **Southern District**
> http://www.flsb.uscourts.gov/

Georgia

> **Middle District**
> http://www.gamb.uscourts.gov/
> wwwgamb/

> **Northern District**
> http://www.ganb.uscourts.gov/

> **Southern District**
> http://www.gasb.uscourts.gov/

Hawaii
http://www.hib.uscourts.gov/

Idaho
http//:www.id.uscourts.gov/

Illinois

> **Central District**
> http://www.ilcb.uscourts.gov/

> **Northern District**
> http://www.ilnb.uscourts.gov/

Southern District
http://www.ilsb.uscourts.gov/

Indiana

> **Northern District**
> http://www.innb.uscourts.gov/

> **Southern District**
> http://www.insb.uscourts.gov/

Iowa

> **Northern District**
> http://www.ianb.uscourts.gov/

> **Southern District**
> http://www.iasb.uscourts.gov/
> webpages/home/default.asp

Kansas
> http://www.ksb.uscourts.gov/

Kentucky

> **Eastern District**
> http://www.kyeb.uscourts.gov/

> **Western District**
> http://www.kywb.uscourts.gov/
> fpweb/

Louisiana

> **Eastern District**
> http://www.laeb.uscourts.gov/

> **Middle District**
> http://www.lamb.uscourts.gov/

> **Western District**
> http://www.lawb.uscourts.gov/

Maine
http://www.meb.uscourts.gov/

Maryland
http://www.mdb.uscourts.gov/default.asp

Massachusetts
http://www.mab.uscourts.gov/

Michigan

> **Eastern District**
> http://www.mieb.uscourts.gov/

> **Western District**
> http://www.miwb.uscourts.gov/

Minnesota
http://www.mnb.uscourts.gov/

Mississippi

> **Northern District**
> http://www.msnb.uscourts.gov/

> **Southern District**
> http://www.mssb.uscourts.gov/

Missouri

> **Eastern District**
> http://www.moeb.uscourts.gov/

> **Western District**
> http://www.mow.uscourts.gov/

Montana
http://www.mtb.uscourts.gov/

Nebraska
http://www.neb.uscourts.gov/

New Hampshire
http://www.nhb.uscourts.gov/

New Jersey
http://www.njb.uscourts.gov/

Nevada
http://www.nvb.uscourts.gov/

New Mexico
http://www.nmcourt.fed.us/bkdocs

New York

> **Eastern District**
> http://www.nyed.uscourts.gov/

> **Northern District**
> http://www/nynb.uscourts.gov/

> **Southern District**
> http://www.nysd.uscourts.gov/

> **Western District**
> http://www.nywd.uscourts.gov/

North Carolina

> **Eastern District**
> http://www.nceb.uscourts.gov/

> **Middle District**
> http:/www.ncmb.uscourts.gov/

Western District
http://www.ncwb.uscourts.gov/

North Dakota
http://www.ndb.uscourts.gov/

Ohio

> **Northern District**
> http://www.ohnb.uscourts.gov/

> **Southern District**
> http://www.ohsb.uscourts.gov/

Oklahoma
Eastern District
http://www.okeb.uscourts.gov/

> **Northern District**
> http://www.oknb.uscourts.gov/

Oregon
http://www.orb.uscourts.gov/

Pennsylvania

> **Eastern District**
> http://www.paeb.uscourts.gov/

> **Middle District**
> http://www.pamb.uscourts.gov/

> **Western District**
> http://www.pawb.uscourts.gov/

Puerto Rico
http://www.prb.uscourts.gov/

Rhode Island
http://www.rib.uscourts.gov/

South Carolina
http://www.scb.uscourts.gov/

South Dakota
http://www.sdb.uscourts.gov/

Tennessee

> **Eastern District**
> http://www.tneb.uscourts.gov/

> **Middle District**
> http://www.tnmb.uscourts.gov/

> **Western District**
> http://www.tnwb.uscourts.gov/

Texas

Eastern District
http://www.txeb.uscourts.gov/

Northern District
http://www.txnb.uscourts.gov/
index.jsp

Southern District
http://www.txs.uscourts.gov/

Western District
http://www.txwb.uscourts.gov/

Utah
http://www.utb.uscourts.gov/

Vermont
http://www.vtb.uscourts.gov/

Virginia

Eastern District
http://www.vaeb.uscourts.gov/

Western District
http://www.vawb.uscourts.gov/
courtweb/enter1.htm

Washington

Eastern District
http://www.waeb.uscourts.gov/

Western District
http://www.wawb.uscourts.gov/

West Virginia

Northern District
http://www.wvnb.uscourts.gov/

Southern District
http://www.wvsb.uscourts.gov/
bankruptcy/index.html

Wisconsin

Eastern District
http://www.wieb.uscourts.gov/

Western District
http://www.wiw.uscourts.gov/
bankruptcy/

Wyoming
http://www.wyb.uscourts.gov/

American Bankruptcy Institute
http://www.abiworld.org

Federal Public Defender (District of Columbia)
http://www.dcfpd.org/

Judicial Panel on MultiDistrict Litigation
http://www.jpml.uscourts.gov/

United States Sentencing Commission
http://www.ussc.gov/

Federal Judicial Center
http://www.fjc.gov/

Resources
http://www.fjc.gov/newweb/jnetweb.nsf/

LII
Cornell Law School
http://www.law.cornell.edu/

The Oyez Project
Northwestern University
http://oyez.nwu.edu

WashLaw
Washington University School of Law
http://www.washlaw.edu/

Internet Legal Research Compass
http://vls.law.villanova.edu/compass/

AKO Titanic Virtual Trial
http://www.andersonkill.com/titanic/
home.htm

Global Legal Information Network
Library of Congress
http://www.loc.gov/law/glin/

Federal Court Clerk's Association
http://www.id.uscourts.gov/fcca.htm

Supreme Court Historical Society
http://supremecourthistory.org/

American Judicature Society
http://www.ajs.org/

FindLaw
http://www.findlaw.com/

Law.com
http://www.law.com/index.shtml

FedLaw
General Services Administration
http://www.thecre.com/fedlaw/default.
    htm

CataLaw
http://www.catalaw.com/

USSC+
http://www.usscplus.com

WESTLAW
http://web2.westlaw.com/signon/
    default.wl?newdoor=true

LEXIS-NEXIS
http://www.lexis-nexis.com/

Understanding the Federal Courts
http://www.uscourts.gov/UFC99.pdf

Chapter 8

Statistics

When people seek government information, it is often for the statistics collected, compiled, and reported by thousands of federal offices, bureaus, and other bodies scattered throughout the country. Indeed, the U.S. government remains the largest producer and distributor of data in the world. Much of it is free to the public and measures nearly every aspect of a citizen's life: health, housing, income, labor and jobs, crime, education, commerce, energy, environment, agriculture, national resources, national economy, recreation, safety, and transportation. According to recent budget estimates, almost seventy federal agencies spend at least $500,000 annually gathering, organizing, and distributing these data. The purpose of this chapter is to identify some of the more prominent Web sites of statistical agencies.

Anyone searching for statistics should determine if what he or she seeks is best found through a set of general statistics that cover a broad topic over a large geographic area (e.g., the number of murders reported from across the United States in 1995) or by a set of specific data related to a smaller geographical area, narrow time period, or particular type of event (e.g., the number of automobile thefts in Chicago, Illinois, during 1997). Before the emergence of the Web, the first place to look for such general and particular information was usually a "fact book," such as the annual *Statistical Abstract of the United States* (**http://www.census.gov/statab/www**), which is the oldest and most comprehensive collection of statistics on American life. By downloading the section on "Law Enforcement, Courts, and Prison" as a portable document file (.pdf), one finds that there were more than 13,000 murders in the United States in 1995. The same document reveals that there were 1,215.1 auto thefts per 100,000 people in Chicago during 1997. Other important general statistical sources include *Health, United States*; *State and Metropolitan Area Data Book*; *Uniform Crime Reports;* and the *Digest of Education Statistics*. Another reason to keep these general information sources in mind is that they are really electronic versions of paper sources readily available in many depository libraries.

Because the Web has vastly increased the level of access to the abundance of federal statistics, the first place to visit might be FEDSTATS (**http://www.fedstats.gov/**), which the Federal Interagency Council on Statistical Policy maintains. Indeed, these general information sources can be found through site's "Statistical Reference Shelf" (**http://www.fedstats.gov/fast.html**). FEDSTATS offers links to federal statistics through two primary ways of searching: by agency or by topic. The agency section gives an excellent summary on what each government body collects (and why it does so), lists the important sources of information of those agencies, and then offers direct links to the data. The "Topic Links—A to Z" feature organizes data sources according to broad subject categories (e.g., agriculture, crime, drugs, and energy). For each category, there is a direct link to an agency (or list of agencies) responsible for data collection on a selected topic(s). For instance, under "Smoking" the National Center for Health Statistics, part of the Centers for Disease Control and Prevention (CDC), offers data sets that support a wide range of research, analysis, and evaluation programs on the effects of smoking (**http://www.cdc.gov/nchs/fastats/smoking.htm**). Some of the links lead to specific data sets, whereas others refer to related sites, such as the CDC's Office on Smoking and Health (**http://www.cdc.gov/tobacco/mission.htm**).

FEDSTATS also has a section called "Statistics by Geography from U.S. Agencies," which is divided into broad subject categories that arrange data sources by geographic area (city, county, federal district, region, state, or other area). For instance, under the topic "Health," there is a link to the *Atlas of the United States Mortality* (**http://www.cdc.gov/nchs/products/pubs/pubd/other/atlas/causes.htm**), which has downloadable maps showing the incidence of heart disease, lung cancer, stroke, motor vehicle injuries, and other specific causes of death around the United States.

Many data collected by the federal government come with qualifications, caveats, or explanations of how the questions were framed or how terms used to describe the conditions are defined. For instance, after a Web site that reports statistics of criminal activity on the nearly six thousand U.S. colleges and universities (**http://ope.ed. gov/security**) was criticized for inconsistencies and the inaccuracy of some of its data,[1] the Department of Education, which manages the site's content, offers the following warning to users on its opening page:

> The institutions provided data presented on this website to the Department using a Web-based data collection tool. The statistics represent *alleged* criminal offenses *reported* to campus security authorities or local police agencies. *Therefore, the data collected do not necessarily reflect prosecutions or convictions for crime.* Because some statistics are provided by non-police authorities, the data are not directly comparable to data from the FBI's Uniform Crime Reporting System which only collects statistics from police authorities. It is important for users of the data on this Web site and in the Department's report to Congress to become knowledgeable about how to categorize and quantify the nature and extent of crime on college campuses in the United States. Valid comparisons are possible only with study and analysis of the conditions affecting each institution.

To reinforce this "quality control" over federal data, an amendment was attached to an obscure section of a large omnibus appropriation act signed into law during the last weeks of the 106th Congress (December 2000). There was no debate, no explanation, and no hearings held on the law. It came to be known as the *Data Quality Act.*[2] Ostensibly the law requires agencies to apply several "policy and procedural guidance . . . for ensuring and maximizing the quality, objectivity, utility, and integrity of information (including statistical information) disseminated by Federal agencies." In October 2001,[3] the Office of Management and Budget published its final guidelines that required all government agencies, as of October 1, 2002, to post these guidelines on their Web sites (see Chapter 1).

THE MAJOR FEDERAL STATISTICAL AGENCIES

Congress, the judiciary, and assorted executive departments provide numerous statistics on assorted topics. What follows are detailed descriptions of some the key federal Web sites.

Economics and Statistics Administration

The Economics and Statistics Administration (ESA; **http://www.esa.doc.gov/**), part of the Department of Commerce, manages the three largest bureaus responsible for the statistics that chronicle, organize, distribute, and explain societal changes throughout the United States, as well as document relationships with other countries around the globe. Political and business leaders use the data from these bureaus (Bureau of the Census, Bureau of Economic Analysis, and STAT-USA) to make both policy and economic decisions that affect millions of citizens every day. Overall, ESA has three primary missions: (1) to maintain the quality and integrity of the overall federal statistical system and make improvements where warranted and feasible, (2) sustain a governmentwide framework of the economy and opportunities that might improve the well-being of all Americans, and (3) support the information and analytical infrastructure necessary to support of the Commerce Department and the executive branch.

In their attempts to meet these primary missions, these three bureaus have a spectrum of policy choices that involve data quality and collecting; these choices often reflect a deeper constitutional struggle between the executive and legislative branches over how to conduct the statistical surveys that will meet the greater needs of American society. For instance, the issue about how much information the federal government needs to collect from citizens to reapportion the congressional districts every ten years has to be resolved in a helpful manner. At the very least, the constitution demands essentially a "head count" of where everyone in the nation is on a particular day every ten years. Since the first census was taken in 1790, other questions about the social, economic, and personal situation of citizens and their households have been added. By the mid-twentieth century, two forms were used by the Census Bureau (statistical programs discussed in more detail later in this chapter), one "short" (to meet the constitutional minimum for congressional reapportionment) and one "long," which was sent to about one of six of the households during the census. It contained all the questions on the short form but included additional detailed questions relating to the social, economic, and housing characteristics of each individual and household. By 2001, conservative elements (along with a Supreme Court decision) challenged the need for the long form. Instead, critics urged the Census Bureau to use the *American Community Survey (ACS)* as a substitute for the long form. The argument for change rests on two points: it is cheaper and it is less intrusive. Supporters for the continued use of the long form argue that there would be demonstrable drop in timeliness, accuracy, geographic coverage, as well as consistency if the *ACS* is used. (For an excellent discussion of this debate, the General Accounting Office issued a report in October 2002; **http://www. gao.gov/new.items/d02956r.pdf**).

Bureau of the Census

The Census Bureau is the largest of the three bureaus, and clearly the world's leading public statistics-gathering agency. Although best known for its responsibility for conducting the decennial census, it regularly applies other types of formal censuses to measure the constantly changing patterns of individual and household demographics, economic conditions, as well as world economic or social conditions. The bureau's specific statistical programs include the following:

- Censuses: These include the population and housing, economic activities, and government entities. As described earlier, the decennial census is the nation's oldest and most comprehensive source of population and housing information. Results are also used to distribute billions of dollars of federal funds each budget cycle. The census data are also by state, local, and tribal governments and by businesses, organizations, and governments. The population and housing census produces the widest range of information available at the smallest geographic levels. In addition, every five years, the bureau conducts an Economic Census that offers a detailed portrait of the nation's economy, which examine aspects of the economy such as agriculture, retail, wholesale, mining, and transportation. Related programs supply information about business ownership. The Census of Governments, conducted at the same time as the Economic Census, covers government organization, public employment, and government finance.

- Demographic Surveys: the bureau, through specific or regular statistical surveys, creates a wealth of primary source of social and economic data. Survey information is used to measure income, poverty, education, health care coverage, crime victimization, computer usage, and as well as other subjects. The bureau also contributes critical data to support the Bureau of Labor Statistics' monthly unemployment rate and the Consumer Price Index.

- Economic Surveys: the bureau provides monthly, quarterly, and annual surveys on the current state of the economy. The majority of these surveys supports the Bureau of Economic Analysis as it updates the nation's gross domestic product accounts. The surveys also provide essential data that the Bureau of Labor Statistics, part of the Department of Labor, uses in its maintenance of the monthly Producer Price Index. The Federal Reserve Board uses the data for input into indices of industrial production and capacity utilization.

- International activities: through various programs, the bureau sustains several international demographic and socioeconomic databases. This activity includes the creation of international demographic, estimates, and projections; special international analyses; and interpretive reports and monographs. The bureau also offers technical advisory services to foreign governments, including developing and implementing statistical programs for censuses and surveys, conducting training, and developing statistical software and methodology.

- General activities: These efforts represent official population estimates and projections, as well as yearly inventories of governmental unit boundaries. Bureau staff are leaders in the areas of research on statistical standards and census and survey methodology, and they contribute to not only improvements in the work of the Census Bureau but also the bodies of statistical, economic, and demographic knowledge. Ongoing research evaluations keep data collection activities relevant.

Since the release of data from the 2000 census, the Web has become the primary method of dissemination for the bureau's information products and services. Because of this, its primary Web pages are some of the most complicated and difficult to navigate without some of the background just outlined. Indeed, the bureau's home page (http://www.census.gov/) lists six general categories in the middle of its screen; some of them are obviously connected to the categories described enumerated here, which the following descriptions attempt to make more clear:

1. Census 2000: this page is perhaps the most complicated (and useful) for users trying to get a basic understanding of the information products and sources generated by the decennial population and housing census.

2. People: this category gives a blend of statistics about population and households in the United States and from around the world. Although many of the data come from the population and housing census, data also come from the bureau's other demographic surveys. For instance, clicking on "Health Insurance" (http://www.census.gov/hhes/www/hlthins.html) reveals different reports giving data on health insurance coverage, uninsured low-income children, methodology explanations, and related sites. There is also a wealth of genealogical information.

3. Business: this page provides access to the 1997 economic censuses and foreign trade statistics. Here visitors to the site can find announcements, press releases, data, background information, and reports.

4. Geography: this categorie includes the TIGER Map Service, "a public resource for generating high-quality, detailed maps of anywhere in the United States, using public geographic data." These "detailed maps on-the-fly" cover many metropolitan areas in the United States. "TIGER," under "Geography," also leads to the LandView, which "reflects the collaborative efforts of the U.S. Environmental Protection Agency, the U.S. Census Bureau, the U.S. Geological Survey, and the National Oceanic and Atmospheric Administration to produce a 'Federal Geographic Data Viewer' that provides the public ready access to published Federal spatial and related data." *Map Stats* (http://quickfacts.census.gov/qfd/index.html) provides a visual profile of each state and its counties, together with companion data on each state, county, and metropolitan area. The *U.S. Gazetteer* (see "Gazetteer" under "Geography") is an excellent resource for linking place names and zip codes to a TIGER map of the area. The bureau also provides "The GIS Gateway" (http://www.census.gov/geo/www/gis_gateway.html),

which "offers connections to many Geographical Information Systems (GIS) resources available on the Internet" (see Chapter 11).

5. Newsroom: this is the bureau's primary Web page for announcing specific publication program, and public information programs. Here are shorter reports and quick summaries of essential data developed by all the Bureau's programs.

6. Special Topics: There are specific links to the overall calendar of census releases, information about the complete files being released from the 1930 census, tools and sources that teachers can use, information about the *American Community Survey*, and more.

The right side of the bureau's home page provides access to latest economic indicators, quick facts about states and countries (facts and maps), a population clock for the nation and the world, and specially featured reports. On the left side, there is "Subjects A to Z," which, in essence, functions as a site map and shows the information seeker the wealth of information available at this site. The *American Factfinder* is an interactive database engine for data from the latest population and housing census. Other options include a sales catalog (**http://www.census.gov/mp/www/Tempcat/ Catalog.html**) and a list of publications (**http://www.census.gov/prod/www/titles. html**).

The "Search" button on the left side of the opening screen enables information seekers to search the site in general, to concentrate on specific collections (press releases, publications, subject matter experts, or other online information), or to conduct a place search, map search, or staff search (employee phone numbers and e-mail addresses. These staff members can assist with specific inquiries.) The Census Bureau works closely with numerous other government agencies and with nongovernmental entities including businesses and nonprofit organizations. The result is a vital information resource for both government and business.[4]

The American Factfinder. This resource provides useful information about communities, the economy, and society. In many ways, this interrelated, and complicated, set of Web pages replaces the traditional printed volumes of the decennial census. Chapter 12 elaborates on this tool and its value.

Economic Census. This important set of Web pages offers general and specific information about the latest economic census, data release schedules, sample forms, questions and answers, the latest results, media resources, news releases, a slide show, related sites, and so on (**http://www.census.gov/epcd/www/econ97.html**). There is discussion of the North American Industry Classification System (NAICS) (see also "Business," described in the list earlier in this section), which has replaced the U.S. Standard Industrial Classification (SIC) system. In addition, the site includes information about how to use economic census data, plans for user conferences, brochures, and a guide.[5]

Demographic and Economic Surveys. This section profiles demographic and economic surveys, some of which the bureau conducts in conjunction with other federal agencies. The demographic surveys (see **http://www.census.gov/main/www/ sur_demo.html**) include *The American Community Survey, American Housing Survey, Current Population Survey, Current Population Survey Supplements, Housing Vacancy Survey, National Level Survey Data, Property Owners and Managers Survey,*

Residential Finance Survey, Survey of Income and Program Participation, Survey of Program Dynamics, and *Women- and Minority-Owned Business Survey.* For each survey, additional information is supplied.

The Economic Surveys (see **http://www.census.gov/main/www/sur_econ.html**) are: *Advance Monthly Retail Sales Survey; Annual Capital Expenditures Survey; Annual Retail Trade Survey; Annual Survey of Communication Services; Annual Survey of Manufactures; Annual Trade Survey; Assets and Expenditures Survey; Business and Professional Classification Survey; Characteristics of Business Owners Survey; Commodity Flow Survey; Education Finance Survey; Farm and Ranch Irrigation Survey; Investment Plans Survey; Manufacturers' Shipments, Inventories, and Orders (M3) Survey; Monthly Retail Trade Survey; Monthly Wholesale Trade Survey; Motor Freight Transportation and Warehousing Survey; Nationwide Truck Activity and Commodity Survey; Plant and Equipment Survey; Quarterly Financial Report; Service Annual Survey; Survey of Plant Capacity Utilization; Survey of Program Dynamics; Transportation Annual Survey; Truck Inventory and Use Survey;* and *Women- and Minority-Owned Business Survey.* Again, additional information is supplied for each survey.

CenStats. CenStats (**http://www.census.gov/apsd/www/censtats.html**) "provides a convenient, easy, point-and-click access to several popular Census Bureau databases including some that . . . [the bureau sells] on CD-ROMs. CenStats' basic functionality is its search and display. That is, the viewer specifies geographic areas, data sets, commodities, etc. and CenStats finds and displays the specific data." Furthermore, "CenStats takes advantage of a standard feature of the Internet by providing direct links between several databases that have common geography (i.e., counties, ZIP code areas, and census tracts)."

Census Briefs. "*Census Briefs* contains articles describing newly issued reports, new data files and software. Developments in census statistical areas are highlighted, with the principal emphasis on demographic, social, housing, and economic data for states and smaller areas. Articles dealing with statistical developments and data use outside the Census Bureau appear regularly along with information about the products available from other Federal agencies." Through this site (**http://www.census.gov/prod/www/abs/briefs.html**), it is possible to view the publication or to go to publication ordering information. By the way, beginning in December 1996, the *Statistical Briefs,* short reports issued occasionally on specific issues of public policy, "were redesigned and reissued as the *Census Briefs.*" For the *Statistical Briefs,* see **http://www.census.gov/apsd/www/statbrief/**; these publications are in Adobe's Portable Document Format (.pdf).

Map Gallery. Through this gallery, the bureau's Geography Division "offers sample map products . . . as part of . . . [a] continuing program of testing a variety of approaches to distributing graphic products" (see **http://www.census.gov/geo/www/mapGallery/index.html**). Some maps are available online, but all of those mentioned can be purchased in paper form; ordering information is provided. Some of the wall maps "are available as a plotted on-demand product."

Citation Patterns for Web-based Census Files. The bureau offers suggestions for how users should cite HTML (hypertext markup language), ASCII (American Standard Code for Information Interchange), .pdf, and ftp (file transfer protocol) files, as well as tables and e-mail messages (see **http://www.census.gov/main/www/citation.html**).

Other Key Sources for Census Information. The *Statistical Abstract of the United States* contains data on social and economic conditions in the United States, and presents selected international data. It is also a "guide to sources of other data from the Census Bureau, other Federal agencies, and private organizations." The bureau, through its Web site (**http://www.census.gov/prod/www/statistical-abstract-us.html**), provides information on ordering a print or CD-ROM copy, and presents some frequently requested tables, state and county profiles, and state rankings from *Statistical Abstract* and *USA Counties*. One could also access the latest version of the *Abstract* online at **http://www.census.gov/prod/www/statistical-abstract-02.html**.

The County and City Data Book "contains the latest official statistics for all 3,141 U.S. countries, 1,078 cities with 25,000 or more inhabitants, and 11,097 places of 2,500 or more inhabitants." The reference source provides "socioeconomic and housing data from the 1990 census and the surveys that update them," "businesses in your city and county," and "median income, tax base, and more than 100 other variables for counties and cities nationwide" (**http://www.census.gov/statab/www/ccdb.html**).

State and Metropolitan Area Data Book reports statistics on social and economic conditions in the United States at the state and metropolitan area levels. It also provides "selected data for component counties and central cities of metropolitan areas" (see **http://www.census.gov/statab/www/smadb.html**).

Lastly, *USA Statistics in Brief,* a supplement to the *Statistical Abstract,* provides national summary data and state population estimates. The Web coverage (**http://www.census.gov/statab/www/brief.html**) extends to population, state population estimates, vital statistics, health, education, law enforcement, communications and transportation, housing, social welfare, government, agriculture, energy, employment, income, prices, business, finance, and foreign commerce.

Bureau of Economic Analysis

The Bureau of Economic Analysis (BEA) produces and disseminates

accurate, timely, relevant, and cost-effective economic accounts statistics that provide government, businesses, households, and individuals with a comprehensive, up-to-date picture of economic activity. BEA's national, regional, and international economic accounts present basic information on such key issues as U.S. economic growth, regional economic development, and the Nation's position in the world economy.

The national economic accounts provide a quantitative view of the production, distribution, and use of the nation's output; one of the most widely known measures is gross domestic product (GDP). BEA also prepares estimates of the nation's tangible wealth and input-output tables that show how industries interact. The regional economic accounts provide estimates and analyses of personal incomes, population, and employment for regions, states, metropolitan areas, and counties. BEA also prepares estimates of gross state product. The international economic accounts encompass the international transactions accounts (balance of payments) and the estimates of U.S. direct investment abroad and foreign direct investment in the United States.

BEA's current national, regional, and international estimates usually appear first in press releases, which are available in a variety of formats. In addition, the "monthly journal of record, the *Survey of Current Business*, pulls together our estimates, analyses, research, and methodology into one comprehensive package." For an overview of BEA's data products, and for a more detailed description of BEA's economic programs, see BEA's *Catalog of Products*.

The Web site (**http://www.bea.doc.gov/**) covers four general areas:

1. National (GDP and related data, articles, and industry and wealth data)

2. International (data, articles, and survey forms)

3. Regional (state and local data, articles, and other products)

4. Bureauwide (e.g., mission, *Catalog of Products,* papers and presentations, phone numbers of agency personnel, and methodology)

The site provides access to the *Survey of Current Business* and offers "tips on using our site."

"The comprehensive revision of BEA's gross state product (GSP) estimates for 1977–98 has been completed. For the first time, the estimates can be accessed interactively, allowing you to specify which GSP components, states or regions, industries, and years you want to see and the format in which the estimates should be displayed." For the steps to follow in search the GSP data, see **http://www.bea.doc.gov/bea/regional/data.htm**. This page also leads to other regional data provided over a long time period.

☞ STAT-USA

Over the past few years, the Department of Commerce has developed a number of Web resources for citizens and businesses to use to access the department's important economic and trade information. For businesses and institutions with a particular interest in economic and trade data, there is STAT-USA (**http://www.stat-usa.gov/**). Although much of the data listed through STAT-USA can be found, often for free, on other government Web sites, STAT-USA organizes the sources in a fashion that delivers information quickly. By the way, a subscription pays for the information's organization, not its production. In this sense, it is a comparable effort to FEDSTATS as an attempt to organize a broad range of statistical information.

The International Trade Library contains close to fifty files that describe how the federal government can assist businesses or individuals in exporting (or importing) their products and services. Under its "State of the Nation" section, STAT-USA gathers the most significant financial indicators produced by at least a half dozen federal agencies. These include, for instance, the *Consumer Price Index, Producer Price Index, Gross Domestic Product,* Housing Starts and Building Permits, New Construction, and New Home Sales. STAT-USA also offers a comparable collection of domestic statistical information called the "State of the Nation Library."

The price of subscription varies: for single users, it is a modest sum per year (see **http://orders.stat-usa.gov/**); there are various fees for site licenses. STAT-USA is free if it is accessed through a terminal at any federal depository library or, in some cases, through the depository institution's Web pages. To find the nearest depository library, use the search engine found at **http://www.gpoaccess.gov/libraries.html**. Anyone accessing the information through a depository library should know that some parts of STAT-USA are inaccessible without a paid subscription.

Bureau of Justice Statistics

The Bureau of Justice Statistics, a part of the Office of Justice Programs in the Department of Justice, "collects, analyzes, publishes, and disseminates information on crime, criminal offenders, victims of crime, and the operation of justice systems at all levels of government." The Web site (**http://www.ojp.usdoj.gov/bjs/**) contains information about the bureau and the criminal justice system, "What's New," "Key Facts at a Glance" (charts and brief statements on crime trends, trends in federal investigations and prosecutions, trends in felony convictions in state courts, corrections trends, and expenditure trends), press releases, publications, data for analysis, a site search, justice records funding, and related links. The site offers statistics about crimes and victims, drugs and crime, homicide trends, criminal offenders, special topics (e.g., *Sourcebook of Criminal Justice Statistics* and *World Factbook of Criminal Justice Systems*), crime and justice data from other sources (e.g., FBI's *Uniform Crime Reports*), corrections, expenditures and employment, courts and sentencing, prosecution, and law enforcement (federal, state, and local).

The data to download include the following:

- Crime and Justice Electronic Data Abstracts: "Aggregated data assembled into spreadsheets from a wide variety of published sources. Intended for analytic use, the files include crime, justice and socio-demographic variables. Many of the files contain data over time and by state, locality, [and] federal district."

- Online tabulations, source data, and codebooks: The data and the supporting documentation (codebooks) are from the National Archive of Criminal Justice Data and the Federal Justice Statistics Resource Center.

Bureau of Labor Statistics

Located within the Department of Labor, the Bureau of Labor Statistics (BLS) is the government's principal fact-finding agency in the area of labor economics and statistics, including employment and unemployment, prices and living conditions, compensation and working conditions, productivity, employment projections, and international data (foreign labor statistics and U.S. import and export price indexes). On the right side of the home page (**http://stats.bls.gov/**), there are the latest numbers for certain indices that the agency collects as well as

- Employment and Unemployment: these reports deal with such topics as mass layoffs, employment projections, job openings, and so on.

- At a Glance Tables: these give quick access to fact and figures dealing with the U.S. economy, regional, state, and local information, as well as data about specific industries.

- Publications and Research Papers: Online Magazines: among those available are *Monthly Labor Review, Compensation and Working, Conditions, Occupational Outlook Quarterly,* and *MLR: The Editor's Desk*, and more.

- Industries: information is available on employment, unemployment rate, employment projects, average hourly earnings, wages by area and occupation, employment costs, employment benefits, and collective bargaining worker safety and health (injuries and illness, and fatalities, and so on).

- Business Costs: items such as Producer Price Indexes, Employment costs, employee benefits, foreign labor costs, and more are available here.

- Geography: reports of all aspects of business and labor conditions are broken down by international, national, regional, state, and local geographic areas, Kid's Page (see Chapter 13).

The left side of this well-organized page covers other statistical sites, and so on. "Data," for instance, covers nine topics:

1. Productivity

2. Safety and Health

3. International

4. Occupations

5. Demographics

6. Other Statistical Sites

7. BLS Information Offices

8. Inflation and Consumer Spending

9. Wages, Earnings, and Benefits

Bureau of Transportation Statistics

The Bureau of Transportation Statistics (BTS), located within the Department of Transportation,

is a statistical agency, a mapping agency [involved with geographic information systems; see Chapter 11], and an organization for transportation analysis. . . . BTS compiles, analyzes, and makes accessible information on the Nation's transportation systems; collects information on intermodal transportation and other areas as needed; and works to enhance the quality and effectiveness of government statistics.

Offering itself as "TranStats: the Intermodal Transportation Database," the Web site offers the user two ways to access significant sources of transportation data. The first is through the "Data Library," which offers a choice of searching through three broad subjects: mode of transportation, by subject, or by federal agency. The second, "In Focus," serves as a quick reference to transportation data as they affect the larger economy. For instance, the links lead to reports on the "Domestic Air: Revenue by

Ton-miles," "Rail Fatalities," "Consumer Price Indices: Air Fares," and "Tonnage of U.S. Waterborne Imports and Exports." On the right side of the screen, a series of graphs and charts offer "at a glance," which provides periodic transportation reports, and a "Mapping Center," which links to a series of mapping and geographic analysis tools. On the left side of the screen, there are links for how to use the information available through the Web site, as well as to products and information services for purchase, and to the National Transportation Library (**http://ntl.bts.gov/**). One of the Bureau's major reports, *The National Household Transportation Survey,* is a household-based travel survey conducted every five years. "Survey data are collected from a sample of U.S. households and expanded to provide national estimates of trips and miles by travel mode, purpose, a host of other characteristics. The survey collections information on daily, local trips and on long-distance travel in the United States."

The BTS's home page (**http://www.bts.gov/nhts/**) also discusses "What's New," the process of data collection, sampling, and the pretest design; provides related links; and so on. Another signification addition to the bureau's information is a collection of data selected through the Data Library links that focus on National Security and Public Safety.

The Commodity Flow Survey (CFS; **http//www.bts.gov/gov/ntda/cfs/**) "obtains data on shipments by domestic establishments in manufacturing, wholesale, mining, and selected other industries. The CFS is conducted as part of the Economic Census by the U.S. Census Bureau in partnership with the Bureau of Transportation Statistics." BTS also provides research, statistics, and analyses in areas pertaining to international transportation, trade, and travel (**http://www.bts.gov/itt**) and the National Transportation Library offers access to a transportation database, TRIS Online (**http://199.79. 179.82/sundev/search.cfm**).

Furthermore, there is a National Transportation Data Archive (**http://www. transtats.bts.gov/**). However, "due to documented security problems and other limitations of earlier versions of Netscape and Internet Explorer, the TranStats Website supports only" Netscape Version 6.1 or higher; and Window Internet Explorer Version 5.5 or higher. "For FREE updates, visit on of the following websites. . . ."

Office of Airline Information. The Office of Airline Information (OAI) provides "uniform and comprehensive financial and market/traffic statistical economic data on individual air carrier (airline) operations and the air transportation industry." OAI consists of three divisions: the Regulations Division, Data Administration Division, and ADP Services Division.

The home page (**http://www.bts.gov/programs/oai**) provides, for instance,

- Taxi-In & Taxi-Out Times (major U.S. airports and carriers)
- On-Time Statistics
- *Statistical Handbook of Aviation* (Federal Aviation Administration)
- Rural Airports List
- Air Traffic Statistics and Airline Financial Statistics
- Fuel Cost and Consumption
- Sources of Air Carrier Aviation Data
- Airframe Cost Report
- U.S. International Air Passenger and Freight Statistics
- Number of Employees Certified Carriers

⬂ Economic Research Service

The Economic Research Service (ERS), an agency within the Department of Agriculture, is the "official source for economic analysis and information on agriculture, food, national resources, and rural development." The home page (**http://www.ers.usda.gov/**) provides information on "a competitive agricultural system," "a safe food supply," "a healthy, well-nourished population," "harmony between agriculture and the environment," and "enhanced quality of life for rural Americas," the *Agricultural Outlook*, the "Latest ERS Products," a site search, "How to . . ." (e.g., "find state facts" and "visit our newsroom"), and "Key Topics." Examples of these topics are crops, food safety, and trade; each of these leads to subtopics and data.

⬂ Energy Information Administration

The Energy Information Administration (EIA), which was created by Congress in 1977, is a statistical agency of the Department of Energy. It provides "policy-independent data, forecasts, and analyses to promote sound policy making, efficient markets, and public understanding regarding energy and its interaction with the economy and the environment." The home page (**http://eia.doe.gov/**) covers "Energy A–Z," "What's New," "About Us/Jobs," "Press Releases," "Kid's Page" (see Chapter 13), "Publications," "Sign up for EMAIL Updates," "Contact Experts," "Energy Links," "Presentations," "Energy Events," and "Privacy/Security." Other choices include information and data by "Geography," "Fuel," and "Sector," as well as "process," "Environment," and "Forecasts." The EIA provides resources on the following topics:

- Petroleum
- Gasoline
- Diesel
- Natural Gas
- Electricity
- Coal
- Nuclear
- Renewables
- Alternative Fuels
- Prices
- State
- International
- Environment

There are also country analysis briefs (with country maps) and various energy analyses.

↗ Internal Revenue Service

The Internal Revenue Service's Tax Stats page (**http://www.irs.ustreas. gov/taxstat/index.html**) offers data files compiled from tax and information returns filed with the IRS. The topics include

- Individual Tax Statistics

- Corporation Tax Statistics

- Partnership Statistics

- Tax Exempt/Employee Plans Statistics

- Estates/Wealth/Gift Statistics

- Employment Taxes

- International Tax Statistics

- Sole Proprietorship Tax Statistics

- Excise Tax Statistics

The site also identifies statistics about the number of returns audited, the total number of returns by type of return, statistical description of the number and kinds of tax returns, as well as a statistical summary of the kinds of assistance the IRS has given to the public in recent years.

↗ National Agricultural Statistics Service

The National Agricultural Statistics Service (NASS) of the Department of Agriculture collects data on "virtually every facet of U.S. agriculture—production and supplies of food and fiber, prices paid and received by farmers, farm labor and wages, farm aspects of the industry. NASS also . . . conducts the Census of Agriculture every five years." Under statistical information, the home page (**http://www.usda.gov/nass**) covers "Publications," "Graphics," "Historical Data," "Search," "State Information," "Statistical Research," and "*Census of Agriculture.*" There is also access to "Today's reports" and the agency's online database. Under agency information, there is "Coming Events and News," "Customer Service," "Other Links," agency contact telephone numbers and personnel, state statistical offices, and the agency Web site for the nation's youth.

Agricultural Graphics (**http://www.usda.gov/nass/aggraphs/graphics.htm**) covers "Crops" (e.g., field crops, county maps, crop weather, and specialty crops), "Livestock" (e.g., cattle, dairy products, and poultry), "Cold Storage: Crops & Livestock," "Economics" (agricultural prices farm labor, grazing feeds, and farms and land on farms), and "Research" (satellite and vegetation imagery). Satellite research is based on the Normalized Difference Vegetation Index (NDVI), which "measures vegetation vigor caused by chlorophyll activity. . . . These data have proven valuable to USDA policy officials in providing geographic location and monitoring information for vegetation conditions in crop areas."

☞ National Center for Education Statistics

The National Center for Education Statistics (NCES), part of the Department of Education, has a Web site (**http://nces.ed.gov/**) that provides statistical charts, quick links (pull-down menus), news releases, "What's New," "Electronic Catalog," "Students Classroom," "Survey & Program Areas," "Encyclopedia of ED Stats," "Quick Tables & Figures," "Global ED Locator," "NCES Fast Facts," and "News Flash"—a service that alerts subscribers about new publications and data, conferences, training programs, workshops, and so on. Some examples of items available under "Encyclopedia of ED Stats," are

- *The Condition of Education,* an annual report to Congress on sixty indicators, "representing a professional consensus on the most significant national measures of the condition and progress of education"
- *The Digest of Education Statistics*
- Education Indicators: An International Perspective
- Youth Indicators

☞ National Center for Health Statistics

The National Center for Health Statistics is part of the Centers for Disease Control and Prevention, Department of Health and Human Services. The home page (**http://www.cdc.gov/nchs/**) offers assorted data (including public-use data files and documentation), "Highlights," facts, publications, vital statistics, a detailed site index (**http://www.cdc.gov/nchs/siteindex.htm**), and so on. The home page also provides clinical growth charts and information about the agency, as well as identifies the services of the Division of Data.

☞ Other

Returning to the Department of Agriculture, the USDA Economics and Statistics System covers topics such as agricultural baseline projections; farm sector economics; field crops; food; inputs, technology, and weather; international agriculture; land, water, and conservation; livestock, dairy, and poultry; rural affairs; specialty agriculture; and trade issues. Most of the "reports are text files that contain time-sensitive information. Most data sets are in spreadsheet format and include time-series data that are updated yearly." The Albert R. Mann Library, Cornell University, hosts the Economics and Statistics System (**http://usda.mannlib.cornell.edu/usda**) and is a partner with the Economic Research Service, the National Agricultural Statistics Service, and the World Agricultural Outlook Board of the Department of Agriculture.

The Economics and Statistics System participates in AgNIC (Agriculture Network Information Center), "a distributed network that provides access to agriculture-related information, subject area experts, and other resources." The AgNIC home page (**http://www.agnic.org**) lists "sponsored resources and activities," including the online reference services of the National Agricultural Library and libraries at some land grant universities. AgNIC covers agricultural and applied economics, animal science, animal welfare, asparagus, blueberry, chili pepper, food and nutrition, forestry, maple syrup, plant genetics, plant science, rangeland management, rural information, sustainable agriculture, technology transfer, turf grass, water quality, and wild blueberry. There is also a link to Cornell University's USDA Economics and Statistics System.

CONGRESSIONAL BUDGET OFFICE

"CBO aims to provide the Congress with the objective, timely, nonpartisan analyses needed for economic and budget decisions and with the information and estimates required for the Congressional budget process." It includes statistical reports on how the federal budget might be affected by natural disasters, health, homeland security, housing costs, labor, and so on. It also offers testimony, official reports, studies, and other tools designed to help legislators and their staff make sense out of trillions of dollars appropriated and spent through the federal budget. For instance, under "Computers & Information Science" (**http://www.cbo.gov/byclasscat.cfm?cat=24**), there are reports dealing with *The Need for Better Price Indices for Communication Investments,* and *The Role of Computer Technology in the Growth of Productivity*. The Web site (**http://www.cbo.gov/index.cfm**) also offers a search engine to locate specific cost estimates within the federal budget going back to 1999.

©Linsay Hernon

SUMMARY

The Web sites discussed in this chapter cover a wide variety of topics. FEDSTATS and its list of "Data Access Tools" (**http://www.fedstats.gov/toolkit.html**), as well as GPO Access (**http://www.library.okstate.edu/gov/govdocs/browsetopics/statisti.html**), identify a variety of statistical sources within the executive branch of government. Both the Bureau of Economic Analysis and the Bureau of the Census have broad mandates for the types of data they collect. The Census Bureau, for example, collects and reports data related to population, housing, retail and wholesale trade, service industries, construction, mineral industries, manufacturing, and state and local governments. The other sites discussed in this chapter tend to have a more specific focus: agriculture, criminal justice, education, energy, health, income tax returns, labor, and transportation. Sites might present maps, including ones that are interactive and enable users to construct basic profiles, and have resources aimed at teaching the nation's youth. Clearly, the amount and variety of information available from the federal statistical system is vast. As a consequence, readers might find Figure 8.1 helpful in an effort to identify some general subjects for which they seek statistics.

Figure 8.1. Selected Subject Guide.

Agriculture and Food

- National Agricultural Statistics Service (Department of Agriculture)
  http://www.usda.gov/nass/

- Economic Research Service (Department of Agriculture)
  http://www.ers.usda.gov/

- Foreign Agricultural Service (Department of Agriculture)
  http://www.fas.usda.gov/

- Centers for Disease Control and Prevention (Health and Human Services)

  - Division of Bacterial and Mycotic Diseases—Food Safety Initiative
    http://www.cdc.gov/foodsafety/default.htm

- National Resources Conservation Service (Department of Agriculture)
  http://www.nrcs.usda/gov/technical/

Crime and Justice

- Bureau of Justice Statistics (Department of Justice)
  http://www.ojp.usdoj.gov/bjs/

- Administrative Office of U.S. Courts
  http://www.uscourts.gov/news.html

- Drug Enforcement Administration (Department of Justice)
  http://www.usdoj.gov/dea/

Figure 8.1. (*Cont.*)

- Federal Bureau of Investigation (Department of Justice)
  http://www.fbi.gov/libref.htm

- Federal Bureau of Prisons (Department of Justice)
  http://www.bop.gov/

- Immigration and Naturalization Service (Department of Justice)
  http://www.ins.usdoj.gov/graphics/aboutins/statistics/index.htm

Demographics and Social Statistics

- Bureau of the Census (Department of Commerce)
  http://www.census.gov/population/www/index.html

Economic Data, National Accounts, International Trade

- Office of the Trade Representative (Executive Office of the President)
  http://www.ustr.gov/index.html

- Council of Economic Advisors (Executive Office of the President)
  http://www.whitehouse.gov/cea/
  - Economic Report of the President:
    http://w3.access.gpo.gov/eop/index.html

- Office of Trade and Economic Analysis (Department of Commerce)
  http://www.ita.doc.gov/td/industry/otea/

- Customs Service (Department of the Treasury)
  http://www.customs.gov/xp/cgov/home.xml

- Bureau of the Census (Department of Commerce)
  http://www.census.gov/cgi-bin/briefroom/BriefRm
  http://www.census.gov/epcd/www/econ97.html
  http://www.census.gov/foreign-trade/www/
  http://www.census.gov/epcd/www/naics.html

Education

- National Center for Education Statistics (Department of Education)
  http://nces.ed.gov/

- National Science Foundation
  http://www.nsf.gov/sbe/srs/stats.htm

Energy, Environment, and Natural Resources

- Energy Information Administration (Department of Energy)
  http://www.eia.doe.gov/
- National Oceanic and Atmospheric Administration (Department of Commerce)
  http://www.nesdis.noaa.gov/
- Geological Survey (Department of the Interior)
  http://www.usgs.gov/
- National Aeronautics and Space Administration
  http://www.earth.nasa.gov/
- Minerals Management Service (Department of the Interior)
  http://www.mms.gov/

- Natural Resources Conservation Service (Department of Agriculture)
  http://www.nrcs.usda.gov/TechRes.html
- Forest Service (Department of Agriculture)
  http://www.fs.fed.us/
- Environmental Protection Agency
  http://www.epa.gov/
  http://www.epa.gov/epahome/Data.html

Foreign Countries

- Federal Research Division (Library of Congress)
  http://lcweb2.loc.gov/frd/cs/cshome.html
- Central Intelligence Agency (Executive Office of the President)
  http://www.odci.gov/cia/publications/factbook/index.html
- Countries/regions (Department of State)
  http://www.state.gov/countries/index.htm
- Human Rights (Department of State)
  http://www.state.gov/g/drl/l
- Economic and Business Affairs (Department of State)
  http://www.state.gov/

Health and Health Care Industry

- National Center for Health Statistics (Department of Health and Human Services)
  http://www.cdc.gov/nchs/

Figure 8.1. (*Cont.*)

- Veterans Health Administration (Department of Veterans Affairs)
  http://www.va.gov/health_benefits/

- Centers for Medicare and Medicaid (Department of Health and Human Services)
  http://cms.hhs.gov/

- Agency for Toxic Substances and Disease Registry (Department of Health and Human Services)
  http://www.atsdr.cdc.gov/atsdrhome.html

- Healthfinder®
  http://healthfinder.gov/

- Agency for Healthcare Research and Quality (Department of Health and Human Services)
  http://www.ahcpr.gov/

- Bureau of the Census (Department of Commerce): Health Insurance Coverage
  http://www.census.gov/hhes/www/hlthins.html

Income/Labor

- Bureau of Labor Statistics (Department of Labor)
  http://www.bls.gov/iif/
  http://www.bls.gov/data/
  http://stats.bls.gov/

- Bureau of Economic Analysis (Department of Commerce)
  http://www.bea.doc.gov/

- Internal Revenue Service (Department of the Treasury)
  http://www.irs.gov/tax_stats/index.html

Military and Defense Resources

- Directorate for Information Operations and Reports (Department of Defense)
  http://web1.whs.osd.mil/peidhome/peidhome.htm

Safety and Emergency Management

- Bureau of Labor Statistics (Department of Labor)
  http://stats.bls.gov/oshhome.htm

- National Highway Traffic Safety Administration (Department of Transportation)
  http://safety.fhwa.dot.gov/facts_data/facts_data.htm

- Federal Emergency Management Agency

http://www.fema.gov/library/femainfo.shtm

- Office of Environment, Safety, and Health (Department of Energy)
  http://tis.eh.doe.gov/portal/home.htm

- Occupational Safety and Health Administration (Department of Labor)
  http://www.osha.gov/oshstats/index.html

- Mine Safety and Health Administration (Department of Labor)
  http://www.msha.gov/stats/STATINFO.HTM

Transportation

- Bureau of Transportation Statistics (Department of Transportation)
  http://www.bts.gov/

- Bureau of the Census (Department of Commerce)
  http://www.census.gov/econ/www/tasmenu.html

NOTES

1. Julie L. Nicklin, "Inconsistencies Mar Web Site on Campus Crime," *The Chronicle of Higher Education* (December 1, 2000): A46.

2. 114 STAT. 2763A-154, *Consolidated Appropriations Act,* 2001 (Public Law 106-554).

3. The rules and regulations have gone through two successive comment periods; see http://www.whitehouse.gov/omb/inforeg/iqg_draft_guidelines.pdf.

4. See "Symposium on the 1997 Economic Census, U.S. Bureau of the Census," *Government Information Quarterly* 15 (1997): 243–380.

5. See "Symposium on the Decennial Census," *Government Information Quarterly* 17 (2000): 93–234.

FEDSTATS
http://www.fedstats.gov/

Data Access Tools
http://www.fedstats.gov/toolkit.html

Statistical Reference Shelf
http://www.fedstats.gov/fast.html

Congressional Budget Office
http://www.cbo.gov/

Computers & Information Science
http://www.cbo.gov/byclasscat.cfm?
cat=24

Department of Agriculture
AgNIC
http://www.agnic.org

Economic Research Service
http://www.ers.usda.gov/

Foreign Agricultural Service
http:www.fas.usda.gov/

Forest Service
http://www.fs.fed.us/

National Agricultural Statistics Service
http://www.usda.gov/nass/

Agricultural Graphics
http://www.usda.gov/nass/aggraphs/
graphics.htm

National Resources Conservation Service
http://www.nncs.usda.gov/technical/

USDA Economic Statistics System
http://usda.mannlib.cornell.edu/usda

Department of Commerce

Economics and Statistics Administration
http://www.esa.doc.gov/

Bureau of Economics Analysis
http://www.bea.doc.gov/

Gross State Product Data
http://www.bea.doc.gov/bea/
regional/data.htm

STAT-USA
http://www.stat-usa.gov/
http://orders.stat-usa.gov/

Bureau of the Census
http://www.census.gov/

CenStats
http://www.census.gov/apsd/www/
censtats.html

Census Briefs
http://www.census.gov/prod/www/
abs/briefs.hml

Citation Patterns for Census Products
http://www.census.gov/main/www/
citation.html

County and City Data Book
http://www.census.gov/statab/www/
ccdb.html

Demographics/Social Statistics
http://www.census.gov/population/
www/index.html

Demographic Surveys
http://www.census.gov/main/www/
sur_demo.html

Economic Census
http://www.census.gov/epcd/www/
econ97.html

Economic Surveys
http://www.census.gov/main/www/
sur_econ.html

GIS Gateway
http://www.census.gov/geo/www/
gis_gateway.html

Health Insurance Coverage
http://www.censs.gov/hhes/www/
hltins.html

Map Gallery
http://www.census.gov/geo/www/
mapGallery/index.html

Map Stats
http://quickfacts.census.gov/qfd/
index.html

Products and Publications
http://www.census.gov/prod/www/
titles.html

State and Metropolitan Area Data Book
http://www.census.gov/statab/www/
smadb.html

Statistical Abstract of the United States
http://www.census.gov/statab/www/
http://www.census.gov/prod/www/
statistical-abstract-02.html

Statistical Briefs
http://www.census.gov/apsd/www/
statbrief/

Transportation
http://www.census.gov/econ/www/
tasmenu.html

USA Statistics in Brief
http://www.census.gov/statab/www/
brief.html

Other
http://www.census.gov/cgi-bin/
briefroom/BriefRm
http://www.census.gov/epcd/www/
econ97.html
http://www.census.gov/foreign-trade/
www/
http://www.census.gov/epcd/www/
naics.html

National Oceanic and Atmospheric Administration
http://www.nesdis.noa.gov/

Office of Trade and Economic Analysis
http://www.ita.doc.gov/td/industry/
otea/

Department of Defense
Directorate for Information Operations and Reports
http://web1.whs.osd.mil/peidhome./
peidhome.htm

Department of Education

College Campus Security
http://ope.ed.gov/security

National Center for Education Statistics
http://nces.ed.gov/

Department of Energy

Energy Information Administration
http://www.eia.doe.gov/

Office of Environment, Safety and Health
http://tis.eh.doe.gov/portal/home.htm

Department of Health and Human Services

Administration on Aging
http://www.aoa.dhhs.gov/aoa/stats/
statpage.heml

Agency for Healthcare Research and Quality
http://www.ahcpr.gov/

Agency for Toxic Substances and Disease Registry
http://www.atsdr.cdc.gov/atsdrhome.html

Atlas of the United States Mortality
http://www.cdc.gov/nchs/products/pubs/
pubd/other/atlas/causes.htm

Food Safety
Centers for Disease Control and Prevention
http://www.cdc.gov/foodsafety/default.
htm

Centers for Medicare and Medicaid Services
http://cms.hhs.gov/

Healthfinder®
http://www.healthfinder.gov/

National Center for Health Statistics
http://www.cdc.gov/nchs/
http://www.cdc.gov/nchs/default.html

    Site Index
    http://www.cdc.gov/nchs/siteindex.
    htm

    Smoking
    http://www.cdc.gov/nchs/fastats/
    smoking.htm
    http://www.cdc.gov/tobacco/
    mission.htm

Department of Interior

Mineral Management Service
http://www.mms.gov/

U.S. Geological Survey
http://www.usgs.gov/

Department of Justice

Bureau of Justice Statistics
http://www.ojp.usdoj.gov/bjs/

Drug Enforcement Administration
http://www.usdoj.gov/dea/

Federal Bureau of Investigation
http://www.fbi.gov/
http://www.fbi.gov/ucr.htm
http://www.fbi.gov/libref.htm

Federal Bureau of Prisons
http://www.bop.gov/

Immigration and Naturalization Service
http://www.ins.usdoj.gov/graphics/abouti
ns/statistics/index.htm

Department of Labor

Bureau of Labor Statistics
http://www.bls.gov/iif/
http://www.bls.gov/data
http://stats.bls.gov/

Mine Safety and Health Administration
http://www.msha.gov/stats/STATINFO.
HTM

Occupational Safety and Health Administration
http://www.osha.gov/oshstats/index.html

Department of State

Countries/Regions
http://www.state.gov/countries/index.
htm

Economic and Business Affairs
http://www.state.gov/

Human Rights
http://www.state.gov/g/drl/1

Department of the Treasury

Customs Service
http://www.customs.gov/xp/cgov/
home.xml

Statistics of Income Program
Internal Revenue Service
http://www.irs.ustreas.gov/tax_stats/
index.html

Department of Transportation

Bureau of Transportation Statistics
http://ww.bts.gov/

Commodity Flow Survey
http://www.bts.gov/ntda/cfs/

International Transportation
http://www.bts.gov/itt

National Household Transportation Survey
http://www.bts.gov/nhts/

National Transportation Data Archive
http://www.transtats.bls.gov/

National Transportation Library
http://ntl.bts.gov/

    TRIS Online
    http://199.79.179.82/sundev.
    search.cfm

Office of Airline Information
http://ntl.bts.gov/

National Highway Traffic Safety Administration
http://safety.fhwa.dot.gov/facts_data/
facts_data.htm

Department of Veterans Affairs
Veterans Health Administration
http://www.va.gov/health_benefits/

Environmental Protection Agency
http://www.epa.gov/
http://epa.gov/epahome/Data.html

Executive Office of the President

Central Intelligence Agency
http://www.odci.gov/cia/publications/
factbook/index.html

Council of Economic Advisors
http://www.whitehouse.gov/cea/index.
html

Economic Report of the President
http://http://w3/access.gpo.gov/eop/

Office of the Trade Representative
http://www.ustr.gov/index.html

Federal Emergency Management Agency
http://www.fema.gov/library/femainfo.
shtm

General Accounting Office
http://www.gao.gov/

American Community Survey report
http://www.gao.gov/new.items/
d02956r.pdf

Government Printing Office

Location of Nearest Depository Library
http://www.gpoaccess.gov/libraries.html

Browse Titles
http://www.library.okstate.edu/govdocs/
browsetopics/statisti/html

Statistics

http://www.library.okstate.edu/govdocs/
browsetopics/statisti.html

Library of Congress

Federal Research Division
http://lcweb2.loc.gov/frd/cs/cshome.html

National Aeronautics and Space Administration
http://www.earth.nass.gov/

National Science Foundation
http://www.nsf.gov/sbe/srs/stats.htm

U.S. Courts

Administrative Office
http://www.uscourts.gov/news.html

Chapter 9

Web Portals and
Electronic Reference Desks

The scale, number, complexity, and quality of programs that the national government manages often overwhelm and confound any serious attempt for Web sites to offer users a simple interface or database engine. One way to address this issue, however, has been the development of Web sites that try to make it easier to find needed information and services among the thousands of government agencies, bureaus, and offices. These sites, called "Web portals" or "gateways," are excellent places to begin (and, in some cases, conclude) a general search, although they have inherent limitations. Another evolving category is *electronic reference service* that government libraries offer to answer general questions that the public poses. The purpose of this chapter is to highlight both Web portals and electronic reference desks or service.

FIRSTGOV

FirstGov (**http://www.firstgov.gov/**) is the primary portal for federal public information, and it is described as "the official gateway to all government information. . . . Our work transcends the traditional boundaries of government and our vision is global—connecting the world to all U.S. government information and services." Developed in the mid-1990s as part of the Clinton administration's "reinventing government" initiative, it is now managed by the General Services Administration. FirstGov provides access to about 27 million federal Web pages and further links to about 24 million other Web pages produced by state, local, regional, tribal, and territorial government Web sites, as well as Internet resources produced by foreign countries and international organizations. FirstGov users can find information through two methods: viewing pages organized by subjects or by using a sophisticated search engine (see Chapter 3).

Based on the same software that powers a commercial search engine (the software was "given" to the federal government by its owner and creator as a way of getting FirstGov started), it is at best an iffy proposition to use when a person searches for information in a general way. "Search Tips" offers guidance to first-time users (**http://www.firstgov.gov/Help/Search_Tips.shtml**). Those tips should be read carefully to ensure that searches are as effective as possible. Furthermore, one must not forget that this feature organizes a search through millions of federal Web pages, and that the results often depend on how well the subject of the search is understood and the kinds of words chosen in conducting that search. As example, using the words "travel advisory Germany" (in the hopes of finding something about the dangers of travel in that European country) turns up more than a thousand matches, and none of the first hundred appear to be relevant. The words "travel warning Germany," however, leads to a list of travel warnings; the Web page of the Department of State's Consular Affairs (**http://travel.state.gov/travel_warnings.html**) is among the first few entries. This example demonstrates how such search engines, although powerful in speed and scope, still cannot distinguish between when the words occur, and when they occur in a context that meets the needs of the information seekers. Obviously, Web searching of this type is still in early days of development. There is also an advanced search capability (**http://www.firstgov.gov/fgsearch/index.jsp**).

Consumers (**http://www.consumer.gov/**), which is arranged by subject (e.g., food, health, home and community, transportation, children, careers and education, technology, product safety, and money), identifies a broad range of online government consumer information from various government bodies (see the twenty-two page list of them at **http://www.consumer.gov/about.htm**); this page also provides links to their Web sites.

Science (**http://www.science.gov/**) "contains reliable information resources selected by the respective agencies as their best science information. Two major types of information are included—selected authoritative science Web sites and databases of technical reports, journal articles, conference proceedings, and other published materials." The Web site offers links to significant scientific resources according to the following categories:

- Agriculture & Food: Food Safety, Gardening, Pesticides, and Veterinary Science

- Applied Science & Technologies: Biotechnology, Electronics, Engineering, and Transportation

- Astronomy & Space: Exploration, Planets, Space Technologies

- Biology & Nature: Animals & Plants, Ecology, Genetics, and Pest Control

- Computers & Communication: Network, Hardware, Software

- Earth & Ocean Sciences: Land, Maps, Natural Disasters, Oceans, and Weather

- Energy & Energy Conservation: Energy Use, Fossil Fuel, Solar, and Wind

- Environment & Environmental Quality: Air/Water/Noise Quality, Cleanup, and Climate Change

- Health & Medicine: Disease, Health Care, Nutrition, and Mental Health

- Math, Physics, & Chemistry: Astrophysics, Chemicals, and Mathematical Modeling

- Natural Resources & Conversation: Ecosystems, Energy Resources, and Forestry Mining

- Science Education: Homework Help and Teaching Aids (All Topics)

FirstGov also groups resources for special groups, including children (**http://www.kids.gov/**), senior citizens (**http://www.seniors.gov/**), and students (**http://www.students.gov/**).

BUSINESS INFORMATION, CONTRACTING SERVICES, TRADE, AND TRANSACTIONS

The U.S. Business Advisor (**http://www.business.gov/**) "exists to provide business with one-stop access to federal government information, services, and transactions. Our goal is to make the relationship between business and government more productive." The site offers a "Business Resource Library," "Agencies & Gateways [Federal Agency business pages and one-stop gateways]," and "How Do I . . . (Find the Answers by Searching Our FAQs),"as well as covering the following topics:

- Business Development

- Financial Assistance

- Taxes

- Laws and Regulations

- International Trade

- Workplace Issues

- Buying and Selling

It is also possible to conduct a search of the site, visit the site map, examine "What's New," and so on.

For business opportunities with the Federal Government, FedBizOpps (**http://www.gedbizopps.gov/**) casts itself as the Web portal for federal procurement opportunities over $25,000. This includes the opportunity for buyers from the government to post their contracting needs directly on the Web site and allow commercial vendors to review the contract needs. A related site, AcqNet.gov (**http://www.acqnet.gov/**), is produced by the Office of Management and Budget's Office of Federal Procurement Policy. AcqNet.gov provides an overview of federal policy statements and reports involving federal acquisitions and contracts.

TradeNet's Export Advisor (**http://www.tradenet.gov/**) "features a range of information and services ranging from tailored links in 'getting started' in exporting to local export contacts searchable by zip code, trade finance information, searchable international business opportunities or trade leads, export answers accessible by keyword search, and an export library with scores of export promotion links." This portal is particularly useful when users do not know the agency or government body that might have the information needed.

DISABILITIES

In late August 2002, President Bush announced a new executive initiative called the "New Freedom Initiative" among federal agencies to build a Web portal for people with disabilities, their families, and others interested or concerned about the disability issues (**http://www.disabilityinfo.gov/**). It offers information and further links about employment, education, housing, transportation, health, income support, technology, community life, and civil rights. (Chapter 12 provides additional discussion of such Web-based resources.)

FEDERAL CONSUMER INFORMATION CENTER (FCIC) AND CONSUMER-RELATED INFORMATION

Established in 1970 within the General Services Administration, the Federal Consumer Information Center (FCIC) in Pueblo, Colorado, (**http://www.pueblo.gsa.gov/**) distributes consumer information to the public. The *Consumer Information Catalog*, that stalwart publication of late-night television commercials, is an inexpensive but helpful guide to everything from fixing an automobile to insulating a house. The catalog can be ordered from the FCIC's Web page (**http://www.pueblo.gsa.gov/cicform.htm**), but a .pdf (portable document format) version can also be download (**http://www. pueblo.gsa.gov.catalog.pdf**). Many of the publications in the catalog can be accessed directly from the FCIC home. This page offers a wealth of news information, pamphlet-type material, links to Web sites, and other information aimed at the consumer. For example, "Links" leads to the topics of "cars," "computers," "education," "employment," "federal programs," "food," "health," "housing," "money," "small business," "travel," "and more." From these topics, there are links to government and nongovernment sites.

An important publication available from the Web site is the *2001 Consumer Action Handbook*, which is available in .pdf, HTML, and .TXT formats and which

provides advice and consumer tips on: car repair, purchase, and leasing; shopping from home; avoiding consumer and investment fraud; home improvement and financing; choosing and using credit cards wisely; and much more. Also included is the Consumer Assistance Directory with thousands of names, addresses, telephone numbers, web site and e-mail addresses for national consumer organizations, better business bureaus, corporations, trade associations, state and local consumer protection offices, state agencies, military consumer offices, and Federal agencies.

Federal Information Center

FCIC's Federal Information Center (FIC), part of the General Services Administration operation and established in 1966, receives nationwide telephone calls from the public (toll-free: 800-688-9889; 800-326-2996 for TTY users) seeking answers to questions about government agencies, programs, and services. FIC's staff either answer directly or refer the caller to the correct office or agency. "Not surprisingly, many asks the same questions. We've gathered answers to some frequently asked topics below. Your question isn't here? Call us." The home page (**http://www.info.gov/**) offers those topics:

- Social Security
- Federal Loans
- Federal Grants
- Freedom of Information
- Work Place Issues
- Federal Employment
- Medicare and Medicaid
- Congress
- Consumer Topics
- Recalls
- Savings Bonds
- Government Publications
- Privacy
- Travel Abroad
- Finding Military Person
- The Draft
- Presidential Greetings
- Order a Flag

Each topic provides answers as well as links to Web pages. For example, "Congress" provides links to members who have home page, and "Government publications" offer general advice about where the public can purchase or read an item.
Children (**http://www.kids.gov/**) provides

educational subjects that you might have in your school. Within each subject, we have also divided the sites into these categories: Government, Organizations, Education, and Commercial. The government sites could be federal, state, or military sites. Government sites generally do not sell anything. They are simply sharing information with visitors. Organization sites are developed by groups that have an interest in a special topic and they want to share their information. Sometimes these sites do sell products. Education sites are developed by schools. They can be developed by colleges/universities or high, middle, or elementary schools. These sites usually do not have products to sell. Commercial sites are developed by businesses. Commercial sites share information, but they also have products to sell.

Press and News Releases (**http://www.pueblo.gsa.gov/call/pressreleases.htm**) provides a gateway to news and press release Web sites throughout the U.S. government.

FOOD SAFETY

FoodSafety.gov (**http://www.foodsafety.gov/**) is a gateway to government food safety information. It offers "News & Safety Alerts," "Consumer Advice," "Kids, Teens, & Educators" (thus complementing Chapter 13), "Report Illness & Product Complaints," "Foodborne Pathogens," "Industry Assistance," "National Food Safety Initiative," "Federal & State Gov't Agencies," "Other Topics," and "Search & Site Index." There are videos, frequently asked questions, materials in different languages, and "Selected Highlights" of key information. The frequently asked questions are arranged by subjects, thereby enabling the consumer to find the sought after information in an efficient manner.

GOVERNMENT BENEFITS

GovBenefits.gov (**http://www.govbenefits.gov/jsp/GovBenefits.jsp**) is a good example of various agencies working together to provide a single portal that identifies possible funding or benefit opportunities for individuals. It presents a database of government benefit programs that is searchable through a series of questions about an individual's particular financial, social, or economic conditions. No personal information (e.g., name and social security number) is requested, and the questions are specific, thereby enabling the user to get some very specific and useful programs from which to choose.

HEALTH INFORMATION

Since 1997, the Department of Health and Human Services launched Healthfinder® (**http://www.healthfinder.gov/**), a consumer information service that offers a wide range of facts and data on health and physical well-being. It includes statistics on the leading causes of death in the United States, the conditions and consequences of smoking, unhealthy diet habits, physical inactivity, and substance abuse.

The site is arranged by the following categories:

- Health Library
- Just For You
- Health Care
- Directory of Healthfinder organizations
- Health News
- Online Checkups

Most important, the portal is a "free guide to reliable health information." Healthgov (**http://www.health.gov/**) is "a portal to the Web sites of a number of multi-agency health initiatives and activities of the Department of Health and Human Services and other Federal departments and agencies." It is coordinated by the Office of Disease Prevention and Health Promotion, which is part of the Health and Human Service Department's Secretary's office.

JOBS AND EMPLOYMENT

In addition to the Web site of the Office of Personnel Management (see chapter 6; **http://www.usajobs.opm.gov/**), two portals (**http://www.americorps.org/**; **http://www.ajb.dni.us/**) offer employment or career opportunities in the government as well as opportunities for community service and volunteer work. In addition to these portals, most government home pages provide career information and opportunities. This is true regardless of the branch of government.

NONPROFIT SECTOR

U.S. Nonprofit Gateway (**http://firstgov.gov/Topics/Nonprofit.shtml**) is a central access point for federal government and agency information resources geared to the nonprofit section. It enables visitors to search more than 530,000 government Web pages, to link to the home pages of executive branch departments and selected independent agencies, to connect to some government clearinghouses and services, and to find management and policy resources related to grants and contracts, nonfinancial information, laws, regulations, forms, public and private partnerships, volunteering, and so on.

RECREATION

Recreation.gov (**http://www.recreation.gov/**) is a partnership among the U.S. Army Corp of Engineers, Bureau of Land Management, Bureau of Reclamation, Fish and Wildlife Service, Forest Service, Tennessee Valley Authority, Federal Highway Administration, and National Park Service. It serves as a portal "for information about recreation on federal lands." Users can find recreation opportunities on public lands by state or recreational activity (biking, climbing, camping, fishing, hiking, winter sports, and wildlife viewing). A search results in the names, locations, and telephone numbers for the specific recreation areas.

RESEARCH AND DEVELOPMENT

Federal Research and Development Project Summaries (**http://www.osti.gov/fedrnd/**) provide access to information about federal research projects located in various departments and agencies. Through this resource, it is possible to gain access to the EnergyFiles Virtual Library (**http://www.osti.gov/energyfiles**), the PrePRINT Network (**http://www.osti.gov/preprint**), and the GrayLIT Network (**http://graylit.osti.gov/**; see Chapter 5 for additional coverage of these sites). The GrayLIT Network contains full-text technical reports for the Department of Energy, Department of Defense, Environmental Protection Agency, and the National Aeronautics and Space Administration.

STUDENTS

There are two major Web portals for students. The first, sponsored by the Department of Education (**http://www.students.gov/**), offers a wide selection of information and further Web resources under the following topics: planning for education opportunities after high school, career development, military service obligations and opportunities, how to pay for education, community services, how do research on government policies and programs, additional resources, as well as resources classified by travel and fun. On the left side of the page are two quick link boxes that offer direct connections to how to file for financial aid, file taxes, finding consumer information, find health information, and safety. The second Web site offers a wealth of information about after school activities for teenagers (**http://www.afterschool.gov/cgi-binh/ home.pl**) that allows students and their parents to search "web sites that let them explore the wealth of information the federal government agencies have to offer whether they are looking for help with their homework; reinforcing a skill they learned in school; researching a school term paper; looking for a job, college or volunteer opportunities; researching an topic just because it is interesting; or they just want to surf." A companion Web site, America'steens.gov, can be found at **http://www.Americasteens .gov/**.

U.S. BLUE PAGES

These online telephone books and directories (**http://www.usbluepages.gov/**) to the federal government are one of the best places to connect to the services and initiatives of the federal government or to seek an answer to a question from a federal agency. The U.S. Blue Pages are an easy-to-use directory that links to various government agencies and federal services. The Web site is organized by topic (e.g., "Elected Officials" and "Money and Taxes"). An interesting feature is that the information provided can be localized. In other words, an option is "Give me local information," which leads to

- My home state is . . .

- My city is . . .

For example, "the state of Alabama and the city of Birmingham" can be combined with the topic of "Elected Officials" to produce a listing of the state's senators and the representative of that areas, together with their home page. Clearly, the Blue Pages enable information seekers to focus on their state and locality. A companion Web page to the Blue Pages can be found as part of the Federal Citizen Information Center. Called the National Contact Center (**http://www.pueblo.gsa.gov/call/ phone.htm**), it offers lists of frequently requested toll-free telephone numbers, as well as numbers to members of Congress, cabinet agencies, and other agencies and commissions.

SUSTAINABLE COMMUNITY DEVELOPMENT

The Energy Efficiency and Renewable Energy Network (EREN) of the Department of Energy (**http://www.sustainable.doe.gov/**) deals with sustainable development, "a strategy by which communities seek economic development approaches that also benefit the local environment and quality of life." Among the topics covered are

- Green Buildings and Development
- Local Use Planning
- Measuring Progress
- Disaster Planning
- Community Energy
- Transportation
- Sustainable Business
- Financing
- Rural Issues
- Resource Efficiency (Air, Water, Materials)

Another offering is the "Top Websites on Sustainable Community Development" (**http://www.ustainable.doe.gov/hotspots.shtml**). There is even customized geographic information service software for measuring community indicators.

EDUCATION

Federal Resources for Educational Excellence (FREE; **http://www.ed.gov/free**) makes federally supported teaching and learning resources easier to locate. The site is more than a collection of resources; it also serves as a collaborative tool that encourages partnerships between educators and government agencies.

IMMIGRATION

The American Immigration Center (**http://www.us-immigration.com/**) discusses visas and becoming a citizen, and it offers forms, services, study guides, a message board, chat room, and other resources.

HOW STANDARDS ARE SET

The National Institute of Standards and Technology (see Chapter 5) has a portal (**http://ts.nist.gov/ts/htdocs/210/gsig/gsig.htm**) that covers conformity assessment and how it affects the daily lives of the public. Conformity assessment involves any method or procedure used to ensure that a product, service, or system follows a set of standards or meets certain requirements. This includes testing, inspection, certification, and accreditation. The purpose is to verify that a particular product meets a given level of quality or safety (e.g., the refrigerator plug that fits into the electronic outlet). If the verification is conducted improperly, the product may malfunction or confuse consumers.

ELECTRONIC REFERENCE DESKS

Another type of comprehensive information service is being forged through partnerships between universities and government agencies, as well as through government libraries. These electronic library "reference desks" answer any and all public questions (through e-mail, forms available on special Web pages, or, in a few cases, through chat services, which allow the librarian and user to communicate through the exchange of real-time text messages). A few examples of this evolving service are (also see the next chapter):

- "Ask a Librarian" (Library of Congress; **http://www.loc.gov/rr/askalib/**)

- "Ask a Librarian" (U.S. Geological Survey; **http://library.usgs.gov/request. html**)

- "Contacts" (Energy Information Administration; **http://www.eia.doe.gov/ contacts/main.html**)

- Electronic Research Collections (ERC; Department of State; **http://dosfan.lib. uic.edu**)

- Virtual Reference Desk (National Library of Education; **http://www.vrd.org/**)

"Ask a Librarian" service, whether operated by the Library of Congress or U.S. Geological Survey (USGS) Library, are designed to meet the following needs (as reflected in the description of the USGS service):

If you are a student, teacher, or researcher, you may use our e-mail reference service for assistance in finding information on geology, hydrology, cartography, biology, paleontology, environmental science and related topics. A USGS reference librarian will attempt to respond within 3 working days. The response may include an answer to your question, a list of resources that will help you find the answer, or a request for clarification.

Many agencies, including the Energy Information Administration (**http://www. eia.doe.gov/contacts/main.htm**), identify personnel who are experts on a particular topic and who can answer queries.

The first three of the examples in the bulleted list are services operated by the government, whereas the last two examples demonstrate how universities (in this case the University of Illinois at Chicago and Syracuse University) work with the agency's public affairs officers to help sort, answer, and archive questions from the public.

ERC is an extension of a seven-year arrangement with the State Department to manage a collection of Web pages featuring historic department news, policy position papers, and other foreign relations information from 1993 to the present. These pages provide immediate, global access to official U.S. foreign policy information and decision making. Updated daily, they include country and issue specific information on sociopolitical situations, economic trends, democracy, human rights, culture, development assistance, environment, terrorism, and more. Speeches, statements, and testimony by the president, secretary of state, and other senior department officials are featured, along with many publications such as congressional reports.

In addition to these official sources of information, librarians at the University of Illinois at Chicago also answer questions from the public that cover a wide range of topics. They developed a series of Frequently Asked Reference Questions (FARQ; **http://dosfan.lib.uic.edu/ERC/refdesk.html**) that cover some of the most popular subjects from the thousands of queries received over the years. Subjects include everything from getting married in a foreign country, getting arrested, and recovering the body of someone who has died overseas, to how long family pets might have to stay in isolation before being allowed back in the United States after extensive foreign travel. The site also contains historical, policy, and directory information.

The Education Department's Virtual Reference Desk (VRD) began as a pilot project between the ERIC Clearinghouse on Information & Technology at Syracuse University and the National Library of Education, with support from the White House Office of Science and Technology. Begun in 1997, the initial project focused on answering questions from the elementary and high school community via the Web. Three years later, the service evolved to answering questions from a broader public. The primary objective was to create an Internet-based question-and-answer service that connects users with individuals who possess specialized subject or skill expertise. Unlike the ERC service, VRD attempts to facilitate the answers to public questions through better communication with affiliated "experts." It creates specific subject-based electronic reference sources. To search the wealth of experts available, check the subject guide found at **http://www.vrd.org/index.shtml**.

As described on the Web site,

When a subject specific service receives questions which are out of its stated scope area, it can forward those questions to the VRD Network for assistance. If a question cannot be addressed by another participating service, it will be handled by one of the VRD Network Information Specialists, a librarian volunteering to respond with suggestions or an answer. The network can accept questions from K–12 students, educators, parents, and others. Each service responds to questions using its own format, policy, and response time. The volunteer librarians with the VRD Network have an intensive training session before taking actual questions from patrons.

These services participate with the VRD Network in question exchanges for

- Ask A MAD Scientist
- AskERIC
- Ask a Space Scientist (NASA)
- Eisenhower National Clearinghouse for Mathematics and Science Education
- Environmental Protection Agency
- Internet Public Library

- Library of Congress's American Memory
- Morris County Public Library (NJ)
- National Museum of American Art
- ScienceLine (from the UK)

SUMMARY

Instead of consulting a general search engine, or when they experience problems in using a Web site of a specific federal agency, information seekers might try any of the portals or gateways discussed in this chapter. Indeed, the advantage of these sites is that information seekers only have to search one location. Some of the highlighted sites only present information, whereas others offer both information and services. At least by using these portals, a person has a clear idea of where to begin to search. That search, however, might also involve services—the kinds of sites discussed in Chapter 10.

Although it does not comprise a portal, the National Biological Information Infrastructure (NBII), which the Center for Biological Informatics of the U.S. Geological Survey developed and maintains, is a worthy inclusion in this chapter. The NBII (**http://www.nbii.gov/**) provides access to data and information related to biology.[1] The home page explains the NBII; "Current Biological Issues," which covers "hot topics" for biological research; "Teacher Resources" ("activities, lesson plans, experiments, projects, resources, and references for classroom and home use," thus complementing Chapter 13); and more.

Finally, a number of libraries, such as those in the federal depository program, may have purchased or acquired government information from a private vendor, such as the Congressional Information Service. Nongovernment "one-stop shopping" services may offer better-organized ways of locating and retrieving information. Given their cost to individual libraries, however, access to them may be limited to their own clientele; thus, these libraries may be unable to accept requests from the general public. Expanding "Ask a Librarian" services over the last few years throughout many libraries suggests that many reference librarians now consider the Web to be equal to their in-person or telephone programs.

NOTE

1. See Ron Sepic and Kate Kase, "The National Biological Information Infrastructure as an E-Government Tool," *Government Information Quarterly* 19 (2002): 407–24.

URL Site Guide for This Chapter

FirstGov
http://www.firstgov.gov/

Search Tips
FirstGov
http://www.firstgov.gov/Help/Search_
Tips.shtml

Advanced Search Capability
FirstGov
http://www.firstgov.gov/fgsearch/
index.jsp

U.S. Nonprofit Gateway
http://www.firstgov.gov/Topics/
Nonprofit/shtml

Travel Warnings and Information Sheets

State Department
http://travel.state.gov/travel_warnings.
html

Portals Aimed at Particular Groups

Kids
http://www.kids.gov/

Individuals with Disabilities
http://www.disabilityinfo.gov/

Senior Citizens
http://www.seniors.gov/

Students
http://www.students.gov/

After School Activities for Teenagers
http://www.afterschool.gov/cgi-binh/
home.pl

AcqNet.gov
http://www.acqnet.gov/

Federal Consumer Information Center
http://www.pueblo.gsa.gov/

Consumer Information Catalog
http://www.pueblo.gsa.gov/cicform.htm
http://www.pueblo.gsa.gov.catalog.pdf

National Contact Center
http://www.pueblo.gsa.gov/call/phone.htm

Press and News releases
http://www.pueblo.gsa.gov/call/
pressreleases.htm

Federal Information Center
http://www.info.gov/

Science
http://www.science.gov/

U.S. Blue Pages
http://www.usbluepages.gov/

U.S. Consumer Gateway
http://www.consumer.gov

Online Information
http://www.consumer.gov/about.htm

FedBizOpps
http://www.gedbizopps.gov/

FirstGov for Worker
http://workers.gov/

U.S. Business Advisor
http://www.busines.gov

TradeNet's Export Advisor
http://www.tradenet.gov

Federal Resources for Educational Excellence
http:///www.ed.gov/free

FoodSafety.gov
http://www.foodsafety.gov/

Healthfinder®
http://www.healthfinder.gov/

Healthgov
http://www.health.gov/

Standards
**National Institute of Standards and
    Technology**
http://ts.nist.gov/ts/htdocs/210/gsig/gsig/htm

American Immigration Center
http://www.us-immigration.com/

Recreation.gov
http://www.recreation.gov/

**Energy Efficiency and Renewable
    Energy Network**
http://www.sustainable.doe.gov/

> **Top Web Sites on Sustainable
>   Community Development**
> http://www.sustainable.doe.gov/
>   hotspots.shtml

EnergyFiles Virtual Library
http://www.osti.gov/energyfiles

**Federal Research and Development
    Project Summaries**
http://www.osti.gov/fedrnd/

GrayLIT Network
http://www.osti.gov/fedmd/

PrePRINT Network
http://www.osti.gov/preprint

Employment

> http://www.usajobs.opm.gov/
> http://www.americorps.org/
> http://www.ajb.dni.us/

GovBenefits.gov
http://www.govbenefits.gov/jsp/
    GovBenefits.jsp

Electronic Reference Service

> **Ask a Librarian**
> http://library.usgs.gov/request.html

Contacts

> **Energy Information Administration**
> http://www.eia.doe.gov/contacts/main.
>   html

> **Electronic Research Collections**
> http://dosfan.lib.uic.edu

>> **Frequently Asked Reference
>>   Questions**
>> Department of State
>> (University of Illinois at Chicago)
>> http://dosfan.lib.uic/ERC/refdesk.html

> **Please Answer Question**
> Energy Information Administration
> http://www.eia.doe.gov/contacts/main.
>   html

> **Virtual Reference Desk**
> National Library of Education
> http://www.vrd.org/

>> **Subject Guide**
>> Virtual Reference Desk
>> National Library of Education
>> http://www.vrd.org/index.shtml

**National Biological Information
    Infrastructure**

> **U.S. Geological Survey**
> http://www.nbii.gov/

Chapter 10

Government Web-based Services

Electronic government is an evolving concept, meaning different things to different people. It has significant relevance to four important areas of governance, however:

1. Delivery of services

2. Providing information

3. Facilitating the procurement of goods and services

4. Facilitating efficient exchanges within and between government bodies

These areas may overlap; services may extend to the public but may also facilitate procurement and efficient exchanges within the federal government and with subnational levels of government. This chapter complements the previous one, showing that the government offers online services to the public and special groups (e.g., agency contractors) and has as its goal the provision of interactive transactions and electronic commerce in a secure environment. Security is essential if transactions involve the transmission of private data such as social security numbers and credit card numbers, and security includes the implementation of encryption procedures to protect e-commerce transactions. Still, issues related to the archival management of electronic records remain unresolved (see Chapter 1).

PRIVACY

Internet privacy encompasses a range of concerns that could affect the provision of services. One is that the Internet makes it easier for government and the private sector to obtain information about consumers and possibly use that information to the consumer's detriment. Such issues focus on the extent to which Webmasters collect personally identifiable information about individuals and share that information with third parties, often without the knowledge or consent of the people concerned.

Another aspect of Internet privacy is the extent to which law enforcement officials monitor Internet activities such as correspondence via e-mail and visits to Web sites. In the wake of the September 11 terrorist attacks, the issue of law enforcement monitoring of Internet activity has become more controversial, with some advocating the need for additional tools for law enforcement to fight terrorism and others warning that basic tenets of democracy, such as privacy and civil liberties, should not be sacrificed in the effort.

With the enactment of the *USA PATRIOT Act* (Public Law 107-56), law enforcement gained additional authority to monitor Internet activity. Civil liberties groups have expressed concern about the potential ramifications of the new act on this and other grounds. They assert that they will monitor law enforcement use of the new powers to determine if any need to be challenged in court.

In summary, Title II of the act

- Expands the scope of subpoenas for records of electronic communications to include records commonly associated with Internet usage, such as session times and duration (Section 210)

- Allows Internet service providers (ISPs) to divulge records or other information (but not the contents of communications) pertaining to a subscriber if they believe there is immediate danger of death or serious physical injury or as otherwise authorized, and requires them to divulge such records or information (excluding contents of communications) to a governmental entity under certain conditions (Section 212)

- Adds routing and addressing information (used in Internet communications) to dialing information to the information that a government agency may capture using pen registers and trap and trace devices as authorized by court order, while excluding the content of any wire or electronic communications (Section 216). The section also requires law enforcement officials to keep certain records when they use their own pen registers or trap and trace devices and to provide those records to the court that issued the order within thirty days of expiration of the order

- Allows a person acting under the color of law to interpret the wire or electronic communications of a computer trespasser transmitted to, through, or from a protected computer under certain circumstances

Section 224 sets a four-year sunset period for many of the Title II provisions, but among the sections excluded from the sunset are Sections 210 and 216.

Although not an Internet privacy issue per se, consumer's identity often arises in the Internet privacy context because of the perception that Social Security and credit card numbers are more readily accessible because of the Internet.

Privacy advocates worry that in this emotionally charged climate, Congress passed legislation that it will later regret. Furthermore, the unresolved question is, "What is the proper balance between national and homeland security and e-government as a means of foster communication and service: government-to- citizen, citizen-to-government; government-to-business, business-to-government, and government-to-government?" Concerns about adequate privacy protection could have chilling consequences on the achievement of the goals of e-government.

SOME TYPES OF SERVICES PROVIDED

A close examination of the previous chapters reveals that government Web sites offer a wide assortment of services to the public, businesses, and other government bodies. One service is a list of frequently asked questions. For anyone using a government site for the first time, such a list may be a time saver and may offer guidance in how to search that site. Another useful feature is a detailed site map that is well laid out and easy to navigate. Such maps may appear as "A–Z" indexes. Other common services are the inclusion of e-mail addresses (as well as telephone and fax numbers) of agency contact personnel, links to related government sites, a list of employment opportunities, and copies of forms for doing business with the agency. Agencies might hold electronic town meetings, press conferences, and other informative sessions; these might be available as Webcasts. Congressional committees also use Webcasts, and both Congress and the agencies might have an archive of previous digital meetings or hearings.

In addition, services include

- Electronic e-mail or notification and updating services (e.g., providing news releases, new publications, or release dates for reports and data sets)

- Subscription services (some free and others fee based)

- Online retail (see Appendix A) and the inclusion of a heading, "Doing Business with [name of agency]" on the opening screen of a home page

- Online forms and instructions explaining how to complete those forms

- The identification of the most frequently requested pages at the Web site (e.g., such as the Department of Housing and Urban Development does with its bookshelves)

- Reference service provided by an agency's library (i.e., answering reference questions (and Ask services) and sending packets of material)

- Personalized information (the ability to inform the agency about what information citizens or businesses seek and to create a personalized page, "My ___")

- A breakdown of a Web site's offering by constituent group (e.g., parent, educator, research, and policy maker)

- Full compliance with Section 508, which deals with disability access (see Chapters 1 and 12)

- Clear guidance about how to solve problems (e.g., deal with a lost passport or benefits)

- Arranging for the receipt of benefits

- Redirecting users from an old to a new Web address (and that redirection actually works)

- Locating nearby services (those of a local, state, or regional office)

- The availability of search engines that permit simple and advanced searching of the site, including its archive

- Availability of information in English, Spanish, and perhaps other languages

- Technical support for business and industry, as well as nonprofit and community organizations

- Clear, visible, and unambiguous access to *Freedom of Information Act* (FOIA) materials and the electronic reading room

- Availability of software to use specialized products (access, view, and download; see Chapter 15)

- Choice of movie format based on file size (large and small versions), desired viewers (same movie in either QuickTime or RealPlayer formats), and movie resolution (which affects file size) based on the speed of the user's connection to the Internet (high resolution for larger file sizes for cable modems and T1 users, medium resolution and average file sizes for fast dial-up modem users, and low resolution with smaller file sizes for slower dial-up use; see Chapter 15)

A Web site should include the prominent display of disclaimers on its opening screen; conformity with the e-government policies set by the Office of Information and Regulatory Affairs, Office of Management and Budget (see Chapter 5); and the use of logical Web addresses that are not too long and complex. Unless information seekers bookmark a Web page or particular source, it might be difficult to key in a "two-inch" address without the use of bifocals and making a keystroke error.

SERVICE BARRIER

As discussed in the preface, the authors of this guide provide frequent updates of the Web addresses in the guide on the publisher's home page. We have also kept a statistical record of those changes in Web addresses (URLs). The first edition contained 985 URLs. Of these, 136 are now dead links (the URL is no longer functional); 205 are "redirected links," which means that the URL has changed but the user is redirected from the old URL to the new one. Most URLs are temporary and later become dead links. Additionally, redirect URLs do not update bookmarks. If a user has bookmarked a redirected URL, the browser bookmark is not updated. In summary, of the 985 addresses, 34.6 percent are either dead or redirected links. In that this percentage covers 1999 to the end of 2002, this finding is probably not surprising.

Turning to the second edition (published in 2001), of the 1,272 addresses, 51 are dead links and 155 are redirected links. Thus, 16.2 percent of the links are either dead or redirected. Note that the numbers and percentages would be higher if we had not checked all Web addresses prior to publication and made the necessary changes at that time.

Clearly, one service barrier that has not been discussed in the general and professional literature is the fact that e-government is very unstable. The three branches of government have made numerous changes to their Web address, and the logic of those changes is not always apparent. (This finding underscores the importance of the frequent updating provided at the publisher's home page.)

Many government Web sites contain "customer surveys," which they invite the public to complete. There is often no detailed explanation of how the data will be used for service improvement. The government could do a great deal more to raise service expectations.[1] On the other hand, however, in our monitoring of government Web sites since 1999, we have witnessed a marked improvement in the display, organization, and retrieval of the information resources and services provided. The government has an incredible amount of information resources, and it is trying to present them to the public logically as well as meet the information needs of specific target groups.

GETTING STARTED

Figure 10.1 is a list of frequently requested services from the government, and the rest of this chapter highlights other examples. A useful starting point is FirstGov, which is discussed in Chapters 3 and 9. This portal identifies numerous online forms, news releases, phone directions, and sources that answer "Questions about Government?," and it identifies a number of online services for citizens (Citizen Gateway), business (Business Gateway), and government (Government Gateway). For example, the Business Gateway includes resources under categories such as "find data and statistics for businesses and about businesses," "find business finance and tax related resources of use to businesses small and large," and "the U.S. government is the world's largest customer." The last category covers "Federal Supply Service," "Women-owned Business Opportunities," "Minority-owned Business Opportunities," and much more. FedForms (**http://www.fedforms.gov/**), provides links to the government's five hundred most-used services and their related forms. Users can go directly to agency Web sites that have forms posted online; some of the forms can be completed online, whereas others must be printed and mailed.

Figure 10.1. Examples of Information Services.

America's Job Bank (Department of Labor)
http://www.ajb.dni.us/
This site offers job listings as well as online resumes of job seekers.

Assistance after a Natural Disaster (Federal Emergency Management Agency)
http://www.fema.gov/
Use this site to locate information on where to find temporary shelters, crisis counseling, or legal counseling. Assistance in applying for help in rebuilding your home is also available.

Auctions (FirstGov)
http://www.firstgov.gov/shopping/auctions/auctions.shtml
This site provides links to online auctions from various agencies. The auctions offer surplus property, furniture, supplies, equipment, and vehicles.

Business Opportunities (Environmental Protection Agency)
http://www.epa.gov/epahome/doingbusiness.htm
Use this site to locate programs for business and industry to participate in or benefit from and resources for small businesses, including compliance assistance and technical help. For access to the Small Business Gateway, see **http://www.epa.gov/smallbusiness/**.

Fig 10.1 (*Cont.*)

Children's Health Insurance Program
http://www.insurekidsnow.gov/

    This site offers information about getting health insurance for children. It offers state-specific information on who is eligible and how to enroll to make sure that children grow up healthy.

Coins (U.S. Mint)
http://www.usmint.gov/
http://catalog.usmint.gov/

    An online catalog, for instance, offers collectible and investment-quality coins (e.g., the state quarters), jewelry, and gifts.

Efficiency (Department of Energy)
http://www.energy.gov/efficiency/index.html

    This site covers "Consumers," "Shoppers Corner," "Builders & Designers," "Business," "Energy Tool-Kit," "Your Community," and "Transportation." The last topic covers "Alternative Fuel Vehicles."

Environmental Hazards (Environmental Protection Agency)
http://www.epa.gov/

    Users can protect their families by finding out about drinking water quality, toxic and air releases, and hazardous waste sites near their homes. Information about water discharge permits and Superfund sites is also available.

FedBizOpps
General Services Administration
http://www.fedbizopps.gov/

    This is a single government point of entry for government procurement opportunities over $25,000. "Government buyers are able to publicize their business opportunities by posting information directly to FedBizOpps via the Internet. Through one portal . . . commercial vendors seeking federal markets for their products and services can search, monitor and retrieve opportunities solicited by the entire federal contracting community."

Federal Resources for Educational Excellence (Department of Education)
http://www.ed.gov/free

    This site provides educational resources for teachers, students, and parents from different federal agencies.

Food Safety (Department of Agriculture)
http://www.foodsafety.gov/

    Learn food safety and handling tips, proper cooking temperature for food, and how to test to see if your kitchen is safe from food-borne illness.

Forms

The Department of Education offers information about finding and applying for financial aid for higher education.
http://www.ed.gov/

Tax form and tax questions answered
Internal Revenue Service
http://www.irs.gov/

Medicare recipients can use a form on the Social Security Administration's (SSA) Web site to apply for a replacement card online. Future services will make it possible for senior citizens to file online for retirement benefits and allow the agency's business partners, doctors, and hospitals to file reports online.
http://www.ssa.gov/

Find online housing discrimination forms (Department of Housing and Urban Development) at this site.
http://www.hud.gov/

Learn how to engage in procurement activities with the General Services Administration.
http://contacts.gsa.gov/

This site is the Gateway to Educational Materials (Department of Education) For lesson plans and educational material, this site provides linkage to more than 140 Web sites.
http://www.thegateway.org

Healthfinder® (Department of Health and Human Service)

http://healthfinder.gov/

This site offers tips on choosing a health plan, a doctor, a course of treatment, or a long-term care facility. It also provides information on health research and different diseases.

Healthier US.gov

http://www.healthierus.gov/

"Information to help Americans choose to live healthier lives": This site offers links to other health sites.

Homebuying Information (Department of Housing and Urban Development)

http://www.hud.gov/

There is a homebuyer's kit, information for home buying or selling, information for tenants, coverage of HUD approved lenders, and more.

INS Case Status Service Online

https://egov.immigration.gov/graphics/cris/jsps/index.jsp

This service of the Immigration and Naturalization Service lets people find the status of their case: "If you have an application receipt number, you can check the status of your case online."

Fig 10.1 (*Cont.*)

Medicate Benefits (Centers for Medicare and Medicaid Services)
http://www.cms.hhs.gov/medicare/
http://www.cms.hhs.gov/medicaid/
Learn about your Medicare benefits, get information about nursing homes in your area, or report suspected Medicare fraud. The site also offers information about Medicaid.

Pension Benefits (Pension Benefit Guaranty Corporation)
http://www.pbgc.gov/
Reunites people with mission pensions and features an online Pension Search Directory to discover if any benefits are owed you.

Retirement (Social Security Administration)
http://www.ssa.gov/
This site allows users to compute their estimated social security benefits, get information for employers on reporting earnings, and obtain a social security number. There are interactive tools to help with investment decisions and guidance about how to avoid Internet fraud.

Smoke-Free Kids (Centers for Disease Control and Prevention)
http;//www.smokefree.gov/
This site encourages the nation's youth not to smoke or to quit smoking.

Starting a Business (Small Business Administration)
http://www.sba.gov/
This site provides information on loans and outreach initiatives for women and minority-owned businesses. It features e-mail counseling and mentoring, on-line educational courses, and a database of contacts for small firms (see also the Small Business Gateway, http://www.epa.gov/epahome/doingbusiness.htm).

TradeNet
http://tradenet.gov/
This site offers an opportunity to create My TradeNet, a personalized version of the U.S. Export Advisor. The service "keeps useful trade sites 'bookmarked' and readily accessible. . . . The site currently features a range of information and services ranging from tailored links in 'getting started' in exporting to local export contacts searchable by zip code, trade finance information, searchable international business opportunities or trade leads, export answers accessible by keyword search, and an export library with scores of export promotion links."

Travel Abroad (Department of State)
http://travel.state.gov/
Download a passport application, get travel trips, and discover where it is unsafe to travel.

Veterans' Information (Department of Veterans Affairs)
http://www.va.gov/
Users of this site can find the closest Veterans' Medical Center and find out for which benefits they may qualify.

EDUCATION

AskERIC (**http://www.askeric.org**) is "a personalized Internet-based service providing education information to teachers, librarians, counselors, administrators, parents, and others throughout the United States and the world." A project of the ERIC (Educational Resources Information Center) Clearinghouse on Information and Technology at Syracuse University, it offers the following:

- The ERIC Question-Answer Service is a "collection of hundred of responses to questions" previously asked as well as an opportunity to receive an answer ("personalized resources relevant to your needs") for questions not in the archives.

- The Resources section on this site contains a collection of "more than 3000 resources on a variety of educational issues," including, for instance, Internet sites, educational organizations, and electronic discussion groups.

- The Question Archive is "a collection of . . . responses to questions received through AskERIC Question & Answer Service. These responses may include ERIC citations, Internet sites, discussion groups, and/or print resource information."

- Teachers nationwide have submitted more than two thousand unique lesson plans, all available online.

- "Search the ERIC Database" allows users access to "abstracts of documents and journal articles on education research and practice" from the print-based *Resources in Education* and *Current Index to Journals in Education*, beginning in 1966.

- The Mailing Lists archive covers education-related discussion groups.

The same ERIC clearinghouse also offers the Virtual Reference Desk[SM] (VRD) (**http://www.vrd.org/**), which is "dedicated to the advancement of digital reference and the successful creation and operation of human-mediated, Internet-based information services. . . . Digital reference, or 'AskA,' services are Internet-based question-and-answer services that connect users with experts and subject expertise. Digital reference services use the Internet to connect people with people who can answer questions and support the development of skills." For a list of those services active with the VRD network in question exchange, see **http://www.vrd.org/index.shtml**.

VRD contains the DIG_REF Listserv (**http://www.vrd.org/Dig_Ref/dig_ref. shtml**), which "is a forum for the growing number of people and organizations answering the questions of users via the Internet. As mentioned in the previous chapter, an increasing number of organizations are creating digital reference services to provide expert information and reference help." Moreover, "DIG_REF seeks to bring together experts who answer questions, as well as librarians, organizations and associations dedicated to meeting the reference needs of their users via the Internet. The list will . . . [address] all aspects of providing question & answer services over the worldwide network, from service creation and implementation to issues of services and quality." A complete list of the Ask services, in addition to AskERIC, may be found at **http://www.vrd.org/locator/subject.shtml**.

A Department of Education site, "Computers for Learning" (**http://www.computers.fed.gov/School/user.asp**), "allows school and educational nonprofits to register to request surplus federal computer equipment. Federal agencies will then use the website to donate computers to schools and educational nonprofits based upon indications of need." The goal is to "place hundreds of thousands of computers in our Nation's classrooms and prepare our children to contribute and compete in the 21st century."

Finally, the Department of Education offers "My Education," a personalized page for subscribers to be alerted of new products and developments (see **http://www.ed.gov/personalize/addMyInformation.jsp**), as well as a "Main Cross-Site Indexing Search Page" (**http://search.ed.gov/csi**) that enables information seekers to conduct a search across the Departments' Web sites.

ELECTRONIC GOVERNMENT AND INFORMATION TECHNOLOGY PROCUREMENT

Electronic government, together with electronic commerce (see Chapters 1, 12, and 14), has generated extensive discussion and a growing literature. Agencies, such as the OMB and the Bureau of the Census, have promoted electronic government through their town meetings or interactive news announcements. Some Web sites present electronic government and may suggest ways to improve it. Other sites include, for instance, the following:

- The General Services Administration's (GSA) has different Web pages (see **http://www.gsa.gov/; http://www.gsa.gov/Portal/home.jsp**) that cover electronic commerce. GSA Advantage Electronic Commerce is an "online electronic ordering system to search for products, review delivery options and place orders" (**https://www.gsaadvantage.gov/advgsa/main_pages/start_page.jsp**).

- Other e-government initiatives, ones not confined to GSA, can be found at **http://www.whitehouse.gov/omb/egov/**.

- The Chief Information Officers Council (**http://www.cio.gov/**) also "plays a key role in directing and leading the strategic management of Federal IT resources" (see Chapter 5). The *E-Government Act of 2002* strengthens its role.

HEALTH CARE

In 1998, the National Library of Medicine (NLM) launched MEDLINEplus, a consumer health Web site (**http://medlineplus.gov/**). It is "designed to assist the public in locating appropriate, authoritative health information resources" on common diseases and conditions (see Chapter 5 and **http://www.nlm.nih.gov/hinfo.html** lists different digital resources). PubMed (**http://www. ncbi.nlm.nih.gov/PubMed**), a service of NLM, "provides access to over 12 million MEDLINE citations back to the mid-1960s and additional life science journals. PubMed includes links to many sites providing full text articles and other related resources" (see **http://www.ncbi.nim. niih.gov/entrez/query.fcgi**).

PubMed Central is "a digital archive of life sciences journal literature managed by the National Center for Biotechnology Information . . . at the National Library. . . . Access to . . . [it] is free and unrestricted." Publishers can encouraged to participate. (For coverage of this and the journals covered, see **http://www.pubmedcentral. nih.gov/**). Making this archive most useful is the inclusion of a table of contents service— a listing of the table of contents for the "latest available issue."

ClinicalTrials.gov covers clinical trials for new medicines (see **http:// clinicaltrials.gov/**). The TOXNET Database (**http://toxnet.nlm.nih.gov/**) is a free system for gaining access to information on toxicology, hazardous chemicals, and related areas.

JOB SEEKING

The Office of Personnel Management (see Chapter 6) maintains USAJOBS (**http://www.usajobs.opm.gov/**), which is the executive branch's main site for employment information. Web sites within all three branches of government frequently provide information on employment opportunities, however. For example, the Department of Energy has an automated recruitment system, DOE Jobs ONLINE (**http://chris.inel.gov/jobs/index.cfm?fuseaction**), that enables prospective candidates to search for jobs using criteria such as location or job title. The department also offers a Web-based map of the United States that uses icons for all its facilities. The job seeker can click on a facility and find out what jobs are available there and learn more about what kinds of work the facility's employees perform.

The Internal Revenue Service provides career information at **http://www.jobs. irs.gov/mn-home.html**). Information is grouped according to the following categories: "Accounting Careers," "Administrative/Clerical," "Business/Finance," "Executive Careers," "Information Technology," "Law Enforcement," and "Other Careers."

POSTAL SERVICES

The United States Postal Service (USPS) offers products and services over the Web (**http://www.usps.com**). These sites provides public information, a store (offering the location of nearby post offices, gifts, shipping supplies, how to calculate postage, stamps, finding zip codes, a complete list of lost or stolen postal money orders, and address changes), and post office (for looking up zip codes, obtaining consumer and stamp information, making address changes, downloading passport applications, finding out about postal rates and fees, calculating the cost of mailing letters and packages, tracking express mail deliveries, locating nearby post offices, and identifying local postal Web sites). The USPS, through its Web site, is targeting the online shipping market as it competes more with other package delivery businesses.

SELECTIVE SERVICE REGISTRATION

In November 1998, the Selective Service activated its online registration site (**http://www.sss.gov/**). Rather than sign up for the potential draft at the post office and waiting a couple of months for a confirmation card, a young man (nearly every male U.S. citizen or alien living in the United States aged 18 through 25 is eligible for the draft) can simply log onto the site and sign up. The online program compares the information entered against the government's social security database. After a match is made, the person receives a registration number and is mailed an acknowledgment card within weeks.

SOCIAL SECURITY

The Social Security Administration (**http://www.ssa.gov/**) offers online services that cover benefits' information and payments. There is also an identification of "online direct services" and "services for businesses." For example, there is a "Social Security number verification service." It is also possible to "check your eligibility for Social Security or SSI benefits," " apply for Social Security retirement, disability, or spouse's benefits," "estimate your benefit amounts," "replace your lost or damaged Medicare card," register a password to obtain "your personal Social Security and SSI information," subscribe to a free electronic newsletter (*eNews*; **http://www.ssa.gov/enews/**), and more (see **http://www.ssa.gov/onlineservices/**).

SUMMARY

In December 2002, nearly 60 percent of two thousand people surveyed in the Pew Internet and American Life Project used the Web regularly and thought that the Internet was a "stable source of information about government services," among other things. They also expected that information to be "reliable." Despite these findings, the public may discover that use of a particular Web site requires their consent to having their information seeking monitored by means of a cookie attachment. Furthermore, e-government is unstable, involves numerous changes to Web addresses, and may provide unreliable information content (see Chapter 1). On the other hand, government on the Web is becoming more service oriented.

Government services are especially rich in the areas of business, compliance with federal paperwork requirements, consumer protection, education, the elderly, health care, travel abroad, electronic government, and veterans' benefits and care. The Internal Revenue Service even permits individuals and businesses to file their tax returns electronically (**http://www.irs.gov/efile/index.html**). Moreover, an increasing number of government bodies offer users access to some of their information resources in Spanish. Service provision is not confined to the executive branch. Examples from other branches include

- Employment opportunities (House of Representatives, **http://www.house.gov/cao-hr/**; U.S. Courts, **http://www.uscourts.gov/employment. html**)

- Members of Congress provide constituent services at their home pages (**http://www.house.gov/house/MemberWWW.html**; **http://www.senate.gov/general/contact_information/senators_cfm.cfm**)

- Mailing labels for the address of members of the House of Representatives (**http://clerk.house.gov/members/index.php**)

- The PACER Service Center (see Chapter 7), which is the "centralized registration, billing, and technical support center for electronic access to U.S. District, Bankruptcy, and Appellate court records" (see **http://pacer.psc.uscourts.gov/**)

© Linsay Hernon

NOTES

1. See Peter Hernon and John R. Whitman, *Delivering Satisfaction and Service Quality* (Chicago: American Library Association, 2001).

2. "Survey Cites Use of Internet to Gather Data," *New York Times*, 30 December 2002, p. C5.

URL Site Guide for This Chapter

Chief Information Officers Council
http://www.cio.gov/

Children's Health Insurance
Program
http://www.insurekidsnow.gov/

Congress

    Constituent Services
    http://www.house.gov/house/
        MemberWWW.html
    http://www.senate.gov/general/contact_
        information/senators_cfm.cfm

    Employment Opportunities
    House of Representatives
    http://www.house.gov/cao-hr/

    Mailing Labels House Members
    http://clerk.house.gov/members/index.
        php

Department of Agriculture

    Food Safety
    http://www.foodsafety.gov/

Department of Commerce

    TradeNet
    http://tradenet.gov/

Department of Education

    AskERIC
    http://www.askeric.org

    Computers for Learning
    http://www.computers.fed.gov/School/
        user.asp

    Federal Resources for Educational
        Excellence
    http://www.ed.gov/free

    Financing College Education
    http://www.ed.gov/

    Gateway to Educational Materials
    http://www.thegateway.org

Main Cross-Site Indexing Search Page
http://search.edu.gov/csi

My Education (personalized page)
http://www.ed.gov/personalize/
    addMyInformation.jsp

Virtual Reference Desk[SM]
http://ww.vrd.org/

    Ask Services
    http://www.vrd.org/locator/subject.
        shtml

    Digital Reference
    http://www.vrd.org/Dig_Ref/dig_
        ref.shtml

    Services
    http://www.vrd.org/index.shmtl

Department of Energy

    Efficiency
    http://www.energy.gov/efficiency/
        index.html

    Job Seeking
    http://chris.inel.gov/jobs/index.cfm?
        fuseaction

Department of Health and Human
Services

    Clinical Trials
    http://clinicaltrials.gov/

    Healthfinder®
    http://healtfinder.gov/

    Healthier US.gov
    http://www.healthierus.gov/

    MEDLINEplus
    http://medlineplus.gov/
    http://www.nlm.nih.gov/hinfo.html
    http://www.nlm.nih.gov/medlineplus/
        criteria.html

PubMed
http://www.ncbi.nlm.nih.gov/entrez/
query.fcgi
http://www.ncbi.nlm.nih.gov/PubMed

PubMed Central
http://www.pubmedcentral.nih.gov/

TOXNET
http://toxnet.nlm.nih.gov/

Centers for Disease Control and Prevention

Smoke-Free Kids
http://www.smokefree.gov

Centers for Medicare and Medicaid Services
Medicare and Medicaid
http://www.cms.hhs.gov/medicare/
http://www.cms.hhs.gov/medicaid

Department of Housing and Urban Development

Home Buying
http://www.hud.gov/

Housing Discrimination Forms
http://www.hud.gov/

Department of Justice

INS Case Status Service Online
Immigration and Naturalization Service
https://egov.immigration.gov/graphics/
cris/jsps/index.jsp

Department of Labor

America's Job Bank
http://www.ajb.dni.us/

Department of State
http://www.state.gov/

Travel Abroad
http://travel.state.gov/

Department of the Treasury

Coins
U.S. Mint
http://www.usmint.gov/
http://catalog.usmint.gov/

Electronic Filings
http://www.irs.gov/efile/index.html

Tax Form/Questions
http://www.irs.gov/

Careers with the IRS
Internal Revenue Services
http://www.jobs.irs.gov/mn-home.html

Department of Veterans Affairs
http://www.va.gov/

Environmental Protection Agency
http://www.epa.gov/

Business Opportunities
http://www.epa.gov/epahome/
doingbusiness.htm

Small Business Gateway
http://www.epa.gov/smallbusiness/

Federal Emergency Management Agency
http://www.fema.gov/

FirstGov
http://www.firstgov.gov/

Auctions
http://www.firstgov.gov/shopping/
auctions/auctions.shtml

FedForms
http://www.fedforms.gov/

General Services Administration
http://www.gsa.gov/

Electronic Commerce
http://www.gsa.gov/Portal/home.jsp

GSA Advantage Electronic Commerce
https://www.gsaadvantage.gov/advgsa/
main_pages/start_page.jsp

Procurement
http://contacts.gsa.gov/

E-Government Initiatives

Office of Management and Budget
www.whitehouse.gov/omb/egov/

FedBizOpps
http://www.fedbizopps.gov/

Judicial Branch

Employment Opportunities
http://www.uscourts.gov/employment.html

PACER Service Center
http://pacer.psc.uscourts.gov/

Pension Benefit Guaranty Corporation
http://www.pbgc.gov/

Securities and Exchange Commission

Online Trading
http://www.sec.gov/

Selective Service
http://www.sss.gov/

Small Business Administration
http://www.sba.gov/

Social Security Administration
http://www.ssa.gov/

Online Services
http://www.ssa.gov/onlineservices/

eNews (newsletter)
http://www.ssa.gov/enews/

USAJOBS

Office of Personnel Management
http://www.usajobs.opm.gov/

U.S. Postal Service
http://www.usps.com

Office of Management and Budget

E-Government Initiatives
http://www.whitehouse.gov/omb/egov/

Chapter 11

Maps, Cartography, and Geographic Information Science and Systems

From the federal government's earliest years, cartography, mapmaking, and geological surveys were essential components to the missions of several federal agencies. Most of these eighteenth- and nineteenth-century geographic efforts focused on either military applications or territorial expansion—principally charting coastal and other navigable waters by the U.S. Navy or Coast and Geodetic Survey, or surveys of the territories west of the Appalachians opened by Lewis and Clark through the Louisiana Purchase of 1803. The Library of Congress' virtual exhibit has many of documents and maps produced by the expedition (**http://www.loc.gov/exhibits/lewisandclark/lewisandclark.html**), and the United States Geological Survey has the Lewis and Clark Home Page (**http://www.usgs.gov/features/lewisandclark.html**).

As the young nation expanded west and south over the North American continent, several generations of scientific explorers added to the nation's wealth of cartography and geographic knowledge. By the mid to late 1800s, the Geographic Survey was producing highly detailed maps and coastal charts. For an excellent summary of the Survey's history, consult *The United States Geological Survey: 1879–1989* (**http://pubs.usgs.gov/circ/c1050/index.htm**). Further economic crises and global conflicts created a greater demand for maps and technological innovations in the geographic sciences during the twentieth century.

These early traditions in cartography and map production are now strengthened by the theories and techniques of geographic information sciences (GISci), as well as the analytical techniques of geographic information systems (GIS). Both GISci and GIS rely on a combination of distributed network of computerized systems and software designed to capture, store, manipulate, analyze, and visualize geospatial data—coded to a particular location or area on Earth's surface (e.g., latitude and longitude, census tract or block number, school district, state or town, zip code, congressional district, or hazardous waste site). Simply stated, geographic information science and systems allow users to detect trends, patterns, or other associations among events, conditions, and factors that otherwise might not be readily apparent through traditional mapmaking or statistical analysis tools. In essence, this type of geospatial analysis is both a tool and a process that integrates, from variety of sources, data about spatial areas and boundaries (geographic coordinate data) and data about conditions (attribute data) that occur within those areas. The software enables users to query, manipulate, analyze, and present these integrated data in ways that reveal patterns or relationships. With such analysis, it is possible to produce maps, create computer models of complex environmental conditions (oil spills, hurricanes, earthquakes), engage in "what if" scenarios (if event X were to take place, how would it affect situation Y), provide customized output to address specific situations, add additional data sets, measure patterns and trends in spatial relationships, and gain more detailed insights into questions that previously might not have been answerable.[1]

Federal agencies use both GISci and GIS to manage natural resources, engage in planning, ensure compliance with regulations, and allocate resources. More precisely, they use geospatial database systems for land-use analysis and planning, land-cover interpretation, map demographic changes and analyses, transportation route or traffic corridor selection, natural hazard assessment, market studies, and global environmental change research, as well as military reconnaissance. Some agencies even use the techniques for the receipt and review of grant proposals. Increasingly, government agencies are working together to build a national spatial information infrastructure. In earlier programs, agencies produced separate maps of the same areas (e.g., the same town could have topographic map from U.S. Geological Survey (USGS), a soil map from the Department of Agriculture, and a coastal map from the Department of Commerce). The idea of a national spatial information infrastructure assumes that all agencies use one base map supported by a database that delivers the different information layers produced by federal agencies. This approach assumes a considerable amount of cooperation and coordination among government bodies, a goal that is more often a hope than reality.

Another consideration for this particular chapter is the chilling effect of the war on terrorism. Without question, as the White House and Congress work through a multitude of responses to the September 11 attacks, a number of cartographic and GIS Web resources have been removed from government Web sites.

CARTOGRAPHIC AND MAPPING AGENCIES

This section identifies agencies with primary or secondary missions in cartography or mapping. Research that these agencies perform supports a broad array of cartographic resources to assure the accuracy of the national geospatial data infrastructure. In short, cartography "consists of a group of techniques fundamentally concerned with reducing the spatial characteristics of a large area—a portion or all of the earth, or another celestial body—and putting it in map form to make it observable" (**http://www2. cr.nps.gov/gis/cartography.htm**).

The agencies included in this chapter, however, are responsible for broader mandates beyond the production and dissemination of map products and services. Thus, the discussion, at times, has a broader focus than the presentation of mapping and GISci, GIS products, and mappings services. This chapter complements Chapter 8 because statistical-gathering agencies may also provide GIS products and services.

⟲ Environmental Protection Agency

The Environmental Protection Agency (EPA; **http://www.epa.gov/**) maintains the *Environmental Atlas*, which "offers an online environmental map collection, links to other important collections, and information to help you understand environmental quality maps, mapping, and environmental information." There are four choices: "USA Maps," "State and Regional Maps," "Learn about Maps and Geological Data," and "About the Atlas." The "USA Maps" feature environmental information collected by the EPA and other federal, state, and local agencies, and they summarize data collected across the United States. These data include analysis of air (air quality), land (landscape and land use), and water (watershed, groundwater, drinking water, and water quality). The state and regional maps link to general maps of a state, environmental-quality maps, agency environmental programs, and state facts. "Learn about Maps and Geographic Data" is a handy tutorial that describes the essentials of maps, cartography, and geographic information systems. A land atlas "contains links to national maps and maps of many aspects of land environment" and covers

- Land resources (landscape types, forest land and ecoregions, and wetlands)

- Land use and cover (predominant cover, agricultural lands, and human settlement)

- Threats to human and ecological health (pesticide use, agriculture, wetland losses, toxic and hazardous waste sites, and land and change)

- Health of the people of the land (life expectancy and mortality from cancer)

The *Environmental Atlas* also contains links to maps produced by other government agencies:

- *State of the Land* (**http://www.nrcs.usda.gov/technical/land/**; Department of Agriculture, Natural Resources Conservation Service), which provides "data on land use and change, soil erosion and soil quality, water quality, wetlands, and other issues regarding the conservation and use of natural resources on non-federal land in the United States"

- National Water Summary on Wetland Resources (**http://water.usgs.gov/nwsum/WSP2425/**; USGS), which "gives a broad overview of wetland resources and includes discussions of the scientific basis for understanding wetland functions and values; legislation that regulates the uses of wetlands; wetland research, inventory, and evaluation; and issues related to the restoration, creation, and recovery of wetlands"

- *Pesticides National Synthesis Project* (USGS), which offers "maps based on state-level estimates of pesticide use rates for individual crops, which have been compiled by the National Center for Foods and Agricultural Policy (NCFAP) for 1991–1993 and 1995, and on county-based crop acreage data obtained from the 1992 Census of Agriculture"

- Water resources (USGS), which makes GIS data available for downloading (The site serves as a node of the National Spatial Data Infrastructure (NSDI) for finding and accessing USGS spatial data related to water resources.)

EPA's EnviroMapper Storefront (**http://www.epa.gov/enviro/html/em/index. html**) "maps several types of environmental information, including drinking water, toxic and air releases, hazardous waste, water discharge permits, and Superfund sites. EnviroMapper also links to text reports." It also has GIS functionality using EPA data for the nation; links tax incentive zones for brownfields ("abandoned, idled, or under-used industrial and commercial facilities where expansion or redevelopment is complicated by real or perceived environmental contamination"); provides statistics, profiles, and trends; and so on.

There are also environmental profiles, "a collection of descriptive statistics that can help evaluate a community's environmental quality, status, and trends." A profile consists of "graphs and brief descriptions that summarize existing information on air quality, drinking water systems, surface water quality, hazardous waste, and reported toxic releases." Profiles are available by state, county, EPA region, or zip code.

Geographical Data Innovations is an "exhibition of projects to collect, analyze, communicate, and use geographical environmental information (**http://www.epa.gov/ ceisweb1/ceishome/atlas/studiesandinnovations.html**). It also includes ECOVIEW Ohio waters, a partnership for access to environmental information.

Department of Defense

As might be expected, the Department of Defense makes extensive use of GIS and the Global Positioning System. The National Imagery and Mapping Agency (NIMA), within the department, "provides Geospatial Intelligence in all its forms, and from whatever source—imagery, imagery intelligence, and geospatial data and information—to ensure the knowledge foundation for planning, decision, and action." Since the war on terrorism was launched, a number of the Web pages described in this section have been seriously altered for public viewing or removed completely from the public's Web space. NIMA's home page (**http://www.nima.mil**) contains the following options:

- Public Affairs

- Support to Our Customers

- Safety of Navigation

- Publications

- NIMA Kids Page

- FOIA [*Freedom of Information Act*] Requests

- NIMA Security Policy

- Links

- Search

- What's Hot!

- About NIMA

- Employment

- Geospatial Intelligence

- Business Opportunities

- FAQ [frequently asked questions]

- Publications

Maps and imagery includes, for instance, products for public sale and to download, as well as digital data, Digital Nautical Chart Public Page, Geodesy and Geophysics Department Home Page.

NIMA is establishing the National Center for Geospatial Intelligence Standards (NCGIS) to address standards and interoperability issues related to technologies, data architecture, and software used by the private sector and the defense, intelligence, and homeland security communities.

National Oceanic and Atmospheric Administration

The National Oceanic and Atmospheric Administration (NOAA) (**http://www. noaa.gov/**), within the Department of Commerce, offers numerous maps and charts related, among others, to the coastline, climate, fisheries, oceans, and weather (see the agency's site map). NOAA's National Ocean Service (NOS) "is the primary civil agency within the federal government responsible for the health and safety of our nation's coastal and oceanic environment." NOS "provides a wide range of products and services, established on the best scientific basis, for the protection of life, property and the environment." In fact, "thousands of private companies and government agencies use NOS services to save the public time and money, and to enrich our quality of life." As the agency Web site explains, "NOS . . . surveys the coast, now using satellites, airplanes, and high-tech computers. But to keep pace with increasing demands for accurate, usable data about the world in which we live, NOS also provides important management and scientific information for wide variety of day-to-day needs which helps keep our coast healthy and the economy moving" (**http://www.nos.noaa.gov/ about/about.html**).

NOS's home page (**http://www.nos.noaa.gov/**) includes a site map, search of the site, information about the agency, "News & Events," "Publications & Products," "Programs Education & Outreach," and so on. A useful feature is "Popular NOS Web Sites," which includes

- Ocean Explorer

- Coastal and Ocean Resource Economics

- Gulf of Mexico Hypoxia Assessment Reports

- Marine Protected Areas

- NOS MapFinder

- National Marine Sanctuaries

- Coast Survey/Nautical Charts

- NOAA Coastal Services Center

- Tidal and Current Information

- Oil and Chemical Releases

- Geodetic Data, Software & Publications

- NOAA Coastal Services Center

The home page also provides access to NOS programs and staff offices, which maintain their own Web sites. Furthermore, there are links to the National Environmental Satellite, Data and Information Service; National Weather Service; National Marine Fisheries Service; Oceanic and Atmospheric Research, career opportunities, and a personnel locator. NOS has photographs and other imagery, as well as the MapFinder home page (**http://oceanservice.noaa.gov/mapfinder/**), which "is a one-stop World Wide Web service that provides direct Internet access to primary NOS imagery and data holdings for coastal photography, nautical charts, coastal survey maps, environmental sensitivity index maps, hydrographic surveys, water level stations, and geodetic control points." A spatial index "allows users to identify specific NOS products."

The Office of Ocean and Coastal Resource Management maintains the

- Coastal Zone Management Program

- National Estuarine Research Reserves

- National Marine Sanctuaries

The Coastal Zone Management Program, a voluntary partnership between the government and coastal states and territories, protects "more than 99 percent of the nation's 95,000 miles of oceanic and Great Lakes coastline." The home page (**http://www.ocrm.nos.noaa.gov/czm/welcome.html**) explains the Program and covers job vacancies, the Coastal Nonpoint Pollution Control Program, state and territory coastal management program summaries, and links to program Web sites.

The National Estuarine Research Reserves (NERRS) "is a protected areas network of federal, state, and local partnerships. . . . Through linked programs of stewardship, education and research, the NERRS enhances informed management and scientific understanding of the nation's estuarine and coastal habitats." The home page (**http://oceanservice.noaa.gov/topics/coasts/reserves/welcome.html**) provides access to research, monitoring, and educational activities, as well as information on the administration of the reserves. There are also links to related home pages.

Within the thirteen sites of the National Marine Sanctuaries (**http://www.sanctuaries.nos.noaa.gov/**),

 you'll discover a vast range of marine creatures, habitats, historical artifacts, and flourishing marine cultures. In one site you might find giant humpback whales, in another the remains of an 18th century shipwreck, and in yet another thriving coral reef colonies or kelp forests.

For the national marine protected areas (MPA), see **http://mpa.gov/**.

Oceanographic Products and Services Division. This division "collects, analyzes and distributes historical and real-time observations and predictions of water levels, coastal currents and other meteorological and oceanographic data." The home page (**http://www.co-ops.nos.noaa.gov/**) offers important notices (database status and selected notices to mariners); "What's New;" products; publications; station locator; benchmarks; observations; predictions; the Physical Oceanographic Real-Time System (PORTS), which "supports safe and cost-efficient navigation by providing ship masters and pilots with accurate real-time information required to avoid groundings and collisions;" information about the division ("address, phone numbers, location map, mission, personnel and organizational setting") ; frequently asked questions; and "About" ("water levels, tides & currents, their measurement, analysis and prediction"). Furthermore, there are links to NOS's programs on "safe maritime navigation, more productive water-borne commerce, and the needs of the National Weather Service, coastal zone management, engineering and surveying communities. The division manages the National Water Level Observation Program and the national network of Physical Oceanographic Real-Time systems in major U.S. harbors."

United States Geological Survey

The U.S. Geological Survey (USGS) provides information to describe and understand the earth. That information pertains to biology, geology, mapping, and water. The Web site (**http://www.usgs.gov/**) provides current information, conference and workshop proceedings, USGS Special Projects Images ("selected images, including volcanoes and other natural features, available from the USGS EROS [Earth Resources Observation Systems Data Center;" **http://edcwww.cr.usgs.gov/**), biology, geology, mapping, water, agency contacts, and searching the USGS database. Fact sheets cover resources, hazards, the environment, and information management; they are also available by state (see **http://water.usgs.gov/wid/indexlist.html**).

One of USGS's major initiatives involves the creation of "The National Map," which

will provide public domain core geographic data about the United States and its territories that other agencies can extend, enhance, and reference as they concentrate on maintaining other data that are unique to their needs. *The National Map* will be a foundation of information to which the private sector can contribute core feature content and to which proprietary datasets can be linked to provide access to higher resolution data, additional (non-base) features, and enriched attribute information. *The National Map* will promote cost effectiveness by minimizing the need to find, develop, integrate, and maintain geographic base data each time they are needed. The viewer/browser for the National Map can be found at **http:// rockys20.cr.usgs.gov/nmmulti/MultiService/viewer.htm**.

"Maps and Other Products" (**http://www.usgs.gov/pubprod/**) covers aerial photographs, digital maps and data, fact sheets and booklets, maps, new products, real-time data, satellite imagery, scientific publications, and software. "National Mapping Information" (**http://mapping.usgs.gov/**) lists interactive sources, the National Spatial Data Infrastructure, products and ordering information, downloadable data, geospatial data standards, regional mapping centers, partnership opportunities, mapping library and publications, related sites, and educational resources for students, parents, and teachers. One of the interactive sources is the *National Atlas of the United States*, which "is designed to promote greater geographic awareness through the development and delivery of products that provide easy to use, views of our national and socio-cultural landscapes." The *Atlas*'s home page (**http://nationalatlas.gov/index.html**) includes *Atlas Maps* (for designing and exploring maps or to view interactive multimedia maps).

The Web site also contains information about the *Atlas* and its development, frequently asked questions, and partnerships with the private sector. "You can follow a link to a fact sheet describing business partnership opportunities. Another link provides an overview of the federal agencies already working on the *National Atlas*."

The Geographic Names Information System (GNIS) "contains information about almost 2 million physical and cultural geographic features in the United States, and references are made to a feature's location by state, county, and geographic coordinates. The GNIS is our Nation's official repository of *domestic* geographic names information. Information about *foreign* geographic feature names can be obtained from the GEOnet Names Server" (**http://164.214.2.59/gns/html/index.html**). Geographic features for Antarctica are covered at **http://geonames.usgs.gov/antform.html**.

The Global Land Information System (GLIS; **http://edcwww.cr.usgs.gov/glis/glis.html**) contains metadata, descriptive information about data sets, and examples of earth science data that can be ordered online. It "contains references to regional, continental, and global land information including land use, land cover, and soils data; cultural and topographic data; and remotely sensed satellite and aircraft data."

The United States Geological Survey has a "National Satellite Land Remote Sensing Data Archive Page" (**http://edc.usgs.gov/archive/nslrsdal**), which is "a permanent government archive containing satellite remote sensing data of the Earth's land surface." The archive reflects "almost 40 years of satellite remote sensing" and contains declassified intelligence satellite photographs. It is also possible to order satellite images, aerial photographs, and cartographic products (EarthExplorer, **http://edcsns17. cr.usgs.gov/cgi-bin/EarthExplorer/phtml/BrowserTest. phtml**).

USGS's Cartography and Publishing Program (CAPP; **http://sr6capp.er.usgs.gov/**) "recommends and coordinates publishing policy for water resource programs and provides cartographic support for reports of national scope." It also "tests and applies emerging technologies in publishing and cartography." CAPP offers databases, maps, and a GIS.

Beginning in 1999, the USGS began a Web site that offers information on water levels and rain prospects. Better known as *Drought Watch*, this site provides frequently asked questions, information resources, definitions, and a current map on drought conditions in the United States (**http://md.water.usgs.gov/drought/**). Finally, most useful are the *Site Map* (**http://www.usgs.gov/sitemap.html**) and the *Index of USGS Web Sites* (**http://www.usgs.gov/network/**).

Some of the other mapping resources of the agency include the following:

- Rocky Mountain Mapping Center (**http://rmmcweb.cr.usgs.gov/**), which conducts mapping activities in the western part of the nation as well as research, and distributes maps, open-file reports, and other products

- U.S. Geological Survey Library (**http://library.usgs.gov/**), which "serves the research needs of USGS scientists . . . and provides information to other organizations and individuals in the areas of geology, hydrology, cartography, biology, and related fields." There is also access to some databases

- Earthshots (**http://edc.usgs.gov/earthshots/slow/tableofcontents**), which are satellite images of environmental change (For those worldwide sites covered, there are also descriptive articles placing the image in context.)

- View USGS Maps and Aerial Photo Images Online (**http://mapping.usgs.gov/partners/viewonline.html**), which links to business and cooperative research and development agreement partners that provide maps and aerial photo images

- Digital Orthophoto Quadrangle (uniform-scale images; **http://www-wmc.wr.usgs.gov/doq/**), which provides images, information about how to obtain the images, software, technical documentation

- "Educational Links" (**http://wwwdlabrg.er.usgs.gov/educational_links.htm**) is part of an educational outreach program "designed to stimulate interest in water resources for teachers and students and encourage individuals to become more aware of basic concepts in the science of water." One option here is "Educational resources for cartography, geography, and related disciplines" (**http://mapping.usgs.gov/www/html/1educate.html**)

- "Related Links" (**http://water.usgs.gov/wid/index-state.html#FL**), which leads to Web sites on South Florida restoration

- Terra Web page (**http://terraweb.wr.usgs.gov/**), which covers terrestrial remote sensing or the gathering of information about the Earth from a distance. This site explains the technique and its applications, as well as presents digital image products

- GISDataWeb Mapping Portal (**http://gisdata.usgs.net/**), which provides public Web map services and interfaces developed at the EROS Data Center and includes data sets, maps, and links

- PHOTOFINDER (**http://edc.usgs.gov/Webglis/glisbin/finder_main.pl?dataset_name=NAPI**), which provides photographs "shot from airplanes flying at 20,000 feet"

☞ Bureau of the Census

As discussed in Chapter 8, the bureau offers interactive software tools and downloadable software (**http://www.census.gov/main/www/access.html**). Furthermore, the bureau identifies selected GIS resources available on the Web, not all of which relate to activities of the federal government (see **http://www.census.gov/geo/www/gis_gateway.html**). This site covers

- Other GIS gateways on the Web

- Some university sites

- Resource collections and documents

- Meta-data ("data about data") sources

- Information servers

- Frequently asked questions

- Usenet newsgroups having discussions related to GIS

There is also a list of geography career resources.

The bureau offers products related to the TIGER (a computerized mapping project for the entire United States) database (see **http://www.census.gov/geo/www/tiger**). LandView III software displays EPA-regulated sites and demographic and economic data from the 1990 Census. This information can be overlaid on the network of U.S. streets, water features, and political and census boundaries.

Bureau of Reclamation

The bureau's mission "is to manage, develop, and protect water and related resources in an environmentally and economically sound manner in the interest of the American public." It has a Reclamation Remote Sensing and Geographic Information Group that specializes in image processing, GIS, global positioning systems, and other spatial technologies. Its Web site (**http://www.usbr.gov/main/**) explains some of its projects, provides some general GIS information, and offers additional Web links.

Bureau of Transportation Statistics

The bureau's (BTS) "Geographic Information Services" (**http://www.bts.gov/gis/index.html**) are a "national resource for transportation spatial data and GIS in transportation . . . information." These services include conferences, discussion, geospatial data sets that can be downloaded), a map gallery, references (abstracts, papers, and citations), links ("state, federal, international, vendors"; "FGDC Ground Transportation Subcommittee"; and "Spatial Data & Information Science Committee") , and National Transportation Atlas Data (NTAD). The set of geospatial data covers "transportation networks, transportation facilities, and other spatial data used as geographic reference." The National Spatial Data Infrastructure (NSDI) "is a first draft of a proposed road data model standard for segmenting and identifying unique road segments. . . . [It] also includes reference documents and a new e-mail list server for sharing comments about the road data model standard." A "Map Gallery" (**http://www.bts.gov/gis/maps**) presents preselected maps showing transportation statistics, national transportation analysis, interstate commodity shipments, and the *American Travel Survey*. For instance, they reflect interstate personal trips to any state; interstate trips represent trips of at least one hundred miles one way. Each map has an easy-to-read legend.

Finally, there are links to state GIS resources, state departments of transportation, federal resources, international resources, organizations, vendors, metropolitan planning organizations, and other resources (**http://www.bts.gov/gis/links**).

↗ Centers for Disease Control and Prevention

The Centers for Disease Control and Prevention offers a bimonthly, electronic newsletter, *Public Health GIS News and Information*, which is available gratis via e-mail to anyone in the public health sector interested in GIS. There is information on public health GIS literature, conferences and meetings, and applications of GIS technology (**http://www.cdc.gov/nchs/about/otheract/gis/gis_publichealth.info.htm**).

↗ Central Intelligence Agency

The Central Intelligence Agency (CIA; **http://www.odci.gov/cia/publications/pubs.html**) provides a list of unclassified maps and publications available for purchase from the Government Printing Office (GPO) and/or the National Technical Information Service (NTIS). For each country map, there is a brief description, the year of publication, the NTIS retrieval number and map number, and the price. Before ordering a map, it is beneficial to check the NTIS database, *FedWorld* (see Chapter 3) or GPO's *Sales Product Catalog* (**http://bookstore.gpo.gov/**) for the current price. A good collection of online CIA maps may be found at the University of Texas library's map collection (**http://www.lib.utexas.edu/maps/index.html**).

↗ Forest Service

Through its national headquarters, the Forest Service (**http://www.fs.fed.us/maps/**) provides visitor maps to national forests and grasslands, as well as specialty maps and topographical maps (from the U.S. Geological Survey). There are also regional maps and information on the Geometronics Service Center, and maps depicting "Where Are the Forests Located?" and "Forest Land Distribution Data for the United States." The Geometronics Service Center works closely with other Forest Service units and federal agencies that engage in geospatial activities (see **http://www.fs.fed.us/gstc/**). The center has a data library that serves agency personnel and, to some extent, other federal and state agencies, private industry, and academia.

The Forest Service offers data to the public, as GIF images and in ARC/INFO format, by forest type (continental United States, Alaska, and Hawaii) and forest density (continental United States; see **http://www.epa.gov/docs/grd/forest_inventory**). There are also meta-data records for both forest density and forest type. In addition, the agency provides GIS maps that depict fire areas; there is even a fire spreadsheet (**http://www.fs.fed.us/r1/ecology/fire2000/index.html**).

↗ Federal Emergency Management Agency

The Federal Emergency Management Agency (discussed in Chapter 6) runs the Mapping and Analysis Center (MAC), which "provides national level . . . GIS . . . support and coordination to the agency. GIS mapping products are available for the latest disasters, along with current and an archive of prior year disasters. This site is limited to presidential declared disasters and tropical storms/hurricanes that have projected landfall on the U.S. or a territory." The site (**http://gismaps.fema.gov/**) also links to the Web sites of the National Weather Service and the National Flood Insurance Program. It posts more than a thousand references to maps on its Web site. Some of the maps tracked past hurricanes and are included in FEMA's map archive. That archive also includes satellite imagery. In addition, FEMA maintains HazardMaps.GOV (**http://www.hazardMaps.gov/**), a "site for public access to online hazard advisory maps of various types, including earthquakes, hurricane, and flood."

National Park Service

The National Park Service (NPS), another agency of the Department of Interior, manages the nation's National Parks. The home page (**http://www.nps.gov/parks. html**) contains park maps and detailed regional and state maps showing park locations. It is possible to search for parks by park name or theme. It also has "Cultural Resources Mapping & Geographic Information Systems" (**http://www2.cr.nps.gov/ gis/cartography. htm**; **http://www2.cr.nps.gov/gis/mapit.htm**), the latter page contains *Open File Reports* that describe completed and ongoing projects that apply GIS technologies to mapping, documenting, and managing cultural resources. One of the reports is a survey of archaeological sites in the Mesa Verde National Park (Colorado). The same page also has brief explanations of GIS and papers such as "Mapping History Using GIS."

The Mapping and Preservation Inventory Tool (MAPIT; **http://www2.cr.nps. gov/gis/mapit.htm**) is a NPS resource for the organization of "historic resource inventories in a computerized database with sophisticated mapping capabilities, and [it] combines information about where historic properties are located with information about how these properties look." MAPIT displays "inventory information as a map, chart, or table." Furthermore, "through a linked database MAPIT can also generate standard survey forms, National Register of Historic Places nomination forms, and other forms used by preservationists—all in a computerized environment."

Natural Resources Conservation Service

The Resource Assessment Division of the National Resources Conservation Service (NRCS; United States Department of Agriculture; **http://www.nrcs.usda.gov/**) offers maps of wetland areas in the United States. The maps may contain pie charts showing different land use categories (see **http://www.nhq.nrcs.usda.gov/land/ index/wetlands.html**) and the map may be available as ASCII, GIF, or postscript files. NRCS has a mapping and spatial data center (**http://www.ftw.nrcs.usda.gov/ncg/ empty.html**) and offers other data resources (see **http://www.ftw.nrcs.usda.gov/ status_data.html**). GIS resources are available at **http://www.cr.nps.gov/map.htm**.

The National Cartography and Geospatial Center is NRCS's mapping and spatial data center. It provides a variety of map products and services and "is the focal point for digital imaging, modern mapping, global positioning systems, geographical information systems, and remote sensing" (see **http://www.ftw.nrcs.usda.gov/ncg/empty.html**).

The Natural Resources Conservation Service of the Department of Agriculture provides maps and statistics on the Wetland Reserve Program. At the national level, the site (**http://www.nrcs.usda.gov/programs/wrp/maps/**) covers total acres enrolled and contracts enrolled. State projects cover Arkansas, Florida, Illinois, Indiana, Louisiana, Minnesota, Mississippi, New York, North Carolina, Oklahoma, and Washington; statistical maps relate to Colusa County, California.

Department of Housing and Urban Development

The Department (HUD) has environmental maps (**http://www.hud.gov/offices/cio/emaps/**) that are part of "a free Internet service that combines information on HUD's community development and housing programs with EPA's environmental data. HUD E-MAPS provides location, type and performance of HUD-funded activities in every neighborhood across the country; and select EPA information on brownfields, hazardous wastes, air pollution and waste water discharges." At **http://www.hud.gov/maps.html**, users can find HUD's On-line Map Library and see departmental "projects in your area."

Federal Communications Commission

The Federal Communications Commission's (FCC) Geographic Information System (**http://uls-gis.fcc.gov/choice.htm**) queries information in FCC databases and displays the results graphically on maps. "The current release of the GIS accesses the Commission's Action and Microwave databases. Future releases will provide access to additional licensing databases." There is information about how to conduct the search and build maps, as well as how to save the data in the license table as standard ASCII text. It is also possible to save a map as an image file.

Federal Highway Administration

The Federal Highway Administration (FHWA), with assistance from the states, is building a GIS, the National Highway Planning Network (NHPN). The FHWA views the network as a planning resource that will include data from the Highway Performance Monitoring System and the National Bridge Inventory (see **http://www.fhwa.dot.gov/hep10/gis/gis.html**). The Federal Highway Administration of the Department of Transportation provides a listing of its Web sites as well as "related sites and resources." Examples of the sites include highway safety, infrastructure (e.g., bridge and pavement technology), stop red light running, and travel management (see **http://www.fhwa.dot.gov/fhwaweb.htm**).

Federal Transit Administration

The Federal Transit Administration's (FTA; **http://www.dot.gov/affairs/ftaind.htm**) National Transit Geographic Information System, once developed, will be "a representative inventory of the public transit assets of the country." Bridgewater State College's GeoGraphics Laboratory, in Bridgewater, Massachusetts, is assisting the FTA in developing the system and "is digitizing transit bus routes from around the country" (**http://www.fta.dot.gov/fta/library/technology/GIS/nt_gis.htm**). For a discussion of the GeoGraphics Laboratory's activities, see **http://geolab.bridgew. edu/home.**

↗ Other

American Memory of the Library of Congress has a historical map collection that spans the years 1500 to 2003 (**http://lcweb2.loc.gov/ammem/gmdhtml/gmdhome. html**). It covers "Cities and Towns," "Conservation and Environment," "Discovery and Exploration," "Cultural Landscapes," "Military Battles and Campaigns," "General Maps," and "Transportation and Communication." For example, the site features maps of Boston, Massachusetts, from the Revolutionary War period into the nineteenth century. Maps in the collection of the National Archives and Records Administration are also available (see **http://www.archives.gov/**). It is possible to order reproductions of maps and aerial photographs from its collection (**http://www. archives.gov/research_room/obtain_copies/maps_and_aerial_photos.html**).

Some additional examples of maps are the following:

- The maps links of the U.S. Fish and Wildlife Service (**http://northeast. fws.gov/moremaps.html**), for instance, provide access to the National Wetlands Inventory

- "Geographic Information Systems & Spatial Data" of the U.S. Fish and Wildlife Service (**http://www.fws.gov/data/gishome.html**) covers wetlands, roads, and topography and offers data, tools, and information

- National Pipeline Mapping System of the Department of Transportation (**http://www.npms.rspa.dot.gov/**) also includes maps on its site.

- Perusal of the search engine of the National Aeronautics and Space Administration discloses numerous resources related to GIS that are not password protected. One example is "GIS News" (see **http://guinan.gsfc.nasa.gov/docs/ asca/gisnews.html**).

FEDERAL GEOGRAPHIC DATA COMMITTEE

The Federal Geographic Data Committee (FGDC) coordinates the development of the National Spatial Data Infrastructure (NSDI), which "encompasses policies, standards, and procedures for organizations to cooperatively produce and share geographic data." The Web site (**http://www.fgdc.gov/**) explains the NSDI and provides other news and metadata (describing "the content, quality, condition, and other characteristics of data"). FGDC's Ground Transportation Subcommittee, which "promotes the coordination of geo-spatial data for ground transportation related activities,"

is sponsoring the development of a conceptual data model standard for identifying road segments as unique geo-spatial features which are independent of any cartographic or analytic network representation. These road segments will form the basis for maintenance of NSDI framework road data . . . and for establishing relationships between road segments and attribute data.

The Subcommittee's Web site (**http://www.bts.gov/gis.fgdc/web_intr.html**) encourages "open discussion of the NSDI Framework Transportation Identification Standard by potential stakeholders in both the transportation and the spatial data communities. In addition to the most current version of the standard, the site provides links to relevant technical reference documents and e-mail correspondence throughout the development process."

SUMMARY

This chapter discusses some government agencies that offer maps and geographic information systems; of course, other agencies may offer similar products. Clearly, the government has an extensive array of mapping and GIS services and products, ranging from the apparently simple to the very complex. Some of the products and services will appeal to the general public, whereas others are aimed at specialized audiences.

FirstGov, in fact, leads to thousands of entries related to geographical information systems. Needless to say, this chapter's treatment has been cursory. Those seeking additional information on GISs should see the following two sites:

- The Bureau of Land Management (Department of Interior) site offers "Meta Data and WWW Mapping Sites" (**http://www.blm.gov/gis/nsdi.html**).

- Bureau of Transportation Statistics (Office of Geographic Information Services, "Federal Resources" (**http://www.bts.gov/gis/links/fed/index.html**) includes "house data on roads, railroads, public transit, navigable waterways, commercial air routes, intermodal connections, and pipelines."

Finally, the Open GIS Consortium, a nonprofit membership organization, addresses the lack of interoperability among systems that process georeferenced data and between those systems and mainstream computer systems (see **http://www.opengis.org/**). It is playing a leading role in seeing what diverse sets of mapping data—stored in incompatible software languages and on different platforms—can be included in an electronic map.

NOTE

1. An example of a question that can be addressed using a GIS is the following: "When chemicals are released accidentally into the air or water, where will they go, how fast, and in what concentrations?" See James M. Smith, "ALOHA Software Gives Quick Answers in Chemical Spills," *Government Computer News* (August 8, 1994): 10. See also Stanley Aronoff, *Geographic Information Systems: A Management Perspective* (Ottawa, Ontario, Canada: WDL Publications, 1989): 2. See also the entire issue of *Journal of Academic Librarianship* 23 (November 1997).

URL Site Guide for This Chapter

Department of Agriculture

Forest Service
http://www.fs.fed.us/maps/

Fire Spreadsheet
http://www.fs.fed.us/r1/ecology/
fire2000/index.html

Geometronics Service Center
http://www.fs.fed.us/gstc/

National Resources Conservation Service
http://ww.ncrs.usda.gov/

Data Resources
http://www.ftw.nrcs.usda.gov/status_
data.html

Mapping and Spatial Data
http://www.ftw.nrcs.usda.gov/ncg/
empty.html

National Cartography and Geospatial Center
http://www.ftw.nrcs.usda.gov/ncg/
empty.html

State of the Land
http://www.nrcs.usda.gov/technical/land/

Wetland Maps
http://www.nrcs.usda.gov/programs/wrp/
maps/

Department of Commerce

GIS Resources
Bureau of the Census
http://www.census.gov/main/www/
access.html
http://www.census.gov/geo/www/
gis_gateway.html

TIGER
Bureau of the Census
http://www.census.gov/geo/www/tiger

National Ocean Service

National Oceanic and Atmospheric Administration
http://www.nos.noaa.gov/

Coastal Zone Management Program
http://www.nos.noaa.gov/ocrm/czm/
welcome.html
http://www.nos.noaa.gov/about/about.
html

MapFinder
http://oceanservice.noaa.gov/
mapfinder/

National Estuarine Research Reserves
http://oceanview.noaa.gov/topics/
coasts/reserves/welcome.html

National Marine Protected Area
http://www.mpa.gov/

National Marine Sanctuaries
http://www.sanctuaries.nos.noaa.gov/

Oceanographic Products and Services Division
http://www.co-ops.nos.noaa.gov/

Spatial Data Explorer
http://mapindex.nos.noaa.gov/

Department of Defense
http://www.defenselink.mil

National Imagery and Mapping Agency
http://www.nima.mil

Department of Health and Human Services

GIS Resources
Centers for Disease Control and Prevention
http://www.cdc.gov/nchs/about/othersact/
gis/gis_publichealthinfo.htm

Department of Housing and Urban Development

Map Library
http://www.hud.gov/maps.html

Environmental Maps
http://www.hud.gov/offices/cio/emaps/

Department of the Interior

Meta-data and WWW Mapping Sites

Bureau of Land Management
http://www.blm.gov/gis/nsdi.html

Bureau of Reclamation
http://www.usbr.gov/main/

Projects, GIS, and Links
http://dataweb.usbr.gov/html/maps.html

National Park Service
http://www.nps.gov/parks.html

Cartography
http://www2.cr.nps.gov/gis/cartography.htm

Cultural Resources Mapping & GIS
http://www2.cr.nps.gov/gis/gispubs.htm

MAPIT
http://www2.cr.nps.gov/gis/mapit.htm

GIS Resources
http://www.cr.nps.gov/map.htm

U.S. Fish and Wildlife Service

Map Links
http://northeast.fws.gov/moremaps.html

GIS and Spatial Data
http://www.fws.gov/data/gishome.html

U.S. Geological Survey
http://www.usgs.gov/

Antarctica
http://geonames.usgs.gov/antform.html

Cartography and Publishing Program
http://sr6capp.er.usgs.gov/

Digital Orthophoto Quadrangle
http://www-wmc.wr.usgs.gov/doq/

Drought Watch
http://md.water.usgs.gov/drought/

EarthExplorer
http://edcsns17.cr.usgs.gov/cgi-bin/EarthExplorer/phtml/BrowserTest.phtml

Earthshots
http://edc.usgs.gov/earthshots/slow/tableofcontents

Educational Links
http://wwwdlabrg.er.usgs.gov/educational_links.htm

Educational Resources
http://mapping.usgs.gov/www/html/1educate.html

EROS Data Center
http://edcwww.cr.usgs.gov/

Fact Sheets
http://water.usgs.gov/wid/indexlist.html

Geological Survey Library
http://library.usgs.gov/

GEOnet Names Server
http://164.214.2.59/gns/html/index.html

GISDATA Web Mapping Portal
http://gisdata.usgs.net/

Global Land Information System
http://edcwww.cr.usgs.gov/glis/glis.html

Index of USGS Web Sites
http://www.usgs.gov/network/

Lewis and Clark Home Page
http://www.usgs.gov/features/lewisandclark.html

Maps and Other Products
http://www.usgs.gov/pubprod/

National Atlas of the United States®
http://nationalatlas.gov/index.html

National Map
http://rockys20.cr.usgs.gov/nmmult
iService/viewer.htm

National Mapping Information
http://mapping.usgs.gov/

**National Satellite Land Remote
Sensing Data Archive Page**
http://edu.usgs.gov/archive/nslrsda/

**National Water Summary on
Wetlands Resources**
http://water.usgs.gov/nwsum/
WSP2425

PHOTOFINDER
http://edc.usgs.gov/Webglis/
glisin/finder_main.pl?dataset_
name=NAPP

Related Links (South Florida)
http://water.usgs.gov/wid/index-state.
html#FL

**Rocky Mountain Mapping
Center**
http://rmmcweb.cr.usgs.gov/

Site Map
http://www.usgs.gov/sitemap.html

Terra Web
http://terraweb.wr.usgs.gov/

**The United States Geological
Survey, 1879-1989**
http://pubs.usgs.gov/circ/c/1050/
index.htm

**View Maps and Aerial Photo
Images Online**
http://mapping.usgs.gov/partners/
viewonline.html

Department of Transportation

GIS Resources

Bureau of Transportation Statistics
http://www.bts.gov/gis/index.html

Map Gallery
http://ww.bts.gov/gis/maps

National Pipeline Mapping System
http://www.npms.rspa.dot.gov/

**Highway Performance and Bridge
Inventory**
Federal Highway Administration
http://www.fhwa.dot.gov/hep10/gis/gis.html
http://www.fhwa.dot.gov/fhwaweb.htm

GeoGraphics Laboratory
Federal Transit Administration
http://www.dot.gov/affairs/ftaind.htm
http://geolab.brdigew.edu/home

Transit Bus Routes
http://www.fta.dot.gov/fta/library/
technology/GIS/nt_gis.htm

Environmental Protection Agency
http://www.epa.gov/

EnviroMapper
http://www.epa.gov/enviro/html/em/
index.html

Environmental Atlas
http://www.epa.gov/ceisweb1/ceishome/
atals
http://www.epa.gov/ceisweb1/ceishome/
sitemap.html

Geographical Data Innovations
http://www.epa.gov/ceisweb1/ceishome/
atlas/studiesandinnovations.html

Executive Office of the President

Central Intelligence Agency
http://www.odci.gov/cia/publications/
pubs.html

CIA Maps (University of Texas)
http://www.lib.utexas.edu/maps/index.html

Federal Communications Commission

GIS Resources
http://uls-gis.fcc.gov/choice.htm

Federal Emergency Management Agency

Mapping
http://gismaps.fema.gov/

HazardMaps.Gov
http://www.hazardmaps.gov/

Federal Geographic Data Committee
http://www.fgdc.gov/

Subcommittee
http://www.bts.gov/gis/fgdc/web_intr.html

FirstGov
http://www.firstgov.gov/

Government Printing Office

Online Bookstore
http://bookstore.gpo.gov/

Library of Congress

American Memory
http://memory.loc.gov/

Historical Map Collections
http://lcweb2.loc.gov/ammem/gmdhtml/gmdhome.html

Lewis and Clark Expedition
http://www.loc.gov/exhibits/lewisandclark/lewisandclark.html

National Aeronautics and Space Administration

GIS Resources
http://guinan.gsfc.nasa.gov/docs/asca/gisnews.html

National Archives and Records Administration
http://www.archives.gov/

Reproductions of Maps and Aerial Photographs
http://www.archives.gov/research_room/obtain_copies/maps_and_aerial_photos.html

Open GIS Consortium
http://www.opengis.org/

Chapter 12

Selected Subjects

To complement the variety of federal information resources and Web sites discussed in previous chapters, this chapter provides a selection of federal information sources and Web sites organized by popular subject areas. At a basic level, few government agencies were ever created to accomplish a single purpose or program; indeed, over time, they often acquire other responsibilities, or Congress or the president have assigned other duties to them. Frequently, a single subject or a group of related subjects is shared among several agencies, offices, and bureaus located in cabinet-level departments and independent agencies, as well as among the legislative and judicial branches of government. For example, a search of government Web pages on the issue of nutrition indicates that no fewer than a dozen agencies detail information about matters such as what and how much to eat; which foods are dangerous; which foods are best for human growth; how agriculture, industry, pollution, and other factors affect the nutrition in foods; and how genetic engineering might affect the nutritional qualities in the food. Search engines, Web portals, and other online tools (discussed in Chapters 3 and 9) are useful starting points for finding information on simple or single topics, but they fail to draw necessary links and associations among government programs when considering more complicated issues.

Furthermore, as with any general subject searching techniques, it is important to frame terms or concepts in a fashion to capture successfully the greatest number of relevant resources. Within public policy, that framing results from knowledge about how laws are created and implemented through specific government policies, as well as from where to look for this information, specifically which sources and government bodies.

The subject areas included in this chapter are not exhaustive; rather, the areas presented are drawn from the authors' collective experience of answering thousands of reference questions about government information over the last thirty years and from discussions in the print and electronic news. Appendix C provides a further list of government Web sites, organized by broad subject headings, and thereby offers the reader more "subject" access to government Web sites and information resources. There is much about the federal government and what it does that confounds anyone who attempts to organize its programs and purposes into distinct categories. With the subjects offered in this chapter and Appendix C, the authors have created categories to enable readers to find some of the more popular (and heavily used) Web sites. For quick reference, this chapter includes the following subjects:

- Business and Trade
- Citizenship, Immigration, and Naturalization
- Country Information, Passports, and Travel
- Decennial Census
- Disabilities and Equal Access
- Endangered Wildlife and Environment
- *Freedom of Information Act*
- Genealogy
- Government Printing and Published Reports
- Grants and Contracting Opportunities
- Health and Medical Resources
- Historic Preservation
- History and Culture
- Intellectual Property & Copyrights
- Patents and Trademarks
- Postsecondary Education Finance
- Rules and Regulations
- Terrorism and Homeland Security

BUSINESS AND TRADE

The government provides a wealth of resources, including data sets, for the business community as well as for anyone interested in trade data. A good first place to check is FirstGov (**http://www.firstgov.gov/**), which provides access to different resources for the business community. FirstGov's Business Gateway (**http://www.firstgov.gov/Business/Business_Gateway.shtml**) links to resources of different agencies of cabinet-level departments and independent agencies. In particular, it offers the following

- Resources for exporters, small businesses, and minority, rural, and women-owned businesses
- Access to online services, laws and regulations, publications for small businesses, resources related to business development, opportunities to buy and sell to the government, local offices of different agencies, and business data
- Resources on international trade, business finances and taxes, and workplace issues

- Frequently asked questions

- Presidential policies and initiatives

From this gateway, information seekers can branch out to the U.S. Business Advisor (**http://www.business.gov/**) and to Department of Commerce (**http://www.commerce.gov/**) and its various agencies, including for instance, the National Technical Information Service (**http://www.nits.gov/**), the International Trade Administration (**http://www.ita.doc.gov/**), the Bureau of Export Administration (**http://www.bea.doc.gov/**), STAT-USA (**http://www.statusa.gov/**), and the Bureau of Industry and Security (**http://www.bxa.doc.gov/**) and its site map (**http://www.bxa.doc.gov/SiteMap.html**).

Other bodies include the Federal Trade Commission (**http://www.ftc.gov/**), the United States International Trade Commission (**http://www.usitc.gov/**), the State Department (**http://www.state.gov/**), the Small Business Administration (**http://www.sbaonline.sba.gov/**), and the Securities and Exchange Commission (**http://www.sec.gov/**).

Examples from the legislative branch include the House Committee on Small Business (**http://www.house.gov/smbiz/**), the Senate Committee on Small Business and Entrepreneurship (**http://wwws.senate.gov/~sbc/**), and the General Accounting Office (**http://www.gao.gov/**).

CITIZENSHIP, IMMIGRATION, AND NATURALIZATION

The dream of becoming a U.S. citizen or seeking permanent resident status remains a goal for tens of thousands of people every year. Before the advent of the Web, finding information, or even official forms required to achieve this status, demanded endless hours of telephone calls, visits to various government agencies, letter writing, or hiring a lawyer specialized in naturalization and immigration practice. Although the Web has not displaced these moments of "chasing paper" through the federal bureaucracy (nor has it removed the need for lawyers at times), it has made the whole process a bit more transparent and accessible. Most interaction with the federal government over the issues of citizenship, naturalization, and immigration involve primarily two agencies: the Bureau of Citizenship and Immigration Services (BCISS), part of the Department of Homeland Security, and the Department of State (see Chapter 5). The essential problem of finding information about citizenship, naturalization, and immigration usually involves two basic issues: first, how does someone determine his or her status (citizen vs. noncitizen); second, how does one find the paperwork and application process if that person wants (or needs) to change his or her status. The following discussion tries to explain some of the more frequently sought sources of information.

The other area of confusion revolves around foreign travel and visas. As discussed in more detail later, the permissions and lengths of stay to which Americans are subject while traveling overseas are determined by the laws and regulations of the countries they visit. The basic document required for travel by most Americans is the passport. For foreign nationals visiting the United States, the Department of State, and, in some cases, the INS, require comparable levels of documentation and restrictions on foreign travelers within the territories governed by the United States.

⬎ Coming to the United States: So Many Paths

The easiest way to become a U.S. citizen is to either be born within the territories of the United States or have a parent(s) who is an American citizen if one is born outside the country. As the Bureau of Citizenship and Immigration Services Web page (**http://www.immigration.gov/graphics/services/natz/citizen.htm**) explains,

A citizen of the United States is a native-born, foreign-born, or naturalized person who owes allegiance to the United States and who is entitled to its protection. In addition to the naturalization process, the United States recognizes the U.S. citizenship of individuals according to two fundamental principles: jus soli, or right of birthplace, and jus sanguinis, or right of blood. The 14th Amendment of the U.S. Constitution guarantees citizenship at birth to almost all individuals born in the United States or in U.S. jurisdictions, according to the principle of jus soli. Certain individuals born in the United States, such as children of foreign heads of state or children of foreign diplomats, do not obtain U.S. citizenship under jus soli.

Certain individuals born outside of the United States are born citizens because of their parents, according to the principle of jus sanguinis (which holds that the country of citizenship of a child is the same as that of his /her parents). The U.S. Congress is responsible for enacting laws that determine how citizenship is conveyed by a U.S. citizen parent or parents according to the principle of jus sanguinis. These laws are contained in the *Immigration and Nationality Act*.

Citizenship gained through naturalization constitutes an application process for those born outside the United States and whose parents are not U.S. citizens or might have relatives who are already citizens. According to the BCIS Web site,

U.S. citizenship is conferred upon a foreign citizen or national after he or she fulfills the requirements established by Congress in the Immigration and Nationality Act. . . . The general requirements for administrative naturalization include:

– A period of continuous residence and physical presence in the United States; residence in a particular BCIS District prior to filing;

– An ability to read, write and speak English;

– A knowledge and understanding of U.S. history and government;

– Good moral character;

– Attachment to the principles of the U.S. Constitution; and

– Favorable disposition toward the United States.

All naturalization applicants must demonstrate good moral character, attachment, and favorable disposition. The other naturalization requirements may be modified or waived for certain applicants, such as spouses of U.S. citizens. (**http://www.immigration.gov/graphics/services/natz/index.htm**).

Information about dual citizenship, or how to renounce U.S. citizenship, is at the State Department's Consular Affairs Web site (**http://travel.state.gov/dualnationality. html** and **http://travel.state.gov/renunciation.html**). These Web pages also offer advice for those seeking guidance on how to adopt a child from overseas, what to do when one marries a foreign national, how to handle a divorce (i.e., legal paperwork) when it happens overseas or involves a foreign national, how handle certificates of record necessary to document an individual's status if born overseas, and what to do if any (or all) of this essential paperwork is missing.

The Most Complicated Path: Permanent Residence

Permanent residence status, for individuals who wish to remain in the United States for longer periods of time (because of work, political asylum, family, etc.) but not seek outright citizenship is the most difficult and political of the immigrant categories. As subsequent events after the terrorist attacks on September 11, 2001, revealed, even individuals with permanent resident status are still subject to various restrictions of how they live, work, leave, or return to the United States. There are several categories, conditions, and exemptions that determine the manner and means of how an individual achieves permanent residency status in the United States. Each is explained at the BCIS Web site (**http://www.immigration.gov/graphics/services/residency/ index.htm**). There are several "paths" to achieve "lawful permanent residency." Keep in mind each path is strewn with obstacles, caveats, exceptions, and, in some cases, political expediency, during the application process. Forms can be found at the INS Web site (**http://www.immigration.gov/graphics/formsfee/forms/index.htm**).

Following is a brief list of possible conditions of how residency is considered.

- If there is a family member already living in the United States who is either a citizen or permanent resident

- If the applicant has a permanent job

- If the applicant creates investment opportunities: 10,000 immigrant visas per year are available to qualified individuals seeking permanent resident status on the basis of their engagement in a new commercial enterprise

- If the applicant has already been granted asylum

- Through a "diversity lottery," which makes 55,000 immigrant visas available to people who come from countries with low rates of immigration to the United States

- Through adoption where the foreign born child is declared an orphan

- Exemptions are allowed for various nationalities, social or political conditions, or other situations recognized by Congress and enacted into law

Outside of these specific conditions, foreign nationals arrive and travel through the United States based on a variety of temporary visas. The State Department is responsible for this documentation and offers its visa information in two categories: immigrant and nonimmigrant status

COUNTRY INFORMATION, PASSPORTS, AND TRAVEL

For American citizens, and a selected number of permanent residents, travel to foreign countries, whether for business or pleasure, is an event that demands much preparation and documentation. Just as the previous section discussed the complexities of citizenship, immigration, and permanent residency, the level of information needed for a safe and rewarding trip overseas can appear equally daunting. Here is an outline of information sources that might prove useful when planning a short trip or an extended stay overseas.

Before an American citizen can leave the United States for extended travel overseas, he or she must obtain a passport. The best Web page to learn about how to apply, change, use, or update this critical document can be found at **http://travel.state. gov/passport_services.html**. Here again, knowing what is needed and where to get the information is critical, especially if the foreign travel involves either children or young adults under the age of 18 or if the applicant was born overseas with at least one parent who is a U.S. citizen. Because this level of documentation, as well as an attempt to correct errors or changes in a current passport, might take longer to complete, it is advisable to leave as much time before the scheduled departure to make sure all the paperwork is in order.

Just as foreign nationals who come to the United States are subject to the rules and regulations of BCIS and State Department, foreign countries employ their own regulations and laws that place restrictions on how long noncitizens can stay in their respective countries, along with the necessary visas and other documents that will be demanded at national borders. One of the best places to find this information about foreign travel is by contacting foreign consular offices in the United States. A list of phone numbers and addresses can be found at **http://www.state.gov/s/cpr/ rls/fco/c5698.htm**. For a list of Web sites hosted by foreign embassies in the United States, take a look at **http://www.state.gov/misc/10125.htm**. Web sites for U.S. embassies and diplomatic missions overseas, which often have much information for U.S. citizens who expect to stay in foreign countries, can be found at **http://usembassy. state.gov/**.

U.S. citizens going abroad can find a significant amount of information about the countries they plan to visit, and what they can bring back into the United States, by consulting the following resources:

- **Travel Warnings and Consular Information Sheets (http://travel.state. gov/travel_warnings.html)** are specific notices, warnings, and advisories issued by the State Department to warn of significant risks and dangers documented in foreign countries by U.S. foreign service personnel serving in the embassies and consulates around the globe. In particular, travel warnings may advise U.S. citizens to avoid travel in particular countries. This site also includes Consular Information Sheets, available for every country, that document specific rules and regulations that govern any "unusual immigration practices, health conditions, minor political disturbances, unusual currency and entry regulations, crime and security information, and drug penalties." If an unstable condition exists in a country that is not severe enough to warrant a Travel Warning, a description of the condition(s) may be included under an optional section titled "Safety/Security." Keep in mind, as well, that the individual Web sites for embassies and consulate offices overseas may have more recent or specific information not regularly updated by the publications represented on this page.

- **Country Background Notes (http://www.state.gov/r/pa/ei/bgn/)** is a series published by the State Department that gives a quick overview of a country's history, culture, economy, and relationship with the United States. The series is useful as a supplement to what one finds in the Consular Information Sheets.

- **Emergency Services to U.S. Citizens Abroad (http://travel.state.gov/acs.html#emr)** offers advice, warnings, and specific services available to U.S. citizens if they should run afoul of local laws or regulations, get sick, run out of money, or have a relative die overseas.

- **Travelers' Health (http://www.cdc.gov/travel/)**: Found among the Web pages that the Centers for Disease Control and Prevention manages, this page offers specific advice on how to protect one's health when traveling through regions of the world with minimal public health facilities (along with specific recommendations for required vaccines and immunizations necessary prior to departure). There are also specific notices of known outbreaks of disease overseas. Information about food and water safety, the special needs of traveling with children or pets, and specific health threats posed by type of transport (cruise ships, air travel, local travel arrangements) is also offered.

- **Travel Information (http://www.customs.gov/xp/cgov/travel/)**: Managed by the Homeland Security's Customs and Borders Protection, these pages tell travelers, citizens and foreign nationals alike, what they can (and cannot) bring in and out of the United States. There is also advice on what products and purchases will be subject to customs fees. It also offers information about specific security concerns at ports of entry, length of delays at the borders for processing, as well as other useful information.

- **APHIS Travel Web (http://www.aphis.usda.gov/travel/)**: This site offers information about animals, plants, and other living things regulated through the U.S. Department of Agriculture.

- **Currency Rates and Exchanges (http://www.fms.treas.gov/intn.html)**: Offered by the U.S. Treasury, this site covers currency rates and exchanges stated in foreign currency units and U.S. dollar equivalents. This page covers all foreign currencies in which the U.S. government has an interest, including receipts and disbursements, accrued revenues and expenditures, authorizations, obligations, receivables and payables, refunds, and similar reverse transaction items.

- **Environmental Laws and Regulations (http://international.fws.gov/)**: Through its international programs, the U.S. Fish and Wildlife Service, part of the Department of the Interior, works multilaterally with many partners and nations in the implementation of international treaties, conventions, and other multilateral projects that seek to conservation of species and the habitats in which they depend. Part of this responsibility includes the oversight of all kinds of wildlife in and out of the United States, which might include scientific exhibitions, circus animals, everyday pets, and hunting trophies.

DECENNIAL CENSUS

Finding, locating, and understanding the wealth of data collected through the U.S. Decennial Census remains one of the greatest challenges to those hundreds of thousands of users every year who surf Census Bureau Web pages in attempts to find and understand the latest information derived from this massive national accounting taken every ten years. In previous decades, the bureau's statistical experts provided both the raw data and analyses through specific reports and volumes published two or three years after the census counts were taken. There is an equally long tradition of library-based information services that sought to help individuals understand how the Census Bureau collects its information and how to understand the various specialized tables, reports, maps, and summaries issued by the government. In other words, anyone seeking to find, use, and understand the social and economic conditions revealed by the census questions enjoyed a great deal of mediation and interpretation. With the Web's emergence, along with political and funding developments after the 2000 Census was taken, these mediating roles of both bureau analysts and librarians have probably been sharply reduced. Now users must understand some of the basics of how census statistics are put together, the definitions and limitations put on data sets, and the specialized geographic and spatial conditions that the bureau uses. In other words, everyone becomes a statistical analyst.

Specifically, the Bureau of Census offers the *American Factfinder* (**http://factfinder. census.gov/servlet/BasicFactsServlet**) as the principal tool to the tables and maps of the 2000 Census. It assumes that users understand (1) the differences among the several "summary tape files" (essentially aggregated tables of the raw data generated by both the long and short census forms) and (2) the arcane and technical use of geographic areas by the census, because the bureau organizes data according to spatial areas that might not conform to more familiar places or political geography that most people use. Furthermore, there is little instruction on how to use the Web pages. Again, going to a depository library and asking for help will go a long way in resolving these difficulties. The Web page does offer several guides and tutorials about how to use its features—simply by clicking on the Help button on the top right hand part of the page.

DISABILITIES AND EQUAL ACCESS

Information pertaining to disabilities is available from all three branches of government. As with other topics included in this chapter, searching for this kind of information draws from a variety of laws, regulations, and programs that focus on disabilities and that cover civil rights, education, employment, housing, health, income support, technology, transportation, and community life. Indeed, the list of laws outlined on the Department of Justice's disability Web site (**http://www.usdoj.gov/ crt/ada/**) shows that several government agencies shape specific federal policies to ensure equal access for individuals with disabilities. This section highlights the relevant laws and the Web sites associated with their oversight or implementation

- The *Air Carrier Access Act of 1986* prohibits discrimination on the basis of disability in air travel and requires air carriers to accommodate the needs of passengers with disabilities.

  The Air Consumer Protection Division, Department of Transportation (DOT; **http://airconsumer.ost.dot.gov/ACAAcomplaint.htm**; **http://airconsumer.ost.dot.gov/publications/disabled.htm**; **http://airconsumer.ost.dot.gov/hotline.htm**). The division performs the following functions: receives informal complaints from members of the public regarding aviation consumer issues; verifies compliance with DOT's aviation consumer protection requirements; provides guidance to the industry and members of the public on consumer protection matters; and makes available to the public information on pertinent consumer matters.

- The *Americans with Disabilities Act of 1990* (ADA) prohibits discrimination based on disability in employment, state and local government services, transportation, public accommodations, commercial facilities, and telecommunications.

  Disability Rights Section, Department of Justice (**http://www.usdoj.gov/crt/ ada/adahom1.htm**). This is the principal agency in the Justice Department responsible for advising and enforcing general aspects of ADA.

  U.S. Department of Transportation, Federal Transit Administration (**http://www. fta.dot.gov/office/civrights/adainfo.html**). It is the principal agency in the DOT with the responsibility to ensure ADA requirements are enforced in terms of mass and public transportation systems.

  Equal Employment Opportunity Commission (**http://www.eeoc.gov/**): This independent agency oversees all laws to ensure the prevention of employment discrimination on the basis of race, color, religion, sex, or national origin, age, gender, disability.

  Federal Communications Commission (**http://www.fcc.gov/cgb/dro/**). The independent agency works to ensure people with disabilities have access to the technology in order to use the public communication spectrum.

- The *Architectural Barriers Act of 1968* is enforced by the United States Architectural and Transportation Barriers Compliance Board (commonly known as the Access Board; (**http://www.access-board.gov/**), an independent federal agency, and requires that federally funded buildings and facilities be accessible to people with disabilities.

- The *Civil Rights of Institutionalized Persons Act* authorizes the U.S. attorney general to investigate conditions of confinement at state and local government institutions such as prisons, jails, pretrial detention centers, juvenile correctional facilities, publicly operated nursing homes, and institutions for people with psychiatric or developmental disabilities.

Civil Rights Division, Special Litigation Section, Department of Justice, (**http://www.usdoj.gov/crt/split/cripa.htm**) is in charge of enforcing this act.

- The *Fair Housing Amendments Act of 1988* prohibits housing discrimination based on race, color, national origin, religion, sex, family status, or disability.

  This act is enforced by the Fair Housing and Equal Opportunity, Department of Housing and Urban Development (**http://www.hud.gov/offices/fheo/disabilities/index.cfm**).

- *Individuals with Disabilities Education Act* (IDEA) requires public schools to make available to all eligible children with disabilities a free appropriate public education in the least restrictive environment appropriate to their individual needs.

  Office of Special Education Programs, Department of Education (**http://www.ed.gov/offices/OSERS/OSEP/**) works to enforce the IDEA.

- The *National Voter Registration Act of 1993* requires all offices of state-funded programs that are primarily engaged in providing services to persons with disabilities to provide all program applicants with voter registration forms, to assist them in completing the forms, and to transmit completed forms to the appropriate state official.

  The Civil Rights Division, Voting Section, of the Department of Justice (**http://www.usdoj.gov/crt/voting/nvra/activ_nvra.htm**) is charged with oversight of this act.

- The *Rehabilitation Act of 1973* prohibits discrimination on the basis of disability in federally funded programs and services, in federal employment, and by federal contractors. It also requires that electronic and information technology that the federal government uses to be accessible to, and usable by, people with disabilities

  The Office of Compliance Assistance, Department of Labor (**http://www.dol.gov/dol/compliance/comp-rehab.htm**) ensures compliance with the *Rehabilitation Act*.

- The *Telecommunications Act of 1996* requires that telecommunications equipment and services be accessible to and usable by people with disabilities, if readily achievable.

  The Federal Communications Commission (**http://www.fcc.gov/cgb/dro/**) is charged with compliance to this act.

- The *Voting Accessibility for the Elderly and Handicapped Act of 1984* requires that registration facilities and polling places for federal elections be accessible to persons with disabilities.

  The Civil Rights Division, Voting Section, Department of Justice (**http://www.usdoj.gov/crt/voting**) ensures compliance to this act.

Aside from these specific enforcement responsibilities, other government Web sites provide additional information. For instance, President George W. Bush, through Executive Order 13217 (**http://www.whitehouse.gov/news/releases/2001/06/20010619.html**), created the multiagency initiative "Community-Based Alternatives for Individuals with Disabilities," on June 18, 2001. The order specifically directs parts of the federal government to assist states and localities to implement swiftly the U.S. Supreme Court decision in *Olmstead v. L.C.* (the court case can be found at the Web site of Supreme Court opinions hosted by the law Cornell University's law school: **http://supct.law.cornell.edu/supct/html/98-536.ZS.html**). The order asserts that "the United States is committed to community-based alternatives for individuals with disabilities and recognizes that such services advance the best interests of the United States." It further directs six federal bodies (the Departments of Justice, Health and Human Services, Education, Labor, and Housing and Urban Development, as well as the Social Security Administration) to "evaluate the policies, programs, statutes and regulations of their respective agencies to determine whether any should be revised or modified to improve the availability of community-based services for qualified individuals with disabilities" and to report back to the president with their findings. The Departments of Transportation and Veterans Affairs, the Small Business Administration, and the Office of Personnel Management, although not included in the order, also joined in the implementation effort. These bodies formed the Interagency Council on Community Living to carry out the order's directives.

DisAbility.gov (**http://www.disAbility.gov/**) is the most direct Web resource to result from this effort, and it "brings information on U.S. federal programs, services, and resources to Americans with Disabilities and their families." Specifically, there is coverage of "hot topics" and issues such as health, housing, income, tax credits, technology, and transportation.

The Social Security Administration offers information on its disability programs (**http://www.ssa.gov/disability/**), and the Bureau of the Census provides data on disabilities (**http://www.census.gov/hhes/www/disability.html**). There is the National Council on Disability, an independent agency that makes recommendations to the president and Congress (**http://www.ncd.gov/**). Another relevant site is that of the Small Business Administration (**http://www.sbaonline.sba.gov/hotlist/disabilities.html**).

ENDANGERED WILDLIFE AND ENVIRONMENT

Anyone interested in this topic will again be confronted by a number of legal and policy choices. For the most part, wildlife and environmental law exists primarily as a matter of legal administration enforced by rules and regulations (see the section of this chapter on "Rules and Regulations"). Furthermore, much relevant information is also available from the executive branch in terms of policy documents, scientific information, and public guides to important national resources. Good examples of this are Web pages from the Departments of Agriculture, Interior, and Energy, as well as the Environmental Protection Agency (EPA).

In the Department of Agriculture, the National Resources and Conservation Service (**http://www.nrcs.usda.gov/**) is the primary program that deals with soil conditions, watershed, land use, protection against erosion, and the development of other conservation technologies. The Department of Interior, through a good number of its subagencies and bureaus, has major responsibilities over the environmental quality and management of the federal public lands ecological protection. In particular, see the Web pages of the U.S. Fish and Wildlife Service (**http://www.fws.gov/**). The EPA (**http://www.epa.gov/**) is the principal agency responsible for the enforcement and scientific basis of many federal pollution, environment, as well as the sundry clean air and water laws. In particular, see the "Topics" Web page (**http://www.epa.gov/ epahome/topics. html**). One of the topics on the EPA page relates to "Ecosystems" and "Endangered Species." The page on endangered species leads to "Recommended EPA Web pages," "Related EPA Topical Pages," and information on "Endangered and threatened species." Finally, the Department of Energy (**http://www.doe.gov/**) contains much information about the effects of large-scale environmental concerns such global warming and environmental damage caused by energy resources, as well as other useful links to related programs. There may also be relevant information from the legislative branch, primarily the appropriate congressional committees, GPO Access, and the General Accounting Office (see Chapter 4).

FREEDOM OF INFORMATION ACT

As discussed in Chapter 1, the *Freedom of Information Act* (FOIA) applies to the executive branch. In specific response to a set of 1996 amendments, the tenets of the basic law were expanded to create online electronic reading rooms designed to offer selected "repeatedly requested" records according to following categories:

- "Final opinions [and] . . . orders" rendered in the adjudication of administrative cases

- Specific agency policy statements

- Certain administrative staff manuals

- Records disclosed in response to a FOIA request that "the agency determines have become or are likely to become the subject of subsequent requests for substantially the same records"

These electronic reading rooms should also guide members of the public to information locator systems agencies might maintain. Furthermore, the public is often informed on how to invoke the act. Figure 12.1 is a selective list of department and agency Web sites on the FOIA. There are many guides to the FOIA. One of the best is *Litigation under the Federal Open Government Laws 2002* (Electronic Privacy Information Center; **http://www.epic.org/bookstore/foia2002/**), which covers the FOIA, the *Privacy Act of 1974*, the *Government in the Sunshine Act*, and the *Federal Advisory Committee Act*. The Office of Information and Privacy of the Department of Justice issues the *Justice Department Guide to the Freedom of Information Act* (**http://www.usdoj.gov/oip.html**).

Figure 12.1. Some *Freedom of Information Act* Web Sites.

Executive Office of the President

National Security Agency **http://www.nsa.gov/docs/efoia/**

Office of Management and Budget **http://www.whitehouse.gov/omb/foia/index.html**

Office of the United States Trade Representative **http://www.ustr.gov/efoia/efoia.html**

Executive Branch Departments and Agencies

Department of Agriculture **http://www.usda.gov/news/foia/main.htm**

Department of Commerce **http://www.osec.doc.gov/oebam/foia25.htm**

Department of Defense **http://www.defenselink.mil/pubs/foi/**

> Air Force **http://www.foia.af.mil/**
>
> Army **http://www.rmd.belvoir.army.mil/FOIAERR.htm**
>
> Marine Corps **http://www.hqmc.usmc.mil/foia/foiaweb.nsf**
>
> Navy **http://foia.navy.mil/**
>
> National Imagery and Mapping Agency **http://164.214.2.59/cda/article/0.2311.3104_59416_114576.00.html**
>
> National Reconnaissance Office **http://www.nro.gov/foia/index.html**

Department of Education **http://www.ed.gov/offices/OCIO/foia/index.html**

Department of Energy **http://www.nv.doe.gov/programs/foia/default.htm**

Department of Health and Human Services **http://www.hhs.gov/foia/**

> Centers for Disease Control **http://www.cdc.gov/od/foia/foi.htm**
>
> Food and Drug Administration **http://www.fda.gov/foi/foia2.htm**

Department of Homeland Security **http://www.dhs.gov/dhspublic/display?theme=48**

Department of Housing and Urban Development **http://www.hud.gov/ogc/foiafree.html**; **http://www.hud.gov/ogc/bshelf2a.html**

Department of the Interior **http://www.doi.gov/foia/**

> Bureau of Indian Affairs **http://www.doi.gov/bia/foia/list.htm**
>
> Bureau of Land Management **http://www.blm.gov/nhp/efoia/index.htm**
>
> Bureau of Reclamation **http://www.usbr.gov/foia/**
>
> Minerals Management Service **http://www.mms.gov/adm/foia.html**
>
> National Park Service **http://www.nps.gov/refdesk/npsfoia.html**
>
> Office of Surface Mining **http://www.osmre.gov/ocfoia.htm**
>
> U.S. Fish and Wildlife Service **http://foia.fws.gov/**

Fig. 12.1. (*Cont.*)

U.S. Geological Survey **http://www.usgs.gov/foia/**

Department of Justice **http://www.usdoj.gov/04foia/index.html**

Drug Enforcement Administration **http://www.usdoj.gov/dea/foia/dea.htm**

Federal Bureau of Investigation **http://foia.fbi.gov/**

Federal Bureau of Prisons **http://www.bop.gov/foiapol.html**

Department of Labor **http://www.dol.gov/dol/foia/main.htm**

Department of State **http://foia.state.gov/**

Department of Transportation **http://www.dot.gov/foia/index.html**

Department of the Treasury **http://www.ustreas.gov/foia/**

Bureau sites **http://www.treas.gov/foia/bureaus.html**

Department of Veterans Affairs **http://www.va.gov/foia/**

Independent Agencies

Central Intelligence Agency **http://www.foia.ucia.gov/**

Environmental Protection Agency **http://www.epa.gov/foia/**

Export-Import Bank **http://www.exim.gov/about/disclosure/foia.html**

Federal Election Commission **http://www.fec.gov/press/foia1a.htm**

Federal Emergency Management Agency **http://www.fema.gov/library/foia01.shtm**

Federal Reserve Board **http://www.federalreserve.gov/generalinfo/foia/**

Federal Trade Commission **http://www.ftc.gov/foia/index.htm**

General Services Administration **http://www.gsa.gov/Portal/content/offerings_ content.jsp?contentOID=113231+contentType+1004+P+I+5=1**

National Aeronautics and Space Administration **http://www.hq.nasa.gov/office/ pao/FOIA/**

National Archives and Records Administration **http://www.archives.gov/research_ room/foia_reading_room/foia_reading_room.html**

National Endowment for the Arts **http://www.arts.endow.gov/learn/FOIA/ Contents.html**

National Endowment for the Humanities **http://www.neh.gov/whoweare/foia main.html**

National Science Foundation **http://www.nsf.gov/home/pubinfo/foia.htm**

Nuclear Regulatory Commission **http://www.nrc.gov/reading-rm/foia/ foia-request.html**

National Transportation Safety Board **http://www.ntsb.gov/info.foia.htm**

Office of Government Ethics **http://www.usoge.gov/pages/about_oge/ foiaguide.html**

Office of Personnel Management **http://www.opm.gov/efoia/index.asp**

Securities and Exchange Commission **http://www.sec.gov/foia.shtml**

Selective Service System **http://www.sss.gov/freedomhome.htm**

Small Business Administration **http://www.sba.gov/foia/**

Social Security Administration **http://www.ssa.gov/foia/**

United States Postal Service **http://www.usps.gov/foia/**

GENEALOGY

Bureau of the Census

Copies of decennial census forms from 1790 through 1930 are available on microfilm for research at the National Archives and Records Administration and several other locations. The primary service that the Bureau of the Census provides related to genealogy is the Age Search Service (**http://landview.census.gov/genealogy/www/agesearch.html**). The bureau "will search the confidential records from the federal population censuses of 1910 to 1990 and issue an official transcript of the results (for a congressionally mandated fee)." However, the information is only released "to the named person, his/her heirs, or legal representatives." Thus,

individuals can use these transcripts, which may contain information on a person's age, sex, race, state, or country of birth, and relationship to the householder, as evidence to qualify for social security and other retirement benefits, in making passport applications, to prove relationship in settling estates, in genealogy research, etc., or to satisfy other situations where a birth or other certificate may be needed but is not available.

This service is available at **http://landview.census.gov/genealogy/www/index. html**.

Through the same Web address, the bureau provides counts of names from the 1990 census, though *Frequently Occurring First Names and Surnames from the 1990 Census* and *Spanish Surname List for the 1990 Census*.

Bureau of Land Management

The Bureau of Land Management's (BLM) Eastern States General Land Office (GLO) has a records automation Web site (**http://www.glorecords.blm.gov/**), which provides "access to federal land conveyance records for the public land states." There is a "database and image access to more than two million Federal land title records for the Eastern Public Land States, issued between 1820 and 1908." "Images of Serial patents, issued between 1908 and the mid-1960's, are currently being added to this Web site." Furthermore, the "site does not currently contain every Federal title record issued for the listed states. . . . Researchers can request certified copies of land patents either electronically or through the mail."

The Federal Land Patent Databases provide "a source of information on the initial transfer of land titles from the Federal government to individuals. In addition to verifying title transfer, this information will allow the researcher to associate an individual (Patentee) with a specific location (Legal Land Description) in time (Signature date)."

"Researchers can request certified copies of land patents either electronically or through the mail by printing a document request form. To search for land patents, enter your local postal code in the text box . . . ; then click Search Land Patents. A series of pages will guide you through viewing and ordering land patents." Finally, the site provides genealogists with "a wealth of additional resources."

National Archives and Records Administration

The Web site of the National Archives and Records Administration (NARA) contains "The Genealogy Page" (**http://www.archives.gov/research_room/genealogy/**), which offers finding aids, guides, and research tools to accommodate users of the agency's regional records service facilities and of the Washington, D.C., research rooms. The page also assists them in conducting research and in requesting records from NARA. Furthermore, there is information about relevant records sets, findings aids, microfilm catalogs, as well as, for instance,

- Genealogical publications

- Genealogy workshops

- News and events

- Genealogical resources on the Web

A microfiche collection contains data from past (1790–1920) federal censuses of the population. The Soundex Machine "is a coded last name (surname) index based on the way a name sounds rather than the way it is spelled. Surnames that sound the same, but are spelled differently, like SMITH and SMYTH, have the same code and are filed together. . . . Knowing a surname's Soundex code is an important first step in research using NARA's census microfilm holdings (1880–1920)" (see **http://www.archives. gov/research_room/genealogy/census.soundex.html**).

United States Geological Survey

The Geographic Names Information System (GNIS) contains information on physical and cultural geographic features in the United States (see **http://geonames. usgs.gov/**). "The Federally recognized name of each feature described in the database is identified, and references are made to a feature's location by state, county, and geographic coordinates." There is reference to the appropriate 1:24,000-scale U.S. Geological Survey (USGS) topographic map on which the name is shown. Included in this database "are defunct features of special interest to genealogists, such as sites of long-forgotten churches and cemeteries."[1]

↗ Other

Ancestry.com, a commercial genealogical publishing company, offers the online "Social Security Death Index" (**http://www.ancestry.com/search/rectype/vital/ssdi/main.htm**), which can be searched by name, social security number, location issued, last known residence, and birth or death date. The index, which is free to subscribers and guests, contains more than 64 million names who received benefits and only provides the month and year for the deceased individual.

GOVERNMENT PRINTING AND OTHER PUBLISHED REPORTS

Although the Web has displaced the primary functions of these traditional sources of printed material, their databases remain a critical link in identifying material that is either not on other federal government Web sites, or published before the Web became so widespread. A search in the Government Printing Office's (GPO) *Catalog of United States Government Publications* (CGP; **http://www.gpoaccess.gov/cgp/index.html**) provides a diverse array of publications. A search, for instance, of "electronic commerce" in this database would show the following record:

Electronic commerce: hearings before the Committee on **Commerce**, House of Representatives, One Hundred Fifth Congress, second session, 1998-.pt. 1. The marketplace of the 21st century; the global electronic marketplace—pt.2. New methods for making **electronic** purchases; investing online—pt.3. Building tomorrow's information infrastructure; doing business online; the future of the domain name system; consumer protection in cyberspace; privacy in cyberspace. United States. Y4.C73/8:105-111. [[109-A-01]].

Rank: 1000 Locate Libraries, [Short Record], [Full Record]

Because the full text is not available online through the GPO, anyone wanting this congressional hearing would have to go to the nearest depository library that is likely to have selected that item, or request a library that does not have the title (either a depository or a nondepository) make an interlibrary loan request. (Click on "Locate Libraries" to find the nearest depository likely to have that item.) Because recent congressional committees may have examined similar issues, relevant information might be contained in unpublished transcripts of congressional hearings (see THOMAS, Chapter 4). Another source of printed reports can be found at the Web sites of the National Technical Information Service (NTIS; **http://www.ntis.gov/**) or its FedWorld (**http://www.fedworld.gov/**). One also needs to consider the national libraries and other sources not necessarily available on the Web (discussed in Chapter 9).

GRANTS AND CONTRACTING OPPORTUNITIES

Both the *Federal Register* (discussed later) and the *Catalog of Federal Domestic Assistance* (*CFDA*) are important resources for anyone seeking grants. The *CFDA* "is a government-wide compendium of Federal programs, projects, services, and activities which provide assistance or benefits to the American public. It contains financial and nonfinacial assistance programs administered by departments and establishments of the Federal government." To "Search the Catalog" see **http://www.cfda.gov/public/faprs.htm**.

Examples of other sources listing funding opportunities include the following:

- Department of Agriculture, which has numerous grants and loans (e.g., **http://www.usda.gov/nonprofi.htm**; See also **http://www.usda.gov/nonprofit.htm**, for its coverage of rural housing loans, grants, and assistance)

- Department of Commerce, which has different pages covering grants (see **http://www.commerce.gov/grants.html**; The National Institute of Standards and Technology (NIST), for example, has a page on "Funding Opportunities" at **http://www.nist.gov/public_affairs/grants.htm**)

- Department of Education, which provides information about funding opportunities (**http://www.ed.gov/funding.html**)

- Environmental Protection Agency, which has pages on environmental education (**http://www.epa.gov/teachers/grants.htm**), research opportunities for scientists and engineers (**http://www.epa.gov/epahome/scifund.htm**), and so on

- Department of Health and Human Services' GrantsNet, which covers departmental and other federal grant programs (**http://www.hhs.gov/grantsnet/roadmap/index.html**)

- Department of Justice, which provides grant information (e.g., Office of Justice Programs; **http://www.usdoj.gov/10grants/index.html**)

- Department of Labor, which offers "Grant and Contract Information" (**http://www.dol.gov/oasam/grants/main.htm**)

- Department of the Interior, which lists departmental and agency grants (**http://www.doi.gov/non-profit/fax.html**). The National Park Service provides "grants to preserve and protect cultural resources nationwide" (**http://www.cr.nps.gov/helpyou.htm**)

- National Endowment for the Arts, which explains its grant-making categories, requests for proposals, deadlines, eligibility, review criteria, and how to apply, as well as providing "information on awards administration for those who have already received a grant or cooperative agreement" (**http://arts.endow.gov/guide**)

- National Endowment for the Humanities, which explains "What We Fund," what to do "If You Have a Grant," and how to go about "Applying for a Grant" (**http://www.neh.gov/grants/**)

- National Science Foundation, which offers assorted grants (**http://www.nsf.gov/home/grants.htm**)

- National Telecommunications and Information Administration (NTIA), which maintains the NTIA NonProfit Gateway (**http://www.ntia.doc.gov/ntiahome/ gateway/nonprofit/gateway.htm**) to provide nonprofit agencies with links to the government (e.g., for grants and assistance)

- Small Business Administration, among other things, identifies contracts (**http://www.sba.gov/expanding/grants.html**)

- Smithsonian Institution's Office of Fellowships and Grants, which explains fellowship, internship, and grant opportunities (**http://www.si.edu/ofg/start.htm**)

The Government Printing Office has a *Subject Bibliography* on "Grants and Awards" (**http://bookstore.gpo.gov/sb/sb-258.html**).

The *Commerce Business Daily* "lists notices of proposed government procurement actions, contract awards, sales of government property, and other procurement information" (see **http://cbdnet.gpo.gov/read-gd.html**). CBDNet "is the Government's official FREE electronic version of the *Commerce Business Daily* (*CBD*). Notices appearing in CBDNet do not satisfy the requirements of Federal Acquisition Rule (FAR) Part 5 until they appear in the printed *CBD*." For information about the *CBD* and conducting a search of CBDNet, see **http://cbdnet.gpo.gov**. The *CBD* is available at **http://cbdnet.access.gpo.gov/index.html**.

HEALTH AND MEDICAL RESOURCES

Numerous government agencies distribute information to individuals to help them make intelligent choices when confronted with critical health care decisions or when looking for health care facilities. Just as it does with other areas of the social and economic lives of its citizens, the federal government not only provides information but also serves to regulate the tools, personnel, and institutions that provide health care services throughout the country. Following is a selected list of Web sites organized by broad topics.

Alternative Medicines

- The National Center for Complementary and Alternative Medicine (**http:// nccam.nih.gov/**) was established to study a group of diverse medical and health care systems, practices, and products that are not presently considered to be part of conventional medicine.

Food Safety and Food Industry Information

- For information on food safety and applied nutrition, see **http://www. cfsan.fda.gov/list.html**. The primary federal Web portal on food safety issues is found at **http://www.foodsafety.gov/**.

General Web Pages on Health

- **http://www.health.gov/** is the primary federal Web portal to multiagency health initiatives and activities of the Department of Health and Human Services and other federal departments and agencies.

- **http://www.healthfinder.gov/** is a key resource for finding the best government and nonprofit health and human services information on the Internet. Healthfinder® links to carefully selected information and Web sites.

- **http://www.nlm.nih.gov/medlineplus/** includes material of general and specific health information selected by the National Library of Medicine for health care professionals and consumers.

Nutrition, Exercise, and Preventative Medicine

- **http://www.nutrition.gov/home/index.php3/** is the primary Web portal on nutrition, healthy eating, physical activity. It provides accurate scientific information on nutrition and dietary guidance.

- **http://nps.ars.usda.gov/programs/programs.htm?npnumber=107** is part of the Department of Agriculture's Agriculture Research Service, "the Human Nutrition Program is to conduct basic and applied research to identify and understand how nutrients and other bioactive food components affect health. The ultimate goal of this food-based agricultural research is to identify foods and diets, coupled with genetics and physical activity, that sustain and promote health throughout the life cycle."

- **http://www.usda.gov/cnpp/** is part of the Department of Agriculture. The Center for Nutrition Policy and Promotion works to promote healthy eating.

- **http://www.fitness.gov/** is sponsored by the President's Council on Physical Fitness and Sports (PCPFS). The Web page is designed to encourage and motivate Americans of all ages to become physically active and participate in sports.

Quality Information on Health Institutions and Services

- **http://www.ahrq.gov/** offers data and research on medical facilities, research, and other health care services. It is operated by the Agency for Health Care Research and Quality.

- **http://www.medicare.gov/Nursing/AboutInspections.asp** is the official government Web site that measures the quality of about 17,000 nursing homes and long-term care facilities.

- **http://www.fda.gov/cder/consumerinfo/DPAdefault.htm** offers information about drugs and other medical devices.

☞ Women's Health Issues

- **http://www.fda.gov/womens/default.htm**: The mission of the Food and Drug Administration's Office of Women's Health (OWH) is to serve as a champion for women's health both within and outside the agency.

- **http://www.cdc.gov/health/womensmenu.htm** gives advice and information about a host of issues facing women and their health care choices.

- **http://www.4woman.gov/**: The National Women's Health Information Center provides a gateway to the vast array of federal and other women's health information resources. "Our site on the Web can help you link to, read, and download a wide variety of women's health-related material developed by the Department of Health and Human Services, other Federal agencies, and private sector resources"

HISTORIC PRESERVATION

Some of the more prominent sites include the

- Advisory Council on Historic Preservation (**http://www.achp.gov/**), which offers both information and images

- Department of Housing and Urban Development (**http://www.hud.gov/offices/cpd/energyenvision/environment/subjects/preservation/index.cfm**), which provides handbooks, press releases, and other types of information

- National Park Service (**http://www.cr.nps.gov/**), which offers an interactive maps, information, and images; other examples are the Historic American Buildings Survey (**http://www.cr.nps.gov/buildings.htm**), the National Register of Historic Places (**http://www.cr.nps.gov/places.htm**), National Historic Landmarks (**http://www.cr.nps.gov/landmarks.htm**), the Heritage Preservation Services (**http://www2.cr.nps.gov/**), and Maritime History and Preservation (**http://www.cr.nps.gov/maritime/**)

- Library of Congress (**http://lcweb.loc.gov/rr/print/catalog.html**) has a collection of online prints and photographs

Additional sites can be found in Subject Bibliography 140: "Buildings, Landmarks and Historic Sites" in the GPO's sales program (see Chapter 4; **http://bookstore.gpo.gov/sb/**).

HISTORY AND CULTURE

The federal government, for all of its other services, remains a virtual treasure trove of historical and cultural artifacts. The principal agency, the Smithsonian Institution (**http://www.si.edu**), as described in Chapter 6, represents the best example of this type of federal function. Through the dozens of national museums, institutes, and centers, the Smithsonian's collections constitute a large part of American national memory and heritage. Other cultural institutions, such as the Library of Congress and the National Archives and Records Administration, are building large collection of digitized material. Furthermore, many executive agencies have funded history offices and historians to document the public artifacts, land, and cultural resources placed under their charge. Some relevant sites include

- American Folklife: **http://www.loc.gov/folklife/afc.html**

- September 11, 2001 Project: **http://www.loc.gov/folklife/nineeleven/nineelevenhome.html**

- Veterans History Project: **http://www.loc.gov/folklife/vets/**

- Civil War Soldiers and Sailors Database: **http://www.itd.nps.gov/cwss/**

- Cultural Resources from the Natural Resources Conservation Service: **http://www.nrcs.usda.gov/technical/cultural.html**

- Explore America's Historic Places: **http://www.cr.nps.gov/nr/travel/**

- Library of Congress American Memory Project: **http://memory.loc.gov/**

- Military History: **http://www.cr.nps.gov/military.htm**

- National Park Museums: **http://www.cr.nps.gov/museum.htm**

- Native American History and Culture: **http://www.si.edu/resource/faq/nmai/start.htm**

- Smithsonian Institution: **http://www.si.edu/**

    African American History and Culture: **http://www.anacostia.si.edu**

    American Social and Cultural History: **http://www.si.edu/resource/faq/nmah/start.htm**

    Center for Folklife and Cultural Heritage: **http://www.folklife.si.edu/**

- U.S. Culture, Society and History: **http://usinfo.state.gov/usa/infousa/homepage.htm**

INTELLECTUAL PROPERTY RIGHTS AND COPYRIGHTS

"Copyright is a form of protection provided by the laws of the United States for 'original works of authorship' including literary, dramatic, musical, architectural, cartographic, choreographic, pantomimic, pictorial, graphic, sculptural, and audiovisual creations." Furthermore,

"Copyright" literally means the right to copy. The term has come to mean that body of exclusive rights granted by statute to authors for protection of their works. The owner of copyright has the exclusive right to reproduce, distribute, and, in the case of certain works, publicly perform or display the work; to prepare derivative works; or to license others to engage in the same acts under specific terms and conditions. Copyright protection does not extend to any idea, procedure, process, slogan, principle, or discovery.[2]

The primary objective of copyright is not to reward the labor of authors but, as the Constitution specifies, to "promote the Progress of Science and useful Arts."[3] As the Supreme Court has declared, "to this end, copyright assures authors the right in their original expression, but encourages others to build freely upon the ideas and information conveyed by a work."[4]

Against this brief background, the Copyright Office is

an office of record, a place where claims to copyright are registered and where documents relating to copyright may be recorded when the requirements of the copyright law are met. The Copyright Office furnishes information about the provisions of the copyright law and the procedures for making registration, explains the operations and practices of the Copyright Office, and reports on facts found in the public records of the Office. The Office also administers various compulsory licensing provisions of the law, which include collecting royalties.[5]

As discussed in Chapter 4, the United States Copyright Office, Library of Congress, maintains a Web site (**http://lcweb.loc.gov/copyright**) that provides, among other resources, "General Information" and "Publications." Here are the application forms, form letters, and information on "Copyright Basics," "Registration Procedures," and "Mandatory Deposit." There is also CORDS (Copyright Office Electronic Registration, Recordation & Deposit System).

PATENTS AND TRADEMARKS

"A patent for an invention is a grant of a property right by the Government to the inventor (or his or her heirs or assigns), acting through the Patent and Trademark Office. . . . What is granted is not the right to make, use, offer for sale, sell or import, but the right to exclude others from making, using, offering for sale, selling or importing the invention."[6] Trademarks or service marks, on the other hand, relate

to any word, name, symbol or device which is used in trade with goods or services to indicate the source or origin of the goods or services and to distinguish them from the goods or services of others. Trademark rights may be used to prevent others from using a confusingly similar mark but not to prevent them from making the same goods or from selling them under a non-confusing mark. Similar rights may be acquired in marks used in the sale or advertising of services (service marks). Trademarks and service marks which are used in interstate or foreign commerce may be registered in the Patent and Trademark Office.[7]

The Patent and Trademark Office (PTO) of the Department of Commerce (**http://www.uspto.gov/**) grants patents for the protection of inventions and registers trademarks. Anyone dealing with patents and the PTO for the first time should examine "General Info" and review the coverage of patents and trademarks. As well, the PTO emphasizes that "understanding the limitations of these Web databases can help you avoid significant problems." Prior to using these databases, the PTO advises, "it is critical that you review . . . [certain] information," which is then specified.

The PTO now takes orders for documents online and provides for their delivery by automatic fax-back within hours (**http://www3.uspto.gov/oems25p/index.html**; **http://www.uspto.gov/oems/index.html**). There are other means of document delivery, and prices vary by delivery method.

Searchers might prefer to consult and rely on the resources and services of a library participating in the Patent and Trademark Depository Library Program.

 To be designated as a Patent and Trademark Depository Library (PTDL), a library must meet specific requirements and agree to fulfill certain obligations. . . . Each PTDL is required to acquire and make freely available to the public a minimum 20-year backfile of U.S. patents. It must protect the integrity of the collection, maintain classification system documents and related publications, and assist the public in efficient use of the collection, and retain all depository items until disposal is arranged through the Patent and Trademark Depository Library Program.

The intellectual property collections of some libraries significantly exceed the core requirements. A significant number have complete backfiles of U.S. patents since 1790.[8]

For information about this program, including a list of participating libraries and other general information, services, and publications, see **http://www.uspto.gov/web/offices/ac/ido/ptdl/ptdlserv.htm.9**

In brief, anyone conducting a patent search should be familiar with the following seven sources that patent and trademark depository libraries have these resources and can provide guidance on their use.

- *Index to the U.S. Patent Classification* (available paper, CD-ROM, or Web)

- *Manual Classification* (paper, CD-ROM, or Web)

- *Classification Definitions* (microfiche, CD-ROM, or Web)

- *Patents BIB CD-ROM or WEST (Web-based Examiner Search Tool) or USPTO Web Patent Database*

- Subclass Listing (CD-ROM)

- *Official Gazette—Patent Section* (paper)

- *Complete Patent Document* (microfilm, paper, CD-ROM, or Web)

A trademark search in at these libraries involves six sources:

- *Goods and Services Manual* (paper, CD-ROM, or Web)

- *International Schedule of Classes* (paper, CD-ROM, or Web)

- *Trademark Manual of Examining Procedure* (paper, CD-ROM, or Web)

- *Design Code Manual* (paper or Web)

- *Trademarks REGISTERED and PENDING CD-ROMs or USPTO Web Trademark Databases*

- *TARR Trademark Status Database* (Web)

Incidentally, the National Agricultural Library's Biotechnology Information Resource (**http://www.nal.usda.gov/bic**), an information center of the USDA's National Agricultural Library, provides "access to selected sources, services, and publications covering many aspects of agricultural technology." For example, it covers biotechnology patents including "selected full-text patents and links to other patent databases."

POSTSECONDARY EDUCATION FINANCIAL AID

The Department of Education is one of the best sites for discovering the current sources of information about how to pay for college or other institutions of higher education. These sources of funding include grants (which do not have to be paid back), work-study programs, and loans (which do have to be repaid). The department's primary Web site on financial aid for students can be found at **http://www.ed.gov/offices/OSFAP/Students/sfa.html**. The page offers information within the following categories:

- Finding Out about Financial Aid: provides general information about the major federal student aid programs (who is eligible and how to apply), tax credits for education expenses, and other federal, state, and private sources of information

- Applying for Federal Student Aid: helps explain and select electronic aid applications that can be processed through the Web page

- Paying Back Your Student Loan: describes specific ways, through federal teacher support programs, that students may use deferments and cancellations if they teach in low-income areas or communities with a shortage of teachers; also includes information about how to consolidate loans

- FSA Ambassador Toolkit: one- or two-page handouts that describe how to apply and pay for college

For an excellent overview of these opportunities, the department offers its annual publication *Funding Your Education*, found at **http://www.ed.gov/prog_info/SFA/FYE/**. In addition, the department has developed a Web portal (**http://studentaid.ed.gov/PORTALSWebApp/students/english/index.jsp**) that describes how individuals can take advantage of existing financial aid programs. A useful feature of this portal is the ability to select information about federal student aid according to levels of education. There are specific pages that target students who attend Graduate School, College, Junior/High School, and Elementary School.

Further funding opportunities can be found through the Web pages of the USA Freedom Corps (**http://www.usafreedomcorps.gov/for_volunteers/awards.scholarships/overview.asp**). Specific scholarships are offered through federal grants to support community volunteers, as well as a longer list of specific funds from various nonprofit organizations. Another site many students, and prospective students, should consider is the new Web portal for government benefits (**http://www.govbenefits. gov/**). By selecting the student category and then answering a forty-question survey, the Web page identifies possible government programs to support further education. Many of these programs, although mentioned on the Department of Education Web sites, provide another way to put together a list of possible resources that directly relate to an individual's situation.

Through the direct support of professional education, benefits in return for service in the government, or international agreements, other government agencies also offer federal funds to support postsecondary educational goals of individuals. Several government agencies subsidized expensive professional education (i.e., teachers and doctors) in return for moving and working in low-income areas or areas that are underserved by these professions (**http://www.hhs.gov/grants/index.shtml#scholarships**). The Department of Defense (**http://www.defenselink.mil**) and the military services offer dozens of programs to support further education opportunity, either as benefits awarded to recruits or the technical education while serving in uniform. The Department of State offers a series of programs that support cultural and educational exchanges through one of its bureaus (**http://exchanges.state.gov/**).

RULES AND REGULATIONS

The three primary sources of law are statutes (see Chapter 4), judicial opinions (see Chapter 7), and administrative rules and regulations, which are commonly known as *administrative law*. Rules and regulations are a means by which agencies implement the provisions of statutory law. Thus, it is important to know what existing rules and regulations say, as well as what agencies propose as new rules and regulations. Proposed rules and regulations are subject to a period of public comment; however, agencies are not bound to make changes based on the comments received.[10]

☞ Code of Federal Regulations

The *Code of Federal Regulations* (CFR) is the codification (subject arrangement) of all general and permanent rules written to implement Public Laws (see Chapter 4). To come into effect, they must be published as final regulations in the *Federal Register* by the issuing department or agency. This database to the CFR is available from GPO Access (**http://www.gpoaccess.gov/cfn/index.html**; **http://www.archives.gov/federal_register/code_of_federal_regulations/code_of_federal_regulations.html**); there is now a "Browse Feature."

As a Beta Test site, the National Archives and Records Administration offers e-CFR (Electronic Code of Federal Regulations; **http://www.access.gpo.gov/ecfr/**), which enables information seekers to search the current CFR. In addition, there are search tips, frequently asked questions, information user information, and updates.

☞ Federal Register

The *Federal Register*, produced by NARA and available online from GPO Access (**http://www.archives.gov/federal_register/index.html**; **http://www.archives.gov/federal_register/publication/about_the_federal_register.html**; **http://www.gpoaccess.gov/fr/index.html**), provides daily coverage of rules, proposed rules, and notices of agencies, as well as executive orders and other presidential documents. There is now a "Browse Feature." It is possible to search this database for material dated 1994 and after. "Documents may be retrieved in ASCII TEXT format (full text, graphics omitted), Adobe Portable Document Format (.pdf; full text with graphics), and SUMMARY format (abbreviated text)."

It is important to check the Web site of executive departments and agencies for proposed rules and regulations. The reasons are twofold: first, the *Federal Register* is not a comprehensive record of proposed rules and regulations,[11] and, second, the *E-Government Act of 2002* mandates that agencies also place such rules and regulations on their Web site.

Regulations.Gov

"Regulations.gov is the U.S. Government Web site that makes it easier for you to participate in Federal rulemaking—an essential part of the American democratic process. On this site, you can find, review, and submit comments on Federal documents that are open for comment and published in the *Federal Register*, the Government's legal newspaper." The site (**http://www.regulations.gov/**) also has related links (e.g., links to agencies' regulatory information pages, executive orders, policy directives from the Office of Management and Budget, and rule tracking information), "Contact Us," and "Help."

TERRORISM AND HOMELAND SECURITY

Terrorism and the issues of homeland security have dominated the news (as well as the political agenda) since mid-September 2001. Trying to find information about what the federal government is doing to wage the war remains difficult. FirstGov (see Chapter 3) has organized a general Web page about how the federal government has responded to the attacks (**http://www.firstgov.gov/Topics/Usgresponse.shtml**). Furthermore, Keven Motes, a librarian at the Oklahoma Department of Libraries, has put together a fairly comprehensive list of relevant government documents in a annotated bibliography, which can be found at **http://www.odl.state.ok.us/usinfo/terrorism/911.htm**.

Another aspect of the war on terrorism has been the growing discussion on civil liberties and privacy. Various initiatives taken by the federal government to reduce the threat of terrorism at home and abroad, a number of people believe have unnecessarily curtailed the basic rights of citizens and others in the name of security. For instance, a research office in the Pentagon (the Office of Information Awareness) has begun to study the possibility of creating a database of networked information called "Total Information Awareness" that will attempt to create links among an individual's personal communications (phone calls, e-mail messages, and Web searches), financial records, purchases, prescriptions, school records, medical records and travel history, in effort to find "patterns" of possible terrorism activity. On another front, the *USA PATRIOT Act*, passed by Congress and signed by President Bush a little over a month after the September 2001 attacks, gives the Justice Department increased capabilities to investigate "potential" terrorist activity through electronic eavesdropping, obtaining personal records from libraries about what individuals might have borrowed, or investigate computer logs or records to reveal Web sites that possible suspects have visited. For a discussion of these issues, one must visit nonprofit and advocacy group Web sites, in particular the American Civil Liberties Union (**http://www.aclu.org**), the Electronic Privacy Information Center (**http://www.epic.org**), OMB Watch (**http://www.ombwatch.org**), and the Electronic Freedom Foundation (**http://www.eff.org**).

Some relevant federal Web sites are the following:

- Central Intelligence Agency: The War on Terrorism, **http://www.cia.gov/terrorism/index.html**

- Department of Defense: Defend America, **http://www.defendamerica.mil/index.html**, and Homeland Security, **http://www.defenselink.mil/specials/homeland/**

- Department of Energy: Capabilities: Homeland Security, **http://www.sandia.gov/capabilities/homeland-security/links.html**

- Department of Health and Human Services: Bioterrorism, **http://www.fda.gov/oc/opacom/hottopics/bioterrorism.html**

- Department of Homeland Security (**http://www.dhs.gov/dhspublic/**): Ready.Gov instructs the public about how to prepare for a threat (see **http://www.ready.gov/**)

- Department of Justice

  - Federal Bureau of Investigation: Awareness of National Security and Issues and Response, **http://www.fbi.gov/hq/ci/ansir/ansirhome.htm**

  - Drug Enforcement Administration (**http://www.usdoj.gov/dea/**)

- Department of State: Global Terrorism Against Terrorism, **http://www.state.gov/coalition/12669.htm**

- White House: America Responds to Terrorism, **http://www.whitehouse.gov/response/**, and The National Strategy for Homeland Security, **http://www.whitehouse.gov/homeland/book/index.html**

- Congress

  - Oversight: House Select Committee on Homeland Security, **http://hsc.house.gov/**

  - General Accounting Office: (reports one on terrorism and on airport security), **http://www.gao.gov/**

The National Technical Information Service of the Department of Commerce maintains a Homeland Security Information Center (**http://www.ntis.gov/hs/**) that arranges information resources by the following categories: "health and medicine," "biological and chemical warfare," "food and agriculture," "preparedness and response," and "safety training package." Additional coverage of terrorism and homeland security are available in the *Congressional Record* and on THOMAS.

The Office of Management and Budget is developing, guidelines to ensure that agencies carry out the laws the protect Americans' privacy, including the *E-Government Act of 2002*. This act "explicitly states that the privacy policies apply to symptoms that are developed or bought by federal agencies"—not those held by the private sector. Clearly, homeland security envolves a balance between security and open acccess and the extent to which government agencies can reach private sector data.[12]

SUMMARY

The U.S. national government has expanded its digital information resources greatly since this guide first appeared in 1999. While increasing the quantity of information resourccs and services available, the government has also improved the relevance of (and ease of access to) its information available through its Web sites. Certain tools such as search engines and Web portals have certainly helped organize this information for the general user, and they provide better means of access. Nonetheless, it must be acknowledged that much of the information generated by the federal government is multisubject and created for a number of policy and enforcement purposes, thereby spreading information gathering and reporting among many bodies in the executive and legislative branches. Using the suggested subject headings in this chapter, as well as those in Appendix C, offers another way to access this wealth of information. (If a reader wishes to suggest other general subject categories to include in future editions of the book, please contact the authors.)

NOTES

1. Judith Schiek Robinson, *Tapping the Government Grapevine: The User-friendly Guide to U.S. Government Information Sources* (Phoenix, AZ: Oryx Press, 1998): 183.

2. United States Copyright Office: A Brief History and Overview" Available: **http://www.loc.gov/copyright/docs/circ1a.html**.

3. United States Constitution, article I, section 8, clause 8.

4. *Feist Publication, Inc. v. Rural Telephone Service Co.*, 499 U.S. 340, 349-350 (1991).

5. United States Copyright Office.

6. "What Is a Patent?" Available: **http://www.uspto.gov/web/offices/pac/doc/general/whatispa.htm**.

7. Ibid.

8. See **http://www.uspto.gov/web/offices/ac/ido/ptdl/ptdlserv.htm**.

9. For an extended introduction to patents and trademarks, see, for instance, Joe Morehead, *Introduction to United States Government Information Sources* (Englewood, CO: Libraries Unlimited, 1999): Chapter 10, 333–72; Robinson, *Tapping the Government Grapevine*, Chapter 7, 69–84.

10. See Peter Hernon, Harold C. Relyea, Robert E. Dugan, and Joan F. Cheverie, *United States Government Information: Policies and Sources* (Westport, CT: Libraries Unlimited, 2002): 225–47.

11. See, for instance, Robert Gellman, "Cost-Saving Move Jeopardizes Federal Register," *Government Computer News* (March 6, 2000): 24.

URL Site Guide for This Chapter

Advisory Council on Historic Preservation
http://www.achp.gov/

Ancestry.com
http://www.ancestry.com/search/rectype/vital/
ssdi/main.htm

Catalog of Federal Domestic Assistance
http://www.cfa.gov/public/faprs.htm

FirstGov
http://www.firstgov.gov/

> **Business Gateway**
> http://www.firstgov.gov/Business/
> Business_Gateway.shtml

> **Responding to Terrorist Attacks**
> http://www.firstgov.gov/Topics/
> Usgresponse.shtml

Congress

> **Committee on Small Business (House)**
> http://www.house.gov/smbiz/

> **Committee on Small Business and Entrepreneurship (Senate)**
> http://www.senate.gov/~sbc/

> **Select Committee on Homeland Security (House)**
> http://hsc.house.gov/

Department of Agriculture

> **Agriculture Research Service**
> http://nps.ars.usda.gov/programs/
> programs.htm?npnumber=107

> **APHIS Travel Web**
> http://www.aphis.usda.gov/travel/

> **Center for Nutrition Policy and Promotion**
> http://www.usda.gov/cnpp/

FOIA
http://www.usda.gov/news/foia/main.htm

Grants
http://www.usda.gov/nonprofi.htm

National Agriculture Library
Biotechnology Information Resource
http://www.nal.usda.gov/bic

National Resources and Conservation Service
http://www.nrcs.usda.gov/

> **Cultural Resources**
> http://www.nrcs.usda.gov/technical/
> cultural.html

Department of Commerce
http://www.commerce.gov/

> **Bureau of the Census**

> **American Factfinder**
> http://factfinder.census.gov/servlet/
> BasicFactsServlet

> **Disabilities**
> http://www.census.gov/hhes/www/
> disability.html

> **Genealogy**
> http://landview.census.gov/genealogy/
> www/agesearch.html
> http://landview.census.gov/genealogy/
> www/index.html

> **Bureau of Export Administration**
> http://www.bea.doc.gov/

> > **STAT-USA**
> > http://www.statusa.gov/

> **Bureau of Industry and Security**
> http://www.bxa.doc.gov/

> > **Site Map**
> > http://www.bxa.doc.gov/SiteMap.html

> **Computer Security Resource Center**
> http://csrc.nist.gov/

FOIA
http://www.osec.doc.gov/oebam/foia25.htm

Grants
http://www.commerce.gov/grants.html
http://www.nist.gov/public_affairs/
grants.htm

International Trade Administration
http://www.ita.doc.gov/

National Institute of Standards and Technology
Funding Opportunities
http://www.nist.gov/public_affairs/
grants.htm

National Technical Information Service
http://www.ntis.gov/

> **FedWorld**
> http://www.fedworld.gov/

> **Homeland Security Information Center**
> http://www.ntis.gov/hs/

NTIA NonProfit Gateway

National Telecommunications and Information Administration
http://www.ntia.doc.gov/ntiahome/
gateway/nonprofit/gateway.htm

Patent and Trademark Office
http://www.uspto.gov/

> **Depository Library Program**
> http://www.uspto.gov/web/offices/
> ac/ido/ptdl.ptdlserv.htm

> **Online Orders**
> http://www3.uspto.gov/oems25p/
> index.html
> http://www.uspto.gov/oems/index.
> html

Department of Defense
http://www.defenselink.mil/

> **FOIA**
> http://www.defenselink.mil/pubs/foi/

> **Air Force**
> **FOIA**
> http://www.foia.af.mil/

Army
FOIA
http://www.rmd.belvoir.army.mil/
FOIAERR.htm

Defend America
http://www.defendamerica.mil/index.html

Homeland Security
http://www.defenselink.mil/specials/
homeland/

Marine Corps
FOIA
http://www.hqmc.usmc.mil/foia/
foiaweb.nsf

Navy
FOIA
http://foia.navy.mil/

National Imagery and Mapping Agency
FOIA
http://164.214.2.59/cda/article/0.2311.
3104_59416_114576.00.html

National Reconnaissance Office
FOIA
http://www.nro.gov/foia/index6.html

Department of Education

> **Financial Aid**
> http://www.ed.gov/offices/OSFAP/
> Students/sfa.html
> http://studentaid.ed.gov/PORTALSWebApp/
> students/english/index.jsp

> **FOIA**
> http://www.ed.gov/offices/OCIO/foia/
> index.html

> **Funding Your Education**
> http://www.ed.gov/prog_info/SFA/FYE/

> **Grants**
> http://www.ed.gov/funding.html

> **Office of Special Education**
> http://www.ed.gov/offices/OSERS/OSEP/

Department of Energy
http://www.doe.gov/

Capabilities: Homeland Security
http://www.sandia.gov/capabilities/
homeland-security/links.html

FOIA
http://www.nv.doe.gov/programs/foia/
default.htm

Department of Health and Human Services

Agency for Health Care Research and Quality
http://www.ahrq.gov/

FOIA
http://www.hhs.gov/foia/

Centers for Disease Control
FOIA
http://www.cdc.gov/od/foia/foi.htm

   Travelers' Health
   http://www.cdc.gov/travel/

   Women's Health Issues
   http://www.cdc.gov/health/
   womensmenu.htm

Food and Drug Administration

   Bioterrorism
   http://www.fda.gov/oc/opacom/
   hottopics/bioterrorism.html

   Drugs and Medical Devices
   http://www.fda.gov/cder/
   consumerinfo/DPAdefault.
   htm

   FOIA
   http://www.fda.gov/foi/foia2.htm

   Food Safety and Applied Nutrition
   http://www.cfsan.fda.gov/list.html

   Women's Health
   http://www.fda.gov/womens/
   default.htm

   GrantsNet
   http://www.hhs.gov/grantsnet/road
   map/
   index.html

   Health.gov
   http://www.health.gov/

Healthfinder®
http://www.healthfinder.gov/

National Center for Complementary and Alternative Medicine
http://nccam.nih.gov/

National Library of Medicine
http://www.nlm.nih.gov/medlinepl
us/

National Women's Health Information Center
http://www.4woman.gov/

Support for Education
http://www.hhs.gov/grants/index.
shtml#scholarships

Department of Homeland Security
http://www.dhs.gov/dhspublic/
http://www.ready.gov/

   FOIA
   http://www.dhs.gov/dhspublic/
   display?theme=48

Department of Housing and Urban Development

Fair Housing and Equal Opportunity
http://www.hud.gov/offices/fheo/
disabilities/index.cfm

FOIA
http://www.hud.gov/ogc/foiafree.html
http://www.hud.gov/ogc/bshelf2a.html

Historic Preservation
http://www.hud.gov/offices/cpd/
energyenvision/environment/
subjects/preservation/index.cfm

Department of the Interior
FOIA
http://www.doi.gov/foia/

Bureau of Land Management
FOIA
http://www.blm.gov/nhp/efoia/index.htm

   Genealogy
   http://www.glorecords.blm.gov/

Bureau of Reclamation
FOIA
http://www.usbr.gov/foia/

Grants
http://www.doi.gov/non-profit/fax.html

Minerals Management Service
FOIA
http://www.mms.gov/adm/foia.html

National Park Service
Civil War Soldiers and Sailors Database
http://www.itd.nps.gov/cwss/

> **FOIA**
> http://www.nps.gov/refdesk/npsfoia.
> html

> **Grants**
> http://www.cr.nps.gov/helpyou.htm

> **Historic Preservation**
> http://www.cr.nps.gov/
> http://www.cr.nps.gov/buildings.htm
> http://www.cr.nps.gov/places.htm
> http://www.cr.nps.gov/landmarks.
> htm
> http://www2.cr.nps.gov/
> http://www.cr.nps.gov/maritime/

Military History
http://www.cr.nps.gov/military.htm

National Park Museums
http://www.cr.nps.gov/museums.htm

Office of Surface Mining
FOIA
http://www.osmre.gov/ocfoia.htm

U.S. Fish and Wildlife Service
http://www.fws.gov/

> **Environmental Laws and**
> **Regulations**
> http://international.fws.gov/

> **FOIA**
> http://foia.fws.gov/

U.S. Geological Survey
FOIA
http://www.usgs.gov/foia/

Geographic Names Information
System
http://geonames.usgs.gov/

Department of Justice

Civil Rights Division
http://www.usdoj.gov/crt/split/cripa.htm
http://www.usdoj.gov/crt/voting
http://www.usdoj.gov/crt/voting/nvra/
activ_nvra.htm

Disabilities
http://www.usdoj.gov/crt/ada/
http://www.usdoj.gov/crt/ada/adahom1.
htm

FOIA
http://www.usdoj.gov/04foia/index.html

Drug Enforcement Administration
FOIA
http://www.usdoj.gov/dea/foia/dea.htm

Federal Bureau of Investigation
Awareness of National Security and
Issues and response
http://www.fbi.gov/hq/ci/ansir/
ansirhome.htm

> **FOIA**
> http://foia.fbi.gov/

Federal Bureau of Prisons
FOIA
http://www.bop.gov/foiapol.html

Grants
http://www.usdoj.gov/10grants/index.
html

Justice Department Guide to the
Freedom of Information Act
http://www.usdoj.gov/oip/oip.html

Department of Labor
FOIA
http://www.dol.gov/dol/foia/
main.htm

Grants
http://www.dol.gov/oasam/grants/
main.htm

Office of Compliance Assistance
http://www.dol.gov/dol/compliance/
comp-rehab.htm

Department of State
http://www.state.gov/

Consular Affairs
http://travel.state.gov/dualnationality.
html
http://travel.state.gov/renunicaiton.html

Immigrant/Non-immigrant Status
http://travel.state.gov/visa_
services.html
http://unitedstatesvisas.gov/index.html

Travel Warnings and Consular Information Sheets
http://travel.state.gov/travel_
warnings.html

Country Background Notes
http://www.state.gov/r/pa/ei/bgn/

Cultural and Educational Exchanges
http://exchanges.state.gov/

Emergency Services to U.S. Citizens Abroad
http://travel.state.gov.acs.html#emr

Embassies and Missions Overseas
http://usembassy.state.gov/

FOIA
http://foia.state.gov/

Foreign Consular Offices in U.S.
http://www.state.gov/s/cpr/rls/fco/
c5698.htm

Foreign Embassies in U.S.
http://www.state.gov/misc/10125.htm

Global Terrorism against Terrorism
http://www.state.gov/coalition/12669.
htm

Services and Information for Americans Abroad
http://travel.state.gov/acs.html

Department of Transportation

Air Consumer Protection Division
http://airconsumer.ost.dot/gov/
ACAAcomplaint.htm
http://airconsumer.ost.dot.gov/
publications/disabled.htm

Federal Transmit Administration
http://www.fta.dot.gov/office/civrights/
adainfo.html

FOIA
http://www.dot.gov/foia/index.html

Department of the Treasury

Currency Rates and Exchanges
http://www.fms.treas.gov/intn.html

FOIA
http://www.ustreas.gov/foia/
http://www.treas.gov/foia/bureaus.html

**Travel Information
U.S. Customs Service**
http://www.customs.gov/travel/travel.
htm

U.S. Culture, Society and History
http://usinfo.state.gov/usa/infousa/
homepage.htm

Department of Veterans Affairs

FOIA
http://www.va.gov/foia/

DisAbility.gov
http://www.disability.gov/

Environmental Protection Agency
http://www.epa.gov/

Endangered Species
http://www.epa.gov/epahome/topics.html

FOIA
http://www.epa.gov/foia/

Grants
http://www.epa.gov/teachers/grants.html
http://www.epa.gov/epahome/scifund.
htm

Executive Office of the President

Central Intelligence Agency
FOIA
http://www.foia.ucia.gov/

The War on Terrorism
http://www.cia.gov/terrorism/index.html

National Security Agency
FOIA
http://www.nsa.gov/docs/efoia/

Office of Management and Budget
FOIA
http://www.whitehouse.gov/omb/foia/
index.html

Office of the United States Trade Representative
FOIA
http://www.ustr.gov/efoia/efoia.html

Export-Import Bank

FOIA
http://www.exim.gov/about/disclosure/
foia.html

Federal Communications Commission
http://www.fcc.gov/cgb/dro/

Federal Election Commission

FOIA
http://www.fec.gov/press/foia1a.htm

Federal Emergency Management Agency

FOIA
http://www.fema.gov/library/foia01.shtm

Federal Employment Opportunity Commission
http://www.eeoc.gov/

Federal Reserve Board

FOIA
http://www.federalreserve.gov/
generalinfo/foia/

Federal Trade Commission
http://www.ftc.gov/

FOIA
http://www.ftc.gov/foia/index.htm

FoodSafety.gov
http://www.foodsafety.gov/

General Accounting Office
http://www.gao.gov/

General Services Administration
http://www.gsa.gov/

Catalog of Federal Domestic Assistance
http://www.cfda.gov/public/faprs.htm

FOIA
http://www.gsa.gov/Portal/content/
offerings_content.jsp?contentOID=
INDENT113231+contentType=
1004+P=I+S=1

Government Benefits
http://www.govbenefits.gov/

Government Printing Office

Catalog of United States Government Publications
http://www.gpoacceess.gov/cgp/index.html

Code of Federal Regulations
http://www.gpoaccess.gov/cfr/
index.html
http://www.archives.gov/federal_register/
code_of_federal_regulations/code_
of_federal_regulations.html

Commerce Business Daily
http://cbdnet.gpo.gov/read-gd.html
http://cbdnet.access.gpo.gov/index.html

E-CFR
http://www.access.gpo.gov/ecfr/

Federal Register
http://www.gpoaccess.gov/fr/index.html
http://www.archives.gov/federal_register
/index.html
http://www.archives.gov/federal_register/
publications/about_the_federal_
register.html

Subject Bibliographies
Online Bookstore
http://bookstore.gpo.gov/sb/

Grants and Awards
http://bookstore.gpo.gov/sb/
sb-258.html

Historic Preservation
http://bookstore.gpo.gov/sb/
sb-140.html

Library of Congress

American Folklife
http://www.loc.gov/folklife/afc.html

September 11, 2001 Project
http://www.loc.gov/folklife/
nineeleven/nineelevenhome.html

Veterans History Project
http://www.loc.gov/floklife/vets/

American Memory
http://memory.loc.gov/

Copyright Office
http://lcweb.loc.gov/copyright

Online Prints and Photographs
http://lcweb.loc.gov/rr/print/catalog.html

National Aeronautics and Space Administration

FOIA
http://www.hq.nasa.gov/office/pao/FOIA/

National Archives and Records Administration

FOIA
http://www.archives.gov/reading_room/
foia_reading_room/foia_reading_
room.html

Genealogy Page
http://www.archives.gov/research_room/
genealogy/

Soundex
http://www.archives.gov/research_room/
genealogy/census/soundex.html

National Council on Disability
http://www.ncd.gov/

National Endowment for the Arts

FOIA
http://www.arts.endow.gov/learn/FOIA/
Contents.html

Grants
http://arts.endow.gov/guide

National Endowment for the Humanities

FOIA
http://www.neh.gov/whoweare/foia/
foiamain

Grants
http://www.neh.gov/grants/

National Science Foundation

FOIA
http://www.nsf.gov/home/pubinfo/
foia.htm

Grants
http://www.nsf.gov/home/grants.htm

Nuclear Regulatory Commission

FOIA
http://www.nrc.gov/reading-rm/foia/
foia-request.html

National Transportation Safety Board

FOIA
http://www.ntsb.gov/info/foia.htm

Nurse Home Quality
http://www.mediccare.gov/Nursing/
AboutInspections.asp

Nutrition.gov
http://www.nutrition.gov/home/
index.php3/

Office of Government Ethics

FOIA
http://www.usoge.gov/pages/about_
oge/foiaguide.html

Office of Personnel Management

FOIA
http://www.opm.gov/efoia/index.asp

Olmstead v. L.C.

Supreme Court Decision
http://supct.law.cornell.supct/html/
98-536.ZS.html

The President's Council on Physical Fitness and Sports
http://www.fitness.gov/

Regulations.Gov
http://www.regulations.gov/

Securities and Exchange Commission
http://www.sec.gov/

FOIA
http://www.sec.gov/foia.shtml

Selective Service System

FOIA
http://www.sss.gov/freedomhome.htm

Small Business Administration
http://www.sbaonline.sba.gov/

Disabilities
http://www.sbaonline.sba.gov/hotlist/dis
abilities.html

Electronic Commerce
http://www.sbaonline.sba.gov/hotlist/
commerce.html

FOIA
http://www.sba.gov/foia/

Grants
http://www.sba.gov/expanding/grants.
html

Smithsonian Institution
http://www.si.edu/

American Social and Cultural History
http://www.si.edu/resource/faq/nmah/
start.htm

Center for Folklife and Cultural History
http://www.folklife.si.edu/

Grants
http://www.si.edu/ofg/start.htm

Native American History and Culture
http://www.si.edu/resource/faq/nmai/
start.htm

Social Security Administration

Disability Programs
http://www.ssa.gov/disability/

FOIA
http://www.ssa.gov/foia/

THOMAS
http://thomas.loc.gov/

United States International Trade Commission
http://www.usitc.gov/

United States Postal Service

FOIA
http://www.usps.gov/foia/

USA Freedom Corps
http://www.usafreedomcorps.gov/for_
volunteers/awards.scholarships/
overview.asp/scholarships_awards.
asp

U.S. Architectural and Transportation Barriers Compliance Board
(Access Board)
http://www.access-board.gov/

U.S. Business Advisor
http://www.business.gov/

White House

America Responds to Terrorism
http://www.whitehouse.gov/response/

Executive Order 13217
http://www.whitehouse.gov/news/
releases/2001/06/20010619.html

The National Strategy for Homeland Security
http://www.whitehouse.gov/homeland/book/index.html

Home Page
American Civil Liberties Union
http://www.aclu.org/

Home Page
Electronic Freedom Foundation
http://www.eff.org/

Home Page
Electronic Privacy Information Center
http://www.epic.org/

Litigation under the Federal Open Government Laws 2002
http://www.epic.org/bookstore/foia2002/

Home Page
OMB Watch
http://www.ombwatch.org

Terrorism Bibliography
Oklahoma Department of Libraries
http://www.odl.state.ok.us/usinfo/terrorism/911.htm

Chapter 13

Web Pages for the Nation's Youth

As shown in Figure 13.1, the U.S. government offers Web sites for the nation's youth, teachers, and parents that are informative, instructional, educational, and, in many cases, intended to be fun. They may provide photographs, animation and characters, graphics (involving pie and bar charts showing trends or facts), coloring books or pictures to color, fact sheets, jokes, puzzles, tours, and games. Some of them urge youth to "get involved" and others speak to parents and educators, for example, by suggesting reading lists and offering classroom exercises, course materials, and course units. Perhaps the most impressive points are that these Web pages exist (the government wants to communicate directly with, inform, and help to educate young people), that the pages are typically aimed at elementary or middle school, and that they enable young people, parents, and teachers to follow up by sending e-mail messages to the agency.

This chapter arranges Web sites by broad subjects. Some sites, however, provide information that cuts across different subjects. Clearly, the goal is to make agencies, their work, and their information resources more understandable and accessible to school-age children and to make resources available for use in the classroom.

AERONAUTICS, SPACE FLIGHT, AND ASTRONOMY

For Kids

This site provides information about the National Aeronautics and Space Administration (NASA), airplanes, Earth and the other planets, space travel, stars and galaxies, and so on. There is a site map, multimedia gallery, hot topics, linkage to NASA television, and frequently asked questions.

Figure 13.1. A List of Web Sites.

Name	Department or Agency	Address
Afterschool.gov	General Services Administration and the Interagency Federal Child Care Council	http://www.afterschool.gov/
Air Force Link Junior	Air Force	http://www.af.mil/aflinkjr/ parents.htm
ARTSEDGE	Kennedy Center for Performing Arts	http://artsedge.kennedy-center. org/
Ben's Guide to U.S. Government for Kids	Government Printing Office	http://bensguide.gpo.gov/
BEP for Kids	Bureau of Engraving and Printing	http://www.moneyfactory.com
BLS Career Information	Bureau of Labor Statistics	http://stats.bls.gov/k12/html/ edu_over.htm
CIA for Kids	Central Intelligence Agency	http://www.odci.gov/cia/ciakids/
Cool Stuff for Young People	Department of Veterans Affairs	http://www.va.gov/kids/ default.asp
CYFERNet Kid's Space	Cooperative Extension Service (Department of Agriculture)	http://www.aces.uiuc.edu/ ~kidspace/ces_office/ces_ office.html
Dr. E's Energy Lab	Office of Energy Efficiency and Renewal Energy	http://www.eere.energy.gov/kids
Earthquakes for Kids	U.S. Geological Survey	http://earthquakes.usgs.gov/ 4kids/
Education, Career Development, and Safety Awareness	Federal Railroad Administration (Department of Transportation)	http://www.fra.dot.gov/public/ edu/index.htm
EIA Kid's Page	Energy Information Administration	http://www.eia.doe.gov/kids/
EPA Student Center	Environmental Protection Agency	http://www.epa.gov/students/
Especially for Kids	National Ocean Service	http://response.restoration. noaa.gov/kids/kids.html
Especially for Kids	U.S. Fish and Wildlife Service	http://www.fws.gov/kids/

Name	Department or Agency	Address
Especially for Kids and Teens	U.S. Maritime Administration (Department of Transportation)	http://www.marad.dot.gov/kids/index.html
The Exhibit Hall	National Archives and Records Administration	http://www.archives.gov/exhibit_hall/index.html
Explorers' Club	Environmental Protection Agency	http://www.epa.gov/kids/
FBI Youth	Federal Bureau of Investigation	http://www.fbi.gov/kids/6th12th/6th12th.htm
FDA Kids	Food and Drug Administration	http://www.fda.gov/oc/opacom/kids
FEMA for Kids	Federal Emergency Management Agency	http://www.fema.gov/kids/
For Kids	National Aeronautics and Space Administration	http://www.nasa.gov/audience/forkids/index.html
For Kids	Department of the Treasury	http://www.treas.gov/kids/
For Kids Only	National Clearinghouse for Alcohol and Drug Information (Department of Health and Human Services)	http://www.health.org/features/kidsarea/index.htm
For Students	Hoover Library (NARA)	http://hoover.archives.gov/students/index.html
Foreign Affairs for Young People	State Department	http://www.state.gov/kids/
Frog Web.gov	National Biological Information Infrastructure	http://www.frogweb.gov/
Fun Activities for Kids!	National Institute of Standards and Technology	http://www.nist.gov/public_affairs/kids/kidsmain.htm
The Further Adventures of KIDD Safety	Consumer Product Safety Commission	http://www.cpsc.gov/kids/kid/safety/mainl.html

Figure 13.1 (*Cont.*)

Name	Department or Agency	Address
Hey, Kids!	Agency for Toxic Substances and Disease Registry	http://www.atsdr.cdc.gov/child/ochheykids.html
HHS Pages for Kids	Department of Health and Human Services	http://www.hhs.gov/kids/
Justice for Kids & Youth	Department of Justice	http://www.usdoj.gov/kidspage/
Kids	Smithsonian Institution	http://www.si.edu/kids/
Kids' Castle	Smithsonian Institution	http://www.kidscastle.si.edu/home.html
Kids Area	National Mental Health Information Center	http://www.mentalhealth.org/kidsarea/
Kids Corner	Energy Information Administration	http://www.eia.doe.gov/kids/kidscorner.html
Kids Corner	Federal Aviation Administration	http://www.faa.gov/education/resource/kidcornr.htm
Kids Corner	National Oceanic and Atmospheric Administration	http://www.nmfs.noaa.gov/kids.htm
Kids' Corner	Census Bureau	http://factfinder.census.gov/home/en/kids/kids.html
Kids in the House	Office of the Clerk, House of Representatives	http://clerkkids.house.gov/
Kids Next Door	Department of Housing and Urban Development	http://www.hud.gov/kids/kids.html
Kids on the Web	Department of the Interior	http://www.doi.gov/kids/
Kids Page	Federal Bureau of Investigation	http://www.fbi.gov/kids/k5th/kidsk5th.htm
Kids Page	Bush Presidential Library	http://bushlibrary.tamu.edu
Kids Page	Truman Library (NARA)	http://www.trumanlibrary.org/kids/index.html

Name	Department or Agency	Address
Kids Page!	Jimmy Carter Library (NARA)	http://www.jimmycarterlibrary.org/kids/index.phtml
KIDS Pages	U.S. Patent and Trademark Office	http://www.uspto.gov/web/offices/ac/ahrpa/opa/kids/index.html
Kids Stuff	Mine Safety and Health Administration (Department of Labor)	http://www.msha.gov/SOLICITOR/KIDS/KIDSPAGE.HTM
Kids, Teens & Educators	Foodsafety.gov (Department of Health and Human Services)	http://www.foodsafety.gov/~fsg/fsgkids.html
Kids World	Peace Corps	http://www.peacecorps.gov/kids/index.html
KIDZ Privacy	Federal Trade Commission	http://www.ftc.gov/bcp/conline/edcams/kidzprivacy/index.html
Kidzzone	Department of Energy	http://www.energy.gov/kidz/kidzone.html
LBJ for Kids!	Johnson Library (NASA)	http://www.lbjlib.utexas.edu/johnson/lbjforkids/main.htm
Learning Bank	Federal Deposit Insurance Corp.	http://www.fdic.gov/about/learn/learning/index.html
Learning Web	U.S. Geological Survey	http://www.usgs.gov/education/
NASA Multimedia Gallery	National Aeronautics and Space Administration	http://www.nasa.gov/multimedia/highlights/index.html
National Zoo	National Zoo	http://natzoo.si.edu/
Nature Watch	Forest Service (Department of Agriculture)	http://www.fs.fed.us/outdoors/naturewatch/default.htm
The NCES Classroom	National Center for Education Statistics (Department of Education)	http://nces.ed.gov/nceskids/
NIEHS Kids' Pages	National Institute of Environmental Health Sciences	http://www.niehs.nih.gov/kids/home.htm
OPIC for Kids	Overseas Private Investment Corporation	http://www.opic.gov/opickids/frameset.htm

Figure 13.1 (*Cont.*)

Name	Department or Agency	Address
Planet Youth	Office of Native American programs (Department of Housing and Urban Development)	**http://www.codetalk.fed.us:80/ planet/planet.html**
Safety City	National Highway Traffic Safety Administration (Department of Transportation)	**http://www.nhtsa.dot.gov/kids/**
Sci4Kids	Agricultural Research Service (Department of Agriculture)	**http://www.ars.usda.gov/is/kids**
Smoke-Free Kids	National Cancer Institute	**http://www.smokefree.gov/**
Specially for Students	National Oceanic and Atmospheric Administration	**http://www.education.noaa.gov/ students.html**
StarChild	National Aeronautics and Space Administration	**http://starchild.gsfc.nasa.gov/ docs/StarChild/StarChild.html**
Students' Corner	Nuclear Regulatory Commission	**http://www.nrc.gov/reading-rm/ basic-ref/students.html**
Students K–12	National Science Foundation	**http://www.nsf.gov/home/ menus/k12.htm**
SUPERFUND for KIDS!	Environmental Protection Agency	**http://www.epa.gov/superfund/ kids/index.htm**
Tvakids.com	Tennessee Valley Authority	**http://www.tvakids.com/**
USDA for Kids	Department of Agriculture	**http://www.usda.gov/news/ usdakids/index.html**
USFA's Kids Page	U.S. Fire Administration	**http://www.usfa.fema.gov/kids/**
VRD Learning Center	National Library of Education	**http://vrd.askvrd.org/index.asp**
Water Science for Schools	U.S. Geological Survey	**http://ga.water.usgs.gov/edu/ navguide.html**
Whitehousekids.gov	White House	**http://www.whitehouse.gov/kids/**
YouthlinK	Social Security Administration	**http://www.ssa.gov/kids**

NASA also has three Web sites devoted to games and puzzles: For Kids Only, **http://kids.earth.nasa.gov/games**; Fun and Games, **http://www.ueet.nasa.gov/StudentSite/funandgames.html;** and NASA Kids, **http://kids.msfc.nasa.gov/Puzzles/.**

Kids Corner

This site of the Federal Aviation Administration includes activities (e.g., crossword and picture maze puzzles, coloring books, and conducting experiments), some of which are aimed at kids aged 5 to 9 and others at youth aged 10 to 12. "Teen Pages" offers other activities, such as "look for a job."

NASA Multimedia Gallery

This site offers photo, video, audio, and arts galleries. The Photo Gallery contains NASA's still images, the Video Gallery is a "guide to digital video and animation related to NASA and space exploration," the Audio Gallery draws together NASA's audio resources, and the Arts Gallery has art works documenting the history of NASA projects and showing advancements in aerospace.

StarChild

StarChild, "a learning center for young astronomers," contains information and images about the solar system, the universe, and space. There are links to additional Web sites covering these three topics. *StarChild* has also been translated into languages other than English (see "Other Languages") .

AGRICULTURE

USDA for Kids, a gateway of the Department of Agriculture, provides links to various Web pages within the department, each of which could have been listed separately in this chapter. The gateway links to the "Farmer's Market," "Weather," "Nature Watch," "Preventing Foodborne Illness," "Backyard Conservation," "Food Guide Pyramid," "George Washington Carver Coloring Book," "Smokey Bear," and "Nature Inquiry." There are even more pages: "Meet the Beagle Brigade," "Food for Thought," "Agriculture for Kids," "Teen Nutrition," "RUS, the Surfin' Squirrel," "Stanley Sta & Pie Chart Pam," "Facts about Agriculture," "S.K. Worm," "History of Agriculture," "Gardening," "Woodsy Owl," "USDA Hall of Fame," "Kids' Science Page," "Natural Resource Conservation Education," "4-H in the USA," "Kid's Corner," "Thermy [the thermometer] for Kids," and "SciKIDS." There are also photographs and "More Cool Links."

S.K. Worm, for instance, provides information about soil and natural resources. Smokey Bear's Official Home Page discusses rules for forest fire safety and prevention, and Woodsy Owl of the Forest Service is an environmental champion, one that motivates kids to form lasting relationships with nature:

Caring, friendly, and wise, Woodsy Owl is a whimsical fellow and he's got his heart set on motivating kids to form healthy, lasting relationships with nature. As Woodsy flies across our land, he encourages youngsters to marvel at and explore the natural world, even in the city. His new motto, "Lend a Hand—Care for the Land," encourages everyone to make a positive difference in the world.

In addition to offering coloring sheets and an activity guide (e.g., teacher training opportunities, questions and answers, and "teacher's guide at-a-glance"), there is an explanation of how to arrange for Woodsy Owl to visit a school or after-school center.

CYFERNet Kid's Space

The Department of Agriculture's Cooperative Extension Service (CES) has icons for "Community Center," "Communications Center," "National Theatre," "Clover Café," "CES Office," "Welcome," and "Library." These choices lead to 4-H information, resources, curriculum, and so forth. There are virtual 4-H clubs and links to other sites in the department.

ALCOHOL AND DRUGS

FDA Kids

See the section of the chapter on Science and Technology.

For Kids Only

This site of the National Clearinghouse for Alcohol and Drug Information, Department of Health and Human Services, is available in both English and Spanish. The intent of the site is to discourage the use of alcohol and drugs through games and visuals. The site also presents educational and science information. Clearly, the resources presented here entertain and educate; in particular, see "Related Internet Links."

THE ARTS

ARTSEDGE

ARTSEDGE of the Kennedy Center for Performing Arts "is a directory of instructional resources available through other websites." The teaching materials ("curricula, lessons and activities") cover "ESL" [English as a second language], "Foreign Language," "Mathematics," "Physical Education," "Science," "Social Studies," "Design Arts," "Language Arts," "Performing Arts," and "Visual Arts." ARTSEDGE, for instance, provides teaching materials, including lesson plans and curriculum Web links.

BUSINESS AND FINANCE

⤳ For Kids

The Department of Treasury site provides access to its education page, which links to other sites. There is a history of the department, taxes, and the mint. There is a virtual tour of the U.S. Treasury Building and an introduction to the department's historic collection, as well as information about savings bonds, coins and gifts, starting a business (i.e., a lemonade stand, a lawn-mowing service, and a band), how employers file their taxes, the dog of the month (from the U.S. Customs Service showing the dog that made the "largest or most notable [drug smuggling] seizure") . Furthermore, kids can "sign-in" for fun and games, and teachers can register for classroom resources.

"Know Your Money," a button, explains counterfeiting and the forgery of U.S. government checks and savings bonds. It also provides facts and trivia about engraving and printing. The "Bond Calculator" explains the redemption values for a savings bond and presents other information compiled by the Federal Reserve Bank of New York. Finally, a "Savings Bond Wizard" "helps you manage your savings bond inventory. This Windows® application allows you to maintain an inventory of your bonds and determine the current redemption value, earned interest, and other information. You can also print your bond inventory."

⤳ Learning Bank

The Learning Bank, a Web site of the Federal Deposit Insurance Corporation, "is presented solely to educate and entertain children, teachers, and parents." It discusses the agency, what a bank does with money, and how a bank makes money. Furthermore, it explains what bank accounts, checking accounts, savings accounts, and loans are. A time line succinctly depicts banking in colonial America and the United States during the 1700s, 1800s, 1900–19, and in each decade from the 1920s through the 1990s. It is possible to send e-mail messages to the agency.

⤳ OPIC for Kids

The Overseas Private Investment Corporation (OPIC), which assists U.S. companies in investing in different countries, maintains OPIC for Kids. This site explains the independent agency, its role and programs. Other features are related links, a photo Safari of wildlife in places in which the agency does business, and information on countries.

CAREER PLANNING

⤳ BLS Career Information

This page of the Bureau of Labor Statistics (BLS) provides information for careers in music and the arts, science, physical education and the outdoors, social studies, mathematics, and reading. There is also a teacher's guide to career information and a list of educational resources from the Department of Labor.

CONSUMER PROTECTION

☞ FDA Kids

This Food and Drug Administration (FDA) site discusses food safety, caring for pets, vaccines, children and tobacco, conducting a FDA investigation, the dangers in medicine cabinets, the teen scene, and a parents' corner. That corner contains articles from the *FDA Consumer* and some Web sites for parents. There are also coloring books, an opportunity to "learn about medical devices from FDA's favorite skeleton," and a link to all pages of the Department of Health and Human Services that comprise "Pages for Kids" (**http://www.hhs.gov/kids/**). These pages may also be of value to parents and teachers.

☞ The Further Adventures of KIDD Safety

The purpose of this site of the Consumer Product Safety Commission is to help "prevent unreasonable risks of injures to children associated with consumer products." There are safety games as well as a quiz and information about safety in the home and when playing outdoors.

COPING WITH NATURAL DISASTERS

☞ FEMA for Kids

This site explains the role of the Federal Emergency Management Agency (FEMA) in helping people cope with "floods, wildfires, hurricanes, tornadoes, earthquakes and winter storms." FEMA also teaches people what to do before or during a disaster. Specific options at the site cover resources for parents and teachers; a library of resources; games, quizzes, and challenges; "Disaster Connection: Kids to Kids"; the disaster area; "Get Ready, Get Set . . ."; "What's Happening Now?"; "Becoming a Disaster Action Kid"; and so on.

☞ USFA's Kids Page

This site of FEMA's U.S. Fire Administration provides facts and games as it educates youth about fire safety and hazards in the home. One game asks users to locate fire hazards in each room of a house, and another covers escape planning from a burning house.

CRIMINAL JUSTICE

⟳ FBI Youth

This site, which complements the Federal Bureau of Investigation's (FBI) *Kids Page* (discussed later), covers grades six through twelve. There are games, adventures, activities of agents and the agency, a history of the agency, and other information.

⟳ Justice for Kids & Youth

Produced by the Department of Justice, this site contains information for young people in grades K to five and six to twelve, as well as for parents and teachers; thus, it overlaps with the other sites covered in this section. That information explains the role of the FBI, presents the list of "10 most wanted" and the inside of a courtroom, encourages kids to get involved in crime prevention, discusses facts about drugs, and highlights civil rights law and history. There is additional coverage of topics under "subjects." Viewed from another perspective, information covers health and safety (including substance abuse prevention), biological and life sciences (learn about DNA testing, fingerprint identification, forensic science, and polygraph testing), criminology (e.g., famous cases), current events and issues, human relations, technology, the government, and U.S. history (e.g., history of the U.S. Marshals and the FBI). There is also information about "Getting Involved in Crime Prevention" and "Internet Dos & Don'ts."

⟳ Kids Page

This FBI page is aimed at kids from kindergarten through fifth grade. It provides information about the agency and its activities. There are also games and a field trip of the FBI.

EDUCATION

⟳ Afterschool.gov

This Web site "offers one-stop access to government resources that support after school programs. The site is designed for anyone who cares about kids 6–18—providers, parents, and kids and teens. You can find information to help you understand the issues that face kids and teens or fund, start and operate an after school program." The information for parents covers a wide range of topics "from child and adolescent development to how to help with homework to Federal parks they can stay in on their east to west coast summer vacation." This site provides community links, planning activities, methods for keeping current, running a program, and current information (e.g., on the West Nile Virus).

☞ Foodsafety.Gov

Foodsafety.gov, which is covered in Chapter 5, has a page that pertains to "Kids, Teens & Educators." There are coloring books, a food safety quiz, games, career profiles, crossword puzzles, word scrambles, and more. There is a "Presenter's Guide for Working with Children from Kindergarten through Grades 3," and many resources intended to assist parents and teachers in educating the youth. There are also frequently asked questions and Web links to state and local government.

☞ The NCES Classroom

This excellent site, provided by the National Center for Education Statistics of the Department of Education, has information on primary and secondary schools throughout the nation, as well as the public libraries and colleges in every state. For example, information seekers can locate any primary and secondary school and obtain enrollment information, as well as the racial and ethnic distribution of the student population. There is also information on how to create a graph and on being a mathematician. Other features include "Word of the Day" and facts, games, quizzes, and other activities. There are also links to the agency and a site index.

☞ VRD Learning Center

This site of the Department of Education covers assorted categories: "Arts," "College/Career," "Foreign Language," "Health," "Mathematics," "Physical Education," "Religion," "Social Studies," "Vocational Education," "Educational Technology," "Biography," "General Education," "Language Arts," "Philosophy," "Reference," and "Training." It is also possible ask a question of the "Experts."

ENERGY AND THE ENVIRONMENT

☞ Dr. E's Energy Lab

Produced by the Office of Energy Efficiency and Renewable Energy, the site covers wind, geothermal, renewable, and solar energy, plus alternative fuels and energy efficiency. There is also an opportunity to ask a question of an energy expert.

☞ Earthquakes for Kids

The U.S. Geological Survey has a number of pages useful for the youth of the world. One of these is Earthquakes for Kids, which discusses the science of earthquakes, "Cool Earthquake Facts," "Latest Quakes," "Today in Earthquake History," and more.

EIA Kid's Page

Energy Ant discusses energy and offers fun facts and information about energy, online resources, milestones (e.g., energy in the United States, 1635–2000), a quiz, "What's New," and classroom resources. There are also links to other Web pages in the Department of Energy that would be of interest to young people.

EPA Student Center

The Environmental Protection Agency (EPA) provides a site map and a dictionary, as well as information about itself and coverage of conservation, ecosystems, water, waste and recycling, human health, air, and "in your neighborhood." There are resources for both teachers and the nation's youth in middle and high school, including "Fun Activities," "Environmental Club Projects," "Environmental Youth Awards," and "Careers, Internships, & Scholarships."

Especially for Kids (National Ocean Service)

This site of the National Ocean Service covers oil spills and hazardous chemical accidents. Among its offerings are experiments, guided tours, an image gallery, instructor's kits, and more.

Especially for Kids (U.S. Fish and Wildlife Service)

This site, produced by the U.S. Fish and Wildlife Service, provides information on endangered species (plants and animals) and explains what can be done to save them. It offers educational materials, slide shows, drawings, coloring books, photographs, access to other Web sites (e.g., for the Mexican Gray Wolf and endangered species), and so on.

The agency also has educator's and student's pages that cover habitats, fish, plants, contacts within the agency, and related links. There is a conservation laboratory as well as videos, maps, training courses, and frequently asked questions (see **http://educators.fws.gov/; http://educators.fws.gov/students.html**).

Explorers' Club

This EPA site, which is aimed at kids from ages five to twelve, covers air and water quality, garbage and recycling, plants and animals, and the environment. There is artwork about ozone depletion and protecting oneself from the sun, life in a polluted area, plants and animals living in water, and water pollution. An activity book covers making Earth a better place to live. There are also games, science rooms, and a trophy case (recognition of kids who work to protect the environment). The site links to the EPA Student Center (discussed above) and the Environment Education Center, which is intended for teachers (**http://www.epa.gov/teachers/**).

Frog Web.gov

This site, which is designed for older students, notes that "amphibians are good 'indicators' of significant environmental changes that may go initially undetected by humans. . . . The worldwide occurrences of amphibian declines and deformities could be an early warning to us of serious ecosystem imbalances." There is access to scientific research, news releases, educational resources, and so on.

Hey, Kids!

Provided by the Agency for Toxic Substances and Diseases Registry (ATSDR), this site presents facts about toxic chemicals and the environment for the nation's youth, parents, teachers, doctors, and nurses. There are also links to assorted Web sites related to "Fun Things from Government Agencies," "Kids' Homes at Government Agencies," and "More for Kids . . . And MORE . . . And MORE for Kids!"

Kids Corner (Energy Information Administration)

Energy Ant serves as the host to this introduction to energy and explains "What Is Energy." The page also provides a "Classroom Connection," an "Energy Quiz," "Fun Facts," "Online Resources," "Contact Info," "About Us," "Milestones," and information about the Energy Information Administration and Energy Ant.

Kids Corner (National Oceanic and Atmospheric Administration)

The National Oceanic and Atmospheric Administration's "many educational activities are distributed across the agency. This site has been designated to help students, teachers, librarians, and the general public access the many educational activities, publications, and booklets that have been produced."

Kids on the Web

This site of the Department of Interior presents wildlife species, a butterfly site, a coloring book, landmark adventures, shorebirds, guidance in learning the Web, coal mining, the Hoover Dam, and so on. The butterfly site, for example, has a coloring page, answers to frequently asked questions, books and videos (including teacher resources), hot links to related sites (e.g., U.S. Patent and Trademark Office's Kids Pages), and a photo gallery. Furthermore, there are fact sheets on different wildlife species.

Kids' Stuff

This site of the Minerals Management Service, Department of the Interior, provides information on safety in mines, quarries, and sand and gravel pits. From a map of the United States, those visiting the site can locate where minerals are mined. There is also coverage of coal mining, related links, and so on. *Kids' Pages*, another site (**http://www.mms.gov/mmskids/**) discusses energy saving, natural resources, the composition of seawater, and historic shipwrecks. The intended audience is both teachers and youth.

Kidzzone

This site of the Department of Energy (DOE) gives the nation's youth information about energy, its users and its conservation, through contests, games, and activities. There is coverage of science, frequently asked questions, a glossary, and so on. There are also links to other DOE Web pages intended for kids.

Nature Watch

Produced by the Forest Service and part of *USDA for Kids* (see section on Agriculture), this site illustrates "watchable nature" as one tours a national forest. There is coverage of fish, plants, and birds and other wildlife, as well as links to nature organizations, school curricula, journals, and newsletters. There are also guides, tours, and lists (e.g., of sites accessibility to those with disabilities).

NIEHS Kids' Page

This site of the National Institute of Environmental Health Sciences (National Institutes of Health) has stories, a coloring book, jokes, word scrambles, brain teasers and riddles, games and surprises (including hidden pictures and words), quotations, related links, and so on. There is also music and an opportunity to sing along. All of the resources relate to science, particularly the effects of the environment on human health.

Specially for Students

This site of the National Oceanic and Atmospheric Administration covers grades six through twelve. A second site, Specially for Kids, is for kindergarteners through fifth graders and provides activities to explore the earth. A third site, "Higher Education Opportunities," is aimed at undergraduate and graduate students who are searching for research opportunities, scholarships, grants, fellowships, and jobs (see **http://www.education.noaa.gov/students.html**).

Students' Corner

This site of the Nuclear Regulatory Commission discusses "Nuclear Reactors," "Radiation," "Emergency Planning," "Radioactive Waste," "Periodic Table of the Elements," "Basic References," "Glossary of Nuclear Terms," "Decommissioning," and more.

➪ Superfund for KIDS!

This EPA site explains the Superfund and offers stories, tips, activities and homework help, and related links. It also covers "What's New."

➪ Tvakids.com

The Tennessee Valley Authority, an independent agency, has Tvakids.com, which discusses the agency's history, working with the agency, green power, electrical safety, "Class Favorites," "Protecting the Environment," "Making Electricity," "Running the River," "For Teachers," and "Cool Stuff."

➪ Water Science for Schools

The U.S. Geological Survey offers a broad range of information about water. There is coverage of rainwater, surface water, groundwater, glaciers and icecaps, water quality, water use, and so on.

ENGRAVING AND PRINTING

➪ BEP for Kids!

The Bureau of Engraving and Printing (BEP) is the largest producer of security documents in the United States. It produces Federal Reserve notes, postage stamps for the U.S. Postal Service, paper currency, and miscellaneous security documents for other government agencies. The site, which is intended for children (aged five to thirteen) and teachers, discusses anticounterfeiting features in the new 1996 and 1999 Series Federal Reserve Notes. There are interactive displays and games.

HEALTH CARE

➪ HHS Pages for Kids

This site provides links to different Web pages within the Department of Health and Human Services aimed at the youth, not all of which have not been highlighted in this chapter.

➪ Kids Area

Kids Area of the National Mental Health Information Center provides information about the mental health services. It explains and provides access to the agency's Knowledge Exchange Network (KEN), offers Internet tips, and has links to other sites.

⤤ Smoke-Free Kids

To discourage smoking among the nation's youth, the National Cancer Institute of the Department of Health and Human Services offers information presented through banners, posters, screen savers, and links.

INTELLIGENCE COMMUNITY

⤤ CIA for Kids

The Central Intelligence Agency's *CIA for Kids* provides information about the history of intelligence, the agency, and the CIA seal; and about the present-day agency. Furthermore, the page provides a test of one's knowledge about geography, word puzzles, an opportunity to "try a disguise" and "break the code," a virtual tour of the agency, and the *World Factbook*, which contains maps and concise profiles of countries.

MAPS, GEOGRAPHY, AND EARTH SCIENCES

Some related sites are available in this chapter under "Energy and the Environment."

⤤ Learning Web

The U.S. Geological Survey offers the *Learning Web*, a collection of educational materials aimed at students, teachers, and explorers that covers mapping and biology, geology, hydrology, and geography on planet Earth. Topics range from satellite images of environmental change, coastal wetlands, geological animations and paper models, water education posters, and water science for schools. There are maps, links to other Web sites (e.g., one for the ecosystem of South Florida), photographs, and so on.

MILITARY

⤤ Air Force Link Junior

Air Force Link Jr. "provides children (ages 6–12) with an educational and entertaining online experience while familiarizing them with the Air Force and its heritage. It provides online activities, reading, language skills and motor skills, as well as general Air Force information." There are also links to sites providing "quality online activities for children."

MUSEUMS

➔ Kids' Castle

Presented by the *Smithsonian Magazine*, this site introduces the diversity of the Smithsonian Institution's collections. There are messages, games, a "Cool Link of the Day," and assorted information on science, animals, personalities, sports, the arts, worldwide occurrences, history, and air and space.

NATIVE AMERICAN CUSTOMS, CULTURE, AND TRADITIONS

➔ Planet Youth

The Department of Housing and Urban Development sponsors this site, which, among its options, covers "Native Customs, Traditions, & Links." There are excellent links to a wide variety of Native American Web sites. There are also online games and so on.

PATENTS

➔ KIDS Pages

Offered by the United States Patent and Trademark Office, there are resources for youth in grades kindergarten through six and grades six through twelve, as well as for "Guiding Lights" (parents, teachers, and coaches).There are games, puzzles, contests, links, events, and a wide assortment of information about patents (e.g., "assisting minor children with patent applications") .

SCIENCE AND TECHNOLOGY

➔ Fun Activities for Kids!

This site of the National Institute of Science and Technology (NIST) illustrates the agency's role to develop and promote measurement, standards, and technology to enhance productivity, encourage trade, and seek to improve the quality of life. The site contains word finders and other games, crossword puzzles, and other activities that show what NIST studies, measures, and seeks to improve to ensure safe and high-quality products.

Sci4Kids

Sci4Kids is a series of stories about what scientists at the Department of Agriculture's Agricultural Research Service (ARS) do. The stories, geared to children between eight and thirteen years old, are based on articles from the monthly *Agricultural Research* magazine and other news reports.

Students—K–12

This site of the National Science Foundation has teaching activities, news, and information. There is also an opportunity to "Ask a Scientist or Engineer, as well as "math challenges," experiments and other activities, coverage of earth science and ocean science, and so on.

SOCIAL STUDIES

Members of Congress may devote part of their Web sites to the nation's youth. The House Committee on Science has a page for the youth under construction (**http://www.house.gov/science/kidspage/index.htm**).

Ben's Guide to U.S. Government for Kids

Ben's Guide introduces how the government works based on information resources available through GPO Access (see Chapter 3). Ben refers to Benjamin Franklin, who serves as a guide to "Core Documents of Democracy" (e.g., the Gettysburg Address and the Federalist Papers), symbols of the government, the three branches of government, what it means to be a citizen, and games (e.g., the "Constitution Crossword," "Presidential Names Word Scramble," and "The 13 Original States Crossword Puzzle") . The resources are tailored to specific age groups, and there are resources for parents and educators. There are also links to other government Web sites created for the youth.

The Exhibit Hall

This home page of the National Archives and Records Administration (NARA) contains the *Charters of Freedom* (Declaration of Independence, Constitution, and Bill of Rights), photographs throughout the twentieth century, and assorted historical documents (e.g., the Louisiana Purchase, a police report on the assassination of Abraham Lincoln, and President Nixon's letter of resignation).

A complementary Web site is "Celebrating America's Freedoms," produced by the Department of Veterans Affairs (**http://www.va.gov/pubaff/celebAm/CAIndex.htm**). It provides information that teachers can use to honor patriotic observations such as Veterans Day. For instance, a Microsoft Word document provides the Pledge of Allegiance and changes made to it in the early part of the twentieth century.

⤴ Foreign Affairs for Young People

This site, which is the Department of State's page for youth, introduces both the Secretary of States and the Department. It also covers "Social Studies," "Career Exploration," a "Photo Gallery," "Arts at State," Interesting Links," travel tips, and news highlights. "Social Studies," for instance, offers a time line of diplomatic history, the secretary's travels, and information about different countries. There is also information about the Model UN Program (**http://www.state.gov/p/io/mdlun/**).

⤴ Kid's Corner

Provided by the Bureau of the Census, this site provides information taken from the American Factfinder (see Chapter 8) and provides facts about each state, quizzes, and information about the agency. The user views the role of the agency as the nation's fact finder and is able to find information on the bureau's home page that is arranged especially for their use.

⤴ Kids

This site of the Smithsonian Institution contains games, quizzes, coloring books, crossword puzzles, and opportunities to make things (e.g., a giant panda mask). It also links to the page for the National Zoo and to *Kids' Castle*, sponsored by the *Smithsonian* magazine, which includes games and other activities.

⤴ Kids in the House

This site of the Office of the Clerk, House of Representatives, is "an interactive center that helps kids learn about the . . . House . . . and its role in lawmaking." There is coverage of the legislative process and its effect on the citizenry. There are also games and other activities.

⤴ Kids Next Door

This site of the Department of Housing and Urban Development offers an opportunity for kids to "learn more about being good citizens." The goal of making kids care is accomplished through giving kids a chance to "see neat things," "visit awesome places," and "meet cool people." Meeting cool people explains volunteer activities and helping the homeless, whereas visiting places involves a field trip that is either "a quick picture tour or our animated tour with sound and motion."

⤴ Kids Stuff

Provided by the Mine Safety and Health Administration of the Department of Labor, this site provides an introduction into high school civics, through its explanation of the three branches of government, guidance in "how a bill becomes law," access to the Constitution and its amendments, the Declaration of Independence, and the

Articles of Confederation. There are also links to related sites, not all of which the government produces.

Kids World

This site of the Peace Corps "explores the globe and [the kids] learn about making a difference." There is coverage of food and friends.

KIDZ Privacy

This site covers privacy rights and tries to educate students about those rights. There is also information and resources for adults, teachers, and the media.

Presidents of the United States

Four presidential libraries administered by the National Archives and Records Administration (NARA) have kids' pages: those for Herbert Hoover (For Students), Harry S. Truman (Kids Page), Lyndon Baines Johnson (LBJ for Kids!), and Jimmy Carter (Kids Page!). These sites introduce the former presidents, the first ladies, the period in history in which the president was in office, his accomplishments, and issues of his presidency. The Hoover Presidential Library and Museum even has some presidential cartoons. The Truman Library, among its offerings, depicts the family tree, provides selected speeches, explains how the president made major decisions, and offers a digital archives (Project Whistlestop) and trivia questions (e.g., "What was Truman's favorite poem?"). The Carter home page, among other inclusions, covers the Camp David Accords, gifts given to the President and Mrs. Carter, "a timeline of young Jimmy Carter," and an explanation of presidential libraries. The Johnson site contains his Great Society speech, his swearing in as president, a "LBJ timeline," an introduction to government civics, fast facts, and coverage of civil rights, education, environment, the war on poverty, and foreign policy during his administration. Clearly, the contents of these sites are aimed at children and teachers. By the way, the Bush Presidential Library has a *Kids Page* under construction.

White House

This site, known as *Whitehousekids.gov*, contains a time line that offers lessons of liberty for the years 1777, 1831, 1886, 1938, and 1948. There are also tours, biographical information, guides for teachers and parents, pictures, information on some historical figures, and so on.

Youthlink

Youthlink of the Social Security Administration consists of "Hot Questions for Cool Teens" and "Social Security Kids Stuff." The former covers "What's Your Number?," "Why Social Security?," "How Does It Work?," "Who Pays?," "How Much?," "How Do I Use It?," "Will It Be There?," "Cool Facts!," "Quizzes," and "Puzzles."

"Social Security Kids Stuff," using animals as tour guides, explains the purpose of social security and who receives the benefits. There are also resources for parents and teachers.

TRANSPORTATION

↗ Education, Career Development, and Safety Awareness

This home page of the Federal Railroad Administration (Department of Transportation) presents railroad history and museums, railroad transportation of today and tomorrow, animation of a train coming at the user through a tunnel, education news, and related Web sites. There are also lesson plans, quizzes and word problems, and problem-solving exercises for mathematics.

↗ Especially for Kids and Teens

The purpose of this site of the U.S. Maritime Administration is "to help ensure that today's generation is prepared to become the transportation workforce of the 21st century." The agency provides career information, a three-dimensional transportation Web site, an interactive project for worldwide transportation, an introduction to lighthouses, information on the role of the Merchant Marine in World War II, and a photograph collection.

↗ Safety City

This site of the National Highway Traffic Safety Administration depicts a city and its highways. There are spots (e.g., town hall, safety school, research laboratory, garage, a theater, and an art gallery) to visit. It is also possible to take a bike tour of the city. Two crash test dummies serve as guides to teach kids about safety. Among the resources available are a quiz about "safety trivia," lesson plans and teaching materials, and so on. In the garage, "you can download all the fonts and valuable plug-ins that make Safety City so exciting!"

VETERANS

↗ Cool Stuff for Young People

This site introduces the Department of Veterans Affairs and provides coverage of "America's Wars," "Lincoln's Second Inaugural Address," and fact sheets. There is also a teacher's page. As previously noted, "Celebrating America's Freedoms" (**http://www.va.gov/pubaff/celebam/caindex.htm**) contains information and activities that teachers can use in connection with patriotic observations. For instance, one activity relates to how the national flag has developed since 1776 and another explains the story behind how the flag became known as "Old Glory."

WILDLIFE IN CAPTIVITY

↗ National Zoo

The site presents highlights, animal photographs, and information about the National Zoo, including feeding times. *Just for Kids*, provided by the Friends of the National Zoo, offers coloring pages, walking tours, games, trivia, and other information and activities (**http://nationalzoo.si.edu/Audiences/Students.cfm**).

SUMMARY

This chapter identifies a number of the Web sites that government agencies maintain for children, students, parents, and teachers. The purpose of these sites is to broaden the public's knowledge and understanding of issues, to encourage the youth to become more sensitive to their surroundings and to become better citizens; to enable kids to learn about different issues and circumstances; to realize various roles that the national government plays; to pursue different career choices; to regard government as a partner in their lives and as supplier of useful information and services; and to provide educational resources to the educational community. For example, *Learn NPS* (**http://www.nps.gov/learn/**) serves both teachers and students interested in the National Parks. At this site, the National Park Service provides curriculum-based learning tools (School Zone); teaching resources, workshops, and skill development (Teacher Zone); online activities and games (Go Zone); and park junior ranger programs (Ranger Zone).

FirstGov for Kids, FedStat's Kids' Pages, and Safe Places to Play merit mention for their identification of additional sites. In effect, they serve as a partial "one-stop shop" for some Web sites aimed at the nation's youth, teachers, and parents. First, FirstGov for Kids (**http://www.kids.gov/**), which the Federal Consumer Information Center, developed and maintains, leads to Web sites organized according to the "Arts," "Careers," "Computers," "Fighting Crimes," "Fun Stuff," "Geography," "Global Village," "Government," "Health," "History," "Homework," "Money," "Music," "Plants and Animals," "Recreation," "Safety," "Science and Math," "Space, "States Sites," and "Transportation."

Kids' Pages, which is available by the FEDSTATS (**http://www.fedstats. gov/kids.html**), provides a table of different agencies "special Web pages for kids in elementary through high school"; in fact, it includes more than forty sites, one of which is Kids Links of the Indian Health Services. The Web pages linked to FEDSTATS include fun facts, games, project ideas, and other information.

Third, Safe Places to Play of the Department of Housing and Urban Development covers the home, people, places, and things. It also links to other sites for the youth, including America's Story of the Library of Congress (LC) (**http://www.americaslibrary. gov/cgi-bin/page.cgi**), which introduces LC's collections on historical figures and history, recreation, and music.

© Linsay Hernon

URL Site Guide for This Chapter

Note: The sites listed in Figure 13.1 are omitted.

America's Story (Library of Congress)

Home Page
http://www.americaslibary.gov/cgi-bin/
page.cgi

Celebrating America's Freedoms

Department of Veterans Affairs
http://www.va.gov/pubaff/celebAm/
CAIndex.htm

Committee on Science

House of Representatives
http://www.house.gov/science/kidspage/
index.htm

Educator's Page

U.S. Fish and Wildlife Service
http://educators.fws.gov/

Student's Page
http://educators.fws.gov/students.html

Environmental Education Center (for Teachers)

Environmental Protection Agency
http://www.epa.gov/teachers/

FirstGov for Kids

Federal Consumer Information Center
http://www.kids.gov/

Higher Education Opportunities

National Oceanic and Atmospheric Administration
http://www.education.noaa.gov/
students.html

Just for Kids

Friends of the National Zoo
http://www.nationalzoo.si.edu/audiences/
Students.cfm

Kids' Pages

FEDSTATS
http://www.fedstats.gov/kids.html

Kids' Pages

Mineral Management Service
http://www.mms.gov/mmskids/

Learn NPS

National Park Service
http://www.nps.gov/learn/

Model UN Program

State Department
http://www.state.gov/p/io/mdlun/

NASA (Games and Puzzles)

For Kids Only
http://kids.earth.nasa.gov/games

Fun and Games
http://www.ueet.nasa.gov/StudentSite/
funandgames.html

NASA Kids
http://kids.msfc.nasa.gov/Puzzles/

Pages for Kids

Department of Health and Human Services
http://www.hhs.gov/kids/

Safe Places to Play

Department of Housing and Urban Development
http://www.hud.gov/kids/safemain.html

Chapter 14

E-Gov Comes to the Federal Government

Harold C. Relyea*

Electronic government, or e-gov, is a concept increasingly used in American public discourse today. Initially, the term was little more than a general recognition of a confluence of information technology (IT) developments and the application and use of these technologies by government entities. Subsequently, it has oftentimes been used as a symbol, an ambiguous reference to both current applications of IT to government operations and to a goal of realizing more efficient and economical performance of government functions. It is a dynamic concept of varying meaning and significance.[1]

BACKGROUND

The conditions contributing to the e-government phenomenon were recognized at least three decades ago. Observations offered by the authors of a report of the Commission on the Year 2000 of the American Academy of Arts and Sciences are informative in this regard. Concerning the executive branch, the report proffered that "[b]y the year 2000, despite the growth in the size and complexity of federal programs, the technological improvement of the computer, closed-circuit TV, facsimile transmission, and so on, will make it possible for the federal bureaucracy to carry out its functions much more efficiently and effectively than it can today, with no increase in total manpower."[2]

The use of information technologies was also seen as having critical importance for the legislative branch, constituting nothing less than "another aspect of congressional reform." Should "Congress continue to deny itself the tools of modern information technology and permit the Executive virtually to monopolize them," said the report, "Congress will ultimately destroy its power both to create policy and to oversee the

*Harold C. Relyea is Specialist in American National Government, Congressional Research Service (Library of Congress, Washington, DC 20540).

Executive." Moreover, it was observed, the "technology revolution . . . promises greater accessibility of senators and congressmen to their constituents, individually and collectively, and vice versa." Indeed, the report warned as follows:

> Communications may become too close and constant, and act as a constricting force. For instance, by 2000 it will be easy to have virtually up-to-the-minute polls of the electorate on any given issue. But where does this instant-opinion development leave the senator and congressman?[3]

Such observations, however, should not obscure recognition that new information technologies have affected government operations in the past, as the following comment, penned in 1910, attests:

> Public officials, even in the United States, have been slow to change from the old-fashioned and more dignified use of written documents and uniformed messengers; but in the last ten years there has been a sweeping revolution in this respect. Government by telephone! This is a new idea that has already arrived in the more efficient departments of the Federal service. And as for the present Congress, that body has gone so far as to plan for a special system of its own, in both Houses, so that all official announcements may be heard by wire.[4]

The author, a respected Canadian editor and writer, also presciently noted that "[n]ext to public officials, bankers were perhaps the last to accept the facilities of the telephone," because "[t]hey were slow to abandon the fallacy that no business can be done without a written record."[5] Subscription to such a "fallacy" constitutes a basis for the concerns of some regarding the paperless transactions of e-government.

POLICY ENVIRONMENT

Various policy instruments support and shape the e-government concept. They seek to promote the use of new IT by government entities with a view to improving the efficiency and economy of government operations, as well as to ensure the proper management of these technologies and the systems they serve, their protection from physical harm, and the security and privacy of their information. These instruments are chronologically identified and summarized in the following sections.

⟳ *Privacy Act*

With the *Privacy Act of 1974,* Congress addressed several aspects of personal privacy protection.[6] First, it sustained some traditional major privacy principles. For example, an agency shall "maintain no record describing how any individual exercises rights guaranteed by the First Amendment unless expressly authorized by statute or by the individual about whom the record is maintained or unless pertinent to and within the scope of an authorized law enforcement activity."[7]

Second, the statute provides an individual who is a citizen of the United States, or an alien lawfully admitted for permanent residence, with access and emendation arrangements for records maintained on him or her by most, but not all, federal agencies.

General exemptions in this regard are provided for systems of records maintained by the Central Intelligence Agency and federal criminal law enforcement agencies.

Third, the statute embodies a number of principles of fair information practice. For example, it sets certain conditions concerning the disclosure of personally identifiable information; prescribes requirements for the accounting of certain disclosures of such information; requires agencies to "collect information to the greatest extent practicable directly from the subject individual when the information may result in adverse determinations about an individual's rights, benefits, and privileges under Federal programs"; requires agencies to specify their authority and purposes for collecting personally identifiable information from an individual; requires agencies to "maintain all records which are used by the agency in making any determination about any individual with such accuracy, relevance, timeliness, and completeness as is reasonably necessary to assure fairness to the individual in the determination"; and provides civil and criminal enforcement arrangements.

Paperwork Reduction Act

Replacing the ineffective *Federal Reports Act of 1942,* the original *Paperwork Reduction Act of 1980* (PRA) was enacted largely to relieve the public from the mounting information collection and reporting requirements of the federal government.[8] It also promoted coordinated information management activities on a governmentwide basis by the director of the Office of Management and Budget (OMB) and prescribed information management responsibilities for the executive agencies as well. The management focus of the PRA was sharpened with the 1986 amendments, which refined the concept of "information resources management"(IRM), defined as "the planning, budgeting, organizing, directing, training, promoting, controlling, and management activities associated with the burden, collection, creation, use, and dissemination of information by agencies, and includes the management of information and related resources such as automatic data processing equipment."[9] This key term and its subset concepts received further definition and explanation in the PRA of 1995,[10] making IRM a tool for managing the contribution of information activities to program performance, and for managing related resources, such as personnel, equipment, funds, and technology.[11]

The evolution of the PRA reflects the beginning of an effort to manage better electronic information and supporting IT. A recodification of the 1980 statute, as amended, the PRA of 1995 specifies a full range of responsibilities for the director of OMB for all government information, regardless of form or format, throughout its entire life cycle. Regarding IT, the director, among other duties, is tasked with

1. Developing and overseeing the implementation of policies, principles, standards, and guidelines for federal IT functions and activities, including periodic evaluations of major information systems

2. Overseeing the development and implementation of certain statutorily specified technology standards

3. Monitoring the effectiveness of, and compliance with, certain statutorily authorized technology directives

4. Coordinating the development and review by the OMB Office of Information and Regulatory Affairs (OIRA) of policy associated with federal procurement and acquisition of IT with the OMB Office of Federal Procurement Policy

5. Ensuring, through the review of agency budget proposals, IRM plans, and other means, both (1) the integration of IRM plans with program plans and budgets for the acquisition and use of IT by each agency and (2) the efficiency and effectiveness of interagency IT initiatives to improve agency performance and the accomplishment of agency missions

6. Promoting agency use of IT to improve the productivity, efficiency, and effectiveness of federal programs, including through the dissemination of public information and the reduction of information collection burdens on the public

Similar responsibilities are specified for the agencies regarding government information, regardless of form or format, throughout its life cycle. With respect to IT, the agencies are tasked with

1. Implementing and enforcing applicable governmentwide and agency IT management policies, principles, standards, and guidelines

2. Assuming responsibility and accountability for IT investments

3. Promoting the use of IT by the agency to improve the productivity, efficiency, and effectiveness of agency programs, including the reduction of information collection burdens on the public and improved dissemination of public information

4. Proposing changes in legislation, regulations, and agency procedures to improve IT practices, including changes that improve the ability of the agency to use technology to reduce burden

5. Assuming responsibility for maximizing the value and assessing and managing the risks of major information systems initiatives through a process that is both (1) integrated with budget, financial, and program management decisions and (2) used to select, control, and evaluate the results of major information systems initiatives.

OMB governmentwide guidance on the implementation of the PRA and related policies is provided in Circular A-130.[12] Appendices address federal agency responsibilities for maintaining records about individuals; cost accounting, cost recovery, and interagency sharing of IT facilities; the security of federal automated information resources; and important key sections of the circular.

✍ *Computer Security Act*

Recognizing the increasing use of computers by federal agencies and the vulnerability of computer-stored information, including personal information, to unauthorized access, Congress enacted the *Computer Security Act of 1987.*[13] The statute requires each federal agency to develop security plans for its computer systems containing sensitive information. Such plans are subject to review by the National Institute of Standards and Technology (NIST) of the Department of Commerce, and a summary, together with overall budget plans for IT, is filed with OMB. NIST is authorized to set security standards for all federal computer systems except those containing intelligence, cryptologic, or certain military information, or information specifically authorized under criteria established by an executive order or statute to be kept secret in the interest of national defense or foreign policy. The statute also mandates a Computer Systems Security and Privacy Advisory Board within the Department of Commerce to identify emerging managerial, technical, administrative, and physical safeguard issues relative to computer systems security and privacy and to advise NIST and the secretary of commerce on security and privacy issues pertaining to federal computer systems, among other duties. Each federal agency is directed to provide all employees involved with the management, use, or operation of its computer systems with mandatory periodic training in computer security awareness and accepted computer security practice.

✍ *Computer Matching and Privacy Protection Act*

Congress amended the *Privacy Act in 1988* to regulate the use of computer matching—the computerized comparison of records for the purpose of establishing or verifying eligibility for a federal benefit program or for recouping payments or delinquent debts under such programs—conducted by federal agencies or making use of federal records subject to the statute. The amendments were denominated the *Computer Matching and Privacy Protection Act of 1988.*[14] A controversial matter for more than 10 years, computer matching had begun in 1977 at the Department of Health and Human Services. The effort, dubbed Project Match, compared welfare rolls in selected jurisdictions with federal payroll records in the same areas. The controversy surrounding this and similar computerized matches pitted privacy protection advocates, who alleged that personally identifiable data were being used for purposes other than those prompting their collection, against those using the technique to ferret out fraud, abuse, and the overpayment of federal benefits. As the practice subsequently became more widespread, controversy over its use grew.

The amendments regulate the use of computer matching by federal agencies involving personally identifiable records maintained in a system of records subject to the *Privacy Act.* Matches performed for statistical, research, law enforcement, tax, and certain other purposes are not subject to such regulation. For matches to occur, a written matching agreement, effectively creating a matching program, must be prepared specifying such details, explicitly required by the amendments, as the purpose and legal authority for the program; the justification for the program and the anticipated results, including a specific estimate of any savings; a description of the records being matched; procedures for providing individualized notice, at the time of application, to applicants for and recipients of financial assistance or payments under federal benefits programs and to applicants for and holders of positions as federal personnel that any information they provide may be subject to verification through the matching program; procedures for verifying information produced in the matching program; and procedures for the retention, security, and timely destruction of the records matched and for the security of the results of the matching program. Copies of such matching agreements are transmitted to congressional oversight committees and are available to the public upon request. Executive oversight of and guidance for matching programs is vested in the director of OMB. Notice of the establishment or revision of a matching program must be published in the *Federal Register* 30 days in advance of implementation.

The amendments also require every agency conducting or participating in a matching program to establish a Data Integrity Board, composed of senior agency officials, to oversee and coordinate program operations, including the execution of certain specified review, approval, and reporting responsibilities.

Agencies are prohibited from reducing, suspending, or terminating financial assistance to an individual without first verifying the accuracy of computerized data used in the matching program and without first giving the individual thirty days to contest the action.

Electronic Freedom of Information Act Amendments

In 1966, Congress enacted the *Freedom of Information Act*[15] (FOIA) to replace the public information section of the *Administrative Procedure Act* (APA), which was found to be ineffective in providing the public with a means of access to unpublished executive agency records.[16] Subsection (a) of the FOIA reiterates the requirements of the APA public information section that certain operational information (e.g., organization descriptions, delegations of final authority, and substantive rules of general policy) be published in the *Federal Register.*

Subsection (b) statutorily establishes a presumptive right of access by any person— individual or corporate, regardless of nationality—to identifiable, existing, unpublished records of federal agencies without having to demonstrate a need or even a reason for such a request. Subsection (b)(1)-(9) lists nine categories of information that may be exempted from the rule of disclosure. The burden of proof for withholding material sought by the public is placed on the government. Denials of requests may be appealed to the head of the agency holding the sought records and ultimately pursued in federal court.

The FOIA was subsequently amended in 1974, 1976, 1986, and 1996, the last alterations being the Electronic Freedom of Information Amendments (E-FOIA), which, among other modifications, confirm the statute's applicability to records in electronic form or formats, require that responsive materials be provided in the form or format sought by the requester, and mandate so-called electronic reading rooms that the public may access online to examine important and high-interest agency records.[17]

Clinger-Cohen Act

The PRA was modified in 1996 by new procurement reform and IT management legislation, which had originated as two distinct bills that were subsequently combined into a single proposal that was attached to a Department of Defense appropriations authorization act. Division D of the statute was denominated the *Federal*

Acquisition Reform Act of 1996;[18] Division E was titled the *Information Technology Management Reform Act of 1996*.[19] The two divisions were later denominated the *Clinger-Cohen Act* in honor of the House and Senate legislators who had proposed the original bills.[20]

Repealing a section of the *Automatic Data Processing Act*,[21] the *Clinger-Cohen Act* makes each agency responsible for its own IT acquisition and requires the purchase of the best and most cost-effective technology available.[22] It also contains several provisions that either amend or gloss provisions of the PRA of 1995 as set out in chapter 35 of Title 44 of the *United States Code* (U.S.C.).[23] Among the amendments is one establishing a chief information officer (CIO) in each agency, replacing the designated senior official originally mandated by the PRA.[24] The *Clinger-Cohen Act* also prescribes additional duties and qualifications of the CIO.

Other *Clinger-Cohen Act* provisions gloss the responsibilities prescribed in the PRA. The capital planning and investment control duties assigned to the OMB director by the *Clinger-Cohen Act* are to be performed, according to that statute, in fulfilling the director's IT responsibilities.[25] Similarly, the director is to "encourage the use of performance-based and results-based management" in fulfilling these same responsibilities. The *Clinger-Cohen Act* requires agency heads, in fulfilling their counterpart IT responsibilities,[26] to "design and implement . . . a process for maximizing the value and assessing and managing the risks of the information technology acquisitions of the . . . agency" and to perform certain prescribed duties. Also, agency heads identify in a required strategic information resources management plan "any major information technology acquisition program, or any phase or increment of such a program, that has significantly deviated from the cost, performance, or schedule goals established for the program."[27]

E.O. 13011: Federal Information Technology Management

Following the enactment of the PRA of 1995 and the *Clinger-Cohen Act,* President Clinton issued Executive Order (E.O.) 13011 on July 16, 1996, to improve federal IT management and promote a coordinated approach to its application and use across the executive branch.[28] The directive prescribes, as a matter of policy, that executive agencies significantly improve the management of their information systems, including the acquisition of IT, by implementing the relevant provisions of the PRA and the *Clinger-Cohen Act*; refocus IT management to support directly their strategic missions, implement an investment review process that drives budget information and execution for information systems, and rethink and restructure the way they perform their functions before investing in IT to support that work; establish clear accountability for IRM activities by creating agency CIOs with the visibility and management responsibilities necessary to advise agency heads on the design, development, and implementation of those information systems; and cooperate in the use of IT to improve the productivity of federal programs and to provide a coordinated, interoperable, secure, and shared governmentwide infrastructure that is provided and supported by a diversity of private sector suppliers and a well-trained corps of IT professionals. Agencies are also directed to establish an interagency support structure that builds on existing successful interagency efforts and provides expertise and advice to agencies; expand the skill and career development opportunities of IT professionals; improve the management and use of IT within and among agencies by developing IT procedures and standards and by identifying and sharing experiences, ideas, and promising practices; and provide innovative, multidisciplinary, project-specific support to agencies to enhance interoperability, minimize unnecessary duplication of effort, and capitalize on agency successes.

The directive details new responsibilities for agency heads, including effectively using IT to improve mission performance and service to the public. Strengthening the quality of decisions about the employment of information resources to meet mission needs through integrated analysis, planning, budgeting, and evaluation processes, is another duty, which includes the following:

- Determining, before making investments in new information systems, whether the government should be performing the function, if the private sector or another agency should support the function, and if the function needs to be or has been appropriately redesigned to improve its efficiency

- Establishing mission-based performance measures for information systems investments, aligned with agency performance plans prepared pursuant to the *Government Performance and Results Act*[29]

- Establishing agencywide and project-level management structures and processes responsible and accountable for managing, selecting, controlling, and evaluating investments in information systems, with authority for terminating information systems when appropriate

- Supporting appropriate training of personnel

- Seeking the advice of, participating in, and supporting the interagency support structure established elsewhere in the order

Additional responsibilities include selecting CIOs with the experience and skills necessary to accomplish the duties prescribed in existing law and policy and involving these officials in appropriate processes and decisions at the highest level of the agency; ensuring that the information security policies, procedures, and practices of the agency are adequate; structuring, where appropriate and in accordance with the Federal Acquisition Regulation and OMB guidance, major information systems investments into manageable projects as narrow in scope and brief in duration as practicable, consistent with the *Clinger-Cohen Act*; and, to the extent permitted by law, entering into a contract that provides for multiagency acquisitions of IT as an executive agent for the government in accordance with OMB direction.

The interagency support structure created by the directive includes the establishment of a CIO Council, which, during the Clinton administration, served as the principal interagency forum to improve agency practices on such matters as the design, modernization, use, sharing, and performance of agency information resources. The council was tasked with developing recommendations for overall federal IT management policy, procedures, and standards; sharing experiences, ideas, and promising practices, including work process redesign and the development of performance measures to improve the management of information resources; identifying opportunities and making recommendations for, and sponsoring cooperation in, using information resources; assessing and addressing the hiring, training, classification, and professional development needs of the government with respect to IRM; and making recommendations and providing advice to appropriate executive agencies and organizations, including OMB, regarding the governmentwide strategic plan required by the PRA of 1995. Its membership consisted of the CIOs and deputy CIOs of twenty-eight specified entities, two representatives from other agencies and six other designated officials, with the OMB deputy director for management serving as the chair.

The role of the council was, by some estimates, eclipsed somewhat with the June 2001 appointment of former Unisys Corporation vice president Mark Forman as OMB associate director for information technology and e-government. Forman took over the leadership of the council; eliminated its security and e-government subcommittees; and created four portfolio teams reflective of the emphases of the Bush administration's citizen-centric electronic government model, arising from the president's August 2001 management reform agenda. New teams were created for government to citizen, government to business, and intergovernmental transactions, and government process improvement. These changes, particularly the disbanding of the security subcommittee, reportedly engendered some dismay within the council.[30] The *E-Government Act of 2002,* discussed later, mandated a new CIO Council to replace the one established by E.O. 13011.

PDD 63: Critical Infrastructure Protection

Concerned about the vulnerabilities of certain critical national infrastructures—including the telecommunications system—to physical and cyber attack, President Clinton, with E.O. 13010 of July 15, 1996, established the President's Commission on Critical Infrastructure Protection.[31] The temporary study panel was tasked with assessing the scope and nature of the vulnerabilities of, and threats to, critical infrastructures; determining what legal and policy issues are raised by efforts to protect critical infrastructures and assessing how these issues should be addressed; recommending a comprehensive national policy and implementation strategy for protecting critical infrastructures from physical and cyber threats and ensuring their continued operation; and proposing any statutory or regulatory changes necessary to effect its recommendations. The commission produced twelve special topical reports and submitted its final report, offering many recommendations, on October 13, 1997.[32]

On May 22, 1998, the White House issued documents concerning Presidential Decision Directive 63 (PDD 63), a security classified policy instrument on critical infrastructure protection resulting from an interagency evaluation of the recommendations of the president's commission.[33] The directive mandated a national coordinator for security, infrastructure protection, and counterterrorism; a National Infrastructure Protection Center at the Federal Bureau of Investigation, which recently was transferred to the new Department of Homeland Security; a National Infrastructure Assurance Council, composed of private sector experts and state and local government officials, to provide guidance for a national plan for critical infrastructure protection; and a Critical Infrastructure Assurance Office to provide support for the national coordinator's work with government agencies and the private sector in developing a national plan for critical infrastructure protection. The centerpiece of the efforts launched with PDD 63 is a national plan to serve as a blueprint for establishing a critical infrastructure protection capability. Version one, the National Plan for Information Systems Protection, was unveiled on January 7, 2000.[34]

Rehabilitation Act Amendments

Among the 1998 amendments to the *Rehabilitation Act of 1973* adopted by Congress is a new subsection requiring federal agencies to procure, maintain, and use electronic and information technology that provides individuals with disabilities,[35] including both federal employees and members of the public, with accessibility comparable to what is available to individuals without disabilities. The Architectural and Transportation Barriers Compliance Board, known as the Access Board (**http://www.access-board.gov/),** was tasked with developing access standards to implement the new requirement. After some delay, these standards were issued on December 21, 2000, for agency compliance by June 2001.[36]

Government Paperwork Elimination Act

Additional amendments to the PRA were enacted in 1998 as the *Government Paperwork Elimination Act* (GPEA). The GPEA makes the director of OMB responsible for providing governmentwide direction and oversight regarding "the acquisition and use of information technology, including alternative information technologies that provide for electronic submission, maintenance, or disclosure of information as a substitute for paper and for the use and acceptance of electronic signatures."[37] In fulfilling this responsibility, the director, in consultation with the National Telecommunications and Information Administration (NTIA) of the Department of Commerce, is tasked with developing, in accordance with prescribed requirements, procedures for the use and acceptance of electronic signatures by the executive departments and agencies. A five-year deadline is prescribed for the agencies to implement these procedures.[38]

The GPEA tasked OMB's director to "develop procedures to permit private employers to store and file electronically with Executive agencies forms containing information pertaining to the employees of such employers."[39] In addition, the director, in cooperation with NTIA, is to conduct an ongoing study of the use of electronic signatures under the GPEA, with attention to paperwork reduction and electronic commerce, individual privacy, and the security and authenticity of transactions. The results of this study are to be reported periodically to Congress.

Finally, electronic records submitted or maintained in accordance with GPEA procedures, "or electronic signatures or other forms of electronic authentication used in accordance with such procedures, shall not be denied legal effect, validity, or enforceability because such records are in electronic form." The act further specifies

> Except as provided by law, information collected in the provision of electronic signature services for communications with an executive agency . . . shall only be used or disclosed by persons who obtain, collect, or maintain such information as a business or government practice, for the purpose of facilitating such communications, or with the prior affirmative consent of the person about whom the information pertains.[40]

Children's Online Privacy Protection Act

Although the Clinton administration and many members of Congress preferred to rely on industry self-regulation for realizing Internet privacy protection, frustration with the industry's slow response regarding minors led to the enactment of the *Children's Online Privacy Protection Act of 1998* (COPPA) as part of the *Omnibus Consolidated and Emergency Supplemental Appropriations Act,* 1999.[41] The statute requires the operator of a commercial Web site or online service targeted at children under the age of thirteen to provide clear notice of information collection and use practices; to obtain verifiable parental consent prior to collecting, using, and disseminating personal information about children under thirteen; and to provide parents access to their children's personal information and the option to prevent its further use. On October 20, 1999, the Federal Trade Commission issued a final rule to implement the COPPA, which went into effect on April 21, 2000.[42] The statute authorizes the commission to bring enforcement actions and impose civil penalties for violations of the rule in the same manner as for its other rules. A June 22, 2000, Web site privacy memorandum from the OMB director to the heads of executive departments and agencies, discussed later, prescribed, as a matter of policy, compliance with the standards set forth in the COPPA by federal agencies and contractors operating on behalf of agencies.

OMB Memoranda: Federal Web Site Privacy

A June 2, 1999, memorandum from the OMB director to the heads of executive departments and agencies directs the posting of clear privacy policies on federal Web sites and provides guidance for this action. Such policies "must clearly and concisely inform visitors to the site what information the agency collects about individuals, why the agency collects it, and how the agency will use it." Also, they "must be clearly labeled and easily accessed when someone visits a web site," according to the memorandum. Agencies are reminded that, pursuant to the *Privacy Act,* they must protect an individual's right to privacy when they collect personal information.

A June 22, 2000, follow-up memorandum was issued by OMB after press disclosures that the National Drug Control Policy Office, an agency within the Executive Office of the President, was secretly tracking visitors to its Web site through the use of "cookies."[43] Addressing this revelation, it said the following:

> Particular privacy concerns may be raised when uses of web technology can track the activities of users over time and across different web sites. These concerns are especially great where individuals who have come to government web sites do not have clear and conspicuous notice of any such tracking activities. "Cookies"—small bits of software that are placed on a web user's hard drive—are a principal example of current web technology that can be used in this way. The guidance issued on June 2, 1999, provided that agencies could only use "cookies" or other automatic means of collecting information if they gave clear notice of those activities.

Because of the unique laws and traditions about government access to citizens' personal information, the presumption should be that "cookies" will not be used at Federal web sites. Under this new Federal policy, "cookies" should not be used at Federal web sites, or by contractors when operating web sites on behalf of agencies, unless, in addition to clear and conspicuous notice, the following conditions are met: a compelling need to gather the data on the site; appropriate and publicly disclosed privacy safeguards for handling of information derived from "cookies"; and personal approval by the head of the agency. In addition, it is Federal policy that all Federal web sites and contractors when operating on behalf of agencies shall comply with the standards set forth in the *Children's Online Privacy Protection Act of 1998* with respect to the collection of personal information online at web sites directed to children.[44]

Electronic Commerce

The convergence of computer and telecommunications technologies has not only revolutionized the storage, retrieval, and sharing of information but also, in the considered view of many, produced an information economy resulting from commercial transactions on the Internet. The federal government is a participant in e-commerce, and statutes such as the GPEA reflect encouragement of this development.

Among the first initiatives in furtherance of government participation in e-commerce was the Clinton administration's June 15, 1995, unveiling of the U.S. Business Advisor (**http://www.business.gov/**), a new online computer service directly linking the federal government to American business. An upgraded and improved version of the U.S. Business Advisor, providing users with one-stop electronic access to more than sixty federal organizations that assist or regulate businesses, was announced on February 13, 1996.

On July 1, 1997, President Clinton released a report, *A Framework for Global Electronic Commerce,* expressing five operating principles that the administration would follow in fostering e-commerce and designating lead federal agencies in key policy areas.[45] These principles are as follows:

- The private sector should lead.

- Governments should avoid undue restrictions on electronic commerce.

- Where government involvement is needed, its aim should be to support and enforce a predictable minimalist, consistent and simple legal environment for commerce.

- Governments should recognize the unique qualities of the Internet.

- Electronic commerce on the Internet should be facilitated on a global basis.

In his remarks announcing the release of the report, the president indicated he was directing all federal department and agency heads to review the policies of their organization that affect global electronic commerce with a view to ensuring that they are consistent with the five core principles of the report.

In a November 29, 1999, memorandum to the heads of executive departments and agencies, President Clinton directed each federal agency, including independent regulatory agencies, to assist a working group on electronic commerce with identifying any provision of law administered by the agencies, and any regulation issued by them, that may impose a barrier to electronic transactions or otherwise impede the conduct of commerce online or by electronic means. They were also tasked with recommending how such laws or regulations might be revised to allow electronic commerce to proceed while maintaining protection of the public interest.

The heads of executive departments and agencies were informed of Clinton administration efforts to address the so-called digital divide in a December 9, 1999, presidential memorandum. The digital divide is a reference to the perceived disparity that results from portions of the population not having the ability to use IT due to a lack of access, skill, or both. Among the actions directed, the memorandum indicated, were the development of a national strategy for making computers and the Internet accessible to all Americans, expansion of the federal community technology centers network to provide low-income citizens with access to IT, encouragement of the development of IT applications that would help enable low-income citizens to start and manage their own small businesses, and use of training to upgrade the IT skills of the American workforce, particularly workers living in disadvantaged urban and rural communities.

A December 17, 1999, memorandum to the heads of executive departments and agencies directed them, among other actions, to make available online, by December 2000, to the maximum extent possible, the forms needed for the top five hundred government services used by the public; to make transactions with the federal government performable online, with online processing, by October 2003; and to promote the use of electronic commerce, where appropriate, for faster, cheaper ordering on federal procurements.

E-Government Act

In late 2000, the PRA was amended with new government information security requirements.[46] These provisions, due to expire automatically, were subsequently replaced by comparable requirements specified in the *E-Government Act of 2002*.[47] With the exception of national security systems, the director of OMB is responsible for overseeing agency information security policies and practices. Each agency must develop, document, and implement an information security program, approved by the director of OMB, providing security for the information and information systems that support its operations and assets. In addition, each agency, in consultation with the director of OMB, must include in its performance plan required by the *Government Performance and Results Act* a description of the time periods and resources that are necessary to implement its security program.[48] Each agency is required to have an annual independent evaluation of its information security program and practices to determine its effectiveness.

In addition to its security provisions, the *E-Government Act* contains a number of management, privacy, and other innovations. Management developments include establishment of an Office of Electronic Government (OEG) within OMB to promote, coordinate, and plan electronic government services and related information life cycle management. A CIO council and an E-Government Fund are statutorily mandated.[49] In addition to managing the e-government fund, the administrator of general services is tasked with creating and promoting a governmentwide program to encourage contractor innovation and excellence in facilitating the development and enhancement of electronic government services and processes. Among other responsibilities, agencies are to develop performance measures that demonstrate how electronic government enables progress toward their objectives, strategic goals, and statutory mandates. The act prescribes a system of Web sites for the federal courts, as well as their minimal information content, and promotes the use of Web sites, electronic submissions, and electronic docketing by regulatory agencies. Programs for federal IT workforce development and public-private sector IT personnel exchange are also mandated.

ISSUES

Amid this policy environment, IT has been, and continues to be, applied to the performance of federal responsibilities with a view to improving the efficiency and economy of government operations. Although controversy continues over the extent of the so-called digital divide, some progress has been made regarding other issues and concerns.[50] IT infrastructure protection will seemingly receive greater attention as a consequence of the establishment of the Department of Homeland Security (**http://www.dhs.gov/dhspublic/**), which devotes an assistant secretary and half of one of its five principal directorates to this area of responsibility. This arrangement may also help focus congressional oversight regarding this matter.

In addition to continuing important information security policy and practice, the provisions of the *E-Government Act* proffer, among other initiatives, promotion of electronic government services, including increased access, accountability, and transparency in federal judicial, and agency regulatory, processes and procedures; improved organization of, preservation of, and public access to government information provided via the Internet; closer attention to personal privacy protection; and, through E-Government Fund allocations, agency development and implementation of innovative uses of the Internet or other electronic methods to conduct activities electronically. These and other efforts mandated by the *E-Government Act* are now getting underway.

There is, as well, a countercurrent of no small magnitude. The terrorist attacks of September 11, 2001, prompted rethinking about various aspects of the internal security, or homeland security, of the United States. The public availability of information of seemingly potential value to terrorists is one such area of rethinking and continuing concern. The concept of homeland security, although defined in the national strategy for homeland security published in July 2002, provides little policy guidance in the form of criteria for determining the potential value of information to terrorists.[51] Various actions, nonetheless, have been taken since the September 11 attacks to regulate or manage information thought to be of possible value to terrorists. Moreover, it seems likely that further efforts will be made in this regard.

George W. Bush, not quite eight months into his presidency when the attacks occurred, had arrived at the office with his own information management agenda, one that called for a reassessment of operative security classification policy and practice, which was initiated prior to the spectacular terrorist events, and one that probably would have resulted in some modification of *Freedom of Information Act* (FOIA) administration even if the September 11 attacks had not occurred. Before the prevailing security classification arrangements could be overhauled, the President extended such authority to the Secretary of Health and Human Services, the head of the Environmental Protection Agency, and the Secretary of Agriculture as a consequence of the important roles their entities play in preparations to combat biological and chemical terrorism.[52]

The Bush administration's FOIA policy, which undoubtedly was being formulated prior to the terrorist attacks, was issued in a October 12, 2001, memorandum from the attorney general to the heads of all federal departments and agencies.[53] The memorandum appeared to ignore the act's presumptive right of records access and seemed to regard the application of its exemptions to the rule of disclosure to be mandatory rather permissive. The memorandum assured readers that the Department of Justice and "this Administration," in addition to being "committed to full compliance with the *Freedom of Information Act,*" were "equally committed to protecting other fundamental values that are held by our society," including "safeguarding our national security, enhancing the effectiveness of our law enforcement agencies, protecting sensitive business information and, not least, preserving personal privacy." The attorney general encouraged each agency "to carefully consider the protection of all such values and interests when making disclosure determinations under the FOIA." Furthermore, the agencies were told, when "making these decisions, you should consult with the Department of Justice's Office of Information and Privacy when significant FOIA issues arise, as well as with our Civil Division on FOIA litigation matters." Readers were assured that "the Department of Justice will defend your decisions unless they lack a sound legal basis or present an unwarranted risk of adverse impact on the ability of other agencies to protect other important records."

The new policy was not well received by users of the act—journalists and public interest organizations, among others—or by at least one congressional overseer. In its March 2002 version of *A Citizen's Guide on Using the Freedom of Information Act,* the House Committee on Government Reform pointedly noted that "the statute requires Federal agencies to provide the fullest possible disclosure of information to the public." Continuing, it said the following:

> The history of the act reflects that it is a disclosure law. It presumes that requested records will be disclosed, and the agency must make its case for withholding in terms of the act's exemptions to the rule of disclosure. The application of the act's exemptions is generally permissive—to be done if information in the requested records requires protection—not mandatory. Thus, when determining whether a document or set of documents should be withheld under one of the FOIA exemptions, an agency should withhold those documents only in those cases where the agency reasonably foresees that disclosure would be harmful to an interest protected by the exemption. Similarly, when a requestor asks for a set of documents, the agency should release all documents, not a subset or selection of those documents. *Contrary to the instructions issued by the Department of Justice on October 12, 2001, the standard should not be to allow the withholding of information whenever there is merely a "sound legal basis" for doing so.*[54]

It was also in March that a memorandum from White House Chief of Staff Andrew H. Card, Jr., to the heads of executive departments and agencies reminded recipients that they and their entities had "an obligation to safeguard Government records regarding weapons of mass destruction." It was accompanied by guidance from the Information Security Oversight Office and the Justice Department's Office of Information and Privacy, in the words of the Card memo, "for reviewing Government information in your department or agency regarding weapons of mass destruction, as well as other information that could be misused to harm the security of our Nation and the safety of our people." The guidance directed the agencies "to safeguard sensitive but unclassified information related to America's homeland security." Failing to define such information, it disingenuously stated that "the *Freedom of Information Act* recognizes the concept by authorizing agencies to withhold from public disclosure several categories of 'sensitive but unclassified' information." It also advised the agencies to follow the attorney general's October 12, 2001, memorandum "by giving full and careful consideration to all applicable FOIA exemptions" and made certain in a question-and-answer exchange that they understood that the Bush administration wanted them to remove from their Web sites information "regarding weapons of mass destruction, as well as other information that could be misused to harm the security of our Nation and the safety of our people."[55]

Subsequently, two federal entities, the Federal Bureau of Investigation (FBI) and the Office of the Secretary of Defense, issued guidance on Web site information management. In a January 17, 2002, advisory, the FBI, after cautioning the agencies that IT has made it easy for Internet users to retrieve "arcane and seemingly isolated information quickly," posed a series of question in an attempt to aid government officials in evaluating the content of their agencies' Web sites:[56]

1. Has the information been cleared and authorized for public release?

2. Does the information provide details concerning enterprise safety and security? Are there alternative means of delivering sensitive security information to the intended audience?

3. Is any personal data posted (such as biographical data, addresses, etc.)?

4. How could someone intent on causing harm misuse this information?

5. Could this information be dangerous if it were used in conjunction with other publicly available data?

6. Could someone use the information to target your personnel or resources?

7. Many archival sites exist on the Internet, and that information removed from an official site might nevertheless remain publicly available elsewhere.

In a January 2003 message, Secretary of Defense Donald Rumsfeld warned that Department of Defense (DOD) Web sites are likely targets of the nation's enemies, mentioned that 1,500 instances of improper posting of information had occurred over the past year, and reminded subordinate commands of DOD policies on Web site information management. Specific guidance advised:

- Verify that there is a valid mission need to disseminate the information to be posted

- Apply the OPSEC [operations security] review process

- Limit details

- Use the required process for clearing information for public dissemination

- Protect information according to its sensitivity

- Ensure reviewing officials and Webmasters are selected and have received appropriate training in security and release requirements in support of DOD Web policy[57]

Many federal agencies removed, or secured, information on their Web sites in the aftermath of the September 11 attacks. Early examples were the Bureau of Transportation Statistics, which restricted access to its National Transportation Atlas Data Base; the Environmental Protection Agency, which removed from its Web site a database with information on chemicals used at 15,000 industrial sites around the country which had been compiled from risk management plans filed with the agency by industries; and the Nuclear Regulatory Commission, which, after briefly closing its Web site, returned with a "bare bones" version.[58] The Government Printing Office ordered federal depository libraries to destroy a CD-ROM containing government survey data on reservoirs and dams in the United States, and other depository holdings were reportedly under scrutiny for similar action.[59] Because each federal department and agency is responsible for the content of its own Web sites, no one in government knows how much information has been removed from, or restricted at, them.[60]

What more can be expected? One answer to that question may be found in section 892 of the *Homeland Security Act of 2002,* which authorizes the president to prescribe and implement procedures by which relevant federal agencies shall share "homeland security information" with other federal agencies, as well as appropriate state and local government personnel. In so doing, the president is directed to "identify and safeguard homeland security information that is sensitive but unclassified."[61] The statute does not define the "sensitive but unclassified" concept. The section raises a number of questions concerning, among other considerations, information delivery and integrity arrangements, the need for and provision of personnel clearances, the detection and punishment of security breaches, and the associated costs for subnational governments, many of which are already financially challenged.[62] It seems unlikely that such information could be protected from disclosure pursuant to the FOI Act because it does not appear to fall clearly within any of that statute's exemptions.

Elsewhere, in section 208 of the *E-Government Act of 2002,* allowance is made for the modification or waiver of a required privacy impact assessment "for security reasons, or to protect classified, sensitive, or private information contained in an assessment." What constitutes "sensitive" information for this section is not evident because the term is neither defined in the statute nor is its relationship, if any, to the "sensitive but unclassified" information mentioned in section 892 of the *Homeland Security Act* explained. Perhaps the president's information-sharing procedures required by the *Homeland Security Act* will prove to be instructive.

As a result of the terrorist attacks of September 11, federal officials, in furtherance of homeland security, are bringing about a change in the balance between the security and the public availability of government information. However, for a number of reasons—voting responsibly, thinking independently, and acting wisely, among others—citizens need information about issues, government programs and policies, and the activities and decisions of public officials. Less information may make it more difficult for citizens and their surrogates, such as the press and public interest groups, to hold government officials accountable. Members of the public may not know what questions to ask, or, if they are able to identify salient issues, they may not be able to obtain the details they need. Nonetheless, these are two benefits—accountability and accessible information—that citizens expect to reap from electronic government. A Hart-Teeter nationwide poll of adults in November 2001, conducted for the Council for Excellence in Government, found that, when asked to name the most important benefit of e-government, 30 percent of the respondents chose accountability and 17 percent selected greater access to information. The remaining respondents chose convenient services (15 percent) and cost-effectiveness (14 percent).[63]

The Council for Excellence in Government is among those who have hailed electronic government as a means to transform government. "Electronic government can fundamentally recast the connection between people and their government. It can make government far more responsive to the will of the people and greatly improve transactions between them. It can also help all of us to take a much more active part in the democratic process."[64]

The removal, or withholding, of what was once considered public information from agency Web sites may thwart the promise of e-government, however. In the aftermath of September 11, the situation may increasingly become one of relative deprivation: expectations may be higher than what agency Web sites are delivering to the public. Although the focus of e-government prior to September 11 was customer service, now it appears to be security.

In early 2002, the Bush administration overhauled the government's portal, *FirstGov,* and released a report, *E-Government Strategy,* recounting the goals of the president's expanding e-government initiative:

- Make it easy for citizens to obtain service and interact with the federal government

- Improve government efficiency and effectiveness

- Improve government's responsiveness to citizens[65]

Work began on the strategy in early August 2001 with the launching of the E-Government Task Force. The report presents a vision and a strategy for e-government; identifies problems that have prevented government from fully realizing the potential of e-government; provides the task force's approach and findings; and discusses recommendations and an implementation strategy. Released before the terrorist attacks, naturally no mention is made of the concerns that have arisen subsequently about the dissemination of public information on agency Web sites, agency efforts to protect information, or the affect such actions might have on the administration's vision for e-government. By publicly presenting two views of e-government—as an avenue to potentially compromising information and as a key means for improving customer service for citizens—the administration is certainly delivering a mixed message. What kind of e-government lies ahead is not the model envisioned by many prior to September 2001.

SUMMARY

Within a brief period of time—largely, the final decade of the twentieth century—the application of new IT to the performance of federal responsibilities, with a view to improving the efficiency and economy of government operations, produced e-government. A few months into the next century, terrorist attacks on the United States prompted rethinking about various aspects of the nation's security. The public availability of information of potential value to terrorists is one such area of rethinking and continuing concern. Information restrictions in furtherance of homeland security have been propounded, thwarting the promise of e-government. Uncertainty prevails regarding the model that will result. The value of that model, however, sweeps beyond efficiency and economy considerations and must ultimately be assessed in terms of self-government: better serving the citizenry and thereby maintaining the continued faith of the American people in their form of government, as guaranteed by the Constitution.

NOTES

1. See Harold C. Relyea and Henry B. Hogue, "A Brief History of the Emergence of Digital Government in the United States," in *Digital Government: Principles and Best Practices,* eds. Alexei Pavlichev and G. David Garson (Hershey, PA: Idea Group Press, 2003): in press.

2. William M. Capron, "The Executive Branch in the Year 2000," in *The Future of the U.S. Government: Toward the Year 2000,* ed. Harvey S. Perloff (New York: George Braziller, 1971): 307.

3. John Brademus, "Congress in the Year 2000," in *The Future of the U.S. Government,* 319–21.

4. Herbert N. Casson, *The History of the Telephone* (Chicago: A. C. McClurg, 1910): 201–202.

5. Ibid., 203.

6. 88 Stat. 1896; 5 U.S.C. 552a.

7. 5 U.S.C. 552a(e)(7).

8. 94 Stat. 2812; 44 U.S.C. 3501 *et seq.*

9. 100 Stat. 3341-336.

10. 109 Stat. 165-166.

11. See David Plocher, "The Paperwork Reduction Act of 1995: A Second Chance for Information Resources Management," *Government Information Quarterly* 13 (1996): 35–50.

12. See *Federal Register* 61 (February 20, 1996): 6428–53.

13. 101 Stat. 1724.

14. 102 Stat. 2507.

15. 80 Stat. 250; 5 U.S.C. 552.

16. 60 Stat. 237.

17. 110 Stat. 3048; 5 U.S.C. 552.

18. 110 Stat. 642.

19. 110 Stat. 679.

20. 110 Stat. 3009-393; the sponsors were Representative William F. Clinger, Jr. (R-PA) and Senator William S. Cohen (R-ME).

21. 79 Stat. 1127.

22. 110 Stat. 186.

23. *The Clinger-Cohen Act* provision (110 Stat. 680) repealed a section (40 U.S.C. 759) that had been appended to the *Federal Property and Administrative Services Act* by the *Automatic Data Processing Act,* which is popularly known as the *Brooks Act*; the repealed provision authorized the administrator of general services to coordinate and provide for the procurement, maintenance, and utilization of federal automatic data processing equipment.

24. 44 U.S.C. 3506.

25. See 44 U.S.C. 3504(h).

26. See 44 U.S.C. 3506(h).

27. 44 U.S.C. 3506(b)(2).

28. 3 *C.F.R.*, 1996 Comp., 202–209.

29. 107 Stat. 285; 31 U.S.C. 115 note.

30. Karen Robb, "Council Shake-Up Startles CIOs," *Federal Times* (October 1, 2001): 4, 18; Thomas R. Temin, "CIO Council Gets New Look, New Direction," *Government Computer News* 20 (October 22, 2001): 10.

31. 3 *C.F.R.*, 1996 Comp., 198–202; according to E.O. 13010, a "cyber" attack involves "electronic, radio-frequency, or computer-based attacks on the information or communications components that control critical infrastructures."

32. President's Commission on Critical Infrastructure Protection, *Critical Foundations: Protecting America's Infrastructures* (Washington, D.C.: Government Printing Office, 1997).

33. A fact sheet, a white paper, and a press briefing transcript on PDD 63 were initially provided by the White House; the full text of PDD 63 is now available at **http://www.fas.org/ irp/ offdocs/pdd/pdd-63.htm**.

34. The full text and executive summary of the national plan are available from the Critical Infrastructure Assurance Office Web site at **http://www.ciao.gov** in the "CIAO Document Library."

35. The *Rehabilitation Act* Amendments of 1998 constituted Title IV of the Workforce Investment Act of 1998, 112 Stat. 936; the electronic and information technology access requirement was appended to the Rehabilitation Act as section 508, 112 Stat 1203, at 29 U.S.C. 794(d); the Rehabilitation Act was originally enacted in 1973, 87 Stat. 355, at 29 U.S.C. 701 *et seq.*

36. Associated Press, Guidelines to Force Federal Agencies to Redesign Web Sites," *Washington Times,* 22 December 2000, p. A5.

37. 44 U.S.C. 3504(a)(1)(B)(vi), as amended.

38. The final version of OMB procedures and guidance for implementing the GPEA was published in *Federal Register* 65 (May 2, 2000): 25508–21, and a memorandum on the preparation and submission of agency plans to implement the statute was issued on July 25.

39. 112 Stat. 2681-750.

40. 112 Stat. 2681-751.

41. 112 Stat. 2681-728; 15 U.S.C. 6501-6506.

42. Federal Register 64 (November 3, 1999): 59888–915.

43. See John F. Harris and John Schwartz, "Anti-Drug Web Site Tracks Visitors," *Washington Post*, 22 June 2000, p. A23; Lance Gay, "White House Uses Drug-Message Site to Track Inquiries," *Washington Times,* 21 June 2000, p. A3.

44. For critique of the OMB memorandum, see Walter R. Houser, "OMB Cookie Memo Crumbles under Its Own Weight," *Government Computer News* 19 (July 24, 2000): 21 and "As It's Written, OMB Policy on Cookies Is Half-baked," *Government Computer News* 19 (November 6, 2000): 27.

45. President's Information Infrastructure Task Force, *A Framework for Global Electronic Commerce* (Washington, D.C.: July 1, 1997). Available from the National Institute of Standards and Technology Web site: **http://www.iitf.nist.gov/eleccomm/ecomm.htm**.

46. 114 Stat. 1654, 1654A-266.

47. The 2000 information security amendments to the PRA were initially replaced by Title X of the *Homeland Security Act,* signed into law on November 25, 2002 (116 Stat. 2135), but these modifications were subsequently superseded by Title III of the *E-Government Act,* signed into law on December 17, 2002 (116 Stat. 2899).

48. The performance plan requirement may be found at 31 U.S.C. 1115.

49. These entities replace the CIO Council established by E.O. 13011 and the e-gov fund proposed by President Bush in his February 2001 *Blueprint for New Beginnings: A Responsible Budget for America's Priorities* (Washington: GPO, 2001), which was realized in the *Treasury and General Government Appropriations Act,* 2002 (115 Stat. 537). The lack of a statutory authorization for the e-gov fund had been a concern of both congressional appropriations committees.

50. See Ariana Eunjung Cha, " 'Digital Divide' Less Clear," *Washington Post,* 29 June 2002, pp. E1–E2.

51. See U.S. Office of Homeland Security, *National Strategy for Homeland Security* (Washington: July 2002): 2, where the following is stated: "Homeland security is a concerted national effort to prevent terrorist attacks within the United States, reduce America's vulnerability to terrorism, and minimize the damage and recover from attacks that do occur."

52. See Alison Mitchell, "Classified Information: Bush Gives Secrecy Power to Public Health Secretary," *New York Times* (December 20, 2001): B6; *Federal Register* 66 (December 12, 2001): 64347; Ibid., 67 (May 9, 2002): 31109; Ibid., 67 (September 30, 2002): 61465.

53. U.S. Department of Justice, Office of the Attorney General, "The Freedom of Information Act," Memorandum for the Heads of All Federal Departments and Agencies, October 12, 2001, Washington, DC. Available: **http://www.usdoj.gov/04foia/011012.htm**.

54. U.S. Congress, House Committee on Government Reform, *A Citizen's Guide on Using the Freedom of Information Act and the Privacy Act of 1974 to Request Government Records,* 107th Congress, 2nd session, H. Rept. 107-371 (Washington, D.C.: Government Printing Office , 2002): 3 (emphasis added).

55. White House Office, Chief of Staff, "Action to Safeguard Information Regarding Weapons of Mass Destruction and Other Sensitive Documents Related to Homeland Security," Memorandum for the Heads of Executive Departments and Agencies, March 19, 2002, Washington, D.C., accompanied by Information Security Oversight Office and Department of Justice, Office of Information and Privacy, "Safeguarding Information Regarding Weapons of Mass Destruction and Other Sensitive Records Related to Homeland Security," Memorandum for Departments and Agencies, undated, Washington, D.C. Available: **http://www.usdoj.gov/oip/foiapost/2002foiapost10.htm**. The version available at this Web site does not include the question-and-answer clarifications accompanying the original documents.

56. U.S. Department of Justice, Federal Bureau of Investigation, National Infrastructure Protection Center, *Internet Content Advisory: Considering the Unintended Audience,* Advisory 02-001 (Washington, D.C., January 17, 2002) Available: **http://www. nipc.gov/ warnings/advisories/2002/02-OOI.htm**.

57. U.S. Department of Defense, Office of the Secretary, "Web Site OPSEC Discrepancies," message to subordinate commands (Washington, D.C., January 14, 2003).

58. Guy Gugliotta, "Agencies Scrub Web Sites of Sensitive Chemical Data," *Washington Post,* 4 October 2001, p. A29; Robin Toner, "Reconsidering Security, U.S. Clamps Down on Agency Web Sites," *New York Times,* 28 October 2001, p. B4.

59. Eric Lichtblau, "Response to Terror; Rising Fears That What We Do Can Hurt Us," *Los Angeles Times,* 18 November 2001, part A, part 1, p. 1; also see Saragail Runyon Lynch, "GPO Recalls of Depository Documents," *Journal of Government Information* 22 (January–February 1995): 23–31.

60. For a public interest group assessment, see OMB Watch, *The Post-September 11 Environment: Access to Government Information* (Washington, D.C., undated). Available: **http://www.ombwatch.org/article/articleprint/213/-1/104**.

61. 116 Stat. 2135 at 2253.

62. Among available criminal punishment authorities is 18 U.S.C. 641 governing stolen or misappropriated government property or records.

63. Council for Excellence in Government, *E-Government: To Connect, Protect, and Serve Us*, (Washington, D.C., undated; released February 26, 2002). Available: **http://www.excelgov.org/techcon/0225poll**.

64. Council for Excellence in Government, *E-Government, The Next American Revolution,* (Washington, D.C., undated): 2 (released September 28, 2000). Available: **http://www.excelgov.org/egovpoll/lindex.htm**.

65. U.S. Office of Management and Budget, Associate Director for Information Technology and E-Government, *E-Government Strategy* (Washington: February 27, 2002): 1. Available: **http://www.whitehouse.gov/omb/inforeg/egovstrategy**

Architectural and Transportation Barriers Compliance Board
http://www.access-board.gov/

Chief Information Officers Council
http://www.cio.gov/

Council for Excellence in Government
http://www.excelgov.org/

Critical Infrastructure Assurance Office

Department of Homeland Security
http://www.ciao.gov/

Department of Homeland Security
http://www.dhs.gov/dhspublic/

Department of Justice

Office of the Attorney General
http://www.usdoj.gov/

FirstGov
http://www.firstgov.gov/

General Accounting Office
http://www.gao.gov/

National Institute of Standards and Technology

Department of Commerce
http://www.nist.gov/

Office of Management and Budget
http://www.whitehouse.gov/omb/

OMB Watch
http://www.ombwatch.org/

U.S. Business Advisor
http://www.business.gov/

Chapter  15

Web Browser Hardware and Software

Most Web sites of the federal government use the hypertext markup language (HTML) to display text because Web browsers can conveniently and easily read it. As the sophistication of government Web sites increases, however, the information formats that the three branches make available digitally increasingly incorporate a variety of text and data table formats, sounds, images, and motion. The capability of someone surfing the Web to view this information successfully depends on the hardware and software installed.

This chapter is not a primer on personal computer workstations. There are literally hundreds of books from which to learn about every general and minute aspect concerning computer workstations. Instead, the chapter reviews the basic technical needs for successful navigation of the majority of government Web sites discussed in this book. Three assumptions, however, are that the reader

- Has some familiarity with connecting to the Internet

- Knows that a "Web browser" is used to navigate the Web and preferably has used one

- Understands the basics of using the operating system on a personal computer workstation (e.g., opening and saving changes to a file)

HARDWARE

Although the maxim of "identify software needs and then choose the hardware needed to run the software" is true, this chapter introduces hardware first. On the Web, it is also true that without the appropriate hardware, a person will not be able to run the software needed to navigate the more sophisticated government Web sites. For the purposes of this chapter, the term *computer workstation* refers to the physical computer case that encloses the system bus and its necessary components, such as random access memory (RAM) and static storage device(s), and the attached monitor, modem, and printer. A computer workstation can be located at home, at a person's place of employment, or somewhere else, such as a library. As everyone knows, computer hardware seems to improve weekly, and the cost of acquiring it decreases monthly. It is impossible to put a suggested configuration in writing without it being out of date by the time the work it appears in print. Therefore, the following only identifies the most important hardware components and discusses the desired characteristics.

- Processor (this is the computer itself, the central processing unit): The general rule is to buy the fastest-processing computer that one can afford. As of 2003, that means an Intel Pentium 4 or equivalent for Microsoft Windows users. Budget-conscious users may also consider Intel's Celeron processors. For Apple Computer users, a PowerPC G4, available on either the popular iMac desktop workstation or the Power Mac G4, is the desired advanced processor. Processor speed is indicated in megahertz (MHz); usually, the higher the speed, the faster the processor, a desirable characteristic.

- RAM: The computer and software use RAM to run applications, and therefore the more RAM that someone has, generally the better the performance. Most computer crashes are a result of "running out of memory"; the more RAM, the less likely that the surfer will have frequent crashes. RAM is inexpensive. The minimum recommended amount is 128 megabytes. The more RAM that is installed, the "faster" the computer will appear to run. This is not because the processor is actually faster; its speed, measured in megahertz, has not changed. The computer processor actually uses RAM to store information. RAM is faster than a hard drive; the more RAM available to the processor, the more programming is stored in RAM, and the result is a seemingly faster processor. The maximum recommendation is 256 megabytes, however; additional performance concerning U.S. government Web pages is incremental above 256 megabytes of installed RAM.

- System bus (the "board" on which the processor, RAM, and other input-output devices are attached): The bus speed (also known as front side bus or FSB) is responsible for the speed at which the aforementioned parts of the computer communicate with each other. The 133-MHz system bus has become a widely available standard, resulting in faster and more efficient workstations. FSB speeds of 400 MHz and 533 MHz are increasingly available. In addition, the system bus expansion capability, the ability to add more devices using slots or connections, is an important consideration for upgrading any computer workstation in the near future. A desktop workstation should give its user expansion possibilities, including PCI- (peripheral component interconnect) and AGP- (accelerated graphics port) specific slots on which to add devices, and one or more shared slots. All computers need at least one USB (universal serial bus) or FireWire (sometimes referred to as a "1394") connection. Some workstations now include both.

- Display (the computer's monitor): Bigger is not always better—the monitor may not fit on the furniture, and too big a screen may increase eye strain. Users may need to upgrade their monitor less frequently than the computer processor if they buy a good screen to start with. A seventeen-inch monitor with at least sixteen inches of viewable area is adequate for Web surfing and graphics. The monitor should be able to display a minimum pixel resolution of at least 800 by 600, displaying millions of colors (sometimes referred to as "high" and "true" colors). The standard resolution is 1,024 by 768. Screen sharpness is measured in dot pitch—the smaller the dot pitch, the sharper the resolution. The maximum dot pitch should be .28 mm; a .26-mm dot pitch yields exceptional resolution. "Flat panel" monitors are available, and their cost has decreased significantly, although they are not as cheap as standard monitors. Furthermore, a monitor with built-in audio speakers is not recommended—the sound from these speakers is not as good as that produced by separate speakers.

- Hard drive (the computer's primary static storage device): The hard drive stores applications, such as word processors and other software, and files that a person creates and downloads. Again, as with the computer processor, buy as large a capacity drive as is affordable. Forty gigabyte hard drives are fairly common and cost less than $100; most desirable is an "Ultra ATA" (which is an IDE interface) with a minimum of 5,400 rotations per minute (rpm); 7,200 rpm is even better because the faster the drive spins, the faster the computer applications will run.

- Graphics accelerator: Although many computers have built-in graphics capability, the computer user may also purchase an AGP-based graphics accelerator card to boost performance. Desirable characteristics include a minimum of 32 megabytes of RAM and the ability to handle three-dimensional (3D) images.

- Sound cards and speakers: A good sound card can be "tweaked" using software in much the same way that a person "balances" a stereo system. As with stereo systems, the better the speakers, the better the sound output. A set of stereo speakers enhances the sound files that a surfer encounters on Web sites. There is no need to spend a great deal; there are many adequate to good sets of speakers for computer workstations that cost less than $50 a set.

- CD-ROM or DVD-ROM drive: This is a necessity for any computer system. Most software is now distributed on CD-ROM. The DVD drives and their backward capability to use CD-ROM discs make them the preferred drive format. Consider a read-writable DVD drive for any new computer.

- Printer (another necessary system component): Printers are inexpensive. All users will want one that can also print color graphics when exploring federal government Web sites. Printers vary widely; the two best measures of quality are "dots-per-inch" (dpi) and "page-per-minute" (ppm) output. A minimally configured printer yields 600 by 600 dpi black text at 10 to 12 ppm; color at 6 ppm. Most of the costs concerning printers are in maintaining them; toner and ink cartridges for printers are expensive compared with the acquisition cost of the printer itself. Prices of laser printers are decreasing; however, the costs, quality, and speed of color ink jet printers make them the better buy for normal use at this time.

- Modem (the device used to connect the computer workstation to the Internet, most often through an Internet service provider [ISP], such as America Online) or network interface card (NIC): Unless a workstation is on a local area network, a user will employ a modem (telephone, cable, or digital subscriber service

[DSL]) and subscribe with an ISP to connect the computer workstation to the Internet. As of 2003, the 56K baud modem using the V.92 specification remains the fastest telephone modem available. If the user has coaxial cable for the home television, cable TV providers may support the use of broadband cable modems to provide access to the Internet. Cable modems can operate at speeds fifty times faster than telephone modems, and people can still watch cable TV while surfing the Web. Furthermore, a cable modem does not use a telephone line. Cable modems and cable modem services are more expensive than most ISP services based on the use of telephone modems. Users may want to install DSL (digital subscriber line) services, which may use their existing telephone lines to connect to the Internet; DSL modems are oftentimes slower than cable TV modems but are faster than standard telephone modems. DSL uses the same telephone wire to connect to the Internet while simultaneously using the telephone for normal voice communications. Both coaxial cable and DSL modems connect to the workstation's NIC using Category 5 Ethernet cabling with RJ-45 ends; a workstation may have an integrated NIC, or an NIC can be purchased and easily installed onto the computer's system bus. A 10/100 megabit per second (Mbps) "Fast Ethernet" NIC is common; a 10/1000 Mbps NIC using the newer "Gigabit Ethernet" link protocol is also available for a few more dollars. Broadband Internet access using a satellite connection is available for home installation (see DIRECWAY; **http://directv.direcway.com**).

WEB BROWSER BASICS

The computer workstation may have various software, such as word processing, spreadsheet, and other applications. To view U.S. government information on the Web, the user will need a Web browser such as Microsoft's Internet Explorer (IE) or Netscape Communicator or Navigator. A Web browser uses a special protocol (hypertext transport protocol; HTTP) to request a specially encoded text document from a Web server. The text document contains special instructions (written in HTML) that inform the browser how to display the document and its contents on the user's monitor. In 2002, Microsoft Internet Explorer was the preferred browser of more than 90 percent of Web users.

Web browsers allow the user to view HTML and other file formats as configured by the browser itself and by the user. Everyone should run the most recent version of the browser because its capabilities are constantly evolving. For example, Microsoft Internet Explorer can be configured to resize images automatically to fit within the browser's window on the monitor, thereby eliminating the need for scrolling to view the entire image. Web browsers can be configured to meet individual needs. To view government Web sites effectively and take advantage of the information content, the Web browser, at a minimum, should be configured to

- Enable Java, which is a popular language used by Web developers to run applications

- Enable frames or tables, which is an HTML-scripted presentation mode that many Web sites use to present information and assist in navigating the site

- Accept cookies, which the government uses as a Web management tool. Under-standing the "whys" and "whats" of cookies is beyond the scope of this chapter. Briefly, a cookie is a small piece of information sent by a Web server to store on a Web browser so it can later be read back from that browser. This can be useful because it allows the Web browser to remember specific information from a fre-quently visited Web site. Examples of cookies in use include a browser storing passwords and user identification numbers for online ordering systems such as Amazon.com (**http://www.amazon.com**). In June 2000, the Office of Manage-ment and Budget advised all federal agencies via memorandum that they were not allowed to use persistent cookies without approval from the agency head.[1] Although federal agency Web sites have tended to cease requiring cookies, many other nongovernmental Web sites require cookies, and individuals may find it inconvenient to have to turn cookies on and off when using their Web browsers (see Chapter 1).

Oftentimes a Web browser has enabled all of the above needs as part of its default configuration. The Web user may choose to turn any or all of these functions off (please refer to the browser's help function to determine the status of these functions).

Let us assume that the browser is minimally configured as suggested above and a connection to the World Wide Web has been made. Now, let us review some basic ac-tivities that users may want to do while traveling through the Web sites discussed in previous chapters. Surfing to a Web site is straightforward. Type in the *u*niform *r*esource *l*ocator (URL) in the "Location," "URL," "Go To," or "Address" text bar found near the top of the screen on Microsoft Internet Explorer or Netscape. Press the "Enter" key on the computer's keyboard; the Web browser connects to the site's Web server, and the page appears. URLs, also known as Web "addresses" and "links," are well known; they oftentimes appear in com-mercial ads in the media, oftentimes as "**http://www.something.com**." Spelling and punctu-ation are important when typing a URL Web address; the URL must be typed exactly. If typed incorrectly, the Web surfer may fail to connect to the Web site (and will receive an er-ror message that the site could not be found) or may end up connecting to an undesired or un-known Web site. The most basic document on the Web is a "Web page." It is a single document that can be viewed without linking to any other document. Characteristically, the Web page has a unique Web address, known as the URL, which oftentimes ends with the ex-tension ".htm" or ".html." Other extensions include ".pdf," ".asp," ".shtml," and ".cfm." A URL or a Web document with the extension ".htm" in the URL refers to an HTML docu-ment, most likely residing on a Web server using a Microsoft Windows operating system. A document with an extension ".html" also refers to an HTML document, most likely residing on a Unix server. Unix is another popular computer operating system that predates the devel-opment of the Windows operating system by Microsoft.

As discussed in Chapter 1, a "Web presentation" is a collection of Web pages de-signed to be linked to each other to convey an idea(s), product(s), or service(s). Web page designers employ numerous Web pages in a presentation instead of a single page in order to facilitate navigation between and among Web pages, and to reduce the time necessary for the viewer to download each page onto the local computer from the Web. A "Web site" may be one Web presentation, or a collection of two or more Web pre-sentations. There may be little, if any, contextual relationship of the Web presentations among and between each other. Or a Web site may include two or more Web presenta-tions that depend on each other for content and context.

A Web site is usually a destination (e.g., **http://www.whitehouse.gov/**) and is anchored by the site's "home page." A home page is the Web designer's preferred starting point for a Web site. It oftentimes serves as the organizing page, like an electronic table of contents, and as the start of the site's navigational buttons linking the home page to one or more Web pages in one or more Web presentations.

Printing Web pages is easy. Once the browser is on the page wanted, one can click on the printer icon that is usually located at the top of the screen for both Microsoft Internet Explorer and Netscape browsers. If the icon is not there, it may have been turned off during configuration. Either turn the icon or task bar on again or go to "File" and use the drop-down menu to print. If the print icon is visible but "faded," then the user has not clicked the mouse button in the correct Web page frame. Put the mouse cursor over the part of the screen to print, and click the left mouse button once. The printer icon should be activated and will no longer be "visible but faded." The page can now be printed by clicking on the printer icon button. Be forewarned that some Web pages are quite lengthy. It is nearly impossible to know how many printed pages the Web page will generate just by looking at it.

Surfers may come across a photograph or other image on the Web that they would like to save. To do so, place the mouse cursor over the image to save. Then, click the right mouse button (hold down the mouse button on a Macintosh). A menu appears. Highlight "save picture as" (or "save image as" if using Netscape) and click once. The operating system will respond and offer an area on the hard or floppy drive as a default for saving the image file. Accept or change the disk area to save the file, change the file name if desired, and then click "OK." The image's file will be saved under the name designated to the area of the hard or floppy drive identified.

Web surfers may also save text or other files, such as application software, through the Web browser. These files are often "downloaded" from the Web site to the hard drive through a process monitored by the workstation's operating system. Fortunately, most Web sites are designed to make the downloading process straightforward and user-friendly. Software is not downloaded to the hard drive unless the user agrees and has approved of the file name and the storage location. Many Web sites also provide instructions on how to install the software and offer helpful hints to troubleshoot problems.

In some cases, the file downloaded is formatted into a vendor-specific document format (e.g., Microsoft Excel or Corel's WordPerfect). If the user does not have the vendor-specific application software on his or her computer workstation, the downloaded file may be unreadable. In some instances, a vendor has created a viewer that allows users at least to read, if not edit, a specifically formatted file. For example, Microsoft makes a viewer available from its Web site (**http://www.microsoft.com/**), which allows users to read a Microsoft Word file (a word processor) or view a PowerPoint presentation even if they do not own the application software.

Viewers

Much of what users see on a Web page appears through HTML, but there are other information formats used on the Web sites that require additional programs, oftentimes referred to as "viewers," "players," and "plugins." Viewers extend the functionality of the Web browser to present information, often adding value to the Web site visit. For instance, most photographs that appear on a Web page are formatted as ".jpg" (usually pronounced "j-peg"). The dot in ".jpg" signifies a file extension, with the name of the file preceding the dot. Therefore, "mars.jpg" is the filename "mars" with a .jpg extension. The extension names are important; they have meaning to the computer workstation's Web browser and operating system. When the computer's Web browser sees the ".jpg" extension, the browser and operating system use application software associated with that extension to execute the format. Most Web browsers are configured to display the .jpg as a photograph within the browser window as part of the default configuration. Another popular image format is a ".gif" (pronounced "jiff"), used most often for drawings and other line graphics. Again, most browsers can internally interpret the .gif and display it within the browser window. As a result, users will not have to do anything with the browser's configuration in order to see a .jpg or .gif.

Most U.S. government Web sites use HTML (as an extension of either ".htm" or .html") for text and .jpg and .gif for images. This is the most basic Web presentation and the most user-friendly because the Web site visitor has to do very little to see and, if so desired, save the information presented. Much information content can be conveyed to users with these file types, and these types comprise the majority of information on the Web sites. U.S. government Web sites also make information available in file formats that require additional software for the browser to interpret the content correctly. Such file formats require the Web browser to acquire and install a "viewer." As an example, many U.S. government Web sites use Adobe's portable document format (.pdf) to display some of their text files. Why would a Web site use the .pdf format over the .htm format? Text displayed in .pdf format appears as it would if photocopied— it is the image of the text rather than just the words of the text. Therefore, a .pdf format enriches the information content by presenting it as originally published. That may include graphics, such as charts, without the need to convert them into a .gif format, as would be the case if the text appeared in HTML format.

Unfortunately, neither Microsoft Internet Explorer nor Netscape browsers can display .pdf files without the Adobe Acrobat Reader, application software that enables users to see a .pdf formatted file. The Adobe Acrobat Reader can be downloaded without cost from Adobe's Web site (**http://www.adobe.com/**); it can then be installed so that the browser recognizes it as a viewer. Then, whenever a .pdf file is requested by the user to be viewed through the browser, the browser recognizes the request as a command to load the Adobe Acrobat Reader software and execute the .pdf file so that it can be read on the computer screen.

U.S. government Web sites are always improving and enriching their information content; the ability to use the content depends on the installed viewers within the Web browser. How do users know when a viewer is needed and where to find it? A viewer program is needed when users try to see (or hear) a file and the browser informs them via a message box that a software application program must be downloaded, the information requested does not appear at all, or it does not appear correct. A browser "wizard," which is an automated online help guide, may provide users with valuable assistance in locating, downloading, installing, and implementing the needed viewer.

To comply with Section 508 of the *Rehabilitation Act of 1973,* as Amended, 36 CFR Part 1194.22(m), federal Web page administrators, designers, or owners will recommend a specific viewer to use with their content and provide a link to a site from which to download the necessary or recommended software. Viewers are most often developed by third-party vendors; oftentimes, they are available through their Web sites at no cost (freeware) or at a cost (shareware or at a stated acquisition cost). In addition to commercial vendors, viewers are sometimes developed and distributed by individuals as freeware or shareware.

In addition, Microsoft Internet Explorer users may visit the Microsoft Web site (**http://www.microsoft.com/**) and use the site's search capability to identify viewers. Netscape users can visit the Web site (**http://www.netscape.com/**) and review the latest plugins for downloading material. Because both Microsoft and Netscape are selective about the viewers available on their Web sites, a third means by which to find viewers is to start with a Web search directory or engine such as Yahoo! (**http://www.yahoo.com**) or Google (**http://www.google.com**). Using the search text bar, type in the desired viewer, such as a "browser movie viewer." The search engine will provide a result list to use. Although this may not be the best way to find viewers, it will likely locate viewers unknown to Microsoft or Netscape or excluded from their Web sites because of agreements with other viewer developers.

Another methodology is to consult an organized list of viewers. The online version of *PC World* (**http://www.pcworld.com/downloads/index/0,00.asp**) magazine lists viewers and other Internet tools that will enhance a browser. ZDNet (**http://downloads-zdnet.com.com/**) is another popular and well-done site that provides downloadable viewers.

In some cases, the browser user will want to visit a viewer developer's Web site to learn about a recommended viewer. Most developers, such as Adobe (Adobe Acrobat Reader at **http://www.adobe.com/**), Macromedia (makers of Shockwave and Flash Player at **http://www.macromedia.com/**), and Apple Computer (QuickTime at **http://www.apple.com/**) maintain informative and easy-to-use Web sites. The developers frequently encourage users to register with them to learn about viewer upgrades through e-mail. Some developers require registration before users may download a viewer.

File Formats

Federal government Web sites require a variety of viewers based on their file requirements. Many of these Web sites offer information content in text, sound, motion, or animation that require third-party viewers not built into either Microsoft Internet Explorer or Netscape. If a viewer is required, the government Web site usually informs the user which viewer is recommended or needed.

Different U.S. government Web sites may recommend different viewers for the same file extension, such as a .wav file. The government does not have a governmentwide recommendation for each type of viewer; such a recommendation is left to each agency. One viewer may handle a multiplicity of file formats (extensions), and a multiplicity of viewers may read a single file extension. A browser can associate only one file extension with one viewer at a time, however. If someone is trying to run a viewer with a particular file format and it does not work, the browser may be using a different viewer than the one recommended by the government site. As a general rule, the browser recognizes (associates) the latest viewer installed over a previously installed viewer. To determine which file extensions are associated with installed viewers, users should review information from their operating system. The review process can be queried through the operating system's online help guides installed on the workstation.

U.S. GOVERNMENT WEB SITES

Over the past five years, costs for personal computer workstations have declined while their processing power has increased, hardware (e.g., sound and monitors) has improved, and new and upgraded software has become generally available. In addition, operating systems (Windows XP and Apple's OS X) have become easier to install and use. Federal government Web sites experiment with, and continue to alter, their page design and Web site usability to take advantage of the improvements in hardware and software. The goal is to expand the resources available to the public and to encourage them to use government information and services.

Web Page Design and Appearance

No page design standards currently apply to federal government Web sites. As a result, these Web sites tend to divide into two general design camps, "true and proven" and those that apply graphic design to make a visual impact. True and proven sites still employ underlined hypertext links that are efficient and effective and that use standard graphics. For example, the Office of Surface Mining (**http://www.osmre.gov/osm.htm**) uses the old fashion "pin" with drop shadow graphics as bullets to draw a user's attention. The Federal Motor Carrier Safety Administration's (**http://www.fmcsa.dot.gov/**) logo is marred by artifacts left over from its creation; these could have been easily removed. Its overall page design appears primitive and amateurish, dating it as old even though the content is clearly current.

Users of federal government Web sites encounter two design contrasts concerning page content density. For example, the appearance of the home page for the Department of Housing and Urban Development (**http://www.hud.gov/**) is dense, whereas the content on the National Park Service's ParkNet's page (**http://www.nps.gov/**) is sparse.

The visual design and appearance of many government Web sites are becoming more professional. The sites use fonts and screen design, rollovers, and animation to gain and keep a user's attention and interest.

Many sites compress fonts and use columns to place as much text as possible on the screen; these designs are intended to reduce or eliminate a user's need to scroll down a Web page. An example is the Internal Revenue Service's home page (**http://www.irs.gov/**), which fits all of its links onto one screen. Other Web sites effectively use color and graphics to break up the text, making it an effective, if not a particularly pleasing, visual experience. An example is the Bureau of Labor Statistics (**http://stats.bls.gov/**), which effectively uses color in section headers to differentiate them from the compressed fonts used to include as many links on its home page as possible.

"Rollovers" are those graphics that change color or the graphic itself when the user's mouse makes contact with (rolls over) the graphic. An example of using rollovers to expand navigation content is the Centers for Medicare and Medicaid Services (**http://cms.hhs.gov/**). A user sees clickable drop-down boxes listing topics when the mouse makes contact with user roles. The Department of Veteran Affairs (**http:// www.va.gov/**) uses rollovers of icons to list the contents of the various pages; this home page is icon-driven rather than text-driven.

A common animation application is the presentation of a rotating set of images, such as photographs. An example may be found on the Drug Enforcement Administration's home page (**http://www.usdoj.gov/dea/**). Often, the capability to view a set of rotating photographs requires the user to install the latest version of Macromedia's Flash viewer. This was a requirement for the rotating photographs on the Federal Railroad Administration's home page (**http://www.fra.dot.gov/site/index.htm**). The Minerals Management Service (**http://www.mms.gov/**) uses Flash to present an opening, animated special effect if the appropriate version of the viewer is installed on the user's workstation.

Unfortunately, not all Web page designs and effects work as intended. For example, the U.S. Surface Transportation Board's home page (**http://www.stb.dot.gov/**) employs a continually changing message marquee under the navigation bar. One cannot click on the text in the marquee box to link to the content of the message, however. Furthermore, the up-down arrows for the message box are useless.

Specialized Software

Federal government Web sites also encourage file downloads so that users may employ third-party software when viewers or application software managed by the Web browser either are inadequate to handle the data properly or do not exist at all. Examples include agency-created data files (often stored in comma- or tab-delimited formats on federal government Web sites) that can be downloaded via the Web browser onto the user's hard drive and then executed offline (opened and read) by spreadsheet software such as Microsoft Excel, and statistical analysis software such as StatView (**http://www.statview.com/**) and SPSS (**http://www.spss.com/**).

Several federal agencies also offer specialized application software for users. For example, the U.S. Geological Survey (USGS) created GEODE (GEO-DATA Explorer; **http://dss1.er.usgs.gov/**) to enable the public to access, view, and download information from geo-spatial databases. GEODE is a Java applet; USGS's Web site can detect if the users' computer can run GEODE; if not, it provides an online help guide to assist them in installing the necessary software. The Environmental Protection Agency's (EPA) Office of Science and Technology provides users with BASINS (Better Assessment Science Integrating Point and Nonpoint Sources; **http://www. epa.gov/OST/BASINS/**). This large downloadable software package integrates a geographic information system (GIS), national watershed data, and state-of-the-art environmental assessment and modeling tools. The National Oceanic and Atmospheric Administration (NOAA) enables Web users to manipulate and display CoastWatch data files (**http://coastwatch.noaa.gov/cw_software.html**). Because CoastWatch data are stored in a special binary format not recognized by normal image display formats, users must first download and install NOAA's CoastWatch Format Software Library and Utilities software package of routines that convert, manipulate, and plot CoastWatch format data files. Other examples of federal-agency-created software made available for use by the public includes the U.S. Census Bureau's EXTRACT program (a general purpose data display and extraction tool that works with Census

Bureau files recorded in dBase format, available at **http://www.census.gov/epcd/ www/extract.html**). Map-It from the USGS (**http://stellwagen.er.usgs.gov/mapit/index. html**) employs the open source Genetic Mapping Tools (GMT) package developed by the Department of Geology and Geophysics at the University of Hawaii and released under the GNU General Public License, which encourages the free distribution and modification of applications software.

WebCasts

An audio-video presentation sent through the Web is referred to as a Webcast. Various government agencies offer Webcast, available either "live" or as a library or archive, to the public. For example, the Department of Housing and Urban Development (HUD) provides live Webcasting of training and public events (**http://www. hud.gov/webcasts/index.cfm**). An audio and video library of past HUD Webcasts are also available for public access at any time. President Clinton recorded his first Internet Webcast at 3:15 p.m. on June 23, 2000, at a private residence in Los Angeles, California, for broadcast at 10 a.m. on June 24.[2] The Bureau of the Census used a Webcast on December 28, 2000, to announce the resident population and apportionment counts as a result of the 2000 Census (**http://www.connectlive.com/events/ census/archive.html**).

A popular type of Webcasts is "streaming." When an audio and video files are "streamed," it means that users can hear or see them without having to wait for the entire file to download. To receive streaming Webcasts, users should have a computer capable of playing sound, at least a 28.8 kilobytes per second connection to the Web, and the appropriate playback software installed in the browser. Most federal government Web sites recommend using the free RealPlayer viewer from RealNetworks in Seattle, WA (**http://www.real.com/**), or Microsoft's Windows Media Player (**http://www. microsoft.com/windows/windowsmedia/download/default.asp**) to view and hear Webcasts.

Interactivity

Federal government Web sites also provide users with interactive functionality, enabling them to create, modify, or customize available information to meet their specific, individual needs. The EPA's Maps on Demand EnviroMapper (**http://www. epa.gov/enviro/html/em/**) is a collection of powerful tools used to map various types of environmental information, including air releases, drinking water, toxic releases, hazardous wastes, water discharge permits, and Superfund sites. One selects a geographic area within EnviroMapper and views the different facilities that are present within that area. It is possible to create maps at the national, state, and county levels, and link them to environmental text reports. EPA's "Dumptown Game" (**http://www.epa.gov/recyclecity/gameintro.htm**) uses Macromedia's Shockwave Player (**http://sdc.shockwave.com/shockwave/download/**) as a browser viewer to watch the images move and change as users interact with the program as the City Manager of Recycle City. The USGS's National Atlas Online (**http://www-atlas.usgs. gov/atlasvue.html**) requires that frames be enabled allowing users to customize maps interactively within a user's Web browser. Shockwave is also required to view the several multimedia maps found on nationalatlas.gov (**http://www-atlas.usgs.gov/atlasvue. html**). The USGS provides users with real-time hydrologic data (**http://waterdata. usgs.gov/nwis/rt**), searchable by state, and then by instrument in rivers, basins, bays, and tidal stations.

Consumer-Orientation: Recognizing User Needs

Federal agencies are increasingly consumer-oriented, using their Web sites to provide visitors with access, viewing, and searching options; the capability to personalize their information usage; and opportunities for two-way communications, rather than presenting information in a "take it or leave it" manner.

Connection Speeds. Federal Web site designers are cognizant that their visitors use a variety of workstations platforms (Intel and Apple), browsers (Microsoft Internet Explorer and Netscape), Internet access speeds (telephone, cable, and DSL modems in addition to local area networks), and workstation-installed software productivity applications (e.g., Microsoft and Corel office suites). As a result, federal government Web sites are making efforts to meet individual needs by providing users with alternatives and choices for viewing information and downloading files based on the speed of their Internet connection and installed viewer. For example, NASA's Video Gallery (**http://www.nasa.gov/multimedia/videogallery/index.html**) provides users with choices of movie format based on file size (large and small versions), desired viewer (same movie in either Quicktime or RealPlayer formats), and movie resolution (which affects file size) based on the speed of the user's connection to the Internet (high resolution for larger file sizes for cable modems and T1 users, medium resolution and average file sizes for fast dial-up modem users, and low resolution with smaller file sizes for slower dial-up users). NOAA's National Environmental Satellite, Data and Information Service's Tropical Satellite Imagery (**http://www.ssd.noaa.gov/PS/TROP/trop-atl.html**) enables users to view Atlantic and Caribbean Tropical Satellite Imagery in a loop, as a pop-up window, or as an image in the same window. The Department of State's video connection page (**http://www.state.gov/misc/10867.htm**) provides users with the latest daily press briefing for download via DSL/cable or dial-up modem, and suggests using the Windows Media Player as the viewer.

Search Engines and Browsing. The search engines for federal agency Web sites have also become more sophisticated. Most Web sites provide users with a search function. In many cases, this search capability enables users to employ Boolean operators (*and*, *or*, *not*) to limit or expand their search results. Users may determine if a Web site enables Boolean by reading the search help tips or guides offered by the agency. An example of a sophisticated search engine can be found at the Department of Transportation, Bureau of Transportation Statistics, TRIS Online (Transportation Research Information Services) (**http://199.79.179.82/sundev/search.cfm**). SciTechResources.gov (**http://www.scitechresources.gov/**) is a site managed by the National Technical Information Service (NTIS) that enables scientists, engineers, and science-aware citizens to conduct a topic search of key government Web sites.

Help and Explanation. Do you remember when help from a Web site primarily related to navigation of the site? There has been continuous improvement in the help guides provided by agency Web sites. Many sites have increased the number of help pages available, and others have created readable and very usable help guides. For example, the National Archives and Records Administration (NARA) provides an online guide, "Getting Started—First Steps," for conducting research work with NARA's holdings (**http://www.archives.gov/research_room/getting_started/getting_started. html**). NOAA provides a tutorial on streaming video—what it is, where to obtain the software, and how to install it (**http://www.broadcast.noaa.gov/getstart.html**). A good example of providing readable explanations of technical issues for the public is that of a ".pdf File" provided by the Library of Congress (**http://thomas.loc.gov/ tfaqs/tfaq15/pdfhelp.html**). The Bureau of Alcohol, Tobacco and Firearms (ATF; **http://www.atf.treas.gov/**) provides detailed technical specifications to apply when visiting its site, including browser versions, screen resolution, and plug-ins. This site also provides a PDF conversion engine (bottom of home page), noting that there may be a problem reading .pdf files when using Microsoft Internet Explorer version 5.0 (and up) in combination with Adobe's Acrobat Reader version 4.0 (**http://www. atf.treas.gov/pdfcon.htm**).

Personalizing the Site Visit. The ability for Web users to personalize their experience with a Web site, such as "My Yahoo!," has migrated to federal Web sites. AccessAmerica for Exporters (**http://tradenet.gov/**) allows frequent users to establish a "My TradeNet" account, a customized version of this site's Export Advisor service. "My TradeNet" (**http://tradenet.gov/**) allows users to collect their favorite parts of Export Advisor and add them to their personalized page, updated whenever the user logs onto the site using their password. The "PrePrint Network" at the Department of Energy (**http://www.osti.gov/preprints/**) has created "PrePrint Alerts" from which users can create personal profiles to match their interests. Users receive notification of new information when it becomes available that matches their saved, online profile. The Department of Education (**http://www.ed.gov/index.jsp**) provides visitors with the opportunity to create a "My.ED.gov" account so that frequent users may bookmark topic-based pages.

Increasing Availability of Full-Text Content. Federal Web sites are increasingly mounting full text from reports and data charts. For example, full-text documents of reports from the Technology Administration of the Department of Commerce are available at **http://www.ta.doc.gov/reports.htm**. The Bureau of Labor Statistics (**http://stats.bls.gov/**) provides site visitors with a table of current statistical information titled "Latest Numbers," which includes the most recent monthly unemployment rate and the U.S. Import Price Index, among others. The Department of Energy's (DOE) Office of Scientific and Technical Information also provides users with persistent URLs to full-text documents. A persistent URL (PURL) is a Web address that does not change; its stability means that users can place a PURL on a Web page with the knowledge that the document will actually be there when another user clicks on the link. The DOE Information Bridge (**http://www.osti.gov/bridge/**) provides PURLs for convenient and free access to full-text and bibliographic records of DOE research and development reports in physics, chemistry, materials, biology, environmental sciences, energy technologies, engineering, computer and information science, renewable energy, and other topics.

Customer Satisfaction and Outreach. To serve their public constituents better, some federal agencies conduct Web-based surveys and use that information, for instance, to improve the design and navigation on their sites and expand content. The

Centers for Disease Control and Prevention, for instance, asks its visitors about their satisfaction with the site (**http://outside.cdc.gov:8091/BASIS/survey/survey/survey/ upf**). Federal agencies also use their Web sites as outreach mechanisms to their users, providing services for the many who cannot visit government offices or are unwilling to deal with the government by telephone or mail. For example, the U.S. Air Force (**https://oaprod.hq.af.mil/saf/pa/misc/listserv.cfm**) encourages visitors to subscribe to news and other information products and services about the branch of the military. The Bureau of Labor Statistics (**http://stats.bls.gov/bls/list.htm**) enables visitors to request that news releases be delivered to them via email. The Department of Energy (**http://www.energy.gov/subscriptions/index.html**) and the Centers for Disease Control and Prevention (**http://www.cdc.gov/subscribe.html**) both provide mail list services via the Internet. The government also uses their Web sites to extend its retail side of agency operations. (Appendix A of this work provides examples of e-government retail that, while generating revenue for the agency, also serves as an outreach mechanism to its clientele.)

An excellent example of outreach is the U.S. District Court for the Eastern District of Pennsylvania (**http://www.paed.uscourts.gov/**). In addition to providing full-text content of documents and opinions, and even a tutorial about Electronic Case Filing (ECF), the site enables a user to install client-side software on their individual workstation for "JUST-ASK," an application that

provides up-to-date information on the status of trials scheduled in the United States District Court for the Eastern District of Pennsylvania seven (7) days a week, twenty-four (24) hours a day, free of charge. All cases scheduled for trial, presently on trial, in the trial pool, and special notices from the Court are included on the system. JUST-ASK also provides a report on the disposition of cases previously listed on the system. Events such as verdicts, settlements, and continuances constantly change the status of cases on the Court's trial list. JUST-ASK immediately reflects the daily status of listings as the information becomes available to the Clerk of Court.

Emerging Roles. Federal agencies are exploring ways to expand their Web-based roles. One example includes the availability of archives of past data. For example, NOAA provides users with "U.S. Climate at a Glance" (**http://lwf.ncdc. noaa.gov/oa/climate/research/cag3/cag3.html**), which archives select climate data for the past one hundred years. Users may select climate data to construct longitude line and bar charts. Department of Transportation (DOT) researchers and the transportation community at large may be interested in the Department's expanding online digital archival collections (**http://dotlibrary.specialcollection.net/**).

Federal Web sites are also becoming more "commercial." The Bureau of the Public Debt Online's site (**http://www.publicdebt.treas.gov/**) includes a billboard with a loop of six rotating frames (on the top left of the page) that, fortunately, a user may start and stop. The U.S. Mint home page (**http://www.usmint.gov/**) requires a Flash player to display its scrolling "latest news" marquee. It, too, includes a rotating set of images that could be described as a billboard.

AND LASTLY . . .

Access to the Web depends on the availability of a computer workstation. Although many homes and businesses have access to the Web, not everyone has direct access to a computer workstation, or one robust enough to surf the Web. One good alternative access point is a local public library that provides Web access through publicly available computer workstations. Additionally, there are more than 1,300 libraries of various types (e.g., public and academic) that are members of the depository library program of the Government Printing Office (GPO). Each of these libraries offers access to the Web as part of its agreement with GPO to serve as a depository. There is at least one depository library in each congressional district. The local public library will be able to identify the depository library for the congressional district (see also the Web site of the Office of the Superintendent of Documents, Chapter 4).

Web browser viewers are a necessity when someone wants the best information content from government Web sites, especially as these sites increasingly provide images and enhanced text, sounds, and motion. The "more viewers the better" is not effective or wise—the more viewers installed on the hard drive, the more likely that the user will have to resolve viewer conflicts. Viewers also consume RAM, which can adversely affect computer workstation performance or, worse yet, result in a workstation crash.

Developers constantly improve their viewers, and new viewers become available all of the time. Cautious users will install and employ those viewers recommended by Web site managers that work best with their information content. The more risk taken, the more likely users will lose the ability to manage the viewers appropriately.

It is also important to be aware of the reality of surfing the Web. The computer workstation hardware and software will significantly influence the Internet experience—the more appropriately configured the workstation for Internet use, the better. The connection to the Internet and its download speeds are directly related to the type of connection used. Local area networks (most often found at businesses and libraries) tend to run faster than computers connected through a telephone line; cable modems, which take advantage of broadband CATV, oftentimes run much faster than modems attached to the telephone system.

Despite all of these potential limitations, the good news is that the thousands of government Web sites are rich in information content and are increasingly using multimedia formats that enhance and enrich the user's experiences. Furthermore, most of this information is free—paid for with taxpayer dollars—and has broad appeal and utility.

NOTES

1. Office of Management and Budget, "M-00-13: Privacy Policies and Data Collection on Federal Web Sites" (June 22, 2000). Available: **http://www.whitehouse.gov/omb/memoranda/m00-13.html**.

2. Weekly *Compilation of Presidential Documents* (July 3, 2000): 1479–80. From the 2000 Presidential Documents Online via GPO Access. Available: **http://frwebgate4.access.gpo.gov/cgi-bin/waisgate.cgi?WAISdocID=00799222433+0+0+0&WAISaction=retrieve**.

URL Site Guide for This Chapter

DIRECWAY
http://directv.direcway.com/

Amazon.com
http://www.amazon.com

Office of Management and Budget

> **"M-00-13: Privacy Policies and Data Collection on Federal Web Sites"**
> http://www.whitehouse.gov/omb/ memoranda/m00-13.html

Microsoft Corporation
http://www.microsoft.com/

Adobe Systems Incorporate
http://www.adobe.com/

Netscape
http://www.netscape.com/

Yahoo!
http://www.yahoo.com

Google
http://www.google.com

PC World
http://www.pcworld.com/downloads/ index/0,00.asp

ZDNet
http://downloads-zdnet.com.com/

Macromedia (makers of Shockwave and Flash Player)
http://www.macromedia.com/

Apple Computer (QuickTime)
http://www.apple.com/

U.S. Office of Surface Mining
http://www.osmre.gov/ osm.htm

Federal Motor Carrier Safety Administration
http://www.fmcsa.dot.gov/

U.S. Department of Housing and Urban Development
http://www.hud.gov/

ParkNet

> **National Park Services**
> http://www.nps.gov/

Internal Revenue Service
http://www.irs.gov/

Bureau of Labor Statistics
http://stats.bls.gov/

Centers for Medicare and Medicaid Services
http://cms.hhs.gov/

Department of Veteran Affairs
http://www.va.gov/

U.S. Drug Enforcement Administration
http://www.usdoj.gov/dea/

Federal Railroad Administration
http://www.fra.dot.gov/site/index.htm

Minerals Management Service
http://www.mms.gov/

U.S. Surface Transportation Board
http://www.stb.dot.gov/

StatView
http://www.statview.com/

SPSS
http://www.spss.com/

United States Geological Survey

GEODE (GEO-DATA Explorer)
http://dss1.er.usgs.gov/

BASINS (Better Assessment Science Integrating Point and Nonpoint Sources)

Environmental Protection Agency
Office of Science and Technology
http://www.epa.gov/OST/BASINS/

CoastWatch

National Oceanic and Atmospheric Administration
http://coastwatch.noaa.gov/cw_
software.html

EXTRACT

Bureau of the Census
http://www.census.gov/epcd/www/
extract.html

Map-It

United States Geological Service
http://stellwagen.er.usgs.gov/mapit/
index.html

Webcasting

Department of Housing and Urban Development
http://www.hud.gov/webcasts/index.cfm

Text of President Clinton's Webcast

http://frwebgate4.access.gpo.gov/cgi-bin/
waisgate.cgi?WAISdocID=
00799222433+0+0+0&WAIS
action=retrieve

Webcast to announce select 2000 Census Data

Bureau of the Census
http://www.connectlive.com/events/
census/archive.html

RealNetworks

http://www.real.com/

Microsoft's Windows Media Player

http://www.microsoft.com/windows/
windowsmedia/download/default.asp

Maps on Demand EnviroMapper

Environmental Protection Agency
http://www.epa.gov/enviro/html/cm/

Dumptown Game

Environmental Protection Agency
http://www.epa.gov/recyclecity/
gameintro.htm

Macromedia's Shockwave Player

http://sdc.shockwave.com/shockwave/
download/

National Atlas Online

United States Geological Survey
http://www-atlas.usgs.gov/atlasvue.html

nationalatlas.gov

United States Geological Survey
http://www-atlas.usgs.gov/atlasvue.html.

Real-time hydrologic data

United States Geological Service
http://waterdata.usgs.gov/nwis/rt

Video Gallery

National Aeronautics and Space Administration
http://www.nasa.gov/multimedia/
videogallery/index.html

Tropical Satellite Imagery

National Environmental Satellite, Data and Information Service
National Oceanic and Atmospheric
Administration
http://www.ssd.noaa.gov/PS/TROP/
trop-atl.html

Video Connection

Department of State
http://www.state.gov/misc/10867.htm

TRIS Online (Transportation Research Information Services)

Bureau of Transportation Statistics
Department of Transportation
http://199.79.179.82/sundev/search.cfm

SciTechResources.gov

http://www.scitechresources.gov/

419

Getting Started — First Steps
National Archives and Records Administration
http://www.archives.gov/research_room/
getting_started/getting_started.html

Tutorial on Streaming Video
National Oceanic and Atmospheric Administration
http://www.broadcast.noaa.gov/
getstart.html

Library of Congress
THOMAS
http://thomas.loc.gov/tfaqs/tfaq15/
pdfhelp.html

The Bureau of Alcohol, Tobacco and Firearms
http://www.atf.treas.gov/
http://www.atf.treas.gov/pdfcon.htm

My TradeNet
AccessAmerica for Exporters
http://tradenet.gov/

U.S. Department of Energy
PrePrint Network
http://www.osti.gov/preprints/

Individualized Service
U.S. Department of Education
http://www.ed.gov/index.jsp

U.S. Department of Commerce
Technology Administration
http://www.ta.doc.gov/reports.htm

Latest Numbers
U.S. Bureau of Labor Statistics
http://stats.bls.gov/

DOE Information Bridge
Office of Scientific and Technical Information
Department of Energy
http://www.osti.gov/bridge/

Satisfaction
Centers for Disease Control and Prevention
http://outside.cdc.gov:8091/BASIS/
survey/survey/survey/upf

Subscriptions
U.S. Air Force
https://oaprod.hq.af.mil/saf/pa/misc/
listserv.cfm

E-Mail Service
Bureau of Labor Statistics
http://stats.bls.gov/bls/list.htm

Mail List Service
Department of Energy
http://www.energy.gov/subscriptions/
index.html

Mail List Service
The Centers for Disease Control and Prevention
http://www.cdc.gov/subscribe.html

Outreach
U.S. District Court for the Eastern District of Pennsylvania
http://www.paed.uscourts.gov/

U.S. Climate at a Glance
National Oceanic and Atmospheric Administration (NOAA)
http://lwf.ncdc.noaa.gov/oa/climate/
research/cag3/cag3.html

Online Digital Archival Collections
Department of Transportation
http://dotlibrary.specialcollection.net/

Online Site
Bureau of the Public Debt
http://www.publicdebt.treas.gov/

Home Page
U.S. Mint
http://www.usmint.gov/

Appendix A.
Examples of E-Government Retail

As this appendix highlights, the government sells numerous items online and generates millions of dollars in online sales. A number of agencies rely on the Office of the Superintendent of Documents at the Government Printing Office for selling publications through its sales programs (**http://bookstore.gpo.gov/**). Other agencies may instead rely on the services of the National Technical Information Service (**http://www.ntis.gov/**) for the distribution of publications, CD-ROM, and other formats. The courts provide a list of statistical publications available from the Superintendent of Documents (see **http://www.uscourts.gov/statpub.pdf**).

GENERAL SITE

The portal FirstGov (**http://www.firstgov.gov/**) provides access to "free government e-mail newsletters" and to "government sales: daily notices, news, announcements and descriptions of important government surplus property and asset sales currently offered across all federal agencies."

EXECUTIVE BRANCH (CABINET DEPARTMENTS)

◁ Department of Agriculture

Foreign Agriculture Service
The FAS offers the U.S. Suppliers Service, which is a searchable database of U.S. exporters and their products. The Department of Agriculture uses the service to help facilitate connecting potential buyers with U.S. suppliers. There are more than five hundred product categories for companies to include in their listing (see **http://ffas. usda.gov/agexport/ussuppinfo.html**).

Forest Service
The Forest Service produces visitor maps for each national forest and grassland, and it provides passes and permits for each forest and grassland (see **http://www. fs.fed.us/maps/**).

⤤ Department of Commerce

The department "has actively pursued the use of the Internet conducting business on-line. Not only do we provide information that is . . . informative, but we also offer the opportunity to apply for fishing permits, export licenses, grants, patents and trademarks" (**http://www.commerce.gov/egov.html**):

- The Trademark Electronic Application System (TEAS) "allows you to fill out a form and check it for completeness over the Internet. Using e-TEAS you can then submit the form directly to the USPTO (U.S. Patent and Trademark Office) over the Internet, making an official filing on-line. Or using PrinTEAS you can print our the completed form for mailing to the USPTO."

- USPTO Electronic Filing System "is [an] electronic system for submitting patent applications, computer readable format (CRF) biosequence listings, and pre-grant publication submissions to the USPTO via the Internet."

- Commerce Opportunities on Line (COOL) is the "Commerce Department's vacancy announcements and application system. It provides a convenient way to search and apply for selected Department of Commerce jobs."

- Simplified Network Application Process (SNAP) allows "the submission of License Applications, Commodity Classification Requests, and High Performance Computer Notices."

- BuyUSA "is an e-marketplace sponsored by the Department of Commerce and IBM that provides trade opportunities for US exporters and international companies."

- NTIA Public Telecommunications Facilities Program "provides online forms and filing information for grants applications."

- NTIA Technology Opportunity Program offers "online forms and grants applications."

- NIST Critical Infrastructure Grants Program allows users to "apply for grants online."

- AESDirect is a site with access to "the U.S. Census Bureau's free, Internet based system for filing Shipper's Export Declaration (SED) information to the Automated Export System (AES). It is the electronic alternative to filing a paper SED, and can be used by U.S. Principal Parties in Interest (USPPIs), forwarders, or anyone else responsible for export reporting."

- The NOAA Fisheries Permit Shop is a site "where you can currently buy initial and renewal permits for Atlantic tunas, update permit information, and report recreational landings of bluefin tuna."

- NOAA National Virtual Data System offers an "online store offering data products from the National Climate Data Center, National Geophysical Data Center, and the National Oceanographic Data Center."

- National Technical Information Service site allows users to "order products from a collection of over 2.5 million scientific, technical, engineering, and related business information materials."

STAT-USA provides authoritative information for the business, economic, and trade community. Its resources are available on subscription (see **http://www.stat-usa.gov/**).

Bureau of Economic Analysis

This statistical agency provides publications and other products, which can be ordered from the Government Printing Office's sales program (see **http://www.bea.doc.gov/bea/uguide.htm**) or from the bureau itself (**http://www.bea.gov**; 800-704-0415 (outside the U.S., call (202) 606-9666). To order by mail, send a check payable to "Economic Analysis, BE-53" (BEA Order Desk, BE-53, Bureau of Economic Analysis, U.S. Department of Commerce, Washington, D.C. 20230). BEA information is also available online through STAT-USA's Web site.

Bureau of Industry and Security

It provides the Simplified Network Application Process (SNAP), for the submission of license applications, commodity classification requests, and high performance computer notices (see **http://www.bxa.doc.gov/SNAP/BasicSNAPInformation.html**).

United States Patent and Trademark Office (USPTO)

For information on the filing fee and other information about the Trademark Electronic Application System (TEAS), see **http://www.uspto.gov/teas/eTEAStechinfo.htm**).

Department of the Interior

Bureau of Land Management

The bureau protects the thousands of wild horses and burros that roam federal lands and auctions them to manage the ranges. Since 1998, this auction and the adoption process can be found at **http://www.adoptahorse.blm.gov/**.

National Park Service

The Web site (**http://www.nps.gov/parks.html**) provides access to individual parks, their bookstores, and maps.

U.S. Geological Survey

This site provides assorted maps and cartographic data (see **http://mapping.usgs.gov/www.products/1product.html**). It also maintains a Business Partner Program that helps customers find retail USGS products: "Digital Cartographic Data," "Digital Satellite Data," "Aerial Photographs," and "Published Products" (**http://rockyweb.cr.usgs.gov/acis-bin/querypartner.cgi**).

Department of State

English Teaching Forum Magazine, which is available for teachers of English outside the United States, is available on subscription at **http://exchanges.state.gov/education/engteaching/eal-foru.htm**.

Department of Transportation

For a discussion of business opportunities and vendor information for online transactions, see **http://www.dot.gov/business.html**.

Department of the Treasury

The department handles auctions at **http://www.ustreas.gov/auctions**. This site also covers "Other Government Auctions:" Department of Defense and the U.S. Army Corps of Engineers, Federal Deposit Insurance Corporation, General Services Administration, Department of Housing and Urban Development, U.S. Postal Service, and the Small Business Administration. The department also sells bills, notes, and bonds at auctions. A Web page (**http://www.savingsbonds.gov/sec/secauc.htm**) "contains links to auction schedules and recent and historical auction results, including rates."

Bureau of Engraving and Printing
The bureau offers uncut currency, portraits, note cards, jewelry, and more (**http://www.publicdebt.treas.gov/**).

U.S. Mint
The mint offers an online catalog that includes collectibles (state quarters, euro coin collection, and other coin sets), coin jewelry, holiday ornaments, clearance sale items, medals, and more (**http://catalog.usmint.gov/**).

INDEPENDENT AGENCIES

American Battle Monuments Commission

"You may request photographs (without charge) of your loved one's headstone or marker located in World War I and II overseas cemeteries; order flowers to be place at a headstone or marker; or a free Honor Roll certificate for a deceased during the Korean War" (**http://www.abmc.gov/abmc5.htm**). Mailed orders only accepted. There is also a "WWII Memorial E-Store," which offers assorted memorial products (**http://www.wwiimemorial.com/store/default.asp?page=products.asp**).

Federal Reserve System

There are publications and FedNotice, announcement of federal reserve speeches and news releases (see **http://minneapolisfed.org/pubs/**.

General Services Administration

The agency's Office of Property Disposal makes available property for sale (see **http://propertydisposal.gsa.gov/property/**). For information about "Buying through GSA," see **http://www.gsa.gov/Portal/displaychannel.jsp?channe;d=13534&cid=2**.

National Aeronautics and Space Administration

The Headquarters Exchange Council offers the Exchange Store that sells clothing with the NASA and other images on them (**http://www.hq.nasa.gov/exchange/clothing/clothing.html**).

National Archives and Records Administration

The presidential libraries have museum stores, perhaps operated by not-for-profit foundations, that sell books, collectibles, clothes, and other items:

- George Bush Presidential Library and Museum (**http://www.museumstore.com/**)

- Jimmy Carter Library and Museum (**http://www.jimmycarterlibrary.org/museum/store/index.phtml**)

- Dwight D. Eisenhower Library and Museum (**http://eisenhower.archives.gov/gift.htm**)

- Gerald R. Ford Library and Museum (**http://www.ford.utexas.edu/museum/catalog.htm**)

- Herbert Hoover Presidential Library and Museum (**http://hoover.archives.gov/giftshop/index.html**)

- Lyndon Baines Johnson Library and Museum (**http://www.lbjlib.utexas.edu/johnson/links.hom/lbjstore.shtm**)

- John F. Kennedy Library (**http://www.jfklibrary.org/store_page02.html**)

- Ronald Reagan Presidential Foundation and Library Museum Store (**http://www.reaganfoundation.org/store/**)

- Franklin D. Roosevelt Presidential Library and Museum (**http://www.fdrlibrary.marist.edu/store.html**)

- Truman Presidential Museum and Library (**http://www.trumanlibrary.org/gifts/catalog.htm**)

National Railroad Passenger Corporation

The agency operates Amtrak, which has a home page for making travel reservations, planning a trip, and so on (**http://www.amtrak.com/**). There is also an Amtrak

Store, which offers apparel, model trains, collectibles, travel bags and totes, toys, games, gift certificates, and other products (**http://store.amtrak.com/**).

Small Business Administration

PRO-Net "is an electronic gateway of procurement information—for and about small businesses. It is a search engine for contracting officers, a marketing tool for small firms and a 'link' to procurement opportunities and important information. It is designed to be a 'virtual one-stop procurement-shop' " (**http://pro-net.sba.gov/ index2.html**).

U.S. Postal Service

Online sales include souvenirs, apparel, the paying and receipt of bills, sending certified mail, customs cards, sending money and letters, and so on (see **http://www. usps.com/**).

OTHER

National Zoo

The gift store offers souvenirs, games, puzzles, apparel, jewelry, books, and videos (**http://store.fonz.org/**).

Smithsonian Institution

One option at the home page (**http://www.si.edu**) is to the SmithsonianStore.com, which sells assorted products, including, for instance, games, puzzles, replicas, and books.

LEGISLATIVE BRANCH

Government Printing Office

As previously noted, the Office of the Superintendent of Documents maintains an online bookstore, which offers selected publications printed by the Government Printing Office. The Sales Product Catalog is the online index to these publications. The Web site (**http://bookstore.gpo.gov/**) also provides ordering information, lists of best-sellers, "New Titles by Topic," and an e-mail alert service. There are also collections of CD-ROMs, emergency response publications, tax products, a regulatory and subscriptions catalog, and so on.

⬩ Library of Congress

The Sales Shop provides books; cards, journals, and stationery; calendars; games and puzzles; clothes, desk accessories, home accessories; kits, crafts, and hobbies; knowledge cards; jewelry; mugs; music; posters; tote bags and umbrellas; and more. Location: 101 Independence Ave., SE, Washington, D.C. 20540. Phone: (888) 682-3557. Fax: (202) 707-5057. E-mail: retail@loc.gov. Web: **http://locstore.com/**.

LC's Photoduplication Service (101 Independence Avenue, S.E., Washington, D.C. 20540; phone: 202-707-5640; Fax: 202-707-5640; E-mail: photoduplication @loc.gov) provides black-and-white or color replicas of a number of historical posters and other items contained in the American Memory collection, as well as other LC collections (see **http://memory.loc.gov/cgi-bin/pprr.pl?c.d,hh,yanker,dwgd.bbcants. lomax.ils.prok**).

JUDICIAL BRANCH

Federal courts charge fees for electronic public access to court records. For the fee schedule, see **http://www.uscourts.gov/Press_Releases/epafee.html**. Furthermore, the Administrative Office of the U.S. Courts provides a PACER Service Center, which is the "Federal Judiciary's centralized registration, billing, and technical support center for electronic access to U.S. District, Bankruptcy, and Appellate court records" (see **http://pacer.psc.uscourts.gov/**).

Appendix B.
Other Useful Web Sites

The Appendix of *United States Government Information: Policies and Sources* (Westport, CT: Libraries Unlimited, 2002), by Peter Hernon, Harold C. Relyea, Robert E. Dugan, and Joan F. Cheverie, covers the "Literature on Government Information Policy," including Internet resources, associations, and organizations. The following list is complementary.

PUBLIC-INTEREST GROUPS

Federation of American Scientists' Project on Government Secrecy, which, among other things, produces the *Secrecy & Government Bulletin* (**http://www.fas.org/sgp/index.html**). There are also links to other government secrecy-related Web sites (**http://www.fas.org/sgp/secrecy.html**) and an important collection of articles related to "Secrecy and Security News."

OMB Watch (**http://www.ombwatch.org/**) "is a nonprofit research, educational, and advocacy organization that monitors executive branch activities affecting nonprofit, public interest, and community groups." It publishes *The OMB Watcher*, an electronic newsletter that covers information policy, including restrictions on access to government information following September 11.

Judicial Watch covers government policies and practices, with an emphasis on the federal courts (**http://www.judicialwatch.org/**).

The Electronic Privacy Information Center (**http://www.epic.org/**), established in 1994, focuses "public attention on emerging civil liberties issues and . . . [protection of] privacy, the First Amendment, and constitutional values. There is access to publications, congressional testimony, legal briefs, reports, and so on (**http://www/epci.org/**).

UNIVERSITIES AND LIBRARIES

Transactional Records Access Clearinghouse (Syracuse University; **http://trac.syr.edu**) contains, for instance, information from "selected federal enforcement agencies": the Federal Bureau of Investigation, Internal Revenue Service, Drug Enforcement Administration, the U.S. Customs Service, and Bureau of Alcohol, Tobacco, and Firearms. The site contains maps, graphs, tables, and other material. The alphabetical and hierarchical lists complement those found on Yahoo!, THOMAS, and other search engines and portals.

Louisiana State University Libraries (**http://www.lib.lsu.edu/gov/fedgov.html**) has an extensive listing of agencies arranged according to the groupings in the *United States Government Manual.*

The University of Memphis library maintains *Uncle Sam MIGRATING GOVERNMENT PUBLICATIONS* (**http://www.lib.memphis.edu/govpubs/mig. htm**), which identifies government publications that enter the Federal Depository Library Program and enables retrieval by title and Superintendent of Documents classification number. This site covers depository publications that have migrated from print to electronic form. Because the *Monthly Catalog of United States Government Publications* (*Catalog of United States Government Publications*) covers numerous publications that are unavailable from government Web sites, *Uncle Sam* has a critical role in making more of those publications available electronically.

Vanderbilt University Library (**http://www.library.vanderbilt.edu/romans/fdtf/**) offers "Frequently Used Sites: Related to U.S. Federal Government Information." There is coverage of "Indexes," "Agencies and Executive Departments," "Agriculture," "Business and Economy," "Census," "Congress," "Consumer Information," "Copyright, Patents, Trademarks," "Crime and Justice," "Education," "Elections," "Energy and the Environment," "Foreign Countries/Comparative Politics," "Foreign Policy/Defense/International Relations," "Health and Welfare," "Laws and Regulations," "Maps and Geography," "Natural Resources," "President," "Science and Technology," "Standards and Specifications," "Statistics," "Supreme Court," "Tax Forms and Publications," "Terrorism," "Travel," "Welfare and Health," and so on.

The University of Michigan Documents Center has a site with which any users of this guide should be familiar (**http://www.lib.umich.edu/govdocs/govweb.html**). Its "Government Resources on the Web" covers federal, foreign, Michigan, state and local governments, and international organizations. Examples of topics included are statistics, politics, "documents in the news," class assignments (e.g., for high school debating groups and guidance on conducting legislative histories). There are also agency directories, bibliographies, coverage of the federal budget, access to executive orders, and other useful information.

PRIVATE SECTOR

EzGov (**http://www.ezgov.com/index_flash.jsp**) provides "the technology and services that enable governments to become more efficient and better serve citizens and businesses through new distribution channels, such as the Internet. . . . EzGov has developed software specifically tailored to meet the unique e-government needs of federal, state and local agency customers."

SOME KEY PUBLIC POLICY NEWSPAPERS AND JOURNALS

Federal Computer Week focuses on recent developments related to U.S. government information policy and the application of information technology. There is coverage of recent developments related to the Web (**http://www.civic.com/fcw/**).

Government Computer News is a good companion for these same topics (**http://www.gcn.com/**).

The Journal of Politics, published by Blackwell for the Southern Political Science Association, covers "American politics, political theory, comparative and international politics" (**http://www.jstor.org/journals/00223816.html**).

Legislative Studies Quarterly "is an international journal devoted to the publication of research on representative assemblies. Its purpose is to disseminate scholarly work on parliaments and legislatures, their relations to other political institutions, their functions in the political system, and the activities of their members both within the institution and outside" (**http://www.uiowa.edu/~lsq/**).

Polity, established in 1984, "is particularly strong in the areas of sociology, politics, and social and political theory. We also have strong and rapidly expanding lists in a range of other fields including gender studies, media and cultural studies, philosophy, literary studies, history, geography, and anthropology." Its contents cover "politics, political theory and international relations" (**http://www.polity.co.uk/**).

Public Administration Review, published by the American Society for Public Administration, covers "public sector management. Articles identify and analyze current trends, provide a factual basis for decision making, stimulate discussion, and make the literature in the field available in an easily accessible format" (**http://www.aspanet.org/publications/par/index2.html**).

Presidential Studies Quarterly "examines domestic and foreign policy decision making, and relationships with Congress as they relate to the American Presidency, through a historical and analytical perspective." The journal, which Sage publishes, is available electronically (**http://thepresidency.org/psq/**).

The Review of Politics, founded in 1939, emphasizes "the philosophical and historical approach to politics" (**http://www.nd.edu/~rop/**).

Social Science Quarterly, issued by Blackwell, "publishes current research on a broad range of topics, including political science, economics, history, geography, and women's studies (**http://www.utexas.edu/utpress/journals/jssq.html**).

The Washington Post (**http://washpost.com/index.shtml**) covers the latest news, politics, and more.

OTHER

Earth's 911 (**http://www.earth911.org/master.asp**) is a joint effort among the Environmental Protection Agency and public and private organizations to provide geographically specific environmental resource and recycling information. There are links to state and local Internet resources, important agency telephone numbers, and zip code searches for nearby recycling centers and household hazardous waste facilities. Visitors to the site can contribute and update information on recycling centers and hazardous waste drop-off stations that are not currently listed.

Environmental Systems Research Institute (ESRI), a California-based GIS software developer, has launched the Geography Network (**http://www.geographynetwork.com**), an Internet portal for map and GIS users and products. There are data from government and commercial sources, and this site is a place to build maps.

Hieros Gamos (HG; **http://www.hg.org/index.html**) is a legal site that provides Web access to the U.S. government, state governments, governments worldwide, law schools, legal associations, prominent law firms, legal publications, legal vendors, services to the legal profession, legal education, law-related discussion group, online law journals, current news, and so on. HG aims "to be the comprehensive starting point for all law and law related information."

Congress.Org (**http://congress.org/congressorg/home/**), a public service of Capitol Advantage, provides information about Congress and legislation. It also provides links to the executive and judicial branches, as well as to state governors.

The National Security Archives (**http://www.gwu.edu/~nsarchiv/**) is an independent, nongovernment research institute and archives at George Washington University. It provides access to a collection of declassified documents obtained through the *Freedom of Information Act.*

The Conference Board (**http://www.conference-board.org/**) addresses issues related to economics and the business environment. The page covers publications, news, membership services, economic indicators, and more.

Congressional Quarterly Press produces a number of reference sources that cover the three branches of the federal government. For example, David T. Canon, Garrison Nelson, and Charles Steward III prepared *Committees in the U.S. Congress 1789–1946* (2002), a four-volume work that covers the history of congressional committee membership. "This reference set details committee organization and membership in Congress from the first session, in 1789 until 1946 when the Legislative Reorganization Act overhauled the committee system" (see **http://www. cqpressbookstore.com**). By the way, Garrison Nelson and Clark H. Benson produced a two-volume companion, *Committees in the U.S. Congress, 1947–1992 (Congressional Quarterly,* 1993–1994).

Appendix C.
Selective Subject List of U.S. Government Web Sites

Selected terms based on the list of subject terms used by U.S. Government Printing Offices, Subject Bibliographies series

Accounting and Auditing

Congressional Budget Office (CBO): **http://www.cbo.gov/**
Federal Accounting Standards Advisory Board (FASAB): **http://www.fasab.gov/**
Financial Report of the United States Government: **http://www.fms.treas.gov/fr/index.html**
General Accounting Office (GAO): **http://www.gao.gov/**
Office of Management and Budget (OMB): **http://www.whitehouse.gov/omb/**

Aerospace

Aerospace (Treasury Department): **http://www.ita.doc.gov/td/aerospace/**
Aerospace Industry (Census Bureau): **http://www.census.gov/econ/www/ip3000.html**
International Aerospace Information Network (IAIN): **http://www.dtic.mil/iain/newindex.html**
National Aeronautics and Space Administration (NASA): **http://www.nasa.gov/**
National Air and Space Museum (Smithsonian Institution): **http://www.nasm.si.edu/**

Africa

Africa (Environmental Sciences Division, Oak Ridge Laboratory): **http://www.esd.ornl.gov/projects/qen/new_africa.html**
Bureau of African Affairs (Department of State): **http://www.state.gov/p/af/**
United States–Sub-Saharan Africa Trade Data (International Trade Commission): **http://reportweb.usitc.gov/africa/trade_data.html**
USAID in Africa: **http://www.usaid.gov/regions/afr/**
Overseas Private Investment Corporation, Investor's Information Gateway (OPIC): **http://www.opic.gov/links/links-afr.htm**

Aging

AgingStats.gov: **http://www.agingstats.gov/**
FirstGov for Seniors: **http://www.seniors.gov/**
NIH Senior Health: **http://nihseniorhealth.gov/**

Agriculture

Department of Agriculture: http://www.usda.gov/
FEDSTATS–Agriculture: http://www.fedstats.gov/programs/agriculture.html
Office of Industrial Technologies (DOE): http://www.oit.doe.gov/agriculture/

AIDS (Acquired Immune Deficiency Syndrome)

Centers for Disease Control and Prevention: http://www.cdc.gov/hiv/pubs/facts.htm
Medline Health Information Medical Encyclopedia: http://www.nlm.nih.gov/
medlineplus/ency/article/000594.htm
AIDSinfo: http://www.aidsinfo.nih.gov/
HIVNET: http://www.ahrq.gov/data/hivnet.htm

Air Force Manuals

National Technical Information Service (NTIS): http://www.ntis.gov/products/families/
airforce_manuals.asp?loc=4-3-4
Air Force Publishing: http://www.e-publishing.af.mil

Air Pollution

MedlinePlus Health Information: http://www.nlm.nih.gov/medlineplus/airpollution.html
Clean Air: http://www.fueleconomy.gov/feg/airpoll.shtml
Centers for Disease Control and Prevention: http://www.cdc.gov/nceh/airpollution/
default.htm
Environmental Protection Agency: http://www.epa.gov/oar/

Alcohol, Tobacco, and Firearms

Bureau of Alcohol, Tobacco and Firearms: http://www.atf.treas.gov/index.htm

American Revolution

John Bull & Uncle Sam (Library of Congress): http://www.loc.gov/exhibits/british/brit-2.
html
Religion and the Founding of the American Republic (Library of Congress): http://
lcweb.loc.gov/exhibits/religion/rel03.html
The American Revolution (Interior Department): http://www.nps.gov/revwar/

The Americas

Bureau of Western Hemisphere (State Department): http://www.state.gov/p/wha/
Science for Global Health, the Americas (National Institutes of Health): http://
www.fic.nih.gov/regional/americas.html
The Americas in World Context (Energy Department): http://www.eia.doe.gov/
emeu/cabs/theamericas.html#world_context
Coming from the Americas (Census Bureau): http://landview.census.gov/prod/
2000pubs/cenbr003.pdf

Aquatic Life

Wetlands, Watersheds, and Oceans (Environmental Protection Agency): http://www.
epa.gov/owow/

Armed Forces

Job Opportunities in the Armed Forces (Bureau of Labor Statistics): http://www.bls.gov/oco/ocos249.htm

Military Career Guide Online (Defense Department): http://www.militarycareers.com/

Today's Military (Defense Department): http://www.todaysmilitary.com/

Arms Control

Under Secretary for Arms Control and International Security (State Department): http://www.state.gov/t/

Nonproliferation, Arms Control and International Security (Lawrence Livermore National Laboratory): http://www.llnl.gov/nai/default.html

Defense Threat Reduction Agency (Defense Department): http://www.dtra.mil/os/dtrom/os_acid.html

Office of Defense Trade Controls (State Department): http://www.pmdtc.org/

Army Corps of Engineers

Corps home page: http://www.usace.army.mil/

Art and Artists

National Endowment for the Arts: http://www.nea.gov

National Endowment for the Humanities: http://www.neh.fed.us

Smithsonian Institute Encyclopedia, Art, Design, and Crafts: http://www.si.edu/resource/faq/art.htm

Asia

Asia and the Near East (Agency for International Development): http://www.usaid.gov/regions/ane/

Bureau of East Asian and Pacific Affairs (State Department): http://www.state.gov/p/eap/

Bureau of South Asian Affairs (State Department): http://www.state.gov/p/sa/

Freer Gallery of Art and Arthur M. Sackler Gallery (Smithsonian Institute): http://www.asia.si.edu/

U.S. Trade Representatives, World Regions: http://www.ustr.gov/regions/asia-pacific/index.shtml

http://www.ustr.gov/regions/china-hk-mongolia-taiwan/index.shtml

http://www.ustr.gov/regions/japan/index.shtml

Background Notes

Department of State, Bureau of Public Affairs: http://state.gov/r/pa/ei/bgn/

Buildings, Landmarks, and Historic Sites

National Building Museum: http://www.nbm.org/home.html

National Historic Landmarks (National Park Service): http://www.cr.nps.gov/landmarks.htm

National Trust for Historic Preservation: http://www.nthp.org/

Business

Small Business Administration: **http:www.sba.gov/**
U.S. Business Advisor: **http://www.business.gov/**

Cancer

National Cancer Institute: **http://www.business.gov/**

Career Education

America's JobBank: **http://www.ajb.org/**

Census of Agriculture

National Agricultural Statistics Service: **http://www.nass.usda.gov/census**

Census of Construction

Census Bureau: **http://www.census.gov/epcd/www/97EC23.HTM**

Census of Governments

Census Bureau: **http://www.census.gov/govs/www/index.html**

Census of Manufactures

Census Bureau: **http://www.census.gov/epcd/www/97EC31.HTM**

Census of Mineral Industries

Census Bureau: **http://www.census.gov/epcd/www/97EC21.HTM**

Census of Population and Housing

Census Bureau: **http://www.census.gov/main/www/cen2000.html**

Census of Retail Trade

Census Bureau: **http://www.census.gov/epcd/www/97EC44.HTM**

Census of Transportation

Census Bureau: **http://www.census.gov/epcd/www/97EC48.HTM**

Census of Utilities

Census Bureau: **http://www.census.gov/epcd/www/97EC22.HTM**

Census of Wholesale Trade

Census Bureau: **http://www.census.gov/epcd/www/97EC42.HTM**

Census Tracts and Blocks (Maps)

Census Bureau: **http://factfinder.census.gov/servlet/BasicFactsServlet**

Census Tracts and Blocks (Publications)

Census Bureau: **http://factfinder.census.gov/servlet/BasicFactsServlet**

Childhood and Adolescence

America's Teens.gov: **http://www.afterschool.gov/kidsnteens2.html**

Ben's Guide to U.S. Government, for Kids: **http://bensguide.gpo.gov/**
FirstGov for Kids: **http://www.kids.gov/**
National Center for Education Statistics, Student's Classroom: **http://nces.ed.gov/
    nceskids/**
(see also Chapter 13)

China

Bureau of East Asian and Pacific Affairs, China (State Department): **http://www.
    state.gov/p/eap/ci/ch/**
Bureau of Public Affairs, Major Reports and other Resources (State Department):
    http://www.state.gov/r/pa/ei/rls/c2671.htm
Tips for Travelers to China (State Department): **http://travel.state.gov/tips_
    china.html**

Citizenship

Citizenship and Nationality (State Department): **http://travel.state.gov/acs.html#cit**
Bureau of Citizenship and Immigration Services: **http://www.immigration.gov/
    graphics/index.htm**

Civil Rights and Equal Opportunity

Civil Rights Division (Justice Department): **http://www.usdoj.gov/crt/**
Commission on Civil Rights: **http://www.usccr.gov/**
Equal Employment Opportunity Commission: **http://www.eeoc.gov/**

Civil War

American Battlefields, Civil War (National Parks Service): **http://www2.cr.nps.
    gov/abpp/civil.htm/**
Civil War at the Smithsonian: **http://civilwar.si.edu/home.html**
Civil War Maps (Library of Congress): **http://memory.loc.gov/ammem/gmdhtml/
    cwmhtml/cwmhome.html**
Selected Civil War Photographs (Library of Congress): **http://memory.loc.gov/
    ammem/cwphtml/**

Coast Guard

Coast Guard home page: **http://www.uscg.mil/uscg.shtm**

Congress

Senate: **http://www.senate.gov/**
House of Representatives: **http://www.house.gov/**
Library of Congress: **http://www.loc.gov/**

Conservation

Natural Resources and Conservation Service (Agriculture Department): **http://www.
    ms.nrcs.usda.gov/**
Educating for Conservation (Fish and Wildlife Service): **http://www.fws.gov/
    educon.html**

Consumer Information

FirstGov (Consumers): **http://www.firstgov/Citizen/Citizen_Gateway.shtml**

Copyright

Copyright Office (Library of Congress): **http://www.loc.gov/copyright/**

Cost of Living

Bureau of Labor Statistics: **http://www.bls.gov/**

Criminal Justice

Bureau of Justice Statistics (Justice Department): **http://www.ojp.usdoj.gov/bjs/**
National Institute of Justice (Justice Department): **http://www.ojp.usdoj.gov/nij/**

Customs, Immunization, and Passports

Consular Affairs (State Department): **http:/www.state.gov/travel/**
Customs Service (Treasury Department): **http://www.customs.gov/**
Immigration and Naturalization Service (Justice Department): **http://www.ins.gov/
   graphics/index.htm**
Traveler's Health, National Center for Infectious Diseases: **http://www.cdc.gov/
   travel/**

Defense and Security

Department of Defense, DefenseLink: **http://www.dod.gov/**
National Security Council: **http://www.whitehouse.gov/nsc/**
National Security Strategy of the United States: **http://www.whitehouse.gov/
   nsc/nss.html**

Diseases

Agency for Toxic Substances and Disease Registry: **http://www.atsdr.cdc.gov/**
Centers for Disease Control and Prevention: **http://www.cdc.gov/**
National Center for Infectious Diseases, Travelers Health: **http://www.cdc
   .gov/travel/**

Earth Sciences

Earth Science Information Center: **http://ask.usgs.gov/**
Geologic Survey, Geology: **http://geology.usgs.gov/index.shtml**
Earth Sciences and Image Analysis: **http://eol.jsc.nasa.gov/**

Economic Development

Commodity Futures Development Commission: **http://www.cftc.gov/cftc/cftchome.htm**
Economic and Rural Development (Agriculture Department): **http://www.nal.
   usda.gov/ric/ruralres/economic.htm**
Economic Development (Housing and Urban Development): **http://www.hud.gov/
   economicdevelopment/**
Economic Development Administration (Commerce Department): **http://www.osec.
   doc.gov/eda/**
Federal Trade Commission: **http://www.ftc.gov/**

Your Town: Designing Its Future (National Endowment of the Arts): **http://www.ins. gov/graphics/index.htm**

Economic Policy

Council of Economic Advisors: **http://www.whitehouse.gov/cea/**

Council of Economic Advisors, Publications: **http://w3.access.gpo.gov/eop/index. html**

The President's Economic Security Plan: **http://www.whitehouse.gov/infocus/economy/**

The Economy

Bureau of Labor Statistics: **http://www.bls.gov/**

Bureau of Economic Analysis: **http://www.bea.gov/**

EconomicIndicators.gov: **http://www.economicindicators.gov/**

Federal Reserve Board: **http://www.federalreserve.gov/default.htm**

Educational Statistics

Education Statistics at a Glance: **http://nces.ed.gov/edstats/**

National Center for Educational Statistics: **http://nces.ed.gov/index.html**

Electricity and Electronics

Consumer Electronics (Census Bureau): **http://landview.census.gov/mp/www/pub/ cir/mscir15j.html**

Electricity Industry (Energy Department): **http://www.eia.doe.gov/fuelelectric.html**

Elementary and Secondary Education

Eisenhower National Clearinghouse (Education Department): **http://www.enc.org/**

Educational Research and Improvement Reports and Studies (Education Department): **http://www.ed.gov/pubs/studies.html**

Research Reports from the National Research and Development Centers (Education Department): **http://research.cse.ucla.edu/**

Employment and Occupations

Occupational Outlook Handbook (Labor Department): **http://www.bls.gov/ oco/home.htm**

Occupational Employment Statistics (Labor Department): **http://www.bls.gov/oes/ home.htm**

Energy

Energy Department: **http://www.energy.gov/**

Engineering

Manufacturing Engineering Laboratory (NIST): **http://www.mel.nist.gov/index.htm**

Directorate for Engineering (National Science Foundation): **http://www.nsf.gov/ home/eng/start.htm**

Electronics and Electrical Engineering Laboratory (NIST): **http://www.eeel.nist.gov/**

Environmental Protection

Environmental Protection Agency: **http://www.epa.gov/**

Council on Environmental Quality: **http://www.whitehouse.gov/ceq/**

Natural Resources Conservation Service (Agriculture Department): **http://www. nrcs.usda.gov/**

Europe

Bureau of European and Eurasian Affairs (State Department): **http://www.state. gov/p/eur/**

Commission on Security and Cooperation in Europe: **http://www.csce.gov/helsinki. cfm**

Europe and Eurasia (Agency for International Development): **http://www.usaid. gov/regions/europe_eurasia/**

Export and Import

Bureau of Labor Statistics, International: **http://www.bls.gov/bls/international.htm**

Foreign Trade Statistics (Census Bureau): **http://www.census.gov/foreign-trade/ www/**

Export-Import Bank of the United States: **http://www.exim.gov/**

Trade Opportunities for U.S. Businesses (Commerce Department): **http://www.commerce. gov/trade_opportunities.html**

Federal Aviation Regulations

Federal Aviation Administration, regulations: **http://www2.faa.gov/index.cfm/ 677/231DC9CF-9892-4D82-B0E12A7A95654717**

Federal Communications Commission

Federal Communications Commission, home page: **http://www.fcc.gov/**

Federal Government

FirstGov, Federal Government: **http://www.firstgov.gov/Agencies/Federal/Federal_ Government.shtml**

Federal Trade Commission

Foreign Trade Commission, home page: **http://www.ftc.gov/**

Financial Institutions

Federal Deposit Insurance Corporation: **http://www.fdic.gov/**

Federal Reserve Board: **http://www.federalreserve.gov/default.htm**

National Credit Union Administration: **http://www.ncua.gov/**

Foreign Affairs of the United States

Department of State, home page: **http://www.state.gov/**

Foreign Country Studies

Library of Congress, Federal Research Division: **http://www.state.gov/r/pa/ho/frus/**

Foreign Relations of the United States

Office of the Historian (State Department): **http://www.state.gov/r/pa/ho/frus/**

Forms

FedForms.gov (General Services Administration): **http://www.fedforms.gov/**

Fossil Fuels

Fossil.Energy.gov (Energy Department): **http://fossil.energy.gov/**

General Accounting Office

General Accounting Office, home page: **http://www.gao.gov/**

General Services Administration

General Services Administration, home page: **http://www.gsa.gov/**

Global Change

Global Change Research Program: **http://www.usgcrp.gov/**

Global Warming (Environmental Protection Agency) **http://yosemite.epa.gov/ oar/globalwarming.nsf/content/index.html**

Grants and Awards (Federal)

GrantsGov: **http://www.grants.gov/**

Health Care

Health.Gov: **http://www.health.gov/**

Higher Education

National Center for Education Statistics, Postsecondary (Education Department): **http:// nces.ed.gov/surveys/SurveyGroups.asp?Group=2**

Office of Postsecondary Education, Programs (Education Department): **http://www. ed.gov/offices/OPE/FIPSE/**

Publications, Postsecondary (Education Department): **http://www.ed.gov/pubs/ studies2.html#Postsecondary**

The Home

Consumer Action Website, Housing: **http://www.consumeraction.gov/caw_housing_ general_tips.htm**

Homeland Security

Department of Homeland Security: **http://www.dhs.gov/dhspublic/**

House of Representatives, Select Committee on Homeland Security: **http:// hsc.house.gov/**

National Strategy for Homeland Security: **http://www.whitehouse.gov/homeland/ book/index.html**

Senate: **http://www.whitehouse.gov/homeland/**

Housing and Development

Federal Housing Finance Board: **http://www.fhfb.gov/**

Housing and Urban Development, home page: **http://www.hud.gov/**

Office of Federal Housing Enterprise Oversight: **http://www.ofheo.gov/**

Immigration and Citizenship

Bureau of Citizenship and Immigration Services: http://www.immigration.gov/graphics/index.htm

Insurance

Consumer Action Website, Insurance: http://www.consumeraction.gov/insurance.htm

Intelligence Community

Central Intelligence Agency: http://www.odci.gov/
National Security Agency: http://www.nsa.gov/

Internal Revenue Bulletins

Internal Revenue Service, Bulletins: http://www.irs.gov/individuals/lists/0,,id=98200,00.html

International Trade

Agency for International Development: http://www.usaid.gov/
Bureau of Economic Analysis, International Accounts (Commerce Department): http://www.bea.gov/bea/di1.htm
Bureau of Labor Statistics: http://www.bls.gov/bls/international.htm
Overseas Private Investment Corporation: http://www.opic.gov/main.htm
Trade and Development Agency: http://www.tda.gov/

Juvenile Crime

Justice Department, justice for youth: http://www.usdoj.gov/kidspage/
Justice Department, youth violence: http://www.usdoj.gov/youthviolence.htm
Office of Juvenile Justice and Delinquency Prevention: http://ojjdp.ncjrs.org/

Labor-Management Relations

Federal Labor Relations Board: http://www.flra.gov/
Labor Department, Employment Standards Division: http://www.dol.gov/esa/olms_org.htm
Merit Systems Protection Board: http://www.mspb.gov/
National Mediation Board: http://www.nmb.gov/

Libraries

Institute of Museums and Library Services: http://www.nmb.gov/
Library of Congress: http://www.loc.gov/
National Commission on Libraries and Information Science: http://www.nclis.gov/

Literacy

National Institute for Literacy: http://novel.nifl.gov/

Maps and Atlases

Library of Congress, Geography and Map Reading Room: http://lcweb.loc.gov/rr/geogmap/gmpage.html

Library of Congress, Map Collections: 1500–2003: **http://lcweb2.loc.gov/ammem/ gmdhtml/gmdhome.html**
Geological Survey, National Mapping Information: **http://mapping.usgs.gov/**
National Atlas of the United States: **http://nationalatlas.gov/index.html**

Marine Corps

Marine Corps, home page: **http://www.usmc.mil/**

Marketing

Business.Gov, Business Advisor: **http://www.business.gov/busadv/**

Mathematics

Computer and Mathematics–Related Occupations (Federal Information Center): **http://www.pueblo.gsa.gov/cic_text/employ/compnmath/oohmath.htm**
What Is Mathematics (Education Department): **http://www.ed.gov/pubs/EarlyMath/ whatis.html**

Mental Health

Center for Mental Health Services, Programs: **http://www.mentalhealth.org/cmhs/**

Middle East

Bureau of Near East Affairs (State Department): **http://www.state.gov/p/nea/**

Military History

Military History, Smithsonian Institution: **http://www.si.edu/resource/faq/nmah/ military.htm**
Military History, National Archives and Records Administration: **http://www.archives. gov/publications/military_history.html**
U.S. Army Military History Institute: **http://carlisle-www.army.mil/usamhi/**

Minerals

Geology and Mineral Sciences, Smithsonian Institution: **http://www.si.edu/resource/ faq/nmnh/mineralsciences.htm**

Minorities

Job Patterns for Minorities and Women in Private Industry (Equal Employment Opportunity Commission): **http://www.eeoc.gov/stats/jobpat/jobpat.html/**
Office of Minority and Women's Health Issues (National Center for Infectious Diseases): **http://www.cdc.gov/ncidod/omwh/**
Office of Advocacy, Women and Minorities (Small Business Administration): **http://www.sba.gov/ADVO/issues.html#wom_min**

Motor Vehicles

FirstGov, State Motor Vehicle Offices: **http://www.firstgov.gov/Topics/Motor_ Vehicles.shtml**

Music

Musical History, Smithsonian Institution: **http://www.si.edu/resource/faq/nmah/music.htm**

Performing Arts Reading Room, Library of Congress: **http://lcweb.loc.gov/rr/perform/**

National Institute of Standards and Technology, home page: **http://www.nist.gov/**

National Park Service Handbooks

National Parks Service: **http://data2.itc.nps.gov/hafe/hfc/salespub-all.cfm**

Naval History

Naval Historical Center: **http://www.history.navy.mil/**

Ship Plans from the Smithsonian Institution: **http://americanhistory.si.edu/csr/shipplan.htm**

Navigation

National Imaging and Mapping Agency, Maritime Safety Information: **http://pollux.nss.nima.mil/index/index.html/**

National Weather Service, Marine and Coastal Weather: **http://www.nws.noaa.gov/om/marine/home.htm**

Nuclear Power

Nuclear Regulatory Commission: **http://www.nrc.gov/**

Energy Information Agency, Nuclear: **http://www.eia.doe.gov/fuelnuclear.html**

Nutrition

Nutrition.Gov: **http://www.nutrition.gov/home/index.php3**

Occupational Outlook Handbook

Occupational Outlook Handbook (Labor Department): **http://www.bls.gov/oco/home.htm**

Occupational Safety and Health

Occupational Safety and Health Administration (Labor Department): **http://www.osha.gov/**

Office of Personnel Management

Office of Personnel Management, home page: **http://www.opm.gov/**

Patents and Trademarks

Patent and Trademark Office: **http://www.uspto.gov/**

Physical Fitness

Medlineplus, Exercise/Physical Fitness: **http://www.nlm.nih.gov/medlineplus/exercisephysicalfitness.html**

President's Council on Physical Fitness and Sports: **http://www.fitness.gov/**

Postal Service

Postal Service, home page: **http://www.usps.com**

Presidents

The American Presidency: A Glorious Burden, Smithsonian Institution: **http://americanhistory.si.edu/presidency/home.html**

The White House: **http://www.whitehouse.gov/**

Presidential Libraries (National Archives and Records Administration): **http://www.archives.gov/**

Radiation

Environmental Protection Agency, Radiation: **http://www.epa.gov/radiation/rrpage/rrpage1.html**

Nuclear Regulatory Commission: **http://www.nrc.gov/**

Energy Information Agency, Nuclear: **http://www.eia.doe.gov/fuelnuclear.html**

Recreation

Recreation.Gov: **http://www.recreation.gov/**

Retirement

Pensions Benefit Guaranty Corporation: **http://www.pbgc.gov/**

Seniors.Gov, Retirement Planner: **http://www.seniors.gov/retirement.html**

Social Security Administration, Benefits Planner: **http://www.ssa.gov/planners/**

Road Construction and Safety

Federal Highway Administration (Transportation Department): **http://www.fhwa.dot.gov/**

National Highway Traffic and Safety Administration (Transportation Department): **http://www.fhwa.dot.gov/**

Russia

Bureau of European and Eurasian Affairs (State Department): **http://www.state.gov/p/eur/ci/rs/**

Safety

Consumer Product Safety Commission: **http://www.cpsc.gov/**

Gateway to Government Food Safety Information: **http://www.foodsafety.gov/**

Hazmat Safety, Office of Hazardous Material Safety (Transportation Department): **http://hazmat.dot.gov/**

National Transportation Safety Board: **http://www.ntsb.gov/**

Occupational Safety and Health Administration (Labor Department): **http://www.osha.gov/**

Occupational Safety and Health Review Commission: **http://www.oshrc.gov/**

School Facilities

School Facility Maintenance Task Force, National Center for Educational Statistics: **http://nces.ed.gov/forum/maintenance.asp/**

Navigating Resources for Rural Schools, School Facilities, Access and Use of Technology, National Center for Education Statistics: **http://nces.ed.gov/surveys/ruraled/SchFacilities.asp**

Scientific Research

Defense Advanced Research Projects Agency (DARPA): **http://www.darpa.mil/**
Center for Scientific Review, National Institutes of Health: **http://www.csr.nih.gov/**
Division of Science Resources Statistics, National Science Foundation: **http://www.nsf.gov/sbe/srs/**

Securities and Investments

Federal Reserve Board: **http://www.federalreserve.gov/**
Securities and Exchange Commission: **http://www.sec.gov/**

Selective Service

Selective Service System: **http://www.sss.gov/**

Small Business

Small Business Administration, home page: **http://www.sba.gov/**

Social Sciences

Social and Economic Sciences, National Science Foundation: **http://www.nsf.gov/sbe/ses/law/start.htm**

Social Security

Social Security Administration: **http://www.ssa.gov/**

Social Welfare

Social Security Online, History Page: **http://www.ssa.gov/history/**
Measuring the Well-Being of the Poor, Economic Research Service (Agriculture Department): **http://www.ers.usda.gov/publications/tb1898/**

Solar Energy

Federal Highway Administration (Transportation Department): **http://www.eere.energy.gov/solar.html**
Space Solar Power (NASA): **http://spacesolarpower.nasa.gov/**

Space Exploration

Liftoff to Space Exploration (NASA): **http://liftoff.msfc.nasa.gov/**
Space Exploration (NASA): **http://adc.gsfc.nasa.gov/adc/education/space_ex/**

Spanish Language Publications

Federal Citizen Information Center, Resources in Spanish: **http://www.pueblo.gsa.gov/spanish/**
Let Everyone Participate, Meaningful Access for People Who Are Limited English Proficient: **http://www.lep.gov/**

Specifications and Standards

National Institute of Standards and Technology: **http://www.nist.gov/**

Statistics

FedStats: **http://www.fedstats.gov/**

Student Financial Aid

Student.gov: **http://www.student.gov/STUGOVWebApp/index.jsp**

Substance Abuse

Substance Abuse and Mental Health Services Administration (Health and Human Services): **http://www.samhsa.gov/**

Drug Enforcement Administration: **http://www.dea.gov/**

Tax Court Reports

United States Tax Court: **http://www.ustaxcourt.gov/ustcweb.htm**

Taxes

Internal Revenue Service: **http://www.irs.gov/**

Teaching

Information for Teachers (Education Department): **http://www.ed.gov/audience/audience.jsp?type=I&top=Teachers**

Regional Educational Laboratories (Education Department): **http://www.ed.gov/prog_info/Labs/**

Telecommunications

Federal Communications Commission: **http://www.fcc.gov/**

National Telecommunications and Information Administration (Department of Commerce): **http://www.ntia.doc.gov/**

Transportation

Transportation Department, home page: **http://www.dot.gov/**

Travel and Tourism

Bureau of Consular Affairs: **http://travel.state.gov/**

Recreation.Gov: **http://www.recreation.gov/**

Traveler's Health, National Center for Infectious Diseases: **http://www.cdc.gov/travel/**

Trees, Forest Management, and Products

Bureau of Land Management (Interior Department): **http://www.blm.gov/nhp/index.htm/**

National Park Service (Interior Department): **http://www.nps.gov/**

Forest Service (Agriculture Department): **http://www.fs.fed.us/**

United States Code

GPO Access Government Printing Office: **http://www.gpoaccess.gov/uscode/index.html**

United States Reports (Supreme Court Decisions)

GPO Access, Government Printing Office: **http://fedbbs.access.gpo.gov/court01.htm**

Utilities

Connecting Rural America, Rural Utilities Service (Agriculture Department): **http://www.usda.gov/rus/**

Federal Communications Commission: **http://www.fcc.gov/**

Federal Energy Regulatory Commission: **http://www.ferc.gov/**

Veterans

Veterans Administration: **http://www.va.gov/**

Vital and Health Statistics

National Center for Health Statistics, National Vital Statistics System: **http://www.cdc.gov/nchs/nvss.htm**

Voting and Elections

Federal Elections Commission: **http://www.fec.gov/**

Waste Management

Office of Solid Waste (Environmental Protection Agency): **http://www.epa.gov/epaoswer/osw/index.htm**

Water Management

Natural Resources Conservation Service, Irrigation Page (Agriculture Department): **http://www.wcc.nrcs.usda.gov/nrcsirrig/**

Natural Resources Conservation Service, Water Science and Technology (Agriculture Department): **http://www.wcc.nrcs.usda.gov/water/quality/wst.html**

Weather

National Ocean and Atmospheric Administration: **http://www.noaa.gov/**

Weights and Measures

National Institute of Standards and Technology: **http://www.nist.gov/**

Wildlife

Fish and Wildlife Service (Interior Department): **http://www.fws.gov/**

National Wildlife Health Center (Interior Department): **http://www.nwhc.usgs.gov/**

Women

Office on Violence against Women (Justice Department): **http://www.ojp.usdoj.gov/vawo/**

National Women's Health Information Center (Health and Human Services): **http://www.4women.gov/**

Women's Bureau (Labor Department): **http://www.dol.gov/wb/**

Government Body Index

Selected Title Index

About the Authors

Peter Hernon is Professor at the Graduate School of Library and Information Science, Simmons College (300 The Fenway, Boston, Massachusetts 02115-5898), where he teaches courses on government information policies, practices, and policies; research methods; the evaluation of library services; and academic libraries. He received his Ph.D. from Indiana University in 1979 and is the author of 39 books and more than 180 articles. He is the founding editor of *Government Information Quarterly,* the former editor-in-chief of the *Journal of Academic Librarianship,* and the co-editor of *Library & Information Science Research.*

Robert E. Dugan is the Director of the Mildred F. Sawyer Library at Suffolk University (8 Ashburton Place, Boston, Massachusetts 02108). During a nearly thirty-year career, he has been an associate university librarian, a state librarian, head of statewide library development, a public library director, and a reference librarian. He was the Webmaster and library director for three years at a mid-Atlantic college before returning to Boston in 1998. He has authored and coauthored four other books and more than fifty articles on topics such as information policy, technology, outcomes assessment, and library management and operations.

John A. Shuler is Documents Librarian/Department Head Documents, Maps, Microforms, and Curriculum Department, University Library, University of Illinois at Chicago (801 S. Morgan St. (m/c 234) Chicago, Illinois 60607–7041). He received his MSLIS from the University of California at Los Angeles in 1983. He has worked as a government documents librarian at the University of Oregon and at Colgate University. He has spoken and written about government information policy and government documents practice. He serves as assistant editor of *Government Information Quarterly,* as column editor for the *Journal of Academic Librarianship's* "Information Policy," and as editor of *Documents to the People*, the American Library Association's Government Documents Roundtable's quarterly publication.